Early Modern Catholicism and the Printed Book

Library of the Written Word

VOLUME 119

The Handpress World

Editor-in-Chief

Andrew Pettegree (*University of St Andrews*)

Editorial Board

Ann Blair (*Harvard University*)
Falk Eisermann (*Staatsbibliothek zu Berlin – Preußischer Kulturbesitz*)
Shanti Graheli (*University of Glasgow*)
Earle Havens (*Johns Hopkins University*)
Ian Maclean (*All Souls College, Oxford*)
Alicia Montoya (*Radboud University*)
Angela Nuovo (*University of Milan*)
Helen Smith (*University of York*)
Mark Towsey (*University of Liverpool*)
Malcolm Walsby (*enssib, Lyon*)
Arthur der Weduwen (*University of St Andrews*)

VOLUME 97

The titles published in this series are listed at *brill.com/lww*

Early Modern Catholicism and the Printed Book

Agents – Networks – Responses

Edited by

Justyna Kiliańczyk-Zięba
Magdalena Komorowska

BRILL

LEIDEN | BOSTON

The proofreading of this publication has been supported by a grant from the Priority Research Area Heritage under the Strategic Program Excellence Initiative at Jagiellonian University.

Cover illustration: Tomasz Treter, Luca Bertelli, Typus Ecclesiae Catholicae, 1574, Kraków, Biblioteka Jagiellońska, Jan Ponętowski's files, folder 149, no. 9041.

The Library of Congress Cataloging-in-Publication Data is available online at https://catalog.loc.gov

Typeface for the Latin, Greek, and Cyrillic scripts: "Brill". See and download: brill.com/brill-typeface.

ISSN 1874-4834
ISBN 978-90-04-53866-5 (hardback)
ISBN 978-90-04-53867-2 (e-book)
DOI 10.1163/9789004538672

Copyright 2024 by Koninklijke Brill NV, Leiden, The Netherlands.
Koninklijke Brill NV incorporates the imprints Brill, Brill Nijhoff, Brill Schöningh, Brill Fink, Brill mentis, Brill Wageningen Academic, Vandenhoeck & Ruprecht, Böhlau and V&R unipress.
All rights reserved. No part of this publication may be reproduced, translated, stored in a retrieval system, or transmitted in any form or by any means, electronic, mechanical, photocopying, recording or otherwise, without prior written permission from the publisher. Requests for re-use and/or translations must be addressed to Koninklijke Brill NV via brill.com or copyright.com.

This book is printed on acid-free paper and produced in a sustainable manner.

Contents

List of Figures and Tables　IX
Notes on Contributors　XII

1　To See the Wood for the Trees
　　Early Modern Catholicism and the Printed Book　1
　　　　Magdalena Komorowska

PART 1
Institutions and Networks

2　Towards the Typographia Vaticana
　　Gregory XIII's Promotion of Printing　17
　　　　Paolo Sachet

3　The 'Primer and Christian Doctrine of Valladolid' (1583)
　　A Multifaceted Publishing Endeavour　37
　　　　Benito Rial Costas

4　A Coordinated Catholic Press
　　The Editing and Dispersal of Nicholas Sander's Schismatis Anglicani,
　　1580–c.1600　52
　　　　Chelsea Reutcke

5　Printing Reformed Plainchant in Papal Rome
　　Giovanni Guidetti, Robert Granjon and the 1582 Directorium Chori　75
　　　　Barbara Swanson

PART 2
Between the Protestant and Catholic Reformations

6　'Write against It, So That They May Return to the Right Faith'
　　Catholic Doctrinal and Polemical Writings in the Early Dutch
　　Reformation (1517–1528)　101
　　　　David Oldenhof

7 Echoes of Worms
Luther's Opponents in Eastern Europe 123
  Maciej Ptaszyński

8 Protestant Books in Jesuit Libraries from Riga, Braniewo and Poznań
Catholic Post-publication Censorship in Practice 143
  Peter Sjökvist

9 Book Collection of a Hinterland Convent in Response to the Lutheran Reformation
The Case of Mid-Sixteenth Century Rakvere (Wesenberg) 180
  Kaspar Kolk

PART 3
Insights into the Collections

10 Italian Religious Orders and Their Books at the End of the Sixteenth Century 199
  Giovanna Granata

11 Books in the Cloister, Books in the Cells
The Augustinians of Santa Maria del Popolo in Rome and Their Book Collections at the End of the Sixteenth Century 220
  Lucrezia Signorello

12 Benedictine Book Acquisitions in Seventeenth- and Eighteenth-Century Bohemia
A Case of Convents in Broumov and Prague 255
  Jindřich Kolda

PART 4
Appropriation of Texts and Books

13 The Earliest Polish Translation of a Jesuit Catechism 275
  Mirosława Hanusiewicz-Lavallee and Robert Aleksander Maryks

14 From Bees to Thieves
The Perception of Writing Practices and Intellectual Property in Early Modern Hungary 288
  Gábor Förköli

PART 5
The Interplay of Word and Image

15 Framing the French Protestant Threat in Richard Rowlands Verstegan's
    Théâtre des cruautés des hereticques de nostre temps (1588)   309
       Claire Konieczny

16 Meditative Emblems in the Polish-Lithuanian Commonwealth
    (1570–1775)   323
       Alicja Bielak

17 Supralibros as a Creed
    Ownership Stamps on Books Belonging to Tomasz Treter, Canonicus et
    Custos Varmiensis   372
       Justyna Kiliańczyk-Zięba

Index   391

Figures and Tables

Figures

2.1 *Kalendarium Gregorianum perpetuum* (Rome: Domenico Basa, 1582). Munich, Bayerische Staatsbibliothek, Chrlg. 328 t   30

2.2 *Officium defunctorum ad usum Maronitarum* (Rome: Domenico Basa, 1585). London, British Library, 753.g.72.(1.)   31

2.3 Ambrose, *Operum … tomus secundus* (Rome: Domenico Basa, 1581). Munich, Bayerische Staatsbibliothek, 2 P.lat. 51-1/2   32

5.1 Lamentations chant for Holy Thursday Matins in Guidetti, *Directorium chori* (Rome 1582)   84

5.2 Robert Granjon's characters for *Novum Testamentum Graece et Latine* (Paris 1549)   88

5.3 Hebrew cantillation symbols in Johannes Reuchlin's *De accentibus et orthographia linguae hebraicae* (Hagenau 1518)   96

8.1 Title page in: Philipp Melanchthon, *Erotemata dialectices continentia fere integram artem, ita scripta, ut juventuti utiliter proponi possint* (Wittenberg: Krafft, 1563). Uppsala University Library, shelf mark: UUB Riga 353   150

8.2 Title page in: Johann Dryander, *New Artznei unnd Practicierbüchlin zu allen Leibs gebrechen* (Frankfurt am Main: Egenolph, 1551). Uppsala University Library, shelf mark: UUB Obr. 42.528 (1)   152

8.3 Title page in: Rudolf Gwalther, *De syllabarum et carminum ratione* (Zurich: Froschauer, 1554). Uppsala University Library, shelf mark: UUB Obr. Qq.554 (9)   154

8.4 Title page in: Hilarius of Poitiers, *Lucubrationes quotquot extant* (Basel: Froben & Episcopius, 1550). Uppsala University Library, shelf mark: UUB Teol. Patres, ensk. lat. fol. (36.103)   155

8.5 Colophon Hilarius of Poitiers, *Lucubrationes quotquot extant* (Basel: Froben & Episcopius, 1550). Uppsala University Library, shelf mark: UUB Teol. Patres, ensk. lat. fol. (36.103)   156

8.6 Last page in: Hilarius of Poitiers, *Lucubrationes quotquot extant* (Basel: Froben & Episcopius, 1550). Uppsala University Library, shelf mark: UUB Teol. Patres, ensk. lat. fol. (36.103)   157

8.7 Title page in: Conrad Gesner, *Physicarum meditationum, annotationum et scholiorum lib. V* (Zurich: Froshauer, 1586). Uppsala University Library, shelf mark: UUB Obr. Qq.81   158

8.8 Colophon in: Philipp Melanchthon, *Ciceronis epistolas, quae familiares vocantur, argumenta* (Leipzig: Rambau & Apel, 1563–1565). Uppsala University Library, shelf mark: UUB Script. Lat. [Cicero] 395: 1–3 (x.368–370)   159

8.9   Title page in: Petrus Ramus, *Institutionum dialecticarum libri III* (Paris: Roigny & David, 1549). Uppsala University Library, shelf mark: UUB Bokband, 1500-t. Nederländerna 3   161
8.10 Johannes Chrysostomos, *Opera* (Basel: Froben & Episcopius, 1530). Uppsala University Library, shelf mark: Teol. patres, ensk. grek. fol. (58.46–48)   162
8.11 Johannes Chrysostomos, *Opera* (Basel: Froben & Episcopius, 1530). Uppsala University Library, shelf mark: Teol. patres, ensk. grek. fol. (58.47–48)   163
8.12 Johannes Chrysostomos, *Opera* (Basel: Froben & Episcopius, 1530). Uppsala University Library, shelf mark: Teol. patres, ensk. grek. fol. (58.47–48)   164
8.13 Johannes Chrysostomos, *Opera* (Basel: Froben & Episcopius, 1530). Uppsala University Library, shelf mark: Teol. patres, ensk. grek. fol. (58.47–48)   165
8.14 Johannes Chrysostomos, *Opera* (Basel: Froben & Episcopius, 1530). Uppsala University Library, shelf mark: Teol. patres, ensk. grek. fol. (58.47–48)   166
8.15 Johannes Chrysostomos, *Opera* (Basel: Froben & Episcopius, 1530). Uppsala University Library, shelf mark: Teol. patres, ensk. grek. fol. (58.47–48)   167
8.16 Title page in: Petrus Ramus, *Scholae in liberales artes* (Basel: Episcopius, 1569). Uppsala University Library, shelf mark: UUB Script. Lat. rec. fol. (29.96)   169
8.17 Preface (p. α3v) in: Petrus Ramus, *Scholae in liberales artes* (Basel: Episcopius, 1569). Uppsala University Library, shelf mark: UUB Script. Lat. rec. fol. (29.96)   170
8.18 P. 452 in: *Novum testamentum Graece et Latine*, ed. Erasmus of Rotterdam (Leipzig: Vögelin & Schneider, 1570). Uppsala University Library, shelf mark: UUB Bib. grek. N.T. (55.69)   173
8.19 Pp. 453–458 in: *Novum testamentum Graece et Latine*, ed. Erasmus of Rotterdam (Leipzig: Vögelin & Schneider, 1570). Uppsala University Library, shelf mark: UUB Bib. grek. N.T. (55.69)   174
11.1 Giovanni Battista Falda, *Piazza del' Popolo abbellita da N. S. papa Alesandro VII* (Rome: Giovanni Giacomo de Rossi, 1665), Amsterdam, Rijksmuseum, RP-P-1957-653-54-1   230
11.2 Augustinus, *Explanatio psalmorum* (Basel: Johann Amerbach, 1489), f. a2r, Viterbo, Central Library of the Augustinian Province of Italy, Inc. 11   235
11.3 Consistency of the book collections of Santa Maria del Popolo and the friars of the convent   245
15.1 A typical spread of the *Theatrum*, pp. 46–47. Special Collections, George Peabody Library, The Sheridan Libraries, Johns Hopkins University, 272 V616 1588 c. 1   311
15.2 A typical spread of the first translation of the *Théâtre*, pp. 52–53. Special Collections, George Peabody Library, The Sheridan Libraries, Johns Hopkins University, 272 V616 1588 c. 1   313
15.3 A typical spread of the second translation of Verstegan's *Théâtre*, n.p. Notice that while the images are lacking, the capital letters linking the text to the

engraving are still present. Special Collections, George Peabody Library, The Sheridan Libraries, Johns Hopkins University, 272 V616 1588 c. 1   314

16.1 Tomasz Treter, *Symbolica vitae Christi meditatio* (Braniewo: Georg Schönfels, 1612), p. 139. Krakow, Biblioteka Jagiellońska, 35699 I   337

16.2 Tomasz Treter, *Symbolica vitae Christi meditatio* (Braniewo: Georg Schönfels, 1612), p. 69. Krakow, Biblioteka Jagiellońska, 35699 I   339

16.3 Paweł Mirowski, *Młotek duchowny w sercach ludzkich tor Chrystusów drelujący* (Gdańsk: Friedrich David Rhete, 1656), f. T1r. Warsaw, Biblioteka Uniwersytecka, Sd.712.788   341

16.4 Hiacynt Sierakowski, *Wieniec różany Królowej Niebieskiej Naświętszej Bogarodzice Panny Maryjej* ([Poznań: Wojciech Regulus], 1644), between pp. 37–38. Warsaw, Biblioteka Narodowa, XVII.3.416   345

16.5 Marcin Hińcza, *Plęsy Aniołów Jezusowi narodzonemu, Naświetszęgo Krzyża tańce* (Krakow: Franciszek Cezary, 1636[1638]), between ff. 142–143. Warsaw, Biblioteka Uniwerystecka, Sd 4g.2.2.31   346

16.6 Mikołaj Krzysztof Chalecki, *Allegoriae albo Kwiecia módł gorących wynalezione dla unurzenia dusze w Bogu* (Vilnius: Leon Mamonicz, 1618), f. B3v. Vilnius, Vilniaus universiteto biblioteka, III 15155   349

17.1 Upper cover of Gregorius I, *Opera omnia*, vol. 1 (Antwerp 1572). Stockholm, Kungliga Biblioteket, KB liste VIII B: 26   378

17.2 Supralibros of Tomasz Treter, upper cover of Jerónimo Osório, *Opera* (Rome 1592), Uppsala Universitetsbibliotek, call no. 1500 t. Polen Fol. 19   379

17.3 Supralibros of Tomasz Treter, lower cover of Jerónimo Osório, *Opera* (Rome 1592), Uppsala Universitetsbibliotek, call no. 1500 t. Polen Fol. 19   380

17.4 Tomasz Treter's seal stamped on a letter of 1569. Olsztyn, Archiwum Archidiecezji Warmińskiej, Ms AB 62   383

17.5 Tomasz Treter's seal stamped on a letter of 1604. Krakow, Biblioteka XX Czartoryskich (Muzeum Narodowe), Ms 1625   384

17.6 Tomasz Treter, *Symbolica vitae Christi meditatio* (Braniewo: Georg Schönfels, 1612), pp. [Gg3v–Gg4r]. Warsaw, Biblioteka Narodowa, SD XVII.3.2721   387

Tables

5.1   Rhythmic values in Giovanni Guidetti's *Directorium chori* (Rome 1582)   83
10.1 List of authors sorted by number of copies   208
10.2 List of authors sorted by the mean of the ROSWs   215
11.1 Book lists of the friars of Santa Maria del Popolo   239
16.1 Meditative emblem collections published in the Polish-Lithuanian Commonwealth (*c.*1569–1775)   354

Notes on Contributors

Magdalena Komorowska
is an assistant professor at the Faculty of Polish Studies, Jagiellonian University in Krakow. Her research focuses on the history of printing in Poland in the late sixteenth and seventeenth century, especially on the milieu of book printers in Krakow and on the relationship between the printed book and the Catholic Reformation. She has published on various aspects of the history of the book in Poland-Lithuania.

Paolo Sachet
is Ambizione Postdoctoral Fellow at the Institut d'histoire de la Réformation, Université de Genève. He has published articles on the impact of printed books on the intellectual history of early modern Europe, co-edited *The Afterlife of Aldus* (2018) and authored *Publishing for the Popes: The Roman Curia and the Use of Printing, 1527–1555* (2020). He is also the editor in chief of AGAPE, a comprehensive database of Greek patristics editions (1460–1600).

Benito Rial Costas
is a professor at the Universidad Complutense de Madrid. His research interests go across book culture and media, historiography, bibliography, digital humanities and typography. He has published in the fields of material bibliography, the sociology of texts, cultural history and literature. His recent publications include an edited collection *Aldo Manuzio en la España del Renacimiento* (2019), and the special issue of *Quaerendo* 'New insights into an old issue: Book historical scholarship on the relationship between the Low Countries and Spain' (2019).

Chelsea Reutcke
received her PhD in Reformation Studies from the University of St Andrews in 2020. Her thesis explored the print networks behind English Catholic books in the late seventeenth century. Her research interests pertain to the production, circulation, and reception of sixteenth and seventeenth-century British Catholic print. She worked for the Bibliography of British and Irish History and for Open Virtual Worlds, which produces digital reconstructions of historic sites.

Barbara Swanson
is an assistant professor at Dalhousie University. She is the author of various articles on Catholic plainchant in the sixteenth and seventeenth centuries,

including on Giovanni Guidetti, female religious, and Counter-Reformation mission. Her interest in book history intersects with visual culture, in particular, how visual aspects of plainchant and its books reflect devotional and reform imperatives.

David Oldenhof
works at the Vrije Universiteit Amsterdam, where he is a research fellow at the HDC Centre of Religious History and affiliated to the University Library as a policy advisor. He graduated from the Radboud University in Nijmegen and was a visiting scholar at the Centre for Medieval Studies at the University of Leeds and at the Centre for Reformation and Renaissance Studies at the University of Toronto.

Maciej Ptaszyński
is a professor at the Institute of History, University of Warsaw. He studied History and Philosophy at the University of Warsaw and Freie Universität Berlin. He has published extensively on the church history and political theories in the early modern times.

Peter Sjökvist
is an associate professor at Uppsala University and is a rare books curator at Uppsala University Library. In his research he has mainly focused on occasional poetry, early modern dissertations, and literary spoils of war. As a curator, he is presently the manager of the project aiming at the identification of books brought to Sweden in the seventeenth century from libraries of a Polish city of Poznań.

Kaspar Kolk
is a researcher at the University of Tallinn and a librarian at the University of Tartu Library. His main areas of research are medieval and early modern book culture, Latin paleography and codicology.

Giovanna Granata
is a full professor at the University of Cagliari. Her main interests include the study of early modern and contemporary private collections, circulation of books in the early centuries of printing and the history of libraries. She is a member of the scientific committees of the research group on 'Private Libraries of Philosophers from the Renaissance to the Twentieth Century' (picus.unica .it), and of the RICI group (Research on the Inquiry of the Congregation of the Index, rici.vatlib.it).

Lucrezia Signorello
is a curator of rare book and manuscript collections at the Malatestiana Library in Cesena and a member of the working group for the *Manus Online* Authority File (ICCU). Her PhD research project is aimed at the identification and reconstruction of the library of the Roman Augustinian convent of Santa Maria del Popolo in the seventeenth century.

Jindřich Kolda
is an assistant professor at the Philosophical Faculty of the University Hradec Králové. His research focuses on the history of early modern female convents, libraries, landscape and art.

Mirosława Hanusiewicz-Lavallee
is a professor and chair of the Department of Early Modern Polish Literature at the John Paul II Catholic University of Lublin and a member of the Polish Academy of Arts and Sciences. She has published extensively on early modern Polish religious and amorous literature, while her recent research focuses on Polish-British literary links in the 1600s–1800s. Her most recent publications include *W stronę Albionu. Studia z dziejów polsko-brytyjskich związków literackich w dobie wczesnonowożytnej* (The Call of Albion. Studies on Early Modern Polish-British Literary Links, 2017).

Robert Maryks
received his PhD from Fordham University and works at the Adam Mickiewicz University in Poznań. He has published widely on the history of the Jesuits, including *The Jesuit Order as a Synagogue of Jews* (Brill, 2010). He is the editor of the *Journal of Jesuit Studies*, Brill's Jesuit Studies book series, Jesuit Historiography Online, and Brill's Research Perspectives in Jesuit Studies.

Gábor Förköli
is a postdoctoral researcher at the Polish Academy of Sciences within the ERC Project 'From East to West, and Back Again: Student Travel and Transcultural Knowledge Production in Renaissance Europe (c.1470–c.1620)' (PI: Valentina Lepri). He received his PhD from the Université Paris-Sorbonne (Paris 4) and the Eötvös Loránd University of Budapest. His interests include political literature, religious anthropology, history of rhetoric, and the uses of excerpts and common place books in early modern hand-written culture.

Claire Konieczny
received her PhD in French Literature from Johns Hopkins University in Baltimore, USA. Her thesis explores the rhetorical manners in which later

Protestant and Catholic reformers attempted to (re)define their respective religions in France in the latter years of the French Wars of Religion.

Alicja Bielak
is a postdoctoral researcher at the Polish Academy of Sciences within the ERC Project 'From East to West, and Back Again: Student Travel and Transcultural Knowledge Production in Renaissance Europe (c.1470–c.1620)' (PI: Valentina Lepri). Her research interests include emblems and knowledge transfer in the early modern period. She works on a monograph devoted to Polish meditative emblems in the 1600s–1800s.

Justyna Kiliańczyk-Zięba
is an assistant professor at the Jagiellonian University in Krakow, Poland. She has published books and articles on book history, emblematics and the history of ideas, as well as edited extensive sixteenth-century texts. Her book *Printers' Devices in the Polish-Lithuanian Commonwealth. Iconographic Sources and Ideological Content* will be published by Brill in 2024.

CHAPTER 1

To See the Wood for the Trees
Early Modern Catholicism and the Printed Book

Magdalena Komorowska

The fact that the Catholic Church in the early modern era made extensive use of the printing press has been highlighted many times, as have been the multifaceted consequences of this decision. Scholars have demonstrated that Catholics produced and used printed materials throughout the early modern period for various purposes, including liturgical, pastoral, missionary, common and individual daily prayer, and controversy. Throughout the era, the religious book in its various forms and functions was predominantly Catholic in large parts of Europe, such as Spain, France, and Italy. In other places, such as the Polish-Lithuanian Commonwealth, it was the zeal of Catholic reformers following Trent and their need for printed materials that significantly contributed to the spread of printing as a craft. In addition, Catholic missionaries disseminated not only printed books but also the technology of their production outside Europe. Studies on these subjects are too numerous to list them all here, and they cover each and every aspect of book production and consumption, from the larger context in which Catholic book culture developed (geographical, cultural, political, economic, scale and scope, etc.) to the printed book as a material object (development, function, form, cost, usage, etc.).[1] Nevertheless,

---

1   The number of books and articles touching more or less directly the problem of the relationship between early modern Catholicism and print is enormous. Therefore, only the most important works will be mentioned here. Two recent collected volumes devoted specifically to Catholic uses of print must be noted as direct attempts to define the connection of Catholics and print as a distinct research field: Natalia Maillard Álvarez (ed.), *Books in the Catholic World during the Early Modern Period* (Leiden: Brill, 2013); Renaud Adam etc. (eds.), *Books and Prints at the Heart of the Catholic Reformation in the Low Countries (16th–17th Centuries)* (Leiden: Brill, 2022). It is also necessary to underscore the work of Alexandra Walsham, whose research focuses mainly on the unique experience of persecuted English Catholicism, but the analysis and conclusions reach beyond this limited context, e.g., Alexandra Walsham, 'Unclasping the Book? Post-Reformation English Catholicism and the Vernacular Bible', *Journal of British Studies*, 42.2 (2003), pp. 142–143; Alexandra Walsham, '"Domme Preachers"? Post-Reformation English Catholicism and the Culture of Print', *Past and Present*, 168 (2000), pp. 72–123; Alexandra Walsham, 'Preaching without Speaking. Script, Print, and Religious Dissent', in Julia Crick, Alexandra Walsham (eds.), *The Uses of Script and Print, 1300–1700*

there have been few attempts to bring these studies together and define a common ground for them, and it is fair to say that when it comes to Catholicism and its connections to print, we have yet to see the wood for the trees.

A necessary common denominator for the aforementioned research is a direct reference to Catholicism, which can be difficult to define in the context of sixteenth-century religious developments. It is rarely considered as a whole, despite its undeniable continuity across the centennial. Rather, it is divided by easily recognizable milestones, such as Luther's breach of unity with Rome or conclusion of the Council of Trent, into a series of distinct occurrences that are considered on their own: the medieval or pre-Reformational Catholicism, the Tridentine or Post-Tridentine Catholicism, the Catholic Reformation, the Counter-Reformation, etc. These prevailing chronological and conceptual divisions are one of the reasons why, for example, the writing and publishing activity of the Brothers of the Common Life or the Dutch Franciscans at the turn of the fifteenth and sixteenth centuries are interpreted as a manifestation of late medieval or pre-Reformation culture, while essentially similar activities undertaken by the Jesuits and other religious groups in the second half of the sixteenth century are seen as typical of the Counter-Reformation or the Catholic Reformation.[2] Meanwhile, in a broader chronological perspective, they could be considered as aspects or occurrences within the framework of early modern Catholic book culture.

(Cambridge: Cambridge University Press, 2004), pp. 211–234. It is also worth mentioning R.S. Miola's introduction in R.S. Miola (ed.), *Early Modern Catholicism. An Anthology of Primary Sources* (Oxford: Oxford University Press, 2007), pp. 1–38. The French context is sketched in Andrew Pettegree, Paul Nelles, Philip Conner (eds.), *The Sixteenth-Century French Religious Book* (New York: Routledge, 2016, first ed. Aldershot: Ashgate, 2001) and Henri-Jean Martin, *Livre, pouvoir et société à Paris au XVIIe siècle* (2 vols., Geneva: Droz, 1969). For Germany, see Wilfried Enderle, 'Die Druckverleger des katholischen Deutschlands. Zwischen Augsburger Religionsfrieden 1555 und Westfälischem Frieden 1648', in Gert Kaiser, Heinz Finger, Elisabeth Niggemann (eds.), *Bücher für die Wissenschaft. Bibliotheken zwischen Tradition und Fortschritt* (München: Saur, 1994). Main features of Catholic publishing after Trent are defined in Ronnie Po-Chia Hsia, *The World of Catholic Renewal 1540–1770* (Cambridge: Cambridge University Press, 2005, first edition 1998), pp. 172–186. It is to be noted that most of the studies refer to the second half of the sixteenth century. For the first half of the century, the studies are far less numerous. Koen Goudriaan's works, together with other important publications, are brought to attention as references further in this and following chapters. Another important work to be mentioned here is: Paolo Sachet, *Publishing for the Popes. The Roman Curia and the Use of Printing (1527–1555)* (Leiden: Brill, 2020).

2 See, for example, Koen Goudriaan, 'The Devotio Moderna and the Printing Press (ca. 1475–1540)', *Church History and Religious Culture*, 93.4 (2013), pp. 579–606. In 2016, the text was included into Goudriaan's collection of essays with a telling title: *Piety in Practice and Print. Essays on the Late-Medieval Religious Landscape* (Hilversum: Verloren, 2016).

As readers may have guessed, this view is based on a concept proposed by historians who see the pre-Reformation Catholicism and the Catholic Reformation as analytical categories within a single framework of early modern Catholicism rather than as independent events.[3] In the context of book history, such an approach, which encompasses occurrences from the late fifteenth to the mid-seventeenth century, is especially appealing as it allows for a comprehensive view. It facilitates the identification of not only certain long-term universal features but also narrower (regional, functional, generic, historical, cultural, etc.) strands within them. Such a framework should bring us closer to answering a set of classic yet fundamental questions about the two-way interaction between Catholicism (as a religion, but also as a cultural factor) and print. First, how and to what extent did Catholicism influence the printing trade and its products in the early modern era? Second, how and to what extent did printed media influence early modern Catholicism? The answer, of course, is far beyond the scope of this brief chapter, due to the subject's vastness and richness, as well as the lack of large-scale planned research in this area thus far. Nevertheless, once such a shift in perspective has occurred, it may turn out that our understanding of the links between Catholicism and the printing press is already greater than one might think.

When conceptualizing the relationship between Catholicism and print, one must take into account, on the one hand, large-scale book production and trade, which ensured the global reach of particular texts and concepts, and on the other hand, printing of vernacular books in small print runs and their local circulation; one must keep in mind the international and officially controlled market of liturgical books, as well as clandestine presses operated by persecuted communities; one must remember not only missionaries who traveled the length and breadth of the world with books as tools of their trade but also nuns who never left monastery walls and used books for their own spiritual formation; not only the clergy and their needs as readers and teachers, but also the roles that books played in the lives of laity, such as shaping of popular piety. Of course, anything that falls between these roughly outlined boundaries must be considered as well. Nevertheless, when read with the intention of getting as complete a picture of the relationship under investigation as

---

3 See, for example, John W. O' Malley, 'Was Ignatius Loyola a Church Reformer? How to Look at Early Modern Catholicism', *Catholic Historical Review*, 77.2 (1991), pp. 177–193; Jaap Geraerts, 'Early Modern Catholicism and Its Historiography. Innovation, Revitalization, and Integration', *Church History and Religious Culture*, 97.3/4 (2017), pp. 381–392; Kathleen M. Comerford, Hilmar M. Pabel (eds.), *Early Modern Catholicism. Essays in Honour of John W. O'Malley, s.J.* (Toronto: University of Toronto Press, 2001); Tadgh Ó hAnnracháin, *Catholic Europe 1592–1648. Centre and Peripheries* (Oxford: Oxford University Press, 2015).

possible, the scattered studies published to date reveal some general features. These can be grouped into three pairs that recur in narratives on early modern Catholicism and encompass the abovementioned phenomena: continuity and change, unity and diversity, and worship and commerce.[4] These pairs should not be interpreted as mutually exclusive, but rather as a reminder that both early modern Catholicism itself and its relationship to print were far from homogeneous.

1   Continuity and Change

One of the most important characteristics of early modern Catholicism was its transitional nature. The starting point can be described, somewhat oversimplifying, as medieval Catholicism, and the direction of the transition as modern Catholicism.[5] Changes, with their dynamism, are usually easier to grasp and define than continuities, but the latter must be acknowledged when mapping the narrative of the relationship between early modern Catholicism and print. To identify these continuities, one must go back to the pre-Reformation period. In the few studies that have attempted an initial synthesis of developments in late fifteenth- and early sixteenth-century printing in the field of religious texts, the period has been interpreted as one of preparation for the Protestant Reformation.[6] This is true to a certain extent. However, if we take into account

---

4   See, for example, Antje Flüchter, 'Translating Catechisms, Translating Cultures. An Introduction', in Antje Flüchetr, Rouven Wirbser (eds.), *Translating Catechisms, Translating Cultures. The Expansion of Catholicism in the Early Modern World* (Leiden: Brill, 2017), pp. 5–17 (question of unity and diversity); Koen Goudriaan, 'The Church and the Market. Vernacular Religious Works and the Early Printing Press in the Low Countries, 1477–1540', in Sabrina Corbellini (ed.), *Cultures of Religious Reading in the Late Middle Ages. Instructing the Soul, Feeding the Spirit, and Awakening the Passion* (Turnhout: Brepols, 2013), pp. 93–116 (for worship and commerce).

5   See O' Malley, 'Was Ignatius Loyola a Church Reformer?', p. 178. O'Malley follows concepts of, among others, Wolfgang Reinhard, expressed, for example, in his 'Reformation, Counter-Reformation and Early Modern State', *The Catholic Historical Review*, 75 (1989), pp. 383–404.

6   See, for example, Jean François Gilmont, 'Introduction', in Jean François Gilmont, Karin Maag (eds.), *The Reformation and the Book* (Aldershot: Ashgate, 1998), p. 6. The compositional schema of essays gathered in this influential volume, which begin with a general background, also tends, perhaps not entirely intentionally, to underscore the fact that by 1517 print culture has been established well enough to successfully promote the ideas of the Protestant Reformation. See also the much debated, yet very influential, work by Elizabeth L. Eisenstein, *The Printing Press as an Agent of Change* (Cambridge: Cambridge University Press, 1980), who included the phrase 'Resetting the Stage for the Reformation' in the title of the chapter devoted to the relationship between Protestantism and print (p. 303ff.).

that Catholics continued to use the printing press throughout the sixteenth century and beyond, the first seventy years of printing must be seen as a period of testing and learning for both printers and the Church regarding how the religious book could function as a printed book, and how the commercial interests of printers could be reconciled with the needs (liturgical, pastoral, devotional, etc.) of the Christian religion. It was then that a religious book culture arose, from which both Luther and his Catholic opponents grew. This culture became a common ground and arena for religious polemic and was far from eradicated by the Protestant Reformation.[7] Such a perspective is, however, uncommon in existing narratives, and one can easily believe that specifically Catholic ways of book usage and production emerged no sooner than the 1530s, mainly in response to the Protestant Reformation.[8]

Apart from the most obvious continuities stemming from the Bible's central role in Christianity and the use of an established set of liturgical books, at least some of the attitudes towards the printed book that emerged in the religious context of the late fifteenth and early sixteenth centuries have proven remarkably enduring.[9] This is perhaps best illustrated by the censorship regulations usually associated with the Tridentine decrees and the establishment of the Congregation of the Index. This association is understandable, given

---

7   Many important remarks are to be found in various works on late fifteenth-century Christianity. The role of books and the early embracing of printing technology by the religious is stressed, for example, in Bert Roest, Johanneke Uphoff (eds.), *Religious Orders and Religious Identity Formation, ca. 1420–1620. Discourses and Strategies of Observance and Pastoral Engagement* (Leiden: Brill, 2016), here especially the *Introduction*, pp. 1–12, and Koen Goudriaan, *The Vineyard of Saint Francis*, pp. 152–170. Their conclusions owe a lot to the previous work by Goudriaan (see, for example, Goudriaan, 'The Church and the Market' and his 'The Devotio Moderna and the Printing Press (ca. 1475–1540)', *Church History and Religious Culture*, 93.4 (2013), pp. 579–606. See also Andrew Pettegree, 'Catholic Pamphleteering', in A. Bamji, G.H. Janssen (eds.), *The Ashgate Research Companion to the Counter-Reformation* (Aldershot: Ashgate, 2013), pp. 109–125. See also Chapter 6 in this volume.
8   See, for example, the first volume of *Histoire de l'édition française* that mentions Catholicism as an agent of book production and dissemination no sooner than in the second half of the sixteenth century and mostly in the Counter-Reformational context. Earlier developments are discussed in a separate chapter devoted to incunabula in general. See Henri-Jean Martin, Roger Chartier (eds.), *Histoire de l'édition française*, vol. 1, *Le livre conquérant: du moyen âge au milieu du XVIIe siècle* (Paris: Fayard, 1989), pp. 223–227, 404–435.
9   On liturgical books, see Paul F. Grendler, 'The Roman Inquisition and the Venetian Press, 1540–1605', *The Journal of Modern History*, 47.1 (1975), pp. 48–65 and Chapter 5 in this volume. For Bibles, see, for example, Kimberly van Kampen, Paul Saenger (eds.), *The Bible as Book*, vol. 2, *The First Printed Editions* (London: British Library – Oak Knoll Press, 1999); Richard Griffiths (ed.), *The Bible in the Renaissance. Essays on Biblical Commentary and Translation in the Fifteenth and Sixteenth Century* (London: Routledge, 2017); Walsham, 'Unclasping the Book?'.

the Council's impetus for controlling the printed matter, both before and after publication, not only in printing houses but also in bookshops and libraries. Nonetheless, it should not be forgotten that the Tridentine decrees merely brought together, refined, and centralized practices that had already emerged in the German universities in the fifteenth century and were officially recognized by the Lateran Council of 1515, resulting in the creation of local indexes of banned books.[10] Continuities can also be noticed in other activities of the Church that were closely tied with books, such as promoting and regulating children's learning to read and write while introducing them to the fundamentals of Christian faith and doctrine. In Spain, for example, these issues were raised and regulated by numerous councils throughout the fifteenth and early sixteenth centuries, and a few decades later, they found their way into Tridentine decrees.[11] Obviously, continuity as defined by these examples is not static, but involves gradual development and sometimes even change.

Change, as understood here, is defined as a clear shift or modification of existing attitudes and practices, as well as the appearance of new ones. A good example of the first type are prayer books such as Books of Hours and the *Hortulus animae*. These books were extremely popular in the first decades of printing, but later they had to be updated or superseded by new collections.[12] On the one hand, it was the changing nature of devotion that led to alterations in the patterns of printed prayer book production; on the other hand, it was the print that enabled certain forms of devotion, both common (e.g. the Forty Hours Devotion) and individual (e.g. rosary and meditation), to spread and rapidly develop.[13] Among the new genres of religious writings published as books, the catechism stands out as an important tool of pastoral care and cultural translation for both Protestants and Catholics.[14] Postils, or sermon collections for Sundays and feast days throughout the year, should be mentioned as well. As a genre of writing, they were deeply rooted in medieval tradition of

---

10   Nelson H. Minnich, 'The Fifth Lateran Council and Preventive Censorship of Printed Books', *Annali della Scuola Normale Superiore di Pisa. Classe di Lettere e Filosofia*, 2.1 (2010), pp. 67–104.

11   See Chapter 2 in this volume. See also John O'Malley, *Trent. What Happened at the Council* (Cambridge, MA: The Belknap Press of Harvard University Press, 2013), pp. 38–42 on the publishing activities by Francisco de Cisneros, bishop of Toledo.

12   Virginia Reinburg, 'Books of Hours', in Pettegree, Nelles, Conner (eds.), *The Sixteenth-Century French Religious Book*, pp. 68–82; Magdalena Komorowska, 'The Counter-Reforming of Polish Prayer Books', *Quaerendo* 47.3–4 (2017), pp. 328–350.

13   Anna P. Pawłowska, 'Emblematyczność w polskich drukach różańcowych', *Terminus*, 14 (2015) 25, pp. 137–157 and Chapter 15 in this volume.

14   Flüchetr, Wirbser (eds.), *Translating Catechisms, Translating Cultures*; Lee Palmer Wandel, *Reading Catechisms, Teaching Religion* (Leiden: Brill, 2016).

preaching, but developed rapidly throughout the sixteenth century. They were published both in Latin and, more importantly, in vernacular languages, by various printers all over Europe and in various formats. Postils had the potential to reach not only their immediate readers but also those who listened to sermons preached (or simply read aloud) in churches.[15] New lay genres of writing that appeared on the market also had an impact on religious ones, as evidenced by the creation of religious emblem collections with various goals and functions.[16]

The nature of the changes differed from place to place and from culture to culture. Some changes must be viewed as more gradual in the context of better-developed book cultures such as France or Italy, and as more distinct, for example, in the eastern parts of Europe. On relatively small book markets, such as Polish-Lithuanian Commonwealth, the period following Trent saw an unprecedented rise in vernacular printed production, the larger part of which must be associated with reformist endeavors of the Catholic Church at the time and their clash with the Protestant Reformation.[17]

2   Unity and Diversity

Another possible way of looking at the evolution of the Catholic book throughout the early modern era is to identify what is universal, or catholic in the literal sense, and what attests to the diversity of the phenomenon. This duality, which has existed in Christianity since its inception, was certainly reinforced as a result of the Council of Trent.

Unity, or at least the pursuit of it, can be demonstrated by the treatment of liturgical books as printing press products. They had been a part of the international book trade for many decades, but with new uniformity promoted by the council, with one version of the Missal and Breviary for each and every clergyman, printing had an obvious role to play. The implementation of one version of these and other liturgical texts on, which can be said without exaggeration, a global scale would be hard to imagine without the printing press that allowed for mass production of uniform books in a limited, and thus easier to control, number of workshops. It is here that the standardizing

---

15   John M. Frymire, *Primacy of the Postils* (Leiden: Brill, 2009).
16   See Chapters 14 and 15 in this volume.
17   Magdalena Komorowska, 'Printing and Post-Tridentine Catholicism in the Polish-Lithuanian Commonwealth', in Elizabeth Dillenburg, Howard Louthan, Drew Thomas (eds.), *Print Culture at the Crossroads. The Book and Central Europe* (Leiden: Brill, 2021), pp. 327–343.

power of print, highlighted not only in printing histories, but also in textual and communication studies, is most evident, because by standardizing texts print brought about a uniformity of rites unheard of before. Of course, there were exemptions and opposition, demonstrating the awareness of sixteenth-century Catholics of the potential and power of printed media.[18] The question of unity vs. diversity corresponds well with the idea of center and periphery and becomes more important in the latter part of the sixteenth century, with Rome promoted as the center of Catholic religion.

Diversity is most visible in smaller-scale local markets, especially in vernacular publications. These were tailored to the needs of local communities. On the one hand, they promoted a universal Catholic message, while on the other, they contributed to the development of vernacular religious cultures. Books published for missionary needs in the New World and the Far East are an obvious example.[19] Practices of translation and adaptation (indispensable tools of cultural translation and exchange in the era) of religious texts were particularly important in multiethnic, multilingual, and multireligious territories, such as Eastern Europe.[20] On the one hand, printed texts helped to define Catholicism after Luther; on the other hand, they clearly demonstrated similarities between Christian denominations and their uses of printing as a medium.[21]

3 Worship and Commerce

The last striking duality that should be briefly mentioned here is a marriage of textual content that, overall, was designed to serve the spiritual, with a craft driven by market principles. Although motivated ideologically, the attempts

---

18 See Chapter 5 in this volume.
19 For a summary, see M. Antoni J. Üçerler, 'Missionary Printing', in Michael F. Suarez, H.R. Wooudhuysen (eds.), *The Book. A Global History* (Oxford: Oxford University Press, 2013), pp. 107–115; see also Ronnie Po-Chia Hsia, *A Companion to the Early Modern Catholic Global Missions* (Leiden: Brill, 2018); Jose Kalapura, 'India Inscribed. Development of Printing Technology in India, 16–18th Centuries', *Proceedings of the Indian History Congress* 68 (2007), pp. 436–463; Martin Austin Nesvig, '"Heretical Plagues" and Censorship Cordons. Colonial Mexico and the Transatlantic Book Trade', *Church History*, 75.1 (2006), pp. 1–37.
20 Peter Burke, 'Cultures of Translation in Early Modern Europe', in Peter Burke, Ronnie Po-Chia Hsia (eds.), *Cultural Translation in Early Modern Europe* (Cambridge: Cambridge University Press, 2007), pp. 7–38.
21 See Chapters 15 and 16 in this volume. For an analogy in art history, see Maria Crăciun, Grażyna Jurkowlaniec, 'Visual Cultures', in Howard Louthan, Graeme Murdock (eds.), *A Companion to the Reformation in Central Europe* (Leiden: Brill, 2015), pp. 412–450.

of the Catholic Church to control printed production were aimed at a 'significant commercial activity' and required approval from secular authorities.[22] Censorship regulations could ruin printers' careers, but when combined with privileges, they could also make considerable fortunes (Venetian and Roman printers, Officina Plantiniana and the Verdussen family in Antwerp, Maternus Cholinus in Cologne, etc.).[23] In some territories, such as the Polish-Lithuanian Commonwealth, the growing activity of Catholic writers after Trent resulted, among other things, in the dissemination of printing across this vast country.[24]

The tension between commercial aspects of printing and the will to spread religious messages is easily observable in the publishing activities of religious orders, as these communities not only formed a large part of the reading public but were also involved in manuscript book production. However, from the first decades after the invention of printing, wherever monks decided to have their own workshops, a number of problems arose.[25] The Jesuits faced similar problems in the second half of the sixteenth century. To begin with, commercial activity such as printing could raise suspicions of greed, which the order wished to avoid. According to Jesuit regulations, books had to be distributed for free, but it was almost impossible to run a press that could not sell its own production. Furthermore, the process of printing itself took time and disrupted the pace of life in a convent. Various Jesuit residencies devised different strategies to deal with these difficulties, ranging from seeking patronage to renting their presses to secular printers to running the workshops themselves despite difficulties. Nevertheless, for the majority of the era, commissioning of books with secular commercial printers proved to be the best solution for religious orders.[26]

---

22 Minnich, 'The Fifth Lateran Council', p. 104.
23 Kristof Selleslach, 'How to Transfer the Officina Plantiniana to the Next Generation. The Instructions of Balthasar Moretus II to His Future Heirs (1659–1673)', *The Golden Compasses*, 98.2 (2020), pp. 205–297; Stijn van Rossem, 'The Bookshop of the Counter-Reformation Revisited. The Verdussen Company and the Trade in Catholic Publications, Antwerp, 1585–1648', *Quaerendo*, 38.4 (2008), pp. 306–321; Stijn van Rossem, *The Verdussens and the International Trade in Catholic Books (Antwerp, Seventeenth Century)*, in Álvarez (ed.), *Books in the Catholic World during the Early Modern Period*, pp. 1–50; Grendler, 'The Roman Inquisition and the Venetian Press, 1540–1605'.
24 Komorowska, 'Printing and Post-Tridentine Catholicism'.
25 Falk Eisermann, *A Golden Age? Monastic Printing Houses in the Fifteenth Century* (Leiden: Brill, 2013), pp. 35–67; Goudriaan, 'The Vineyard of St Francis', pp. 152–171.
26 See Lorenzo Mancini, 'La Politica Tipografica Della Compagnia Di Gesù. Una Rete Transnazionale Di Committenza e Distribuzione?', *Nuovi Annali Della Scuola Speciale per Archivisti e Bibliotecari*, 33 (2019), pp. 105–130; Jerzy Kochanowicz, *Początki piśmiennictwa jezuickiego w Polsce. Studium z historii kultury* (Wrocław: Wydawnictwo Naukowe

The share of Catholic books in commercial printed production in large parts of Europe is unquestionable. However, the precise nature of the relationship, in addition to economy and legal regulations, which are often entangled with politics, remains largely unknown.

4   Agents, Networks, and Responses

On the general background sketched above, various narrower paths and threads, defined mostly by book historical methodologies, can be followed. These allow for a different kind of insight, focusing on the medium, its production, and its role in the society more than on the message. It does not mean that the latter is forgotten; rather, when framed in a broader context, it takes on an additional dimension. With this volume, we aim to provide such a dimension to the messages conveyed by Catholic writers and received by Catholic readers in the early modern period.

The volume as a whole highlights three aspects of the relationship between Catholicism and printed media: the question of agency in the production and dissemination of Catholic texts and books, the role of networks in these processes, and the response on the part of readers and users. In terms of agency, specific chapters demonstrate different types of individuals and institutions involved, from the papal curia and the pope himself to dioceses and bishops, religious orders, and lay individuals. The role of networks can be seen on various levels: from the network of the church's institutions and officials to transnational networks of individuals united by a common goal of publishing and disseminating particular books. Reader and user responses are traced mostly through libraries and translation and adaptation processes, which are viewed as a link in the chain of textual production and dissemination.

The chapters in Part 1, which focus on the role of the Catholic hierarchy and transnational Catholic networks in the publication and circulation of books, directly address the problem of agency. The involvement of the institutional Church in publishing endeavors is demonstrated on two levels: the papal curia and a particular diocese, here represented by Valladolid. In Chapter 2, Paolo Sachet shows the process that led to the establishment of the Typographia Vaticana, an official papal printing house. In Chapter 3, Benito Rial Costas demonstrates how Catholic hierarchy could be involved in the creation of primers. The contrast is striking and illustrates the diversity of Catholic books:

Dolnośląskiej Szkoły Wyższej, 2012); special issue of *Journal of Jesuit Studies*, 10 (2023) devoted entirely to the topic of the Jesuits and print.

whereas the popes were primarily interested in supporting the production of costly volumes in non-European scripts or chant books (the publishing process included designing and cutting new typefaces), the chapter of Valladolid aimed at providing inexpensive reading matter to the local community. Chapter 4 shows the power of a transnational Catholic network in the context of book production and dissemination. Chelsea Reutcke provides a multifaceted analysis of this phenomenon based on the action of the Jesuits to popularize Nicholas Sander's work throughout Europe. Chapters from other parts of the book complete this picture with more detail. Histories of particular texts or the developments of new genres (especially in Parts 2 and 4) indicate the characteristics of local literary cultures and bring to light individuals (mainly priests and friars, but also secular authors and printers) who were responsible for the creation and circulation of Catholic religious publications such as polemics, prayer books, hagiographies, and emblem collections.

Part 2 not only addresses the question of early Catholic reactions to the Protestant Reformation, but also demonstrates the semiofficial, and to a large extent, the local character of this response. In Chapter 6, David Oldenhof, by analyzing early anti-Protestant polemical texts published in the Netherlands, tells the story of their authors and readers, not only clerics but also lay people keenly interested in doctrinal questions. In Chapter 7, Maciej Ptaszyński reflects on how the Diet of Worms shaped early response to the Lutheran Reformation in Poland, demonstrating the role of various media and people in the process: from early Protestant preachers who prepared the ground for the polemic by criticizing the clergy, through the king's ban on publication and dissemination of Luther's books, to the publication of the first anti-Lutheran texts by Polish Catholic hierarchy and their role.

Chapters 8 and 9 introduce convent libraries to the equation. Peter Sjökvist focuses on how books written by Protestant authors were made useful in Jesuit libraries in the Polish-Lithuanian Commonwealth. Jesuits, who were rightfully regarded as one of the major forces of the Catholic Reformation, could be surprisingly open when it came to using prohibited books in their own libraries. Readers of banned books stored in the library, on the one hand, used scissors and black ink to tangibly and visibly distance themselves from the authors' confessional views, but on the other hand they were vitally interested in any useful knowledge they could find in the texts. Another view of a Catholic library is offered by Kaspar Kolk, who focused on a Franciscan convent library in Rakvere (Wesenberg). The history of library acquisitions throughout the sixteenth century illustrates the gradual shift from pre-Reformation Catholicism, focused on preaching the Gospel and fostering devotion, to post-Tridentine Catholicism characterized, among other things, by its fiercely anti-Protestant stand. While in Sjökvist's text the college library is depicted as a place where confessional divisions can be overcome in the pursuit of practical knowledge, in Kolk's chapter it becomes a Catholic outpost in the predominantly Protestant region.

The central theme of Part 3 is insight into libraries. In Chapter 10, Giovanna Granata discusses the preliminary findings of the Ricerca sull'Inchiesta della Congregazione dell'Indice (RICI) project. The analysis of a fragment of the massive database illustrates the project's potential for generating and answering questions about the circulation of religious books in religious orders in sixteenth-century Italy. Thanks to the already gathered data, it is possible to not only analyze individual collections but also identify general patterns by which these collections were created. While Granata provides a breath-taking overall perspective, Lucrezia Signorello offers a detailed case study of one particular collection – the library of the Augustinian convent in Rome (Chapter 11), and Jindřich Kolda discusses the models of book acquisitions in male and female Benedictine convents in Bohemia (Chapter 12).

The chapters in Part 4 mainly focus on the creation and translation of popular Catholic texts, how these texts were written or compiled, and how they functioned in regions where different denominations met within the framework of a relatively small local culture. Mirosława Hanusiewicz-Lavallee and Robert Maryks narrate the Polish translation of a popular Jesuit Catechism, Diego de Ledesma's *Doctrina christiana* (Chapter 13). Gábor Förköli demonstrates the cross-confessional potential of some religious books and the beginnings of the concept of intellectual property in the context of interdenominational disputes in Hungary (Chapter 14).

The final part of the volume focuses on the interplay between words and images, which are crucial for many religious publications of the late-sixteenth and seventeenth centuries. Claire Konieczny presents the anti-Protestant use of image through the example of Richard Verstegan's *Theatrum crudelitatum* (Chapter 15). Alicja Bielak defines and analyzes the predominantly Catholic type of emblem books conceived as guides for individual meditation (Chapter 16). In the final chapter, Justyna Kiliańczyk-Zięba shows how an emblematic composition used on a book cover could become an individual expression of Catholic faith.

Geographically, the chapters cover a wide range of European territories, from the South to the North and from the West to the East. The point of gravity is shifted to the East, focusing on the region where Catholicism (Roman, and since 1596, also Greek or Uniate) coexisted with other Christian denominations (Protestant and Orthodox) as well as religions (Judaism and to a smaller extent also Islam). This part of Europe is particularly interesting due to religious tolerance and the aforementioned diversity in ethnicity and language.

This complexity offers a chance to observe how both boundaries and common grounds for religions, cultures, and languages were created and maintained as well as crossed and destroyed. For Catholicism, there is a distillation of the most important components and characteristics, showing the continuities and universalities, change, and diversity. It pertains to Catholic book production as well.

Despite the undeniable richness of the early modern Catholic book culture, it is still the affinity between the printing press and Protestantism that has become a powerful commonplace of early modern studies. This concept entered historiography and literary history through Protestants themselves relatively early on, in the late sixteenth century, becoming established over time and gaining a permanent place in scholarly discourse.[27] The Protestant Reformation has been considered as a media event that revealed the true potential behind print as a means of communication and as such has dominated narratives in histories of printing and religious controversy in early modern Europe.[28] So much so that most scholars who address Catholics' use of the printing press begin with a reference to these Protestant-centered narratives and, more or less explicitly, attempt to show the other side of the coin rather than depict a distinct phenomenon worthy of attention on its own.[29] The present volume will serve its purpose if it consolidates the view of early modern Catholic book culture as an autonomous field of investigation and encourages further research and discussion.

Acknowledgement

The research for this chapter has been supported by a grant from the Priority Research Area Heritage under the Strategic Programme Excellence Initiative at Jagiellonian University.

---

27   See Gilmont, Maag (eds.), *The Reformation and the Book*, pp. 1–2; Pettegree, 'Catholic Pamphleteering', p. 109; Walsham, 'Unclasping the Book?', pp. 142–143.
28   See for example Johannes Burkhardt, *Das Reformationsjahrhundert. Deutsche Geschichte zwischen Medienrevolution und Institutionenbildung 1517–1617* (Stuttgart: Kohlhammer Verlag, 2002), who follows the course set by many previous publications; Pettegree, 'Catholic Pamphleteering', pp. 109–111.
29   The power of the narrative is confirmed by the fact that the introductory essays to the most recent volumes devoted to early modern Catholic books and prints are written along these lines; see Álvarez (ed.), *Books in the Catholic World*; Adam etc. (eds.), *Books and Prints at the Heart of the Catholic Reformation*.

PART 1

Institutions and Networks

∴

CHAPTER 2

Towards the Typographia Vaticana

Gregory XIII's Promotion of Printing

Paolo Sachet

In the often-neglected history of the use of printing by the sixteenth-century Catholic hierarchy, Rome offers a unique perspective. Long before the Typographia Vaticana was established in 1587, the papacy tried to set up an official press in the Eternal City. Cardinal Marcello Cervini made some innovative attempts in the early 1540s, and in 1561 Pius IV appointed Paolo Manuzio as director of a papal press which was soon strangled by bureaucratic and financial problems.[1] This paper focuses on the pontificate of Gregory XIII (1572–1585), a period of crucial reconfiguration for the Church's effort to deploy the Roman publishing system for its own purposes. On the one hand, highly competitive printshops presented themselves as official enterprises and a few ambitious plans to harness printing were submitted to the curia; on the other, a papal press was secretly functioning. By analysing these initiatives, this paper will shed light on the continuities with Cervini's and Manuzio's undertakings and the novelties that helped lay the groundwork for the establishment of the Vatican Press.

1 A Pope with Many Achievements

Before delving into Gregory XIII's innovative use of printing, some background information on his papacy should be provided. It took less than twenty-four hours to elect the curial jurist Ugo Boncompagni as Pope Gregory XIII at the conclave in May 1572. As the internal battle against Italian heterodoxy had

---

1 See Paolo Sachet, *Publishing for the Popes. The Roman Curia and the Use of Printing (1527–1555)* (Leiden: Brill, 2020) and Francesco Barberi, *Paolo Manuzio e la Stamperia del Popolo Romano (1562–1570). Con documenti inediti* (Rome: Cuggiani, 1942). The latter study can be integrated with a few later essays discussed in Paolo Sachet, 'Il contratto tra Paolo Manuzio e la Camera Apostolica (2 maggio 1561). La creazione della prima stamperia vaticana privilegiata', *La Bibliofilía*, 114.2 (2013), pp. 245–261, and his '*In aedibus Populi Romani apud Paulum Manutium*. La prima tipografia papale tra limiti attuativi e conflitti istituzionali', *Rivista Storica Italiana*, 132.1 (2020), pp. 181–205.

largely been won under his predecessor, Gregory was able to set his sights on the international scene.[2] During his papacy, there was an active evangelisation policy in the Spanish New World, Africa (Ethiopia) and east of the Balkans, including Russia and as far as China, Japan and the Philippines, as well as a concerted attempt to return large swathes of Christendom to Catholicism, from Scotland to the southern regions of the Holy Roman Empire. These elaborate, but often ineffective, diplomatic efforts were accompanied by a failed attempt to maintain Pius V's anti-Turkish alliance following the Christian victory at Lepanto in 1571. The new pope also tried to communicate with the Eastern churches and the Patriarch of Constantinople in the hope of reuniting them with Rome and persuading them to join the Holy See in its fight against the Ottomans.[3]

Gregory XIII continued the process of centralisation of the curial bureaucracy and the emancipation of the pope from the constraints of the College of Cardinals, which had begun under his predecessors.[4] This body had been gradually losing the influence it had through the consistory, while the personal power of curial cardinals was being diminished by assigning them demanding administrative duties. Both permanent and temporary cardinal congregations were established to deal with urgent businesses or long-term goals, the most famous of which was the tribunal of the Roman Inquisition, established in 1542. With regard to papal policy on printed books, in 1572 Gregory formally approved the Congregation of the Index set up by Pius V a year earlier. For

---

2   As a paradigmatic example of the inquistorial activity in the central decades of Cinquecento, see Massimo Firpo and Dario Marcatto (eds.), *Il processo inquisitoriale del cardinal Giovanni Morone. Nuova edizione critica* (3 vols., Rome: Libreria Editrice Vaticana, 2011–2015).

3   The most updated biography is Agostino Borromeo, 'Gregorio XIII', in *Enciclopedia dei papi*, III (Rome: Istituto dell'Enciclopedia italiana, 2000), pp. 180–202, with earlier bibliography, also available online at https://www.treccani.it/enciclopedia/gregorio-xiii_%28Enciclopedia-dei -Papi%29/. More recent investigations have privileged the pope's patronage, including Vernon Hyde Minor, Brian Anthony Curran (eds.), *Art and Science in the Rome of Gregory XIII Boncompagni (1572–1585)*, cluster of *Memoirs of the American Academy in Rome*, 54 (2009), pp. 1–118; Claudia Cieri Via etc. (eds.), *Unità e frammenti di modernità. Arte e scienza nella Roma di Gregorio XIII Boncompagni, 1572–1585* (Pisa: Serra, 2013); Yvan Loskoutoff, *Une arte de la Réforme catholique*, II: *La symbolique du pape Grégoire XIII (1572–1585) et des Bomcompagni* (Paris: Honoré Champion, 2018); Valentina Balzarotti, Bianca Hermanin (eds.), *Gregorio XIII Boncompagni. Arte dei moderni e immagini venerabili nei cantieri della nuova* Ecclesia (Rome: Efesto, 2020).

4   Paolo Prodi, *Il sovrano pontefice: un corpo e due anime. La monarchia papale nella prima età moderna* (Bologna: il Mulino, 2006, new edition), together with Giampiero Brunelli, *Il Sacro Consiglio di Paolo IV* (Rome: Viella, 2011) and Elena Bonora, *Roma 1564. La congiura contro il papa* (Rome and Bari: Laterza, 2011). See also the detailed overview provided by Miles Pattenden, 'The College of Cardinals', in Mary Hollingsworth etc. (eds.), *A Companion to the Early Modern Cardinal* (Leiden: Brill, 2020), pp. 23–39.

over twelve years, this committee, led by Cardinal Guglielmo Sirleto, made strenuous efforts to reform the list of prohibited books and carry out expurgations intended to make several publications acceptable to Catholic readership. Despite its intense activity, the committee failed to produce a definitive result because a proposal for a new index submitted in 1584 did not receive papal approval. Nevertheless, the cardinals frequently gave informal instructions to local inquisitors, encouraging them to take a firmer stance than the relatively mild Tridentine Index permitted. With Sirleto at the helm, the Congregation of the Index, along with the Holy Office, re-embraced many stern ideas championed by Paul IV and Pius V: preventing the circulation of heretical publications while simultaneously expanding the list of books subject to prohibition, castigating literary texts, emending Catholic authors and limiting access to the Bible, biblical commentaries and Scripture-based popular works.[5]

During Gregory XIII's pontificate, Counter-Reformation attitudes became increasingly entrenched in Roman culture.[6] Between 1572 and 1585, in line with the pope's programme of active proselytising, Rome advanced its claims to be the international centre of the Christian religion. Four national colleges, for Hungarian, English, Greek and Maronite clergy, were established in the city between 1577 and 1584. In 1577, the pope also promoted the College of the Neophytes, an institution for recently converted Jews and Muslims. Plans for Armenian, Polish and Serbian institutes were drawn up but not put into action.[7] The new colleges and institutes relied on the Jesuit Collegio Romano for their academic courses, but the Collegio was in an unstable economic

---

5   See Paolo Simoncelli, 'Documenti interni alla Congregazione dell'Indice (1571–1590). Logica e ideologia dell'intervento censorio', *Annuario dell'Istituto Storico Italiano per l'età moderna e contemporanea*, 35–36 (1983–1984), pp. 189–215, at pp. 204, 211–215; Gigliola Fragnito, *La Bibbia al rogo. La censura ecclesiastica e i volgarizzamenti della Scrittura (1471–1605)* (Bologna: il Mulino, 1997), pp. 111–142; eadem, 'Guglielmo Sirleto prefetto della Congregazione dell'Indice (1571–1585)', in Benedetto Clausi and Santo Lucà (eds.), *Il 'sapientissimo calabro'. Guglielmo Sirleto nel V centenario della nascita (1514–2014): problemi, ricerche, prospettive* (Rome: Università degli Studi di Roma Tor Vergata, 2018), pp. 45–61; and, more broadly, her *Rinascimento perduto. La letteratura italiana sotto gli occhi dei censori (secoli XV–XVII)* (Bologna: il Mulino, 2019) alongside Amedeo Quondam, *Una guerra perduta. Il libro letterario del Rinascimento e la censura della Chiesa* (Rome: Bulzoni, 2022).
6   Borromeo, 'Gregorio XIII', pp. 194–197.
7   See Giovanni Pizzorusso, 'Le lingue a Roma. Studio e pratica nei collegi missionari nella prima età moderna', *Rivista Storica Italiana*, 132.1 (2020), pp. 248–271; Aurélien Girard, 'Le Collège maronite de Rome et les langues au tournant des XVIe et XVIIe siècles: éducation des chrétiens orientaux, science orientaliste et apologétique catholique', ibid., pp. 272–299. To appreciate further Gregory XIII's innovative approach, see Antal Molnár, Giovanni Pizzorusso and Matteo Sanfilippo (eds.), *Chiese e* nationes *a Roma. Dalla Scandinavia ai Balcani (secoli XV–XVIII)* (Rome: Viella, 2017) as well as Matthew Coneys Wainwright, Emily Michelson (eds.), *A Companion to Religious Minorities in Early Modern Rome* (Leiden: Brill, 2021).

situation, due to unfulfilled promises of funding from earlier popes. To address this issue, Gregory XIII provided it with a large endowment, for which he was hailed as its true founder.[8] Indeed, the whole Society of Jesus flourished under this pope because of the similar approaches taken towards evangelisation on a global scale and communication strategies, most notably the use of moveable type.

The pope also backed the recently formed Oratory of St Filippo Neri, a religious institute deeply involved in cultural and educational matters. In 1575, the Oratorians, as they were popularly known, were confirmed as a Catholic congregation and were given the Church of Santa Maria in Vallicella. It was here that in 1592 they were to establish a press to continue the publication of a Counter-Reformation landmark: the *Annales ecclesiastici* by Cesare Baronio, who would succeed Neri as the superior of the Oratorians in 1593.[9]

Gregory's renewed efforts to harness printing for the sake of the papacy are a good fit for this line of action. His first, nearly contemporary biographer proudly described how the pope 'established in Rome a press for publishing books of Christian doctrine in every language' to be widely disseminated.[10] And yet, his direct involvement with moveable type has largely been overlooked, alongside a few other projects that theoretically and practically set the stage for the establishment of the Vatican Press by Sixtus V.

---

8   Ricardo García Villoslada, *Storia del Collegio Romano dal suo inizio (1551) alla soppressione della Compagnia di Gesù (1773)* (Rome: Pontificia Università Gregoriana, 1954), pp. 133–154. In recognition of Gregory XIII's crucial support, the Collegio Romano later took the name 'Pontificia Universitas Gregoriana'.

9   On this printing enterprise, which lasted less than four years, see Giuseppe Finocchiaro, *Cesare Baronio e la Tipografia dell'Oratorio. Impresa e ideologia* (Florence: Olschki, 2005).

10 Marcantonio Ciappi, *Compendio delle heroiche et gloriose attioni, et santa vita di papa Greg. XIII* (Rome: Giovanni Martinelli, 1591), USTC 822022, p. 25: 'Eresse in Roma la stampa di tutte le lingue per fare stampare la dottrina christiana et altre compositioni de' santi Padri, per mandarne in tutte le parti et a tutte le nationi del mondo, per augumento et grandezza della nostra vera sacrosanta fede catolica. Ordinò alli custodi della Biblioteca Vaticana che usassero ogni diligenza di cercare per le librarie et stamparie di Roma libri rari d'ogni facultà per ampliatione di detta biblioteca a utilità publica.' See also similar notes by Cardinal Tolomeo Gallio, Gregory's powerful secretary, in Alberto Tinto, 'Per una storia della tipografia orientale a Roma nell'età della Controriforma', *Accademie e biblioteche d'Italia*, 41 (1973), pp. 280–303, at p. 294, n. 16 and Giampietro Maffei, *Degli annali di papa Gregorio XIII pontefice massimo*, ed. by Charles Cocquelines, (2 vols., Rome: Mainardi, 1742), I, pp. VI, 249, 322–325, 372–373; II, pp. 65–66, 76–77, 141–142, 147, 149, 159–160, 184, 477.

2 The *Stampatore Camerale* and the Stamperia del Popolo Romano

In the first year of his reign, Gregory XIII handled the administrative side of printing, focusing on the dissemination of numerous papal pronouncements with both local and global impact. The heirs of Antonio Blado (his widow Paola and their sons) were granted a monopoly over these ephemeral publications, which, in reality, the family had been exercising for almost four decades through the initially ambiguous title of *stampatore camerale*.[11]

The pope also tried to address the issues related to publishing proper books. For this reason, Pius IV had invited Paolo Manuzio, one of the most renowned humanist printers of the time, to Rome in 1561, and entrusted him with a newly established official press. Everything had been planned for the enterprise to command the maximum credibility. However, significant financial and organisational challenges promptly arose, and they worsened once Manuzio made the decision to quit in 1570. At first, Gregory thought of removing the press, by then known as the Stamperia del Popolo Romano, from the ineffective control of the Roman Commune, which was reluctantly bearing the running costs on behalf of the curia. The poor quality of the publications produced by the Stamperia under the management of Manuzio's unworthy successor, Fabrizio Galletti, was regarded as an embarrassment to the church. In 1573, however, the officers of the Commune persuaded the pope to confirm the Stamperia's privilege over the edition of the revised Breviary and to relaunch the press as a partnership of booksellers, led by Domenico Basa, a highly skilled printer and publisher.[12] In the same year, Paolo Manuzio, the former director of the Stamperia who had returned to Rome from Venice, was approached about establishing a new papal publishing house that would issue books expurgated by the Congregation of the Index. The plan, however, fell thorough due to the slow pace of the expurgation process, as well as Paolo's usual indecisiveness

---

11 Rome, Archivio di Stato, *Bandi*, vol. 5, no. 76. A previous bull by Pius V in April 1567 confirmed the salary to the heirs of Antonio Blado, dead two months earlier: Valentino Romani, 'Tipografie papali. La Tipografia Vaticana', in Massimo Ceresa (ed.), *Storia della Biblioteca Apostolica: II: La Biblioteca Vaticana tra riforma cattolica, crescita delle collezioni e nuovo edificio (1535–1590)* (Vatican City: Biblioteca Apostolica Vaticana, 2012), pp. 261–279, at p. 265. For the prolonged ratification of the office of *stampatore camerale*, see Sachet, *Publishing for the Popes*, pp. 26–39.

12 Anna Maria Giorgetti Vichi, *Annali della Stamperia del Popolo Romano (1570–1598)* (Rome: Istituto di studi romani, 1959), pp. 15–30. Significantly, Basa's partners (Giorgio Ferrari, Girolamo Franzini, Sebastiano De Franceschi, Antonio Lanza, as well as, initially, Brianza Brianzi and Marco Amadori) were all foreign dealers who had recently moved to Rome.

and poor state of health.[13] In any case, the idea of establishing a press to parallel the activity of the Congregation of the Index was premature and unrealistic. Although some major works were examined and corrected in the following decades, the only index of expurgated books ever issued did not appear until 1607, under the authority of the Master of the Sacred Palace, and was quickly withdrawn in response to criticism.[14]

The situation became more complicated after Manuzio's death in 1574. Printers and booksellers based in Rome, joined together in a confraternity since 1566, realised how much money could be made from the privileges over the church's institutional publications, as well as from the forthcoming expurgated editions. The Stamperia's decline encouraged them to compete for this promising (and seemingly durable) share of the market. This resulted in the fragmentation of the papacy's printing efforts in Rome; however, in long term, it stimulated the rise of new institutional presses and a division of labour and specialisation among the Roman publishing houses linked to the papal court.

The Stamperia soon proved to be inadequate for the needs of the church under Gregory XIII, despite the change in management from Galletti to the partnership led by Basa. Until 1585, amid legal squabbles and a considerable waste of money, it struggled to publish a new edition of the *Corpus Iuris Canonici* sponsored by the pope, some revised devotional books, a handful of juridical and theological pamphlets and a few inquisitorial publications

13 Paolo illustrated the proposal to his son Aldo in a letter dated on 17 October 1573 and published in Paolo Manuzio, *Lettere ... copiate sugli autografi esistenti nella Biblioteca Ambrosiana*, ed. by Antoine-Augustin Renouard (Paris: J. Renouard, 1834), p. 302: 'Qui vorrebbono a tutti i modi metter una stampa di cose di humanità, e di quei libri, che l'Indice prohibisce, che tutta via si purgano. Me ne ha dato più battaglie la Congregatione di quattro Cardinali [i.e., at the time, Guglielmo Sirleto, Arcangelo de' Bianchi, Vincenzo Giustiniani and Felice Peretti, later elected pope as Sixtus V] che sono deputati con altri Teologi alla purgatione de sudetti libri. E vorrebono pur me, non con la condicione, che già haveva, ma per sopraintendente, senza altra cura. E dicono che lo fanno per l'auttorità del nome mio. Ho negato e nego per diversi aspetti: e batto su questo chiodo, che mi lascino venir a Venetia a correger l'opere mie, come certamente giudico esser necessario. Morone quasi acconsente, Sirletti mi è contrario, con Alciati, et altri, temendo ch'io non torni, e pur glielo prometto. Ma questo è in mano di Dio. Perché son vecchio, e malsano, e vorrei hormai un stato quieto, che nissun mi commandasse.'

14 Vittorio Frajese, *Nascita dell'Indice. La censura ecclesiastica dal Rinascimento alla Controriforma* (Brescia: Morcelliana, 2008), pp. 102–107, 205–208, and Gigliola Fragnito, '"In questo vasto mare de libri prohibiti et sospesi tra tanti scogli di varietà et controversie". La censura ecclesiastica tra la fine del Cinquecento e i primi del Seicento', in Cristina Stango (ed.), *Censura ecclesiastica e cultura politica in Italia tra Cinquecento e Seicento. VI Giornata Luigi Firpo: atti del convegno, 5 marzo 1999* (Florence: Olschki, 2001), pp. 1–35, reprinted in Gigliola Fragnito, *Cinquecento italiano. Religione, cultura e potere dal Rinascimento alla Controriforma*, ed. by Elena Bonora, Miguel Gotor (Bologna: il Mulino, 2011), pp. 325–364, esp. pp. 345–364.

directly related to the Holy Office. The critical edition of St Jerome's collected works, begun under Manuzio in 1565, was also completed.[15]

Blado's heirs were the first to capitalise on the Stamperia's problems. Stepping out of their zone of competence (i.e., administrative publications), they issued some large books on behalf of the curia, including the supplementary instruction about the *Corpus Iuris*; the new Gregorian calendar; a pioneering collection of papal letters from the time of Gregory VII onwards; and a number of patristic editions, such as the works by Anastasius of Sinai, John Chrysostom, Pachomius the Great and Anselm of Canterbury.[16]

3 Four Ambitious Proposals

To address such fragmented editorial activity, four detailed projects for the establishment of papal presses were presented to Gregory XIII shortly after Manuzio's demise. This suggests a renewed interest on the part of the papacy in finding a new solution to the church's institutional printing needs, as its collaboration with the Stamperia del Popolo Romano became increasingly problematic. It is worthwhile to briefly discuss all projects.

Around 1574, the curia received a proposal to set up a centralised Catholic press in Rome dedicated to printing in Cyrillic for the Serbian and partly Croatian churches that were now under the Ottoman Empire. The proposal came from the Serbian printer and nobleman Giovanni Vincenzo Vuković (Italianised as della Vecchia), whose father, Božidar (or Dionigi), was a pioneer in Serbian printing and the founder of the first Serbian press in Venice in 1519. Vincenzo inherited the family firm and ran it until 1561.[17] For over a half-century, father and son had been the main suppliers of liturgical books to the Serbian Orthodox church. In his proposal, Vuković emphasised the importance of establishing a Serbian college in Rome, cleverly connecting the

---

15 See the catalogue in Giorgetti Vichi, *Annali della Stamperia*, esp. pp. 72–96.
16 USTC 805081, 820846, 805471, 809205, 836498, 836505, 845978.
17 Franz Leschinkohl, 'Venedig, das Druckzentrum serbischer Bücher im Mittelalter', *Gutenberg-Jahrbuch*, 31 (1957), pp. 116–121; Corrado Marciani, 'I Vuković tipografi-librai slavi a Venezia nel XVI', *Economia e storia*, 19 (1972), pp. 342–362; *Tre alfabeti per gli slavi: catalogo della mostra allestita nella Biblioteca Vaticana per l'undicesimo centenario della morte di san Metodio* (Vatican City: Biblioteca Apostolica Vaticana, 1985), pp. 71–74. Without any legal justification, Vincenzo claimed the title of the extinguished Serbian Despotate. Recent scholarship, however, has suggested that he and his father were not even Serbian and merely pretended to hold this nationality for commercial motives; they were probably either Italian or Greek. See the Serbo-Croatian literature cited by Krassimir Stantchev, 'Due cinquecentine slave di area croata ritrovate nella Biblioteca Civica di Vicenza', *Slovo*, 58 (2008), pp. 1–19, at p. 15, n. 39.

need for Serbian books not only to the interminable war against the Turks, but also to the attempts by Protestant propaganda to penetrate into this area.[18] Nevertheless, Gregory XIII was sceptical that the Eternal City was the best place for such an enterprise. Vuković then proposed Ancona, the harbour of the Papal States on the Adriatic Sea and historically well-connected to Dalmatia. Vuković offered to supply the printing machinery, woodcuts and fonts, while Francesco Zanetti, who belonged to a family of Greek printers in Venice and had recently moved to Rome, was mentioned as a suitable printer. It is unknown why the proposal was rejected yet again, though an anonymous curial advisor attacked the project on the grounds that it was not economically viable.[19]

In the mid-1570s, Giovanni Carga and Erennio Cervini each submitted plans for the exploitation of printing in support of the papacy's cultural policy. Rather than a papal press, however, they envisaged the involvement of the entire Roman printing system in the publication of the church's revised texts of sacred and biblical literature, in accordance with the fourth decree of the Council of Trent.[20] Very little is known about the background to these pro-

18 For Protestant printing in the Serbo-Croatian world, see: Hermann Ehmer, 'Primus Truber, Hans Ungnad von Sonnegg und die Uracher Druckerei 1560–1564', in Lorenz Sönke etc. (eds.), *Primus Truber, 1508–1586. Der slowenische Reformator und Württemberg* (Stuttgart: Kohlhammer, 2011), pp. 201–216; Silvano Cavazza, 'Libri luterani verso il Friuli: Vergerio, Trubar, Flacio', in Giuliana Ancona, Dario Visintin (eds.), *Venezia e il Friuli. La fede e la repressione del dissenso: omaggio ad Andrea Del Col* (Montereale Valcellina: Circolo culturale Menocchio, 2013), pp. 31–55; and Luca Ilić, Marija Wakounig, 'The Dream of a Border-Crossing Bible. A Study of Ungnad, Trubar, Vergerio, Konzul, and Their Co-Workers', in Elizabeth Dillenburg etc. (eds.), *Print Culture at the Crossroads. The Book and Central Europe* (Leiden: Brill, 2021), pp. 288–306.

19 Tinto, 'Per una storia', pp. 287–288. Despite being unnecessarily cautious in identifying the promoter of the plan as Vincenzo Vuković (ibid., p. 300, n. 79) and therefore overlooking the importance of his role in the project, Tinto provides a clear account of the proposal, relying on documents mostly drawn from the papers of Guglielmo Sirleto, the cardinal protector of the Serbian nation, in the Vatican Apostolic Library (henceforth BAV) and Archive (henceforth AAV). For the wider context, see *Tre alfabeti*, pp. 99–124 and Laura Lalli, 'La fortuna dei caratteri glagolitici e cirillici sotto l'egida dei papi, tra Cinque e Seicento', in Alessandro Scarsella (ed.), *Glagolitsa. Studi slavistici di storia del libro in Italia* (Milan: Biblion, 2021), pp. 97–112.

20 An indication of the importance of Carga's proposal is that at least four contemporary copies survive: MSS Vatican City, BAV, Vat. lat. 3944 and 6792 as well as AAV, *Misc.*, *Arm. XI*, vol. 93; *Congr. Concilio, Positiones*, vols. 1–2. Paul Maria Baumgarten, *Die Vulgata Sixtina von 1590 und ihre Einführungsbulle. Aktenstücke und Untersuchungen* (Münster: Aschendorff, 1911), pp. 141–150, gives a diplomatic transcription, which should be consulted together with the additional and insightful comments in Paul F. Grendler, *The Roman Inquisition and the Venetian Press, 1540–1605* (Princeton: Princeton University Press, 1977), pp. 234–236 (also dwelling on a kindred project put forward to Sixtus V by the Modena physician Antonio Castelvetro) and David L. d'Avray and Julia Walworth, 'The Council of Trent

posals, and it is also unknown whether (and, if so, how) the pope responded to them. Both plans allude to an ongoing debate in the higher echelons of the curia, which would necessitate extensive archival research to verify and elucidate. Nevertheless, it is worth mentioning that both Carga and Cervini were prominent figures in the Roman hierarchy. Carga had been involved in papal administration, with ever-increasing responsibilities, since the pontificate of Paul IV and had assisted the head of Gregory XIII's secretariat. The latter experience inspired him to draft yet another innovative proposal for the archival preservation of curial papers. Carga was also an accomplished Latin poet.[21] Erennio Cervini, the nephew of Cardinal Cervini (pope Marcellus II) and a pupil of Sirleto, was a respected papal administration consultant who worked with the Congregation of the Index. It was not by chance that his proposal was addressed to Cardinal Sirleto.[22]

The fourth plan concerning the Catholic Church's policy towards the use of printing, specifically in Greek, is related to the preparatory works for the official publication of the Greek acts of the Council of Florence of 1439 and for the establishment of a Greek papal college in the 1570s. The Jesuit Giovanni Domenico Traiani and the learned bishop of Anagni, Gaspare Viviani, proposed the original idea for a Greek papal press, including a prospective editorial programme.[23] This plan may have come close to being put into action by

---

and Print Culture. Documents in the Archive of the *Congregatio Concilii*', *Zeitschrift für Kirchengeschichte*, 121 (2010), pp. 189–204. The latter was revised in Julia Walworth, 'The *Congregatio Concilii* and a Proposal for a Vatican Press in the 1570s', in Cristina Dondi etc. (eds.), *La stampa romana nella città dei papi e in Europa* (Vatican City: Biblioteca Apostolica Vaticana, 2016), pp. 235–246. Erennio Cervini's proposal is preserved in MS Vatican City, BAV, Vat. lat. 6207, ff. 215r–217v and was discussed in Simoncelli, 'Documenti interni', pp. 205–207.

21 Theodor von Sickel, 'Römische Berichte: I', *Sitzungsberichte der philosophisch-historischen Classe der Kaiserlichen Akademie der Wissenschaften*, 133 (1896), pp. 1–141, at pp. 104–108, is still fundamental for our knowledge of Carga's biography; see also M. Gabriella Cruciani Troncarelli, 'Carga, Giovanni', in *Dizionario biografico degli italiani*, XX (Rome: Istituto dell'Enciclopedia italiana, 1977), pp. 86–88.

22 Despite his prominence at the time, there is no biography of Erennio Cervini, whose name is barely mentioned even in the studies on his illustrious relatives, not only Marcellus II but also Robert Bellarmine. As the nephew of a pope, he was highly regarded in the Roman curia, especially by churchmen associated with the Cervini family: e.g., Girolamo Seripando wrote to Sirleto in November 1562 (MS Vatican City, BAV, Vat. lat. 6189 (1), f. 136r): 'Mi piace ch'el signor Herennio sia ritornato in Roma, perché con la sua presentia et virtuose maniere ci tiene viva la memoria di Papa Marcello che sia in gloria'.

23 Vittorio Peri, 'La Congregazione dei Greci (1573) e i suoi primi documenti', in Giuseppe Forchielli, Alfonso M. Stickler (eds.), *Collectanea Stephan Kuttner*, III (i.e., *Studia Gratiana*, 13) (Bologna: Institutum Gratianum, 1967), pp. 131–256, at pp. 195–210, and his *Ricerche sull'Editio princeps degli atti greci del Concilio di Firenze* (Vatican City: Biblioteca Apostolica Vaticana, 1975), pp. 64–66, 158–161; on Viviani, see ibid., pp. 58–67.

Gregory XIII. In January 1577, the Greek scholar Piero Vettori wrote enthusiastically to Sirleto, being delighted that the pope had decided to set up a Greek college, with a 'bella stamperia di libri latini e greci' attached to it.[24] In the end, however, only the college and the church of St Athanasius were established.

4 Tackling Greek Printing

The concerns of Traiani and Viviani were genuine: there had been no committed Greek publishers in Rome since the demise of Cervini's enterprise. This could be why Francesco Zanetti, mentioned above in relation to Vukovič's plan, moved from Venice to Rome around 1572. He started out as a copyist for some cardinals and for the Vatican Library. In June 1573, he signed a letter to Vettori as 'copyist, Greek and printer' and used Domenico Basa's shop as an address, which indicates that Zanetti was working for him.[25] As we have seen, Vukovič stated a year later that Zanetti was willing to relocate to Ancona to set up a papal press printing in Cyrillic. Instead, Zanetti partnered with the printer Bartolomeo Tosi in Rome, and launched his own firm in 1577, employing the Greek typeface designed by Pierre Haultin.[26] He published patristic and biblical literature, either in the original language or in Latin translation, often collaborating with Basa. For the first time, Greek books intended for

---

24   MS Vatican City, BAV, Vat. lat. 6185, f. 207r, reported in Peri, *Ricerche*, p. 162. Vettori also mentioned a congratulatory letter which he had written to the pope; this is presumably MS Vatican City, BAV, Reg. lat. 2023, f. 380r–v, published in Piero Vettori, *Epistolarum libri X. orationes XIII. et liber de laudibus Ioannae Austriacae* (Florence: Giunta, 1586), USTC 863134, pp. 190–191. If so, the date '1 November 1577' should be read as 1576, i.e., two months before Vettori's letter to Sirleto.

25   MS London, British Library, Add. 10273, f. 336v: 'Egli è circa un anno che sono qui a Roma ... Servitore, Francesco Zanetti scrittore, greco e stampatore scrisse. [Post scriptum:] Le littere s'hanno a indirizare alla botega de messer Domenego Basa libraro del Ziglio'.

26   Evro Layton, *The Sixteenth Century Greek Book in Italy. Printers and Publishers for the Greek World* (Venice: Istituto ellenico di studi bizantini e postbizantini di Venezia, 1994), pp. 158–159, 522, 526–527, for his early printing activity in Venice, his fonts and his kinship with the Venice-based Greek printers Bartolomeo, Camillo and Cristoforo Zanetti. On his little-known work as a copyist in Rome and Florence, see Anna Gaspari, 'Le "mani" di Camillo Zanetti: il caso di scriba C (sigma), "occidental arrondi" e Francesco Zanetti', in Vasili Atsalos and Niki Tsironi (eds.), *Actes du VIe Colloque International de Paléographie Grecque, Drama 21–27 Septembre 2003* (Athens: Hellenike Hetaereia Bibliodesias, 2008), I, pp. 347–358; III, pp. 1089–1098 (tables), and her 'Francesco Zanetti stampatore, copista e "instaurator" di manoscritti greci', in Daniel Galadza etc. (eds.), ΤΟΞΟΤΗΣ. *Studies for Stefano Parenti* (Grottaferrata: Monastero Esarchico, 2010), pp. 155–175. See also Fernanda Ascarelli, Marco Menato, *La tipografia del '500 in Italia* (Florence: Olschki, 1989), pp. 121–123, 132–133; Gian Lodovico Masetti Zannini, *Stampatori e librai a Roma nella seconda metà del Cinquecento. Documenti inediti* (Rome: Palombi, 1980), *ad indicem*.

Greek-speaking readers were printed outside of Venice.[27] This was part of the policy of assimilation and regulation of minority communities in Italy using the Byzantine rite, which was pursued, with varying degrees of flexibility, by Pius IV, Pius V and Gregory XIII.[28]

Although Zanetti's firm remained a private enterprise, it was dependent on papacy's commissions, which can be seen as a practical solution adopted by Gregory XIII to the church's lack of a means to publish works in Greek, as lamented by Viviani. Zanetti's first publication was, in fact, the Greek acts of the Council of Florence, followed by the Greek translation of the Tridentine decrees and the Gregorian calendar, a compendium of Bessarion's monastic rules for the Basilian monasteries in southern Italy and the profession of faith for Catholic Greeks.[29] Zanetti also worked with the Stamperia del Popolo Romano on the Greek editions of a few works by Theodoret and Chrysostom.[30] In addition to works in Greek, Zanetti's press published: several Latin treatises by Jesuits and a few textbooks for the Collegio Romano; Bellarmine's Hebrew grammar and some books of the Hebrew Bible in the original language, with the assistance of Vittorio Eliano, a converted Jew and printer; three religious texts in early Serbo-Croatian, including a translation of the Psalms; and the profession of faith in Arabic for Eastern Christians seeking to re-establish communion with the Holy See, using the 1566 font of the Collegio Romano.[31]

---

27 On the Venetian publications for the Greek communities, see Layton, *The Sixteenth Century Greek Book*.

28 On the subject, see Vittorio Peri, *Chiesa Romana e 'rito greco'. G.A. Santoro e la Congregazione dei Greci (1566–1596)* (Brescia: Paideia, 1975), esp. pp. 15–103, including a useful analysis of the terms 'Italo-Greeks' and *ritus Graecus*.

29 Ἡ Ἁγία καὶ Οἰκουμενικὴ ἐν Φλωρεντίᾳ γενομένη Σύνοδος (Rome: Francesco Zanetti, 1577), USTC 829948. On this edition, see Peri, *Ricerche*. See also USTC 861064, 820862, 812768, 805765.

30 Giorgetti Vichi, *Annali della Stamperia*, pp. 91–92.

31 Robert Bellarmine, *Institutiones linguae Hebraicae* ... (Rome: Francesco Zanetti, 1578), USTC 852728; *Liber Genesis* (Rome: Francesco Zanetti, 1579), USTC 805391; *Quinque volumina Cantica: Ruth, Threni, Ecclesiastes, Esther* (Rome: Francesco Zanetti, 1580), USTC 805530; *Liber Psalmorum* (Rome: Francesco Zanetti, 1581), USTC 805649. See also Carla Casetti, 'Eliano, Vittorio', in *Dizionario biografico degli italiani*, XLII (Rome: Istituto dell'Enciclopedia italiana, 1993), pp. 475–477. *Pochorni i mnozii inii Psalmi Davidovi* (Rome: Francesco Zanetti, 1582), USTC 805715; Aleksandar Komulovic, *Nauch Charstians chiza Slovignschi Narod v vlaasti iazich. Dottrina christiana per la natione illirica nella propria lingua* (Rome: Francesco Zanetti, 1582), USTC 762020; Juan Polanco, *Isprauniich za erei ispouidniici, i za pochornih, prenesen Slatinschoga iazicha, v Slouignschii. Breve direttorio, per sacerdoti confessori, e per penitenti tradotto da lingua latina, nella illirica* (Rome: Francesco Zanetti, 1582), USTC 762339. These publications should be reconsidered in light of Zanetti's earlier involvement in Vuković's project for a Cyrillic press in Ancona. It is also worth noting that, between 1530 and 1531, the Zanetti family press had printed Glagolitic publications issued in Rijeka (Fiume) at the expense of the bishop of Modruš Šimun Kožičić: Stantchev, 'Due cinquecentine', p. 5. For the Arabic confession

5 The Polyglot Papal Press: A Concealed Enterprise

Gregory XIII's plan for proselytising the East could not rely solely on the limited resources of Zanetti's relatively small printing house. It required a specialist press capable of producing a steady stream of Catholic publications, translated not only into Greek but also into Semitic and Slavic languages (Hebrew, Arabic, Syriac and Karšuni, Armenian, Serbo-Croatian). Another pressing issue was the revision and publication of the Antiphonary, Gradual and other liturgical books of Gregorian chant. Large-scale production of sheet music, however, necessitated a specialist musical press, with skilled manpower.

The first evidence of curial plans for a new papal press appears in relation to these two projects in late 1577. In October, the revision of the liturgical books of Gregorian chant was entrusted to Giovanni Pierluigi da Palestrina and Annibale Zoilo, two renowned composers of sacred music. However, the publication of these works was met with immediate opposition by King Philip II of Spain, who was reportedly concerned about its impact on the Spanish printing industry.[32] Nevertheless, according to the correspondence of Philip's ambassadors in Rome, the pope allocated 100,000 ducats to the new papal press at the end of 1577. In comparison to the meagre 2,000 ducats which Pius IV had allotted to setting up his printing firm in 1562, this impressive sum indicates Gregory XIII's zeal for the endeavour, as well as his correct understanding of the financial commitment required for its success. Along with the revised choral books, the new papal press was expected to publish corrected editions of the Bible in several languages for distribution by missionaries (Jesuits, in particular).[33]

By May 1578, the press had been set up in a Roman palace, with Domenico Basa as its manager.[34] While the reform of Gregorian chant books became

---

of faith see USTC 805533. On the re-uses of the Jesuit Arabic, see Tinto, 'Per una storia', pp. 284–286 and esp. p. 285 for what appears to be the only known copy of an anti-Islamic treatise probably issued by Zanetti or the Collegio Romano about 1580: Vatican City, BAV, R.G.Oriente.v.341(int.1). I am indebted to Laura Lalli for checking this booklet on my behalf.

32   Tinto, 'Per una storia', pp. 280–281; and, on the reform of Gregorian chant, see his *La Tipografia Medicea Orientale* (Lucca: Pacini Fazzi, 1987), pp. 61–66, as well as the more recent account by Robert Prowse, 'The Council of Trent and the Reform of the Gregorian Chant', *Sacred Music*, 136 (2009), pp. 35–46. See also Chapter 5 in this volume.

33   Barberi, *Paolo Manuzio*, p. 36, n. 2. See the *avviso* of 17 February 1580, in MS Vatican City, BAV, Urb. lat. 1408, f. 22r, cited in Tinto, 'Per una storia', p. 293, n. 9.

34   Tinto, 'Per una storia', p. 281, esp. n. 8, argues convincingly that the location was the house of Pomponio Cotta, later in possession of Virgilio Crescenzi and sometimes called the 'casa del Bellhomo'. Giorgetti Vichi, *Annali della Stamperia*, pp. 45–46, incorrectly refers to the palace, close to Piazza S. Eustachio, as the venue of the Stamperia del Popolo Romano. The donation of the palace directly to Basa is confirmed by a later memo; see Peri, *Ricerche*, p. 152.

stalled due to Philip II, the multilingual publication of religious books for the purpose of proselytising continued. The focus was entirely on the East, especially Muslim and Orthodox regions. According to a curial memo from the end of the sixteenth century, printing in Arabic and Armenian would be used for propaganda aimed at Turks and Persians, while Serbian was best suited to address Christians serving as Janissaries in the Turkish army, and Greek for the Orthodox church in Russia.[35] Another anonymous memo from around 1580 expressed the hope that Hebrew, Syriac and Ethiopic would also be used for Catholic printing with an objective of proselytising Christian Eastern communities.[36] The ultimate goal of the pope was to publish an official multilingual edition of the Bible, replacing the Antwerp Polyglot, printed by Christophe Plantin between 1568 and 1573, and challenging early Protestant attempts in the field of Oriental scholarship.[37] Such an ambitious endeavour required outstanding technical skill and linguistic expertise. So, in 1577, the pope hired the renowned French punch-cutter Robert Granjon to design the requisite typefaces. Almost three years later, the firm began publishing ground-breaking works in Oriental languages.[38]

It should be noted, however, that the polyglot papal press was not given a name of its own to distinguish it from Basa's private workshop. The imprint on the title pages of some twenty publications that can be tracked back was usually 'Ex typographia Dominici Basae' or 'Ex officina Dominici Basae', often in combination with different versions of Gregory XIII's coat of arms (Figs. 2.1–3).

---

35   Peri, *Ricerche*, pp. 153–154. The memo is preserved among Vivani's papers, in MS Rome, Biblioteca Vallicelliana, K 17.

36   Giorgio Levi Della Vida, *Documenti intorno alle relazioni delle chiese orientali con la S. Sede durante il pontificato di Gregorio XIII. Appendice* (Vatican City: Biblioteca Apostolica Vaticana, 1948), p. 49. See also H.D.L. Vervliet, 'Robert Granjon à Rome 1578–1589. Notes préliminaires à une histoire de la typographie romaine à la fin de XVIe siècle', *Bulletin de l'Institut historique belge de Rome*, 38 (1967), pp. 177–231, at p. 188, no. 2, who gives a more precise date.

37   Sara Fani and Margherita Farina (eds.), *Le vie delle lettere. La Tipografia Medicea tra Roma e l'Oriente* (exhibition catalogue, Florence, Biblioteca Medicea Laurenziana, 2012–2013) (Florence: Mandragora, 2012), p. 45. See also R.J. Wilkinson, 'Emmanuel Tremellius' 1569 Edition of the Syriac New Testament', *Journal of Ecclesiastical History*, 58 (2007), pp. 9–25 and his 'Syriac Studies in Rome in the Second Half of the Sixteenth Century', *Journal for Late Antique Religion and Culture*, 6 (2012), pp. 55–74.

38   A Malabar font (Indic or more precisely Tamil) was also apparently envisaged; see Cardinal Santori's diary entry for October 1580, quoted by Tinto, 'Per una storia', p. 295, n. 24. No editions using this font, probably never cast, have so far come to light. On the earliest typographical efforts in Malabar, see Denis E. Rhodes, *The Spread of Printing. Eastern Hemisphere: India, Pakistan, Ceylon, Burma and Thailand* (Amsterdam: Van Gendt, 1969), p. 15. For another overview, including early European attempts, see Kamil V. Zvelebil, *Companion Studies to the History of Tamil Literature* (Leiden: Brill, 1992), pp. 151–152.

FIGURE 2.1 *Kalendarium Gregorianum perpetuum* (Rome: Domenico Basa, 1582), USTC 820843. Munich, Bayerische Staatsbibliothek, Chrlg. 328 t.

FIGURE 2.2
Officium defunctorum ad usum Maronitarum (Rome: Domenico Basa, 1585), USTC 820911. London, British Library, 753.g.72.(1.)

It is therefore difficult to determine which editions resulted from Basa's own efforts and which were due to the editorial programme of the papal endeavour, especially for the few editions of Latin patristics. The same was likely to hold true for contemporary readers.

A plausible explanation for this apparently deliberate ambiguity can be found in a later note among Gaspare Viviani's papers, in which the pope is said to have undertaken Oriental printing 'in that secret manner which it is prudent to adopt in such an enterprise, so as to avoid the many contrary points of view put forward to His Holiness at the time'.[39] The annotator (possibly Viviani himself) seems to have regarded Oriental, and specifically Arabic, printing not only as a useful strategy for proselytising, but also as a matter of state, requiring strict confidentiality.

---

39 MS Rome, Biblioteca Vallicelliana, K 17, f. 111r–v, also transcribed in Peri, *Ricerche*, pp. 152–153: 'Fu concetto molto bene inteso da Papa Gregorio XIII l'introdurre in Roma non solo la stampa greca, ma anco li charatteri Arabici, Chaldei, Armeni et Illirici; però con molta spesa della Sede Apostolica si fece condurre di Francia il Grangion, eccellentissimo intagliatore. Si diede uno palazzo al Basa dove fu eretta la stampa et per molti anni si attese a fare intagliare et gettare polzoni in dette lingue, et fu anco cominciato a stamparsi in Arabo, secondo il modo che fu giudicato espediente per la dilatatione della Religione Christiana et per altri rispetti importanti [etiam in materia di stato]. *Et tutto passava con quel segreto modo che in tal opera prudentemente si deve tenere per schifar molti contrarii all'hora esposti a Sua Santità* [da me spiegati e riferiti].' The emphasis is mine.

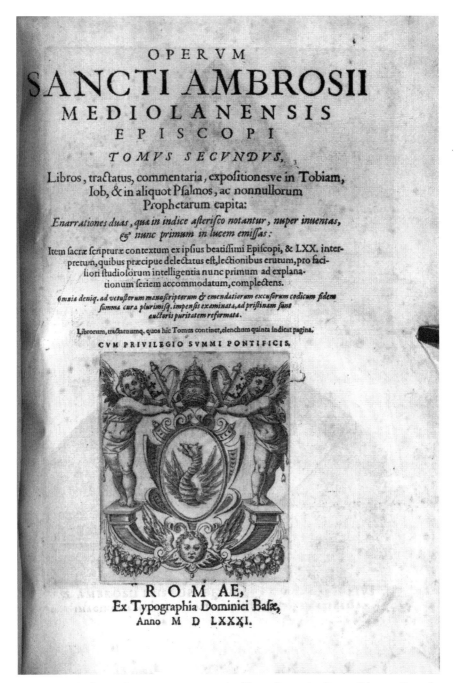

FIGURE 2.3 Ambrose, *Operum ... tomus secundus* (Rome: Domenico Basa, 1581), USTC 809058. Munich, Bayerische Staatsbibliothek, 2 P.lat. 51-1/2

6 Supporters and Competitors

Even so, the establishment of the polyglot papal press must have entailed a number of consultations within the curia. In a memo to Cardinal Giovanni Morone around 1580, Giovanni Carga claimed credit for the enterprise's success, and asked for financial compensation as the initiator of the project.[40] It is also known that Gaspare Viviani participated in the endeavour as an intermediary for Cardinal Sirleto and Cardinal Santori, as well as an expert in Oriental languages.[41] As Basa's former partner, Zanetti was also clearly involved in the papal polyglot press;[42] and his dedication to Gregory XIII in his 1581 Greek edition of Chrysostom provides further evidence.[43] In addition, the rent on his workshop (near S. Giacomo degli Spagnoli) was paid by the pope in 1582 and 1584.[44] After all, Zanetti was the only printer in Rome to have a Greek typeface available.

Finally, some evidence suggests that the Jesuits, whose press in the Collegio Romano was by no means suitable for large-scale religious propaganda, endorsed the initiative. First and foremost, they were the primary distributors of the papal press's publications in their missions around the world. Secondly,

---

40   Describing his earlier proposal and the three-year-old enterprise by Basa as practically a 'stamparia pontificia', he claimed to have successfully introduced institutional printing by the Church in Rome without any remuneration. Vatican City, AAV, *Misc.*, *Arm. XI*, vol. 93, ff. 98r–99v. Despite Tinto's doubts in 'Per una storia', pp. 282, 293–294, the connection of this memo to the polyglot papal press seems obvious.

41   Peri, *Ricerche*, pp. 62–63, and Tinto, 'Per una storia', p. 295, n. 24.

42   It is worth noting that the Basa and Zanetti families continued to collaborate in the following decades. Not only did Basa involve Luigi Zanetti, one of Francesco's sons, in the management of the Oratorian press, but later partnerships between the families were established in Rome (Bernardo Basa, Francesco Zanetti himself and later his son Antonio), as well as in Venice (Isabetta Basa and Daniele Zanetti). See Saverio Franchi and Orietta Sartori, 'Zannetti (Zanetti)', in *Dizionario biografico degli italiani*, C (Rome: Istituto dell'Enciclopedia italiana, 2020), pp. 529–533.

43   John Chrysostom, Ὁμιλίαι δέκα διάφοροι … (Rome: Francesco Zanetti, 1581; two different quarto imprints), USTC 836506–836507, sigs +2r–+4r. An autograph copy is in MS Vatican City, BAV, Vat. lat., 6792, ff. 331r–332r, transcribed by Gaspari, 'Francesco Zanetti', pp. 168–169, with erroneous identification of the related printed editions. Tinto, *La Tipografia Medicea*, p. 5, n. 3 mentioned the manuscript dedication in Vat. lat. 6792 as if it were a proposal by Zanetti for establishing a polyglot press, though the text correctly referred to Gregory XIII's multilingual printing enterprises as great achievements of the immediate past. Rather than a proposal, this was in fact an encomium of the recently accomplished papal projects.

44   Valentino Romani, 'Per una storia dell'editoria romana tra Cinque e Seicento. Note e documenti', *Annali della Scuola speciale per archivisti e bibliotecari dell'Università di Roma*, 15–16 (1975–1976), pp. 23–64, at p. 39, n. 36.

in 1579 there was a proposal to set up a multilingual Catholic bookshop in the Polish-Lithuanian Commonwealth and sell 'missals, breviaries, graduals, antiphonaries, catechisms and other church books in great number for a cheap price' in Slavic-speaking regions.[45] Basa, no doubt on behalf of the polyglot papal press, would supply all the books in partnership with the Giunta of Florence. Antonio Possevino, who was then on a delicate diplomatic mission in North-East Europe, devised the project. When the proposal was rejected by the pope as not financially sustainable, Possevino tried in vain to obtain a copy of the Cyrillic typeface in Vilnius, Krakow and Kolozvár (now Cluj-Napoca).[46] Lastly, the commissioning of Granjon's Syriac typeface and the polyglot press's publication of a Syriac Catechism and profession of faith seem to have resulted from the pleas to the pope by Jesuits, who, after their missions to the Maronite Lebanese community in 1578 and 1580, emphasised how helpful Syriac printing (*stampa caldea*) would be to these Christians.[47]

In the later chapters of the story, at the end of Gregory XIII's papacy, another important character appeared on the stage. He was Cardinal Ferdinando de' Medici, later Grand Duke of Florence. The cardinal founded the so-called Medici Oriental Press in support of, and later in competition with, the polyglot papal press. Set up in Rome in 1584, under the auspices of the pope, the press was in fact entirely funded by de' Medici, its sole owner. The Orientalist scholar Giovanni Battista Raimondi, appointed as manager, and the former Jacobite patriarch Ignatius Naʿmatallah lent their full intellectual support to the initiative.[48] In contrast to the missionary and proselytising goals of the polyglot papal press, the Medici firm had clear commercial objectives. Its founder and collaborators believed that they could make good money by selling their Oriental language publications in the Near East, from Ethiopia to the Ottoman and Persian Empires, which appeared to be an untapped market for printed books, apart from recent attempts made by the polyglot papal press. The Medici press's first publication, a ground-breaking Arabic translation of the Gospels, was not published until 1590–1591; and its plans proved to be far too ambitious given

---

45 Vatican City, AAV, *Segr. Stato, Polonia*, vol. 16, f. 96r, as cited by Tinto, 'Per una storia', p. 289.
46 Ibid., pp. 289–291.
47 Tinto, *La Tipografia Medicea*, pp. 71–72.
48 On Naʿmatallah, who came to Rome in 1577 to discuss the union of his church with Rome, see Levi Della Vida, *Documenti intorno alle relazioni*, pp. 1–113, and *Le vie delle lettere*, pp. 57–63. On Raimondi, see ibid., pp. 54–56; Robert Jones, 'The Arabic and Persian Studies of Giovan Battista Raimondi (c.1536–1614)', MPhil dissertation, Warburg Institute, University of London, 1981, now available in his *Learning Arabic in Renaissance Europe (1505–1624)* (Leiden: Brill, 2020), pp. 177–242; and Mario Casari, '"Et questo bene et perfettamente parlare quanto all'homo sia possibile …". Filosofia naturale del linguaggio di Giovanni Battista Raimondi', *Rivista Storica Italiana*, 132.1 (2020), pp. 228–247.

that the areas it hoped to penetrate were not yet interested in printed books as vessels of knowledge. After several years of operating in the red, the press stopped publishing books at the end of the sixteenth century and, shortly after Raimondi's death in 1614, it shut down completely.[49]

Nevertheless, it is important to stress how this enterprise is connected to Basa's polyglot papal press. Not only did the two printing houses share typographical material and personnel, including key figures such as the punch-cutter Granjon, but Basa also supplied the Medici press with paper and other goods. Moreover, some of the earliest Medici publications had Basa's name. On the basis of these facts, Alberto Tinto argued convincingly that the two Oriental presses were, for all intents and purposes, one and the same firm from 1583 to 1585.[50] This view is confirmed by a later note, datable to between 1588 and 1591, and almost certainly written by Gaspare Viviani, who collaborated with both presses and owned the palace that was the second location of the Medici press.[51] This well-informed account of Oriental printing in Rome in the last quarter of the sixteenth century makes no distinction between the press entrusted to Basa and the Arabic publications undertaken by the Medici press.[52]

7 Novelty and Continuity under Sixtus V

As closing remarks, it seems appropriate to contrast Gregory's polyglot press with the Typographia Vaticana established by Sixtus V in 1587 in the magnificent new location built for the papal library in the Cortile del Belvedere.[53] The

---

49   For Arabic Gospels, see USTC 806525, 801540. See *Le vie delle lettere* and the bibliography cited there, as well as: H.D.L. Vervliet, 'Robert Granjon'; his 'Cyrillic and Oriental Typography in Rome at the End of the Sixteenth Century. An Inquiry into the Later Work of Robert Granjon, 1578–1590', in his *The Palaeotypography of the French Renaissance* (Leiden: 2008), pp. 433–480; and Caren Reimann, 'Ferdinando de' Medici and the *Typographia Medicea*', in Nina Lamal etc. (eds.), *Print and Power in Early Modern Europe (1550–1800)* (Leiden: Brill, 2021), pp. 220–238. For a typographical analysis of the press's Syriac fonts, see J.F. Coakley, *The Typography of Syriac. A Historical Catalogue of Printing Types (1537–1958)* (London: Oak Knoll Press and the British Library, 2006), pp. 40–45, 158–160.
50   Tinto, *La Tipografia Medicea*, pp. 11–25 (esp. p. 20), 29, 34, 41, 43.
51   Ibid., p. 10.
52   Peri, *Ricerche*, pp. 152–153.
53   Insightful accounts of the press are given by Maria Iolanda Palazzolo, 'Una stamperia per il papa. La Tipografia Vaticana di Sisto V', *Rivista Storica Italiana*, 132.1 (2020), pp. 206–227 and Giampiero Brunelli, 'Tipografia Vaticana e *Congregatio XIV*. Focus sugli anni sistini', in *Nuovi inediti su Sisto V. Per le celebrazioni del V Centenario della nascita di Felice Peretti*

latter enterprise was given a loan of 20,000 ducats at a fixed interest rate of six per cent. Sixtus once again chose Basa as a manager, who, along with Zanetti, had stood out throughout Gregory XIII's pontificate as the Rome-based printer most favoured by the curial establishment and the pope himself. With the new pope (then Cardinal Felice Peretti), Basa and Zanetti had already worked together in publishing Ambrose's collected works on behalf of Gregory XIII.[54] The shared staff is certainly the most visible sign of continuity between the two projects, though the timing between the disappearance of the first and the emergence of the second is also telling, with the polyglot press *de facto* outliving Gregory under Basa's shrewd leadership.[55]

As for their editorial programme, Gregory's polyglot press was concerned with Oriental printing, while the Typographia Vaticana mainly handled patristic and biblical literature, much like the papal press set up by Pius IV and run by Manuzio until 1570. Despite the change in focus, it is worth noting that all these areas of interest have common roots: they can easily be traced back to the multifaceted projects undertaken in the middle of the Cinquecento by Cardinal Marcello Cervini.[56]

To be sure, Gregory and Sixtus took very different approaches to foreign affairs, with the latter preferring to play within the European scenario, to the detriment of Gregory's global aspirations.[57] Their patronage, particularly the presses they established, mirrored such differences. Yet it is hard to believe that the Vatican Typography did not emerge from the remains of Gregory's polyglot enterprise and that the increasingly centralised exploitation of printing pursued until the mid-1580s did not pave the way for the regulative interventions promoted by Sixtus in this crucial field for the church's communication policy.

1521–2021 (Ascoli Piceno: Fas, forthcoming), which I was able to consult thanks to the author's generosity.

54   USTC 809058. The fifth volume was issued in 1585, already under Sixtus as pontiff, while the sixth and final appeared in 1587 with the imprint of the Vatican Press.
55   Tinto, *La Tipografia Medicea*, p. 104.
56   Sachet, *Publishing for the Popes*, esp. pp. 41–184, 208–210.
57   See, e.g., Silvano Giordano, 'Sisto V', in *Enciclopedia dei papi*, III, pp. 202–222 and Maria Antonietta Visceglia (ed.), *Papato e politica internazionale nella prima età moderna* (Rome: Viella, 2013), *ad indicem*. New insights into his cultural policy are to be found in the ongoing edition of Vincenzo Catani (ed.), *Roma, l'Italia e l'Europa durante il pontificato di Sisto V. Gli 'Avvisi' dal 1585 al 1590* (Teramo: Palumbi, 2020) and in Filip Malesevic, *Inventing the Council inside the Apostolic Library. The Organization of Curial Erudition in Late Cinquecento Rome* (Berlin: De Gruyter, 2021).

CHAPTER 3

The 'Primer and Christian Doctrine of Valladolid' (1583)

A Multifaceted Publishing Endeavour

Benito Rial Costas

This article studies the role played by Christian doctrine primers, and specifically by the so-called *Cartilla y doctrina cristiana* of Valladolid, in the Spanish Catholic Reform or Counter-Reformation. In 1577, the Spanish Inquisition prohibited some primers and indicated that some of these kinds of books went against the teachings of the church, ordering the seizure of those in circulation and banning their sale and use. After 1577, it became necessary for the Spanish Crown to provide a new primer for teaching children to read. In 1578, a proposal for a Christian doctrine primer, free of religious errors, was sent to Philip II, and in 1583, the King gave privilege to the Chapter of Valladolid for reviewing, printing and distributing a new doctrine primer to teach children in Castile. The primers were entitled *Cartilla y doctrina Cristiana* (Primer and Christian doctrine) and were known from that moment on as the 'Primer and Christian doctrine of Valladolid'. This article analyses the history and content of this publication. The first part explains what primers, doctrines and Christian doctrine primers were. The second part describes some deficiencies of printing and selling the new primers. The third part disentangles some aspects of this enormous publishing business and the tools that the Chapter of Valladolid possessed to control it.

1 Teaching Christian Doctrine and the First Letters to Children

In the Iberian Peninsula, the first reference to the obligation of teaching Christian doctrine was made at the Council of Coyanza, which gathered at Villa de Don Juan in 1055. From this time on, councils and synods, such as those of Toledo (1323), Coria (1462), Talavera (1498) and Calahorra (1553), continually highlighted the importance of teaching Christian prayers and doctrine to people. The church was especially concerned about the education of children. It soon began to see the relationship between teaching to read and teaching to pray, and it began to make reference to the teaching doctrine at schools and the procedures for surveying it. The synodal constitutions of Alcala of 1480 established that in all churches, there was to be a cleric or a parish clerk who could teach the children of the parish how to read, write, sing and develop good habits. In 1492, the Synod of Jaen established that sacristans had to give lessons to the children of the parishioners and stated that whoever set up a school should try to do it near the church and educate the children about the doctrine. In 1499, the Synod of Santiago de Compostela obliged the sacristans to teach reading and writing to children and dictated that reading should be taught with the articles of faith and the Commandments. In 1497, the Synod of the Canary Islands also stated that sacristans should be teachers and catechists and that they should teach children to read, write and count. The same narrative was consistently repeated during the sixteenth century. The synodal constitutions of Coria of 1537 remarked that the clergy had to be sure that children's teachers taught Christian doctrine in their schools on a daily basis and that parishioners compelled teachers to do so. One of the agreements adopted by the Council of Trent, whose sessions began in 1545, was that churches should be responsible for teaching grammar to children. In 1553, the Synod of Calahorra insisted that teachers who taught children to read had to compel them to read the Christian doctrine aloud.[1]

However, it is not yet clear what education was given in Castilian primary and parish schools because teaching methods and tools were often adapted to particular circumstances and specific demands. The teaching of the first letters to children had some different features in parish and private schools, and various texts were used for this purpose. Primers, non-religious broadsheets and religious booklets were common. Primers contained the tools for learning the alphabet, the syllabary and, in some cases, some basic grammar or general guidelines for writing. Prayers, religious texts, *romances* and stories such as

---

1   José Sánchez Herrero, 'La legislación conciliar y sinodal hispana de los siglos XII a mediados del XVI y su influencia en la enseñanza de la doctrina cristiana', *Revista Española de Teología*, 46 (1986), pp. 181–213. See also José Sánchez Herrero, 'Los concilios provinciales y los sínodos diocesanos españoles, 1215–1550', *Quaderni di Studi Classici e Medievali*, 3 (1981), pp. 113–181, and 4 (1982), pp. 111–197; José Sánchez Herrero, 'Los catecismos de la doctrina cristiana y el medio ambiente social donde han de ponerse en práctica (1300–1550)', *Anuario de Historia de la Iglesia*, 3 (1994), pp. 179–196; María Luisa Calero Vaquera, 'La "Cartilla para enseñar a leer en romance" (h. 1564) de Juan Robles', in Pablo Cano López etc., *Actas del VI Congreso de Lingüística General: Santiago de Compostela* (Madrid: Arco Libros, 2007), III. 2745–2746; Betsabé Caunedo del Potro, 'Primary Education in Medieval Castile', *Imago Temporis: Medium Aevum*, 13 (2019), p. 252; See Benito Rial Costas, 'Catechesis and Christian Doctrine in the Iberian Parishes of the Late Middle Ages', in Angelika Kemper, Christian Domenig (eds.), *Wissen in mittelalterlichen Gemeinschaften: Diskurse, Ideale, soziale Räume* (Berlin: Peter Lang Verlag, 2022), pp. 135–154.

Crónica del Cid, Los siete sabios de Roma and *Infante don Pedro y Abad don Juan* were often used to practice the notions learned in primers.[2]

Primers and doctrines were two very different kinds of works with different contents, purposes and readers. Primers were the most basic text used for teaching people how to read. Doctrines were elementary catechetical works and were often used by priests to teach the main prayers and the most important principles of Christian doctrine. What I call 'Christian doctrine primers' were the result of a process of mixing the teaching of the first letters and the doctrinal principles or *vice versa*. Christian doctrine primers were also a mixture of primers and doctrines. On the one hand, these works combined the teaching of reading with the teaching of doctrine. On the other hand, they blended the teaching of the alphabet and syllabary with religious texts for reading training. Christian doctrine primers were a kind of work that had a twofold goal: the teaching of the first letters through Christian doctrine and the teaching of Christian doctrine while learning to read. Their aim was not only a matter of learning to read but also to learn Christian doctrine and to read it.[3] Despite the discussions in the synods about the urgency to establish

---

2   For example, in 1578, in the inventory of a teacher, García Beltrán de la Peña, there were listed primers, 'books of San Alejo', two 'small books of contemplation', some paper, ink, a framed poster with 'thick round letters' and other tools probably also used for teaching. María del Carmen Álvarez Márquez, 'La enseñanza de las primeras letras y el aprendizaje de las artes del libro en el siglo XVI en Sevilla', *Historia, Instituciones, Documentos*, 22 (1995), p. 48, p. 50. See also Víctor Infantes, *De las primeras letras. Cartillas españolas para enseñar a leer de los siglos XV y XVI: Preliminar y edición facsímil de 34 obras* (Salamanca: Universidad de Salamanca, 1998), pp. 36–37. For some insights into learning to read in the sixteenth century, see for example Piero Lucchi, 'La Santacroce, il Salterio e il Babuino. Libri per imparare a leggere nel primo secolo della stampa', *Quaderni Storici*, 38 (1978), pp. 596–601; Jean-Paul Le Flem, 'Instruction, lecture et écriture en Vieille Castille et Extrémadure aux XVIe–XVIIe siècles', in Lucienne Domergue (ed.), *De l'alphabetisation aux circuits du livre en Espagne XVI–XIX siecles* (Paris: Centre National de la Recherche Scientifique, 1987), pp. 30–34; León Esteban y Ramón López Martín, *La escuela de primeras letras según Juan Luis Vives. Estudio iconografía y textos* (Valencia: Universitat de València, 1993), p. 47; Francisco M. Gimeno Blay, 'Aprender a escribir en la Península Ibérica. De la Edad Media al Renacimiento', in Francisco M. Gimeno Blay, Armando Petrucci (eds.), *Escribir y leer en Occidente* (Valencia: Universitat de València, 1995), pp. 125–144; Antonio Viñao Frago, 'Alfabetización y primeras letras (S. XVI–XVII)', in Antonio del Castillo, Armando Petrucci (eds.), *Escribir y leer en el siglo de Cervantes* (Barcelona: Gedisa, 1999), p. 67; Caunedo del Potro, 'Primary Education in Medieval Castile', p. 252.

3   José Sánchez Herrero, 'La enseñanza de la doctrina cristiana en algunas diócesis de León y Castilla durante los siglos XIV y XV', *Archivos Leoneses. Revista de estudios y documentación de los Reinos Hispano-Occidentales*, 59–60 (1976), p. 159. See also Luis Resines, *La catequesis en España. Hstoria y textos* (Madrid: BAC, 1997), pp. 227–230; Infantes, *De las primeras letras*, pp. 36, 38.

one single doctrine, there was not a single text or a single Christian doctrine primer until 1583, but rather a series of them. Pre-1583 Christian doctrine primers did not coincide in their text, structure or language. However, all clearly highlighted that they were intended to teach children to read, regardless of the school or parish, and, in addition to the alphabet and syllabary, all included the main prayers and some basic Christian principles.[4] This content was normally divided into two main sections. The first section or part included at least the alphabet and a syllabary. The second section or part was a Christian doctrine that included at least some prayers.

2 A New Christian Doctrine Primer: *La cartilla y doctrina de Valladolid*

Christian doctrine primers brought together two very different works with varied purposes and risks: monetary and doctrinal. On the one hand, primers, as necessary school books, were a major publishing business, were printed by thousands and were an important source of income for authors, printers and booksellers. On the other hand, doctrines were basically religious and catechetical works and at times contained mistakes in dogma. A single text approved by the church was clearly needed.[5] In response to the Protestant Reformation, the Castilian Inquisition inspected lay and religious texts and, therefore, the texts used for learning to read. The authorities did this out of fear that such texts presented a way to spread allegedly erroneous or Reformation ideas pernicious and contrary to the teachings of the Catholic Church. For example, in 1577, the Castilian Inquisition ordered the prohibition of some Christian doctrine primers that contained a chapter entitled 'Castigo y doctrina de Caton' (Cato's punishment and doctrine) and indicated that some of these kinds of books were going against the teachings of the church, 'especially those printed

---

4 Christian doctrine primers lacked a well-established structure and content, and in addition to the alphabet, syllabary and prayers, some included grammatical concepts, brief notions of writing, secular pedagogic texts or doctrinal readings. See, for example, Infantes, *De las primeras letras*, pp. 15, 17, 20, 34–45, 50; María del Carmen Álvarez Márquez, *La impresión y el comercio de libros en la Sevilla del quinientos* (Seville: Universidad de Sevilla, 2007), p. 329.

5 Primers were subject to some general Castilian policies for printing and selling books. Antonio Viñao Frago, 'Aprender a leer en el Antiguo Régimen: cartillas, silabarios y catones', in Agustín Escolano Benito (ed.), *Historia ilustrada del libro escolar en España. Del Antiguo Régimen a la Segunda República* (Madrid: Fundación Germán Sánchez Ruipérez, 1997), p. 150.

by Juan de la Plaza in Toledo'. They ordered the seizure of items in circulation and prohibited their sale and use.[6]

Given that Christian doctrine primers were not only doctrines but also primers, these drastic seizures and prohibitions had immediate consequences for booksellers and printers due to the financial damage resulting from the confiscations. Primers were a good business. They were in great demand, they were cheap to produce and they had large profit margins. After the provisions of 1577, it was necessary to provide an alternative to the banned Christian doctrine primers while avoiding the danger of repeating the mistakes in the religious content. Publishing an official text and monopolising its production and distribution seemed to be a good idea.[7] The *Cartilla y doctrina cristiana* of Valladolid was the culmination of this project.

It seems that after 1577, it became necessary for the Crown to provide a new Christian doctrine primer for teaching children to read. In 1578, a proposal for the same, free of religious errors, was written by Sebastián Pérez de Aguilar and sent to Philip II, who scrupulously revised it.[8] Pérez de Aguilar's text would fulfil the need for a standard and single Christian doctrine primer. It was to be the only authorised text for learning to read, and it was to be used in all Castilian schools, allowing the Crown to control any doctrinal risks and excesses. In September 1583, Philip II gave an exclusive privilege for three years to the Chapter of Valladolid for reviewing, printing and distributing Christian doctrine primers to teach children in Castile. The primers were entitled *Cartilla y doctrina cristiana* (Primer and Christian doctrine) and were known from that moment on as the 'primer and doctrine of Valladolid'. Printing and selling the

---

6 Archivo Histórico Nacional (afterwards AHN), Inquisición de Valencia, Leg. 6, n. 2. This document was mentioned by Henry Charles Lea, *A History of the Inquisition of Spain* (London: Macmillan, 1906–1907), III. 531. *Castigo y ejemplos de Catón* was a poem and moral catechism that was used to teach doctrine to children since the Middle Ages. See Antonio Rodríguez Moñino, *Los pliegos poéticos de Oporto (siglo XVI)* (Madrid: Joyas Bibliográficas, 1976), p. 15.

7 A similar strategy was being deployed for liturgical books. See, for example, Benito Rial Costas, 'International Publishing and Local Needs. The Breviaries and Missals Printed by Plantin for the Spanish Crown', in Matthew McLean, Sara Barker (eds.), *International Exchange in the European Book World* (Leiden: Brill, 2016), pp. 15–30; Benito Rial Costas, 'Book Market and Surveillance. The Distribution of Plantin's Tridentine Liturgical Books in Sixteenth-Century Castile', in Benito Rial Costas (ed.), *New Insights into an Old Issue. Book Historical Scholarship on the Relationship between the Low Countries and Spain (1568–1648)*. Special issue of *Quaerendo*, 48.4 (2018), pp. 339–355.

8 See José Luis Gonzalo Sánchez-Molero, 'En torno a los orígenes de la "Cartilla de Valladolid"', *Pliegos de Bibliofilia*, 28 (2004), pp. 44–45. Sebastián Pérez de Aguilar, Bishop of Osma, also wrote a *Doctrina christiana* (Burgos, 1586) and a treatise on the sacramentos (Burgos, 1588), USTC 341037 and 341039.

new work was only possible with the licence of the Prior and the Chapter of Valladolid:[9]

> The King: Since on behalf of you, the Prior and Chapter of the Collegiate Church of Valladolid, a report was sent to us saying that the work of the said church had been begun for many years and because it was very costly, it could not be finished ... you asked and begged us to grant you a privilege for the time that we would want to be able to print and sell the primers in which the children learn to read in these our Kingdoms with prohibition that no one else could do it without having your order and authorisation. ... For which reason We give you license and authorisation so that for a time and space of three years ... the person who has your authorisation ... may print and sell the said primer. And we hereby grant license and authority to any printer of these our Kingdoms that you may name, so that for this time they may print it, with the condition that after it is printed, before it is sold, you bring it to our Council together with the original ... which is initialled on each page and signed at the end by Alonso de Vallejo ... so that it may be corrected ... and that you may be charged for each volume to be sold, so that you may have and have printing presses for the printing of the said primers in Burgos, Valladolid, Salamanca, Madrid and Seville. And we command that during the said time no person, without your permission, may print, sell the said primer or any other. ... Dated in Madrid on the twentieth day of the month of September of one thousand five hundred and eighty-three years.[10]

---

[9] Although the privilege was initially granted for only three years, it remained in force through successive extensions until the first quarter of the nineteenth century. During the sixteenth century, extensions were granted in 1586, 1588, 1590, 1593 and 1598. The purpose of this exclusive privilege was to raise funds to complete the construction of a new church in Valladolid. This document was noted and transcribed by Mariano Alcocer Martínez, *Catálogo razonado de obras impresas en Valladolid, 1481–1800* (Valladolid: Imprenta de la Casa Social Católica, 1926), pp. 882–883. See also Calero Vaquera, 'La "Cartilla para enseñar a leer en romance"', pp. 2747–2748; Jaime Moll Roqueta, 'La cartilla et sa distribution au XVII ème siècle', in Lucienne Domergue, (ed.), *De l'alphabetisation aux circuits du livre en Espagne XVI–XIX siecles* (Paris: Centre National de la Recherche Scientifique, 1987), pp. 311–332; Álvarez Márquez, 'La enseñanza de las primeras letras', p. 48; Infantes, *De las primeras letras*, p. 38; Fermín de los Reyes Gómez, *El libro en España y América. Legislación y censura (siglos XV–XVIII)* (Madrid: Arco Libros, 2000), I. 75, 77; and Álvarez Márquez, *La impresión y el comercio de libros*, p. 329.

[10] Alcocer Martínez, *Catálogo*, pp. 882–883.

By a privilege of His Majesty dispatched in Madrid on twentieth September, one thousand five hundred and eighty-three, it is ordered that to teach children in these kingdoms to read, only this primer be used ... and that it be printed and sold by the Collegiate Church of Valladolid for three years for [the construction of] its building. And without the permission of the prior and chapter of the said church, no person can print this primer or any other. ... And to provide the said church with an abundant supply of primers, it must have printing presses in Burgos, Valladolid, Salamanca, Madrid and Seville.[11]

The process for editing, reviewing and publishing the new Christian doctrine primer had been clearly established, and *Cartilla y doctrina cristiana* supposedly provided a new standardised text for teaching children to read. The first part of the work included the alphabet and a syllabary, as had, for example, the Christian doctrine primers printed in Antwerp in 1574 and in Toledo in 1577.[12] The second part or doctrine of this work, consistent with the reasons that led to the prohibition of primers in 1577, followed the structure and model of the Tridentine Hours and Catechism. This part included the Creed in Latin and Spanish, the Articles of Faith, the Commandments of God in Latin and Spanish, the Commandments of the Church, the Sacraments, the Works

---

11 *Cartilla y doctrina christiana examinada y aprovada por el ilustrissimo y reverendíssimo señor don Gaspar Quiroga*, (Seville: Alonso de la Barrera, 1584), USTC 342804, IV. London, The British Library, 1481.b.42(1).

12 *Cartilla y doctrina christiana en la qual se contiene todo lo que el christiano es obligado a saber, creer y obrar, y de lo que se deve apartar para no peccar* (Antwerp: Christophe Plantin, 1574), USTC 440430. Copy in Museum Plantin-Moretus, MPM A 497; *Cartilla para mostrar a leer a los niños con la doctrina christiana que se canta 'Amados Hermanos'* (Toledo: Francisco Guzmán, 1577), USTC 337149. Copy in Biblioteca de la Real Academia Española, RM-4872. *Cartilla y doctrina christiana* printed in Antwerp in 1574, followed a Christian doctrine primer printed in Castile in 1549 (USTC 346731). Antwerp's doctrine, like that of 1549, contained in the first part the alphabet and a syllabary. The second part or doctrine was presented in the form of a dialogue between the teacher and the child. In this doctrine, the fundamental questions of the doctrine were reviewed, with the inclusion of the prayers in Spanish, together with other traditional contents, traditionally presented separately in previous primers. At the end of this dialogue were added in Latin the Pater Noster, the Hail Mary, the Creed, the Salve and the Confession, the Confession in Spanish, the Magnificat and the Gospel of St John in Latin, and the prayers 'Bless me God the Father' and 'The Peace of Our Lord' closing the doctrine. *Cartilla para mostrar a leer a los niños* (Toledo: Francisco de Guzmán, 1577) USTC 337149, followed a Christian doctrine primer published in Castile in 1526: *Cartilla para mostrar a leer a los moços* (Toledo, Miguel de Eguía, c.1526), USTC 1793001. As did the Antwerp's Christian doctrine primer, the first part of this work included the alphabet and a syllabary. The second part included some prayers alternating Latin and Spanish, the Confession of the Mass, 'the Christian doctrine which is sung', Beloved Brethren, the Sacraments and the mortal sins.

of Mercy, the Virtues, the Gifts and Fruits of the Holy Spirit, the Beatitudes, the Mortal Sins, the Enemies of the Soul, the Powers of the Soul and the Corporal Senses. These texts were followed by prayers: the Pater Noster, the Holy Mary, the Salve, the Confession and the Bowing of the Cross, all in Latin and Spanish.[13] However, it does not seem that there was a wholly rigid official text, since the surviving copies, printed in Seville in 1584 and in Valladolid in 1584 and in 1588, show some differences.[14] It seems that each publisher or printer enjoyed a certain freedom in the format and content of the primers or, at least, the original model was flexible and versatile depending on the circumstances or minor differences were overlooked to a certain extent.

3   The Printing and Selling of the New Christian Doctrine Primer

The privilege given by Philip II required the Chapter of Valladolid to make agreements for the printing of the new Christian doctrine primer in Seville, Madrid, Salamanca, Valladolid and Burgos. This was probably intended to guarantee supply throughout Castile and reduce transport costs. It is known that 300,000 Christian doctrine primers were printed in Seville, 100,000 copies in Valladolid, 50,000 in Salamanca, 48,500 in Madrid and 37,500 in Burgos. By centralising in Valladolid the administration of Christian doctrine primers but printing them in several other cities and distributing them along Castile, the Chapter of Valladolid had to have a network of agents from whom booksellers purchased the books for retail sale. The Chapter of Valladolid assigned the administration of the printing and marketing of Christian doctrine primers to agents who, in turn, delegated those tasks to other people, especially the selling of the books throughout a specific town or region. The Chapter of Valladolid's agents were authorised to arrange the printing of the primer with a specific printer, certify the copies by signing them and sell them for the price established by the Crown.[15]

---

13   See also Álvarez Márquez, 'La enseñanza de las primeras letras', p. 48.
14   *Cartilla y doctrina christiana examinada y aprovada por el ilustrissimo y reverendíssimo señor don Gaspar Quiroga* (Seville: Alonso de la Barrera, 1584), USTC 342804. Copy in London, The British Library, 1481.b.42(1); *Cartilla y doctrina christiana examinada y aprovada por el ilustrissimo y reverendíssimo señor don Gaspar Quiroga* (Valladolid: Diego Fernández de Córdoba, 1584), USTC 1793002. Cuenca, Diocesan Archive, folder 829, file 79; *Cartilla y doctrina christiana examinada y aprovada por el ilustrissimo y reverendíssimo señor don Gaspar Quiroga* (Valladolid: Diego Fernández de Córdoba, 1588), USTC 1793003. Cuenca, Diocesan Archive, folder 819, file 7496.
15   This network may have varied in its extension during the almost two and a half centuries that the privilege was in force. Álvarez Márquez, *La impresión y el comercio de libros*, pp. 329–330.

The agreement between the Chapter of Valladolid, Juan de Naveda and García de Neira for printing and selling the primer provides important information about how this process functioned and what several shortcomings it had. Three months after the concession of the privilege, in December 1583, the Chapter of Valladolid made an agreement with Juan de Naveda and his nephew to manage the printing of the primer for the three years of the privilege and to receive 300,000 copies to distribute them in Andalusia. Pedro García de Neira, a neighbour of Seville, was designated by the Chapter of Valladolid to make agreements with printers, buy paper and deliver it to them, receive the printed books, have them signed by Fray Ignacio de Jesús and deliver them to Naveda.[16] In August 1584, Neira, in the name of the Chapter of Valladolid, notified Naveda that the latter had already received 95,500 primers and offered to deliver the remaining 204,500 copies to him to comply with the agreement Naveda had made with the Chapter of Valladolid.[17] Naveda responded to Neira's claim and offer, stating that he was not obliged to receive the said 204,500 copies because the Chapter of Valladolid had not respected, and had even altered, the terms of the agreement signed with him, that, therefore, nobody wanted to buy them and that he had already informed the Chapter of Valladolid and Neira about the problems and his concerns. Naveda stated three main reasons for not taking the contested items. First, in the agreement that he had signed with the Chapter of Valladolid, it had been agreed that the primers delivered to him had to be printed well and on good paper, and this requirement had not been met. Naveda argued that the copies had been printed badly and on poor-quality paper and that children could not read them. Second, the agreement had been signed before the price of the primers had been fixed; each primer consisted of two sheets (and not of one sheet as was common) and once the price was fixed, each sheet was appraised at four maravedis and not at two maravedis as was customary, resulting in a very high price. Third, he had already asked that no more primers be printed, following the 95,000 that he had already received,

---

16   María del Carmen Álvarez Márquez provides a detailed account of the expenses for printing the 300,000 Christian doctrine primers in Seville. Álvarez Márquez, *La impresión y el comercio de libros*, pp. 336–337.

17   This agreement was invalidated by another made in October 1584. In October 1584, Naveda and his nephew owed 668,500 maravedis for 95,400 Christian doctrine primers they had received from a printer in Seville at seven maravedis each; 325,000 for 50,000 Christian doctrine primers they had received from Valladolid, at six and a half maravedis each; and 337,500 maravedis for the Christian doctrine primers they had received from Salamanca. This amounted to 1,331,000 maravedís, which they were obliged to pay in three installments. In 1584, the Seville printer Alonso de la Barrera printed 200,000 Christian doctrine primers for Pedro García de Neira. The Seville printer Francisco Pérez printed the remaining 100,000. Álvarez Márquez, *La impresión y el comercio de libros*, pp. 330–331, 333.

because they could not be sold. He had also asked that their prices be lowered and that the primers be reduced to one sheet to remedy the inconveniences.

Everything suggests that Naveda's complaints were heard. His commercial relations with the Chapter of Valladolid continued; the distribution of the remaining 204,500 primers was given to Neira and the price of each copy and their number of sheets were reduced. In February 1585, Naveda, naming himself the treasurer of the Holy Crusade in the archbishopric of Seville, received a letter of indebtedness from the Seville printer Alonso de la Barrera for 1,500 primers Barrera had sold to Naveda at eight maravedis each. In March 1585, Neira received the power of attorney from the Chapter of Valladolid for the administration and sale of copies in the archbishopric of Seville and in all of Andalusia. He was given 204,500 primers, the ones that Naveda had not wanted to take and, one year later, in February 1586, he sold 2,000 of them to Seville bookseller Pedro López de Haro at six maravedis each. In September 1586, Naveda registered 52,600 primers sent by the Inquisition to be distributed in Peru.[18]

Other agents took charge of the administration and sale of the new primer in Seville in the following years, with the usual complex network of delegates and book retailers. For example, in June 1586, the Chapter of Valladolid gave power of attorney to Juan Bautista de Espinosa to manage its distribution. In March 1587, Espinosa sold 3,000 primers to Seville book merchant Juan Hidalgo at three and a half maravedis each to sell them in Seville. In October 1587, Espinosa delegated to Lucas de Belorado the expedition, administration and sale of primers in the archbishopric of Seville and in the bishoprics of Badajoz, Cádiz, Granada and Jaen for the years 1587 and 1588 at the price of no more than four maravedis each. In September 1588, Seville printer Alonso de la Barrera was in charge of the administration and sale of the new primer, committing himself to sell 200,000 copies of one sheet each in the archbishoprics of Seville and Granada, in the bishoprics of Cádiz, Cordoba, Coria, Guadix, Jaen and Málaga, in the vicariate of Lepe, in the duchy of Feria and in the town of Zafra. In 1589, Málaga book merchant Alonso de la Huerta was in charge of selling primers in the bishopric of Málaga and Juan García was in charge of selling them in Seville. In 1590, Juan de León, was in charge of selling their sale in Medina Sidonia and its jurisdiction. In 1593, Baeza book merchant Antonio de la Vega was in charge of selling in Baeza, Úbeda and Cazorla. Córdova book

---

18 Cartilla y doctrina christiana examinada y aprovada por el ilustrissimo y reverendíssimo señor don Gaspar Quiroga (Seville: Alonso de la Barrera, 1584) was sold for eight maravedis. Moll Roqueta, 'La cartilla et sa distribution', pp. 313–314. See also Álvarez Márquez, La impresión y el comercio de libros, pp. 330–335, 339.

merchants Miguel Rodríguez and Francisco Roberto were in charge of selling them in the bishopric of Cordoba during the same period.[19]

4   Business as Usual: Dealing with the Monopoly

As with the monopoly of printing, distributing and selling Spanish Tridentine liturgical books, production, supply and distribution problems were also frequent with Christian doctrine primers.[20] It was probably assumed that by centralising the administration of the primer, the dissemination of one single and approved text would be guaranteed; that by printing them in different Castilian cities, shortages would not exist; that by signing each printed copy, any attempt to sell non-certified copies would be avoided; and that by fixing their price, abuses would not occur. None of these assumptions proved correct. As Juan de Naveda was already asserting in 1583, the Chapter of Valladolid was not always able to manage the production and distribution of the primer; sometimes, shortages occurred and copies were printed poorly; the signing of each copy slowed their distribution and increased their price; and the official price was not always respected since transportation and distribution costs increased it considerably.[21] For example, it is noteworthy that in 1588, Seville printer Alonso de la Barrera, being in charge of the administration and sale of 200,000 primers, was authorised by the Chapter of Valladolid to print and sell as many copies as he wished in addition to the 200,000 already agreed, but the Chapter of Valladolid required that no copy could be sold that was not signed. Barrera assured the Chapter of Valladolid that there would not be any shortage, and the Chapter of Valladolid established that it would pay the cost of the signing process and would take any unsold copies of the 200,000.[22] Complaints about the high price of the primer were also common, and in the agreements

---

19   Juan Bautista de Espinosa named his brother Alonso de Espinosa as his universal heir in his will in 1588. In February 1593, a new agreement was signed between Alonso de Espinosa and the printer Alonso de la Barrera for the printing and administration of Christian doctrine primers from December 1592 to September 1595 at the price of four maravedis for each primer of one sheet. Álvarez Márquez, *La impresión y el comercio de libros*, pp. 338–339, p. 342, pp. 344–347.
20   Rial Costas, 'International Publishing and Local Needs', pp. 15–30.
21   In 1583, the price was fixed at four maravedis, although when they were cut and sewn the price increased to six maravedis, and to eight when they had a parchment cover. Calero Vaquera, 'La "Cartilla para enseñar a leer en romance"', pp. 2747–2748.
22   The copies had to be signed by the Carmelite friar, Alonso de la Cruz, or by who had been appointed by the Chapter of Valladolid for that purpose. Álvarez Márquez, *La impresión y el comercio de libros*, pp. 343–344.

between the Chapter of Valladolid and its agents for the distribution of the new text, it was often stated that the primer had to be sold at a price fixed by the Crown.[23]

In the following years, a number of booksellers, printers and book merchants began to explore new publishing strategies to escape the monopoly, began to offer new and better products to the book market and regained the huge profits that the production and sale of primers offered. A noteworthy petition was made by the Seville bookseller Baltasar de los Reyes to the City of Seville for printing a new primer around 1590. Baltasar de los Reyes asked the City of Seville for a licence or permission to publish a primer or abc that he had written (no mention was made of a doctrine or of a Christian doctrine primer), arguing that the high price of the previous primers had impeded many children from going to school and informing the city of his willingness to help poor widows:

> I say that I want to give poor children, for the love of God, an abc, made by my hand, because they do not go to school because a primer costs ten maravedis, and poor widows do not have ten maravedis to give for a primer. Therefore, I beg Your Mercy, for the love of God, to order to give me the said license [to publish it] so that no one can prevent me from doing so. Also, I ask Your Mercy diligently to order to demand the Cortes to lower the [the price] of the [Christian doctrine] primers.[24]

It is not known if a licence was granted to Baltasar de los Reyes by the City of Seville, but it is well known that the Chapter of Valladolid was attentive to and vigilant about the exploitation of new commercial strategies that could undermine its profits and affect its monopoly. In the renewal of the privilege to the Chapter of Valladolid of 1593, it was stated:

> And in so many traces and inventions of printers and other persons, who print books with the title of Christian doctrine, or catechisms, putting in them the abc and the other principles necessary to learn to read and

---

23 Álvarez Márquez, 'La enseñanza de las primeras letras', p. 339.
24 Joaquín Guichot y Parodi, *Historia del Excmo. Ayuntamiento de la Muy Noble, Muy Leal, Muy Heróica e Invicta Ciudad de Sevilla* (Seville: Tipografía de la Región, 1896), II. 314; Richard L. Kagan, *Universidad y sociedad en la España moderna* (Madrid: Tecnos, 1981), p. 62. It is also mentioned by Álvarez Márquez, 'La enseñanza de las primeras letras', p. 51; Álvarez Márquez, *La impresión y el comercio de libros*, p. 335; and María del Carmen Álvarez Márquez, *Impresores, libreros y mercaderes de libros en la Sevilla del Quinientos* (Zaragoza: Pórtico, 2009), II. 229. See also Resines, *La catequesis en España*, p. 232.

the Christian doctrine, that the [Christian doctrine] primers of the said church are not being used and had come to decrease the said alms.[25]

It is important to note that the complaints, litigations and disputes of Chapter of Valladolid against those new works and publishing strategies were financial in nature and not religious. They focused on Christian doctrine primers as works for teaching how to read, not as doctrines or catechetical works. One of the first of the Chapter of Valladolid's lawsuits must have been over the printing of the work 'Catón con el abc y el beaba al principio' (Cato with the abc and the *beaba* at the beginning) of 1584. On 27 June 1584, the Seville book merchant Alonso de la Mata had been granted royal privilege to print a primer entitled this way. It seems that the work was effectively published, since it is known that the Chapter of Valladolid filed a lawsuit before the Royal Council for what the Chapter of Valladolid understood as a work that undermined its exclusive privilege for printing Christian doctrine primers.[26] It can be argued that the Royal Council itself had broken the privilege given to the Chapter of Valladolid on September 1583 by granting another privilege to Mata in June 1584, but it is difficult to believe that the Council was unaware of the privilege granted to the Chapter in 1583. As an alternative, it is also possible that the Royal Council perceived Mata's Cato and Christian doctrine primers as two very different works. Indeed, they were probably very different texts and works, but the Chapter of Valladolid's monopoly over primers and, therefore, an unavoidable school booklet meant control over a huge publishing business and the consequent profits. The Chapter of Valladolid's lawsuit against the edition of Gaspar Astete's *Interrogaciones para la doctrina christiana en forma de diálogo entre el maestro y el discípulo* (Questions about Christian doctrine by way of a dialogue between a teacher and a disciple) printed in Madrid in 1589 and in Alcalá de Henares in 1595 seems to confirm this pattern. Astete's work was a famous Christian doctrine published many times during the sixteenth century and afterwards. However, Astete's doctrine was never a danger as far as the teachings of the church were concerned. Indeed, the Chapter of Valladolid's lawsuit against Astete's work was not filed for its religious teachings, but for the inclusion of a primer in the edition of Astete's doctrine printed in Alcalá de Henares

---

25   Luis Resines, 'Astete frente a Ripalda. Dos autores para una obra', *Teología y Catequesis*, 58 (1996), p. 126.
26   The work was probably published between July 1584 and April 1585. On 5 May 1585, Mata gave power of attorney to Diego del Castillo and Gaspar de Zárate. An agreement was reached between Mata and the Prior and the Chapter of Valladolid. Álvarez Márquez, 'La enseñanza de las primeras letras', p. 73; Álvarez Márquez, *La impresión y el comercio de libros*, pp. 93–94, p. 188, pp. 332–333.

in 1595, which, from the Chapter of Valladolid's viewpoint, was an infringement of its privilege. A licence for printing Alcala's edition of Astete's work was granted to Alcala bookseller Gaspar de Buendía on 11 June 1595.[27] That same year, Sebastián Martínez printed around 650 copies of Astete's work, but they were never marketed. In 1595, the Chapter of Valladolid filed a complaint against Hernán Ramírez, Valladolid bookseller and printer, María Ramírez and Juana Martínez de Angulo, daughter of Sebastián Martínez, because they were responsible for publishing it. In 1596, the copies were seized by royal decree, and it was ordered that new editions of Astete's work with a primer could not be published:[28]

> I criminally denounce Hernán Ramírez, bookseller and printer, neighbour of this city, and all others who appear to be guilty. And counting the case of this, my complaint ... I say that ... the said neighbours, without fear of God and in disregard of the fault and in great damage and prejudice on my part and in violation of the royal privileges ... by which I was given privilege so that I could have the primers printed and printed in these kingdoms to teach the children and that no other person could print or sell them under the penalty of the said privileges. ... And the said defendants have craftily and secretly printed and sold the said primers ... in doing which ... they have committed a grave crime worthy of punishment. I ask your Majesty and for the investigation of the aforesaid provisions and orders ... to visit personally the printing offices and bookstores of the aforementioned, and of any others, and that the doctrines and primers found on them be seized and confiscated, and that they be imprisoned and that they are to be proceeded against with all remedy and rigor.[29]

---

27 A licence had been given to Madrid bookseller Francisco Enríquez for printing the same work in 1589 and in 1590. See Archivo General de Simancas (afterwards AGS), Consejo Real de Castilla, 478-5 and 478-5(19). A reference to the license granted to Buendía can be found in AGS, Consejo Real de Castilla, 478-5(12). These documents were mentioned and transcribed by Resines, 'Astete frente a Ripalda', pp. 101–103, 120. Gaspar Astete, *Interrogaciones para la Doctrina Christiana en forma de diálogo entre el maestro y el discípulo* (Madrid: widow of Querino Gerardo, 1589), USTC 1793004. AGS, Consejo Real de Castilla, 478-5(3).

28 *Interrogaciones para la Doctrina Christiana en forma de diálogo entre el maestro y el discípulo* (Alcalá de Henares: Sebastián Martínez, 1595), USTC 1793005. AGS, Consejo Real de Castilla, 478-5(3). See Resines, 'Astete frente a Ripalda', pp. 89–96, p. 107.

29 'Complaint made by the Chapter of Valladolid against Hernán Ramírez, María Ramírez and Juana Martínez de Angulo for printing a primer'. AGS, Consejo Real de Castilla,

> You know that having seen by those of our council the lawsuit ... about the complaint ... made by the Prior and Chapter of ... Valladolid, against Hernán Ramírez, bookseller, and others about the printing of a book of doctrine and dialogue with written in them the *beabá* and *abecé*, against the privilege that the said church has with a prohibition against printing or selling it ... they ordered ... to seize the doctrines that have been printed with a primer ... and that you do not consent that they can be printed with ... the said primer, nor that those already printed can be sold.[30]

Many questions remain unanswered regarding the Christian doctrine primers and the role they played in the history of the Spanish Catholic Reform. In this article, I suggest that the history of the said primer and of the *Cartilla y doctrina cristiana de Valladolid* goes far beyond Counter-Reformation ideas and goals and that logistical and economic issues also played an important role. I have tried to disentangle some of the intricacies of this enormous publishing business to present the control that the Spanish Crown and church exercised over the texts used for teaching children to read, the administrative failures of the Chapter of Valladolid for printing and selling the new primer, and the oversight and control it exercised over any danger to its profits.

478-5(2). This document was mentioned and transcribed by Resines, 'Astete frente a Ripalda', pp. 95–96.

30 'Condemnation of Hernán Ramírez, María Ramírez and Juana Martínez de Angulo for printing a doctrine, containing a primer'. AGS, Consejo Real de Castilla, 478-5(20). This document was mentioned and transcribed by Resines, 'Astete frente a Ripalda', p. 107.

CHAPTER 4

A Coordinated Catholic Press

The Editing and Dispersal of Nicholas Sander's Schismatis Anglicani, *1580–c.1600*

Chelsea Reutcke

Originally published in 1585, Nicholas Sander's *De origine ac progressu schismatis Anglicani* offered the first printed Catholic account of the English Reformation from Henry VIII down to the current year of Elizabeth I's reign.[1] The octavo book established England's break with Rome as the result of Henry's lust and wickedness. As a polemical piece, it effectively filled a void in the writings on English Church history, responding to Protestant claims like John Foxe's *Actes and Monuments*. However, its primary audience was not those in England but rather Continental Catholics. Emerging at a time of amplified persecution in England, the *Schismatis Anglicani*'s assertions of the queen's illegitimacy and its chronicling of anti-Catholic cruelty sought to justify the militant suppression of Protestantism. It was quickly translated directly or adapted by authors for local histories and contexts so that Sander's arguments appeared in French, Spanish, Portuguese, Italian and German (and later, Polish).[2] Despite this, there was no extant English translation until the nineteenth century. Over the final decade of the sixteenth century, it became the standard Catholic source for this history, and by 1592, Robert Persons, head of the English Jesuit Mission, wrote, 'I find it printed againe in Latin almost in euery [*sic*] state' and the translations 'I am tolde are many'.[3]

---

1 Cologne [Rheims]: s.n., 1585, USTC 640960/A&R no. 972. Note: in addition to the USTC numbers, for Catholic books, this article will also include the numbers from Allison and Rogers catalogues: A.F. Allison and D.M. Rogers, *The contemporary printed literature of the English counter-reformation between 1558–1640: an annotated catalogue* (Brookfield, VT: Scolar Press, 1989–1994), 2 vols.
2 Adaptation here signifies an expanded and altered translation credited to an independent author but recognised as having derived the bulk of its text from Sander.
3 Robert Persons, *An Aduertisement written to a secretarie of my L. Treaturers of Ingland* ([Antwerp]: s.n., 1592), USTC 441442/A&R no. 264, p. 7. (Note: Allison & Rogers attribute this to Joseph Creswell.)

Born to a Catholic family in Surrey, England in c.1530, Nicholas Sander was already a prominent polemicist when he died in 1581.[4] He established connections throughout the Continent by advising the pope on English affairs, representing English pensioners before the Spanish king and serving as an aid to Cardinal Stanislaus Hosius at the Council of Trent.[5] His most famous work at the time of his death, *De visibili monarchia* (1571), supported the pope's deposing power over Queen Elizabeth.[6] He died in a failed Irish uprising against the queen.[7] In his militancy, Sander was a few years ahead of his contemporaries, which might explain part of the delay in his work going to press. What then made his history of the Anglican schism the default narrative was the coordinated and deliberate efforts of members of continental Catholic networks. After Sander died with his manuscript incomplete, the secular priest (later Cardinal) William Allen and the Jesuit Robert Persons took up the *Schismatis Anglicani* as propaganda on the evils and invalidity of the Elizabethan regime, as well as a more global warning against heresy and indulgent rulers. In doing so, they worked closely with Catholic priests, rulers and laymen across Europe, especially the Jesuits.

This article explores all the major editions, translations and adaptations in the first fifteen years of its printed existence. In doing so, it shows the coordinated international effort spearheaded by Allen and Persons, with support from the Society of Jesus and Continental post-Tridentine leaders, to print, promote and circulate Nicholas Sander's *Schismatis Anglicani*. The group produced multiple iterations and translations of the work to appeal to audiences in Catholic strongholds of Europe, particularly in those areas whose rulers had pledged support for an invasion of England. With Elizabeth appearing as the defender of Protestant Europe, Robert Scully argues that the Catholic powers set aside their own disputes and their concern over Philip's European hegemony to support the Spanish endeavour against England.[8] This included Spain, (Guise-support in) France, the Papal States and Bavaria. Sander's book served as a call-to-arms about England, a warning to those with Protestants in their

---

4   Christopher Highley, *Catholics Writing the Nation in Early Modern Britain and England* (Oxford: Oxford University Press, 2008), pp. 24–32.
5   J.H. Pollen, 'Dr. Nicholas Sander', *The English Historical Review*, 21 (1891), pp. 36–37.
6   *De visibili monarchia ecclesiae libri octo* (Louvain, 1571), USTC 406212/A&R no. 1013. New editions emerged in 1572, 1578, 1580 and 1592 printed in Louvain, Antwerp and Würzburg. The text defended the papal bull of excommunication against the queen issued in 1570.
7   Highley, *Catholics Writing*, pp. 37–40.
8   Robert Scully, '"In the Confident Hope of a Miracle". The Spanish Armada and Religious Mentalities in the Late Sixteenth Century', *The Catholic Historical Review*, 89 (2003), pp. 643–654.

realms and a caution to those seeking to emulate Henry VIII. At the same time, this article highlights this network's awareness of the highly malleable nature of Sander's text, which allowed it to comment on local concerns, in addition to raising support for the English enterprise. While retaining the same recognisable core narrative, the purposeful use of dedications, expansions or contractions as well as the choices of format, language and genre made Sander's history relevant to as many readers as possible. This allowed the *Schismatis Anglicani* to serve many goals at once: to call for an English invasion, to instigate a papal crusade across Europe and to shore up readers' personal resistance to heresy. Taken together, the collaborative efforts behind the various Latin editions, translations and vernacular adaptations demonstrate the existence of vital networks across Catholic Europe that understood the power of print and the persuasiveness of a narrative that was both uniform and highly adaptable.

Though still a minor figure in English historiography, Sander's work has become increasingly referenced in discussions of Catholic print and Reformation historiography and is well known to most scholars of continental polemics.[9] The most significant voices have been those of Christopher Highley and Victor Houliston, who established the importance of the *Schismatis Anglicani* in polemical battles against Protestants and highlighted Person's input.[10] While these works focus on the benefits of the core text, this article aims to break down these various editions, demonstrating the perhaps paradoxical cohesion and variability across the works. Towards this end, this article explores the context and alterations behind the editions, translations and adaptations of Sander's history through to the end of Elizabeth's reign.

The article begins with a brief exploration of the author and book, the first two Latin editions (and the Allen–Persons party) and the Ribadeneira adaptation. Of these, Pedro de Ribadeneira's contributions have received significant

---

9   David Lewis, 'Introduction', in Nicholas Sander, *Rise and Growth of the Anglican Schism*, trans. David Lewis (London: Burns & Oates, 1877); Pollen, 'Sander', pp. 36–47; Paul Arblaster, *Antwerp & the World. Richard Verstegan and the International Culture of Catholic Reformation* (Louvain: Cornell University Press, 2004); Victor Houliston, *Catholic Resistance in Elizabethan England. Robert Persons's Jesuit Polemic, 1580–1610* (Aldershot: Ashgate, 2007); Thomas McCoog, 'Construing Martyrdom in the English Catholic Community, 1582–1602', in Ethan Shagan (ed.), *Catholics and the 'Protestant Nation'. Religious Politics and Identity in Early Modern England* (Manchester: Manchester University Press, 2005), pp. 95–127.

10   Christopher Highley, 'A Pestilent and Seditious Book'. Nicholas Sander's '*Schismatis Anglicani* and Catholic Histories of the Reformation', *Huntington Library Quarterly*, 68 (2005), pp. 151–171; Victor Houliston, 'The Missionary Position. Catholics Writing the History of the English Reformation', *English Studies in Africa*, 54 (2011), pp. 16–30.

scholarly attention.[11] Studies on Ribadeneira emphasise the Spanish character of his work, but this article also stresses where it fits into the international narrative by placing it alongside the other translations. As a result, the rest of this article covers the still comparatively obscure iterations: the 1591 Italian adaptation, the 1587 French translation, the 1586–1588 Latin editions from Ingolstadt and the 1594 German translation. These sections will demonstrate why these editions deserve similar attention to what Ribadeneira's has received. In placing the various versions of Sander alongside each other, this article seeks to balance the local and international contexts to demonstrate how each iteration fits into the agendas of the English militant priests and the revived Catholic League. Taken together, the early Catholic use of Sander's Reformation history encapsulates the international networks of post-Tridentine Catholic Europe, their goals and their methods.

1   Origins

Sander had been steadily writing and gathering sources for his history throughout the 1570s. According to Freddy Dominguez, Sander had originally presented a manuscript copy of his history in 1573 while residing in Spain. However, at the time, the king had agreed to suppress the work to keep open diplomatic channels with England.[12] While Sander had previously written about papal infallibility and Catholic suffering under Elizabeth, his *Schismatis Anglicani* adopted a far more hostile tone to its subject matter.[13] Attacking the royal supremacy, he depicted Henry's church as a selfish schismatic innovation, not even able to claim descent from Wycliffe, Luther or Calvin. 'Whither, then, did you go when you went out of the Roman Church?' Sander asked. 'It was to yourself'.[14] Sander framed the king's marriage to Anne as one of the foundations of the Church of England, arguing that it was built upon the worst of sins. He conflated heresy and Elizabeth, stating that Anne and Henry's marriage 'opened a door to every heresy' and birthed 'that evil thing', which drove out the Christian church.[15]

---

11   Spencer J. Weinreich (ed., trans.), *Pedro de Ribadeneyra's 'Ecclesiastical History of the Schism of the Kingdom of England'* (Leiden: Brill, 2017). See also Freddy C. Domínguez, 'History in Action. The Case of Pedro de Ribadeneyra's *Historia Ecclesiastica del Scisma de Inglaterra*', *Bulletin of Spanish Studies*, 93.1 (2016), pp. 13–38.
12   Freddy C. Dominguez, *Radicals in Exile. English Catholic Books During the Reign of Philip II* (University Park, USA: Penn State University Press, 2021), p. 25.
13   *De visibili monarchia ecclesiae libri octo*.
14   Note: All quotes come from the 1877 Lewis translation. Sander, *Anglican Schism*, p. 106.
15   Ibid., p. 101.

In what became the claim most attacked by Protestants, Sander stated that Elizabeth was the child of an 'incestuous marriage', as her mother was Henry VIII's daughter.[16] Though rumours of an affair between Elizabeth Boleyn and Henry VIII had circulated since the 1530s, Sander expanded it to make Anne the product of this liaison.[17] In doing so, he revoked any argument of godly preference for the English reformers by locating their Reformation's origins in an abomination.

While many of the arguments responded to the Church of England's self-perception and promotion, its intended audience was educated 'foreigners that are unversed in our affairs'.[18] Although there was a note of manuscript copies reaching England in 1583 and a reference to the work being 'Englished' in 1596, no English translation emerged until the nineteenth century.[19] Given the propensity with which Sander had written in English in the 1560s, his choice of Latin for his history was deliberate to make it more accessible to a variety of Continental audiences. He constructed the narrative following contemporary standards for the genre, including documenting his sources where possible. As with other sixteenth-century histories, he depicted an actively intervening God, with England declining into ruin as divine punishment for the actions of its rulers.[20] In other words, he intended his book to be a scholarly, albeit inflammatory, piece designed to spur the learned and influential into action. However, Sander died in 1581, before his manuscript could be completed. At the time of his death, it only covered the reigns of Henry, Edward and part of Mary.

After Sander's death, the manuscript was passed to the seminary priest Edward Rishton in Rome to finish it. The first edition of *Schismatis Anglicani* appeared in print in late 1585, with an anonymous imprint listing the city of Cologne. This was a false imprint for Jean de Foigny's press in Rheims. At the

---

16   Ibid., pp. 23–28, 101.
17   William Peto and George Throckmorton referenced Henry as 'meddling' with Elizabeth, Mary and Anne Boleyn in the 1530s, claims which were repeated in the manuscript works of Nicholas Harpsfield and William Rastell, whom Sander heavily cited. 'Sir George Throckmorton to [Henry VIII], 1537' in *Letters and Papers, Foreign and Domestic, Henry VIII, Volume 12 Part 2, June–December 1537*, ed. James Gairdner (London: Her Majesty's Stationery Office, 1891), pp. 332–333; Nicholas Harpsfield, *A Treatise on the Pretended Divorce between Henry VIII and Catharine of Aragon*, ed. Nicholas Pocock (Camden Society: London, 1878); Nicholas Harpsfield, *The Life and Death of Sir Thomas Moore*, ed. Elsie Vaughan Hitchcock, R.W. Chambers (EETS: London, 1932).
18   Highley, 'Pestilent and Seditious Book', p. 155.
19   CSPD, Eliz I, 1595–1597, p. 339.
20   Joseph H. Preston, 'English Ecclesiastical Historians and the Problem of Bias, 1559–1742', *Journal of the History of Ideas*, 32 (1971), p. 219.

time, Rheims served as the temporary location of the English College of Douai, founded by Cardinal Allen, and Foigny had been responsible for the Douai-Rheims Bible and several other English Catholic works. Nevertheless, subsequent editions and translations repeatedly reiterate the text's provenance as Cologne.[21] Rishton added the final book on Elizabeth, showcasing her most recent aggressions from the perspective of one who had suffered first-hand. Rishton had spent five to six years imprisoned in the Tower of London for his missionary work before being banished from England on pain of death.[22] This provided a perspective that Sander, despite his suffering in Ireland, could not, while delivering on the promised horrors Sander had set up in describing Elizabeth's origins.

In addition to retaining the fake origin of the first edition, all subsequent editions and most translations included Rishton's preface, crediting him for completing the work. However, the book covers the months after Rishton's own death in 1585, indicating that there were other editors at play. These contributions most likely came from Allen and Persons, who are near-universally recognised as the editors of the second, enlarged and most significant edition produced in Rome in 1586.[23] Allen and Persons were almost certainly present from the onset of preparing Sander's incomplete manuscript for print. In his preface, Rishton described having been given the manuscript by a man he named as Jodocus Skarnkert and whom Houliston suggests was Allen, head of the English Mission.[24] David Lewis, meanwhile, suggested that Rishton received the manuscript from Persons, with whom he had travelled for a time before his mission to England.[25] It was principally the efforts of these men that set into motion the wide-ranging dispersal and adaptation of Sander's narrative; they would take a compelling and scandalous narrative and expand, disperse and adapt it into a bestseller.

---

21 Dominguez discusses the significance of Cologne as a chosen false city in *Radicals in Exile*, pp. 31–34.
22 Highley, 'Pestilent and Seditious Book', p. 155.
23 Thomas Mayer, 'A Sticking-Plaster Saint? Autobiography and Hagiography in the Making of Reginald Pole', in Thomas Mayer, D.R. Woolf (eds.), *The Rhetorics of Life-writing in Early Modern Europe. Forms of Biography from Cassandra Fedele to Louis XIV* (Ann Arbor: University of Michigan Press, 1995), p. 212; Victor Houliston, 'Fallen Prince and Pretender of the Faith. Henry VIII as seen by Sander and Persons', in Thomas Betteridge, Thomas S. Freeman (eds.), *Henry VIII and History* (Burlington: Routledge, 2012), p. 121.
24 Houliston, 'Fallen Prince', p. 121.
25 Lewis, 'Introduction', p. xiv.

2 The Allen–Persons Project

When they took on the project of Sander's text, Allen and Persons combined their knowledge of book-selling strategies with the breadth of their clerical network to enhance the appeal of the work to as many audiences as possible. Scholars have long acknowledged both men's involvement, but the multifaceted ways in which they shaped the text continue to be added to. Allen and Persons travelled together from Rheims to Rome in late 1585, their movements aligning with the printing schedule for the first and second editions. The surviving manuscript of Sander's history features copious annotations by Persons on the first 46 folios, and the Jesuits worked to gather additional material for the second edition's expansion. Meanwhile, Persons credited sections, particularly regarding universities in book two, to Allen.[26] Both men had long known Sanders, with Allen referring to him as 'my special friend', and understood the utility of a Catholic history of the English Reformation.[27]

Allen and Persons were not only prolific writers, but they also consistently engaged in and oversaw Catholic printing operations on the Continent and at secret presses in England, as well as smuggling operations to bring texts to English readers.[28] As such, they knew how to effectively 'sell' Sander's text to as wide an audience as possible. The second edition, printed in Rome in 1586, featured letters of Persons and Allen, an extensive list of Tudor martyrs, and the 'Tower Diary', an account by the seminary priest John Hart, protégé of Allen, of his imprisonment in the Tower of London from 1580 to 1585.[29] Hart arrived in Rome a week after Persons and Allen and likely created the diary either by the request of the two priests or to salvage his reputation after he had agreed to spy on Allen for the English crown.[30] Anne Dillon refers to the inclusion of the Tower Diary as 'a masterstroke' from a man who 'understood

---

26 Pollen, 'Sander', pp. 42–45; Houliston 'Missionary Position', pp. 18–19.
27 P. Renold (ed.), *Letters of William Allen and Richard Barrett, 1572–1598* (CRS: London, 1967, Catholic Record Society, 58), p. 10.
28 For more on the collaborations between Allen and Persons, see Thomas H. Clancy, *Papist Pamphleteers. The Allen-Persons Party and the Political Thought of the Counter-Reformation in England, 1572–1615* (Chicago: Loyola University Press, 1964); Mark Netzloff, 'The English Colleges and the English Nation. Allen, Persons, Verstegan, and Diasporic Nationalism', in Ronald Corthell etc. (eds.), *Catholic Culture in Early Modern England* (Notre Dame: University of Notre Dame Press, 2007), pp. 236–260; Peter Holmes, 'The Missing "Allen-Persons" Cases of Conscience', *British Catholic History*, 32 (2014), pp. 1–20.
29 USTC 854487/A&R no. 973. Here and further in the subsequent footnotes the USTC numbers are used to identify new editions of Sander's work.
30 Mordechai Feingold, 'The Reluctant Martyr. John Hart's English Mission', *Journal of Jesuit Studies*, 6 (2019), pp. 647–649.

the book-buying market on the continent'.³¹ This account provided graphic details of the 'instruments of torture and their use', executions and governmental attempts to coerce Catholics into conformity.³² With this and Rishton's account, the editors adapted Sander's providential history for use in polemics of martyrologies. It was this second edition that became the standard for the translations and the other Latin editions, with the French translation describing itself as 'selon la copie latine de Rome'.³³

Allen and Person inserted contemporary European events to illustrate the direct threat a heretical England posed to Christendom. The final book contained several examples of Elizabeth aiding heretics beyond her borders, including siding with Protestant rebels in Scotland and France and supporting the 'reprobate' William of Orange in Flanders.³⁴ The book further turns these actions into a conspiracy, with the queen hoping 'that all the Catholic sovereigns being fully occupied with their own affairs' would not be able to interfere in England.³⁵ She became a threat not just to England but to all of Christendom. Armed with manuscript copies and the first two editions, Allen and Persons worked to circulate the text to key allies across continental Europe. On May 20, 1586, the same month it came out of the press, Persons sent a copy of the Roman edition to Don Juan Idiaquez, Philip II's secretary of state. He wrote in the accompanying letter:

> We are sending to your Excellency ... a book on the English Schism, in which towards the end can be seen what has been said in defence of His Majesty's interests. I am confident that ... you will not let those men [i.e. English exiles] be entirely lost to you, who are serving you so faithfully.³⁶

The letter summarises what Allen and Persons saw in the text: a means to flatter or inspire Catholic leaders and to remind the world of how those of the 'true faith' in England or exiled abroad were suffering. The frequent republication of *Schismatis Anglicani* in the 1580s was largely tied to preparing 'public opinion in Catholic Europe for the enterprise of the Spanish Armada'.³⁷

---

31   Anne Dillon, *The Construction of Martyrdom in the English Catholic Community, 1535–1603* (Aldershot: Ashgate, 2002), p. 81.
32   Ibid.
33   USTC 6011/A&R no. 893, titlepage.
34   Sander, *Anglican Schism*, p. 289.
35   Ibid, pp. 288–289.
36   Leo Hicks SJ (ed.), *Letter and Memorials of Father Robert Persons, s.j., Vol. I (to 1588)* (CRS: London, 1942, Catholic Record Society 39), pp. 277–278.
37   Houliston, 'Missionary Position', p. 19; Robert Bireley, *The Counter-Reformation Prince. Anti-Machiavellianism or Catholic Statecraft in Early Modern Europe* (Chapel Hill: University of North Carolina Press, 1990), pp. 112–115.

However, the priests also saw the text as a means to shore up the strength of Catholicism against the threat of Protestantism. As Rishton exclaimed, 'I write this that other nations ... may learn how heresies begin and grow, and be on their guard ... against pestilences of this kind'.[38] This wider goal can be seen in the chosen printing format of the *Schismatis Anglicani*, as well as the continued push to make the history accessible in more places and to more people. The octavo format made the printed book more portable. Combined with the lack of red-lettering, embedded woodcuts or engravings and minimal ornamentation all lowered the printing costs and increased the audience pool. Most future iterations of the *Schismatis Anglicani* preserved this format.

The two English priests also began encouraging, funding and guiding translation and adaptation efforts to expand the readership even more. Crucial to the success of the *Schismatis Anglicani* and demonstrating the truly intertwined nature of post-Reformation Catholic printing, other Counter-Reformation figures, particularly Jesuits, lent their support as well. These figures included the Superior General of the Jesuits, Claudio Acquaviva and the Jesuit Pedro de Ribadeneira, who adapted it for Spanish audiences.[39] Indeed, Jesuit enthusiasm for the project was so strong that their influence could be seen even in those editions without specific links to Allen or Persons. Letters from Cardinal Reginald Pole, which had been in the possession of Cardinal Stanisław Hosius, with whom Sander travelled and served, were donated to the cause.[40] Powerful leaders like Philip II and Henri I, Duke of Guise, also lent financial support. The remainder of this article will trace the numerous iterations that Sander's work took on over the next two decades and how they demonstrate the cohesion of communication and goals shared across Catholic Europe. Connected through the Catholic networks behind the texts to the international aims, subsequent editions to the 1586 Roman version were also connected to the local climates through the use of dedications, language and additions.

3 The Spanish Sander: Pedro de Ribadeneira's *Historia eclesiástica*

By far the most well-known and influential of the iterations of Sander's *Schismatis Anglicani* is the Spanish adaptation by the Jesuit Pedro de Ribadeneira. *Historia eclesiástica del scisma* first appeared in Madrid in 1588 and was the result of the networks and collaboration between Ribadeneira and Persons, encouraged

---

38   Robert Bireley, *The Counter-Reformation Prince*, p. 268.
39   Houliston, 'Missionary Position', p. 18.
40   Ibid.

by Acquaviva.[41] A significant polemicist for the proposed Spanish invasion, Ribadeneira and his *Historia* joined in the propaganda campaign leading up to the Spanish Armada. However, the book's continued re-publication as Armada dreams faded pointed to its wider relevance, combining Spanish pride with a sincere desire to re-Catholicise England.

Ribadeneira had maintained an interest in England since his visit in 1558, which had coincided with Elizabeth's ascension, and had been working on his own history of the English Reformation.[42] For years, he had corresponded and collaborated with Sander and Persons and had even met Nicholas Sander while the latter was in Madrid.[43] It was natural, therefore, for Persons to seek out his fellow Jesuit and present him with Sander's manuscript, a move supported by the Superior General, Acquaviva. In 1588, Acquaviva sent Persons to Spain to open the English College of Valladolid, placing the English Jesuit in a useful place to oversee Ribadeneira's final product. Moreover, in 1593, he provided material for Ribadeneira's second volume. Acquaviva hoped it would strengthen the 'English Party' in Spain, especially as invasion plans routinely stalled.[44] This influence also made the Spanish adaptation a strongly pro-Jesuit text, emphasising their contributions and leadership in a move that foresaw the complications of the Archpriest Controversy in 1598. Around the same time, Acquaviva and Ribadeneira worked on a uniform history of the Jesuit order.[45] *Historia ecclesiástica* therefore showcased the combined efforts of the English Catholic and Jesuit networks.

The English Catholics sought out not only Ribadeneira's skills but also Spanish influence. The use of vernacular opened up the book to the Spanish public, and it was widely distributed across Philip II's territories. In the year of the Armada alone, it was printed in Madrid, Saragossa, Valencia, Barcelona, Lisbon and Antwerp, some cities receiving multiple reprints that same year.[46] The relative plainness of the first edition, octavo in format like the Latin

---

41 USTC 337767/A&R no. 993.
42 Spencer J. Weinreich, 'England in the Margin. Providence and Historiography' in *Pedro de Ribadeneyra's Historia ecclesiastica del scisma del reyno de Inglaterra*, in *Jesuit Intellectual and Physical Exchange between England and Mainland Europe, c.1580–1789* (Leiden: Brill, 2018), pp. 263–286.
43 Jodi Bilinkoff, 'The Many "Lives" of Pedro de Ribadeneyra', *Renaissance Quarterly*, 52 (1999), pp. 180–181.
44 Houliston, 'Missionary Position', p. 19.
45 Gómez Díez, Francisco Javier, 'Espiritualidad ignaciana y primera historiografía jesuíta. Pedro de Ribadeneira', *Cauriensia*, 11 (2016), p. 571.
46 (Madrid) USTC 337766/A&R no. 994; (Saragossa) USTC 337768/A&R no. 998; (Valencia) USTC 337769/A&R no. 999; (Barcelona) USTC 343225/A&R no. 997; (Lisbon) USTC 440419/A&R no. 995; (Antwerp) USTC 440419/A&R no. 1008.

editions, indicates its intention for a wider reading public than just the king and Habsburg court. This audience also explains the direction the adaptation took. Without the looming threat of a Protestant ruler or 'Calvinist poison', it sought instead to win Spanish support for action against England by highlighting the history of the two countries' connections. Textually, Ribadeneira expanded the history to the current year to include Francis Drake's recent attack on Cadiz and Mary Stuart's execution as further testaments to Elizabeth's cruelty. Meanwhile, his expansion of the life of Catherine of Aragon made her a more dramatic foil for Anne Boleyn. He also explored Mary Tudor's reign in more depth, using her marriage to Philip II in 1554 as a means to praise the king. These additions reminded Spaniards of their intertwined past with, and therefore their responsibility towards, England while simultaneously presenting the current threat Elizabeth represented to their kingdom's prosperity.

Other audiences were also catered to. Philip viewed his eventual attempted invasion of England as a crusade befitting the successor of the Catholic Monarchs.[47] Reflecting this, dedication praised the lineage of Catholic Monarchs from which Philip II and his son descended, contrasting them with the 'bestia fiera' Henry VIII and his two Protestant children.[48] Other expansions worked to place the history in a global Catholic narrative, highlighting Spain's (and the Jesuits') role in safeguarding Christianity.[49] Ribadeneira frequently recognised Sander's efforts throughout his text, frequently stating 'todo esto dize Sandero', meaning 'all this said Sander'.[50] This move allowed Ribadeneira to credit his sources (and perhaps deflect negative reactions) while building the history of the English schism as a history of the fight for Christendom. Though its core remained Sander's history, Ribadeneira adapted the *Schismatis Anglicani* for Spanish and wider Catholic audiences, a crucial alteration for coming events.

While English exiles and Catholic powers had been plotting an invasion of England for years, Ribadeneira's *Historia* specifically sought to generate support for the upcoming launch of the Spanish Armada in the summer of 1588. To enforce a cohesive message, other Armada propaganda featured Sander's contributions as well. William Allen's pamphlet for English audiences repeated Sander's most salacious claim, describing Elizabeth as 'a bastard, conceived and born by incestuous adultery'. The sheets accompanied the Armada and were to be released after its successful landing. Demonstrating how the

---

47   Geoffrey Parker, 'The Place of Tudor England in the Messianic Vision of Philip II of Spain', *Transactions of the Royal Historical Society*, 12 (2002), pp. 170, 173–176.
48   USTC 337767/A&R no. 993, pp. 181–182.
49   Weinreich, *Ribadeneyra's historia ecclesiastica*, pp. 30–38, 58–65.
50   USTC 337767/A&R no. 993, e.g., pp. 79–80.

histories influenced each other, the pamphlet also stated that Elizabeth was 'troublesome to the whole body of Christendom', a stance reiterated in the later editions of Sander.[51] Moreover, the Latin editions of Sander printed after 1600 featured an appendix from Ribadeneira's history.[52] Despite the Armada's failure, both Sander and Ribadeneira's texts maintained their popularity. A second volume of the *Historia* emerged in 1593, with several reprints of both volumes occurring throughout the 1590s as the Spanish mood recovered from despair into renewed confidence. Spain attempted two more armadas in 1596 and 1597, and invasion hopes did not fade until Elizabeth's death in 1603. Even beyond this year, Sander and Ribadeneira's narrative continued to set the tone of continental opinion of England and showcased Spain's fortitude against heresy.

The following editions and adaptations should be viewed in this same Armada framework, with those from 1586 to 1588 intended to win international support for the endeavour and those from after the 1588 Armada's failure deployed to revive the dream of an invasion of England by any European power. At the same time, they fit into the pan-European calls for a crusade against heresy while simultaneously responding to regional needs. This flexibility allowed for their continued relevancy after the 1590s.

4   Italian Tributes to Allen: Pollini's *Storia Ecclesiastica*

While Ribadeneira's adaptation was influenced by Persons, Allen potentially assumed patronage of the Italian iteration. In 1591 in Florence, the Dominican friar, Girolamo Pollini, adapted the text into Italian under the title *Storia ecclesiastica della riuoluzione d'Inghilterra*. The Italian adaptation serves as a reminder that non-Jesuit priests were involved in popularising Sander's narrative. According to a letter from Lord Darcy to Lord Burghley, Pollini 'had the most parts of his instruccions from the Cardinall Allen'.[53] Pollini dedicated his book to Allen, then based at the English College of Rome, and credited him for

---

51   William Allen, *A Declaration of the Sentence and Deposition of Elizabeth*, quoted in Robert Miola (ed.), *Early Modern Catholicism. An Anthology of Primary Sources* (Oxford: Oxford University Press, 2007), USTC 441441/A&R no. 770, pp. 77–78.

52   The title expanded to specifically mention Ribadeneira: *Vera Et Sincera Historia Schismatis Anglicani, De eius Origine ac Progressu, Tribus libris fideliter conscripta, ab R.D. Nicolao Sandero Anglo, Doct: Theologo; aucta per Eduardum Rishtonum. Nunc postremum Appendice ex R.P. Petri Ribadeneirae libris, auct* (Cologne: s.n., 1610), USTC 2106907, 2015541, 2002616/A&R no. 977; (Cologne: s.n., 1628) USTC 2033509/A&R no. 978.

53   Carlo M. Bajetta (ed.), *Elizabeth I's Italian Letters* (New York: Palgrave MacMillan, 2017), p. 173. Bajetta disputes Allen's involvement.

providing additional information on English affairs. Doing so not only opened up the story of the schism to a wider Italian audience but also drew that audience's attention to the presence and work of the English exiles in Rome. The timing also coincided with Allen's attempts to have the pope renew Elizabeth's excommunication.[54]

Although Elizabeth requested that the Duke of Tuscany suppress it, the text re-emerged again in 1591 from the same Florentine printing firm, the Giuntas, only in Bologna, which was under papal control.[55] The queen's outrage likely emerged from seeing the text's effectiveness in the failed Armada. Allen wrote to the duke and Spanish ambassador to Rome, complaining about the men who had stopped further printing of the book.[56] The Italian adaptation likely promoted the first printed response, John Cowell's anonymous *Antisanderus* (1593).[57] When the queen again protested against the book, publication simply transferred to Rome, where it was printed in 1594, the same year Allen died, under the patronage of Clement VIII's bookseller, Giovanni Angelo Ruffinelli, and dedicated to the pope.[58] Ruffinelli would also print a 1602 abridgement of Pollini in the Florentine dialect by Bernardo Davanzati.[59] This returned the publication of the Italian adaptation to the same city that had produced the authoritative Latin edition in 1586. Moreover, the dual link to the papacy (printer and dedication) highlighted Sander's defences of papal supremacy and infallibility, a useful reminder to the surrounding city-states. Despite Elizabeth's active protests against the history, Allen and his associates used their network to switch between safe printing cities and continued to produce the text for Italian audiences.

Like Ribadeneira, Pollini expanded Sander's history to over 800 pages to cover recent events and Italian contexts. In doing so, he drew on documents held at the English College of Douai. In adapting the work in the aftermath of the failed Armada, the death of the Guises, and the declining health of the leaders of the English Mission, history of the English schism took on a more dramatic visual tone. Throughout, Pollini amplified the tone of previous writers,

---

54 Ibid., p. 184.
55 USTC 850206/A&R no. 990; USTC 850207/A&R no. 991. There is evidence that the Florence edition copies were mostly seized. For the Bologna copy, see Dennis E. Rhodes, 'A Curious Giunta Imprint', *The Library*, s6-X:3 (1988), pp. 242–246.
56 Bajetta, *Elizabeth I's Italian letters*, p. 186.
57 USTC 512334.
58 USTC 850208/A&R no. 992. This edition was divided into four rather than five books.
59 Bernardo Davanzati, *Scisma d'Inghilterra sino alla morte della reina Maria* (Rome: Giovanni Angelo Ruffinelli, 1602), USTC 4030220/A&R no. 985. Another edition emerged the same year in Milan, USTC 4034277/A&R no. 986.

using even more bombastic prose to paint a vivid picture for the audience.[60] He also maintained a dismissive tone towards the intelligence of the English (Protestants). In other areas, he copied directly from Sander. For instance, when discussing Anne Boleyn's parentage, Pollini translated Sander's paragraph near-verbatim, concluding that 'el Re (e non d'alcun altro in somma) Anna era figliuola' (Anne was the daughter of the king – and not anyone else in short).[61]

It is interesting that it was the Italian rather than the French or Spanish adaptations that caused the greatest stir. Although Elizabeth's letter cited the slanders made against her mother, these had been present since Sander's original manuscript. Perhaps the issue instead lay with Pollini's commentary on contemporary events. Like Rishton, Pollini was explicit about his desired goal: to oppose Elizabeth and stir up people to drive out heresy. He expanded on Mary Tudor's reign, celebrating her marriage to Philip and praising his character. Then, in the final book, Pollini greatly expanded upon Elizabeth's treatment of Mary Stuart beyond what even Ribadeneira accomplished. His account also drew on Adam Blackwood's history of the queen, which, as will be seen below, itself used Sander as a source. The dedication praises Allen's efforts to oppose the queen's regime. Perhaps this praise of (at the time) still-living actors against Elizabeth proved to be too much. The 1594 edition and the 1602 abridgement by Davanzati both curtailed some of Pollini's more virulent rants, but, as with Ribadeneira's *Historia*, it became the core source for Italian accounts of the English Reformation going forward.[62]

While the 1594 edition emerged in the safety and support of Rome, the 1591 Florence edition faced scrutiny from within and without the city. This prompts the question of why Florence was chosen as the site of publication. The simplest answer is that it was the location of Pollini. However, there might have been a secondary purpose: to sway the Duke of Tuscany, still subject to Philip II, back to the English cause. While his brother (d. 1587) had previously pledged troops and funds to the 'English enterprise', Ferdinando de' Medici maintained

---

60 Fabio Battista, 'Staging English Affairs in Early Modern Italy. History, Politics, Drama', PhD thesis, The City University of New York, 2019, pp. 68–71; Michael Wyatt, *The Italian Encounter with Tudor England. A Cultural Politics of Translation* (Cambridge: Cambridge University Press, 2005), pp. 102–108.
61 USTC 850206/A&R no. 990, pp. 22–23.
62 Another Italian derivation of Sander cites both Pollini and Ribadeneira as its main sources: Angelo Galioto, *Relatione dello scisma anglicano, e del glorioso martirio del B.P.F. Giouanni Foresta Francescano Osseruante* (Palermo: Giovanni Antonio De Franceschi, 1597), USTC 831529/A&R no. 1010, p. 162/*X3r.

friendly relations with both Elizabeth and Henri IV (r. 1589).[63] Certainly, texts circulated beyond the cities that printed them, but the Sander iterations always had multiple goals. Through his adaptation, Pollini cautioned the duke on his alliance, highlighted the contributions and sufferings of English exiles like Allen and Sander, and flattered the Pope through a reminder of the latter's powers.

5   The Guise Translation in the French Wars of Religion

Although the Ribadeneira and Pollini versions show direct involvement from Allen and Persons, their influence can be detected more circumspectly in France. The first vernacular translation of Nicholas Sander's *Schismatis Anglicani* emerged after July 1587 in French, entitled *Les trois livres de Nicolas Sander*.[64] It was published in the context of the French Wars of Religion, with the powerful Guise family fighting against the perceived leniency towards Protestants of the king, Henri III. Just a few years earlier, the king had named the Huguenot Henri of Navarre as his successor, prompting the reconstitution of the radical Catholic League by the Duke of Guise. While the first editions of the *Schismatis Anglicani* required a Latin-literate audience, this vernacular translation sought to stir up public outrage and pressure Henri III to end his association with Elizabeth. Many exiled Catholics had already been working with the League to oust Henri III for his friendly diplomacy with Elizabeth and opposition to Spanish influence.[65] When Elizabeth signed off on the execution of Mary Stuart, former queen of France, in February 1587, the timing was perfect for a French translation of the many evils of the English queen and her Protestant governance.

In contrast to the other iterations, this text did not receive royal support but was instead 'produced with Guise support' and likely printed in Paris, although the imprint does not list the city.[66] Funding came from Charles Lorraine,

---

63   *CSP Venice*, 1581–1591, pp. 131, 284, 290, 551; 1592–1603, pp. 21, 41.
64   Nicolas Sander, *Les trois livres* ([Paris]: s.n., 1587), USTC 6011/A&R no. 983. The translator's preface to the reader signs off with the date 9 July 1587.
65   See Katy Gibbons, *English Catholic Exiles in Late Sixteenth-Century Paris* (London: Boydell Press, 2011), pp. 43–45, 56, 84, 89; Alexander Wilkinson, *Mary, Queen of Scots and French Public Opinion, 1542–1600* (Basingstoke: Palgrave MacMillan, 2004), pp. 109–117, 126–125.
66   Gibbons, *English Catholic Exiles*, p. 107. Adams suggests Louvain as the place of publication for the copy held at Cambridge, perhaps based on Sander's longstanding publication history in that city: H.M. Adams, *Catalogue of Books Printed on the Continent of Europe, 1501–1600, in Cambridge Libraries* (London: Cambridge University Press, 1967), p. 198, S293.

Cardinal de Vaudemont. Though Lorraine was Henri III's brother-in-law, he aligned himself with his Guise relatives. The impetus for the translation was also credited to 'Gentilzhommes Anglois refuguis de la foy catholique' (English gentlemen refugees of the Catholic faith), with the translator listed as I.T.A.C., which one source suggests was the pseudonym for an Englishman named John Thornhull.[67] This very overt joining of forces was the boldest declaration of English Catholic involvement in circulating the text to various ports and reaffirmed the book as a warning to French Catholics of the dangerous future that could be in store for them. League pamphleteers had exiles in their ranks as writers, collaborators and consumers, and it was not a stretch to place Allen and Persons among the *gentilzhommes Anglois*.

The Jesuits had a strong alliance with the House of Lorraine, strengthened by the opening of a new Jesuit college in the 1570s–1580s. Guise support had enabled Allen to set up his college in Rheims and establish a Jesuit university in Normandy. This, combined with the Duke of Guise's concern for Mary Stuart's imprisonment, prompted Persons to meet with him from 1581 through to 1587.[68] Most importantly, the Guises, the Spanish king, the Jesuits and the Allen-Persons party had an ongoing alliance to secure their realms from Protestantism. Towards this end, Persons and Allen had also met with the Duke of Guise frequently in the early 1580s, hoping to plan an invasion of England in coordination with the Spanish king.[69] Having already realised the polemical potential of Sander's history, and with propaganda efforts already underway to sway the French public against the king, his heir and the Huguenots, France was the perfect launching ground for the first vernacular edition.

In one text, the book reminded the public of the new and old atrocities committed by Elizabeth I and drew comparisons between Henry VIII and Henri III, the latter of whom was also painted as a heretic and sexual deviant by pro-League pamphleteers.[70] It followed the 1586 Roman edition faithfully, with minor expansions, including four sonnets by the translator. Even without significant changes, the book's content was connected to French concerns. As mentioned, Henry VIII's reign served as a stand-in for the disasters awaiting

---

67 Joseph Gillow, *A Literary and Biographical History, or Bibliographical Dictionary of the English Catholics. From the Breach with Rome, in 1534, to the Present Time* (London: Burns and Oates, 1885), p. 427.
68 Allen, *Letters and Memorials*, pp. xxxiv–xl.
69 Ibid., pp. xlv–xlix. Philip also aided the League's efforts to disillusion the public regarding Henri III, particularly over the fear of heretical succession: Gibbons, *Catholic Exiles*, pp. 90–92.
70 Keith Cameron, 'Henri III: The Anti-Christian King', *Journal of European Studies*, 40 (1974), pp. 152–156, 162.

France if Henri III continued to rule. Meanwhile, the final entries in book three on Elizabeth's reign and the appendices specifically called out the mistreatment of Mary Stuart and Henri III's friendship with the English queen, including his acceptance of the Order of the Garter in 1585.[71]

Moreover, the translator made use of the paratext to continue the original history's chronology. In the section describing Mary's imprisonment, printed marginalia reflected the timing of the translation with the note 'ceste annee 1587, la Royne Elizabeth a fait decapiter [Marie Royne d'Escosse]'.[72] Mary's death altered French attitudes towards her situation from disinterest to outrage. The paratext makes use of this anger to shift the book's message from restoring the Scottish queen to avenging her. To French audiences, the text presented the dangers of Protestant succession, Elizabeth's encroachment in the affairs of their ruler and the torment that would strike all Catholics if Calvinism continued to spread. Despite presenting a recent history, the book heavily reflected current events.

The translation was enough of a success that a second edition emerged within a few months, although this one was more circumspect in its origins. Gone was the attribution to Cardinal de Vaudemont and the English gentlemen. Instead, its imprint claims that the book was printed in Augsburg by Hans Mark.[73] However, this imprint is most likely false. Neither the Universal Short Title Catalogue nor the VD 17 catalogue contain any other references to Hans Mark, and he is not listed in Christoph Reske's dictionary of German printers.[74] Moreover, the artificial intelligence image recognition project, *Ornamento*, linked the printer's mark to that of Paris-based printer Abel L'Angelier.[75] The

---

[71] USTC 6011/A&R no. 983, pp. 224–226, 262; Wilkinson, *Mary, Queen of Scots*, p. 78. The book had a similar response in Poland, where there had been fear that the king would emulate Henry VIII by establishing a national church and setting aside his wife. See Martin Murphey, 'Robert Abercromby, S.J. (1536–1613) and the Baltic Counter-Reformation', *The Innes Review*, 50 (1999), pp. 59–60; Clarinda E. Calma, 'Sixteenth-Century Rare Books on and by English Recusants in the Libraries of Kraków', *Kultura i Polityka*, 10 (2011), pp. 156–160.

[72] 'This year 1587, Queen Elizabeth had decapitated Mary Queen of Scotland', USTC 6011, p. 225.

[73] USTC 9681/A&R no. 981.

[74] Christoph Reske, *Die Buchdrucker des 16. und 17. Jahrhunderts im deutschen Sprachgebiet* (Wiesbaden: Harrassowitz, 2015); *The Universal Short Title Catalogue* (USTC), https://www.ustc.ac.uk/; *Verzeichnis der im deutschen Sprachraum erschnienenen Drucke des 17. Jahrhunderts* (VD 17), http://www.vd17.de/. Allison and Rogers also conclude the imprint is false: A&R no. 981.

[75] *Ornamento*, https://ornamento.ucd.ie/. Thanks to Dr Drew Thomas for his assistance with this search. The same woodcut is found in the contemporary text printed by L'Angelier:

titlepage changes would reflect the censorship efforts from 1586 against works that might damage Henri's alliance with England and again hint at the effectiveness of the history.[76]

While the first two Latin editions of the *Schismatis Anglicani* had signalled a shift in rhetorical stance from Allen, the emergence of the French translation was far more calculated. The *Trois livres* appeared as one of many well-timed attacks on Elizabeth and Henri III in 1587–1588, responding to both the death of Mary Stuart and the approaching Armada launch. The title page's description of the English exiles recalled the broadsheet attributed to Richard Verstegan, *Breifve description des cruautéz que les Catholiques endurent en Angleterre pour le foy*.[77] The broadsheet's images reappeared in 1587 at the churchyard of Saint-Séverin, coinciding with the release of the French translation. Parallel publications, such as Adam Blackwood's French histories of the life and death of Mary Stuart, drew on Sander as a source, reinforcing his narrative.[78]

The French translation, combined with the other pamphlets and displays against the monarch, had their intended effect: in May 1588, the Parisians drove the king from the city, and the Duke of Guise, coordinating with the Spanish ambassador, looked to assume control. Things seemed to be going according to plan, as the escalation of tensions in Paris was also meant to distract the French public from siding against the planned invasions of England from Spain.[79] However, despite the care and coordination that had gone into it, its impact was cut short by the assassination of the Duke of Guise and his brother in December 1588. While the messages still stood, the primary force behind the production and circulation of the translations ended. However, the 1594 Italian edition might have been prompted by the entrance of Henri IV into Paris; even though the new king had converted to Catholicism, his rule was still opposed by the Catholic League and its allies. Meanwhile, as in Spain, French writers incorporated Sander's narrative into their histories and commentaries on current events.

Francisco Lopez de Gómara, *Voyages et conquests du capitaine Ferdinand Courtois* (Paris: Abel L'Angelier, 1588), USTC 8933.

76 Wilkinson, *Mary, Queen of Scots*, p. 113.
77 (Paris, 1583/4) USTC 75136/A&R no. 1285.
78 Adam Blackwood, *Martyre de la royne d'Escosse* (Edinburgh [Paris]: s.n. 1587), USTC 343/A&R no. 98/1; ([Paris]: s.n., 1588), USTC 5991/A&R no. 98.2. It was followed by *La Mort de la Royne* ([France]: s.n, 1588), USTC 344/A&R no. 99. They were merged into *Histoire et martyre de la royne d'Escosse* (Paris, 1589), USTC 5989/A&R no. 100.
79 Wilkinson, *Mary, Queen of Scots*, pp. 106–108.

6 Imperial Editions: The Printer, the Archbishop and the Duke

Not every edition was the direct result of Persons and Allen; however, they still demonstrated coordination across the post-Trent Catholic Continent and the ubiquitous influence of the Jesuits. From the late 1580s to the 1590s, three Latin editions and one German translation emerged from Ingolstadt and Salzburg, respectively.[80] Combined with the 1600-abridged German translation printed in Munich, this area of the Holy Roman Empire was therefore the greatest producer of Sander's work outside of Spain and perhaps even the Papal States.[81] Bavaria was another key site where Jesuits had worked to support Counter-Reformation activities, and the Duke of Bavaria, Wilhelm V, had been taking strong action against heresy in the bordering principalities. As Dillon points out, in Europe, Catholic action incidentally created Protestant martyrs, including in the Low Countries and the Huguenots in France.[82] The English Catholic martyrs thus became Europe's response to Protestant martyrologies. As a result, many individuals were motivated to put forth local editions and translations. The archbishop and the Bavarian duke, dubbed 'the Pious', were known for their hard-line stance against Protestantism; they had intervened to halt Calvinism in both Cologne and Inner Austria.[83] They were also willing to form alliances with other Catholic kingdoms.[84]

In 1586, the German printer, Wolfgang Eder, produced a Latin edition in Ingolstadt, a major centre of Jesuit scholarship. As the dedicatory epistle reveals, Eder undertook the printing and circulation of the work at his own expense ('ut typis at, impensis meis quam primum evulgaretur') to further the mission and literary efforts of re-Catholicising Europe.[85] Licensed by the Emperor and dedicated to George von Kuenburg, the Archbishop of Salzburg, a Catholic diocese in Hapsburg hereditary lands, the Ingolstadt edition underwent reprints in 1587 and 1588.[86] Eder was one of the top Catholic polemical

---

80   Latin translations: (1585) USTC 678008/A&R no. 974; USTC 678009/A&R no. 975; USTC 678007/A&R no. 976. German translation: USTC 704959/A&R no. 984.
81   Johann Mayr, *Kurtzer Bericht Aller gedenckwürdigen Sachen so sich in Engelland* ... (Munich, 1600), USTC 671040/A&R no. 989.
82   Dillon, *Construction of Martyrdom*, p. 82.
83   Regina Pörtner, *The Counter-Reformation in Central Europe* (Oxford: Oxford University Press, 2001), pp. 71, 81–90. Between 1583 and 1588, the duke joined with Philip II to install Ernst of Bavaria as Prince-elector-archbishop of Cologne.
84   The Inner-Austria schemes drew on assistance from the Emperor, the Spanish king and the Pope, although the help often fell short, particularly when it was financial. Ibid., pp. 83, 86.
85   USTC 678008/A&R no. 974, *3r.
86   Despite the death of Kuenburg in January 1587, his name remains in the dedications of the 1587 and 1588 prints: USTC 678009/A&R no. 975, USTC 678007/A&R no. 976.

printers of Ingolstadt, with several influential connections, including those among the Jesuits and rulers. Eder had been in business since 1577 and had received a loan from the Jesuit-affiliated university in Ingolstadt in 1578. Holding an imperial printing privilege since 1582, he also received a loan to save him from bankruptcy from the Duke of Bavaria in 1593.[87] As in the French translation, Eder's edition served as a warning of tolerating Protestantism and as encouragement to the archbishop to continue to act. He praised Kuenburg for driving Protestants from Salzburg and setting up a Franciscan monastery there.[88] Although he did not name Persons or Allen, he repeatedly referenced the 1586 Roman edition, and his version follows it closely and includes the Tower Diary and index of martyrs.[89] Given the number of Jesuit connections, it would be no surprise if one of them had passed the text on to Eder, or perhaps he had acquired a copy at a book fair. Regardless, Eder clearly understood both Persons' and Allen's mission in circulating the text and the effective call-to-arms the book contained.

A few years later, in 1594, the same year as the Italian edition, a German translation of Sander's book was printed in Salzburg, dedicated to Wilhelm V, of the house of Wittelsbach, and done by a courtier at the Bavarian Court, Johann Heller. Printed by Conrad Kürner, the court printer, in black letter, the titlepage of *Warhaffte Engelländische Histori, in wellicher was sich, besonder in Religionssachen ...* called for the strengthening of the Catholic face against the flourishing poison of Calvinism.[90] The German translation changed the format from octavo to quarto and compressed the final book on Elizabeth. Instead, the focus was on the reproduction of papal bulls and letters from Catherine of Aragon and English missionaries, highlighted through shifts in fonts. English Catholics increasingly sought out the patronage of the Wittelsbachs over the 1590s, especially after the death of Philip II in 1598.[91] This might help explain the desire for a German translation, and the Spanish king's death might have prompted a second, abridged German adaptation that appeared in Munich in 1600, which combined Sander's history with several others.[92]

The timing and location of the Ingolstadt editions fit into the pattern of using Sander's history in the short term to support the 'English enterprise', while the

---

87   Reske, *Die Buchdrucker*, pp. 422–423. Many thanks to Dr Jessica Farrell-Jobst for her assistance and insight regarding the German sources.
88   USTC 678008/A&R no. 974: *4r–*5v.
89   USTC 678008/A&R no. 974: titlepage, *3r–v.
90   USTC 704959/A&R no. 984.
91   Thomas McCoog, 'Spoils of War? The Edict of Restitution and Benefactions to the English Province of the Society of Jesus', in Kelley, Thomas (eds.), *Jesuit Intellectual and Physical Exchange*, p. 187.
92   USTC 671040/A&R no. 989.

Duke of Bavaria was in the orbit of the English priests. Several English Jesuits had already formed close ties to the area: Edmund Campion spent two weeks at the Duke of Bavaria's court and the future head of the English Mission, Jasper Heywood, was stationed there in the 1570s.[93] Moreover, the duke had strong ties to both the Allen–Persons party and the other continental patrons of the English mission and the *Schismatis Anglicani*. In 1583, Cardinal Allen requested and received funds from the duke for the English College of Douai (then in Rheims), and that same year, Wilhelm pledged German troops for a proposed Spanish invasion of Scotland and then England to reclaim Mary Stuart's throne.[94] He also offered for his brother to lead the Spanish army.

Given Bavaria's willingness to invade England and lead Counter-Reformation activities elsewhere, it makes sense that Jesuits, and those working for them, would be inspired to make the most out of Sander's narrative, as had been done in France and Spain. Regardless of whether Persons or Allen were involved, the forces surrounding and praised in the imperial iterations showcase the legacy of the Jesuit and noble patronage of Sander. That being said, the rapidity by which Eder funded and put out his edition in the same year as and following the Rome 1586 edition points to a more direct connection in the network of those invested in the 'English enterprise'.

7   Conclusion

In the French Nuncio's letter to the Cardinal of Como in 1583 regarding the English enterprise, he lists aid to the English cause (as well as a bid to reclaim Scotland) from the Spanish king, Guise family and the Duke of Bavaria.[95] He described a force composed of Spanish, Italian, German and French troops. It is no coincidence that these figures and their states were also responsible for producing the key iterations of Nicholas Sander's *Schismatis Anglicani*. The dedications targeted major Counter- or Catholic Reformers, while the choices of languages and printing cities aimed for areas of strong Catholic sentiment (and stronger anti-Protestant feeling). More specifically, the earliest editions all emerged from editors or cities highly involved in the Spanish plan to retake Elizabeth's England for Catholics, timed to coincide with various invasion attempts. Placing these early editions alongside each other highlights an

---

93   Dennis Flynn, 'The English Mission of Jasper Heywood, S.J.', *Archivum Historicum Societatis Iesu*, 54 (1985), pp. 45–49.
94   Allen, *Letters and Memorials*, pp. 187, 416–418.
95   Ibid., pp. liv–lv.

expansive network of clergy, supported by printers, patrons and laymen working towards the multiple goals of saving England, restoring Catholic Europe and protecting against further encroachments by Protestantism.

The mutability of Sander's narrative allowed for wide distribution throughout the continent. Changes in dedications, expansions and even paratext made the story of England the story of Christendom's fight against heresy. As a result, each iteration was shaped both for the local contexts in which the text was printed and for a larger continental audience. Translations into French, German, Spanish and Italian expanded the readership to the populace of Catholic strongholds who read parallels to their own countries' situations in Sander's history. In Spain, it praised the Catholic Monarchs and the Jesuits; in France, it warned against Huguenot sympathies and the direction of Henri III's rule; in the Holy Roman Empire, it called for the continuation of the re-Catholicising mission; and in Italy, it attempted to thwart a pro-Elizabethan alliance and bolster papal order. At the same time, the core of the text, including its most salacious accusations about Anne, Henry and Elizabeth, remained intact. Printed predominantly as an octavo book with minimal ornamentation, it was financially accessible to a wide range of audiences. It was not designed as a tributary text for a select few, but rather a widely circulating book, first among the Latin-literate, and then, quickly, among the vernacular publics. Its tailored relevancy and the active efforts involved in the dispersal of this text transformed it into a keystone work.

After Elizabeth's death, the history's value in justifying invasion had waned. The next Latin edition emerged in Cologne in 1610, the year Robert Persons died.[96] After another Latin edition appeared in 1628 in Cologne, there was an absence of new editions for the next several decades.[97] However, the many iterations of Sander's narrative succeeded in creating a uniform history of the Reformation that could be found repeated in most Catholic histories and increasingly refuted in those by Protestants. Sander's work undermining the Church of England remained relevant, and during the religious turmoil of the late seventeenth century, new editions and translations emerged in Spain, Portugal, France and Poland. Moreover, for the rest of the early modern (and modern period), it became a key source for even more histories, plays and novels of the English Reformation.

Having died with his work unfinished, Sander's history was shaped and deployed by a group of Catholics who understood the book-buying market and knew where they would get the best response. The various editions were never

---

[96] USTC 2106907, 2015541, 2002616/A&R no. 977. Note: USTC includes multiple variants.
[97] USTC 2033509, 2033620/A&R no. 978.

the sole work of English hands alone but rather the result of international networks. Led by Cardinal William Allen and Robert Persons, the editors strategically cultivated and spread the messages of the *Schismatis Anglicani*, making it relevant to European audiences. They played into the demand and power of accounts of English Catholic suffering and used it to justify the intervention of foreign rulers in England and harsh measures on the continent. There was care and deliberation behind the choices in every edition, whether it was the language or dedicatee chosen or the material added. The result of these networks was the creation of a uniform, yet locally nuanced, and popular continental Catholic view of the Reformation, or rather Schism, in England, based on the collaborative work of many priests under the collective name of 'Sander'.

Acknowledgement

This article is an expansion of the research first conducted for my master's dissertation (St Andrews, 2014).

CHAPTER 5

Printing Reformed Plainchant in Papal Rome
Giovanni Guidetti, Robert Granjon and the 1582 Directorium Chori

Barbara Swanson

The reform of the Roman Breviary and Missal in 1568 and 1570 initiated a series of liturgical changes with widespread implications for plainchant. Both the Breviary and Missal included a brief selection of plainchants; but more pointed efforts to align plainchant with the new liturgical requirements would begin in the 1570s, most famously when Gregory XIII commissioned papal composers Giovanni Pierluigi da Palestrina and Annibale Zoilo to update texts and melodies for the office, mass and psalms. Although Palestrina and Zoilo seem to have completed a significant portion of this work, the project was abandoned in 1578, in part due to intervention from Philip II of Spain.[1] In 1582, however, the celebrated French typographer Robert Granjon printed the *Directorium chori*, a portable octavo volume of office chants edited by Vatican cleric Giovanni Guidetti, which may have been related to the original commission.[2] Scholars in the nineteenth century were especially concerned with a possible relationship, in part because of renewed interest in both Palestrina and plainchant. Possible justifications for such a connection included Guidetti's relationship to Palestrina, the dedication to the Vatican Basilica and Gregory XIII's papal privilege.[3]

---

1 There is some evidence that Palestrina continued to advocate for the project and pursue publication on his own. See Richard J. Agee, 'Ideological Clashes in a Cinquenceto Edition of Plainchant', in Ann Buckley, Cynthia J. Cyrus (eds.), *Music, Dance, and Society. Medieval and Renaissance Studies in Memory of Ingrid G. Brainard* (Kalamazoo: Medieval Institute Publications, 2011), pp. 144–146.
2 Giovanni Guidetti, *Directorium chori ad usum sacrosanctae Basilice Vaticanae, et aliarum Cathedralium, et collegiatarum ecclesiarum collectum opera Ioannis Guidetti Bononiensis, eiusdem Vaticanae Basilicae clerici beneficiati, et sanctissimi domini nostri Gregorii XIII capellani* (Rome: Robert Granjon, 1582), USTC 83548.
3 Among the nineteenth-century authors who associated Guidetti with the 1577 commission or positioned him as an inheritor of Palestrina's work, see Giuseppe Baini, *Memorie storico-critiche della vita e delle opera di Giovanni Pierluigi da Palestrina* (Rome: Società tipografica, 1828) II. 100–102, 115–116; and Amédée Gastoué, *Le graduel et l'antiphonaire romains* (Lyon: Janin Frères, 1913), p. 170.

Scholars today still associate the *Directorium chori* with the original commission, even though no study has yet investigated the connection, including between Guidetti's *Directorium*, papal-led publishing initiatives and Granjon's involvement.[4] As I will demonstrate, Guidetti and Granjon were both engaged in projects supported by Gregory XIII for dissemination abroad. In the case of Guidetti, a Vatican cleric active in the papal chapel, this took the form of multiple liturgical volumes, newly edited with extensive prefatory material by Guidetti, which were intended for Vatican use but also by priests and cantors working in Protestant regions and Jesuit missions. Granjon also worked in Vatican circles but as a typecutter of foreign language alphabets for publications destined for the Far East, to convert non-Christians and also establish stronger ties with the eastern church. Given that Guidetti's *Directorium* used an unusual musical notation with no clear precedent in printed musical volumes, Granjon was an ideal collaborator – because of his celebrated skills as a type designer and cutter, as well as his proximity to Gregory's mission-oriented work.[5]

1   Codifying Liturgical Plainchant in Print: 1568–1577

Long a staple of liturgical worship, plainchant gained renewed attention in the sixteenth century as a vehicle for confessional identity and for reform. In Protestant regions, for example, plainchant was increasingly either translated, edited, significantly supplemented or replaced with vernacular congregational psalms and hymns. This was certainly the case in Lutheran Germany. Plainchant continued to be sung but in non-traditional ways: in vernacular translation as in Thomas Müntzer's *Deutsch evangelisch Messe* (1524); by priests alone with the congregation singing hymns; textually and melodically

---

4   On more recent associations between the *Directorium* and Gregory XIII's original commission, see Allan W. Atlas, 'Music for the Mass', in James Haar (ed.), *European Music 1520–1640* (Woodbridge: Boydell Press, 2006), p. 114; Nicholas Baragwanath, *The Solfeggio Tradition. A Forgotten Art of Melody in the Long Eighteenth Century* (Oxford: Oxford University Press, 2020), pp. 46–47; Peter Bennett, *Music and Power at the Court of Louis XIII. Sounding Liturgy in Early Modern France* (Cambridge: Cambridge University Press, 2021), p. 196, in a chapter entitled 'Plainchant and the Politics of Rhythm'.

5   Although a related notation appears in Johannes Reuchlin's *De accentibus et orthographia linguae Hebraicae*, the musical notation was handwritten, even though the rest of the volume was printed. See Johannes Reuchlin, *De accentibus et orthographia linguae Hebraicae libri tres* (Hagenau: Thomas Anshelm, 1518), USTC 62887.

modified; or versified and barely recognisable as plainchant.[6] In England, the plainchant for the mass was translated by John Merbecke for use in Anglican liturgies, with melodies truncated for rhetorical force.[7] At the same time, metrical psalm-singing replaced or supplemented plainchant recitation in worship, including before and after sermons, morning prayer and evening prayer. Metrical psalms were also sung outside of worship to express anti-Catholic sentiments and affirm a Protestant identity. At the defeat of the Catholic Spanish Armada in 1588, for example, celebrations included metrical psalm singing.[8] Catholic mission priests in England took offense to these new musical forms, with the Jesuit John Gerard preferring the sound of his chains in an English prison to the metrical psalm singing (and bawdy songs) sung by his fellow prisoners.[9] Thus, while some Protestant reformers maintained continuity with earlier church practices through plainchant, others found new musical means for expressing their Protestant identity.

Despite this complex relationship to plainchant in Protestant worship, liturgical chant retained priority of place in the Catholic liturgy, functioning as a marker of spiritual authenticity and of confessional identity. Still, there were different approaches and emphases. In 1578, for example, Phillip II of Spain and his correspondents in Rome noted the long history of the plainchant tradition and emphasised the need to protect longstanding melodic practices and local traditions.[10] By contrast, Duke Wilhelm V of Bavaria sought the most up-to-date plainchant volumes from Rome in his communication with Vatican

---

[6] For an excellent study of approaches to plainchant in the Lutheran Reformation, including Thomas Müntzer's *Deutsch evangelisch Messe*, see Marianne Gillion, 'Interconfessional Implications. Printed Plainchant in the Wake of the Reformation', *Music & Letters* (November 2021, pp. 657–686), https://doi.org/10.1093/ml/gcab024. For earlier studies addressing plainchant and versification, as well as the metrical psalm tradition, see Robin A. Leaver, *'Goostly Psalmes and Spirituall Songes'. English and Dutch Metrical Psalms from Coverdale to Utenhove 1535–1566* (Oxford: Clarendon Press, 1991); and Robin A. Leaver, *Luther's Liturgical Music. Principles and Implications* (Grand Rapids, MI: William B. Eerdmans, 2007).

[7] Hyun-Ah Kim, *Humanism and the Reform of Sacred Music in Early Modern England. John Merbecke the Orator and the Booke of Common Praier Noted* (Aldershot: Ashgate, 2008), pp. 139–202.

[8] Beth Quitslund, *The Reformation in Rhyme. Sternhold, Hopkins, and the English Metrical Psalter, 1547–1603* (Aldershot: Ashgate, 2008), pp. 239–273, especially p. 247.

[9] John Gerard, *The Autobiography of a Hunted Priest*, trans. Philip Caraman (New York: Pellegrini & Cudahy, 1952), p. 77.

[10] For transcriptions and translations into Italian of the letters between Don Fernando de las Infantas, Philip II, Giovanni di Çuñiga, and Gregory XIII, see the appendices of Carlo Respighi, *Nuovo studio su Giovanni Pier Luigi da Palestrina e l'emendazione del Graduale Romano* (Rome: Desclée, Lefebre, 1899), pp. 121–134.

clerics and his attempts to solidify a Catholic presence in Bavaria.[11] In these two cases, the difference in emphasis clearly reflected the degree to which those practices were threatened: little in Catholic Spain but significantly in Bavaria, where Protestants formed a distinct minority despite prohibitions on Reformation practices.[12] Plainchant provided a clear link to early church practices and Catholic identity, with varying degrees of emphasis on tradition and contemporary renewal.

Amid the diversification of confessional identities and worship practices, codifying and disseminating the liturgy in print became an important way to foster and revitalise Catholic liturgical practices, including plainchant. The Breviary of 1568 and Missal of 1570 provide a case in point. During the final session of the Council of Trent, a papal commission was struck to revise both volumes.[13] Priorities included a more streamlined liturgical year with fewer commemorations of saints, facilitating (in part) easier use by clergy across regions and with different levels of training.[14] The Breviary was complete less than five years after the initial commission, and its use was advised for all Catholic dioceses despite many errors, which were corrected in later editions.[15]

Both the Breviary and Missal included a small selection of notated plainchants. In most cases, the chant texts were either updated (often shortened or lengthened) or the chants were assigned new liturgical uses. The Breviary, for example, included select notated plainchants for a range of feasts, including *Simile est regnum caelorum grano sinapis* for the sixth Sunday after Epiphany (Benedictus antiphon) and *Non me permittas* for the feast of St Andrew (first

---

11   Raphael Molitor, *Die nach-tridentinische Choral-Reform zu Rom* (Leipzig: Leuckart, 1901) II. 6–7.

12   On Protestant-Catholic tensions in Bavaria, see Philip M. Soergel, *Wondrous in His Saints. Counter-Reformation Propaganda in Bavaria* (Berkeley: University of California Press, 2018), pp. 8–9, 75–78.

13   For a useful overview of this process with attention to the impact on plainchant reforms, see Mariannae Gillion, 'Retrofitting Plainchant. The Incorporation and Adaptation of "Tridentine" Liturgical Changes in Italian Printed Graduals', *Journal of Musicology*, 36.3 (2019), pp. 333–335.

14   For an overview of these priorities, see, for example, Christopher S. Black, *Church, Religion and Society in Early Modern Italy* (New York: Bloomsbury, 2004), pp. 23–25. See also Gillion, 'Retrofitting Plainchant', pp. 332–335.

15   Prior to this decree, the use of a particular breviary was at the discretion of an individual diocese, with no single breviary mandated for use by all. See Simon Ditchfield, *Liturgy, Sanctity and History in Tridentine Italy* (Cambridge: Cambridge University Press, 2002), pp. 26–30. Note that the adoption of the new Roman breviary was left to the local councils. Dioceses and orders were exempted if they could prove that their form of the office was approved and celebrated for at least two hundred years.

antiphon, third nocturn).[16] *Simile est regnum caelorum grano sinapis* was for the newly introduced but rarely needed sixth Sunday after Epiphany (usually superseded by Septuagesima Sunday, except in the case of a late Easter).[17] In the case of *Non me permittas*, the Breviary version included an additional phrase ('et me ad te venire jubeas'), which is absent in earlier versions of the same chant.[18] Although both of these examples illustrate minor changes to traditional plainchant usage, textual and liturgical changes to the Breviary as a whole had widespread impact on plainchant volumes, including because of the addition and removal of numerous saints.[19] Philip II, for example, noted in a letter to his ambassador in Rome that chant books throughout Spain had been amended to conform to the Breviary and Missal of Pius V.[20]

Chant books published by Giunta's Venetian press in 1572 provide insight into the initial impact of the Breviary and Missal on plainchant prints. For example, Giunta's 1572 *Antiphonarium*, *Graduale* and *Psalterium* lack internal changes to content and structure and thus appear continuous with preconciliar chant books. However, each begins with a list of amendments required to align the volumes with the Breviary and Missal.[21] The lengthy lists indicate new liturgical usages for existing chants, textual revisions and new verses for

16   Other chants included the Benedictus and Magnificat antiphons for feasts, ranging from Rogation II, the Saturdays before the eighth, tenth and eleventh Sundays after Pentecost, and a Benedictus antiphon for the sixth feria. The only other significant feasts with newly assigned plainchants were Trinity Sunday (Matins responsory chant) and the Invention of the Holy Cross (Matins responsory chant).

17   In the Cantus Database, *Simile est regnum caelorum grano sinapis* is assigned to the sixth Sunday after Epiphany in only one source: the Portuguese P-BRS Ms. 032 (with Cantus ID a00079), dated in the early sixteenth century. Benedictus antiphons with different texts for the sixth Sunday after Epiphany occur in just over ten sources in Cantus. See Debra Lacoste etc., *Cantus. A Database for Latin Ecclesiatical Chant*: cantusdatabase.org/feast/1647 (note that within this retrieved list, F-SO 596, MA Impr. 1537, and D-Gsta AB III 9 do not include Benedictus antiphons).

18   For example, earlier sixteenth-century antiphonals lack this additional phrase for *Non me permittas* (Cantus ID 003923), including the Salzinnes Antiphonal from ca. 1554 (CDN-Hsmu M2149.L4, cantusdatabase.org/chant/271718) and the Münster Antiphoner of 1537 (MA Impr. 1537, cantusdatabase.org/chant/389840).

19   For examples of such changes implemented in later chant volumes (i.e. the addition and subtraction of text and select musical additions), see Gillion, 'Retrofitting Plainchant', pp. 340–365.

20   Letter from Philip II to his ambassador Giovanni de Çuñiga, 10 January 1578 (Arch d. Amb. D. Spagna pr. i. s.s., tom. VI, p. I, fol. 138), in Respighi, *Nuovo studio*, p. 129.

21   Marco Gozzi, 'Le edizioni liturgico-musicali dopo il Concilio', in Marco Gozzi, Danilo Curti (eds.), *Musica e liturgia nella riforma tridentina* (Trento: Castello del Buonconsiglio, 1995), pp. 40–43. See also Marianne Gillion, '*Cantate Dominum Canticum Novum*? A Re-Examination of "Post-Tridentine" Chant Revisions in Italian Printed Graduals', in Wim

Introits, among other changes. For example, the list for the 1572 Gradual indicates that for St Stephen's Day, the chant *Etenim sederunt* should begin not with 'etenim' but with 'sederunt'. Similarly, the offertory for the Sunday within the octave of Epiphany should omit the repetition of 'Jubilate Deo omnis terra'. Such lists allowed printers to quickly and efficiently update a volume with little impact on its internal structure and content, as well as minimal visible impact on plainchant tradition.

Gregory XIII's brief on chant reform (25 October 1577) marked a decisive shift of approach. Whereas the reformed Breviary and Missal necessitated new liturgical placements and some textual changes, the reform initiated by Gregory XIII would change the melodic aspect of plainchants, essentially overhauling hundreds of chants. According to the brief, the goals not only included alignment with Pius V's Breviary and Missal but also applied humanistic principles to plainchant, including the elimination of 'superfluities', 'barbarisms' and 'obscurities'.[22] In practice, this meant reducing long melismas and aligning textual accents with melodic inflection, even changing melodic contours to more clearly reflect modal principles.[23] Similar issues were discussed during the Council of Trent sessions on music, although not specifically in the context of plainchant and only in broad terms. For example, in the September 1562 session, it was agreed that any words spoken or sung during the liturgy should be intelligible, and that lascivious content be removed (applying more to polyphonic music with secular musical themes).[24] Claiming clear responsibility for the chant reform, Gregory XIII noted that the project be undertaken with 'full and unrestricted jurisdiction and power by virtue of our apostolic authority'.[25]

Gregory XIII entrusted this major reform initiative to two composers closely aligned with the Vatican, Giovanni Pierluigi da' Palestrina (choirmaster for the Cappella Giulia) and Annibale Zoilo (singer in the Cappella Sistina), as well as their choice of skilled musicians if such might hasten the completion of the

---

François, Violet Soen (eds.), *The Council of Trent. Reform and Controversy in Europe and Beyond* (Göttingen: Vandenhoeck and Ruprecht, 2018), pp. 159–182.

22   Gregory XIII, 'Brief on the Reform of Chant', 25 October 1577 in Molitor, *Die nachtridentinische Choral-Reform* I. 297–298; translated in Oliver Strunk, Leo Treitler (eds.), *Source Readings in Music History* (New York: Norton, 1998), pp. 374–375.

23   Infantas specifically mentions the first two of these when expressing his concerns about the revision to Philip II. See Fernando de las Infantas to Philip II, 25 November 1577 (Archivio d. Ambasciata di Spagna presso la Santa Sede, tom. VI, parte I, fol. 134a), in Respighi, *Nuovo studio*, p. 122.

24   Craig A. Monson, 'The Council of Trent Revisited', *Journal of the American Musicological Society*, 55.1 (2002), pp. 1–37.

25   Gregory XIII, 'Brief on the Reform of Chant', in Strunk, *Source Readings in Music History*, p. 375.

project. Palestrina was specifically charged with reforming the Graduals, and Zoilo charged with the Antiphonarium and Psalterium. Although Palestrina appeared to have completed chants for the Temporale, the project encountered political complications within months of its inception. On 25 November 1577, Fernando de las Infantas informed Philip II of the chant renewal project and enumerated multiple potential problems: the project falsely presumed corruption of the plainchant tradition, and if the volumes made it into print, they would be mandated for use throughout all regions (as with the Breviary and Missal).[26] This letter initiated at least four further letters between Infantas, Phillip II, the Spanish ambassador in Rome and Gregory XIII. The message was clear: the project compromised the integrity of plainchant tradition (arguably dating back to St Gregory the Great) and risked introducing more errors than it remediated. Infantas and Philip II were also clearly concerned about the cost to Spanish churches, cathedrals and religious, which had already implemented reforms from the new Breviary and Missal into existing chant books and should not be tasked with further emendations.

Although rarely discussed in histories of plainchant, the issue of print recurs in both the brief from Gregory XIII and the Spanish letters. The pope, for example, asserted that printers had been guilty of disseminating faulty chants, noting negligence and possible wickedness. He did not specify the nature of this potential wickedness, but likely meant profit-mongering and confessional indifference (i.e. printers more concerned with business than promoting Catholic orthodoxy in the ideological war against Protestantism). Holding printers to such moral standards was certainly not uncommon, and confessional declarations by printers proliferated, especially among Catholics. For example, when Giovanni Battista Raimondi became director of the Typographia Medicea in 1584, Raimondi himself noted the importance of promoting the Catholic faith in print ('all'Aumento della fede').[27]

The Spanish letters also expressed concerns about print, but relative to Catholic orthodoxy and change. The intensification of reform through print put pressure on religious institutions to keep pace – to purchase new books and implement new liturgies, thus updating long-ingrained practices. For example, in his first letter to Phillip II, Infantas noted that newly printed plainchant volumes would destroy long-held traditions and undermine local collections.[28]

26   Letter from Infantas to Philip II, 25 November 1577, in Respighi, *Nuovo studio*, pp. 121–125.
27   See the founding documents for the Medici Press (ASF, MM 719_1, f. 1r), cited in Caren Reimann, 'Ferdinando de' Medici and the Typographia Medicea', in Nina Lamal etc. (eds.), *Print and Power in Early Modern Europe 1500–1800* (Leiden: Brill, 2021), p. 223.
28   Letter from Infantas to Philip II, 25 November 1577 (134b), in Respighi, *Nuovo studio*, p. 123.

Phillip II's response to the Spanish ambassador in Rome similarly emphasised the perils of reprinting such significant volumes so shortly after implementing by hand the revisions required by the new Breviary and Missal.[29] Such tensions and controversy reveal how the renewal of confessional identity in print was not uniformly valued among Catholics and, in this case, may have slowed the progress of change. To this effect, the Spanish letters to Gregory XIII clearly advised against the creation of a new printing house, whether to publish plainchant or as a polyglot press. Given the widely recognised power of Philip II in papal Rome, it is no wonder that the plainchant reform project was abandoned, likely inhibiting Gregory XIII regarding plans for a new press and newly printed chant volumes. But as Miles Pattenden has demonstrated (and as I will explore shortly), the papacy frequently conceded on the surface with Philip II's requests but found ways to realise their own priorities all the same.[30]

2 Guidetti and the Legacy of the 1577 Commission

Within four years of Gregory XIII's cancelled plainchant project, Vatican cleric Giovanni Guidetti edited the chants of the Divine Office with extensive directions for use, resulting in the 573-page *Directorium chori* of 1582. Part chant book, part manual, the *Directorium* simplified the daily celebration of the liturgical offices by providing incipits and select full chants, including sung items not typically found in an Antiphonal. Chants were organised in a performance-oriented style, by office and in liturgical order, rather than separated into different books or section of by chant type. In other words, notated antiphons, psalm incipits and hymns were provided in order of use for a specific office, rather than in separate volumes (antiphons in one book, hymns in another and psalms in yet another). As specified by Guidetti in the dedication and directions for use, the book would especially benefit cantors and the weekly officiant (*hebdomadarian*) of the daily offices, guiding the choice of plainchants, the approach to declamation and the distribution of sung elements among priests, cantors and choir. Given its small size (octavo), it could be used for personal reference before a liturgy but also kept near-to-hand in a church or chapel for quick and subtle use by a new cantor or cleric. The

---

29 Letter from Philip II to his ambassador Giovanni de Çuñiga, 10 January 1578 (Arch d. Amb. D. Spagna pr. i. s.s., tom. VI, p. I, fol. 138), in Respighi, *Nuovo studio*, pp. 129–131.

30 Miles Pattenden, 'Rome as a "Spanish Avignon"? The Spanish Faction and the Monarchy of Philip II', in Piers Baker-Bates, Miles Pattenden (eds.), *The Spanish Presence in Sixteenth-Century Italy. Images of Iberia* (New York: Routledge, 2014), pp. 65–84.

compilation of multiple chant types into a single volume clearly fulfilled conciliar mandates to streamline liturgical celebrations, ensure ceremonial dignity and facilitate uniformity of worship, while also standardising the offices around the newly published Breviary.

The *Directorium* was equally notable for its musical aspects, especially the application of four rhythmic values to all chant genres using an idiosyncratic notation based on semi-circular figures over pitches. As visible in Table 5.1, a semibreve (diamond-shaped note) indicated half a pulse (tempora); the breve (square note) indicated a single pulse; a breve under a semicircle was equivalent to a modern dotted note; and a breve topped by a fermata indicated two pulses. A breve and semibreve could further be united under a larger slur, indicating a re-articulated vowel, which Guidetti described as if singing 'Do-ominus'. The goal of the notation was to improve the delivery of text by imparting a ceremonial, speech-like quality.[31] Guidetti noted frequently in his prefatory material that the singer should use an elevated tone (*sublimi tono*) and that using the *Directorium* would help to remediate inept and clamorous singing.[32]

When applied to recitational chants in particular, the note values mimicked Latin prosody and facilitated more rhetorical declamation. This aspect of the volume becomes immediately clear by applying Guidetti's rhythmic values,

TABLE 5.1   Notational symbols in Guidetti's *Directorium chori*, 1582

Symbol	Value	Description
◆	½ tempus (semibreve)	*Celeries est percurrenda* (quickly)
■	1 tempus (breve)	*Tempus unum*
■◆	1½ tempora followed by ½	*Paolo tardius* (more slowly)
⌒■	2 tempora	*Magis est protrahenda* (prolonged)
⌒◆	Rearticulation	*Cum decore et gratia* (with beauty and grace)

---

31   For a fuller explication of this desired speech-like quality, see Barbara Swanson, 'Speaking in Tones. Plainchant, Monody, and the Evocation of Antiquity in Early Modern Italy' (PhD Diss., Case Western Reserve University, 2013), pp. 24–63.
32   See, for example, Guidetti, *Directorium chori* (1582), f. A4v.

such as in the opening of the Lamentations chant for the second nocturn of Matins on Holy Thursday (see Figure 5.1). The Hebrew syllable 'Mem' is sung to five pitches, with Guidetti's notation elongating the first and fourth. The effect is a slightly inflected musical gesture that might otherwise be sung with equal emphasis on each pitch. There are also multiple examples of speech-like inflections, including the dotted rhythms at 'misit', 'ossibus', 'erudivit' and 'expandit'. This rhythmicised approach itself was not entirely new. Paris de Grassis (1470–1528), papal master of ceremonies during the pontificates of Julius II and Leo X and an important source of information on Vatican music and ceremony in the early sixteenth century, provided select notated examples of prosodic chant recitation in his *Ceremonial for Cardinals* (1505), as well as advice on singing with appropriate affect.[33] But comparison of this work with the *Directorium* shows not only that Guidetti applied this principle more thoroughly (to the entirety of the sung offices) but also with more extensive rhythmicisation, including the addition and frequent use of 'dotted' rhythms.[34] Guidetti also frequently realigned pitches to alter the accentuation of text and omitted select pitches to improve declamation, thereby improving the clarity of textual delivery.

FIGURE 5.1   Lamentations chant for Holy Thursday Matins in Guidetti, *Directorium chori* (Rome 1582)

---

33   Paris de Grassis, 'De tonis sive tenoribus', 1505, Vat. lat. 5634/2, fol. 67v–90r, *Biblioteca Apostolica Vaticana*; discussed in James M. Borders, 'Rhythmic Performance of *Accentus* in Early Sixteenth-Century Rome', in Marco Gozzi, Francesco Luisi (eds.), *Il canto fratto. L'altro gregoriano* (Rome: Torre d'Orfeo, 2005), pp. 385–405.

34   For further comparison, see Swanson, 'Speaking in Tones', pp. 59–61.

Although Guidetti is little-known today beyond his edited chant volumes, his significance within Vatican circles should not be underestimated. A set of synod proceedings in 1589 mentions the *Directorium* alongside the *Pontificale Romanum*, an essential resource for papal ceremonies.[35] In the same proceedings, Guidetti is mentioned alongside de Grassis, which suggests that Guidetti occupied a comparable role in the later sixteenth century. A year later, Guidetti was named in a published document describing the installation of an ancient obelisk in St Peter's Square, a significant event in Sixtus V's plans to remake Rome in the image of the ancient Roman Empire.[36] Furthermore, Guidetti cultivated relationships with leading patrons and nobility, as evidenced in the dedications of his publications.[37] For example, Guidetti corresponded with Duke Wilhelm V of Bavaria (with advice about chant books), travelled to Bavaria after Wilhelm requested Roman priests to provide liturgical guidance and also dedicated his 1586 Passion chants to the duke.[38] When Guidetti issued a second edition of the *Directorium* in 1589, he dedicated it to another powerful Catholic figure, Cardinal Pallotta, who was a close associate of Gregory's successor, Sixtus V, and a notable supporter of Palestrina's earlier plainchant reforms.[39]

Given Guidetti's role in Vatican ceremonial proceedings, his recognised expertise as a chant reformer, his chaplaincy to Gregory XIII and the date of the *Directorium*, it bears asking whether the *Directorium* was an attempt to fulfil the brief of Gregory XIII and if Guidetti inherited Palestrina's work or

---

35 *Synodus Dioecesana sub admodum ill. et reverendissantissimo domino, d. Philippo Sega episcopo Placentiae* (Piacenza: Giovanni Bazachi, 1589), USTC 848129, p. 85.

36 *Della trasposizione dell'obelisco Vaticano et altre fabbriche di nostro signore Papa Sisto V* (Rome: Domenico Basa, 1590), USTC 4035051.

37 According to Nele Gabriels, dedications to such prominent patrons helped garner public respect for an author's work by aligning it with the prestige and principles of a well-known figure. Nele Gabriels, 'Reading (Between) the Lines. What Dedications Can Tell Us', in Ignace Bossuyt etc. (eds.), *Cui dono lepidum novum libellum. Dedicating Latin Works and Motets in the Sixteenth Century* (Leuven: Leuven University Press, 2008), pp. 73–78.

38 Molitor, *Die nach-tridentinische Choral-Reform*, II. 6–7. For a useful discussion of Wilhelm V's challenges and Catholic agenda in Bavaria, see W. David Myers, *'Poor Sinning Folk'. Confession and Conscience in Counter-Reformation Germany* (Ithaca: Cornell University Press, 1996). For the volume of chants, see Giovanni Guidetti, *Cantus ecclesiasticus passionis Iesu Christi secundum Matthaeum, Marcum, Lucam, et Ioannem, iuxta ritum capellae sancti domini nostri papae ac sacrosanctae Basilicae Vaticanae a Ioanne Guidetto Bononiensi in tres libros divisus* (Rome: Alessandro Gardane, 1586), USTC 835482.

39 Molitor, *Die nach-tridentinische Choral-Reform*, II. 13. For the volume of chant, see Giovanni Guidetti, *Directorium chori ad usum omnium Ecclesiarum tam Cathedralium quam collegiatarum nuper restitutum et nunc secundo in lucem editum* (Rome: Francesco Coattino, 1589), USTC 835485.

somehow brought it to fruition. Notably, Guidetti thanked Palestrina in the prefatory material to the *Directorium*, indicating that Palestrina reviewed and approved of the volume's contents. A later volume of Guidetti's chants even included musical settings by Palestrina (in a harmonised style known as *falsobordone*).[40] Both were active in Vatican liturgical life: Guidetti as papal chaplain and Palestrina as choirmaster of the Cappella Giulia, with Guidetti dedicating the *Directorium* to the choirs of the Vatican Basilica as a reflection of Vatican musical practices.[41] Although Palestrina is thought to have worked on chants for the mass rather than the offices, this does not preclude communication of common principles between Palestrina and Guidetti or the codification of Vatican-wide practices in the *Directorium*, as Guidetti stated.

Correlations also exist between Guidetti's dedication of the volume and the 1577 brief. Although Gregory XIII never mentioned rhythmicised chants, both Guidetti and Gregory outlined three main priorities: (1) to correct other chant volumes by 'revising' and 'purging' in the case of Gregory XIII and 'restoring' and 'expunging' in the case of Guidetti; (2) to align with the new Breviary and Missal; and (3) to restore devout praise. Both also vehemently criticised current and recent practices ('barbarisms' and 'wickedness' in the case of Gregory XIII; 'confused' and 'negligent' ones in the case of Guidetti). Further, both had a clear sense of the importance of the work and that it served an urgent need. Guidetti's edited chants further reflect the very amendments that Infantas noted in the fledgling chant reforms of Palestrina, notably the alignment of musico-textual accents and the reduction of melismas.

A connection between Guidetti and Gregory XIII probably began before Gregory's papal rule (1572–1585). Born in Bologna in 1530, Guidetti moved to Rome in his early 40s, likely at the invitation of Gregory, who was also Bolognese and known for conferring favours on his compatriots.[42] Guidetti became a

---

40 Giovanni Guidetti, *Cantus ecclesiasticus officii maioris hebdomadae iuxta ritum capellae sanctissimi domini nostri papae ac Basilicae Vaticanae collectus et emendatus, a Ioanne Guidetto Bononiensi eiusdem Basilicae perpetuo clerico beneficiato nunc primum in lucem editus* (Rome: Alessandro Gardano, Francesco Coattino, Giacomo Tornieri, 1587), USTC 835483.

41 The entry on Palestrina in the *New Grove Dictionary of Music and Musicians* suggests what I argue here: that Guidetti's chant book codified what was already in practice in Palestrina's Cappella Guilia. See Lewis Lockwood, Noel O'Regan, Jessie Ann Owens, 'Palestrina', in Stanley Sadie (ed.), *The New Grove Dictionary of Music and Musicians* (29 vols., Oxford: Oxford University Press, 2001), XVIII. 942.

42 On Gregory XIII and his Bolognese relationships, see Nicola Courtright, *The Papacy and the Art of Reform in Sixteenth-Century Rome. Gregory XIII's Tower of the Winds in the Vatican* (Cambridge: Cambridge University Press, 2004), pp. 5–25.

papal chaplain soon after on 27 November 1575.[43] Although his specific duties are not known, Guidetti was described as a close companion of the popes in the papal privilege to the 1582 *Directorium chori*, the only one of Guidetti's publications to appear during Gregory's rule.[44] Other clerics held papal chaplaincies along with Guidetti, each with varying honours and roles, including the privilege of assisting the pope during mass in his private chapel, reciting the offices and rosary with the pope and functioning as papal confidante.[45] As such, Guidetti would have had close contact with Gregory XIII and was likely aware of his various reform projects.

3   Robert Granjon, Gregory XIII and Innovations in Plainchant Type

During his pontificate, Gregory XIII clearly prioritised the dissemination of Catholic materials in print, implicating, in principle, volumes like the *Directorium*. As already discussed, plans to print reformed plainchants fell through, due in part to pressure from Philip II (who also discouraged the creation of a specifically papal press for foreign language publication). Despite this, Domenico Basa fulfilled the role of unofficial papal printer as early as 1577 (later becoming director of the Stamperia Vaticana), beginning with multilingual publications for dissemination to the East, whether to proselytise or to re-establish relationships with the eastern churches. Robert Granjon was soon hired to create foreign type, later working for the Medici Press and continuing to work for Basa.[46]

Before his arrival in Rome, Granjon had distinguished himself as one of the foremost typecutters in Europe. In addition to creating an elegant italic typeface that surpassed any previous French versions, he developed a cursive

---

43   See Baini, *Memorie storico-critiche*, II. 116. According to Baini, Guidetti replaced the recently deceased Francesco Tosti.

44   Guidetti, *Directorium chori* (1582), f. A2r: 'familiarem et continuum comensalem nostrum specialibus favoribus'.

45   See 'Chaplain, Papal', in Philippe Levillain, John O'Malley (eds.), *The Papacy. An Encyclopedia* (New York: Routledge, 2001), pp. 300–302.

46   See Paolo Sachet, 'Publishing for the Popes. The Cultural Policy of the Catholic Church Towards Printing in Sixteenth-Century Rome' (PhD diss., The Warburg Institute University of London, 2015). Note that Sachet's book (with the same initial name) does not include the commentary found here on Gregory XIII and Granjon. See also Evelyn Lincoln, 'Printers and Publishers in Early Modern Rome', in Pamela M. Jones etc. (eds.), *A Companion to Early Modern Rome 1492–1692* (Leiden: Brill, 2019), p. 552.

script particular for French, called *civilité*.[47] He developed a comparable *civilité* typeface for music that imitated hand-written note heads, which suggested a carefully rendered autograph version of the musical repertoire.[48] His musical tablature also showed inventiveness, as he used a single impression process of placing the tablature letters between rather than across the tablature lines and used delicate curves for the lowercase letters.[49] Granjon also created numerous typefaces for foreign alphabets, including Syriac for the Polyglot Bible of Plantin (1568–1572) and Greek for a New Testament in both Greek and Latin (1549) (see Figure 5.2).[50]

Once in Rome, Granjon quickly became the pope's favourite for creating foreign-language typefaces. For example, Granjon created an Armenian that Gregory XIII approved directly during a personal audience on 10 September 1579. In a letter dated 2 October that same year, Cardinal Santoro praised Granjon as a 'singular engraver', referring to his work on the Armenian characters.[51] In addition to a single folio demonstrating the script in 1579 and bearing the

FIGURE 5.2
Robert Granjon's characters for *Novum Testamentum Graece et Latine* (Paris 1549)

---

47 Rémi Jimenes, *Les caractères de civilité. Typographie & calligraphie sous l'ancien régime, France, XVIe–XIXe siècles* (Chambery: Atelier Perrousseaux, 2011), pp. 17–18.
48 Kate van Orden, *Materialities. Books, Readers, and the Chanson in Sixteenth-Century Europe* (New York: Oxford University Press, 2015); Kate van Orden, 'Robert Granjon and Music', in Craig A. Monson and Roberta Montemorra Marvin (eds.), *Music in Print and Beyond: Hildegard von Bingen to The Beatles* (Woodbridge, Suffolk: Boydell & Brewer, 2013), pp. 11–35.
49 For an example of Granjon's tablature and related discussion, see van Orden, 'Robert Granjon and Music', pp. 18–19. For all Granjon's music founts, see Hendrik Vervliet, *Robert Granjon, Letter-cutter 1513–1590. An oeuvre-catalogue* (New Castle, DE: Oak Knoll Press, 2018), pp. 154–163.
50 Hendrik Vervliet, 'Robert Granjon à Rome. Notes préliminaire à une histoire de la typographie Romaine à la fin du XIVe siècle', *Bulletin de l'Institut Historique Belge à Rome*, 38 (1967), p. 183.
51 Arch. Vat., Arm. LII, 17, f.265, cited in Vervliet, 'Robert Granjon à Rome', p. 191: 'Di Roberto Francese intagliatore di caratteri singolarissimo che vuol baciare i piedi a Sua Santità'.

names of both Gregory XIII and Granjon, Granjon's Armenian characters were used for a 1584 printing of the Gregorian calendar for the Armenian patriarch Azarias and multiple other works. When Cardinal Ferdinando de' Medici established the Medici Press in 1584, he hired Granjon to create further foreign typefaces, including another Arabic.[52] Aware that Granjon's abilities were valued throughout Europe, Gregory secured access to Granjon's designs by forbidding the punches from leaving Rome. He also paid Granjon generously with 300 scudi for a complete alphabet.[53]

Granjon printed Guidetti's *Directorium* within four years of his arrival in Rome amid his growing renown in Vatican circles. Other than an Arabic cosmography and four individual sheets (created to showcase his typefaces and often bearing the papal coat of arms), Granjon printed no other known works during his Roman years, let alone with music.[54] Since Granjon was not known to have his own printing equipment, what he did print was likely accomplished using the printing press and types of Basa (the unofficial Vatican printer until the early 1580s). It was indeed common in the challenging Roman publishing market for printers to collaborate, including sharing their means of production.[55] To this effect, the Arabic cosmography indicates Granjon as printer on the title page, but Basa in the colophon, and the volume as a whole is typically attributed to Basa as publisher-printer.[56] As well, Granjon seems to have shared Basa's coat of arms for Gregory XIII in the sample sheet of

---

52   On this aspect of Granjon's work, see chapter 3 (European Printing and Arabic) of J.R. Osborn, *Letters of Light. Arabic Script in Calligraphy, Print and Digital Design* (Cambridge: Harvard University, 2017).

53   Hendrik D.L. Vervliet, *Cyrillic and Oriental Typography in Rome at the End of the Sixteenth Century. An Inquiry into the Later Work of Robert Granjon* (Berkeley: Poltroon Press, 1981), p. 34. Note that although this was originally published in French as 'Robert Granjon à Rome', the English version has additional content, especially related to Guidetti and Granjon.

54   Vervliet, *Cyrillic and Oriental Typography*, pp. 24–25. For the Arabic cosmology, see Jean-Charles Ducène, 'Le *Hortus rerum mirabilium* (Rome 1584–1585). Une cosmographie arabe oubliée', *Zeitschrift der Deutschen Morganländischen Gesellschaft*, 156.1 (2006), p. 81. Granjon's role is indicated on the title page of the *Hortus* in Arabic as 'printed in Rome-the-Great by Robert Granjon of Paris in the year 1584 of the incarnation'. For an Arabic transliteration, see Vervliet, *Robert Granjon, Letter-cutter 1513–1590*, p. 81. Translated here from the French from J.Th. Zenker, *Manuel de bibliographie orientale* (Leipzig: Guillaume Engelmann, 1866), p. 120. Ducène further notes that it was printed on Basa's press with characters made by Granjon.

55   For various examples of this, see Suzanne Cusick, 'Valerio Dorico. Music Printer in Sixteenth-Century Rome' (PhD diss., University of North Carolina at Chapel Hill, 1975), pp. 9–10, 38–39. This dissertation was printed by UMI Research Press in 1981 under the same title.

56   See, for example, Ducène, 'Le *Hortus rerum mirabilium*', pp. 81–83.

Arabic typography (indicating 'Rob. GranIon Parisien. Typographus Incidebat Romae'), suggesting indeed that Granjon used Basa's materials when executing a print.[57]

Such clear associations indicate that Granjon likely printed the *Directorium* using Basa's equipment. To this effect, Gregory's coat of arms on the title page of the *Directorium* exactly matches the coat of arms used by Basa for Lorenzo Frizzoli's *Sacellum Gregorianum*, even though it differs from an earlier coat of arms used by both Granjon and Basa (the dragon faces left rather than right, as well as other small variants).[58] As already mentioned, such collaboration (or borrowing) was common in Rome as a way of mitigating financial risks. A printer might be paid a flat fee by another printer-publisher to physically produce a volume. Or, a printer could rent the means of production from a more established printer-publisher and produce the volume with the expectation of sharing profits directly with the author, among other possible arrangements. Given the high cost of musical type, it was especially common for a less established printer to rent or borrow a musical typeface. For example, Sistine Chapel singer Antonio Barré borrowed or rented musical typeface from papal printer Antonio Blado for Barré's fledgling music printing business in the 1560s.[59]

In the case of the *Directorium*, however, it seems more likely that Granjon used Basa's equipment, including an existing text type, but designed and cut the musical type himself.[60] Guidetti's notation was unique in the history of printed musical notation and could only be executed with a newly cut type. Although fermatas over select pitches occurred in other printed music, Guidetti's system required semicircles as well as fermatas over numerous pitches as an integral part of the typeface. Given Granjon's previous expertise designing and cutting innovative musical typefaces (i.e. the musical *civilité* and his tablature), Granjon was a clear choice and possibly the only choice. Music printing was

---

57 To compare Basa's coat of arms for Gregory XIII and that used by Robert Granjon for the Arabic character sheet, see the title page of the 1584 Armenian calendar (with Granjon's type) and Granjon's 1580 *Arabici Characteres* in Vervliet, *Cyrillic and Oriental Typography*, pp. 15, 31.

58 See Laurentii Frizolii, *Sacellum Gregorianum* (Rome: Dominici Basae, 1582), available from Google Books: https://books.google.ca/books/about/Sacellum_Gregorianum_Laurentii _Frizolii.html?id=swADibCTlcoC&redir_esc=y (accessed June 2022).

59 Cusick, 'Valerio Dorico. Music Printer', pp. 37–39.

60 As a notable scholar of Granjon's work and histories of sixteenth-century print, Vervliet stated something similar. He noted, 'I can discern no reason why Granjon himself felt impelled to patronize this publication', elaborating on what appears to be a stock typeface for the text. He wondered if Granjon was compelled to create the typeface by the relative absence of music printers in Rome. Vervliet, *Cyrillic and Oriental Typography*, p. 49.

hardly a large industry in Rome. Basa printed a very small number of music-related works, but between the demise of Valerio Dorico's firm in the 1570s and the emergence of the Alessandro Gardano and Francesco Coattino partnership in 1583, there was relatively little music printing in Rome. Typefaces often came from Venice and were as expensive as foreign alphabets (the very alphabets that Granjon was making for Vatican-related publications), given the similar skills required to cut them.[61]

Regarding Granjon's role as typecutter, it is important to consider the work involved in creating the type. Although the musical notation resembled the square and lozenge-shaped notes of other plainchant editions, the addition of semi-circular figures and the small octavo dimensions of the *Directorium* introduced a variety of questions for a typecutter. Would the semi-circular figures be cut independently, becoming small individual pieces of type placed over relevant pitches? Or would each note-head be cast with and without the semi-circular signs to ensure alignment between notes and semicircles in the printing process? Cursory examination shows that Granjon cast each note-head with staff lines and semicircle as a single piece of type, which facilitated alignment and pitch accuracy in a single-impression process. This certainly would have simplified the printing of long chants, such as the Lamentations, which used as many as 121 semicircles, including single and double fermatas; even the slight misalignment of such figures could negate Guidetti's intended musical effect.[62] To that end, Granjon's semi-circular figures show the work of a careful hand: the fermata sits directly over the relevant pitch, touching and lightly crossing the top line of the staff. The dot sits in the exact same plane as the staff line, thus requiring a slight but visible space on either side to distinguish the dot from the line itself. Even Vervliet, who disdained the print quality of the *Directorium* as a whole, noted the excellent execution of these markings.[63] Notably, Granjon's type was reused in the two subsequent editions of the *Directorium* produced during Guidetti's lifetime, in 1589 and 1591. Granjon himself did not print the volumes as he was in ailing health as of 1588 and died in the spring of 1590. Both later editions were entrusted to Francesco

---

61   On the sourcing of musical typefaces for Roman music publications, see Cusick, 'Valerio Dorico. Music Printer', pp. 99.
62   For the Lamentations chant, see Guidetti, *Directorium chori* (1582), pp. 184–187, available from Google Books: https://www.google.ca/books/edition/Directorium_chori_ad_vsum_sacrosanctae_B/WfwPMbYrvMUC?hl=en&gbpv=1 (accessed March 2022).
63   Vervliet, *Cyrillic and Oriental Typography*, pp. 34–35. Granjon's plainchant type for a 1588 *Missale Romanum* published by Basa exhibits a similar low print quality. See Vervliet, *Robert Granjon, Letter-Cutter*, p. 162.

Coattino, who began publishing music in Rome in 1583 but clearly had access to Granjon's type.[64]

Given the mutual connection of Granjon, Guidetti and, by extension, Basa to Vatican reform-minded initiatives, it bears asking whether the *Directorium* fell under the auspices of Gregory XIII's many sponsored print projects. The first sign would be the coat of arms for Gregory XIII on the title page. It was common for papal-sponsored volumes (or their presses more generally) to bear a papal coat of arms. For example, Olaus Magnus, the Rome-based publisher and former primate of Sweden, published two editions of Johannes Magnus' *Historia de omnibus Gothorum et Sueonumque regibus* in 1554 – one with the coat of arms of Pope Julius III on the title page, recognising his financial patronage of the press and its proselytising goals.[65] In such cases, papal sponsorship was implied if not directly stated. To this effect, Basa's publications for the pope usually bore Gregory's coat of arms alongside Basa's own imprint ('*Ex typographia Dominici Basae*'), sometimes with and sometimes without overt statements of papal approbation. This ambiguity could be purposeful, with Paolo Sachet citing Gaspare Viviani's 'secret manner', which allowed the pope to avoid direct association with controversial viewpoints.[66] In exchange, papal subsidies and sponsorship offset the risks and costs of printing reform-minded volumes in an unpredictable market and ensured that such works would reach fruition.[67]

The pope's interest in the *Directorium* is further suggested by Gregory XIII's printer's privilege, featured as a prefatory letter at the beginning of the volume.

---

64 Coattino's publication of Guidetti's volumes, including with his business partner Alessandro Gardano and their frequent collaborator Jacopo Tornieri, is worth its own study. Coattino, Gardano and Tornieri printed all of Guidetti's volumes after 1582: *Cantus ecclesiasticus passionis* (Rome: Alessandro Gardano, 1586), USTC 835482; *Cantus ecclesiasticus officii maioris hebdomadae* (Rome: Jacopo Tornieri, 1587), USTC 835483; *Praefationes in cantu firmo, iuxta ritum Sanctae Romanae Ecclesiae, emendatae, et nunc primum in lucem editae a Ioanne Guidetto Bononiensi Basilicae principis apostolorum de urbe clerico beneficiato* (Rome: Giacomo Tornieri, 1588), USTC 835484; *Directorium chori ad usum omnium ecclesiarum, iam cathedralium quam collegiatarum, nuper restitutum, & nunc secundo in lucem editum* (Rome: Francesco Coattino, 1589), USTC 835485; *Directorium chori ad usum omnium Ecclesiarum nuper restitutum et nunc tertio in lucem editum* (Rome: Francesco Coattino, 1591), USTC 835486.

65 See Paolo Sachet, *Publishing for the Popes. The Roman Curia and the Use of Printing (1527–1555)* (Leiden: Brill, 2020), p. 199.

66 BVR, K 17, f. 111r–v, cited in Sachet, 'Publishing for the Popes', p. 60 fn. 90: 'con quel segreto modo che in tal opera prudentemente si deve tenere per schifar molti contrarii all'hora espositi a Sua Santità'.

67 For examples of such sponsorship, including of Dorico, Blado and Manuzio, see Cusick, 'Valerio Dorico. Music Printer', pp. 11–19.

The letter is lengthier than a comparable privilege from Sixtus V for Guidetti's *Cantus ecclesiasticus maioris hebdomadae* of 1587, in part because of more personal remarks and more extensive references to protecting the printed contents.[68] For one, the privilege refers in a familiar way to Guidetti as a close member of the Vatican community and offers protection to Guidetti should he be censured 'on whatever pretext or for whatever reason', as if anticipating a controversial response like that which followed the 1577 commission.[69] The contents and approach of the *Directorium* are described at some length, noting their benefit to the public. Gregory also specifically notes the typeface within his papal privilege.[70] As already described, the typeface was innovative, as was the notation itself. Most probably, by mentioning it specifically, Gregory XIII included it among the Granjon designs that merited papal protection and which were not to leave Rome.[71]

The mission-oriented aspect of the *Directorium* also bears consideration alongside Gregory XIII's print activities and the bulk of Granjon's Vatican-related work to create foreign-language types. As an upright octavo musico-liturgical manual, the *Directorium* was well-suited to Catholic missions abroad by priests and other religious, including for educational purposes and frequent use.[72] Numbering 573 pages and measuring 154 × 104 mm, the thickness of the

---

68 For a transcription and English translation of the Sixtus V privilege, see Swanson, 'Speaking in Tones', pp. 275–278. Transcription of other Guidetti-related prefatory materials can be found here as well, with English translations by Catherine Gunderson.

69 Guidetti, *Directorium chori* (1582), A2v: 'Quavis occasione, vel causa latis'.

70 Guidetti, *Directorium chori* (1582), f. A2v: 'missionis typorum, librorum, et operum tibi irremisibiliter applicandorum respectivem ... quoties contraventum fuerit auctoritate, et tenore premissis districius inhibemus'.

71 To this effect, thirty-two punches and thirty-nine matrices are registered in a 1595 inventory of the Typographia Vaticana, alongside those for foreign types, for which Granjon was known. Alberto Tinto indicates in his copying of the inventory records for the Typographia Vaticana that the chant punches and matrices were for Guidetti's chant volume (with no attribution to Granjon). Given that Granjon worked for the same press, it makes sense that these would indeed be Granjon's. That said, Mary Kay Duggan suggests that these were commissioned from Granjon for Palestrina's unfinished Gradual, which underscores the longstanding ambiguity between Palestrina's original commission and Guidetti's work. See Alberto Tinto, 'Di un inventario della Tipografia Vaticana (1595)', in Giorgio de Gregorio, Maria Valenti (eds.), *Studi di biblioteconomia e storia del libro in onore di Francesco Barberi* (Rome: Associazione Italiana Biblioteche, 1976), pp. 547–549; Mary Kay Duggan, *Italian Music Incunabula. Printers and Type* (Berkeley: University of California Press, 1992), pp. 25, 28.

72 On the use of octavo volumes in teaching, see Samuel J. Brannon, 'Books about Music in Renaissance Print Culture. Authors, Printers and Readers' (PhD diss., University of North Carolina at Chapel Hill, 2016), p. 185. Jane Bernstein notes that upright octavo was often used for popular works (such as *canzone alla napolitane*): Jane Bernstein, *Music Printing*

volume was minimised by using thin paper, making the book easily carried and transportable. Containing primarily chant incipits, the volume assumed memory of the church's plainchant tradition and would not likely circulate unmediated among the uninitiated but rather among priests and cantors seeking to ensure the latest in Catholic orthodoxy.

The missionary significance of Guidetti's edited volumes is suggested not only in the *Directorium* but also in his various other publications. For example, in the *Directorium*, Guidetti remarked that the 'church is waging war in the world', implying that the *Directorium* provided one of many possible weapons.[73] In a 1586 book, he specified even more clearly that 'the sacred practices of the Roman rite' should be 'transferred into the nations and diligently observed', presumably with his books.[74] Posthumous editions of the *Directorium* were even printed for Jesuit use.[75] Notably, an edition of the 1582 *Directorium* appears in a seventeenth-century inventory of religious books belonging to the Jesuit missionary and bishop of Japan, Diogo Valente, during his term in the Portuguese colony of Macau (1623–1633). Macau was a known stopping place for Jesuit missionary priests en route to mainland China, where such book collections contributed to the missionary project.[76] Guidetti was clearly aware of the mission-related potential of his works, and the books were used to that end within and beyond his lifetime. Given Guidetti's missionary zeal and Granjon's role in mission-oriented printing efforts, it thus seems likely that Granjon was invited to design and cut the type for Guidetti because it was in keeping with Granjon's ongoing role with Gregory XIII's print projects, and because the *Directorium* was an important publication that needed his skill and expertise.[77]

---

in Renaissance Venice. The Scotto Press, 1539–1572 (New York: Oxford University Press, 1998), pp. 65–67.

73 Guidetti, *Directorium chori* (1582), f. A4r: 'S. Mater Ecclesia, donec in terris militat, necessitatibus urgeatur'.

74 Guidetti, *Cantus ecclesiasticus passionis* I. †4r, dedication to Serenissimo D. D. Guilielmo: 'Quo in genere illam quoque cogitationem suscipere dicitur, ut qui sacrorum ritus Romae in primis celebres, ac probati habentur eos istuc transferri curet, diligenterque per omnes suae ditionis Ecclesias observari'.

75 Giovanni Guidetti, *Directorium chori ad usum omnium ecclesiarum cathedralium, & collegiatarum a Ioanne Guidetto olim editum, et nuper ad novam romani Breviarii correctionem ex praecepto Clementis 8. impressam restitutum, & plurimis in locis auctum, & emendatum* (Rome: Andrea Fei, Vincenzo Castellano, 1615), USTC 4022026; and Marzio Ercoleo, *Cantus omnis ecclesiasticus ad Hebdomadae maioris* (Mutinae: Haeres Cassiani, 1688).

76 For the role of the books within this collection and the *Directorium* in particular, see Noël Golvers, 'The Library Catalogue of Diogo Valente's Book Collection in Macao (1633). A Philological and Bibliographic Analysis', *Bulletin of Portuguese-Japanese Studies*, 13 (2006), pp. 8, 17, 39.

77 For a related set of associations between Granjon, Gregory XIII, the Jesuits and publication for mission, see Sachet, 'Publishing for the Popes', pp. 60–63.

But why use this unusual notation at all? Justifying his reforms, Guidetti presented his notation and editing as a revival of ancient practices. He noted that he was guided by early Church Fathers and that he was recovering an 'ancient rite' ('antiqui ritu').[78] In one such instance, Guidetti mentioned the influence of old ('vetustis') chant volumes from the Vatican, as if these ancient practices were simply older versions of Catholic chant.[79] But he also interspersed ancient Greek and Hebrew musical references in his prefaces. In his 1591 *Directorium*, for example, he used the example of Pythagoras to declare the potential power of Christian musical arts. In the same volume, he referenced King David as a model of music's power and importance within Judeo-Christian worship traditions.[80]

Hyun-Ah Kim has suggested that Guidetti modelled his unusual notation on a handwritten notated version of Hebrew cantillation found in Johannes Reuchlin's *De accentibus et orthographia linguae Hebraicae* of 1518 (see Figure 5.3).[81] Notably, Reuchlin also used semi-circular figures over pitches, albeit sixty years earlier than Guidetti. Reuchlin's notation was itself not ancient but developed by another German scholar, Johann Boeschenstein, for transcribing Hebrew biblical cantillation.[82] That said, Reuchlin linked the notation not only to Hebrew cantillation practice but also to ancient Greek recitation, noting how in more ancient practices like these, signs over notes facilitated expressive declamation, including syllable emphasis, textual division and textual meaning.

If the visibility of these semi-circular signs created an aura of antiquity within the volume, they further signalled the rhetorical potential and power of

---

78 Biblioteca Apostolica Vaticana Reg. lat. 2076: 'Ipse chori veras leges modulosque docebo Antiqui ritu, quo cecinere Patres. Prisca damus, ne spernere tamen, quae prisca fuere Dissita, iuncta simul fecimus esse nova'.

79 Guidetti, *Directorium chori* (1582), f. A5r–v: 'Ac licet in Musicis notis collocandis, coniungendis, separandis, augendis, expungendis cum vetustis Vaticanae nostrae Basilicae, tun recentioribus Antiphonarijs, ac Psalterijs'.

80 Guidetti, *Directorium* chori (1591), preface: 'quod recte exemplo Pitagorae comprobatur, quem dicunt iratos animos musicae harmonia placidos reddidisse ... ad quod saepe nos David propheta invitat: Omnes gentes (inquit ille) plaudite manibus, iubilate Deo in voce exultationis. et alibi: Cantate Dominum canticum novum'.

81 Kim, *Humanism and the Reform of Sacred Music*, pp. 152–154, 180. How Guidetti would have encountered Reuchlin's notation is unclear, although Reuchlin was highly regarded within and beyond the early sixteenth century as an important Christian Hebraicist. The celebrated music theorist Gioseffo Zarlino, for example, quoted extensively from Reuchlin's *De accentibus* in his own 1588 theory treatise *Sopplimenti musicali*, although he neglected to identify his source.

82 Eric Werner, 'Two Obscure Sources of Reuchlin's *De accentibus et orthographia linguae Hebraicae*', *Historia Judaica*, 16 (1954), pp. 47–52.

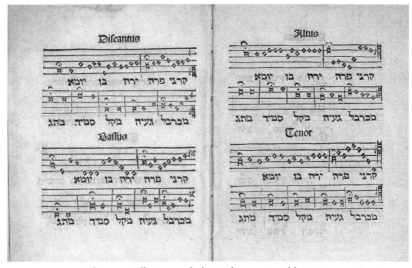

FIGURE 5.3 Hebrew cantillation symbols in Johannes Reuchlin's *De accentibus et orthographia linguae hebraicae* (Hagenau 1518)

plainchant.[83] To this effect, Guidetti urged in his prefaces that religious prayers should be 'recited not ineptly and with confused clamour but with modulated voices and the highest sweetness of musical harmony'. He was concerned that 'all the functions of the choir be exercised correctly and praiseworthily' and performed 'with grace and dignity'.[84] He identified his *Directorium* as a resource for teaching 'ministers of the choir the way of regulating and moderating the voice', and noted that 'sacred words must be enunciated in a lofty tone (*sublimi tono*) and brought forth towards the established ways in like manner to the ancient rite of the church'.[85] A poem about the *Directorium* (likely by Guidetti) emphasises this yet further, linking his musical innovations with ancient ideals:

83 On this connection between ancient rites and modulated voice, see Swanson, 'In Search of the Word', pp. 42–50.
84 Guidetti, *Directorium chori* (1582), f. A4r: 'Hinc denique institutum, ut religiosae preces, non inepto, et confuso clamore, sed modulatis vocibus, et summa cum Musicorum concentuum suavitate reciterentur … ut omnia Chori munia rite, ac laudabiliter exerceant … cum gratia aliqua, et dignitate'.
85 Guidetti, *Directorium chori* (1582), f. A5r: 'Merito igitur liber hic Directorium chori appellabitur, seu quod regendae, ac moderandae vocis viam chori ministris ostendit, seu quod regendae, ac moderandae vocis viam chori ministris ostendit, seu quod Hebdomadarij maximè, et cantorias exercentium usui deservit, ad quos totum chori officium dirigere pertinet'. See also f. A4v: 'Atque ut caetera omittam, et ad id quod propositi mei est veniam, in Sacrosancta nostra Vaticana Basilica, ceterisq. omnibus seu Cathedralibus, seu Collegiatis Ecclesijs, ministrantibus in Choro apparet, nihil frequentius usu venire, quàm ut eis sacra verba sublimi tono enuncianda, et ad certos modos iuxta veterem Ecclesiae ritū proferenda sint'.

I myself shall teach the true rules and measures of the choir
in the ancient rite, by which our Forefathers sang;
We offer the ancient music: do not spurn that ancient music
which has been remote, for we have caused the new to be joined with it.[86]

Notably, although the 1589 and 1591 editions of the *Directorium* all used the same symbols and Granjon's musical type, a posthumous edition in 1604 omitted the notational symbols and instead used more standard plainchant notation. In the prefatory material, the editor (Joanne Francisco Massano, a beneficed priest of St Lorenzo in Damaso) justified the changed notation by mentioning the absence of such marks in other ancient and learned precedents, suggesting that Guidetti's notation from 1582 was understood by his contemporaries as a sign of an ancient lineage but that this same effect could be accomplished with other means.[87] Published by Stefano Paulino, it may also be the case that the printer did not have access to Granjon's type.

4   Conclusions

The printing of plainchant in Rome reflects the changing priorities of ruling popes between 1568 and 1582, but also the vagaries of counter-Reformation politics and the gradual development of papal printing initiatives. From the conservative integration of plainchant into the reform-minded Breviary and Missal to Guidetti's innovative rhythmicised chant melodies, we see very different approaches to reform, including plainchant texts, melodies and liturgical use. Whereas the earlier efforts focused primarily on liturgical placement and minor textual or slight melodic modification, later efforts addressed the melodies themselves. In the case of Gregory XIII's commission to Palestrina and Zoilo, this proved controversial for both musical and political reasons, with Philip II intervening in Gregory's publishing project.

---

86   Biblioteca Apostolica Vaticana Reg. lat. 2076: 'Ipse chori veras leges modulosque docebo Antiqui ritu, quo cecinere Patres. Prisca damus: ne sperne tamen quae prisca fuere Dissita, iuncta simul fecimus esse nova'.

87   Ioanne Francisco Massano (ed.), *Directorium chori ad usum omnium ecclesiarum cathedralium & collegiatarum, a Ioanne Guidetto olim editum & nuper ad novam Romani Breviarii correctionem ex praecepto Clementi VIII* (Rome: Stefano Paolini, 1604), USTC 4030244. Directions for use: 'Atque hoc est discrimen, quod habent notae Musicae, quas in nova hac Directorij, impressione apposuimus, expedire enim arbitrati sumus totum hunc cantum tribus his tantummodo notis comprehendere, tum quia illis usi sunt artis Musicae veteres, et doctissimi Magistri, tum etiam, quia in antiquis et recentoribus libris hae solum reperientur, et ipsemet Directorij Auctor in officio Maioris hebdomadae, ac in alijs a se editis libris, illis usus est'.

How Guidetti's *Directorium* relates to Gregory's failed plainchant project may never be known with certainty. However, the evidence discussed in these pages suggests that Gregory XIII supported Guidetti's project, albeit in subtle ways: from his printing privilege for the *Directorium*; to the coat of arms on the title page, which frequently graced papal projects; to Granjon's involvement as Rome's celebrated, if newly arrived, typecutter; and as a subtle subversion of Philip II's earlier power play, by endorsing if not commissioning a chant revision project. Guidetti's prefaces to the *Directorium*, alongside those for his later works, certainly aligned with Gregory's zeal regarding the dissemination of an authoritative Catholicism in print. To that end, Guidetti's references to an ongoing religious war and the need to recover musico-liturgical dignity confirm a proselytising approach, comparable to Gregory's own focus on missions abroad.

Granjon's involvement in the *Directorium* has puzzled many scholars, since the volume as a whole lacks the finesse of Granjon's other projects. That said, even Vervliet acknowledged the care required to cut the musical type for such a small volume, specifically the semi-circular figures. Although the musical notation in the *Directorium* hardly exploited the range of Granjon's skills, it was unique enough to require a skilled typecutter and valuable enough to its creator and supporters to merit the significant time and effort required to create it. Although likely costly to produce (as with any musical typeface), the ultimate value of the notation was its potential to elevate the delivery of the plainchant melodies and thus contribute to the revitalisation of Catholic liturgy and the codification of new approaches for the Church in Rome and beyond.

PART 2

Between the Protestant and Catholic Reformations

∴

CHAPTER 6

'Write against It, So That They May Return to the Right Faith'

Catholic Doctrinal and Polemical Writings in the Early Dutch Reformation (1517–1528)

David Oldenhof

A thriving field of scholarship has emerged devoted to the printed religious books that were available in the Low Countries during the fifteenth and early sixteenth century.[1] Koen Goudriaan, for example, discovered that friars from the Franciscan order were early adopters of the printing press, which they regarded as a valuable instrument in their missionary endeavours. In the period before the Reformation, an astonishing 148 books were published by these mendicants.[2] That the Franciscans were among the first to see the potential of the press is unsurprising, as the mendicant orders had already influenced the urban religious landscape significantly by stimulating the laity to participate in religious activities such as reading.[3] Following the increased demand for religious books, printing workshops flourished in the Low Countries, as religious printing was mostly a commercial affair.[4] From 1477 until 1520, printers provided this market with a steady stream of religious books and faced little

---

1 Bert Roest, 'Franciscan Religious Instruction in the Low Countries, c.1520–1560', *Ons Geestelijk Erf*, 85 (2014) 4, pp. 292–310, 292–293; Wim Francois, 'De Leuvense theologen en de eerste gedrukte bijbels in de volkstaal (1522–1533). Een feitelijk gedoogbeleid?', *Trajecta. Tijdschrift Voor de Geschiedenis van Het Katholiek Leven in de Nederlanden*, 11 (2002) 3, pp. 244–276; Koen Goudriaan, 'Het sint-agnesklooster en de moderne devotie', *Ons Geestelijk Erf*, 81 (2010) 1, pp. 17–37; Hans Kienhorst, 'Mystiek op schrift in vrouwenkloosters uit de traditie van de moderne devotie. Een oriënterende vergelijking van drie collecties: Arnhem, Geldern en Maaseik', *Ons Geestelijk Erf*, 81 (2010) 1, pp. 38–63.
2 Koen Goudriaan, 'The Church and the Market. Vernacular Religious Works and the Early Printing Press in the Low Countries, 1477–1540', in Sabrina Corbellini (eds.), *Cultures of Religious Reading in the Late Middle Ages. Instructing the Soul, Feeding the Spirit, and Awakening the Passion* (Turnhout: Brepols, 2013), pp. 93–117, 113.
3 John Van Engen, 'Multiple Options. The World of the Fifteenth-Century Church', *Church History*, 77 (2008), pp. 257–284.
4 Jan Luiten Van Zanden, Eltjo Buringh, 'Book Production as a Mirror of the Emerging Medieval Knowledge Economy, 500–1500', in Jan Luiten van Zanden (ed.), *The Long Road to the Industrial Revolution. The European Economy in a Global Perspective, 1000–1800* (Leiden: Brill, 2009), pp. 69–91.

restrictions by the authorities.[5] Bestselling books and popular genres included meditations on the life and Passion of Christ and 'mirrors' of Christian life, such as *Kerstenspiegel* (Christian mirror) by the Franciscan Dirk Coelde, *Spieghel der volcomenheid* (Mirror of perfection), printed in 1488 by Gerard Leeu and *Boexken van der Missen* (Book of the mass) by the Observant Franciscan Gerrit van der Goude.[6]

Bibles were part of this rich landscape of religious printing and the number of printed editions is impressive. Forty editions of vernacular Bibles were published in the Low Countries before the Reformation started, and during the three decades after 1517, eighty more editions of the vernacular Bible were circulated. Unlike in England, where vernacular Bibles were readily linked with the Lollard heresy by church authorities, and unlike in France, where vernacular Bible reading was outlawed because of the perceived reformist threat, vernacular Bibles were part of the fabric of Dutch religious life throughout the later fifteenth and sixteenth century.[7] The idea that the Dutch clergy enthusiastically provided the laity with religious texts is now widely shared among historians who study the fifteenth and sixteenth century.[8] These insights are part of a historiographical re-examination of the western European religious landscape of the fifteenth and early sixteenth century, and many recent studies have successfully nuanced earlier interpretations of the late-medieval church as being in a weak and critical condition at the turn of the sixteenth century.[9] For example, scholars like John Bossy and Eamon Duffy demonstrated that the laity played a substantial role in pre-Reformation England's rich and diverse religious life.[10]

---

5 Goudriaan, 'The Church and the Market', p. 115.
6 Peter Van Dael, 'Two Illustrated Catechisms from Antwerp by Petrus Canisius', in Koen Goudriaan (eds.), *Education and Learning in the Netherlands, 1400–1600. Essays in Honour of Hilde de Ridder-Symoens* (Leiden 2004), pp. 277–296; Clemens Drees (ed.), *Der Christenspiegel des Dirk Koelde van Munster* (Werl: Dirk Coelde Verlag, 1954); Benjamin de Troeyer, 'Bio-bibliografie van de minderbroeders in de Nederlanden vóór het jaar 1500. Dirk van Munster', *Franciscana*, 25 (1971); Gerrit van der Goude, *Dat boexken vander missen* (Antwerp: Adriaen van Berghen, 1504), USTC 438148.
7 August den Hollander, 'De Nederlandse bijbelvertalingen, 1522–1545', *Bibliotheca Bibliographica Neerlandica*, 33 (1997), pp. 7–22.
8 Andrew Gow, 'Challenging the Protestant Paradigm. Bible Reading in Lay and Urban Contexts of the Later Middle Ages', in Th.J. Heffernan, Th.E. Burman (eds.), *Scripture and Pluralism. Reading the Bible in the Religiously Plural Worlds of the Middle Ages and Renaissance* (Leiden: Brill, 2005), pp. 161–191.
9 Jacques Toussaert, *Le Sentiment religieux, la vie et la pratique religieuse des laïcs en Flandre maritime et au 'west-hoeck' de langue flamande aux XIVIe, XVe et début du XVIe siècle* (Paris: Plon, 1963), p. 606.
10 John Bossy, *Christianity in the West, 1400–1700* (Oxford: Oxford University Press, 1985); Eamon Duffy, *The Stripping of the Altars. Traditional Religion in England, c.1400–c.1580* (New Haven, CT: Cambridge University Press, 2005).

However, these insights have not altered a key interpretation of religious instruction during the first decades of the sixteenth century: the idea that the laity had very few explicit printed religious teachings at their disposal that dealt with the topics that would be contested during the Reformation. The belief that the Dutch clergy were somehow 'unable' to doctrinally defend their faith comes from Catholic scholars in the 1940s, such as L.J. Rogier, who judged the nature of the doctrinal religious teachings of the fifteenth and early sixteenth century according to post-Tridentine criteria, a period when the dogmatic position of the Catholic Church became more explicitly formulated.[11] However, modern studies reveal that this interpretation is still prevalent. In 2006, Judith Pollmann wrote that the clergy in the Low Countries were unable and unwilling to write doctrinal texts for the laity, as they wrote 'almost exclusively in Latin, for an audience of priests and theologians'.[12] She argued that one of the defining reasons for the success of the Reformation was this lack of instructional texts to equip the laity with arguments to counter reformist critiques. In her monograph *Catholic Identity and Revolt in the Netherlands, 1520–1635*, published in 2011, she concluded that the available books were purely devotional in nature with little to help the reader counter reformist arguments. Furthermore, the clergy would have consciously kept the laity 'in the dark' about arguments voiced by reformist authors in attempt to keep the debate within academic circles.[13] As a consequence, the laity would have been unable to defend their faith, which in turn, according to Pollmann, resulted in weak resistance to Protestantism and the iconoclastic events of 1566.[14]

The present paper questions this interpretation of the availability of religious teachings and anti-reformist publications during the first decades of the sixteenth century. It does so by exploring several books, either by Dutch authors or translated into the Dutch vernacular, that were published between 1517 and 1528. Publications by Dutch clerical authors from this period reveal many, often conflicting strategies to deal with the challenges of the emerging reformist authors and their rapidly spreading texts. The books that will be discussed in this paper show a strong preoccupation with instructing the laity and with debunking reformist arguments in detail. It will be argued that, during the 1520s, at least some clerical authors felt forced to react in print to

---

11 Lodewijk J. Rogier, *Geschiedenis van het Katholicisme in Noord Nederland in de 16de en 17de eeuw* (Amsterdam: A'dam, 1948), pp. 5–15.
12 Judith Pollmann, 'Countering the Reformation in France and the Netherlands. Clerical Leadership and Catholic Violence 1560–1585', *Past & Present*, 190 (2006), pp. 83–120, 100.
13 Judith Pollman, *Catholic Identity and the Revolt of the Netherlands, 1520–1635* (Oxford: Oxford University Press, 2011), p. 47.
14 Pollmann, *Catholic Identity*, p. 47.

the circulation of Lutheran books. They started to publish or translate instructional texts in which the Dutch reader could find many arguments to counter reformist critiques and learn about the contested topics and controversies of their time.

1 Theological Debates and the Laity: The Indulgence Controversy

Introducing educated readers to contemporary theological debates was not a novelty during the Reformation. The Franciscans and Carthusians had a well-established printing tradition and used the printing press to publish both devotional and instructional texts.[15] One such work that introduced the laity to a complex theological controversy was a treatise called *Hier begint een boecxken lerende hoe dat een mensche zijn gebet ordineren sal om aflaten te verdinen* (Here starts a book that teaches how a person should pray in order to earn indulgences), published in 1517 in Leiden by Lucas van der Hey.[16] He was a Franciscan friar from the province of Holland, and his ministry spanned a wide area in the Netherlands.[17] The work was written in the form of a dialogue between a nun and a priest, a genre primarily aimed to instruct monks and nuns but which found its way into the literature of lay instruction.[18] It was a popular tool for spreading religious messages, and both clerical and reformist authors wrote in this literary form. A well-known example of this is the book by the spiritualist David Joris, called *Twesprake tuschen een meister ende sijn disciple* (Dialogue between a master and his disciple).[19] During the sixteenth century, these sets of questions and answers evolved into the catechisms that became an important tool in the repertoire of religious instruction.[20]

It is not surprising that texts about indulgences were published around 1517, as buying indulgences was intensely popular among the laity, even though the theology of indulgence was in no way a fleshed-out theory. Even the theological faculty of Paris complained that this way of talking about achieving

---

15 Goudriaan, 'The Church and the Market', p. 100.
16 Lucas van der Hey, *Hier begint een boecxken lerende hoe dat een mensche zijn gebet ordineren sal om oflaten te verdinen* (Leiden: Jan Severs, 1518), USTC 420623.
17 Benjamin de Troeyer, *Bio-bibliographia franciscana neerlandica saeculi XVI, 1: Pars bio-graphica* (Nieuwkoop: B. de Graf, 1969), pp. 25–26.
18 Bert Roest, 'Franciscans between Observance and Reformation. The Low Countries (ca. 1400–1600)', *Franciscan Studies*, 63 (2005), pp. 409–442, 422.
19 David Joris, *Twesprake tuschen een meister ende sijn discipel* (Rostock: Ludwig Dietz, 1550), USTC 412552.
20 Lee Palmer Wander, *Reading Catechisms, Teaching Religion* (Leiden: Brill, 2016), p. 11.

salvation was too mechanical.[21] This striking discrepancy between the lack of theological foundation and the great popularity of buying indulgences among the laity alarmed many theologians; Martin Luther's *Ninety-five theses* was one contribution to this much larger debate.[22]

The text by Van der Hey dealt with many different aspects of indulgences. The first part was theoretical, explaining the scriptural basis and theology of indulgences. It directly confronted the concerns posed by critics. The second part of the book was mostly devotional, and the third part functioned as a prayer guide. It is not possible to pinpoint Van der Hey's target audience, but a lay readership is very plausible, as the addressed criticisms on indulgences were predominantly voiced by lay people. For example, Van der Hey wrote that 'evil Christians, who speak about indulgences, are saying that the papists' only concern is money, and that they gladly shave the poor people and take the money out of their purses'.[23] It was mostly the urban laity who voiced these criticisms, as there was a widespread concern among the urban elite that their money would flow to Rome in the form of church taxes and indulgences.[24]

One of the main theological arguments Van der Hey developed in his treatise was the role of the saints in the treasury of the church, a storage of 'grace' from which indulgences had their origin. He explained that the saints, because of their unjustly endured suffering and death, substantially contributed to this treasury. The grace was so abundant that it could be distributed to Christians through the indulgences.[25] To position himself in a theological debate, he wrote, 'there are doctors, that are also great in theology, that say that the treasure of the Holy Church is not filled by the merits of the saints ... but is filled only by the merits of the Son of God'.[26] To counter this viewpoint, Van der Hey

---

21   David Bagchi, 'Luther's Catholic Opponents', in Andrew Pettegree (eds.), *The Reformation World* (London: Routledge, 2000), p. 18.

22   Theodor Dieter, Wolfgang Thönissen, *Der Ablassstreit. Dokumente, ökumenische Kommentierungen, Beiträge. Abteilung 1: Dokumente zum Ablassstreit* (Leipzig: Evangelische Verlagsanstalt, 2021), p. 24.

23   'Ende oeck mede een quaet kersten mensche dye opten aflaet spreeckt seghende. Tis al ghecimeer daer en sijn aflaten tis alleyn den papen omt gelt te doen dat si gaern souden die arme luyden scheren ende tgelt uut den buydel crigen', Van der Hey, *Hier begint een boecxken*, p. 25.

24   Reinhold Kiermayr, 'How Much Money Was Actually in the Indulgence Chest?', *The Sixteenth Century Journal*, 17.3 (1986), pp. 303–318.

25   Van der Hey, *Hier begint een boecxken*, p. 10.

26   'Soe vintmen sommige doctoren die oec groot sijn inder godheit dye seggen dat die schat vander heiliger kercken en is niet doer die verdiente der heilighen want si sijn geloont boven haer verdienten mer die schat der heyligen kercken comt alleen doer dat verdiente van die soon gods', ibid., p. 9.

cited established theological authorities and carefully introduced these figures and their arguments to his reader. On the role of the saints in indulgences, he quoted Peter de Palude and pointed to where these arguments could be found in de Palude's books, as if encouraging the reader to look it up and read the source text itself. Van der Hey wrote that De Palude had argued that the saints' accomplishments were greater than their guilt and that they suffered more than they deserved. Therefore, they generated more merit than they needed themselves, and this overabundance of merit contributed to the treasure of the Holy Church and thereby can help 'poor people' with their salvation.[27]

The careful and nuanced treatment of this theological debate, in which the author explored both sides of the argument in detail, suggests not only that his readers were both informed and literate but also that informing his Dutch readers on contemporary theological debates preceded the Reformation. Van der Hey's work challenges Pollmann's claim that Catholic authors wrote in a deliberately inaccessible style to keep theological debates out of the public sphere.[28]

2 Searching and Testing Strategies

During the years after the publication of Van der Hey's treatise on indulgences, the controversy that had started with the publication of Luther's *Ninety-five theses* rose to great heights. Lutheran writings started to spread widely throughout the Low Countries, and many Catholic theologians felt forced to respond. The Dutch Catholic response has not been studied in detail, but the German situation has been examined extensively by David Bagchi.[29] In the German countries, the publication of the *Ninety-five theses* resulted in an all-out pamphlet war, which lasted until 1525. During this propaganda campaign, both clerical authors and early sympathisers of Luther used the printing press vigorously to spread their respective messages. Around sixty Catholic authors were involved, mostly German secular priests and friars from the mendicant orders.[30] Although the Franciscans were the smallest group of these 'controversialists', they did manage to out-publish the Dominican authors. This can be partly explained by the early adoption of the printing press by the Franciscans, by which they knew how to exploit its capabilities.[31] However, the

---

27 Ibid., pp. 20–21.
28 Pollmann, 'Countering the Reformation in France and the Netherlands', p. 100.
29 David Bagchi, *Luther's Earliest Opponents. Catholic Controversialists, 1518–1525* (Minneapolis: Fortress Press, 1991).
30 Bagchi, 'Luther's Catholic Opponents', p. 99.
31 Goudriaan, 'The Church and the Market', p. 100.

Catholic texts were far outnumbered by pamphlets published by Luther's early supporters. For every single book or pamphlet that their opponents wrote, they published five.[32]

This should not be interpreted as evidence that there lacked skilled writers who could adequately respond to Luther. Most Catholic controversialists wrote only one work. One of the reasons for this was that these authors were both disliked by the early reformers as well as by the Roman Curia. The Roman Curia was very suspicious of authors who published without its consent, and these early authors all published independently. Sometimes, these controversialists were even blamed for the Reformation, labelled as having magnified a debate that had begun as a small issue from a minor theologian in Germany. For some time, the curia believed that the debate would have passed without much notice had these clerical authors not responded so fiercely.[33]

As stated, the printing realm was mostly commercial in nature, without much interference by clerical and secular authorities. Groups like the Franciscans had also established their own printing traditions. This all influenced the decentralised responses to the early reformers until the late 1520s. The situation changed with the many proclamations for publishers and printers by both the papacy and by major Catholic secular rulers. As a result, all publishers had to deal with censorship, which sometimes hindered rather than helped the Catholic cause. For example, reformist books continued to flow into the country from publishing centres such as Emden, which could work without censorship restraints.[34]

These tensions, as well as attempts by clerical writers to respond effectively to the challenges posed by reformist authors, are reflected in the many different approaches that can be observed in books from the Low Countries published during the 1520s. Some clerical orders chose to refrain from mentioning Luther because of the fear that preaching and writing about him would only increase interest in his ideas. They had to show to the laity why Luther was in error without eliciting curiosity. Some authors, therefore, published instructional materials that dealt with issues raised by dissidents like Luther without mentioning the dissenter explicitly. Thomas Herentals, a Franciscan friar from Leuven, published such a catechetical work to defend the faith, called *Den speghel des kersten levens* (The mirror of the Christian life), which explained the theology of the sacraments to the laity and equipped them with a deeper understanding

---

32   Bagchi, 'Luther's Catholic Opponents', p. 99.
33   Ibid., p. 100.
34   Guido Marnef, 'The Netherlands', in David M. Whitford (ed.), *Reformation and Early Modern Europe. A Guide to Research* (Kirksville: Truman State University Press, 2008), p. 119.

so they would be less vulnerable to reformist criticism.[35] Another Franciscan from Leuven, Franciscus Titelmans, published *Den schat des kerstens gheloof* (The treasure of the Christian faith) in 1530. It consisted of thirty-two contemplations on the Christian faith, dealing with topics such as the Eucharist, the role of good works in justification and the Virgin Mary.[36] It is easy for scholars to be misled by its devotional character, as many contemplations share an instructional approach.

Neither Thomas Herentals nor Franciscus Titelmans mentioned Luther or other early reformers in their works, and thus they cannot be classified as polemics. This lack of explicit refutations by the Franciscan friars can be partly explained by an official Franciscan strategy that prohibited mentioning Luther and his teachings.[37] However, these two friars both published religious instructional materials on topics that were contested by reformist authors, and they did so with the explicit aim to render the reader less vulnerable to critiques. This should be considered when reviewing the instructional publications available to the Dutch reader during the first decades of the Reformation.

3   The Power of Tradition: Johannes Eck

Among the first signs of a centralised response during the decentralised pamphlet war was an influential publication by Johannes Eck (1486–1543), a Dominican professor from Ingolstadt. This work was called *Enchiridion locorum communium adversus Lutherum et alios hostes ecclesiae* (Handbook of commonplaces against Luther and other enemies of the church).[38] It was extraordinarily successful in the decades after its publication and went through 116 reprints in just 50 years.[39] Eck, who was one of the earliest and fiercest adversaries of Luther, had already engaged in a written dispute with Luther in 1518. This resulted in the famous Leipzig disputation in the summer

---

35   Thomas Herentals, *Den speghel des kersten leuens beslutende tverclaers vanden thien gheboden Gods, ende vanden vii sacramenten der heleger kercken* (Antwerp: Symon Cock, 1532), USTC 400519; Bert Roest, 'Franciscan religious instruction in the Low Countries, c.1520–1560', *Ons Geestelijk Erf*, 85.4 (2014), pp. 292–310.

36   Franciscus Titelmans, *Den schat des kersten gheloofs* (Antwerp: Symon Cock, 1532), USTC 403862.

37   Bert Roest, 'Dutch Franciscans between Observance and Reformation', pp. 409–442, 436.

38   Johannes Eck, 'Enchiridion locorum communium adversus Lutherum et alios hostes ecclesiae', ed. Pierre Fraenkel (Münster: Aschendorffsche Verlagsbuchhandlung, 1979).

39   Jared Wicks, 'Controversial Theologians', in Hans Hillerbrand (ed.), *Oxford Encyclopedia of the Reformation* (New York: Oxford University Press, 1996), pp. 420–423.

of 1519.[40] During this debate, Eck forced Luther to admit that his attack on the pope's authority was in line with the critiques of the condemned theologian Jan Hus. Thereby, Luther implied that Jan Hus had been right, and that the council of Konstanz had wrongfully condemned Hus. Partly because of Eck's efforts, the official condemnation of Luther by Pope Leo X followed in the papal bull *Exsurge Domine*.[41]

This papal condemnation did not stop the pamphlet war and publication efforts of individual Catholic authors who tried to provide an answer to Luther's widely circulating works. They started to print refutations in which they aimed to show Luther's errors and portray him as dangerous to both the church and society.[42] (Later in this chapter, a Dutch example of such a work will be studied in depth.) However, this fierce and combative approach did not seem to be very successful. In 1524, Cardinal Legate Lorenzo Campeggio suggested to Eck that, instead of focusing on confrontational anti-Lutheran writings, it would be more fruitful to write a comprehensive account of all the topics that had come under attack by reformist authors. This resulted in *Enchiridion*, which would be translated into different languages, namely German, French and Dutch.[43] The Dutch version was the first translation of the *Enchiridion* that appeared on the European market. In 1530, five German translations appeared, and four French translations were published in 1551.[44] The Dutch version of this work was printed in 1527 in Delft by Cornelis Henricsz Lettersnijder.[45] While the Dutch translator is unknown, it is clear that he regarded the text as an effective antidote against Lutheran teachings.[46]

The translated work bore the title *Hier beghint een corte declaracie ende antwoert teghen zomighe articulen der lutheranen* (Here starts a short declaration and answer against some articles of the Lutherans).[47] Even though the book contained strong anti-Lutheran content, it was quickly banned by the

---

40   Erwin Iserloh, 'Johannes Eck', in *Katholische Theologen der Reformationszeit* (1991) I. 65–71.

41   Scott Dixon, *The Reformation in Germany* (Oxford: Oxford University Press, 2002), pp. 26–32.

42   Wicks, 'Controversial Theologians', pp. 420–423.

43   Jared Wicks, 'Martin Luther in the Eyes of His Roman Catholic Opponents', *Oxford Research Encyclopedia of Religion*, https://oxfordre.com/religion/view/10.1093/acrefore/9780199340378.001.0001/acrefore-9780199340378-e-276 (access: 29 March 2017).

44   Eck, *Enchiridion locorum communium*.

45   Johannes Eck, *Hier beghint een corte declaracie ende antwoert teghen zomighe articulen der lutheranen* (Delft: Doen Pietersz, 1527), USTC 420954, p. 2.

46   August den Hollander, 'De edities van het Nieuwe Testament door de Delftse Drukker Cornelis Henricsz. Lettersnijder', *Dutch Review of Church History*, 75.2 (1995), pp. 165–187.

47   Eck, *Hier beghint een corte declaracie*, p. 1.

council of Holland.[48] This was a difficult decision for the council, as several high-ranking clerics in Amsterdam regarded the book highly. The council even asked the court at Brussels for advice in a letter from 12 May 1527.[49] However, the fear that the book would contribute to the spread of Lutheran ideas was ultimately the deciding factor in forbidding citizens from buying, owning or selling the book.[50] The fear that Eck's work would spread Lutheran ideas was so strong that the council sent no less than four bailiffs into every part of the country to proclaim its ban.[51] Cornelis Henricsz Lettersnijder was never punished for printing this work, but several instances are known of Flemish civic authorities publicly burning books by Johannes Eck.[52] It is unknown what exact work they burned, but the nervous reactions of the civic Dutch authorities, followed by the official ban of *Enchiridion*, indicate that a version of this book might have been thrown into the fire. The book being among the first 'semi-official' responses to Lutheranism, and the fact that it provoked such a response from the authorities, provide valuable insights into the dynamics of religious reading and printing during the early Reformation.

The government feared that the laity would be influenced by Lutheran ideas. Indeed, Eck's publication indicated that he targeted a lay readership: 'we have made this for the simple folk, and for those who worry about many things but who have no time to read great books'.[53] In the foreword, the translator also encouraged lay people to carry the book with them: 'it is called *Enchiridon*, which means handbook in Greek, because every person should carry it with him'.[54]

The handbook consisted of twenty-eight chapters, each devoted to a subject that had come under attack. These subjects included mass, purgatory and the relation between faith and good works. The number of chapters would increase in the years after the book's initial publication, as Eck continuously refined his work and made it reflect the most current topics.[55] The book's structure was

---

48   Den Hollander, 'De edities van het nieuwe testament', p. 170.
49   Ibid., p. 171.
50   Maria Elizabeth Kronenberg, *Verboden boeken en opstandige drukkers in de Hervormingstijd* (Amsterdam: Van Kampen & Zoon, 1948), p. 22.
51   Kronenberg, *Verboden boeken en opstandige drukkers*, p. 22.
52   Pollman, *Catholic Identity*, p. 51.
53   'Ende men sal weten dat wi dit gemaect hebben voer den simpelen ende voer den ghenen die met veel dingen becommert sijn ende geen tijt en hebben dye grote boecken te lesen', Eck, *Hier beghint een corte declaracie*, p. 185.
54   'Ende dit boecxken is ghenoemt int griecx Echchriridion ende na dat Duyts een hantboecxken/om dat elck mensche dat stedelijc in der hant ende bi hem sal hebben of draghen', ibid., p. 7.
55   Eugène Honée, review of Johannes Eck, 'Enchiridion locorum communium adversus Lutherum et alios hostes ecclesiae (1525–1543)', ed. Pierre Fraenkel, *Dutch Review of Church History*, 61.2 (1981), pp. 224–227.

systematic. First, Eck stated the official position of the church on each subject by referring to papal teachings and proclamations of church councils. After elucidating the official teachings, he defended contemporary church practices and counter-argued against reformist authors with such words as 'against this, the heretics argue'. After this, he provided up to eight points of critique for each theme.[56] Eck's translator introduced these refutations in the following manner:

> Against these heresies, Johannes Eck has written a good and profitable book in Latin, which contains twenty-seven articles by which the common folk has been deceived. His book summarises these arguments of the Lutherans and thoughtfully debunks these arguments with references to scripture.[57]

A prominent theme in the book was the guidance of the church by the Holy Spirit. To Eck, this was why the church had the authority to establish new laws and set rules for Christians. To argue this, he cited many passages from the Gospel.[58] As the Spirit's guidance was the driving force behind ecclesiastical history and church tradition, Eck stressed that there could be only one single, uniform Christian church. He eagerly exploited the divisions among early reformers to show that the Holy Spirit was not present among them. He wrote, 'they argue all the time and contradict each other … Karlstadt against Egranus, Luther against Zwingli'.[59] Pointing to the disagreements among early reformist writers was a tactic that other clerical polemicists deployed as well, as demonstrated by the anonymous Dutch author of *Een redelijck bewijs* (A thoughtful proof), published in 1528.[60] This suggests that these clerical polemicists initially expected the new branch of heresy to be a tightly connected network with a clear religious identity.

---

56 'Hier teghen argueren die ketteren', Eck, *Hier beghint een corte declaracie*, p. 154.
57 'Ende seer gheleerde doctoer inder gofheyt Meester Joannes Eckius doer verlichtinghe ende sterckinghe des heyligen gheest heft hi tegen dese ketterien een schoen ende profitelic boecxken ghemaect in latijn welck besluyt xxvii sonderlinge articulen waer doer datter ghemeen volc meest wert verleyt ende bedrogen. Dit boecxken roert cortelicken die ghemeen argumenten der lutheranen ende het doet seer suverlijck die argumenten te niet ende solveertse met reden ende scrifturen', ibid., p. 6.
58 Ibid., p. 17.
59 'Die Lutheranen maken nieuwe twisten ende si zijn also wel malcanderen contrarie als si ander menschen contrarie zijn / want Carolstadius ende Egranus ende Luther ende Swinglius die gevoelen tegen malcander', ibid., p. 18.
60 Anonymous, *Een redelijck bewijs ende verwinninghe der dolinghen ghesayt door een feninich boecxken toeghescreven ses prochianen der Lutersschen secten* (Antwerp: Willem Vorsterman, 1527), USTC 400473.

After Eck explained why it was evident that the church had the authority to establish new practises, he revealed several Lutheran arguments against this. He explained Luther's principle of *sola Scriptura* and tried to show inconsistencies in Luther's reasoning. He wrote, 'Jesus has not written a book, nor did he command that. He did not say "Go and write" but, "go and preach the Gospel to all creatures"'.[61] Therefore, according to Eck, it was futile to only turn towards the Bible for Christian instruction, as church tradition should be consulted as well.

Eck must have assumed that in the daily lives of his readers, *sola Scriptura* was an often-heard statement. By explaining these arguments against Luther's propositions, Eck provided his reader with ready-to-use arguments to counter the *sola Scriptura* argument. He also gave them a counter question to ask:

> How would you know that the Gospels and the letters of Paul are a part of Scripture if the church had not told you so? Why do you believe the Gospel of Mark, who did not see Christ, but not the Gospel of Nicodemus, who heard and saw him? ... What else is this if not a humble profession that the church had the authority and power to judge Scripture.[62]

Eck also pointed to inconsistencies in the Lutheran arguments regarding the introduction of new religious practices. He wrote:

> The church had Sunday ordained as Sabbath day without reference in Scripture ... Jesus told his disciples to baptise in the name of the Trinity but in the Acts of the Apostles, we read that the early church changed this by baptising in the name of Jesus.[63] See what power the church has over Scripture?[64]

---

61 Mk 16:15.
62 'Wanneer dat een ketter wil spreken of argueren tegen die insettingen ende gewoenten des kercs, soe samen hem vragen met at wapenen dat hi tegen die kercke vechten wildan sal hi seggen met die heylige scrift/met die vier Evangelien met die brieven van sinte Pouwels. Soe machmen daer tegen segghen. Hoe weet ghi dat die Evanglien ende die brieven van sinte Paulus die heylige scrift is anders dan dat die kercke u dat geseyt heeft. Waer om geloeft ghi dat Evangelie dat Sinte Marcus gescreven heeft te wesen die heilige schrift die christum niet gesien heeft / ende niet dat Evangelium dat Nicodemis gescreven heeft. Die nochtans Christum gesien ende gehoert heeft .... anders dan dat ghi oetmoedeliken belijt die autoriteyt des kercs heeft die scriftuer te oerdelen ende te onderscheyden', Eck, *Hier beghint een corte declaracie*, p. 20.
63 Mt 28:19; Ac 2:37–41.
64 'Nochtans so heeft die kercke den Sabbot verwandelt inden sondach doer hoer eygen autoriteyt / daar ghi nochtands gheen scrift of en hebt ... Christus heeft geseyt tot zijn discipulen. Gaet ende leert alle menschen ende doopt hoer inden naem des vader / Des

As he did in the Leipzig disputation, Eck connected Lutheranism to earlier forms of heresy.[65] He wrote in his introduction that 'the filth of old heresies is sprayed again on the field of the Holy Church and has deceived thousands of people'.[66] This interpretation of Lutheranism as a modern version of older heresies was popular among clerics during the first years of the Reformation. For example, during the Provincial Council of Sens in 1528, Luther's teaching on justification by faith and the emphasis of men's impotence to achieve salvation by will were condemned as modern forms of Manicheism.[67]

In the final chapter of his book, Eck explained his reasons for this indisputable condemnation of Lutheranism. For him, it was a slippery slope because the tradition of the church would seem to be negotiable. He wrote, 'our ancestors, under guidance of the Holy Spirit, have proclaimed the truth during councils. Those matters are no longer under debate and should not be scrutinised again, so that evil people will find no reason to fight what once has been decided'.[68] Ultimately, all the chapters of Eck's *Enchiridon* provided the same answer to every point of reformist critique, namely that there was no compromise possible on a single issue. The official position of the church was to be defended at all costs. Giving in to a single criticism would be to imply that doctrine was negotiable.[69]

4   Framing Lutheranism

Cardinal Legate Lorenzo Campeggio suggested that Eck write his *Enchiridon* as a means to rise above pamphlet warfare. Through this pamphlet warfare, individual Catholics wrote strong-worded refutations to show Luther's errors

---

soens ende des heylighen geest … nochtand soe heeft die kercke int beghinsel dese forme verwandelt / dopende inden naem Jesu Christi … Siet wat macht heeft dan die kercke over die scriftuer!', Eck, *Hier beghint een corte declaracie*, pp. 21–23.

65   Jonathan Mumme etc. (eds.), 'Luther at Leipzig. Martin Luther, the Leipzig Debate, and the Sixteenth-Century Reformations', *Studies in Medieval and Reformation Traditions*, 218 (2019), p. 19.

66   'Ende die dreck der ouder ketterie weder om inden acker der heyliger kerc uutgespogen ende veel dusent menschen begrogen ende inder siele jammerliken vermoert', Eck, *Hier beghint een corte declaracie*, p. 6.

67   John W. O'Malley, *Trent. What Happened at the Council* (Cambridge, MA: Cambridge University Press, 2013), p. 66.

68   'Onse voervader hebben geordineert doer ingevingen des heiligen geests der wanneer eens een concilium vergadert geweest is tegen enige ketterie ende der die christelike ende apostelike waerheit daer vercundicht is / so en sal men niet gehengen datmen daerna der selfde sal dederop een nieuwe ondersoeken / opdat des bose menschen geen oersake en geven an te vechten dat eens wel geset is.' Eck, *Hier beghint een corte declaracie*, p. 183.

69   Ibid., p. 183.

and portray him as dangerous to both the church and society.[70] An example of such publication efforts from the Low Countries comes from an anonymous clerical author from Antwerp who encountered a group of parishioners who were meeting to discuss a reformist book. The anonymous author did not mention whether these parishioners had read a book written by Luther himself or another publication by a dissident writer. This phenomenon of lay urban reading groups stemmed from a late-medieval practice. It is often hard to find out what exactly these groups were reading, but it was a common practice to read devotional books such as *Meditationes vitae Christi* or of saint's lives.[71] Guido Marnef wrote that 'at these small gatherings, Bible passages were read and discussed and dissident religious ideas were voiced'.[72] Although one must be careful of linking these groups too closely with the unfolding Reformation, they were not ignorant of the religious concerns of the day, as the Antwerp parishioners clearly demonstrate.

In response to the reformist publication that the parishioners were reading, the parish priest wrote a book in the Dutch vernacular. It was printed in Antwerp in 1527 by Willem Vorsterman, bearing the title *Een redelijck bewijs ende verwinninghe der dolinghen ghesayt door een feninich boecxken toeghescreven ses prochianen der Luterschen secten* (A thoughtful proof and victory over the errors sown by an evil book, dedicated to six parishioners of the Lutheran sect).[73] It responded directly to the dissident reformist book, with the author quoting entire passages from it. He wrote:

> From the book that they have read together, I have taken a chapter which I aim to write against. And when I have shown how greatly they have erred, they will drop all the other chapters as well. And to show how much they have erred, I will copy their own words.[74]

The author started the books by explaining why his refutation was so urgently needed. Official and unofficial book burnings were frequent in the Low Countries

---

70 Wicks, 'Controversial Theologians', pp. 420–423.
71 Sabrina Corbellini, 'Beyond Orthodoxy and Heterodoxy', p. 43.
72 Guido Marnef, 'The Netherlands', p. 345.
73 Anonymous, *Een redelijck bewijs ende verwinninghe der dolinghen ghesayt door een feninich boecxken toeghescreven ses prochianen der Luterschen secten* (Antwerp: Willem Vorsterman, 1527), USTC 400473.
74 'Uut huer boexcken / dat si tsamen ghebIasen hebben heb ik een capittel ghenomen daer ic sonderlighe tegen scriven willen / ende als ic betoent sal hebben hoe grotelijkc dat si daer in ghedoelt hebben / so sullen al te lichtelijc al die andere capittelenen vallen ende versmelten. Ende om dat te verstane hoe si dolen / so sal ic huers selfs woorde setten', Anonymous, *Een redelijck bewijs*, p. 3.

during the 1520s, but by 1527, our author saw that they had a very limited effect. He wrote: 'Luther and his Lutherans spread more evil with their Dutch books ... than with their Latin works. ... I have obtained one of these corrupted books, which is reprinted so often that there is no point in burning it'.[75] Book burnings had clearly not stopped the massive spread of reformist works, and this led him to a new strategy: 'write against it, also in Dutch ... to make the people once more return to the right faith'.[76]

The author displayed a great knowledge of Lutheranism and its critiques of the church, which he gathered by reading reformist works and anti-reformist polemics. He demonstrated this knowledge using rhetorical tropes and anti-Lutheran arguments that he shared with writers such as Johannes Eck. He also encountered many religious discussions in his immediate surroundings. He mentioned these discussions explicitly; for example, he described a discussion at a dinner table where a merchant was asked, 'what virtues have you seen in Lutheranism that attracted you?'.[77]

Two main elements appear in the anonymous author's book: namely, a doctrinal refutation of the reformist book and personal attacks on Luther, whom he often referred to as the 'Pope of Wittenberg'. The priest often points to this 'church of Wittenberg' as if it had a distinct religious entity, even though the emerging Lutheran confessional identity was far from established in the 1520s. Our author, therefore, either feared the dissident people as a well-connected, sectarian group, or simply used it as a rhetorical strategy.

The author of *Een redelijck bewijs* spent a lot of ink to frame Luther and his followers as a sinful sect of runaway monks and nuns, thieves, criminals and brothel owners. These people, 'who earlier had occupied themselves with prayer and praised and loved God, now visit whores, drink, party and gamble'.[78]

---

75 'Aenghemerct dat Luther / ende sijn Lutherianen / veel meer quats ende fenijns in de wereld ghestroyt hebben / door duytsche boecxkens die so onder dat ghemeyn volc gesayt hebben: dan doer die latijnsche boecken die sie gemaeckt hebben. ... So ist want my cortelic een fennich boexcen in mijn hant comen is vol corruptien sijnde / dwelc mi dochte niet nut verbernt / wantter doch gheprint waren dies ghelijcke', ibid., pp. 2–3.

76 'Ic en soude daar eerst wederomme wat teghen ghescreven hebben oock in duytsche om ... eenich behulp mocht sijn om wederomme ten rechten gelove te comen', ibid., p. 2.

77 'Ick neme god te ghetughe dat ick aen een tafele geweest bin / daer een vermaert coopman ooc over tafel was mer was een luteriaen. ... hem wart ghevraecht wat duechden dat hi in die lutheriaenschap toch gesien hadden dat hem daer toe trocke', ibid., p. 130.

78 'Als wi sien in veel geestelike uutgelopen moicken nonnen en priester die voortijts hem selven becommerden met god te bidden / te loven / te dancken / ende te contempleren na die .h. scrifturen die nu anders niet en doen dan hoereren / drincken / houveren clappen / spelen / ende ydelheid voort setten ende sonder ophouden oerdelen ende achterclappen', ibid., p. 54.

He described them all as misled and tempted by Luther, who now 'serves his own belly instead of Christ'.[79] The author emphasised Luther's sexual bestiality, clearly in reference to his marriage to Katharina von Bora in 1525.[80] The author also implied that Luther's parishioners followed his example to engage in illegitimate marriages. He wrote:

> Luther is now mostly concerned with matters of the world and how he should please his whores. He is neither her husband and neither is she his housewife … but they live in a doglike and unchristian state. I can image, dear parishioners, that you have engaged yourself in such marriages as well.[81]

These ad-hominem attacks on morality established a connection between a perceived sinful lifestyle and dissident religious ideas. Our author linked sinfulness with the Lutheran concept of *sola gratia* and claimed that this idea was purposefully devised to excuse sinful behaviour, as good deeds would not matter for an individual's salvation.[82] The principle of justification by faith alone was considered by the author as a cover-up tactic for sins. He wrote, 'they seek nothing else than the freedom of the flesh'.[83] For example, he cited what the aforementioned merchant at the dinner table had said about what had attracted him to Lutheranism. The merchant, according to the cleric, had stated, 'even if adultery is committed, why would that matter? … Christ gave the souls their righteousness. Therefore, it does not matter whether we are good or evil'.[84] The author used this dialogue to assert that Luther fulfilled what Jude the Apostle had written about people who 'are so evil that they extend God's grace to the carnal inclination of man'.[85]

---

79 'Wie en dient der dere Jesu Christo niet / mer hueren Buyc dan Luther', ibid., p. 56.
80 Albrecht Classen and Tanya Amber Settle, 'Women in Martin Luther's Life and Theology', *German Studies Review*, 14.2 (1991), pp. 231–260, 232.
81 'Luter, die nu besorcht moet sijn van dingen der weerelt aengaende / ende hoe hy sijnder hoeren / niet sijnder huysvrouwen behagen sode moghen / want hi noch huer man en is;noch si sijn huysvrouwe:maer … in hondelinken ende onkerstelijken staet. Ick can wel dincken mijn heeren prochianen / dat ghi oocal desghelicks huweliken gedaen hebt', *Een redelijck bewijs*, p. 56.
82 Ibid., p. 19.
83 Ibid., p. 54.
84 'Al isser overspel ghesciet wat can dat maken? … Christus geeft der sielen sijn goetheit. … so en isser toch geen belanc ane / oft wij goet ofte quaet sijn', ibid., p. 132.
85 Ibid., p. 54.

Our author further explained that the Lutherans were so divided because their ideas were not founded on inspiration from the Holy Spirit but on the desires of the flesh.

> Look at Luther's church. It is divided and factitious. Luther writes against Karlstadt, Karlstadt against Luther, Zwingli against Oecolampadius, Hubmaier against Zwingli. ... Some deny baptism, the other wants to innovate it, some write against statues while Luther defends them. One believes in the sacrament of bread, the other in its accident, for the next it is just a sign and for some none of this. This is the 'sustainable' church of Wittenberg.[86]

Such divisions among the early reformist writers provided clerical polemicists with an opportunity to portray the whole movement as illegitimate, as described in Eck's *Enchiridion*. Eck and the anonymous author explain these divisions slightly differently. For Eck, they were a natural symptom of a religious movement that countered the official church teachings. The anonymous priest went one step further, explaining the teachings not only against the church and the Holy Spirit but as based on the desires of the flesh, and therefore bound to be divided.

In a complex argumentation, the anonymous author connected the Lutheran 'church' with a contemporary political issue: namely, the threat of Ottoman invasion. Europeans had only just been defeated by the Ottomans in Mohacs in 1526, so the memory of this event was still very fresh when the book was published.[87] Our author argues that Luther's attack on the church was fundamentally a plot to bring down Christianity and to give way to the Ottomans. He claimed that Luther would have aimed to destroy the papacy by posing no opposition against the Turks and would have rendered the European people too weak to defend themselves.[88] He wrote, 'what else can we conclude in truth and in faith, that Luther is a forerunner of Mohammed and the Turk, and

---

86 'Seker toe eender twistegen ende ghedeylder kercken. Luter scrijft teeten carolostadius, Carolostadius tegen hem, Des ghelijcxs ooc zwinglius ende oecolampadius / wederomme Balthasart scrijft tegen zwinglius ... die eene seet dat tdoepsel niet en is / dander wilt vernieuwen. De sommighe scriven tegen die beelden, Luther bescermse. Die eene ghelovet tsacrament int broot / dander int accident / de sommigehen int teeken de sommige niet met allen. Dit is die gheduerige kercke van wittenberge', ibid., p. 17.
87 János B. Szabó, 'The Ottoman Conquest in Hungary. Decisive Events (Belgrade 1521, Mohács 1526, Vienna 1529, Buda 1541) and Results', in Pál Fodor (ed.), *The Battle for Central Europe* (Leiden: Brill, 2019), pp. 263–275, 270.
88 Anonymous, *Een redelijck bewijs*, p. 29.

that even John the Baptist has never prepared the way for the Lord as Luther does for the law of Mohammed'.[89] The anonymous author established this connection between the Ottomans and the Lutheran controversy by arguing that Luther's goal was to bring Mohammed to the papal throne to cover up his own sinful lifestyle under Ottoman law. He wrote that the Lutherans would say,

> welcome, dear law of Mohammed. We have long waited for you and called for you. We have undone our Christianity before you came, and your way is prepared. Because of you, we can freely cover our sinful lifestyle. We had spoken of Christ, but no one has obscured him more and made him forgotten. We have ordered new laws in Christ's name, but never was there any law which broke away more from Christ and which was more united with your law than these. Come freely, your chair is prepared.[90]

This framing indicates his perception of the Ottomans and of Islamic law as impure and as legitimising sinful behaviour. Because the author of *Een redelijck bewijs* framed the Lutheran position of *sola gratia* as justifying sin because of the freedom it allowed, he was able to draw parallels with the rise of the Ottomans. Furthermore, he was not the only polemicist to do so. In *Enchiridion*, Eck wrote that some Lutherans would 'rather have the Turkish dog as lord than Emperor Charles'.[91] Other Catholic authors pointed in their polemics towards the content of Luther's *Pro declaratione virtutis indulgentiarum*. In this text, Luther explained his fifth thesis, in which he argued that the pope could only remove the penalties that he himself had imposed. Therefore, Luther argued, the authority of the pope did not include things like natural disasters, murders

---

89   'Wat conen wi anders ghevinden ooc in der waerheit ende inden ghelove / dan dat luter een gherechtighe voorlooper is machomets ende des turckxs;ende dat baptista noyt den wech des heeren hadt en bereyde dan luter en doet der wet van machomets', ibid., p. 133.

90   'Mer sullen seggen willcome lieve Machometse wet wi hebben lange na u verlanct ende nae u geroepen ons kersten wesen is ons al afgeleert eer ghi comen zijt uwen wech is wel bereet nu mogen wi voertane vrijlijck ons vuylheyt onder u bedecken. Wi hebben Christus tot noch toe al inden mont gehad mer niemant en wasse oyt die op christum meerder roof ghehaelt heeft meer verdonckert en heeft ende heeft doen verghen. Wij hebben een nieuw wet ghestelt in christus name mer noyt en wasser gheene geordineert die meer van christus wet ghetrocken heeft ende tot uwer wet gevoecht heeft. Comt vrij inne uwen stoel is bereet', ibid., p. 135.

91   'Al hoe weld at sommighe Lutheranen verkeert zijnde / op dat si sonder anxt of verse hoer ketterien souden mogen voertbrengen / so souden si liever over een heer willen hebben den hondt der Turcken / dan den edelen ende godliken Keyser Carolum / keyser van Romen ende een christen coninck van Spaengien', Eck, 'Hier beghint een corte declaracie', ibid., p. 8.

and invasions by Turks and Tartars. To call for war against the Turks out of the authority of the papacy was therefore unlawful.[92] This was, perhaps purposefully, misunderstood by his critics, who thought that Luther meant that it was sinful to resist the Turkish invasion at all. This provided them with polemical arguments to make the European reader mistrusting of Luther.[93]

Another aim of *Een redelijck bewijs* was to show why Luther was wrong on theological grounds. As discussed, the reformist book questioned whether the church had the right to make new laws and commandments that were not mentioned in Scripture, stating that 'the papists invent to their liking commandments not mentioned in Scripture and make rules that according to them are equal to the Word of God'.[94] According to Luther, the church had no right to do so because 'Jesus had closed the Gospel with His death'.[95] Our author then argued that the Bible was not a complete collection of what the apostles and Paul had written and preached, and thus the Catholic tradition should be consulted.[96] According to the author, the claim of *sola Scriptura* was also invalid because the introduction of new regulations could be found in the Bible, and that only the church could continue this practice.[97] He wrote, 'if Paul had changed the church teachings during his own life, how much more has needed to be changed within the church since then, especially since it is so large nowadays?'.[98] He ironically addressed the reformers by stating, 'ask Paul why he, who was a human, made commandments which are not found in one of the four Gospels'.[99] This rhetorical strategy of providing the laity with counter questions to reformist arguments, as Eck did in his work, was a popular strategy among early polemicists in their attempt to equip the laity with tools to use in their own religious debates.

---

92 Martin Luther, *Disputatio D. Martini Lutheri theologi, pro declaratione virtutis indulgentiarum* (Basel: Adam Petri, 1517), USTC 639278.

93 George W. Forell, 'Luther and the War against the Turks', *Church History*, 14.4 (1945), pp. 256–271, esp. 258, fn. 35 on the letter to Johann Rinck (1530). Desiderius Erasmus, *The Correspondence of Erasmus. Letters 2204–2356 (August 1529–July 1530)*, transl. Alexander Dalzell, annotat. James M. Estes (Toronto: University of Toronto Press 2015), p. 232.

94 'Die papisten onderwinden huer eene evangelische spraecke … dat si na huaren behagen buyten dat godlijc woort geboden ende insettingen te maken hebben na huerder meynungen den godliken leeringen ende gheboden ghelijck gehouden souden worden', *Een redelijck bewijs*, p. 44.

95 'Ghelijc eene die stertf sijn testament besluyt met sijnder dood', ibid., p. 50.

96 Ibid., p. 100.

97 Ibid., p. 121.

98 'Heeft Paulus na den tijt sijn leere verandert noch levende / hoe vele te meer is dat der h. kercken van node nu in dese tijde daer die kerstenheyt soe groot is', ibid., p. 49.

99 'Men mochte sinte Pauwels vraghen waeromme hi die een mensche was / insettinghen maecte buyten der evangelien', ibid., p. 50.

After discussing the claim of *sola Scriptura*, our author described why it was foolish of Luther to base his offensive against the church on Scripture itself. After all, Scripture itself had received its canonisation from the church.[100] How then, the author asked, could one fight the church with these same Scriptures? He also pointed to inconsistencies in the Lutheran treatment of Scripture by stating that the Lutherans had rejected parts of Scripture that did not align with their ideas.[101] The author wrote: 'In Deuteronomy and in Proverbs, it is stated that one cannot add or remove anything from the Bible.[102] So, what about those who eliminate entire books from Scripture? Is that not taking away from the Word?'.[103] This was likely an allusion to Luther's rejection of the deuterocanonical books. The priest was able to use this rejection to connect Luther with older heresies, just as Eck had done. The author mainly pointed to the Manicheans, who had also rejected parts of Scripture 'because it did not fit their heresy'.[104]

The author of *Een redelijck bewijs* dealt with very similar subjects to Eck in *Enchiridion*. This is unsurprising, as *Enchiridion* aimed to cover all aspects of Catholicism that had received criticism by reformers and dissidents during the early sixteenth century. These many similarities also reveal something of Eck's influence in the Low Countries, as demonstrated by the praise given to *Enchiridion* by high-ranking clerics in Amsterdam.[105] However, there are also important differences. The anonymous cleric's often-implicit criticism of individual popes and high-ranking church officials differed greatly from Johannes Eck's approach. Eck did not tolerate any criticism towards the church and its authority. The anonymous parish priest, in contrast, took a critical stance towards church officials. On the issue of abuses among the church hierarchy, for example, the anonymous author compared Christ to a carpenter who is 'strong enough to sustain the head of his church, even when this head is often sick'.[106] Furthermore, he did not defend abuses of Papal power and even agreed with Lutheran criticisms on this topic, stating that

---

100 Ibid., p. 60.
101 Ibid., 60.
102 Dt 4:2; Pr 30:5–6.
103 'Maer hier loepen op die woorden Deutheronomii IIII ende XII ende proverbium XXX. Die de Lutherianen voor huer nemen ende doen daer so grotelijck teghen. In die boecken staet bevolen als wi vore ghedeclareert hebben dat neimant totter wet af / oft toe doen en sal. Waer bliven si dan die gehele ende vele boecken nemen vander scrifturen. Is dat niet den woorden gods afnemen?', *Een redelijck bewijs*, p. 61.
104 'Ende dan vinden sij sommege scriftueren die huer niet en dienen tot hueren errueren', ibid., p. 60.
105 Den Hollander, 'De edities van het Nieuwe Testament', p. 171.
106 'Al sijn die hoofden somtijts cranc geweest die timmerman in starc ghenoech', Anonymous, *Een redelijck bewijs*, p. 22.

they bring up the abuses that are in the church … I say they are not in the church but in its head and its members, and principally in its head. I don't defend them but pray to our lord that He will give the grace to correct our leaders and members.[107]

This was strikingly different from Eck, who cited a list of Scriptural references to claim that the powers of contemporary popes were fully justified.[108] It is not surprising to see such divergent viewpoints on issues such as papal power, as this was a strongly debated topic among clerics in the fifteenth and early sixteenth centuries, especially among conciliarists who claimed that church councils should have more power than the pope.[109]

Overall, *Een redelijck bewijs* demonstrated a multi-layered strategy to keep the laity loyal to the church. It contained personal attacks on the sinful nature of Luther and his followers, and it used polemical frames to discredit the entire Lutheran 'sect' by linking it to the Ottomans. However, the book shows that these personal attacks did not exclude doctrinal instruction.

5 Conclusion

The 1520s were characterised by the search for an appropriate strategy by Catholic clerics to counter the challenges posed by Lutheran writings in a quickly changing and tense religious and political climate. Different Catholic clerics chose different approaches, and some Catholic orders abstained from mentioning Luther and his ideas for fear that hearing reformist ideas would elicit curiosity among the laity. This fear led anti-Lutheran polemics to be banned, as was the case with *Enchiridion* by Johannes Eck. Franciscans such as Franciscus Titelmans and Thomas Herentals did, however, publish instructional and devotional texts that indirectly dealt with the critiques of early reformist writers.

Explicit polemics that dealt with reformist arguments were still part of the publishing landscape of the Low Countries, however. The anonymous parish priest from Antwerp cited entire passages from a book by Luther, and Johannes Eck addressed countless Lutheran arguments in his *Enchiridion*. Both authors

---

107 'Dat si opbrengen die abusien die in die kercke sijn: niet in die kercken; mer in huer hoofden ende leden ende principalic in die hoofden/die ic niet genomen en hebben te onsculdighen / mer bidde onse heren dat hi ons gratie gheve in ons allen in hoofden ende leden beteren', ibid., p. 78.
108 Eck, *Hier beghint een corte declaracie*, p. 54.
109 Francis Oakley, 'Conciliarism at the Fifth Lateran Council?', *Church History*, 41.4 (1972), pp. 452–463.

countered Luther's claims by referring to both Scripture and church tradition. They did not keep their lay readers 'in the dark' about Lutheranism, as Judith Pollmann claimed.[110] Rather, the two anti-Lutheran polemics framed Lutheranism as the newest branch of an age-old heresy. They also provided the laity with arguments against reformist critiques to deploy in everyday life.

The two texts reveal strong differences in attitude regarding reforming the church itself. Johannes Eck was not inclined to agree with any critique of the structure or practices of the church; he referred to the Bible to counter even the slightest criticism of the church's wealth and power. In contrast, the anonymous parish priest criticised individuals who abused the ecclesiastical structure. This shows that the Dutch religious landscape in the early sixteenth century was characterised by a multitude of viewpoints towards reforming the church. These debates, and the extent to which the laity participated, deserve thorough study, especially because the break with the church was by no means a certainty for reformers in the 1520s.

---

110   Pollmann, *Catholic Identity*, p. 47.

CHAPTER 7

Echoes of Worms

Luther's Opponents in Eastern Europe

Maciej Ptaszyński

1   'Here I Stand'

The Reichstag in Worms (1521) is regarded as one of the main dates in the birth of the Reformation. It was there that Martin Luther allegedly uttered the famous words 'Here I stand', which became a symbol of rebellion against the established order and a declaration of individual independence.[1] Luther's supporters in Worms carried out a very effective campaign to promote his image, also making use of the talent of Lucas Cranach. As early as December 1520, Luther was depicted as a clergyman and even a martyr or saint.[2] After the proceedings of the Diet, a woodcut by Hans Baldung that portrayed Luther in a halo with the Holy Spirit was placed on the *verso* of the title page of the account of the Diet of Worms.[3] This composition was modelled on an early portrait by Lucas Cranach the Elder and supplemented by a dove motif.[4] Cranach's portrait bore the inscription: 'Luther left an eternal image of his own mind / but Lucas' wax manifests his passing features'.[5]

---

[1]   On the events at Worms and Luther's words in light of historical accounts: Martin Brecht, *Martin Luther* (Stuttgart: Calwer, 1981) I. 439; Heinz Schilling, *Martin Luther: Rebell in einer Zeit des Umbruchs* (München: Beck, 2012), 223. I am grateful to the anonymous reviewer of this chapter for pointing out the difference between the content of the historical sources and the version conveyed in confessional polemics and historiography.

[2]   Paul Kalkoff (ed.), *Die Depeschen des Nuntius Aleander vom Wormser Reichstage 1521* (Halle: Niemeyer, 1886), pp. 34–35.

[3]   *Acta res gestae D. Martini Lutheri in comitiis principum Wormaciae anno MDXXI* (Strasbourg: Johann Schott, 1521), USTC 608615, 608616; see also: London, British Museum, items no. 1845, 0809.1486 (Hieronymus Hopfer); no. 1903,0408.21.

[4]   Robert W. Scribner, *For the Sake of Simple Folk. Popular Propaganda for the German Reformation* (Oxford: Clarendon Press, 1997), pp. 17–19; Joseph L. Koerner, *The Reformation of the Image* (London: Chicago University Press, 2004), pp. 114–124; Grażyna Jurkowlaniec, Maciej Ptaszyński, 'Ptaki reformatorów', in Piotr Borusowski etc. (eds.), *Ingenium et Labor. Studia ofiarowane Profesorowi Antoniemu Ziembie z okazji 60. urodzin* (Warsaw: Uniwersytet Warszawski–Muzeum Narodowe w Warszawie, 2020), pp. 119–128.

[5]   'Aeterna ipse suae mentis simulacra Lutherus Exprimit, at uultus cera lucae occiduos MDXX'; London, British Museum, no. 1854,1113.232.

At Worms, the emperor forbade preaching Luther's views or disseminating his works. Further, Luther himself was sentenced to banishment. The imperial edict, signed on 26 May 1521, echoed the papal bulls *Exsurge Domine* and *Decet Romanum Pontificem*, which had been published in Rome between 1520 and 1521 and gradually reached European courts. The Worms edict portrayed Luther as a heretic and rebel who attacked the clergy and criticised the sacraments, calling on his followers to 'wash their hands in priestly blood' ('ir Hende in der Prieste Blud zu waschen', 'ad lavandas sibi in sacerdotum sanguine manus').[6]

We can identify at least three consequences of these intertwined events related to the Diet of Worms. First, the earliest anti-Lutheran legislation was enacted in the Reich and neighbouring territories, with some cases leading to the persecution and breaking up of Reformation foci. Second, this persecution sometimes had the paradoxical effect of forcing preachers to change their places of ministry frequently, which furthered the spread of Reformation ideas. Third, the clash at the Reichstag set in motion a powerful media machine that made Luther a true hero in mass imagination. All these phenomena and processes have already been the subject of scholarly reflection.[7]

The following chapter raises questions about these processes in Central and Eastern Europe. To date, not many researchers have paid much attention to this part of the Continent, even though Luther's speech in Worms echoed there too. This chapter argues that the Worms events both influenced the course of the Reformation in these regions and helped shape anti-Reformation reactions. The remainder of the chapter focuses on the Kingdom of Poland, with emphasis on regional connections to the Baltics. First, the chapter gives an overview of the early Reformation in these areas; then, it characterizes Andrzej Krzycki (Andreas Cricius), one of the main anti-Lutheran polemicists in early Reformation Poland. Of Krzycki's anti-Reformation works, the chapter focuses on his most famous treatise, *Encomia Lutheri*, published in 1524 and containing direct references to the events at Worms.

---

6 Peter Fabisch, Erwin Iserloh (eds.), *Dokumente zur Causa Lutheri* (Münster: Aschendorff, 1991) II. 484–565, here: 518–19. The phrase appears in: Sylvester Mazzolini (Prierias), *Epitoma responsionis ad Martinum Luther ab ipso Martino Luthero editum* (Wittenberg: Melchior Lotter, 1520), USTC 652930, ed. in: WA VI. 347, l. 22–27.

7 Christopher W. Close, 'Der Reichstag zu Worms und das Heilige Römische Reich', in Alberto Melloni (ed.), *Martin Luther. Ein Christ zwischen Reformen und Moderne (1517–2017)* (Berlin: De Gruyter, 2017), pp. 327–342; Joachim Knape, *1521. Martin Luthers rhetorischer Moment oder die Einführung des Protests* (Berlin: De Gruyter, 2017); Markus Wriedt, Werner Zager (eds.), *Martin Luther auf dem Reichstag zu Worms. Ereignis und Rezeption* (Leipzig: Evangelische Verlagsanstalt, 2022); Thomas Kaufmann, *'Hier stehe ich!' Luther in Worms: Ereignis, mediale Inszenierung, Mythos* (Stuttgart: Anton Hiersemann KG, 2021); Philip K. Haberkern, *Patron, Saint, and Prophet. Jan Hus in the Bohemian and German Reformations* (New York, NY: Oxford University Press, 2016), p. 152.

2 The Effects of Worms

Luther's fame went before him. Evidence shows that news of the friar's critiques of indulgences reached many corners of Europe as early as 1517 or 1518. However, it was only with the emergence of itinerant preachers that the Wittenberg teaching reached wider circles, going beyond academics and church workers. Between 1521 and 1523, the first itinerant preachers arrived in towns along the Baltic coast. The mechanism of their preaching is well illustrated by the story of Premonstratensian congregation friars in Białoboki (Belbuck) in the Pomeranian Duchies, which were part of the Reich.

One of the first to bring news of Luther and the events at Wittenberg to Pomerania was Peter Suawe (1496–1552). Himself a Pomeranian, he studied in Leipzig and then, after the disputation of 1519, moved to Wittenberg. Suawe was among those who accompanied the reformer to Worms in 1521 and participated in his staged abduction after the Diet of the Reich.[8] He then returned to Pomerania and began teaching at the monastery in Białoboki, which was then led by Abbot Johann Boldewan (1485–1533), who was open to the cause of Church reform.[9] To the monastic circle belonged Johannes Bugenhagen, a teacher in nearby Trzebiatów (Treptow), who soon made direct contact with Luther.[10]

Soon, the publication of the first anti-Reformation edicts forced many friars to leave the congregation. In April 1521, Bugenhagen arrived in Wittenberg and became a close associate of Luther. Boldewan soon followed to the main hub of the Reformation. The others (Johannes Äpinus, Johannes Kuricke, Bernhard Dedelow, Christian Ketelhut, Andreas Knopke or Georg von Ueckermünde) decided to go to different corners of northern Europe, from Riga to Rostock. Continuing their journey, they then ended up in Stralsund, where in May 1523 Ketelhut preached his first sermon and was soon joined by other preachers.[11] Almost at the same time, Jakob Hegge spoke in Gdańsk (Danzig). Confessional historiography assumed that his sermon, delivered on 22 June 1522, marked the beginning of the Reformation in the city. Then in 1523, preachers sent by Luther arrived in Königsberg: Johannes von Briesemann, Paul Speratus and

---

8   Martin Brecht, *Martin Luther* (Stuttgart: Calwer, 1981) I. 427, 450.
9   Walter Paap, 'Kloster Belbuck um die Wende des 16. Jahrhunderts', *Baltische Studien, Neue Folge*, 16 (1912), pp. 1–73.
10 Otto Vogt (ed.), *Dr. Johannes Bugenhagens Briefwechsel* (Stettin: Saunier, 1888), p. 8.
11 Date on the epitaph in the church of St Nikolai in Stralsund. DI 102, Inschriften Stadt Stralsund, Nr. 177 (†) (Christine Magin), from: www.inschriften.net, https://nbn-resolving.de/urn:nbn:de:0238-di102g018k0017706 (accessed: 27th March 2023).

Johannes Amandus.[12] In the same year, Paul von Rhode became active in Szczecin (Stettin), Joachim Slüter (Jochim Slyter) preached Reformation sermons in Rostock and Heinrich Never began preaching in Wismar.[13] Over time, more and more Reformation sympathisers joined municipal authorities. In Stralsund it was Roloff Möller, in Szczecin Hans Stoppelberg, in Gdańsk Hans Nimptsch, in Toruń (Thorn) Johann Seyfried and in Rostock Johann Oldendorp, who later collaborated with Jürgen Wollenwever in Lübeck. Some defended the ideas they believed in, and others owed their careers to widely popular slogans. With the entry of the Reformation supporters into the municipal authorities, Reformation themes surfaced in correspondences between cities. Not only did the city councils turn to Wittenberg for preachers, but they themselves shared clergymen who preached the new doctrine.

Preachers spoke in almost all major cities. The backdrop to these activities were numerous social conflicts, culminating in the urban revolts at the turn of the fifteenth to the sixteenth century. The beginnings of the Reformation were thus often entangled in a course of events that inextricably linked social and religious issues.[14] After the Stralsund riots in 1525, the Catholic clergy repeated the accusations familiar from the Edict of Worms: Protestant preachers allegedly had called on the citizens of Stralsund to 'wash their hands in the blood of the priests'.[15] At the same time, however, the region lacked the typical structural elements to provide momentum for the Reformation movement in the Reich. There was no Protestant university in the entire region; the nearest universities, in Greifswald, Rostock, Frankfurt an der Oder or Krakow, were not only Catholic but also attracted very few humanists who might sympathise with the Reformation.[16] There were often no printing houses even in large cities, and those operating were controlled by bishops and the secular authorities. The only historically tangible mechanism for the spread of the Reformation was the word of the preachers. They were able to operate thanks to a network of supporters, which enabled the preachers to constantly change location.

---

12   Bernhart Jähnig, *Preußenland, Kirche und Reformation. Geplantes Zusammenspiel von geistlicher Macht und weltlicher Herrschaft* (Berlin: LIT Verlag, 2019).
13   See Eberhard Völker, *Die Reformation in Stettin* (Cologne: Böhlau, 2003) and Karl Schmaltz, *Kirchengeschichte Mecklenburgs* (3 vols., Schwerin: Bahn, 1935–1952).
14   Heinz Schilling, 'The Reformation in the Hanseatic Cities', *Sixteenth Century Journal*, 14 (1983), pp. 443–456.
15   Maciej Ptaszyński, 'Words Spoken and Unspoken. Preachers and the Baltic Reformation in the Younger Europe', in Mirosława Hanusiewicz-Lavallee, Robert A. Maryks (eds.), *Defining the Identity of the Younger Europe* (Leiden: Brill, 2023).
16   Paul W. Knoll, *'A Pearl of Powerful Learning'. The University of Krakow in the Fifteenth Century* (Leiden: Brill, 2016).

3   The Anti-reformation Response and Andrzej Krzycki

Territorial rulers reacted to the spread of the Reformation with scepticism and even hostility. In Saxony, George the Bearded published the first anti-Lutheran edicts even before Rome issued its bull against Luther.[17] Similarly, King Sigismund I of Poland issued the first anti-Protestant edict on 4 May 1520 and another on 24 July, a year before the bull *Exsurge Domine* appeared in print in Krakow and before Emperor Charles V issued the Edict of Worms.[18] Over the next two decades, the king of Poland issued more than twenty anti-Lutheran edicts.[19] The edicts were primarily directed against the importing, printing and sale of Luther's writings, and over time the spreading of the reformer's views was also banned. Anti-Protestant polemics also began to be printed at the same time as the edicts.

Among the most important authors of the polemics and edicts in Poland was Andrzej Krzycki (1482–1537).[20] He came from an aristocratic family associated with the closest circle of Cardinal Frederick Jagiellon (1468–1503).[21] He received his first ecclesiastical dignity in 1501 thanks to the patronage of the Bishop of Poznań, Jan Lubrański (1456–1520). He owed his rapid career also to the support of his uncle, Piotr Tomicki, who from 1515 had been the bishop of Przemyśl. A year later as vice-chancellor, Tomicki became the righthand

---

17   Christoph Volkmar, *Reform statt Reformation. Die Kirchenpolitik Herzog Georgs von Sachsen, 1488–1525* (Tübingen: Mohr Siebeck, 2008), pp. 79, 564–567; Doreen von Oertzen Becker, *Kurfürst Johann der Beständige und die Reformation (1513–1532). Kirchenpolitik zwischen Friedrich dem Weisen und Johann Friedrich dem Großmütigen* (Cologne: Böhlau Verlag, 2017), pp. 222–246.

18   The original of the edict from 4 May 1520, not recorded in the Royal Chancery Registers (*Metrica Regni Poloniae*), is in the State Archives in Gdańsk [hereafter APG], 300D, 5a, no. 935. The edict from 24 July is in: Archiwum Główne Akt Dawnych, Metryka Koronna [hereinafter: MK], vol. 35, pp. 59–60, ed. in: Oskar Balzer (ed.), *Corpus iuris Polonici* (St Petersburg: s.n., 1908) III. 583–584, no. 237.

19   Maciej Ptaszyński, 'Czy reformacja w Polsce była luterańska? O polemikach antyluterańskich w Polsce w pierwszej połowie XVI wieku', *Odrodzenie i Reformacja w Polsce*, 63 (2019), pp. 5–62.

20   Stefan Zablocki, 'Andrzej Krzycki', in Emanuel Rostworowski (ed.), *Polski Słownik Biograficzny* (Wrocław: Zakład Narodowy im. Ossolińskich – Wydawnictwo PAN, 1970), XV. 544–549; Witold Wojtowicz, *Szkice o poezji obscenicznej i satyrycznej Andrzeja Krzyckiego* (Szczecin: Wydawnictwo Naukowe Uniwersytetu Szczecińskiego, 2002), pp. 170–185; Leszek Barszcz, *Andrzej Krzycki – poeta, dyplomata, prymas* (Gniezno: Tum, 2004); Natalia Nowakowska, 'Lamenting the Church? Bishop Andrzej Krzycki and Early Reformation Polemic' in: A. Suerbaum etc. (eds.), *Polemic: Language as Violence in Medieval and Early Modern Discourse* (Farnham: Ashgate 2015), pp. 223–236.

21   Natalia Nowakowska, *Church, State and Dynasty in Renaissance Poland. The Career of Cardinal Fryderyk Jagiellon (1468–1503)* (Aldershot: Ashgate, 2007).

man of King Sigismund I. He served as the chief architect of the policy for the Krakow court until his death in 1535.[22] Thanks to Tomicki's support, Krzycki quickly climbed the career ladder: in 1510 he became the provost of Środa, in 1512 a member of the Krakow Chapter and in 1515 the king's secretary, meaning he joined the highest circles of the kingdom's central administration and the monarch's closest aides. Accumulating numerous ecclesiastical dignities and offices, Krzycki managed the Diocese of Poznań after Lubrański's death (June 1520) until Tomicki took over (July 1520). Finally, he obtained the bishopric of Przemyśl in 1522 and the bishopric of Płock in 1527. Despite having strong support and being close to the court, Krzycki's efforts to obtain further ecclesiastical honours were not always successful; he strove for the richer bishopric of Poznań in vain. The culmination of a long journey through ecclesiastical institutions was the archbishopric of Gniezno, which Krzycki received in 1535, two years before his death.

Krzycki owed his success to both his aristocratic background and Tomicki's patronage, as well as his own talent. Educated at, among others, the University of Bologna, he was considered by his contemporaries to be the most gifted Latinist. Leonard Cox, a humanist who resided in Krakow for a long time, counted him among the most eminent humanists involved with the University of Krakow.[23] Krzycki's outstanding abilities were often praised in the correspondence of humanists.[24] His talent was regularly used to add splendour to court ceremonies. Krzycki used his pen to grace the wedding of Sigismund I to Barbara Zapolya in 1512 and then to mourn the queen's death in 1515.[25] When the king remarried in 1518 to Bona Sforza, Krzycki honoured the

---

22 Anna Odrzywolska-Kidawa, *Biskup Piotr Tomicki (1464–1535). Kariera polityczna i kościelna* (Warsaw: Semper, 2004).

23 Leonard Cox, *De laudibus Celeberrimae Cracoviensis Academiae* (Krakow: Hieronim Wietor, 1518), USTC 240358, f. b3r-v; on Cox, see Andrew Breeze, 'Leonard Cox, a Welsh Humanist in Poland and Hungary', *National Library of Wales Journal*, 25 (1988), pp. 399–410.

24 Tytus Działyński (ed.), *Acta Tomiciana. Epistole, legationes, responsa, actiones, res geste serenissimi Principis Sigismundi Primi, Regis Polonie et Magni Ducis Lithuanie* (Poznań: L. Merzbach, 1855), IV. 298: Jost Ludwig Decius to Piotr Tomicki, Krakow, 10 May 1518: 'nam quis Andrea Cricio, nepote tuo concentu moduloque auditus unquam dulcior? quis Hieronymo Balbo doctior? Laurentio Corvino quis venustior? Ursino Gasparo quis facundior? Dantisco Joanne quis eleganti ubertate copiosior? Agricolaque quis gravior esse poteri?'.

25 Andrzej Krzycki, *Epitalamion Sigismundi regis et Barbarae regine Polonie* (1512) and *Deploratio immaturae mortis Barbarae* (1515), in: Kazimierz Morawski (ed.), *Andreae Cricii Carmina* (Krakow: Academiae Litterarum Cracoviensis, 1888), pp. 21–27, 57–60; Mirosław Brożek (ed.), *Szesnastowieczne epitalamia łacińskie w Polsce* (Krakow: Księgarnia Akademicka, 1999).

celebrations with a poetic contest with Jan Dantyszek (Joannes Dantiscus) and Rudolph Agricola.[26] His works also praised the king's glory after his military victories, namely in 1512 in a clash with the Tatars and in 1515 after his victory over Moscow at Orsha.[27] Finally, in 1525 Krzycki justified to Christian Europe King Sigismund's acceptance of the homage from Prince Albrecht of Prussia, the first Lutheran ruler in Europe.[28] The work was a rationalisation of the policy pursued by the royal court and was immediately published in print and distributed to European centres of power.[29]

One of the recipients of this treatise was Erasmus of Rotterdam, with whom Krzycki exchanged letters. Erasmus praised Krzycki as the greatest poet and spoke favourably of him in letters to his friends.[30] In return, Krzycki not only sent expensive gifts to Basel but in December 1525 also invited Erasmus to Poland, praising him as an outstanding theologian.[31] This letter is the only surviving example of Krzycki's correspondence with Erasmus. It attracted the interest of researchers because in the invitation, the bishop promised Erasmus the support of the king, a position at the university and access to a printing

26 Andrzej Krzycki, *Epitalamium divi Sigismundi Primi Regis et inclytae Bonae* (Krakow: Jan Haller, 1518), USTC 240630; reprinted in: Morawski (ed.), *Andreae Cricii Carmina*, pp. 62–75; Zygmunt Wojciechowski, *Zygmunt Stary (1506–1548)* (Warsaw: Państwowy Instytut Wydawniczy, 1979, p. 137; see poems in: *Acta Tomiciana*, IV. 276–297.

27 *Encomium divi Sigismundi* (1512) and *Ad divum Sigismundum … post partam de Moscis victoriam* (1515), in: Morawski (ed.), *Andreae Cricii Carmina*, pp. 30–35, 36–41; *Cantilena de victoria e Moscis parta*, in: ibidem, pp. 42–53; *Cantilena de victoria Moscitica in laudem Sigismundi regis Poloniae*, in: ibidem, pp. 56–57.

28 A. Krzycki, *Ad Joannem Antonium Pulleonem Baronem Brugii, nuntium apostolicum in Ungaria, de negotio Pruthenico epistola* (Krakow: Hieronim Wietor, 1525), USTC 240098; Henryk Damian Wojtyska (ed.), *Acta Nuntiaturae Polonae* (Rome: Fundatio Lanckoroński, 1990) II. 185–194; *Acta Tomiciana*, VII. 249–256, A. Cricius to G.A. Buglio, Krakow [1 May 1525].

29 Maciej Ptaszyński, 'Religiöse Toleranz oder politischer Frieden? Verhandlungen über den Religionsfrieden in Polen-Litauen im 16. und 17. Jahrhundert', in Johannes Paulmann etc. (eds.), *Unversöhnte Verschiedenheit. Verfahren zur Bewältigung religiös-konfessioneller Differenz in der europäischen Neuzeit* (Göttingen: Vandenhoeck & Ruprecht, 2016), pp. 161–178.

30 P.S. Allen etc. (eds.), *Opus Epistolarum Desiderii Erasmi Roterodami* (Oxford: Oxford University Press, 1934) VIII. 400–405, no. 2299, Erasmus to Crostóbal Mexía, Freiburg 30 March 1530: 'In eadem Polonia est Andreas Critius, episcopus Plocensis, qui me frequenter et humanissimis litteris et eruditissimis carminibus recreat exitatque'.

31 Feliks Kopera, 'Dary z Polski dla Erazma z Rotterdamu w historycznym muzeum bazylejskiem', *Sprawozdania Komisyi do Badania Historyi Sztuki w Polsce*, 6 (1898), pp. 110–138; Konstanty Żantuan, 'Erasmus and the Cracow Humanists. The Purchase of his Library by Łaski', *The Polish Review*, 110 (1965), pp. 10–11. See also Allen (ed.), *Opus*, VI. 236–239, no. 1652. Cricius to Erasmus, Krakow [20] December 1525: 'proinde horum studiorum et prisce illius cultoris theologie evo nostro principem et assertorem meum Erasmum non potui iampridem, quantumlibet mihi de facie ignotum, non impense amare et suspicere'.

house. Krzycki describing his own works as 'follies' was also an important element of the letter. As the bishop-poet explained, he had been forced to publish the works to silence the critics who had attacked him for defending Erasmus' position and some of Luther's theses.[32]

The accusation that Krzycki defended Luther's position may come as a surprise, since part of the tasks delegated to him as royal secretary and then as bishop was to prepare anti-Protestant edicts and polemics. As in the case of the Worms edict, legal acts prohibiting the preaching of Reformation ideas were issued in Poland by the king and on his behalf, not by the Sejm or on behalf of the estates. Therefore, the edicts concerned the area of the king's immediate jurisdiction, and the nobility, as a social group enjoying judicial immunity since the fifteenth century and participating in the legislative process since the beginning of the sixteenth century, could demand release from these prohibitions. The legal status of the documents could also have been undermined by the fact that the royal officials did not enter all edicts into the Royal Chancery Registers (*Metrica Regni Poloniae*), where they were required to copy all documents signed by the king.

Undoubtedly, the preparation of documents was the exclusive responsibility of the royal chancery, including king's secretaries such as Krzycki. In fact, in his letter of July 1523, Krzycki provided a detailed description of the origins of the edicts.[33] To interpret his testimony, however, it is necessary to put the anti-Protestant legislation of the royal court into context. Indeed, in 1523 the royal chancellery issued at least three general decrees against the Reformation: 7 March, 21 August and 5 September. In addition, a separate edict was also issued on 23 November.[34]

The first of these edicts was issued by the king in March during the Sejm, sitting in Krakow from February to April 1523.[35] The atmosphere of the meeting was extremely tense. The king came from Vilnius and, with the help of the voivodes, wanted to persuade the nobility to pass additional taxes for the

---

32   Ibid., p. 237: 'Verum mihi displicet sane eas nenias ad te, virum tantum, perlatas, que quodam modo invito mihi exciderunt. Nosti enim, mi Erasme, quam hoc seculo nullus angulus suis censoribus et vitilitigatoribus non abundet, quantumque istiusmodi sive crabrones sint sive etiam scarabei exhibere soleant negotii bonis viris, etiam summatibus. Eorum morsus clandestinos neque ego vitare potui, quod et tua semper omnia et Luteri nonnulla que initio recte monuisse videbatur, interdum tueri solebam'.
33   Balzer (ed.), *Corpus iuris Polonici*, IV/1. 21–28.
34   Ibid.
35   Wacław Uruszczak etc. (eds.), *Volumina constitutionum* (Warsaw: Wydawnictwo Sejmowe, 2000) I/1. 381–385, no. 31.

defence against the Tartar invasions.[36] The senate, consisting of the highest officials of the kingdom and the bishops, supported the king's efforts. The nobility deputies, on the other hand, demanded a 'correction of the laws', involving the realisation of royal obligations as well as the implementation of state privileges.

These demands, called 'executive' (from Latin '*executio*'), were formulated by the nobility during the Sejms of Toruń (1519) and Bydgoszcz (1520), convened by Sigismund in the face of the war with the Teutonic Order.[37] The threat of war and the need to pass new taxes meant that the deputies could express their demands more forcefully. In 1519, Bishop Tomicki reported to Bishop Jan Konarski that the deputies 'by their custom present their demands before agreeing to any taxes'.[38] And so, the nobility then presented forty demands in writing, among which was the demand to charge the Catholic clergy with a war tax.[39] The Sejm of 1520 in Bydgoszcz was held in a war camp (*campestraliter*), which led the deputies to agree to pass taxes for enlisting the army in exchange for promises from the king that their demands would be considered at the next Sejm.[40] A year later (1521–1522) at the next tumultuous Sejm, however, the matter was not resolved. Therefore, in 1523, Bishop Tomicki feared that the nobility at the Sejm in Krakow would again demand that the clergy be charged with the costs of war expeditions and the defence of the country.[41] Moreover, news of a

---

36   Działyński (ed.), *Acta Tomiciana*, VI. 264–265, no. 227, Sigismund to palatines, Krakow 10 May 1523: 'In conventu preterito cum nihil decerni potuerat pro defensione regni et stipendio Tartaris dando et intelligeremus, quam inutilis sit et omni statui perniciosa generalis motio bellica, decrevimus secreto consilio cum primariis consiliariis nostris, ut in iis conventibus, quod ad consulendum de ordine proficiscendi ad bellum indiximus, fierent per palatinos motu proprio ipsorum non nostro nomine tractatus cum nobilitate de aliquo alio modo defensionis quam per bellicam motionem tam noxiam'.

37   Wacław Pociecha, 'Walka sejmowa o przywileje Kościoła w Polsce w latach 1520–1537', *Reformacja w Polsce*, 2 (1922), pp. 161–184.

38   Działyński (ed.), *Acta Tomiciana*, V. 123, no. 119, Piotr Tomicki to Jan Konarski [1520]: 'quod usque huc ad nullum effectum perductum propter difficultatem, quam nuncii terrarum more suo faciunt extorquere volentes prius sua petita, quam ad aliquam contributionem consentiant'.

39   Ibid.: 'Sed nuncii terrarum per hos omnes dies nos articulis suis occuparunt, quos, etsi prohibiti fuerunt scribere, tamen scripserunt supra quadraginta, inter quos potissimi sunt: ... Spirituales iam darentur et coequarentur illi in expeditione bellica nobilitati et alia multa'.

40   Działyński (ed.), *Acta Tomiciana*, VI. 7.

41   Działyński (ed.), *Acta Tomiciana*, VI. 203–204, no. 182, Piotr Tomicki to Chapter of Poznań [1523]: 'quia haud dubie dni. seculares venient ad ipsum conventum bene instructi, quo nos sui argumentis et instantia eo adigerent, ut equaliter cum illis onus defensionis ferremus, ad quid nos non adeo sumus obligati, presertim habitis aliis oneribus nostris non modicis'.

riot in larger cities such as Toruń and Gdańsk was reaching Krakow. The bishops were concerned that the social friction was underpinned by Reformation influences that undermined social order.[42]

Very little is known about the proceedings of the short Krakow Sejm of 1523. However, historiography has passed on a story of an attempt on the king's life, said to have taken place on 5 May, and which may have reflected the heated atmosphere of the Sejm.[43] It was during the first weeks of proceedings, on 7 March, that the king signed the anti-Lutheran edict. In this document, the monarch recalled his earlier decrees of 1520, which banned the import and sale of Luther's works under penalty of confiscation and exile. News reached the monarch that these works were being sold in Krakow and Luther's views publicly propagated despite the royal prohibitions.[44] The king, as guardian of unity and peace ('unitas et tranquillitas'), again forbade the 'open or clandestine importing, selling and buying of the works of the said Luther or his associates', as well as the propagation and defence of Luther's views under penalty of confiscation of goods and burning of written works.[45]

What led up to the preparation and issuing of this edict, like the course of the Sejm, remains unknown. Certainly, the document was prepared hastily, as indicated by both its laconic nature and the repetition of the contents of the edicts of 1520. The tenor of the document was also unchanged: Luther was still not branded a heretic, the prohibition applied primarily to his works ('opera cuiusdam Martini Luteri') and the imposed punishment was very mild. The monarch explicitly mentioned Krakow in the document, which also impacted the townspeople in Poland as a social group. After the turbulent course of the Sejm, the monarch was careful not to further stir up the sentiments of the nobility, but he still sought to strengthen the bishops' support of the throne.

---

42 Maciej Ptaszyński, *Reformacja w Polsce a dziedzictwo Erazma z Rotterdamu* (Warsaw: Wydawnictwo Uniwersytetu Warszawskiego, 2018), pp. 96–117, 180–207.

43 Wojciechowski, *Zygmunt*, p. 190, fn. 23.

44 Balzer (ed.), *Corpus Iuris Polonici* IV/1. 3: 'intelleximus tamen, quod comperiuntur in hac regia nostra civitate Cracoviensi, qui opuscula eiusdem Luteri invehere et ad venundandum exponere et manifeste illud doma latiferum profiteri ac tueri in offendiculum bonarum metium hominumque perturbationem ac contemptum auctoritatis et mandate nostri non formidant'.

45 Ibid.: 'praeserti publico edicto nostro statuimus, ut nullus aliqua opera praedicti Luteri aut eius sequacium ad hoc regnum nostrum et dominia nobis subiecta invehere, vendere et emere palam vel occulte audeat, nec invecta habeat, legat, aut illud pestiferum dogma praedicet, approbet et tuetur, sub poena huiusmodi libellorum et operum Luteri eiusque sequacium et illius, qui praemissa ausus fuerit, incendii et concremationis bonorumque confiscationis et amissionis'.

Four months after issuing this edict, Andrzej Krzycki wrote a letter to his patron, Bishop Piotr Tomicki, describing the events taking place at the royal court.[46] Reportedly, it was the archbishop of Gniezno, Jan Łaski, who called on the royal secretaries present at court to prepare a new decree against the Lutherans. Due to the incompetence of the pseudo-scholars and friars, this work turned into a farce.[47] It was then that archbishop was to approach Krzycki, asking him to prepare a document, which Krzycki did, convinced, as he writes, that everything was being done in the king's name and in accordance with the law.[48] However, according to the letter, the document was not signed at the time. Krzycki only sent a draft asking Tomicki for comments and corrections.[49]

Since two almost identical-sounding anti-Lutheran edicts were published on 22 August and 5 September, we can assume that Krzycki wrote about a preliminary version of one of these documents. Before analysing the content of the edict, however, it is worth elucidating the context of this communication. Krzycki was a relative and protégé of Tomicki who had been in acute conflict with Archbishop Łaski for several years. The scope of this aristocratic feud, well-documented in several printed pamphlets, extended to encompass the direction of the Krakow court's politics. Eventually, Tomicki, as vice-chancellor, succeeded in removing Łaski from influence over the king and court politics in the 1520s. During this conflict, both Krzycki and Tomicki referred to the archbishop in contemptuous terms, portraying him as talentless yet deceitful. For example, in a letter from July 1523 on the anti-Lutheran edict, Krzycki called him 'a hydra'. Therefore, the story of the nearly failed initiative should be treated *cum grano salis*.

The edict of 22 August 1523, to which Krzycki contributed, was also issued by the king during the Sejm, which was then meeting in Piotrków.[50] The Sejm became the battleground for a clash between the nobility's representatives

---

46   Działyński (ed.), *Acta Tomiciana*, VI. 291–292, no. 253, Krzycki to Piotr Tomicki, Krakow, 4 July 1523.
47   Ibid.: 'Conduxerat etiam nos omnes, qui sumus hic tam spirituales quam seculares consiliarios in pretorium de statuendo modo inquisitionis adversus Lutheranos, aderat et ingens doctorum et monachorum examen inibique quantis ineptiis quantisque et quam longis monologiis ea commedia sit acta, scribi satis non potest'.
48   Ibid.: 'Rogavit me impense, ut ejusce actus aliquas literas conficerem, quod onus subii libens vel ea causa, ne ipse actus noster derídiculo esset omnibus. Scripsi igitur, ut mihi videbatur nomine regio et legi sue Mti. annuenti et approbanti totum non gravatim'.
49   Ibid.: 'mitto copiam Rme. Dominationi vre., ut priusquam imprimi detur, dignaretur rescribere, si quid addendum, minuendum, mutandumve illi videretur, quod ut faciat citra moram plurimum illam rogo et obsecro'.
50   AGAD, MK, vol. 37, f. 496; AGAD, MK, vol. 43, f. 247; print in Działyński (ed.), *Acta Tomiciana*, VI. 289–290, no. 248; Balzer (ed.), *Corpus Iuris Polonici*, IV/1. 28–31, no. 9.

and the king, backed by the Senate and bishops. The debates were disrupted by a dispute between the nobility from two regions of Poland, Lesser Poland and Greater Poland, and a conflict over the dignities and offices held by the political elite incompatible with the relevant laws (*incompatibilia*).[51] Additionally, news of social friction in the towns of Pomerania, where Protestant preachers were already active, disrupted the proceedings. Before the Sejm in Krakow and during the Sejm in Piotrków, representatives of all the warring parties came to the king from Toruń and Gdańsk.[52] On the top of that, letters sent by the diplomat (and, in a few years, bishop) Jan Dantyszek, who visited Luther in Wittenberg, circulated during the Sejm.[53] Dantyszek extensively described a meeting with the reformer that took place in a convivial atmosphere, although, he added, Luther insulted the bishops and rulers. In his report, Dantyszek noticed that the reformer's face reflected the ideas expressed in his books.[54]

The tone of the proceedings can be discerned in the anti-reform edict of 22 August, which opened with a lament at the plebeians' ('humanis vulgi') predilection for novelties. It was thus the duty of the sovereign to 'pluck the tares from the field' ('zizaniam ex agro amputari ac eradicari'). The king, as a Christian ruler ('pro officio Christiani principis'), was obliged to defend the Christian religion as established by the saints, administered by the church, handed down by the ancestors and defended by the tribute of blood against heresy.[55] The monarch therefore forbade the importing, printing or selling of books and sermons by Luther and his associates ('libri Lutheri cuiusdam eiusque sequacium quorumcunque'). Under the pretext of preaching Christian freedom and pointing out the inevitable errors of the clergy ('pretextu libertatis

---

51 Działyński (ed.), *Acta Tomiciana*, VI. 338, no. 304, Piotr Tomicki to Queen Bona, Piotrków, 30 October 1523; ibid., pp. 338–339, no. 305, Piotr Tomicki to Jan Boner, Piotrków, 30 October 1523; ibid., pp. 339–340, no. 306, Piotr Tomicki to Jan Konarski, Piotrków, 30 October 1523.

52 Ptaszyński, *Reformacja*, p. 99f.

53 Anna Skolimowska etc. (eds.), *Corpus of Ioannes Dantiscus' Texts and Correspondence* [online], no. 186, Jan Dantyszek to Piotr Tomicki, Krakow, 8 August 1523 ('Qui non Romae pontificem et Vitenbergae Lutherum vidissent, vulgo nihil vidisse crederentur'). From: http://dantiscus.al.uw.edu.pl (accessed: 27th March 2023).

54 Ibid.: 'Talem habet Lutherus vultum, quales libros edit. ... Quis sit aliis in rebus, libri eius clare eum depingunt'.

55 Balzer (ed.), *Corpus Iuris Polonici* IV/1. 29, no. 9: 'nos pro officio christiani principis eam ipsam religionem a sanctis patribus ordinatam ac per sanctam Romanam ecclesiam directam, nobisque ac maioribus nostris per manus traditam, ac per nos denique et gentes nostras multo sanguine et clarissimis, gratia Dei, victoriis hactenus defensam, etiam a labe heretica, his temporibus in vicinia emergente, integram et immaculatam in regno et dominiis nostris conservare volentes'.

christiane, pretextu vitiorum ordinis ecclesiastici et scandalorum, quae in hominibus fieri necesse est'), the reformer spread his views to the plebeians ('vulgus'). To prevent the spread of these errors, the king sent his officials to Krakow to search the houses of the townspeople and subject printing houses and bookshops to inspection. Other cities were to follow suit. However, the question of the sanction with which these restrictions were imposed is an open research question because the royal document is known from dozens of historical records.

The oldest version of this document is believed to be an entry in the Royal Chancery Registers.[56] The royal chancellor or, in his absence, the vice-chancellor exercised control over the Registers. It should be recalled that the vice-chancellor at the time was Bishop Tomicki, who was not only present at the Sejm in Piotrków but also, despite his illness and old age, an active participant in the deliberations. This version of the document provided for a very severe sanction: burning at a stake and confiscation of property ('sub poena concremacionis et bonorum omnium confiscacionis'). It is worth noting that researchers have found no evidence of this document's expedition from the Royal Chancery. In other words, officials of the royal chancellery entered a copy of the document in the Registers, but today we do not have any original document bearing the royal signature and seal. Furthermore, four years later, in 1527, the document (in the same form and with the same date, August 22, 1523) was re-entered into the Royal Chancery Registers, prompting one to wonder if the Chancery was intending to re-announce or remind of it.[57]

Another version of this document can be found in Bishop Tomicki's private collection of correspondence, called *Acta Tomiciana*. The collection was compiled by Tomicki's secretary, Stanisław Górski (1497–1572).[58] In the early modern era, this multi-volume collection of manuscripts has been copied many times and survives in several copies. It also contains the anti-Lutheran August edict (admittedly undated). The copies, however, describe the sanctions imposed differently: one as exile and confiscation of property ('sub pena exilii et confiscationis bonorum omnium') and one as death penalty and confiscation ('sub pena capitis et confiscationis bonorum omnium').[59]

---

56 AGAD, MK, vol. 37, f. 496–467.
57 AGAD, MK, vol. 43, f. 125–126.
58 Ryszard Marciniak, *'Acta Tomiciana' w kulturze politycznej Polski okresu odrodzenia* (Warsaw: Państwowe Wydawnictwa Naukowe, 1983).
59 Działyński (ed.), *Acta Tomiciana*, VI. 289–290, no. 248 and VIII.145–146, no. 112.

4 Anti-reformation Praise

At the same time, the anti-Lutheran edict in question appeared in print alongside Krzycki's letter to the king. Later, it was published by Archbishop Jan Łaski in 1527 and 1528, thus ensuring its lasting presence in anti-Protestant literature.[60]

At the beginning of 1524, Krzycki published in Krakow a pamphlet entitled *Encomia Lutheri* (The Praise of Luther).[61] The text, printed by Hieronim Wietor (Hieronymus Vietor), opened with King Sigismund's anti-Lutheran edict of 22 August 1523, here quoted without date.[62] The sanction referred to in this version of the document was the death penalty and confiscation of goods ('sub poena capitis et confiscationis bonorum omnium'), the same that appears in some manuscript accounts from Bishop Tomicki's collection. From then on, only this sanction would appear in printed versions of the edict.

The core of the work was a letter to King Sigismund I, whom Krzycki addressed as Bishop of Przemyśl. According to Krzycki, the history of the church knew innumerable examples of heresy, the sources of which were egoism and pride ('sensu suo et spiritu superbie') and the aim of which was to break up the unity of the church and 'rock the boat' ('naviculam obruere'). All heretics in the history of the church took their inspiration from the Bible and 'spread their poison' under the pretext of preaching the Word of God.[63] This was also the case with Luther, whose intentions were so noble and whose conduct so gentle and in accordance with Christian ideals, that it was hard to imagine anything more impertinent, shameless, deceitful, and repulsive: not only did he deride kings as executioners, jesters, and impostors; popes as antichrists, pimps, and idols; and temples as brothels, but he also slandered and insulted the saints and Mary.[64] Luther's idea of the priesthood of all the

---

60   Jan Łaski, *Statuta nova* (Krakow: Maciej Szarfenberg, 1528), USTC 240844, k. HH2v: 'sub pena capitis et confiscatione bonorum omnium'.
61   Andrzej Krzycki, *Encomia Luteri* (Krakow: Hieronim Wietor, 1524), USTC 240741.
62   Ibid., f. A2r–3r.
63   Ibid., f. A4r: 'Inter tot autem, ac tam varios, qui hactenus fuerunt hereticos, nemo fuit qui non ex Evangelio Basim doctrine sue statuisset, non verbis dei pretextum, et illicem veneni sue fecisset'.
64   Ibd. f. A4r: 'sicuti in presens agit, novum sui anguli numen: Lutherus, quod ita humiliter, ita caste, ita mansuete et pacifice, juxta doctrinam Christi et Apostolorum, tractat, ut nihil arrogantius, nihil impudentius, nihil seditiosus ac virulentius dici vel excogitari possit, ut qui nedum reges carnicifices, scurras et nebulones; Pontifices antichristos, lenones, et idola vocet, que potestates, quales sunt, a deo tamen sunt, et templa dei immortales, que ipse Christus suam domum testatur, lupanaria appellat; sed et sanctos, atque adeo ipsam

faithful ('sacerdotes omnes ex equo facit') abolished the distinction between priests and laity and thus deprived the priesthood of forbearance, humility and poverty. Luther used the slogans of Christian liberty ('libertas Christiana') to abolish all order and all obedience, which after all (according to Krzycki) should also be shown to corrupt authority. Moreover, the reformer defended greed and the plundering of church property to encourage the laity to partake in pillage and desecration.[65]

Luther founded his position on a very radical criticism of the transgressions of the clerical state. 'He paints the morals of the clergy in very dark colours, as if the people could be or were blameless', as evidenced by the words of Christ (Mt 26:31–35, Mk 14:29–31, Lk 22:33–34, J 13:36–38) or the fate of the Apostles.[66] Radical demands opposed the Word and the primacy of Peter established by Christ (Mt 16:18–19). As Krzycki ironically notes, Luther used to 'humbly' say, 'the pope will fall and Luther will stand firm', denying the function of the vicar of Christ, whom he called as his patron, contrary to the biblical account (J 21:1–17).[67] Moreover, Luther not only attacked superiors and ecclesiastical authority but also demanded the abolition of church property, contrary to the injunction to give to God what belongs to God and to the emperor what belongs to the emperor (Mt 22:21). He also called to abolish ceremonies and established laws, abolish fasts and prayers, condemn the vows of chastity and the celibacy of the clergy and demand the abolition of religious orders and congregations.[68]

Luther deliberately made all these claims seem more serious by calling himself a Doctor of the Church, a preacher or an evangelist.[69] 'He claims to have received his doctrine from heaven, like the apostle James, pure, peaceful, humble, accessible, full of mercy and bearing good fruit, neither controversial, nor hypocritical. However, it turns out to be demonic, treacherous, virulent

---

deiperam virginem lingua sacerrima, ut ex plerisque eius argumentis constat, vilipendit ac elevat'.
65 Ibid.: 'Avaritiam et rapinas spiritualium praetendit, ut laicos, quos illis oppido infestos scit, ad rapinas et sacrilegium inducat'.
66 Ibid, f. A4v: 'Mores ecclesiasticorum miris coloribus depingit ac incessit, quasi absque vitiis homines esse possint, aut fuerint: etiam hi pauci quos Christus sibi delegerat, ut pote[m] quorum alii illum vendiderunt, alii abnegarunt, reliqui ab omni fide post passionem illius a lapsi fuerunt, et quasi non doceat Apostolus pontificem offerre debere pro semetipso, quemadmodum pro populo, cum eadem sit infirmitate circumdatus'.
67 Ibid., f. B1r: 'Licet ipse dicat spiritu humilitatis et intellectu. Papa cadet et Lutherus stabit'.
68 Ibid., f. B2r.
69 Ibid., f. B2r–v: 'Vocat se doctorem, vocat ecclesiasten, vocat evangelistam; cum scriptum sit; nemo assumat sibi honorem, nisi fuerit vocatus a deo; vocatur autem a deo quisquis ab his quos deus prefecit; non a semet ipso vocatur'.

and very contentious'.⁷⁰ Moreover, his position was full of contradictions and mutually exclusive elements; he spoke of bringing about the decline of the Church and religious life but found applause among the crowd for whom Luther, like a new Delphic oracle, proclaimed enigmatic freedom.⁷¹ The crowd of Luther's followers regarded as evangelical only those truths that came out of Luther's mouth and from under his pen in Wittenberg. But how could he reconcile this popularity with the biblical saying that no one is a prophet in his own country (Mt 13:57; Mk 6:4; Lk 4:24; Jn 4:44)?⁷²

Summing up this argument full of irony and depicting Luther as a staunch heretic and dangerous populist, Krzycki added that he took the reformer's views directly from his writings. 'For, as Erasmus [of Rotterdam] remarked, no one portrayed Luther better than he himself' as an angry Hekuba.⁷³ However, to explain the true nature of his doctrine, Krzycki referred to Jesus' words in the Gospel of Matthew (7:16), which states that we can recognize prophets, true or false, by their fruits. In contrast to images showing Luther as guided by the Holy Spirit and raising his eyes piously to heaven, Krzycki described the reformer as owing his fame to the hatred of the laity for the clergy and the curiosity of the mindless mob for news.⁷⁴

---

70   Ibid., f. B2v: 'Doctrinam suam doctrinam e coelis se habere iactat; quam cum Jacobus Apostol. castam; pacificam; modestam; tractabilem; plenam misericordie et fructibus bonis, absque diiuidicatione et simulatione testetur. Demoniamcam vero seditiosam; amarulentam et contentiosam plane apparet, cum scribat Lutherus se provocatum ad maledicta; quibus totus scatet; ex quo spiritu, et quali homini doctrina hec sua prodeat; cum ex abundantia cordis os loquatur; et cum qualis virsitalis oratio'.

71   Ibid., f. B3r: 'Numina celestia nephariis in contemptum. Et bona spiritualium harpyis in predam dat. Vulgusque omne libertate; quam asserit Christiana a legibus et obedientia missum facit, et alia huiusmodi scelerum ac turbarum lactari, quibus fit; ut hic novus evangelista; noc novum Pythii oraculum habeat tot diversa farine adoratores'.

72   Ibid., f. B3v: 'Evangelium hoc solum putant, quod et quatenus Lutherus doceat, ceterum quod in ecclesia canitur, cum nihil aliud, quam hoc, vel ad illlud pertinens canatur, aut legatur; credunt esse meras nugas et nenias. Hoc egregio oraculo gaudet et nobilitatur specula orbis Wittenberg, in quo si quid divini aut prophetici videretur, acceptus illi non esset Lutherus: cum nemo propheta acceptus sit in patria; siquidem verba Christi sunt vera'.

73   Ibid., f. B4r: 'quod et decus literarium Erasmus censet: ut nemo melius Lutherum quam semetipse conficiat: inconstantia videlicet: et maledicentia sua: qua in omnes passim: ceu furens illa Hecuba fertur'.

74   Ibid.: 'Sed ut manifestum sit tandem hinc et inde, Lutherum non spiritu sancto, quo plenus videri vult, non doctrina, qua turget, et os in celum point, non ulla sanctimonia: qua fingitur a suis famigeratum esse: sed odio secularium quorundam in ecclesiasticos, studio rerum novarum imperiti vulgi, insolentia, ac libidine apostatarum, cupiditate prede et sacrilegii improborum hominum, neque horum omnium quod scribat Lutherus intelligentium, eo illuviem hanc elatam, ut merito diceri hi omnes possint'.

The purpose of Krzycki's argument, which was in a way a commentary on the king's anti-Lutheran edict, was obviously to demonstrate the duty of secular and ecclesiastical authorities to act against heresy. The essence of the parable of the tares (Mt 13:24–30) lay, in the bishop's view, not only in the fact that heresy must accompany the church until the final judgment but also in the underlying message that heresy could not reign over the church.[75] Therefore, in the conclusion of his long epistle, Krzycki called on the king to defend both his kingdom and the Christian world, which were threatened not only from outside by Turks or Tartars but also by domestic enemies: the new heretics ('a domesticis hostibus Apostatis et hereticis').

The Krakow edition of this short but highly eloquent epistolary treatise was also embellished with short poems to provide commentary or illustrate the argument. The authors of these paratexts included the bishop's nephews Jan Krzycki, Piotr Rydzyński and Stanisław Słomowski, as well as Piotr Potulicki (Petrus Potulicius), Feliks Ciesielski (Felix Ceselius), Piotr Sadowski (Petrus Sadovius), Paweł Głogowski, Jan Ostroróg, Jost Ludwig Decius, Mattheus Conorovius (Maciej Konarzewski?) and Joannes Tirvesius.[76] The authors were either closely tied by family colligations with Krzycki or stayed at Tomicki's court to soon take up clerical positions. The two most important poems, *In imaginem Lutheri* (On the Image of Luther) and *Conditiones boni Lutherani* (The Lutheran Commandments), have been attributed to Krzycki himself.

Both of Krzycki's poems can be read as poetic illustrations to the letter. *Conditiones* are a parody of the Ten Commandments and constitute a call to break all the rules of religious life. A good Lutheran should challenge priests, disregard fasts, prayers, religious rites and other customs. He should also disregard the Bible, rulers and scholars, and value himself most highly, being a good impostor ('bonus impostor'). He should call his opponent, who wishes to preserve the rites, laws and faith, a papist ('papistam').

Krzycki's poem on the image of the reformer followed a similarly ironic style. Luther addresses the reader in the first person, boasting that he argued against the Church Fathers, the decisions of councils and accepted customs ('conciliis, patribus, mori contraria scribo'). Under the pretext that Christ had

---

75   Ibid, f. A3r: 'Necesse sit usque ad diem iudicii, quod etiam Apostolus testatur: hereses venire, ut et vitia que succrescunt, et ea que ab initio iusta et pia ratione statuuntur, ac tempore, ut sunt humana ingenia, in abusum abeunt, tali conflictatione purgentur, ac reticiantur, quod tamen nunquam absque ingenti aliqua inactura et perturbatione rei Christiane venire solebat. Et proinde recte pestes iste divinis ac humanis legibus damnantur et puniuntur'.

76   Jacek Wiesiołowski, 'Z kórnickiego kodeksu Corpus Cricianum', *Pamiętnik Biblioteki Kórnickiej*, 15 (1979), p. 242, fn. 11.

abolished the Law, any norm could be broken ('Christi effero leges, praetextu quarum carpere cuncta licet'). Luther himself resorted to libels ('maledicta', 'impura lingua') and thus gained universal applause. In his homeland, he was worshipped more than Christ, depicted in a halo and with the Holy Spirit ('Pingit et hanc faciem, radios, santamque columbam'), even though no one could be a prophet in his own country ('acceptus patriae nemo prophaeta suae'). This word-painted image of Luther in a halo with a dove was undoubtedly a reference to Cranach's depictions known from the Diet of Worms, where the reformer was shown in monastic robes with a Bible in his hand.

Krzycki's original work fits well into the anti-Lutheran polemic of the first half of the 1520s. Luther was portrayed primarily as a heretic and a revolutionary, speaking out against the church and tradition and thereby undermining the foundations of social order. The reformer's views were acclaimed by the mob, who looked for an excuse to plunder. It is apparent, therefore, that Krzycki formulated his criticism from the point of view of the academic community of the time. He invoked the words of Erasmus and also used irony, which at times makes it difficult to comprehend the message. It is perhaps for this reason (in addition to the telling title) that the work found its way onto the index of prohibited books in 1557.[77]

Before it was on the list of forbidden books, however, the Krakow edition of 1524 received a very lively response. It was immediately reprinted in Dresden, Regensburg and Cologne.[78] Interestingly, the printers omitted the anti-Lutheran royal edict. It was instead published that same year in Speyer under a different title.[79] For thirty years Krzycki's work was part of the mainstream of European polemical literature.

---

[77] Jesús Martínez de Bujanda (ed.), *Index des livres interdits*, VIII: *Index de Rome 1557, 1559, 1564. Les premiers index romains et l'index du Concile de Trente* (Sherbrooke: Centre d'Études de la Renaissance, Université de Sherbrooke, 1990), no. 009, p. 213.

[78] For Dresden and Regensburg editions, see VD16 2478; 2479; for Cologne edition see Electronic Database for the Estreicher Bibliography (EBBE), 146785; 146786 (https://www.estreicher.uj.edu.pl).

[79] The Speyer edition from 1524 was entitled: *Epistola Andree Cricii et Edictum Regis Polonie in Martinum Luterum* (USTC 651484). The author of the preface was the humanist Ferenc Bácsi (Franciscus Bachiensis), who was soon to be among Jan Zapolya's supporters. Bálint Lakatos, 'Bachiensis, Franciscus (Ferenc Bácsi, Bachy, de Bachya)', in *Companion to Central and Eastern European Humanism* [forthcoming].

5 Conclusion

The events of the Reichstag in Worms and the Edict of Worms reverberated beyond the borders of the Reich. On the one hand, they translated into an increase in the popularity of the steadfast reformer, while on the other, they triggered repression that forced the greater mobility of the preachers of the new doctrine. The result was a wave of early public appearances by these preachers in Baltic cities, which historiography has presented as the birth of the Reformation. These actions corresponded with local social conflicts and, thus, sparked a wave of criticism. Among the accusations made against the preachers by their Catholic opponents, we can hear the echo of those already formulated in the edict of Worms, including the alleged incitement to wash one's hands in the blood of priests.

The urban conflicts and the early efforts of the preachers also forced a response from the secular authorities, who probably reacted to requests for intervention from a part of the urban and ecclesiastical elite. Krzycki's participation in the creation of the edicts shows that the anti-Lutheran legislation was drafted by intellectual elites whose education had already been strongly influenced by humanism and Erasmus of Rotterdam. It can be argued that, in contrast to the first anti-Reformation edicts of 1520–1522, the second wave depicted a more complex picture of the early Reformation and Luther himself. In Poland, an example of such an elaborate anti-Lutheran decree was the August 1523 edict by Krzycki, considered at the time to be the most prominent Latinist and correspondent of Erasmus of Rotterdam.

Krzycki's edict was commissioned by the archbishop of Gniezno but was probably modified several times by humanists and clerics gathered around the court. A trace of such work on the document was the change in the range of sanctions envisaged: from the stake to the death penalty to the punishment of exile. Some wordings of the act (e.g. 'under the pretext of Christian liberty') betrayed familiarity with the reformer's writings and anti-Lutheran polemics. At the same time, however, the edict confirmed that Luther's views ('poison in honey') were rapidly gaining popularity. The plebeians ('vulgus') were particularly interested in the new doctrine.

The edict of 1523 projected a rather unambiguous social profile: *de iure* and *de facto*, it primarily targeted the cities and characterised the groups threatened by 'heresy' as the lowest social strata. It described the Reformation itself as a revolutionary event that undermined social order. This profile of the document was probably both a product of historical circumstances, an echo of polemics and edicts (from papal bulls to the Edict of Worms) and, perhaps in part, a legacy of the humanist and elite formation of the authors of the decree.

When Krzycki included the edict in his literary polemic against the reformer's views a year after its publication, the events of the Reichstag in Worms and the Wittenberg propaganda that arose around them were his most powerful point of reference. This framework of the text may also have been the reason for its popularity in the Reich, where the edict, originally published in Krakow, was immediately reprinted many times. Krzycki's treatise thus provides evidence that the echoes of the Reichstag in Worms first reached Poland, then made their way back to the Reich.

Acknowledgement

The article was written thanks to the generous support of the Alexander von Humboldt Foundation during the author's research stay at the Leibniz Institute of European History in Mainz.

CHAPTER 8

Protestant Books in Jesuit Libraries from Riga, Braniewo and Poznań

Catholic Post-publication Censorship in Practice

Peter Sjökvist

The confessional conflicts between Protestants and Catholics in the early modern period involved books in many different ways. The Protestant Swedes, for instance, saw the taking of literary war spoils as a way of depriving their Catholic enemies of their intellectual armoury. At Uppsala University Library, where most of the books looted by the Swedish Army ended up in the first half of the seventeenth century, the less useful Catholic books were stored separately from the remaining collections. The Catholics, among other things, listed forbidden books in the *Index librorum prohibitorum* and developed several kinds of censorship strategies. Much has already been written concerning these strategies, but many details in actual practice remain to be investigated and described. Based on empirical evidence, both theoretical statements and terminology must be problematised and reconsidered. In this article, the aim is to contribute to such a discussion by studying the traces and noticing the absence of traces of postpublication censorship practices in Protestant books from the Jesuit Colleges libraries of Riga, Braniewo and Poznań, which are still extant at Uppsala University Library. Most importantly, too-inattentive usage of the concept of *damnatio memoriae* will be questioned, and the importance of including both books with and without material signs of censorship when describing the practice will be stressed. But we start with a short historical background and say a few words on Catholic post-publication censorship in more general terms.

1   Jesuit Libraries as Literary Spoils of War at Uppsala

Uppsala University Library was founded by the Swedish King Gustavus II Adolphus (r. 1611–1632) by decrees of 1620 and 1621; at the same time, it received the royal book depot from Stockholm as a donation.[1] This was a good start, but

---

1   About the books at Uppsala from the Royal book depot, see Otto Walde, 'Konung Sigismunds bibliotek och Gustaf Adolfs donation 1620–1621. Ett bidrag till Upsala universitetsbiblioteks äldsta historia', *Nordisk tidskrift för bok- och biblioteksväsen* 11 (1915), pp. 317–332; and Åke

many more books would be needed if the library were to match the grand ambitions of the university, and the annual sum given from the king that was reserved for book purchases was far from satisfactory. In the following years, however, the library would grow substantially enlarged by collections that were taken as spoils of war by the Swedish king and were thereafter donated to Uppsala.

This donating of literary war booty to Uppsala commenced in 1622 with the library of the Jesuit college of Riga, which had been confiscated and brought to Stockholm in the previous year. The process continued through 1626 with the library of the Jesuit college of Braniewo and the chapter library of Frombork. In the 1630s, Catholic book collections from Würzburg und Mainz came to Uppsala and, later, from libraries in the Czech lands. In 1693, books from religious institutions in Poznań, among others from the Jesuits, finally came to Uppsala. These had been taken in the 1650s but had until then been privately owned by the nobleman Claes Rålamb (1622–1698), who had been the Swedish officer in Poznań of the highest rank. The result, thus, is that three Jesuit college libraries (as well as books from several other early modern Catholic institutions) are today part of the collections of Uppsala University Library.[2] Not all of them were kept in Uppsala until our time. Many volumes have left the library over the centuries through duplicate auctions and disposals, but today, many thousands of books remain at Uppsala.[3] However, the historic construction of the collections

---

Davidsson, 'Gustav II Adolfs bokgåvor till akademien i Uppsala', in Sven Lundström (ed.), *Gustav II Adolf och Uppsala universitet* (Uppsala: Uppsala universitet, 1982), pp. 93–110.

[2] On literary spoils of war in Sweden, see especially Otto Walde, *Storhetstidens litterära krigsbyten. En kulturhistorisk-bibliografisk studie* (2 vols., Uppsala: Almqvist & Wiksell, 1916–1920). For their reception at Uppsala, see Peter Sjökvist, 'On the Order of the Books in the First Uppsala University Library Building', *Journal of Jesuit Studies*, 6 (2019), pp. 315–326; Peter Sjökvist, 'The Reception of Books from Braniewo in the 17th-century Uppsala University Library', *Biblioteka*, 24 (2020), pp. 101–116; and Peter Sjökvist, 'Useful Literary Spoils of War from Riga at Uppsala University Library', in Jonas Nordin, Gustavs Strenga & Peter Sjökvist (eds.), *The Baltic Battle of Books. Formation and Relocation of European Libraries in the Confessional Age (c.1500–c.1650) and their Afterlife* (Leiden: Brill, 2023), pp. 197–213. A catalogue of the Braniewo collection was published in 2007; see Józef Trypućko, *The Catalogue of the Book Collection of the Jesuit College in Braniewo Held in the University Library in Uppsala*, eds. Michał Spandowski, Sławomir Szyller (3 vols., Uppsala–Warsaw: Uppsala universitetsbibliotek–Biblioteka Narodowa, 2007). A catalogue of the Riga-collection was published in 2021, see Laura Kreigere-Liepiņa etc. (eds.), *Catalogue of the Riga Jesuit College Book Collection (1583–1621). History and Reconstruction of the Collection* (Riga: Latvijas Nacionālā bibliotēka, 2021). Modern catalogues of the Poznań spoils are being created presently. As regards the Polish collections in Uppsala, see also Peter Sjökvist, 'Polish Collections at Uppsala University Library: A History of Research', in Dorota Sidorowicz-Mulak, Agnieszka Franczyk-Cegła (eds.), *Książka dawna i jej właściciele* (Wrocław: Ossolineum, 2017) II. 237–244. For information on the Poznań project, see Peter Sjökvist, 'Books from Poznań at the Uppsala University Library', in Jacek Puchalski etc. (eds.), *Z badań nad książką i księgozbiorami historycznymi. Polonika w zbiorach obcych* (Warsaw: Polskie Bractwo Kawalerów Gutenberga, 2017), pp. 319–327.

[3] See Peter Sjökvist, 'Litterära krigsbytens öden i Sverige', *Biblis 89* (Våren 2020), pp. 20–26; Polish version: 'Losy księgozbiorów zagrabionych w czasach wojen szwedzkich w XVII w.',

can still be discerned by extant seventeenth-century lists of books from Riga, Braniewo and Poznań, made both in Poland and Sweden.

In Lutheran Sweden in the seventeenth century, the state was officially anti-Catholic, the pope was regularly compared with Antichrist and the Jesuits were characterised as his cunning and deceitful followers.[4] Looting Jesuit libraries was explicitly mentioned by the Lutheran authorities as a way to weaken the intellectual forces of their enemies. At the same time, the library of Uppsala University, which was meant to educate loyal servants to the state administration and clergymen to the Lutheran Church, was now filled with books from learned Catholic institutions. However, being a Catholic library did not mean that all it contained was useless in a Lutheran context. In the taken collections, we can, for instance, find the classics, works of the Church fathers, and books on medicine, mathematics and Roman law, in addition to the confessional Catholic books in theology (liturgical and devotional books, sermons, controversial literature, etc.). A number of books authored or edited by Protestants can also be found among the looted Jesuit libraries.

In Uppsala, many Catholic books were placed on the lower storage floor of the building of two floors, which used to house the library from 1627. The classification system from Braniewo was even kept there in the theological sections and applied to all Catholic books on the lower floor, while on the upper floor, the space used as the University library, books were arranged according to the four faculties (that is, the subject areas of theology, law, medicine and arts). Around 1640, when the first library catalogues were compiled, almost half of the entire stock consisted of books looted from Catholic libraries. At about the same time, there were laments in the University Council that the library lacked several important works by Protestant authors. It is a fact, thus, that several titles in the limited number of Protestant works at hand by then at Uppsala had come there with the books looted from Catholic institutions.

2   Post-publication Censorship

Against the background that several Protestant books at Uppsala had come as part of Catholic libraries, it must also be noted that some of these books contain flagrant material evidence of the confessional conflict of the time.[5] Copies of

---

in Dorota Sidorowicz-Mulak, Agnieszka Franczyk-Cegła (eds.), *Kolekcje prywatne w zbiorach książki dawnej* (2 vols., Wrocław: Ossolineum, 2020), I. 252–264.

4   Peter Sjökvist, 'Litterära krigsbyten i Uppsala och deras användning. En kontroversteologi', in *Lychnos. Annual of the Swedish History of Science Society* (2020), pp. 259–268.

5   In addition, we know that heretical books have sometimes been stored separately from the others at these Jesuit colleges. In an account book from Braniewo, still extant at Uppsala

books by prohibited authors or with forbidden content found in Catholic collections from this period have sometimes been manipulated or censored to blur, distort or hide certain unwanted information, such as the name of an author, editor, dedicatee, printer or printing place. Some copies were censored more thoroughly, entire text passages were deleted or cut out or leaves were removed from the book.[6] The technical term for such material manipulations, already employed in early modernity, is expurgation (from Latin *expurgare* – 'to purge'). We also meet traces of such censorship in the copies from the Jesuit colleges of Riga, Braniewo and Poznań that are now at Uppsala.[7] Notice, however, that the word 'sometimes' was chosen in both previous categories on purpose, since only a minority of the books that were concerned by it in theory, i.e. that should be censored according to the Catholic Church authorities, were affected by it in practice at these three Jesuit colleges. This circumstance has often been overlooked in discussions of Catholic post-publication censorship (which was executed to enable the continued usage of useful books with heretical content or written by authors considered heretics) of the authors, printers, printing places and subjects this concerned, as well as of possible ways of understanding the material practice. When studying censorship in practice, however, a full picture must include all forbidden books, both the

---

University (UUB H 169), we notice an expense 31 January 1569 'pro factura armarij pro libris haereticis' (for the making of a safe for heretical books). See Walde, *Storhetstidens litterära krigsbyten*, I. 57. In the Jesuit college of Poznań, a special room for prohibited books was arranged in 1653. Jacek Wiesiołowski, 'O najstarszej bibliotece poznańskich jezuitów w świetle zachowanych w Szwecji katalogów bibliotecznych', *Kronika Miasta Poznania*, 4 (1997), p. 131.

6 As stressed by William H. Sherman, with a reference to Elaine Whitaker, censorship is generally one of the most common among Renaissance readers' interactions with texts. William H. Sherman, *Used books. Marking Readers in Renaissance England* (Philadelphia: University of Pennsylvania Press, 2008), p. 16. On censorship and the Catholic Church, see e.g. Georg Haven Putnam, *The Censorship of the Church of Rome and its Influence upon the Production and Distribution of Literature* (2 vols., New York: Benjamin Blom, 1907); Gigliola Fragnito (ed.), *Church, Censorship, and Culture in Early Modern Italy* (Cambridge: Cambridge University Press, 2001); Ugo Baldini, Leen Spruit (eds.), *Catholic Church and Modern Science. Documents from the Archives of the Roman Congregations of the Holy Office and the Index* (Rome: Libreria Editrice Vaticana, 2009); Peter Godman, *The Saint as Censor. Robert Bellarmine between Inquisition and Index* (Leiden: Brill, 2000); and Francisco Bethencourt, *The Inquisition. A Global History, 1478–1834* (Cambridge: Cambridge University Press, 2009), pp. 221–236. For an example of a kind of expurgation in a Protestant context, see Jeremy J. Smith, 'Thomas Becket. *Damnatio Memoriae* and the Marking of Books', *International Journal for the Study of the Christian Church*, 20.3–4 (2020), pp. 271–273.

7 The censorship of books in the Catholic Church used three main methods: *censura praevia*, by examinition before publication; *expurgatio*, by purging and eliminating peccant expressions and names after publication; and *prohibitio*, by banning published books. Godman, *The Saint as Censor*, p. 3. On censorship as purification, see Jennifer Helm, *Poetry and Censorship in Counter-Reformation Italy* (Leiden: Brill, 2015), pp. 17–18.

expurgated ones and those that have been left untouched, although they could be expected to contain expurgations.[8]

The act of blurring or distortion of the names of an author, printer or printing place was already at the time, and still is among modern historians, normally considered a case of a *damnatio memoriae* ('condemnation of memory'), by which the name of a condemned person, place or notion should never be mentioned but be left to oblivion.[9] This practice has its roots in antiquity and has a long history in the church in relation to excommunication.[10] An early instance, for example, is the synod of Reisbach in 798, when it was said about an excommunicated person that nothing should be written in his memory after his death.[11] In the edict of Worms, it was explicitly stated that the books by Martin Luther should be removed from the memory of all human beings. Allegedly, at the Council of Trent, the name of Martin Luther was never even to be mentioned or expressed aloud.[12] The phrase *auctores damnatae memoriae* can also be found in editions of the *Index librorum prohibitorum*. Therefore, official ecclesiastical early modern sources confirm that the memories of the prohibited heretical authors were seen as condemned and should be left to oblivion.[13] However, while some authors and books should be completely forbidden according to the ecclesiastical authorities, it would often suffice to purge or to expurgate others in order to continue using them. This could be

---

8   The same argument, regarding the necessity to make a difference between postpublication censorship in theory and practice, is made in Francisco Malta Romeiras, 'Putting the Indices into Practice. Censoring Science in Early Modern Portugal', *Annals of Science*, 77.1 (2020), pp. 71–95.
9   Recently in Hannah Marcus, *Forbidden Knowledge. Medicine, Science, and Censorship in Early Modern Italy* (Chicago: Chicago University Press, 2020), pp. 191–197, although her idea of what end a *damnatio memoriae* serves is not representative of modern historians. I argue against Marcus below, but her book remains a very valuable contribution on this topic.
10 See Christoph Schreiter, Johann Heinrich Gerlach, *Dissertationem juridicam de damnatione memoriae* ... (Leipzig: Fleischer, [1689]), USTC 2700727, f. E1v: 'Excommunicatio eo respectu ad fines praesentis materiae accedere putatur, dum ignominiam existimationisque jacturam Reus utrobique patitur ... estque inter poenas canonicas seu Ecclesiasticas omnium gravissima et maxime formidabilis ... imo Judicis intentione, quae quidem in memoriae damnatione perpetuam ac irrevocabilem infamiam efflagitat ....'
11 Jacques le Goff, *History and Memory* (New York: Columbia University Press, 1992), p. 73.
12 Daniel Olivier, *Luthers Glaube. Die Sache des Evangeliums in der Kirche* (Stuttgart: Klett-Cotta, 1982), p. 143.
13 For example *Index auctorum damnatae memoriae, tum etiam librorum, qui vel simpliciter, vel ad expurgationem usque prohibentur, vel denique iam expurgati permittuntur* (Lisbon: Craesboeck, 1624), USTC 5015927. Marcus, *Forbidden Knowledge*, pp. 192–194. Literature on the *Index* is huge. For a very brief overview of the *Index* and its influence, with references to several classics on the subject, see e.g. Michiel van Groesen, *The Representations of the Overseas World in the De Bry Collection of Voyages (1590–1634)* (Leiden: Brill, 2008), pp. 281–283.

done by the deletion of a single word or name or longer passages.[14] The method, as described by Juan Bautista Cardona (1511–1589), a Spanish bishop in the first generation of censors, in his *De expungendis haereticorum propriis nominibus etiam de libris, qui de religione ex professo non tractant* (On erasing the own names of the heretics even from the books that do not explicitly treat religion) from 1576, aimed to solve the problem of how to damn what was unsuitable and preserve what was useful in already published books, which had been created by the fifth and eighth rules of the *Index*. These concern cases when books have authors considered heretics but when nothing of their own is invented, such as lexica, concordances and indices, and in books in which the main argument is good, but where instances of heresy or impiety occur. According to Cardona, these must be expurgated until they become permitted reading.[15]

3 The Cases: Jesuit Libraries from Riga, Braniewo and Poznań

In my investigations, however, it has been difficult to see any consistent material practice or underlying principle of expurgation in the Protestant books from the Jesuit colleges of Riga, Braniewo and Poznań still extant at Uppsala. Sometimes, all controversial names have been deleted, sometimes only one or two, sometimes the same name has been deleted in one instance but not in another, occasionally even on the same page, and sometimes names have been deleted only partially, while remaining fully legible to the reader. Often, such expurgations even take place in books written by authors in the first class of the *Index*, which are of the kind that should be completely avoided. Similar observations of an inconsistent practice have been made in the expurgated books of other Catholic libraries, so there is nothing exceptional here.[16] But most importantly, in two-thirds of the books with forbidden Protestant authors or editors from the Jesuit colleges of Braniewo and Poznań, roughly estimated, there are no signs of

---

14 Marcus, *Forbidden Knowledge*, pp. 52, 208, among others. The reading permits, granted more and more generously towards the end of the sixteenth century, usually had expurgation as a condition, see Marcus, *Forbidden Knowledge*, pp. 134, 146, 150; and Nick Wilding, 'Science and the Counter-Reformation', in Alexandra Bamji etc. (eds.), *The Ashgate Research Companion to the Counter-Reformation* (Farnham: Ashgate, 2013), p. 331.
15 Juan Bautista Cardona, *De expungendis haereticorum propriis nominibus etiam de libris, qui de religione ex professo non tractant* (Rome: De Angelis, 1576), USTC 818877, pp. 5–6, 9–10; Godman, *The Saint as Censor*, pp. 106–107.
16 E.g. Marcus, *Forbidden Knowledge*, pp. 183, 217; Malta Romeiras, 'Putting the Indices into Practice', pp. 72, 84. For a discussion of disagreements and diversity in the opinions of the censors, see Sara Miglietti, 'The Censor as Reader. Censorial Responses to Bodin's *Methodus* in Counter-Reformation Italy (1587–1607)', *History of European Ideas*, 42.5 (2016), pp. 707–721.

expurgations at all.[17] In the books from the Jesuit college of Riga, the proportion of expurgated books is even smaller. This brings into question whether *damnatio memoriae* really is the most proper term when trying to explain the material practice concerning Protestant literature at these Jesuit colleges, although previous historians have usually considered it in similar cases. *Damnatio memoriae* as a concept has been used to describe cases when expurgations of names have been made in the books quite generally, regardless of the circumstance that it has long ago been noticed that these have been made inconsistently. Seemingly, however, those cases have not been taken into account when the same rule applied and when the memory of the name in question was condemned but when there were no expurgations at all. So, since a true *damnatio memoriae*, when all heretical names are deleted, is rarely there, and since a partial *damnatio memoriae* would be against the concept itself, how can we understand these cases? To refine this term, a closer look is necessary at the Protestant literature and extant expurgations from the Jesuit colleges of Riga, Braniewo and Poznań.

As mentioned, there is a difference between the three Jesuit libraries at Uppsala as far as expurgations of names of authors, editors, printers and printing places are concerned. In the extant collection of the Jesuit college of Riga, no less than approximately 13% of 717 titles have a Protestant connection in the form of a Protestant author or editor.[18] In some cases, it cannot be fully certain that the books had really been owned by the college. In one of the books with a somewhat doubtful Jesuit provenance, the only example of a material strategy to cover a theologically controversial name is found, thereby distorting it with ink on the title page.[19] In the copy of Philipp Melanchthon's *Erotemata dialectices* (1563), the printing place *Vitebergae* has been made illegible, while both the names of the author and the printer have been left intact.[20]

The symbolic importance of Wittenberg as the centre and origin of the Lutheran movement was surely great, but fifteen more books in the Riga collection

---

17   Malta Romeiras has noted a very similar low percentage (37%) of expurgated books in his corpus of forbidden books from the Biblioteca Nacional de Portugal, see Malta Romeiras, 'Putting the indices into practice', p. 81.
18   The high number of Protestant titles mirrors the circumstance that the surrounding region of Riga was not Catholic to the same degree as the ones of Braniewo and Poznań. See further Reinis Norkārkls, 'The Riga Jesuit College and Its Book Collection', in Laura Kreigere-Liepiņa etc. (eds.), *Catalogue of the Riga Jesuit College Book Collection*, pp. 90–111. I have used the criterion of the known Protestant religious views of the author or editor to label a book as Protestant throughout this article. Admittedly, books produced in and by typically Protestant places and printers were expurgated too sometimes, even though the authors or editors were not explicitly Protestant, but these publications have not been included in the account here.
19   As regards ink as an expurgatory method, see Marcus, *Forbidden knowledge*, pp. 183–188.
20   Philipp Melanchthon, *Erotemata dialectices continentia fere integram artem, ita scripta, ut juventuti utiliter proponi possint* (Wittenberg: Krafft, 1563), USTC 653634, title page. Shelf mark: UUB Riga 353.

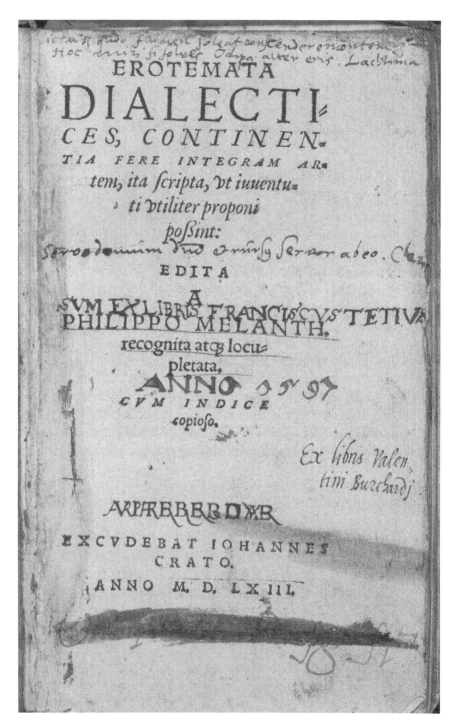

FIGURE 8.1   Title page in: Philipp Melanchthon, *Erotemata dialectices continentia fere integram artem, ita scripta, ut juventuti utiliter proponi possint* (Wittenberg: Krafft, 1563). Uppsala University Library, shelf mark: UUB Riga 353

explicitly mention Wittenberg as the printing place; however, these have been left untouched. Melanchthon's status as one of the greatest Lutheran heroes ensured that he was counted in the *prima classis* of the *Index* among the authors whose books it was forbidden to publish or to own or read once published.[21]

In two copies with Protestant authors or editors from Riga, prefaces have also been removed from the books.[22] Such is the case with the *In librum Psalmorum interpretatio* by Johann Bugenhagen (1485–1558), printed by Adam Petri in Basel 1524, in which both the title page and the preface of Martin Luther and Philipp Melanchthon have been cut out.[23] Another is the *Hortulus animae* of Georg Rhau (1488–1548), printed by him in Wittenberg 1548, where the title page and the preface of Martin Luther are missing.[24] More than 90 books in the Riga collection have a Protestant author or editor, but only three of these have been expurgated or censored. Under these circumstances, is it really fair to talk about a *damnatio memoriae* in practice in one case of the distorted Wittenberg when the same city and so many other names are left intact in other copies? Why condemn the memory of Wittenberg but not of Melanchthon on the same page? More examples of this inconsistency can be seen in books from Braniewo.

Approximately only 5% of the 2,632 titles from Braniewo books still extant in Uppsala have a Protestant connection in the form of a Protestant author or editor.[25] Approximately one-third of these books contain material manipulation that is obviously caused by conflicting religious views or confessional disagreement. Mostly, this consists of a deletion of details concerning the author, editor, printer or printing place. In a few cases, more extreme measures have been taken with parts of the text to ensure illegibility.

Some examples will help demonstrate the variations in this practice. The first is a medical book, in which the name of Euricius Cordus (1486–1535) has been carefully singled out and blurred on the title page.[26]

---

21 E.g. *Index librorum prohibitorum* (Cologne: Cholinus, 1576), USTC 665526, ff. A5r, C6v. (A copy from this edition was part of the spoils from Braniewo. Shelf mark: Obr. 57.99 (2).)

22 I thank Laura Kreigere-Liepiņa at the National Library of Latvia for having directed my attention to these cases. See Marcus, *Forbidden Knowledge*, pp. 179–181, for more examples of cutting out leaves as a method of expurgation.

23 Johann Bugenhagen, *In librum Psalmorum interpretatio* (Basel: [Petri], 1524), USTC 667604. Shelf mark: UUB Riga 99.

24 Georg Rhau, *Hortulus animae. Lustgarten der Seelen* ([Wittenberg: Rhau], 1548), USTC 664284. Shelf mark: UUB Riga 65.

25 Andrew Pettegree's claim in *The Book in the Renaissance* that the Braniewo library 'consisted exclusively of Catholic works' is thus incorrect. Neither can titles from Braniewo in secular subjects and ancient authors like Cicero and Vergil be labelled as Catholic works, and there are several of this kind among the books from Braniewo. Andrew Pettegree, *The Book in the Renaissance* (New Haven: Yale University Press, 2010), p. 329.

26 Johann Dryander, *New Artznei unnd Practicierbüchlin zu allen Leibs gebrechen* (Frankfurt am Main: Egenolph, 1551), USTC 1793006, title page. Shelf mark: UUB Obr. 42.528 (1).

FIGURE 8.2   Title page in: Johann Dryander, *New Artznei unnd Practicierbüchlin zu allen Leibs gebrechen* (Frankfurt am Main: Egenolph, 1551). Uppsala University Library, shelf mark: UUB Obr. 42.528 (1)

Admittedly, Cordus was Lutheran and had openly adhered to the ideas of the Reformation. However, Johann Dryander (1500–1560) was his disciple and Hieronymus Bock (1498–1554) was a Lutheran clergyman, but they have both been left intact. Did the owner of the book only know the confession of Euricius Cordus but not of the others? Or did he consider the expurgatory duty fulfilled only with the deletion of one? Admittedly, Cordus was the only one of them whose *Opera omnia* were prohibited in any sixteenth-century index, while another work by Dryander is listed there, but none by Hieronymus Bock.[27]

The next case makes a stronger impression. The name of the reformed author Rudolf Gwalther (1519–1586) from Zurich has here been erased in a book on metric and poetics, as well as the reformed printing place Zurich, the printer Froschauer and even the year 1554 in the imprint.[28]

The printer's name, deleted in the imprint, can nevertheless still easily be seen on the printer's device in the middle of the title page. Why erase the printer's name in one place but leave it fully legible right next to it if his memory was condemned? A similar case is provided by a copy of the Basel edition of Hilarius from 1550, which was previously owned by the Jesuit College of Poznań.[29]

Both Erasmus of Rotterdam, Martin Lipsius and the printer's device of Froben have been left untouched on the title-page, while the printing place has been blurred. In the colophon of the same book, however, both Basel, Froben and Episcopius have been deleted, while the printer's device on the following page is untouched.

Like this, it continues. In a book on physics, Conrad Gesner's (1516–1565) name has been distorted, while both Zurich and Froschauer are fully legible in the imprint.[30]

In three volumes containing Melanchthon's commentary on Cicero's letters, all title pages have been cut out, while the printing place Leipzig has been deleted in the colophon, but the names of printer and publisher are left intact.[31]

---

27 Jesús Martínez de Bujanda, *Index des livres interdits*, vol. 10: *Thesaurus de la littérature interdite au XVIe siècle. Auteurs, ouvrages, éditions avec addenda et corrigenda* (Sherbrooke: Éditions de l'Université de Sherbrooke, 1996), pp. 137, 158.

28 Rudolf Gwalther, *De syllabarum et carminum ratione* (Zurich: Froschauer, 1554), USTC 631656, title page. Shelf mark: UUB Obr. Qq.554 (9).

29 Hilarius of Poitiers, *Lucubrationes quotquot extant* (Basel: Froben & Episcopius, 1550), USTC 626451, title page, colophon, last page. Shelf mark: UUB Teol. Patres, ensk. lat. fol. (36.103).

30 Conrad Gesner, *Physicarum meditationum, annotationum et scholiorum lib. v* (Zurich: Froshauer, 1586), USTC 624830, title page. Shelf mark: UUB Obr. Qq.81.

31 Philipp Melanchthon, *Ciceronis epistolas, quae familiares vocantur, argumenta* (Leipzig: Rambau & Apel, 1563–1565), USTC 666015, colophon. Shelf mark: UUB Script. Lat. [Cicero] 395: 1–3 (x.368–370).

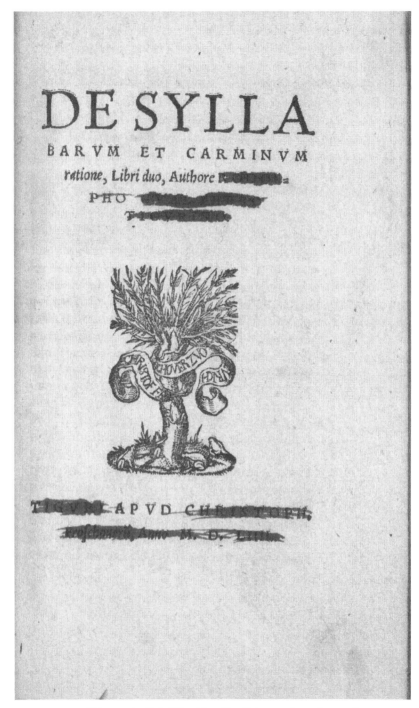

FIGURE 8.3 Title page in: Rudolf Gwalther, *De syllabarum et carminum ratione* (Zurich: Froschauer, 1554). Uppsala University Library, shelf mark: UUB Obr. Qq.554 (9)

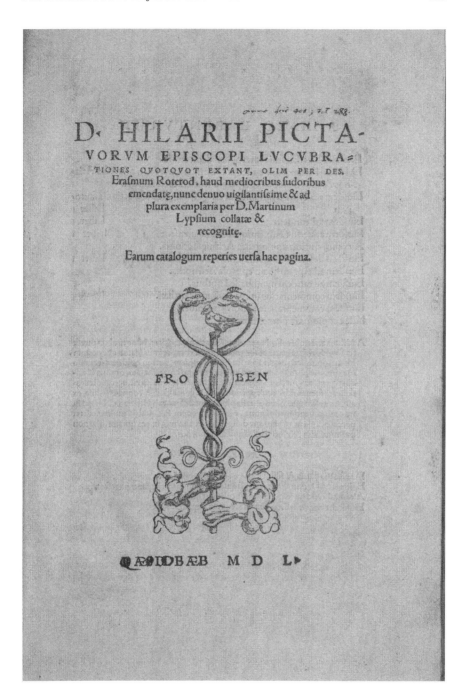

FIGURE 8.4   Title page in: Hilarius of Poitiers, *Lucubrationes quotquot extant* (Basel: Froben & Episcopius, 1550). Uppsala University Library, shelf mark: UUB Teol. Patres, ensk. lat. fol. (36.103)

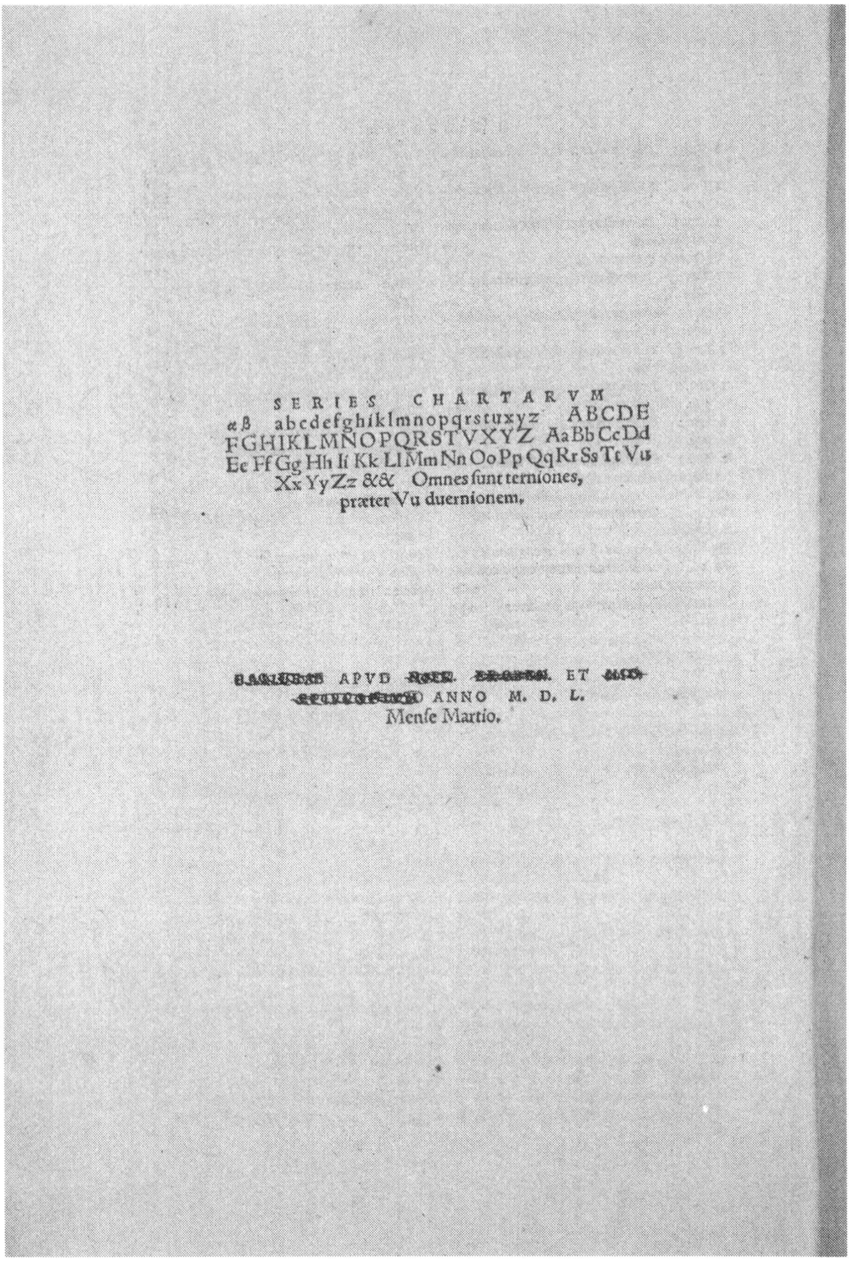

SERIES   CHARTARVM
αβ abcdefghiklmnopqrstuxyz ABCDE
FGHIKLMNOPQRSTVXYZ AaBbCcDd
Ee Ff Gg Hh Ii Kk Ll Mm Nn Oo Pp Qq Rr Ss Tt Vu
Xx Yy Zz &&   Omnes sunt terniones,
præter Vu duernionem.

~~BASILEAE~~ APVD ~~HAER.~~ ~~BROSENI.~~ ET ~~NIC.~~
~~EPISCOPIUM~~ ANNO M. D. L.
Mense Martio.

FIGURE 8.5   Colophon Hilarius of Poitiers, *Lucubrationes quotquot extant* (Basel: Froben & Episcopius, 1550). Uppsala University Library, shelf mark: UUB Teol. Patres, ensk. lat. fol. (36.103)

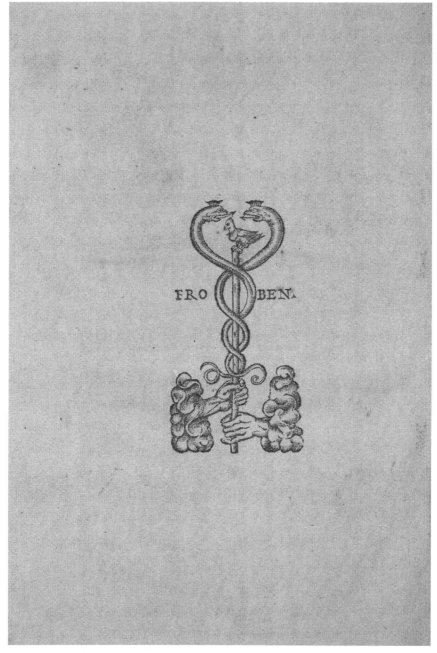

FIGURE 8.6 Last page in: Hilarius of Poitiers, *Lucubrationes quotquot extant* (Basel: Froben & Episcopius, 1550). Uppsala University Library, shelf mark: UUB Teol. Patres, ensk. lat. fol. (36.103)

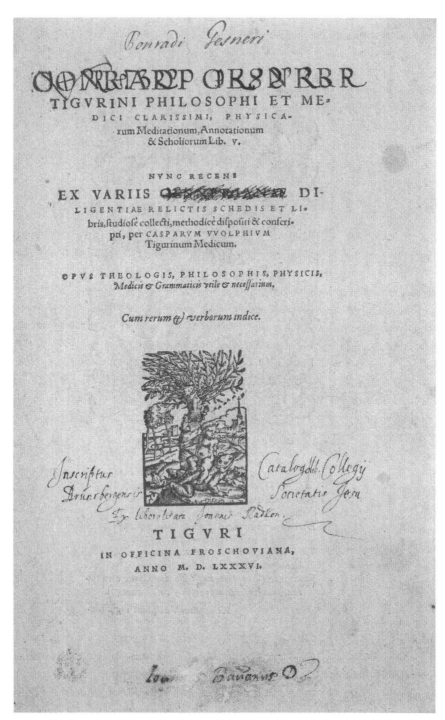

FIGURE 8.7   Title page in: Conrad Gesner, *Physicarum meditationum, annotationum et scholiorum lib. v* (Zurich: Froshauer, 1586). Uppsala University Library, shelf mark: UUB Obr. Qq.81

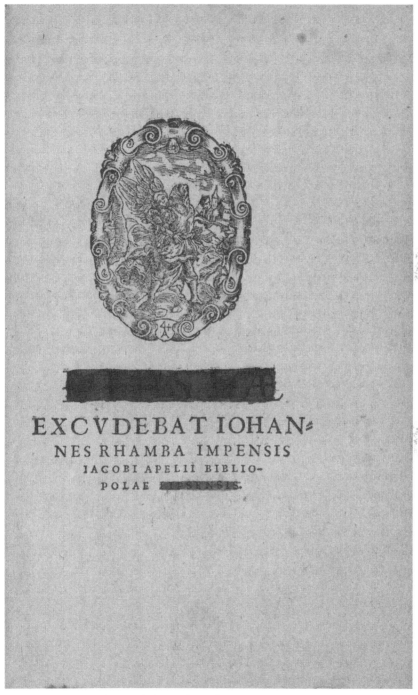

FIGURE 8.8   Colophon in: Philipp Melanchthon, *Ciceronis epistolas, quae familiares vocantur, argumenta* (Leipzig: Rambau & Apel, 1563–1565). Uppsala University Library, shelf mark: UUB Script. Lat. [Cicero] 395: 1–3 (x.368–370)

In a book containing the dialectics of Petrus Ramus (1515–1572), previously owned by Andrzej Frycz Modrzewski (ca. 1503–1572) and the Polish Bishop Stanisław Karnkowski (1520–1603), only a simple stroke in the author's name is applied, leaving it symbolically erased but still easily legible for everyone.[32]

In volumes from the Jesuit college of Poznań containing the works of Chrysostomos printed by Froben in Basel 1530, there are no expurgations at all in the second volume. In the fourth, however, both printing place and printer have been crossed out, in the imprint, in the printer's device, in the colophon and on the page following it, while in the fifth volume, the printer and printing place have been erased in the imprint but are left untouched in the printer's device on the title page. In the colophon, nothing has been changed.[33]

The books from Poznań at Uppsala have yet to be fully catalogued in a way that allows detailed research on provenance.[34] Of the books that have been catalogued thus far, however, a rough estimation suggests that there are approximately 5% books with Protestant authors or editors in this collection. Physical interventions of the same inconsistent kind can seemingly be found to a similar degree as in the books from Braniewo. The names of the authors that have been expurgated in at least one copy observed from these three Jesuit colleges at Uppsala include Wolfgang Anemoecius, Hartmann Beyer, Théodore de Bèze, Johann Bugenhagen, Joachim Camerarius, Euricius Cordus, Thomas Erastus, Valentin Erytraeus, Erasmus of Rotterdam, Georg Fabricius, Johannes Thomas Freig, Conrad Gesner, Rudolph Goclenius, Matija Grbic, Rudolf Gwalther, Ulrich van Hutten, Melchior Junius, Bartholomaeus Keckermann, Heinrich Knaust, Reinhard Lorich, Conrad Lycosthenes, Philipp Melanchthon, Jacob Micyllus, Andreas Misenus, Sebastian Münster, Wolfgang Musculus, Michael Neander, Johannes Oecolampadius, Willibald Pirckheimer, Georgius Pletho, Petrus Ramus, Stefan Reich, Erasmus Sarcerius, Jacob Spiegel, Johannes Sturm and Jodocus Willich.

Many of the above are well-known Protestant characters, and Erasmus of Rotterdam, Philipp Melanchthon and Johann Sturm certainly receive the most deletions. The title Elector of Saxony, as well as the names of some other Protestant princes, have also sometimes been deleted, especially when addressed as dedicatees, as has the phrase *piae memoriae* (in fact, the very opposite of *damnatae memoriae*) twice when it refers to deceased Reformers. The latter supports the idea that the memory of these persons is at stake.

---

32   Petrus Ramus, *Institutionum dialecticarum libri III* (Paris: Roigny & David, 1549), USTC 150352, title page. Shelf mark: UUB Bokband, 1500-t. Nederländerna 3.

33   These three volumes are the only ones still extant. Johannes Chrysostomos, *Opera* (Basel: Froben & Episcopius, 1530), USTC 626163, II. IV. V. title pages and colophons. Shelf mark: Teol. patres, ensk. grek. fol. (58.46–48).

34   A project to catalogue the books from Poznań is ongoing, see footnote 2.

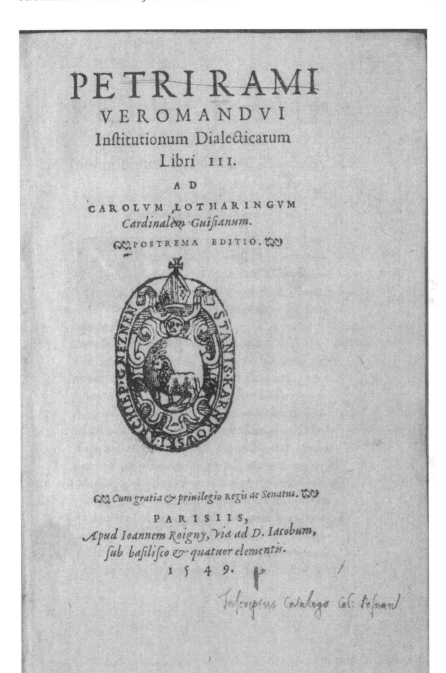

FIGURE 8.9   Title page in: Petrus Ramus, *Institutionum dialecticarum libri III* (Paris: Roigny & David, 1549). Uppsala University Library, shelf mark: UUB Bokband, 1500-t. Nederländerna 3

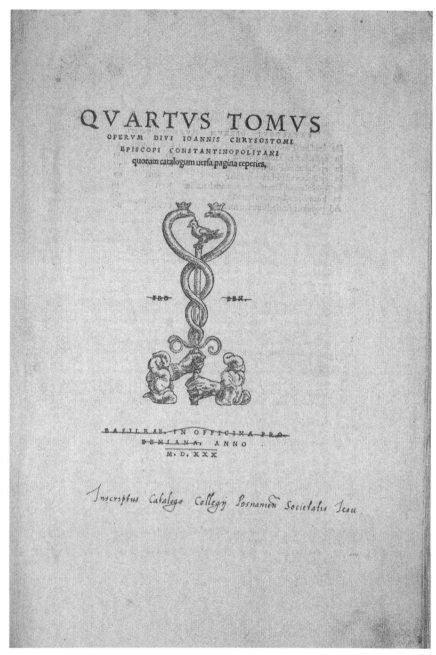

FIGURE 8.10   Johannes Chrysostomos, *Opera* (Basel: Froben & Episcopius, 1530). Uppsala University Library, shelf mark: Teol. patres, ensk. grek. fol. (58.46–48)

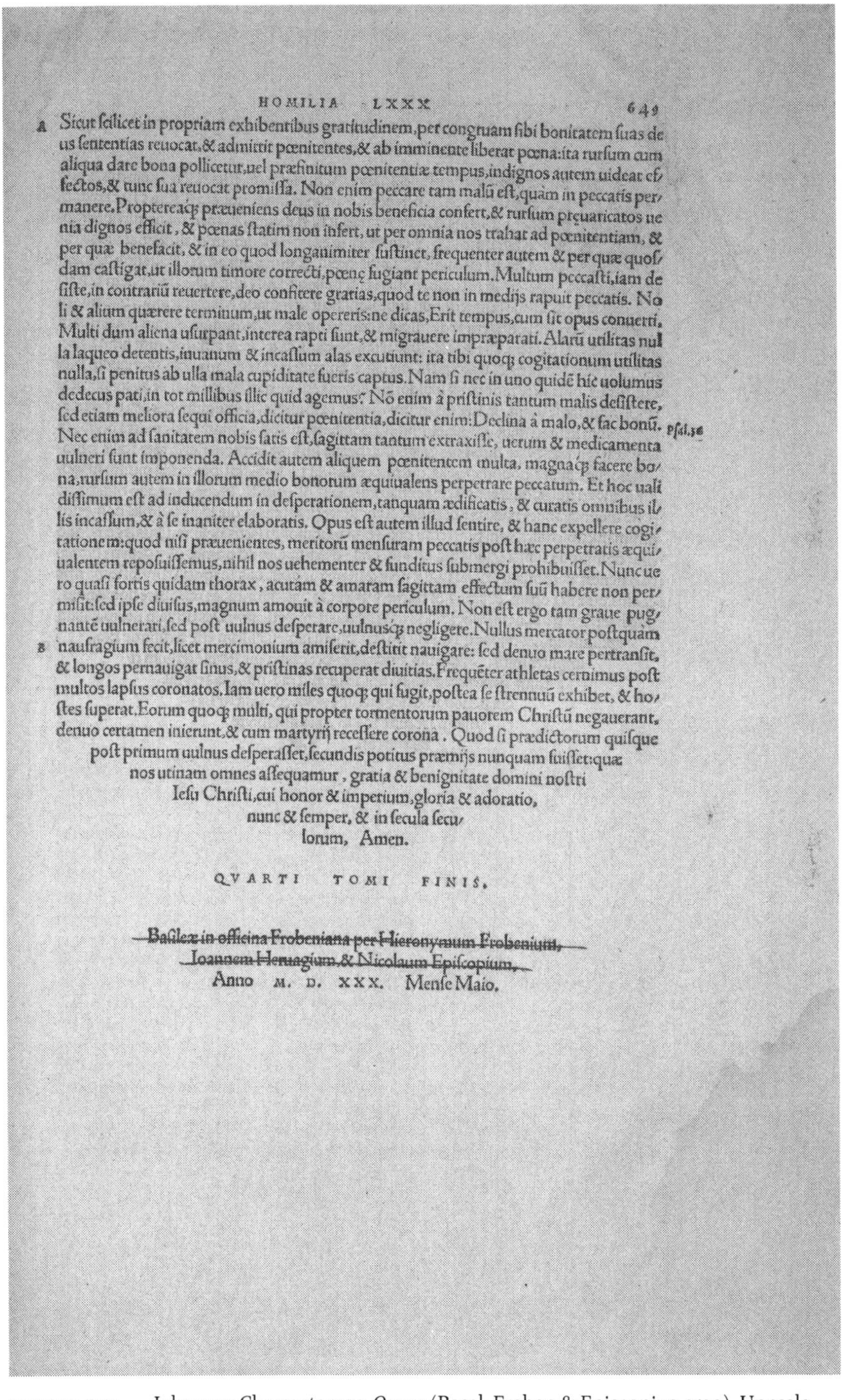
HOMILIA LXXX 649

A Sicut scilicet in propriam exhibentibus gratitudinem, per congruam sibi bonitatem suas de
us sententias reuocat, & admittit pœnitentes, & ab imminente liberat pœna: ita rursum cum
aliqua dare bona pollicetur, uel præfinitum pœnitentiæ tempus, indignos autem uideat ef-
fectos, & tunc sua reuocat promissa. Non enim peccare tam malũ est, quàm in peccatis per-
manere. Proptereaq; præueniens deus in nobis beneficia confert, & rursum prçuaricatos ue
nia dignos efficit, & pœnas statim non infert, ut per omnia nos trahat ad pœnitentiam, &
per quæ benefacit, & in eo quod longanimiter sustinet, frequenter autem & per quæ quos-
dam castigat, ut illorum timore correcti, pœnę fugiant periculum. Multum peccasti, iam de
siste, in contrariũ reuertere, deo confitere gratias, quod te non in medijs rapuit peccatis. No
li & alium quærere terminum, ut male opereris: ne dicas, Erit tempus, cum sit opus conuerti.
Multi dum aliena usurpant, interea rapti sunt, & migrauere impræparati. Alarũ utilitas nul
la laqueo detentis, inuanum & incassum alas excutiunt: ita tibi quoq; cogitationum utilitas
nulla, si penitus ab ulla mala cupiditate fueris captus. Nam si nec in uno quidẽ hic uolumus
dedecus pati, in tot millibus illic quid agemus? Nõ enim à pristinis tantum malis desistere,
sed etiam meliora sequi officia, dicitur pœnitentia, dicitur enim: Declina à malo, & fac bonũ. Psal. 36
Nec enim ad sanitatem nobis satis est, sagittam tantum extraxisse, uerum & medicamenta
uulneri sunt imponenda. Accidit autem aliquem pœnitentem multa, magnaq; facere bona, rursum autem in illorum medio bonorum æquiualens perpetrare peccatum. Et hoc uali
dissimum est ad inducendum in desperationem, tanquam ædificatis, & curatis omnibus illis incassum, & à se inaniter elaboratis. Opus est autem illud sentire, & hanc expellere cogitationem: quod nisi præuenientes, meritorũ mensuram peccatis post hæc perpetratis æqui-
ualentem reposuissemus, nihil nos uehementer & funditus submergi prohibuisset. Nunc ue
ro quasi fortis quidam thorax, acutam & amaram sagittam effectum suũ habere non per-
misit: sed ipse diuisus, magnum amouit à corpore periculum. Non est ergo tam graue pug-
nantẽ uulnerari, sed post uulnus desperare, uulnusq; negligere. Nullus mercator postquam
B naufragium fecit, licet mercimonium amiserit, destitit nauigare: sed denuo mare pertransit,
& longos pernauigat sinus, & pristinas recuperat diuitias. Frequẽter athletas cernimus post
multos lapsus coronatos. Iam uero miles quoq; qui fugit, postea se strennuũ exhibet, & hostes superat. Eorum quoq; multi, qui propter tormentorum pauorem Christũ negauerant,
denuo certamen inierunt, & cum martyrij recessere corona. Quod si prædictorum quisque
post primum uulnus desperasset, secundis potitus præmijs nunquam fuisset: quæ
nos utinam omnes assequamur, gratia & benignitate domini nostri
Iesu Christi, cui honor & imperium, gloria & adoratio,
nunc & semper, & in secula secu-
lorum, Amen.

QVARTI TOMI FINIS.

~~Basileæ in officina Frobeniana per Hieronymum Frobenium,~~
~~Ioannem Heruagium & Nicolaum Episcopium,~~
Anno M. D. XXX. Mense Maio.

FIGURE 8.11 Johannes Chrysostomos, *Opera* (Basel: Froben & Episcopius, 1530). Uppsala University Library, shelf mark: Teol. patres, ensk. grek. fol. (58.47–48)

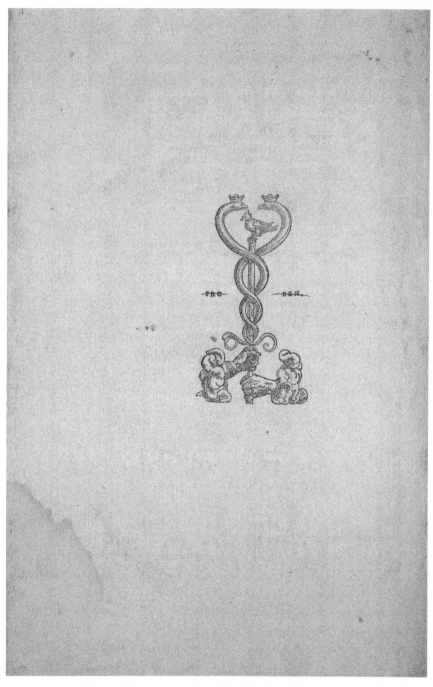

FIGURE 8.12 Johannes Chrysostomos, *Opera* (Basel: Froben & Episcopius, 1530). Uppsala University Library, shelf mark: Teol. patres, ensk. grek. fol. (58.47–48)

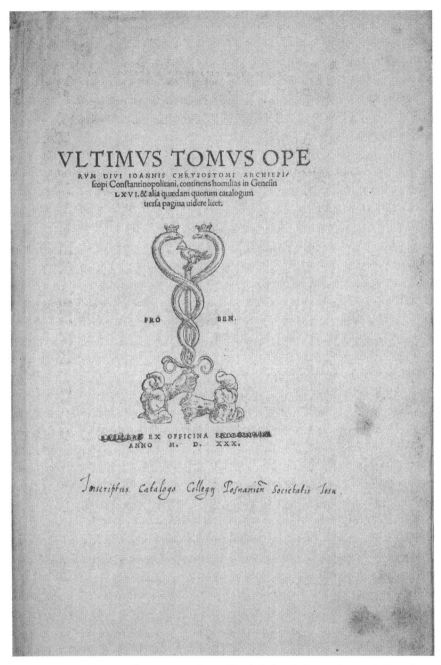

FIGURE 8.13   Johannes Chrysostomos, *Opera* (Basel: Froben & Episcopius, 1530). Uppsala University Library, shelf mark: Teol. patres, ensk. grek. fol. (58.47–48)

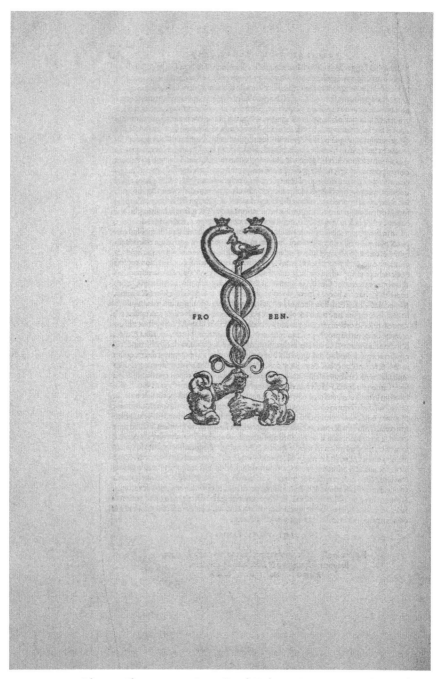

FIGURE 8.14   Johannes Chrysostomos, *Opera* (Basel: Froben & Episcopius, 1530). Uppsala University Library, shelf mark: Teol. patres, ensk. grek. fol. (58.47–48)

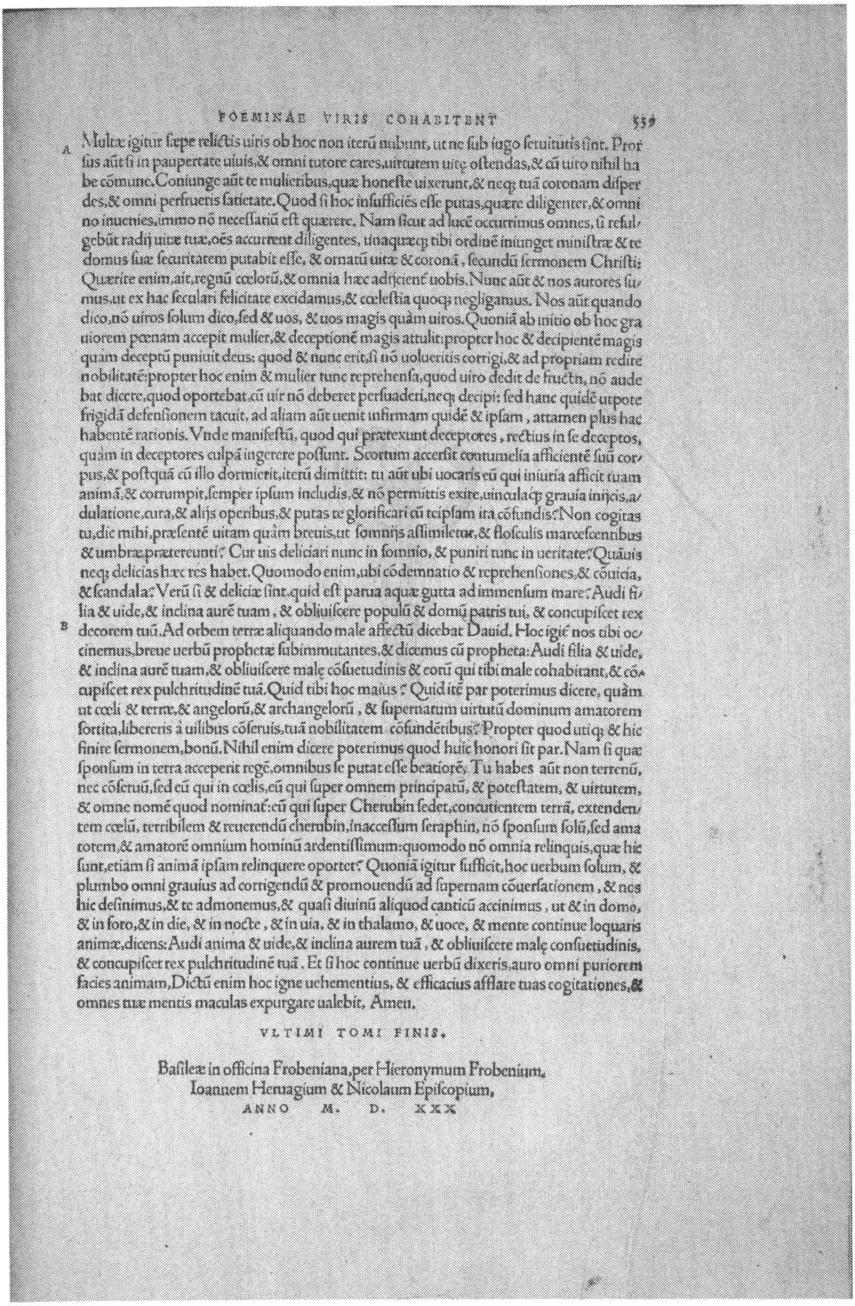
FOEMINAE VIRIS COHABITENT 559

A Multæ igitur sæpe relictis uiris ob hoc non iterũ nubunt, ut ne sub iugo seruitutis sint. Prorsus aũt si in paupertate uiuis,& omni tutore cares,uirtutem uitę ostendas,& cũ uiro nihil habe cõmune.Coniunge aũt te mulieribus,quæ honeste uixerunt,& neq; tuã coronam disperdes,& omni perfrueris satietate.Quod si hoc insufficiẽs esse putas,quære diligenter,& omnino inuenies,immo nõ necessariũ est quærere. Nam sicut ad lucẽ occurrimus omnes, si refulgebũt radij uitæ tuæ,oẽs accurrent diligentes, unaquæq; tibi ordinẽ iniunget ministræ & te domus suæ securitatem putabit esse, & ornatũ uitæ & coronã , secundũ sermonem Christi: Quærite enim,ait,regnũ cœlorũ,& omnia hæc adijcient̃ uobis.Nunc aũt & nos autores sumus,ut ex hac seculari felicitate excidamus,& cœlestia quoq; negligamus. Nos aũt quando dico,nõ uiros solum dico,sed & uos, & uos magis quàm uiros.Quoniã ab initio ob hoc grauiorem pœnam accepit mulier,& deceptionẽ magis attulit;propter hoc & decipientẽ magis quàm deceptũ puniuit deus: quod & nunc erit,si nõ uolueritis corrigi,& ad propriam redire nobilitatẽ:propter hoc enim & mulier tunc reprehensa,quod uiro dedit de fructu, nõ audebat dicere,quod oportebat,cũ uir nõ deberet persuaderi,neq; decipi: sed hanc quidẽ utpote frigidã defensionem tacuit, ad aliam aũt uenit infirmam quidẽ & ipsam , attamen plus habentẽ rationis. Vnde manifestũ, quod qui prætexunt deceptores , rectius in se deceptos, quàm in deceptores culpã ingerere possunt. Scortum accersit contumelia afficientẽ suũ corpus,& postquã cũ illo dormierit,iterũ dimittit: tu aũt ubi uocaris eũ qui iniuria afficit tuam animã,& corrumpit,semper ipsum includis,& nõ permittis exire,uinculaq; grauia inijcis,adulatione,cura,& alijs operibus,& putas te glorificari cũ teipsam ita cõfundis? Non cogitas tu,dic mihi,præsentẽ uitam quàm breuis,ut somnijs assimiletur,& flosculis marcescentibus & umbræ prætereunti? Cur uis deliciari nunc in somnio, & puniri tunc in ueritate? Quãuis neq; delicias hæc res habet.Quomodo enim,ubi cõdemnatio & reprehensiones,& cõuicia, & scandala? Verũ si & deliciæ sint,quid est parua aquæ gutta ad immensum mare? Audi filia & uide,& inclina aurẽ tuam , & obliuiscere populũ & domũ patris tui, & concupiscet rex
B decorem tuũ.Ad orbem terræ aliquando male affectũ dicebat Dauid. Hoc igit̃ nos tibi occinemus,breue uerbũ prophetæ subimmutantes,& dicemus cũ propheta: Audi filia & uide, & inclina aurẽ tuam,& obliuiscere malę cõsuetudinis & eorũ qui tibi male cohabitant,& cõcupiscet rex pulchritudinẽ tuã.Quid tibi hoc maius ? Quid itẽ par poterimus dicere, quàm ut cœli & terræ,& angelorũ,& archangelorũ , & supernatum uirtutũ dominum amatorem sortita,libereris à uilibus cõseruis,tuã nobilitatem cõfundẽtibus? Propter quod utiq; & hic finire sermonem,bonũ.Nihil enim dicere poterimus quod huic honori sit par.Nam si quæ sponsum in terra acceperit regẽ,omnibus se putat esse beatiorẽ. Tu habes aũt non terrenũ, nec cõseruũ,sed eũ qui in cœlis,eũ qui super omnem principatũ, & potestatem, & uirtutem, & omne nomẽ quod nominat̃:eũ qui super Cherubin sedet,concutientem terrã, extendentem cœlũ, terribilem & reuerendũ cherubin,inaccessum seraphin, nõ sponsum solũ,sed amatorem,& amatorẽ omnium hominũ ardentissimum:quomodo nõ omnia relinquis,quæ hic sunt,etiam si animã ipsam relinquere oportet? Quoniã igitur sufficit,hoc uerbum solum, & plumbo omni grauius ad corrigendũ & promouendũ ad supernam cõuersationem , & nos hic desinimus,& te admonemus,& quasi diuinũ aliquod canticũ accinimus , ut & in domo, & in foro,& in die, & in nocte , & in uia, & in thalamo, & uoce, & mente continue loquaris animæ,dicens: Audi anima & uide,& inclina aurem tuã , & obliuiscere malę consuetudinis, & concupiscet rex pulchritudinẽ tuã . Et si hoc continue uerbũ dixeris,auro omni puriorem facies animam,Dictũ enim hoc igne uehementius, & efficacius afflare tuas cogitationes,& omnes tuæ mentis maculas expurgare ualebit, Amen.

VLTIMI TOMI FINIS.

Basileæ in officina Frobeniana,per Hieronymum Frobenium,
Ioannem Heruagium & Nicolaum Episcopium,
ANNO M. D. XXX

FIGURE 8.15 Johannes Chrysostomos, *Opera* (Basel: Froben & Episcopius, 1530). Uppsala University Library, shelf mark: Teol. patres, ensk. grek. fol. (58.47–48)

Worth noticing, however, is that several of these names, including Rudolph Goclenius, Melchior Junius and Bartholomaeus Keckermann, are not listed in any sixteenth-century *Index*.[35] In those cases, the owner of the book has followed the principle of the *Index* but made the decision to expurgate.

The erased printing places and printers are mostly well-known Protestant strongholds and publishers. Printing places include Basel, Gdańsk, Frankfurt an der Oder, Frankfurt am Main, Görlitz, Hannover, Leipzig, Marburg, Mühlhausen, Strasbourg, Tübingen, Wittenberg and Zürich. Among the printers are Antonius, Apel, Bryling, Egenolph, Episcopius, Faber, Fritsch, Froben, Froschauer, Gronenberg, Hantzsch, Herwagen, Jobin, Oporinus, Perna, Petri, Rambau, Rihel, Steinmann, Vögelin and Wyssenbach. Among the printing places, neither Gdańsk nor Mühlhausen are represented in any sixteenth-century *Index*.[36] Among the printers, neither Antonius nor Apel nor Gronenberg can be found.[37] Moreover, when looking at the subjects of the books where expurgations have been found, it is striking but reasonable that the number of theological books and Bibles is rather small: Subjects are Bibles (III), Bible commentaries, church fathers (VI), classical authors (XIV), classical commentaries (III), grammar (vi), law, mathematics, medicine (II), pedagogy, philosophy (iii), prayers, physics (iv), poetics (iv), proverbs (iv) and rhetoric (x).

As it appears, erasing names was often practiced in books used in teaching and in fields other than theology. In addition, the expurgations have often been made in privately owned copies, which happened to end up in an institutional library. Books by Protestants on secular subjects were, of course, generally more useful at Jesuit institutions than those on theological subjects. The pedagogical achievements of Protestant characters like Philipp Melanchthon and David Chytraeus also made their publications attractive in practice in Catholic contexts, although the authors were placed in the first class of the *Index*.[38]

Interesting as these instances of expurgated names are and the reasons and purposes worth pondering upon, there are also cases where we find a deletion of parts of the text. We find striking examples of deletion in the Jesuit collections at Uppsala, although these tend to be the exception to the rule. For example, a copy of the *Scholae in liberales artes* from 1569 by Petrus Ramus, whose *Opera omnia was* forbidden in the *Index*, although this very edition was not listed there.[39] On the title page, the author's name has been deleted, the printing place distorted and the printer left intact. At the end of the preface,

---

35   Bujanda, *Index des livres interdits*, pp. 49–418.
36   Ibid., pp. 35–39.
37   Ibid., pp. 753–789.
38   Cf. Marcus, *Forbidden Knowledge*, p. 32.
39   Bujanda, *Index des livres interdits*, p. 332.

FIGURE 8.16 Title page in: Petrus Ramus, *Scholae in liberales artes* (Basel: Episcopius, 1569). Uppsala University Library, shelf mark: UUB Script. Lat. rec. fol. (29.96)

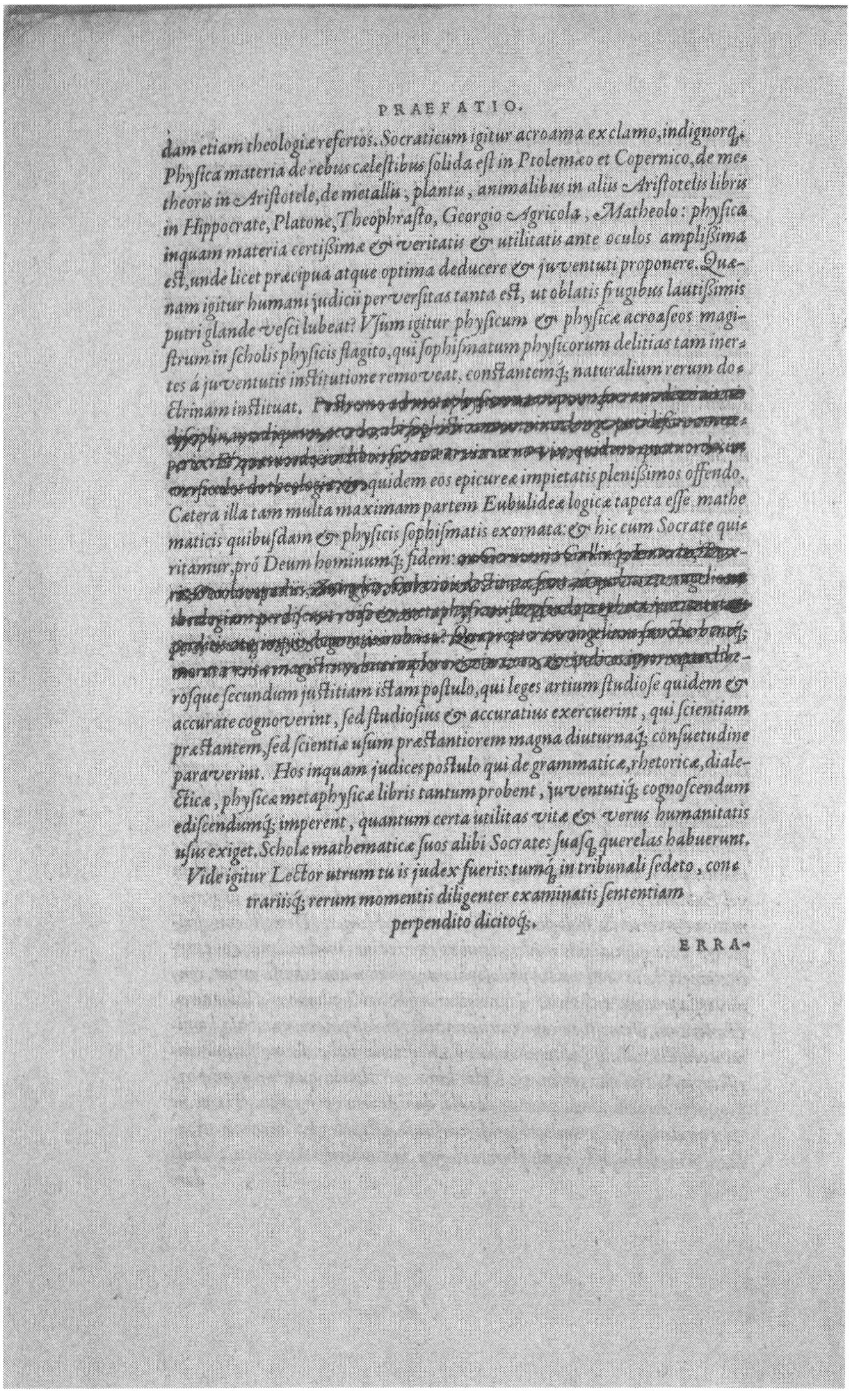

PRAEFATIO.

dam etiam theologiæ refertos. Socraticum igitur acroama exclamo, indignorq; Physica materia de rebus cælestibus solida est in Ptolemæo et Copernico, de mes theoris in Aristotele, de metallis, plantis, animalibus in aliis Aristotelis libris in Hippocrate, Platone, Theophrasto, Georgio Agricola, Matheolo: physica inquam materia certissima & veritatis & utilitatis ante oculos amplissima est, unde licet præcipua atque optima deducere & juventuti proponere. Quænam igitur humani judicii perversitas tanta est, ut oblatis frugibus lautissimis putri glande vesci lubeat? Vsum igitur physicum & physicæ acroaseos magistrum in scholis physicis flagito, qui sophismatum physicorum delitias tam inertes à juventutis institutione removeat, constantemq; naturalium rerum doctrinam instituat. ~~..~~
~~..~~
~~..~~
~~............................~~ quidem eos epicureæ impietatis plenissimos offendo. Cætera illa tam multa maximam partem Eubulideæ logicæ tapeta esse mathematicis quibusdam & physicis sophismatis exornata: & hic cum Socrate quiritamur, pró Deum hominumq; fidem: ~~..~~
~~..~~
~~..~~
~~..~~
~~..~~ liberosque secundum justitiam istam postulo, qui leges artium studiose quidem & accurate cognoverint, sed studiosius & accuratius exercuerint, qui scientiam præstantem, sed scientiæ usum præstantiorem magna diuturnaq; consuetudine paraverint. Hos inquam judices postulo qui de grammaticæ, rhetoricæ, dialecticæ, physicæ metaphysicæ libris tantum probent, juventutiq; cognoscendum edicendumq; imperent, quantum certa utilitas vitæ & verus humanitatis usus exiget. Scholæ mathematicæ suos alibi Socrates suasq; querelas habuerunt. Vide igitur Lector utrum tu is judex fueris: tumq; in tribunali sedeto, contrariisq; rerum momentis diligenter examinatis sententiam perpendito dicitoq;.

ERRA-

FIGURE 8.17   Preface (p. α3v) in: Petrus Ramus, *Scholae in liberales artes* (Basel: Episcopius, 1569). Uppsala University Library, shelf mark: UUB Script. Lat. rec. fol. (29.96)

two passages have been erased in ink. Since the book has no known previous owner before the Jesuit college of Braniewo, it is possible that the expurgation has been made there, but we cannot say whether it was made by a user of the book or by anyone working for the college.[40]

One of the paradoxes of censorship is that both contemporary and modern readers are likely more interested in what has been deleted than in what has not.[41] The preface here is typical of Ramism and stresses the importance of utility in teaching; the author accordingly ridicules the status of Aristotle in the schools of the time and wants to take side with Socrates when revealing the absurdities of the sophists, which here refer to the scholastic Aristotelians. However, some statements are simply too provocative. Just as Renaissance readers often read with a pen in hand in order to write down memorable passages of all kinds to keep in commonplace books, the pious user of the books could now eliminate those that were heretical with their pens.[42] The first deleted lines thus read:

> Postremo ad metaphysicam tamquam sacram divinitatis disciplinam aliquam accedo, ubi sophisticam omnium longe putidissimam reperio. E quatuordecim libris [Aristotelis] sic antea vix ac ne vix quidem quatuordecim versiculos de theologia [quidem eos Epicureae impietatis plenissimos offendo].[43]

Some intact lines follow, and the author states that the rest of the books are mostly adorned with mathematical and physical sophisms. Then, there is a new passage with deleted lines:

> [hic cum Socrate quiritamur ...] an Germania Galliaque Luteris, Buceris, Oecolampadiis, Zuingliis, Calvinis destitutae sunt, a quibus evangelicam theologiam perdiscant, nisi et metaphysicus iste pseudopropheta juventutem perditis atque impiis dogmatis imbuat? Quapropter evangelium

---

40   Petrus Ramus, *Scholae in liberales artes* (Basel: Episcopius, 1569), USTC 681989, title page and preface (f. α3v). Shelf mark: UUB Script. Lat. rec. fol. (29.96).
41   See Marcus, *Forbidden Knowledge*, p. 183. An *Index expurgatorius* could thus in practice also serve as a kind of commonplace book and guide to works that were especially desirable to collect and preserve, as stressed by Thomas James in a preface of 1627 addressed to the curators of the Bodleian Library. Putnam, *Censorship of the Church of Rome*, I. 12–13.
42   Marcus, *Forbidden Knowledge*, pp. 93–95.
43   'Thereafter I approach metaphysics, as some kind of sacred discipline belonging to divinity, where I find that the sophistic one is the far most rotten of all. From the fourteen books [of Aristotle] as mentioned before I hardly, and not even hardly, come upon fourteen lines regarding theology, [and these are indeed full of Epicurean impiety]', Petrus Ramus, *Scholae in liberales artes*, f. α3v. All translations are my own.

sanctae beneque moratae vitae magistrum huc imploro et invoco, et judices incorruptos libe – [rosque ... postulo].⁴⁴

What we see is a violent attack on the metaphysics of Aristotle (*metaphysicus iste pseudopropheta*), and indirectly at Aristotelian scholasticism, which someone has wanted either to save other users of the book from seeing or to state pious disapproval on his behalf and for himself.⁴⁵

Another example of expurgation concerns the New Testament of Erasmus, printed in Basel in 1570.⁴⁶ On the title page, Erasmus's name has been erased and the printer and the printing place have been distorted in ink. Further deletions have been made in the texts explaining the arguments of the different Bible books. In the letter to the Romans, for instance, three different sections have been erased on the first page, in addition to Erasmus's name in the page heading, while the following three leaves have been cut out.⁴⁷

Someone, probably the Kasper Ilmanowski, who inscribed the copy saying he had bought the book in Krakow 1577, disagreed with how Erasmus describes and criticises Jerome's treatment of Paul's double name, Paulus and Saulus, as inconsistent.

> Sed alteram opinionem minus probabilem facit, quod Lucas hoc ipso, quod modo citavimus, capite scribit, Saulus, qui et Paulus, repletus Spiritu sancto, haud obscure declarans eum binominem fuisse, priusquam Sergius a Paulo esset conversus. Alteram plane refellit, quod cum aliis aliquot locis, tum in eodem capite Saulus dicitur iam Christi praedicans Evangelium ... Proinde mihi vero propior [videtur Origenis opinio] ... Quod tamen Hieronymus cum alicubi in aliis reprehendat, hic sibi permittit, opinor, ut in re non admodum seria.⁴⁸

---

44 '[Here we really wonder with Socrates ...] if Germany and France are abandoned by the Lutherans, Bucerians, Oecolampadians, Zuinglians and Calvinians, from whom they learn evangelical theology, if not this metaphysical pseudoprophet too would infect the youth with perverse and impious dogmas. For this reason, I implore and invoke the gospel as the master of a holy and well-mannered life, and [I call for] incorrupt and free judges', ibid.

45 Criticism on the Aristotelian tradition, including the scholars that were still adhering to it, was of course innate to Ramism. For some more examples, see e.g. Hans Helander, *Neo-Latin Literature in Sweden in the Period 1620–1720. Stylistics, Vocabulary and Characteristic Ideas* (Uppsala: Acta Universitatis Upsaliensis, 2004), pp. 445–447, with further references.

46 For an overview of Erasmus in the *Index*, see Putnam, *Censorship of the Church of Rome*, I. 328–340.

47 *Novum Testamentum Graece et Latine*, ed. Erasmus of Rotterdam (Leipzig: Vögelin & Schneider, 1570), USTC 678679, pp. 452, 453–458. Shelf mark: UUB Bib. grek. N.T. (55.69).

48 'But the second opinion he considers less probable, since Lucas in this very chapter, which we recently quoted, writes: Saul, who is also called Paul, was filled with the Holy Spirit,

FIGURE 8.18 P. 452 in: *Novum testamentum Graece et Latine*, ed. Erasmus of Rotterdam (Leipzig: Vögelin & Schneider, 1570). Uppsala University Library, shelf mark: UUB Bib. grek. N.T. (55.69)

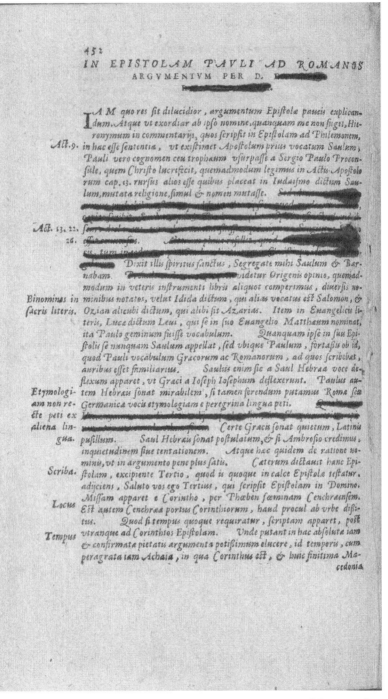

FIGURE 8.19   Pp. 453–458 in: *Novum testamentum Graece et Latine*, ed. Erasmus of Rotterdam (Leipzig: Vögelin & Schneider, 1570). Uppsala University Library, shelf mark: UUB Bib. grek. N.T. (55.69)

It is worth stressing here that this book was completely forbidden, according to the *Index*. This is a translation of the New Testament made by an author of the first class, which would be of little use but of great danger to readers.[49] It has been expurgated in the passage demonstrating the inconsistency of St Jerome and kept nevertheless.

The last example also concerns an edition of Erasmus's New Testament. The edition from 1531 had a preface written by Erasmus's fellow in Basel, Johannes Oecolampadius.[50] In the copy that came to Uppsala from Poznań, the leaves containing this preface have been cut out from the book, while the names of the printing place and printer have been deleted with ink in the imprint. The body of the book containing the Greek text, however, is still there. We do not know, in this case, the names of any previous owners, if there were any. It has already been mentioned that prefaces were removed from some of the copies in the Riga Jesuit College Library and other examples can be found in volumes from Poznań.[51] But in this case, a preface by an author in the first class of the *Index* has been removed in a book edited by an author in the first class of the *Index*.

4   Censorship in Practice and the Concept of Damnatio Memoriae

What is observed, then, with these books, where particular leaves have been completely removed, perhaps at the Jesuit college, is the censorship of offensive heretical content. Entire sections have been taken away to make sure no readers have access to them. In examples where single sentences or parts of a text have been deleted in ink, expurgations of the most offensive expressions and statements are observed. The aim was to make it possible to continue using the books, even though they were listed in the *Index*.

In the first examples, however, concerning the inconsistent expurgation of names and places in titles and imprints, we cannot say that we meet instances of *damnatio memoriae*. The deletions are simply too rare in cases where we

---

clearly stating that he had two names, before Sergius had been converted by Paul. He refutes the second completely, since Saul is told already to be preaching Christ's Gospel both in some other instances and in the same chapter. ... Hence, Origen's opinion seems more appropriate to me. ... But while Jerome reproaches this in others in other places, he allows himself to do so here, I think, although in a case that is not too serious', ibid.

49   *Index librorum prohibitorum* (Cologne: Cholinus, 1576), USTC 665526, f. A6v.
50   Shelfmark: UUB Bib. grek. N.T. (55.91).
51   See e.g. shelfmark: Teol. patres, ensk. grek. fol. (59.29), with Wolfgang Musculus's edition of Gregory of Nazianzus, *Opera, quae quidem extant, omnia, tam soluta quàm pedestri oratione conscripta* (Basel: Herwagen, 1550), USTC 640596.

would have expected them to be, and the consistency and quality of deletions (often very easy to see through) begs the question of whether deletion was really intended. If a *damnatio memoriae* is, in theory, what the *Index* officially proclaims concerning forbidden authors, sometimes even explicitly in its title, this practice looks quite different. Contrary to how the concept has been used in previous research, seemingly trying to understand and reconcile the term *damnatio memoriae* in theory with the many inconsistencies that she, too, has noticed in the practice of these expurgations, Hannah Marcus suggests that oblivion was actually *not* what a *damnatio memoriae* wanted to achieve in cases like these, but rather the opposite. The condemned authors should stay in memory, she claims, but as dishonoured heretics. Thus, the names had to be both deleted and undeleted, that is, punished and remembered at the same time.[52]

But here it is impossible to follow her. Although the Latin term *damnatio memoriae* can, in principle, also mean 'damnation to memory' (*memoriae* as a forensic genitive, referring to the punishment) instead of 'damnation of memory' (*memoriae* as an objective genitive, referring to what is condemned), as Marcus writes, it is only the latter translation that is possible when dealing with *damnatio memoriae* and expurgation. Oblivion is punishment, not memory. In all five early modern examples that Marcus reports on when discussing the matter, the words used are [*auctor*] *damnatae memoriae* ('[an author] of a condemned memory'), and this phrase cannot be translated in two ways.[53] It is memory that is condemned, for the forensic genitive would have needed [*auctor*] *damnatus memoriae* ('[an author] condemned to memory').[54] Another argument against Marcus, in addition to the linguistic one, concerning what an expurgatory *damnatio memoriae* intended to achieve, we find in the explicit

---

52 'Unlike prohibited content removed from the books, the removal of authors' names and infliction of *damnatio memoriae* was not intended to teach readers to forget who wrote the books. Indeed, the damnation of memory (or damnation to memory; the Latin can be translated both ways) was intended to recall the errors of Protestants and to repeatedly and ritually dishonor them. ... In most cases, expurgation of the author's name represented this memorialisation of damnation. ... Instead of damning the memory of Protestant authors to be forgotten, the defacement of names, images and works instead reminded readers that these heretics and their works had been punished. ... Even though books by heretical authors were kept in Catholic libraries, they were retained only in their altered, punished states', Marcus, *Forbidden Knowledge*, pp. 194, 197.
53 Ibid., pp. 192–194.
54 As a point of reference, it should be noted that Schreiter (praes.)/Gerlach (resp.), *Dissertationem juridicam de damnatione memoriae* ... uses the concept of *damnatio memoriae* thirty-nine times in the text. Four of these have the gerundive genitive (*memoriae damnandae*) with a noun, but none has the forensic genitive.

statements on the matter in Juan Bautista Cardona's abovementioned treatise. We read there two of several instances stating a similar idea:

> Multo igitur minus haereticorum nomina, quorum memoria damnata etiam est, sunt conservanda in titulis et inscriptionibus librorum, sed potius omnino expungenda.

> Non congregabit Dominus conventicula impiorum, nec memor erit nominum eorum per labia sua. Hoc est, ad aeterna supplicia condemnabit, et memoriam eorum sempiterna oblivione obruet, ita ut ipsa nomina penitus ignorentur. Quemadmodum Catholici iustique viri memoria, bonorum sanctorumque nomen perpetuo celebratur; ita haeretici impiique hominis memoria damnanda est, et omnino extinguenda.[55]

The aim of a *damnatio memoriae* here is oblivion and that the names of heretics should be completely erased. Instead of saving the term in this context by understanding the Latin without historical support and against important authoritative voices from the time, we should try to find alternative explanations for the very inconsistent practice.[56] Moreover, Marcus claims that books by heretical authors were only kept in Catholic libraries if they were expurgated; however, as we have seen above, that is not true. Less than a third of the books by Protestant authors or editors still extant in the libraries from the Jesuit colleges of Riga, Braniewo and Poznań contained expurgations of some kind.[57] Seemingly, Marcus only took the books that were actually expurgated into account in her study, and this would severely limit its validity concerning post-publication censorship in practice.[58] Such an investigation must

---

[55] 'Much less the names of heretics, whose memory is even condemned, must thus be kept in the titles and headings of books, but they must rather be completely blotted out', Cardona, *De expungendis haereticorum propriis nominibus*, p. 17. 'The Lord will not gather assemblies with impious men, and he will not remember their names by his lips. That is, he will condemn them to eternal punishment, and he will bury their memories in everlasting oblivion, so that their very names are completely unknown. Just as the names of good men and saints are forever celebrated in the memory of a Catholic and righteous man, the memory of a heretic and impious man must be condemned and completely extinguished', ibid., p. 93.

[56] To her credit, Marcus suggests several of these herself. We will follow her line of thought at the end of this text.

[57] The same is the case with the Portuguese collection studied by Malta Romeiras. See footnote 14.

[58] Marcus, *Forbidden Knowledge*, p. 168. This is stated even clearer in Hannah Marcus, 'Expurgated Books as an Archive of Practice', *Archive Journal*, 2017, www.archivejournal

pay attention to all books in Catholic libraries that were forbidden in theory, i.e. also to those books that do not bear any signs of expurgation.[59]

5 Concluding Remarks

From the perspective of the Lutheran library at Uppsala, it could seem to be an irony of destiny, not only that so many books from the Catholic collections were of limited use at Uppsala but also that they were often there in several copies. Among the useful books in the looted collections were, of course, those by Protestant authors or editors. But when opening these, the users sometimes saw evident signs of the confessional conflict; that is, traces from previous owners taking confessional distance from those responsible for a book that they still considered worth owning and reading. It is important, then, to acknowledge that books by prohibited authors and with Evangelical content can still be found in Catholic libraries from Riga, Braniewo and Poznań, both with and without expurgations. In a third part of them, physical manipulations made it possible to use them in an environment other than the first intended. Or, in essence, in the words of William H. Sherman on how books in the Renaissance continuously survived when times changed:

> There are useful reminders of the fact that many books outlived the contexts for which they were originally produced, remaining meaningful and/or useful to readers who were willing to update them.[60]

One way for a Catholic reader to use a book by a forbidden author or with offensive ideas in the period of confessional conflict was by making a material statement against him in the book itself to adjust and update it for a new

---

.net/essays/expurgated-books-as-an-archive-of-practice (access: 17.04.2023): 'Examining expurgated books as normative sources about the practice of censorship, in essence, opens a new archive for the study of the control of books as intellectual and material objects'. However, expurgated books can only be sources for the study of expurgation. For a study on the practice of censorship, forbidden books without any signs of expurgation must be taken into account as well. In addition, this widening of the source material would make it easier to find relevant books in library catalogues, although the number of hits would surely increase. Only searching for expurgated books is often problematic today, since such details are usually lacking or inadequately described in catalogues.

59 Supporting a claim of diversity in the practice is the fact that there was not only one Catholic approach to science and learning at the time. See Michael Edwards, 'Intellectual Culture', in Alexandra Bamji etc. (eds.), *The Ashgate Research Companion*, p. 302.

60 Sherman, *Used Books*, p. 92.

context. This is, after all, the main purpose of expurgations. The complete *damnatio memoriae* was then, in practice, less necessary than signs of disapproval in an act that also served as self-definition. A simple material manipulation could enable scholars and students to consult useful books that were written by heretics and condemned in the *Index*, while at the same time stating their own confessional identity. However, we should not exaggerate. The impression is that the confession of the author mattered more to the ecclesiastical authorities than to the readers who were interested in science, teaching and recent discoveries, and to those who needed prohibited books by skilled and distinguished scholars of another confession for their professional work.[61] In fact, it seems to have mattered so little that more than two-thirds of the books were left completely without expurgations in the Jesuit college libraries of Riga, Braniewo and Poznań, although we know that in those cases the forbidden volumes were sometimes kept in separate rooms or shelves.

---

61   See Marcus, *Forbidden Knowledge*, pp. 50, 56–58, 66–68, 197.

CHAPTER 9

Book Collection of a Hinterland Convent in Response to the Lutheran Reformation

The Case of Mid-Sixteenth Century Rakvere (Wesenberg)

Kaspar Kolk

In the summer of 1522, the first evangelical preachers in medieval Livonia were recorded. This historical region roughly corresponds to today's Estonia and Latvia.[1] By 1525, Livonia's three major cities, Riga, Tallinn (Reval) and Tartu (Dorpat), decided to adopt Lutheranism.[2] In small towns and rural areas, the shift towards Protestantism took several decades. At least formally, the territorial rulers (i.e. the Livonian branch of the Teutonic Order and the prince-bishops) also remained Catholic until Livonia's medieval political structures collapsed due to attacks from Russian, Swedish and Polish-Lithuanian armies between 1558 and 1561. Outside the large cities and the courts of the rulers, which were the primary sources of documentary and narrative evidence, little is known about religious controversies and conflicts between the old and new faiths.

---

1   For the history of medieval Livonia (not to be confused with 'Livonias' of other periods), see e.g. Anti Selart, Matthias Thumser (eds.), *Livland – eine Region am Ende der Welt? Forschungen zum Verhältnis zwischen Zentrum und Peripherie im späten Mittelalter* (Cologne: Böhlau, 2017); Karsten Brüggemann etc. (eds.), *Das Baltikum. Geschichte einer europäischen Region*, vol. 1: *Von der Vor- und Frühgeschichte bis zum Ende des Mittelalters* (Stuttgart: Hiersemann, 2018); Anu Mänd, Marek Tamm (eds.), *Making Livonia. Actors and Networks in the Medieval and Early Modern Baltic Sea Region* (New York: Routledge, 2020). For the early history of the Reformation in Livonia, the most essential is still Leonid Arbusow, *Die Einführung der Reformation in Liv-, Est- und Kurland* (Leipzig: Heinsius, 1921), pp. 185–438; for more recent scholarship, see Juhan Kreem, 'Die Reformationszeit', in Karsten Brüggemann etc. (eds.), *Das Baltikum. Geschichte einer europäischen Region*, Band 1: *Von der Vor- und Frühgeschichte bis zum Ende des Mittelalters* (Stuttgart: Hiersemann, 2018), pp. 432–462, esp. 434–450; Sergiusz Michalski, 'Hölzer wurden zu Menschen. Die reformatorischen Bilderstürme in den baltischen Landen zwischen 1524 und 1526', in Matthias Asche etc. (eds.), *Die baltischen Lande im Zeitalter der Reformation und Konfessionalisierung: Livland, Estland, Ösel, Ingermanland, Kurland und Lettgallen. Stadt, Land und Konfession 1500–1721* (Münster: Aschendorff, 2012), IV. 147–162.
2   Place names are given according to current English usage; if different, the traditional German equivalents for places in the Baltics, which dominated earlier research literature, are added in brackets at first mention.

This study examines surviving books from the Franciscan friary in the small town of Rakvere (Wesenberg). This rare corpus provides a unique opportunity to explore religious and intellectual trends in a Catholic enclave within an increasingly Lutheran environment. The books offer a glimpse into how a monastic institution functioned in mid-sixteenth century Livonia. This study aims to analyse the remaining book holdings of the Rakvere convent from its beginnings in the early sixteenth century, particularly its developments in book acquisition immediately after the Lutheran Reformation during the second quarter of the sixteenth century. The research will contribute to a more comprehensive understanding of the religious aims pursued and the activities performed in a mendicant convent operating in prevailingly rural surroundings under the increasing pressure of Protestantism.

1 Rakvere: The Newest Mendicant Friary of Medieval Livonia

Two mendicant orders, the Dominicans and the Franciscans, arrived in medieval Livonia shortly after the region's conversion to Christianity. Dominican friaries were established in Riga (1234), Tallinn (1229?/1246) and Tartu (before 1300). Franciscans were first mentioned in Riga in 1238.[3] After a centuries-long standstill, the spread of Franciscan convents was revived by the Observant reform in the order. The convent of Riga was reformed in 1463, and between 1466 and 1500 five new houses of Observant Friars were established. The last Franciscan friary in medieval Livonia, the convent of Rakvere was founded between 1503 and 1508.[4] In the Franciscan province of Saxonia, the *custodia*

---

3 Gertrud von Walther-Wittenheim, *Die Dominikaner in Livland im Mittelalter. Die Natio Livoniae* (Rome: Istituto Storico Domenicano, 1938), pp. 7–13; Tiina Kala, *Jutlustajad ja hingede päästjad. Dominiiklaste ordu ja Tallinna Püha Katariina konvent* (Tallinn: Tallinna Ülikooli Kirjastus, 2013), pp. 70–79; Rafał Kubicki, 'Mendicant Orders in Medieval Prussia and Livonia. Pastoral Activities in Towns', *Acta Historica Universitatis Klaipedensis*, 33 (2016), pp. 123–146, p. 130; Kaur Alttoa, 'Kloostritest keskaegses Tartus', in Kaur Alttoa, *Tartu: piiskopi- ja hansalinnast Emajõe Ateenaks. Kirjutisi Tartu vanemast ehitusloost* (Tartu: Ilmamaa, 2017), pp. 172–198, here pp. 179–180; Leonhard Lemmens, 'Geschichte der Observantenkustodie Livland und Preußen', *Beiträge zur Geschichte der sächsischen Franziskanerprovinz vom Heiligen Kreuze*, 6 (1913), pp. 5–67, esp. 12; Leonhard Lemmens (ed.), *Urkundenbuch der alten sächsischen Franziskanerprovinzen*, vol. 1: *Die Observantenkustodie Livland und Preussen* (Düsseldorf: Schwan, 1913), no. 1. The article by Hans Niedermeyer, 'Die Franziskaner in Preußen, Livland und Litauen im Mittelalter', *Zeitschrift für Ostforschung*, 27 (1978), pp. 1–31, does not add anything new about the developments in Livonia.
4 Lemmens, 'Geschichte', pp. 19–23.

of Livonia (later: Livonia and Prussia) was first mentioned in 1472.[5] Surviving sources are scarce, so little is known about the history and spirituality of the Livonian *custodia* and its individual convents. Livonia's most influential mendicant convents in Riga, Tallinn and Tartu were all dissolved in 1524–1525, their belongings confiscated and the friars expelled from the cities. However, most of the remaining monastic houses, particularly in smaller centres, managed to survive. In 1543, the corporations of the nobility decided that all the remaining monastic institutions should be preserved to provide 'non-Germans' (i.e. the rural Estonian and Latvian population) with pastoral care.[6] Eventually, these too were closed or destroyed during the Livonian Wars (1558–1583). The wars also caused the end of the Livonian principalities and the collapse of the political system in its entirety.

The Battle of Smolino between Russian and Livonian troops in 1502 was the catalyst for establishing a Franciscan convent in Rakvere. Livonian Master of the Teutonic Order Wolter von Plettenberg and his allies vowed to found the new convent out of gratitude for their victory in the battle.[7] In the medieval period, Rakvere was a small town of just a few hundred inhabitants in the shadow of its overlord's castle, the Teutonic Order. There were no monastic establishments in the area until the early sixteenth century. A Dominican friary in Narva (close to the Russian border, a hundred kilometres to the east) was planned slightly later in 1520, but it never functioned properly, and the friars were driven out of town in 1524.[8] The nearest monastic foundations to Rakvere, as well as cathedral chapters, were in or outside the cities of Tallinn and Tartu, roughly a hundred kilometres to the west and south, respectively. While it has not been determined how many friars were in Rakvere, evidence shows that no other location within one hundred kilometres had more than one or two educated people. It is not known exactly when the friars arrived, or when the convent's buildings were ready for the friars to move in. The friars' origins also remain unclear. Only five or six friars are known by name in the convent's entire history.[9] Initially, the friars likely moved to Rakvere from other convents in Livonia and Saxonia. In or before 1526, during the ardent years of the Reformation in Livonia's major cities, a fire broke out in the convent

---

5 Ibid., p. 21.
6 Ibid., 'Geschichte', p. 35; Kreem, 'Die Reformationszeit', pp. 458–459.
7 Leonid Arbusow (ed.), *Liv-, Est- und Kurländisches Urkundenbuch, II/3, 1506–1510* (Riga, Moscow: J. Deubner, 1914), no. 64; see also *Liv-, Est- und Kurländisches Urkundenbuch, II/2, 1501–1505* (Riga, Moscow: J. Deubner, 1905), no. 545.
8 Kala, *Jutlustajad*, pp. 333–339.
9 Leonid Arbusow, 'Livlands Geistlichkeit vom Ende des 12. bis ins 16. Jahrhundert. Dritter Nachtrag', *Jahrbuch für Genealogie, Heraldik und Sphragistik*, 1911–1913 (1914), pp. 1–432, 354–355.

from unknown causes.[10] Later, the convent's buildings were destroyed during the capture of Rakvere by Russian troops in 1558; the convent ceased to exist shortly thereafter.[11] This is virtually all the information provided by textual sources about the history of the convent.[12]

Some of Livonia's smaller towns (Narva, Viljandi/Fellin, Pärnu/Pernau) became Lutheran in 1525–1526, but nothing is known about the conversion to Lutheranism or possible tumults among the lay population of Rakvere during the early years of the Reformation.[13] By 1544 at the latest, the town's only parish church had a Lutheran minister.[14] Much the same applies to the surrounding rural parishes. The exact years are unknown, but there were several instances in the late 1530s, 1540s and early 1550s of Lutheran ministers in the parishes.[15] In the countryside, the switch to Lutheranism most often depended on local nobility who held the right of patronage in the parish churches.

2   Franciscan Libraries around the Baltic Sea in the Early Sixteenth Century

During the Lutheran Reformation (roughly the second quarter of the sixteenth century), most of the mendicant convents in the countries surrounding the Baltic Sea were dissolved. At least within the limits of the Franciscan province of Saxonia, the belongings of the convents, including their books, were recorded in inventory lists during or after their secularisation.[16] No such lists

10   Lemmens, *Urkundenbuch*, no. 324.
11   Lemmens, 'Geschichte', pp. 53–54.
12   For an overview of the history of the convent, see Eduard Pabst, 'Das Franciscanerkloster zu Wesenberg', *Beiträge zur Kunde Ehst-, Liv- und Kurlands*, 1 (1873), pp. 31–19; Lemmens, 'Geschichte', pp. 23, 53–54; Jaan Tamm, *Eesti keskaegsed kloostrid* (Tallinn: Eesti Entsüklopeediakirjastus, 2002), pp. 60–63.
13   Joachim Kuhles, *Die Reformation in Livland. Religiöse, politische und ökonomische Wirkungen* (Hamburg: Kovač, 2007), pp. 154–155; Inna Põltsam-Jürjo, 'Über die Reformation in der livländischen Kleinstadt Neu-Pernau', in Arno Mentzel-Reuters and Klaus Neitmann (eds.), *Preussen und Livland im Zeichen der Reformation* (Osnabrück: Fibre, 2014), pp. 199–211; Kreem, 'Die Reformationszeit', p. 436.
14   Liivi Aarma, *Põhja-Eesti kogudused ja vaimulikkond 1525–1885*, 1. raamat: *Põhja-Eesti kirikud, kogudused ja vaimulikud, Matriklid 1525–1885* (Tallinn: Aarma Maja, 2005), p. 96.
15   The earliest dated mentions of Lutheran ministers in rural Virumaa (the area surrounding Rakvere) are from Kadrina (1535), Viru-Jaagupi (1542) and Lüganuse (1546); see Aarma, *Põhja-Eesti kogudused*, pp. 91, 93, 103. In all these cases, the years given are the latest possible dates of adopting Lutheran rites and preaching in those locations.
16   For a comprehensive overview of the inventory lists, as well as of the surviving book collections from Saxonia, see Volker Honemann, 'Bücher und Bibliotheken der Saxonia von ihren Anfängen bis zur Reformation', in Volker Honemann (ed.), *Geschichte der*

survived from Livonia, which was part of the province of Saxonia, or from the Nordic countries, which constituted the Franciscan province of Dacia.[17] A list of books (numbering approximately 350) from Braniewo (Braunsberg) is the only surviving list from Prussia, the region within the Holy Roman Empire that was closest to Livonia and which formed the other part of the *custodia* of Livonia and Prussia in the province of Saxonia. A list of the books of the convent of Zalewo (Saalfeld) in Prussia was drawn up in the modern era.[18]

Saxonia's inventory lists and preserved book collections from some of its convents provide detailed insights into the book holdings of the convents in the early printed book era. The lists indicate that convent libraries normally comprised approximately three to six hundred volumes. It should be noted that many of these lists counted only the chained books in the library, not the books used by or belonging to individual friars; nor did they include liturgical volumes.[19] The contents of the libraries were rather uniform and were dominated by biblical commentaries, patristic and medieval theology and collections of sermons, often exactly the same texts. Most of the libraries also contained books on both canon and, to a lesser extent, civil law, liberal arts, medicine and science.[20] Since many of the convents in the northern parts

sächsischen Franziskaner-Provinz, vol. 1: *Von den Anfängen bis zur Reformation* (Paderborn: Ferdinand Schöningh, 2015), pp. 521–601, esp. pp. 543–571.

[17] From the Scandinavian countries, apart from a few single books, only the remains of two Franciscan book collections have survived; see Jørgen Nybo Rasmussen, *Die Franziskaner in den nordischen Ländern im Mittelalter* (Kevelaer: Butzon & Bercker, 2002), pp. 26–28; see also Birgitte Langkilde, *Libri monasteriorum Danicorum mediae aetatis – index ad tempus compositus* (Copenhagen: Statsbiblioteket, 2005), pp. 22–23, 37, 49–53; Jaakko Tahkokallio, 'Fransiskaanit', in Tuomas Heikkilä (ed.) *Kirjallinen kulttuuri keskiajan Suomessa* (Helsinki: Suomalaisen Kirjallisuuden Seura, 2010), pp. 277–286; Wolfgang Undorf, *From Gutenberg to Luther. Transnational Print Cultures in Scandinavia 1450–1525* (Leiden: Brill, 2014), pp. 127–128, 179–180.

[18] Honemann, 'Bücher und Bibliotheken', pp. 545, 549–550; Franz Hipler, 'Analecta Warmiensia. Studien zur Geschichte der ermländischen Archive und Bibliotheken', *Zeitschrift für die Geschichte und Altertumskunde Ermlands* 5.13–16 (1870–1874), pp. 316–488, here pp. 383–389; Ernst Deegen, *Geschichte der Stadt Saalfeld in Ostpreussen* (Mohrungen, 1915), pp. 211, 220–223.

[19] Normally only a minority of the books would be chained in a Franciscan library; most of the convent's books could be borrowed by the friars or even outsiders. See K.W. Humphreys, *The Book Provisions of the Medieval Friars 1215–1400* (Amsterdam: Erasmus Booksellers, 1964), pp. 102–111.

[20] An analytical survey of the contents of these collections as a single corpus has not been written; my observations are based on Honemann, 'Bücher und Bibliotheken', pp. 550–581, and the editions of individual inventory lists: first of all Eva Schlotheuber, *Die Franziskaner in Göttingen. Die Geschichte des Klosters und seiner Bibliothek* (Werl: Dietrich-Coelde-Verlag, 1996), pp. 137–184; Luitgard Camerer, *Die Bibliothek des Franziskanerklosters*

of the Holy Roman Empire had already been dissolved during the late 1520s or in the 1530s, very little is known about the post-Reformation books they contained.[21] Within the province of Saxonia, we only know that the convent of Brandenburg owned a considerable quantity (almost forty items) of post-Reformation controversial literature. In the province of Cologne, the convent of Grünberg possessed nearly twenty such books.[22]

3 Mendicants and the Book in Medieval Livonia

Most of what survives of pre-Reformation Franciscan book culture in medieval Livonia comes from the convent of Riga. Nicolaus Busch and Albert Bauer identified four manuscripts and about forty printed volumes, mostly incunabula, which certainly or highly probably originate from the friary of Riga. The books were included in the newly established post-Reformation municipal library of Riga after the dissolution of the convent in 1524.[23] Nowadays, they are held in the University of Latvia Academic Library. Almost all the surviving books are religious (bibles with or without commentary, the Church Fathers, medieval scholastic theology and devotional works), but with surprisingly few sermons or preaching aids. The few non-religious works include two small texts on medicine, two books on civil law and one on canon law, *Speculum historiale* by Vincent de Beauvais, a book on chess and a manuscript of the fables of Anonymus Neveleti. The newest of the books were printed in the first two decades of the sixteenth century and as such bear no mark of the religious controversies soon to erupt.

Slightly more is known about the Dominican libraries of medieval Livonia. Approximately ten manuscripts and thirty printed books survive from the Dominican friary of Tallinn; a dozen more books that had once been acquired

---

    in Braunschweig (Braunschweig: Waisenhaus Buchdruckerei, 1982), pp. 14–21; Frank Ivemeyer, *Nah am Wasser gebaut – Das Franziskanerkloster St. Katharinen in Rostock* (Rostock: Andere Buchhandlung, 2013), pp. 109–149; Hipler, 'Analecta Warmiensia', pp. 384–389 (Braniewo); Deegen, *Geschichte der Stadt Saalfeld*, pp. 220–223 (Zalewo); Wilhelm Dersch, 'Die Bücherverzeichnisse der Franziskanerklöster Grünberg und Corbach', *Franziskanische Studien*, 1 (1914), pp. 444–471 (Franciscan province of Cologne); Gerhardt Powitz, *Die Bibliothek des Franziskanerklosters in Frankfurt am Main. Kirchliches und städtisches Bibliothekswesen im Übergang vom Mittelalter zur Neuzeit* (Frankfurt am Main: Klostermann, 1997), pp. 110–123 (province of Strasbourg).

21 Honemann, 'Bücher und Bibliotheken', pp. 540–584.
22 Ibid., pp. 573, 576; Dersch, 'Die Bücherverzeichnisse', pp. 444–471.
23 Nicolaus Busch, *Nachgelassene Schriften, Bd. 2, Schriften zur Bibliotheks- und Büchergeschichte* (Riga: s.n., 1937), pp. 80–91.

can be found in the preserved documents of the convent records.[24] Sixteen books have been preserved from the Dominican convent of Riga.[25] Late medieval sermon collections and preaching aids prevail in the collection from the convent of Tallinn, as can be expected of a mendicant library. Medieval theological and devotional literature was also ever-present. Surprisingly, no volume of biblical literature survived; the convent's liturgical books are represented by a single printed martyrology. A few law books (both civil and canon) from both convents were preserved. The only book that can be termed humanistic, the *Epistolae familiares* by Enea Silvio Piccolomini (Pope Pius II), survived from the convent of Riga; it previously belonged to the Dominican convent of Tartu, one of just two extant books once owned by that friary.[26] One of the last books acquired by the Dominicans of Tallinn early in 1525, immediately before the dissolution of the convent, was *Malleus Ioannis Fabri in haeresim Lutheranam*, an early controversial writing against Lutheranism.[27] This suggests that to the very end, the friars did not lose hope against the challenge of evangelical preaching.[28]

4 Books from the Franciscan Convent of Rakvere

The history of identifying the books connected to the Franciscan friary in Rakvere deserves a brief overview.[29] No inscriptions or any other early six-

---

[24] Gotthard von Hansen (ed.), *Katalog des Revaler Stadtarchivs* (Reval: s.n., 1896), pp. 1–7; Tiina Kala, *Euroopa kirjakultuur hiliskeskaegsetes õppetekstides. Tallinna dominiiklase David Slipperi taskuraamat* (Tallinn: Tallinna Linnaarhiiv, 2001), pp. 106–117; Kala, *Jutlustajad*, pp. 212–218; Tiina Kala, *Mittelalterliche Handschriften in den Sammlungen des Stadtarchivs Tallinn und des Estnischen Historischen Museums* (Tallinn: Tallinna Linnaarhiiv, 2007); Kaspar Kolk, 'Eesti kloostrite raamatud enne ja pärast reformatsiooni', in Piret Lotman (ed.), *Reformatsioon – tõlked ja tõlgendused* (Tallinn: Eesti Rahvusraamatukogu, 2019), pp. 71–112, here pp. 83–95.

[25] Busch, *Nachgelassene Schriften*, pp. 86–89. Fifteen more volumes of printed books originating from monastic establishments survive in Riga, but it has been impossible to determine which monastery or convent they once belonged to; see ibid., pp. 89–91.

[26] Kolk, 'Eesti kloostrite raamatud', pp. 78, 94–95, 104.

[27] The book bought by the Dominicans did not survive; it should have been: Johann Faber, *Mallevs Ioannis Fabri ... in haeresim Lutheranam ...* (Cologne: Peter Quentel, Johann Soter, 1524), USTC 674753; see Kala, 'Jutlustajad', p. 215; Kolk, 'Eesti kloostrite raamatud', p. 94.

[28] Kala, *Euroopa kirjakultuur*, p. 108.

[29] Various aspects of the Rakvere convent's book collection have been discussed in two articles in Estonian, namely Kaspar Kolk, 'Vana Tallinna raamatukogu kolm allikat: komplekteerimisest 16. sajandil', *Tuna. Ajalookultuuri ajakiri*, 2017.3, pp. 10–29, here pp. 20–24; and Kolk, 'Eesti kloostrite raamatud', pp. 95–102.

teenth-century ownership marks in the books point to a Franciscan owner. Only three volumes contain the brief notation 'Wesenberch 1564' on their title pages or flyleaves, dating apparently from the very year 1564. The inscription marks the year of their arrival in Tallinn, in the city library at St Olaf's church. Three more volumes bear a provenance note, such as 'Wesenberg' or 'è Biblioth. Wesenbergens. 1564', in the inventory of St Olaf's Library in Tallinn, which was composed by the librarian Heinrich Bröcker in the mid-seventeenth century.[30] The same kind of inscription may have been present on the title pages or flyleaves of those three volumes too, but the books have since lost their original flyleaves and one has also lost its title page. The books may also have been listed as originating from Rakvere in an earlier list of books known to Bröcker but not extant at present.

In the earliest catalogue of Tallinn's incunabula published in 1912, Theodor Kirchhofer was the first to tentatively connect those books with the Franciscan convent in Rakvere, with no detailed discussion.[31] A few years later, Leonid Arbusow espoused this identification, and it has been adopted since then.[32] To be fair, such is a bold assumption, since those early, pre-Reformation books (see below) might have belonged to any clerical owner in the area of Rakvere; nothing compels us to connect them exactly to the Franciscan friary. The post-Reformation books that were identified later by their bindings are what connect the whole collection to a Catholic owner from the 1530s and 1540s, which in the context of Rakvere would most probably mean the Franciscans.

Each of the six volumes that were known earlier has a different binding, likely the result of where the books originated. Five of the volumes each contain one publication, printed between 1478 and 1518. The sixth volume combines editions of the works of two church fathers: those by St Ambrose, printed in 1515; and by St Augustine, from 1539.[33] The binding decoration of this copy

---

30 Heinrich Bröcker, *Verzeichnüs derer Bücher, so von der alten Revalschen Bibliothec, sent Ao. 1552. überblieben, und jetzo, in S. Olai Kirche, annoch vorhanden sind* (Tallinn University Academic Library, Msc V-2901), fol. 4r–5r.
31 Theodor Kirchhofer, Otto Greiffenhagen, 'Verzeichnis der in zwei Revaler Bibliotheken und im Stadtarchiv vorhandenen Inkunabeln', *Beiträge zur Kunde Est-, Liv- und Kurlands*, 7 (1912), pp. 64–85, 66, 69, 72.
32 Arbusow, *Die Einführung*, p. 75; Lemmens, 'Geschichte', p. 53; Hellmuth Weiss, 'Zur Bibliotheksgeschichte Revals im 16. und 17. Jahrhundert', in *Syntagma Friburgense. Historische Studien Hermann Aubin dargebracht zum 70. Geburtstag am 23. 12. 1955* (Lindau, Konstanz: Thorbecke, 1956), pp. 279–291, 282; Tiiu Reimo, 'Book Collection of the "Old Tallinn Library" (alte Revalsche Bibliothec)', in Lea Kõiv, Tiiu Reimo (eds.), *Books and Libraries in the Baltic Sea Region from the 16th to the 18th Century* (Tallinn: [Tallinna Linnaarhiiv, Tallinna Ülikooli Akadeemiline Raamatukogu], 2006), pp. 37–47, 45.
33 For the bibliographical details of each book, see below.

coincides with the binding pattern of seven more volumes preserved in the same collection at St Olaf's Library. Tanned calfskin covers the solid wooden boards of all eight volumes, lavishly decorated with blind-tooled ornament. Fragments of parchment manuscript used as pastedowns cover the interiors of the boards. Since the stamps used on these bindings are otherwise unknown, and the ornament was executed in a somewhat amateur manner, the bookbinding historian Endel Valk-Falk, who first established the common origins of the set of bindings, suggests that they were all bound at the convent in Rakvere. The binder may have been one of the friars there.[34] These volumes were all bound (or in some instances, probably rebound) during the 1530s and 1540s. These post-Reformation Catholic books and their contents provide firmer ground for inferring that there probably was no other institution or individual in Rakvere during those years besides the friary who could have owned such a collection. All the volumes are currently kept at the Tallinn University Academic Library, the inheritor of the St Olaf's Library collection.

A total of thirteen volumes containing twenty-one publications remain in the small corpus. The books do not have the chains (or the traces of them) that would have been expected of books coming from a monastic library. Perhaps no need was felt to fasten the books with chains in the new-fashioned library of a recently founded convent, in an age when printed books had become exceedingly numerous. Or, perhaps the surviving books did not belong to the convent's common library but instead were in the private use of one or several friars.[35] The evidence does not tell us the location of these books within the

---

34 Endel Valk-Falk, 'Niguliste kiriku järelejäänud raamatutest, mis anno 1660 Oleviste kiriku raamatukogule üle antud, ja teistest annetustest, mille provenients tõendab nende kuuluvust Püha Nikolause kiriku raamatukogule', in Endel Valk-Falk, *Verba volant, scripta manent. Jutt lendab tuulde, kirjutatu jääb: valik raamatuajaloo-alaseid uurimuslikke kirjutisi autori redaktsioonis* (Tartu: Tartu Kõrgem Kunstikool, 2008), pp. 128–154, here pp. 134–139. The present author has added two further volumes to the five volumes identified by Valk-Falk in Kolk, 'Vana Tallinna raamatukogu', p. 21, and Kolk, 'Eesti kloostrite raamatud', pp. 97–98 (see the latter also for descriptions of the stamps used in the decorations of all the bindings). In other parts of the Franciscan province of Saxonia, at least the convents of Brandenburg, Cottbus, Freiberg and Stadthagen had their own bookbinding workshops; see Konrad von Rabenau, 'Von Büchern und Bibliotheken. Bucheinbände aus Franziskanerklöstern der Ordensprovinz Saxonia', in Roland Pieper (ed.), *Geschichte der Sächsischen Franziskaner-Provinz, Bd. 5, Kunst. Von den Anfängen bis zur Gegenwart* (Paderborn: Ferdinand Schöningh, 2012), pp. 541–556, esp. pp. 547–553.

35 Normally only the reference collection of a mendicant library had chains; see Rabenau, 'Von Büchern und Bibiliotheken', pp. 552–553; Neslihan Şenocak, 'Circulation of Books in the Medieval Franciscan Order. Attitude, Methods and Critics', *The Journal of Religious History*, 28 (2004), pp. 146–161, here pp. 148–149.

convent.[36] There are no liturgical books among the surviving volumes. These were probably kept in other locations, such as the sacristy or, in the case of the friars' private breviaries, in their cells.[37]

Six of the thirteen volumes can be called 'pre-Reformation', meaning that the books were published prior to the 1520s. Each of these volumes contains one book. Four of the books are incunabula, printed in the fifteenth century, which indicates that they are older than the convent itself. These are the *Institutes* of Justinian, the Latin *Bible*, the *Sermons* of Meffreth and *Aristotle* in Latin.[38] Ptolemy's *Geography* in Latin (1507) was published around the years when the convent was erected.[39] A volume of Jerome's *Letters* was printed a

---

36 On the position of the books in the Franciscan order and their different locations within the convents, both in general and in Germany, see e.g. Schlotheuber, *Die Franziskaner in Göttingen*, pp. 101–116; Honemann, 'Bücher und Bibliotheken', pp. 521–540. Two classical studies cover mainly the earlier period and focus on Italy: Humphreys, *The Book Provisions*, pp. 46–66, 99–118; Francesco Costa, 'Biblioteche francescane medievali. Tipologie, contenuti, vicende storiche', in Gino Maria Zanotti (ed.), *Archivi – biblioteche, beni e centri culturali. Assisi – Sacro convento di S. Francesco. Atti del convegno. 19–21 settembre 1990* (Assisi: Centro studi C.I.M.P, 1991), pp. 215–283.

37 No complete medieval liturgical manuscript survives in all of Estonia, although they were doubtless numerous in the Middle Ages. Only fragments used as book covers or wrappers in the early modern era have survived. For liturgical books in medieval Livonia and the documentary evidence concerning them, see Tiina Kala, 'Keskaegse Liivimaa kirikliku kirjasõna hulgast ja laadist', in Piret Lotman (ed.), *Konfessioon ja kirjakultuur* (*Eesti Rahvusraamatukogu Toimetised, 15, Raamat ja Aeg, 4*) (Tallinn: Eesti Rahvusraamatukogu, 2016), pp. 13–40, here pp. 24–28. The same can be observed in the Nordic countries: in Norway and Finland, the number of surviving complete manuscripts is insignificant but fragments, predominantly liturgical, are numerous; see e.g. Tuomas Heikkilä, Åslaug Ommundsen, 'Piecing together the past. The accidental manuscript collections of the North', in Åslaug Ommundsen, Tuomas Heikkilä (eds.), *Nordic Latin Manuscript Fragments. The Destruction and Reconstruction of Medieval Books* (New York: Routledge, 2017), pp. 1–23, esp. pp. 4–8; see the whole volume for Nordic manuscript fragments in general. For the few surviving liturgical books of the Scandinavian Franciscans, see Rasmussen, *Die Franziskaner*, p. 27.

38 Justinianus, *Institutiones cum glossa ordinaria* (Venice: Jacobus Rubeus, 20 July 1478), USTC 993884, inventory note: *Wesenberg*; *Biblia Latina* (Nuremberg: Anton Koberger, 6 August 1479), USTC 740066, inventory note: *è Bibl. Wesenb. 1564*; Meffreth, *Sermones de tempore et de sanctis. P. 2. De tempore pars estivalis* ([Basel: Nikolaus Kessler, before 11 July 1486]), USTC 747149; Aristoteles, *Opera* [*Latine*] (Venice: Johannes and Gregorius de Gregoriis for Benedictus Fontana, 1496), USTC 997543, inventory note: *è Biblioth. Wesenbergens. 1564*.

39 Claudius Ptolemaeus, *In hoc operae [!] haec continentur Geographia Cl. Ptholomaei a plurimis viris utriusque linguae doctiss. emendata: & cum archetypo graeco ab ipsis collata* (Roma: Bernardino Vitali, Evangelista Tosini, 1507), USTC 851474, inscription: *Wesenberch 1564*, inventory note: *èx Biblioth. Wesenbergensi*.

decade later.[40] Five of the books have different bindings that originate from different parts of Europe. The books were also printed in different parts of Europe (Germany, Italy and France). The sixth book, by Meffreth, belongs to the Rakvere bindings. This incunabulum was probably rebound half a century later. It can be inferred that these early acquisitions arrived in Rakvere from several places; they could have been bought from the second-hand market or received from other Franciscan friaries to build up the convent's library. Of the remaining seven volumes, all with a similar binding pattern (as mentioned above), two contain one late pre-Reformation book bound together with another, much later book. A preacher's manual by Pelbartus of Temesvar, entitled *Stellarium coronae benedictae Virginis Mariae*, and *De officiis* by St Ambrose were also published in the decade following the establishment of the convent of Rakvere.[41] It is possible that the books remained unbound until the late 1530s, or they may have been rebound, such as after the fire that occurred in the convent in 1526.

Looking at these eight early books, we see the remains of a typical late medieval monastic library, though not particularly Franciscan, or even any specific clerical library.[42] There is a Latin bible and two of the most common Church Fathers (St Jerome and St Ambrose), followed by two collections of sermons by the mid-fifteenth-century German priest Meffreth and the contemporary late-fifteenth-century Hungarian Franciscan Pelbartus, both extremely widespread in those years.[43] Next comes a basic text of civil law (*Institutes* of Justinian), a complete work of Aristotle in Latin and, at the end, Ptolemy in Latin, both the text and the maps. The last volume, the most exclusive in the collection, hints at humanism.

Books on sciences were rare in early Franciscan libraries; however, by the early sixteenth century, they were occasionally available even in the convents of the province of Saxonia. The Franciscans of Göttingen and Braunschweig

---

40   Hieronymus, *Epistolae* (Lyon: Jacques Sacon, 1518), USTC 155366, inscription: *Wesenberch 64*, inventory note: *Wesenberg, 1564*.

41   Pelbartus de Temesvar, *Stellarium corone benedicte Virginis Marie in laudem eius pro singulis predicationibus elegantissime coaptatum* (Lyon: Bernard Lescuyer, Nuremberg: Johann Koberger, 1514), USTC 694648, a lost copy; Ambrosius, *Tres officiorum libri totam vivendi rationem complectentes* (Leipzig: Jakob Thanner, 1515), USTC 640316.

42   On the choice of books in Franciscan convents in Germany, see e.g. Honemann, 'Bücher und Bibliotheken', pp. 550–584; Schlotheuber, *Die Franziskaner in Göttingen*, pp. 116–184.

43   According to the USTC, the seven editions of Meffreth from the early 1480s to 1496 survive in at least 718 copies. By combining the data of USTC and ISTC, we see that the number of editions of different preaching compendia by Pelbartus from 1497/98 to 1521 is 72, and 1,437 known copies have been registered. However, many copies of at least the early sixteenth-century editions have not yet been entered into these international databases.

had books on astronomy, and those of Braniewo in Prussia also had Ptolemy's 'Cosmographia et Geographia'.[44] The books on civil law were already slightly more common in large early Italian Franciscan libraries and sometimes present also in the early sixteenth-century Saxonian friaries.[45] In general, the picture is not particularly conservative or old-fashioned. Scholastic authors or earlier medieval sermon collections, so typical in late medieval monastic libraries, have not survived altogether. The extant corpus is fairly small, but perhaps a modern library of a new monastic establishment aiming at preaching the word of God among the local population did not need the same volume of scholastic texts as previous centuries required.

5 Post-reformation Books from Rakvere Convent

The most recent of the 'pre-Reformation' books were printed sometime between 1514 and 1518. We do not know of any books from Rakvere from the entire next decade. It is possible that they simply did not survive. Alternatively, there may have been few books to begin with because the traditional main trade routes led through the newly protestant cities of Tallinn, Tartu and Riga. Perhaps new routes for the Catholic book trade had not yet been established. The oldest surviving 'post-Reformation' books were printed in 1531 and the acquisitions continued for the next ten years to come.

We possess a total of thirteen books published from 1531 to 1541 in seven volumes. Two of these, as mentioned, were bound together with older books. After 1541, the new acquisitions disappeared again. It is probable that the convent was already falling out of use around that time because most of the local

---

44 Humphreys, *The Book Provisions*, p. 118; Schlotheuber, *Die Franziskaner in Göttingen*, pp. 127, 181; Camerer, *Die Bibliothek*, p. 19; Hipler, 'Analecta Warmiensia', p. 389.

45 The convents of Assisi (1381), Bologna (1421) and Florence (1426) all had several volumes on civil law; see Humphreys, *The Book Provisions*, pp. 107–108, 112–113. In sixteenth-century Saxonia, the convent of Braunschweig had the entire *Corpus juris civilis* and some medieval commentaries, but the *Corpus* likewise belonged to a minor convent in Weida; see Camerer, *Die Bibliothek*, pp. 20–21, 28–29; Schlotheuber, *Die Franziskaner in Göttingen*, p. 130. Individual parts of the *Corpus* were owned by at least the convents of Rostock (*Digesta* and *Institutes*), Braniewo (*Infortiatum*) and in Livonia, Riga (*Codex Justinianus*), see Sandra Groß, 'In altissima paupertate altissimas divitias sapientiae thesaurizatas. Die Bibliothek des Rostocker Franziskanerklosters im Spiegel des Visitationsprotokolls von 1566', in Sebastian Roebert etc. (eds.), *Von der Ostsee zum Mittelmeer. Forschungen zur mittelalterlichen Geschichte für Wolfgang Huschner* (*Italia Regia*, 4) (Leipzig: Eudora-Verlag, 2019), pp. 485–496, here pp. 489–490; Hipler, 'Analecta Warmiensia', p. 387; Busch, *Nachgelassene Schriften*, p. 82.

elites had converted to Lutheranism, and becoming a friar was no longer a career option for local young men. The influx of friars from other countries had also ceased because the nearest German-speaking regions and the areas around the Baltic Sea had almost exclusively converted to Lutheranism as well.

An almost complete shift in the choice of books is evident after the Reformation arrived in Livonia. Out of thirteen publications, only three older works are from earlier centuries: a collection of homilies attributed to Haimo, an epitomised volume of St Augustine and *The Golden Legend* by Jacobus de Voragine.[46] These books were among the most common literature used for preaching and religious learning of the time. Augustine and *The Golden Legend* were extremely common in medieval book collections, both in the age of incunabula and centuries prior. The works edited by Haimo (or Haimos) became numerous in the 1530s.[47] The rest of the works are entirely contemporary, having been written after Luther and in many instances in reaction to Luther or Lutherans. The topics of the books are theology, anti-Protestant polemics and homiletics. Everything is religious: no law, science, philosophy or humanist books survived. Anyone familiar with the German Catholic theologians of the second quarter of the sixteenth century would immediately recognise most of the authors of these books.

The only non-German post-Reformation author is the Spanish Minorite Alfonso de Castro. Castro is represented by his early principal work *Adversus omnes haereses*.[48] The treatise was one of the first surveys of heresies to treat

---

[46] Haimo Altissiodorensis, *D. Haymonis Episcopi Halberstattensis Homiliarum sive concionum popularium in evangelia de tempore & Sanctis ... pars utraque ... Adiectae sunt eiusdem Haymonis homiliae aliquot ...* (Cologne: Johann Prael, 1536), USTC 626114, a lost copy; Aurelius Augustinus, *Omnium operum Divi Aurelii Augustini, Episcopi Hipponensis, Epitome, primum quidem per Iohannem Piscatorium compendiaria quadam via collecta, Nunc autem diligentius recognita ...* (Cologne: Melchior von Neuß, 1539), USTC 679360; Jacobus de Voragine, *Legenda sanctorum. Opus aureum quod legenda sanctorum vulgo nuncupatur* (Lyon, Jacques Moderne apud Jacques Giunta, 1540), USTC 124706. Although they appear first in my discussion, they all belong among the latest of the books.

[47] Augustinus is the most frequent individual author in the indexes to *Mittelalterliche Bibliothekskataloge Deutschlands und der Schweiz, 1–4,3* (Munich: Beck, 1969–2009); the Golden Legend survives in more medieval manuscripts than almost any other individual work. In the fifteenth century, it was one of the most frequently printed works as well; see Uwe Neddermeyer, *Von der Handschrift zum gedruckten Buch: Schriftlichkeit und Leseinteresse im Mittelalter und in der frühen Neuzeit; quantitative und qualitative Aspekte, 1–2* (Wiesbaden: Harrassowitz, 1998), p. 737; for the editions of Haimo(s), see the USTC.

[48] Alfonso de Castro, *Adversus omnes haereses libri XIIII* (Paris: Josse Bade, Jean de Roigny, 1534), USTC 187349. On Castro's heresiology, see Daniela Müller, 'Ketzerei und Ketzerbestrafung im Werk des Alfonso de Castro', in Frank Grunert and Kurt Seelmann (eds.), *Die Ordnung der Praxis. Neue Studien zur Spanischen Spätscholastik* (Berlin: De Gruyter, 2011), pp. 333–348.

Luther as one of the foremost representatives of the persistent flow of heretics, starting from late antiquity and continuing to the contemporary era. As such, it had an enormous impact on the heresiology of the entire sixteenth century. As a counsellor to Emperor Charles v, Castro also strongly influenced attempts to re-catholicise Germany. From Rakvere, we possess the first edition of the book, printed in Paris. The treatise was later reprinted in Germany on several occasions.

All the remaining contemporary Catholic books are by German authors and were printed in Germany. Berthold Pürstinger, the resigned Bishop of Chiemsee, was likely the least known of the authors.[49] His treatise on Holy Mass, entitled *Tewtsch Rational über das Ambt heiliger mess*, is the only German-language book we possess from Rakvere.[50] German, or often Low German, was likely the main language of most of the friars in Rakvere, the local nobility and many of the town's people. Pürstinger's main work, *Theologia Germanica*, attempted to give a comprehensive account of Catholic theology in German to counter Luther's similar works from the Protestant side. The copy in Rakvere, however, was in Latin.[51]

Georg Witzel was a prolific writer who converted to Lutheranism but then back to Catholicism. He is represented by two minor controversial works, a collection of sermons and a major work entitled *Hagiologium*, which details his version of the lives of saints from the earliest origins of the world to the more recent era.[52] Witzel adopted a milder view of reconciliation and of bringing Lutherans back to the unity of the church. This view might also have applied in medieval Livonia, where debate was not yet definitively settled. His *Hagiologium* was inspired by humanist spirituality; he focused not on the miracles but rather the virtues of the saints.[53]

---

49   On Pürstinger, see Christian Greinz, 'Berthold Pürstinger. Bischof von Chiemsee (1465–1543)', *Mitteilungen der Gesellschaft für Salzburger Landeskunde*, 54 (1904), pp. 273–328.

50   Berthold Pürstinger, *Tewtsch Rational über das Ambt heiliger Mess* (Augsburg: Alexander Weißenhorn I, 1535), USTC 696368.

51   Berthold Pürstinger, *Theologia Germanica in qua continentur articuli de fide, evangelio, virtutibus et sacramentis. Quorum materia iam nostra tempestate controverti solet* (Augsburg: Alexander Weißenhorn I, Martin Silbereysen, 1531), USTC 696755.

52   Georg Witzel, *Confutatio calumniosissimae responsionis Iusti Ionae, id est, Iodoci Koch, una cum assertione bonorum operum* (Leipzig: Nickel Schmidt, 1533), USTC 624716; Georg Witzel, *Homiliae aliquot ab Adventu usque in Quadragesimam, & praeterea a Dominica XIII. usque ad Adventum* (Leipzig: Nikolaus Wolrab, 1538), USTC 663988; Georg Witzel, *Conquestio de calamitoso in praesens rerum Christianarum statu* (Leipzig: Nikolaus Wolrab, 1538), USTC 624807; Georg Witzel, *Hagiologium, seu De Sanctis Ecclesiae. Historiae Divorum toto terrarum orbe celeberrimorum, è sacris scriptoribus, summa fide ac studio congestae ...* (Mainz: Franz Behem, 1541), USTC 661478.

53   David J. Collins, *Reforming Saints. Saints' Lives and Their Authors in Germany, 1470–1530* (New York: Oxford University Press, 2008), pp. 131–132.

Friedrich Nausea, the court preacher of the Archduke of Austria (later the Holy Roman Emperor) Ferdinand I, who later left the court to become the Bishop of Vienna, can also be viewed as a supporter of reconciling and reuniting Lutherans with the Catholic Church. Of his works, the Franciscans of Rakvere owned a copy of the homilies for the whole liturgical year.[54] We have from Rakvere only a minor theological treatise on the ordination of priests and the Eucharist by Johannes Cochlaeus, another prolific author and one of the most influential polemicists of his time.[55] Hermann V von Wied, the Archbishop of Cologne, initially made an institutional reconciliation attempt.[56] The decrees of his provincial synod held in 1536 survived with the books from Rakvere.[57] As is well known, Hermann was later converted to Lutheranism and tried to carry out a Lutheran reform in his diocese but was opposed by the chapter and ultimately deposed.

The attempt to compare this small set of post-Reformation books with contemporary Franciscan libraries in the central areas of northern Germany reveals that remarkably little can be established about such book collections from other convents. Many of the convents in Saxonia, once furnished with large libraries, were dissolved by the late 1520s and 1530s. For the most part, next to nothing is known about whether they contained post-Reformation controversial literature.[58] Of the friary libraries examined by Volker Honemann, we know only that Brandenburg owned nearly forty items of controversial literature that had been acquired up to the early 1530s.[59] In the neighbouring Franciscan province of Cologne, the convent of Grünberg possessed almost twenty polemical books, although it was dissolved already in 1528.[60] Admittedly, the selection of controversial books and authors in the convents of Brandenburg, Grünberg and Rakvere differed greatly from each other. Johannes Cochlaeus is the only author attested in Rakvere who also appears

---

54   Friedrich Nausea, *Evangelicae veritatis Homiliarum centuriæ quatuor* (Cologne: Peter Quentel, 1534), USTC 658294.

55   Johannes Cochlaeus, *De ordinatione episcoporum atque presbyterorum, et de Eucharistiae consecratione, quaestio hoc tempore pernecessaria* (Mainz: Franz Behem, 1541), USTC 630810.

56   On Hermann von Wied, see Andreea Badea, *Kurfürstliche Präeminenz, Landesherrschaft und Reform. Das Scheitern der Kölner Reformation unter Hermann von Wied* (Münster: Aschendorff, 2009).

57   Hermannus von Wied, Johann Gropper, *Canones concilii provincialis Coloniensis. Sub reverendiss[imo] In Christo patre ac d[omi]no, D. Hermanno S. Colonien[sis] ecclesiae Archiepiscopo ... Anno 1536. Quibus adiectum est encheridion Christianae institutionis* (Cologne: Peter Quentel, 1537/1538), USTC 617849.

58   See Honemann, 'Bücher und Bibliotheken', pp. 540–584.

59   Ibid., pp. 573, 576.

60   Wilhelm Dersch, 'Die Bücherverzeichnisse', pp. 444–471 (edition of the inventory).

in one of the other two convents (Grünberg). The lists from Brandenburg and Grünberg have only slightly more overlap, despite being more contemporaneous with each other in containing books only from the 1520s (and, in the case of Brandenburg, also from the early 1530s), while the surviving books from Rakvere all come from the period between 1531 and 1541. Even taken together, the three lists are likely not sufficiently representative of the period's Catholic controversial literature in its entirety. The strong bias towards contemporary Franciscan authors detected in the Brandenburg collection was not present in Rakvere, for example, where the only post-Reformation Franciscan author was Alfonso de Castro.

With such books, three focuses can be determined for the post-Reformation collection from Rakvere. The first is preaching, based on collections of sermons and homilies, lives of saints and examples from both the earlier medieval period and the more recent decades after the Lutheran Reformation. Second is liturgical and sacramental theology, an especially volatile issue in the initial era of the Protestant-Catholic controversy, to which the writings of contemporary theologians precisely attested. Thirdly are the explicitly anti-Protestant polemics as could be expected in strongly Lutheran surroundings. The collections give no indication that the Rakvere friars considered joining the Lutheran reformers themselves; no book bears witness to an interest in Protestant theology. Of course, the friars may have possessed controversial Lutheran writings to keep themselves informed of their opponents' views. If they did, however, those pamphlets would not have been valued enough to be bound with the solid bindings used to preserve books for the long term. Books of secular learning, letters or science from that period did not survive either. The reason may partly be the same: minor works with mainly educational objectives were not considered to be worthy of valuable binding. Of course, with such a small corpus of preserved literature, one cannot tell which books the friars did *not* have; we can only conclude that they did not abandon their task of preaching and providing pastoral care, and that they acquired the most recent Catholic theological writings to be prepared for debates with the surrounding Lutherans. Unfortunately, there are almost no marks of use inside the books. Therefore, we cannot tell in what ways the texts were used, whether they were studied in depth or what may have attracted the attention of the friars.

6   Conclusion

The small collection of books from the Franciscan convent in Rakvere is one of the very rare instances, not only from Livonia but from the entire Franciscan province of Saxonia, of surviving post-Reformation Catholic books (or entries of such books in the inventories). The few remaining pre-Reformation books from the Rakvere friary represent a typical mendicant library, or even more broadly, a typical clerical library of the period. All these books could be found in many, or at least some, of the other convents in the province of Saxonia. What makes the collection exceptional is its post-Reformation books. Since we know next to nothing about the preaching or pastoral work, nor of spiritual or devotional life in the monastic establishments in medieval Livonia during the second quarter of the sixteenth century when Lutheranism gradually gained more ground, this collection of post-Reformation books gives us valuable insight into the spiritual perspectives of a hinterland convent. We can conclude that Franciscans in Rakvere continuously informed themselves of spiritual means that were useful for preaching and for confuting Protestantism. The books that they owned would have been useful both for preaching to the laity and for acquiring theological learning. Several authors, whose texts were owned in Rakvere, stressed bringing Lutherans back to the unity of the Catholic Church. This would also have been an important problem for the friars in Rakvere. Notably, works of personal devotion and biblical literature from that period have not survived. Non-religious literature (arts, law, science and medicine) likewise are missing. We can infer that with the help of books, at least initially, the Franciscans attempted to find their way in an increasingly Lutheran environment. Still, we do not know anything about the possible outcome of Franciscan efforts in Rakvere. After the early 1540s, no new books were known to be added to the libraries. In the late 1550s, the Franciscan convent, which was the last Catholic institution in the area, ceased to exist.

Acknowledgement

Work on this article was supported by Estonia Research Council Grant PRG1276.

PART 3

Insights into the Collections

CHAPTER 10

Italian Religious Orders and Their Books at the End of the Sixteenth Century

Giovanna Granata

At the end of the sixteenth century, the censorial machine set up by the Roman Church had reached fearsome and impressive proportions, making the repressive system increasingly complex. The control of books and reading was the responsibility of two cardinal congregations, the Holy Office and, from 1571, the Congregation of the Index, the latter in charge of updating the list of prohibited books and facilitating its enforcement. In forty years, three 'official' Roman lists had been published, prohibitions had become increasingly nuanced and the shadow of suspicion was widening: not only were specific books and authors to be banned outright, but there were also books to be expurgated, whole categories of works to be taken under surveillance and general rules to be eventually applied to different cases.[1]

At the apex of this process, soon after the publication of the third Roman *Index* in 1596, the negotiations between the Congregation of the Index and Italian religious orders over the control of their books took place in an atmosphere of fear, uncertainty and mutual distrust.

---

1   The bibliography on ecclesiastical censorship in sixteenth-century Italy is extraordinarily vast and is even more increasingly growing in the new millennium, due to the opening of the Roman archives of the Inquisition and the Index in 1998; on the new impetus for studies on censorship resulting from this chance see Gigliola Fragnito (ed.), *Church, Censorship and Culture in Early Modern Italy* (Cambridge: Cambridge University Press, 2001). The first *Index Librorum Prohibitorum* was prepared by the Holy Office and published in 1559; the second, ratified by the assembly of bishops in the Council of Trent, was published in 1564; the third *Index* was promulgated by Clement VIII in 1596. For the commented and annotated text of the sixteenth-century *Indices*, see Jesús Martinez de Bujanda (ed.), *Index des livres interdits* (Sherbrooke, Quebec: Centre d'Études de la Renaissance; Geneva: Droz, 1984–1996). On the complex preparatory phases of the Roman *Indices*, see Vittorio Frajese, *Nascita dell'Indice. La censura ecclesiastica dal Rinascimento alla Controriforma* (Brescia: Morcelliana, 2006) and, more recently, Robin Vose, *The Index of Prohibited Books: Four Centuries of Struggle over Word and Image for the Greater Glory of God* (London: Reaktion Books, 2022). On the problems associated with the principle of expurgation, introduced by the Tridentine Index of 1564, see Hannah Marcus, *Forbidden Knowledge. Medicine, Science, and Censorship in Early Modern Italy* (Chicago and London: University of Chicago Press, 2020).

In such a framework, these negotiations took a new and unexpected direction, thus leading to unpredictable results. By a sort of paradoxical effect, they do not return to the negative implications of Roman censorship, requisitions, burnings and losses, but rather memory preservation. The reason for this shifting perspective is now quite familiar to historians.[2] Eager to assert their jurisdictional prerogatives, religious orders hesitated to respond to the Congregation's demands. As they notably claimed to be unable to identify forbidden or suspected books present in their libraries, the Congregation took a different course and, to avoid any misunderstanding, asked them to list all their books. This decision broke any attempts by religious orders to escape the request. So, in a very short time, between 1598 and 1603, Italian convents and monasteries sent to Rome an impressive number of lists, describing myriad books found in common libraries or in use by friars and monks.

It is not clear whether the Congregation of the Index checked these lists for the presence of prohibited books. However, they have been preserved for centuries and are now essentially collected in the Vatican Library, making it possible to learn about a vast network of religious libraries now largely lost.[3]

Religious libraries have a key role in preserving cultural heritage. A strong continuity marks their institutional history and finds confirmation in their stratified collections; nevertheless, they have also experienced deep caesuras,

---

2 The reasons and phases of the contrast between religious orders and the Congregation of the Index has been by now comprehensively reconstructed; the milestones are Romeo De Maio, *I modelli culturali della Controriforma. Le biblioteche dei conventi italiani alla fine del Cinquecento*, in Romeo De Maio, *Riforme e miti nella Chiesa del Cinquecento* (Naples: Guida, 1973), pp. 365–381; Marc Dykmans, 'Les bibliothèques des religieux d'Italie en l'an 1600', in *Archivum Historiae Pontificiae*, XXIV (1986), pp. 385–404 to which studies by Gigliola Frangnito should be added, particularly her 'L'applicazione dell'Indice dei libri proibiti di Clemente VIII', *Archivio storico italiano*, CLIX (2001), pp. 107–149, and works by Roberto Rusconi, starting from his 'Les bibliothèques des ordres religieux en Italie à travers l'enquête de la Congrégation de l'Index. Problèmes et perspectives de recherche', in B. Dompnier, M.-H. Froeschlé-Chopard (eds.), *Les religieux et leurs livres à l'époque moderne* (Clermont Ferrand: Presses Universitaires Blaise Pascal, 2000), pp. 145–160. The documentation on the inquiry and relationships between the Congregation of the Index and regular Orders is kept in the Archive of the Congregation for the Doctrine of the Faith where the Archive of the Congregation of the Index was stored at the moment of its suppression in 1917, see De Maio, *I modelli culturali della Controriforma*. This documentation is now published in Alessandro Serra (ed.), *La Congregazione dell'Indice, l'esecuzione dell'Index del 1596 e gli Ordini regolari in Italia. Documenti* (Vatican City: Biblioteca Apostolica Vaticana, 2018).

3 The main set of surviving inventories has been transferred from the Archive of the Congregation of the Index to the Vatican Library in 1917 (see note 2) and is described by Marie Madelaine Lebreton, Luigi Fiorani, *Codices Vaticani Latini 11266–11326. Inventari di biblioteche religiose italiane alla fine del Cinquecento* (Vatican City: Biblioteca Apostolica Vaticana, 1985).

either in conflict with secular and political authorities or for more internal reasons: periods of decadence and depletion, shifting cultural paradigms, and the new impetus given to pastoral activities or meditative practices. In such a process, libraries of religious orders have been continuously reshaped. Indeed, they have a pre-eminently functional character and are quite far from the bibliophilic model of book collecting, typical, for example, of early modern private libraries. Many of their books, thus, were lost not only as a result of external events but also because they were damaged and not replaced, or because they were no longer useful and were therefore replaced by others.

For this reason, an *a posteriori* historical reconstruction of these libraries (i.e. based on surviving books) can only provide a partial view and risks being poor, which makes the analysis of historical inventories and catalogues all the more essential. Many studies are now focused on this 'diachronic' approach, which is prolific in analysing single cases.[4] It misses, however, a second aspect typical of religious libraries: they are not only functional in terms of their role but also geographically 'distributed'. Religious orders, under the control of more or less centralised forms of government, are organised in local communities, deeply rooted in their respective countries. This makes their settlements a kind of territorial system and their libraries something similar to modern library networks.

Thus, studying these libraries as individual cases, without knowing the context, again risks being unsatisfactory, and it may be seen as just a beginning, since to evaluate their collections it is necessary to broaden the analysis and look at the network. Not only should inventories be studied in chronological series, but large collections of coeval book lists are also needed for a comprehensive approach based on a global analysis of data.

This is exactly what we are provided with by the results of the negotiations between the Congregation of the Index and Italian religious orders at the end of the sixteenth century, a period of crucial transformations from the cultural point of view as well. Several parameters are acting simultaneously: the impetus of Roman Catholicism after the Tridentine Council, the new economy of the book world after the consolidation of the printing press, and the shifting of the library paradigm from the medieval sedimentary models towards the

---

4 Bibliography on this topic is too vast to be mentioned and is increasingly growing, due to the progress of archival search. See, for example, Fiammetta Sabba (ed.), *La libraria settecentesca di San Francesco del Monte a Perugia: non oculis mentibus esca* (Perugia: Fabrizio Fabbri, 2015). On the integration of the analysis of surviving books and historical inventories see, among others, the remarks by Rosa Marisa Borraccini, *Introduzione*, in Rosa Marisa Borraccini (ed.), *Dalla notitia librorum degli inventari agli esemplari. Saggi di indagine su libri e biblioteche dai codici Vaticani latini 11266–11326* (Macerata: EUM, 2009), pp. XI–XXV.

challenges of the early modern public library. An overall view of the book collections owned by religious libraries, highlighting their characteristics and internal fractures, is key to fully understanding how these changes have acted, assessing their impact and evaluating their effects.

1 Toward a Quantitative Approach

Over the centuries, the massive number of book lists sent by religious orders to the Congregation of the Index has been partially lost, but their quantity remains impressive. In addition, other materials are gradually emerging from other archival fonds.[5]

The religious orders to which the data belong are more than thirty; convents or monasteries involved, from the north to the south of Italy, are approximately 2,200; their book lists amount to about 9,500.[6] Generally, for each religious house, the books, either in common libraries or in use to friars and monks, are analytically described, and bibliographic details are of good quality, due to the rules imposed by the Congregation of the Index, so it is possible to identify a large part of the items, even if sometimes misleading references and errors are to be taken into account.[7] Thus we have, if not a complete survey

---

5   The Vatican corpus it is not comprehensive of data from Jesuits and Dominicans; some of the orders included are only partially documented and several convents or entire provinces are missing, see Dykmans, 'Les bibliothèques des religieux d'Italie en l'an 1600', and Lebreton-Fiorani, *Codices Vaticani Latini 11266–11326*. Other materials found in different institutions, probably as a result of the complex history of the original collection, have recently been added to the Vatican lists, notably the lists of Minims, of the Capuchins of the province of Siracusa, of the Camaldoli Hermitage, of the Oratorian library of Santa Maria in Vallicella at Rome, see bibliography in Rosa Marisa Borraccini, Giovanna Granata and Roberto Rusconi, 'A proposito dell'inchiesta della S. Congregazione dell'Indice dei libri proibiti di fine '500', *Il capitale culturale. Studies on the Value of Cultural Heritage*, 6 (2013), pp. 13–45: 17, http://riviste.unimc.it/index.php/cap-cult/article/view/400.

6   Monastic Ordres: Carthusians, Cistercians, Camaldoleses, Camaldoleses of Monte Corona, Vallombrosans, Benedictines of Montevergine, Celestines, Olivetans, Benedictines of Cassino. Hermit Congregations: Hermits of St Jerome, Hermits of St Jerome of Fiesole, Poor Hermits of St Jerome of the Congregation of Blessed Peter of Pisa. Mendicant Orders: Augustinians, the Brethren of St Ambrose ad Nemus and St Barnabas, Carmelites, Cruciferi, Franciscans (Conventuals, Observants, Reformed Observants, Capuchins, Third Order), Minims, Servites. Canons (of the Lateran; of Santo Spirito of Venice; of San Giorgio in Alga, of San Salvatore). Clerks Regular: Barnabites, Caracciolini, Oratorians, Somascan Fathers, Theatines.

7   An examination of the indexing practices based on the lists of the Regular Canons is performed by Gianna Del Bono, 'Le liste delle congregazioni dei Canonici regolari Lateranensi e dei Canonici regolari di San Salvatore. Struttura, ordinamento e stile citazionale', *La*

of Italian religious libraries, at least a vast, homogeneous, and accurate sample of their library network, particularly suitable for a systematic analysis of the documentation. The use of such quantitative data would, of course, be impossible without the support of an automatic information retrieval system. This is the aim of the database *Le biblioteche degli Ordini regolari in Italia alla fine del secolo XVI*, which was launched at the beginning of the new millennium and has recently been updated with a new interface and improved functionalities.[8]

The main concern of this database is not to make inventories available in electronic format for surveys on individual libraries. Studies of this kind are desirable, and this is, in fact, a well-developed line of research that looks at the documentation of the Congregation of the Index insofar as it attests to the early stage of specific book collections.[9]

However, the primary purpose of the database is rather to shift the focus of the investigation towards the whole network of libraries of religious orders and to relate data from their book lists, making it possible to conduct a broad and wide-ranging examination of the ocean of available information.

Bibliofilía, 121.3 (2019), pp. 451–479. On misleading and deceptive items, see Roberto Rusconi, 'The Devil's Trick. Impossible Editions in the Lists of Titles from the Regular Orders in Italy at the End of the Sixteenth Century', in Flavia Bruni, Andrew Pettegree (eds.), *Lost Books. Reconstructing the Print World of Pre-Industrial Europe* (Leiden: Brill, 2016), pp. 310–323.

8   The database (cited as RICI in the following) is available at https://rici.vatlib.it/. The project, coordinated by Roberto Rusconi, started in 2001. After a preparatory phase, the first overall results were presented to scholars and librarians in a conference held in Macerata in 2006, the proceedings of which were published in Rosa Marisa Borraccini, Roberto Rusconi (eds.), *Libri, biblioteche e cultura degli Ordini regolari nell'Italia moderna attraverso la documentazione della Congregazione dell'Indice* (Vatican City: Biblioteca Apostolica Vaticana, 2006) where the general features of the database are also illustrated, see Giovanna Granata, 'Struttura e funzionalità della banca dati Le biblioteche degli ordini regolari in Italia alla fine del secolo XVI', ibid., pp. 285–308). The new interface was launched in June 2021.

9   Several studies of this type were carried out within the RICI project by the closest collaborators. See the bibliography, updated to 2012, published as an appendix to the essay by Borraccini, Granata, and Rusconi, 'A proposito dell'Inchiesta'. It is not possible to bring it further up to date but some conferences and their proceedings can be mentioned: Livia Martinoli, Ugo Fossa (eds.), *Le fonti per la storia camaldolese nelle biblioteche italiane e nella Biblioteca Apostolica Vaticana* (Rome: Biblioteca nazionale centrale di Roma, 2015), pp. 7–39 (papers by Roberto Rusconi, Samuele Megli and Rosa Marisa Borraccini); Riccardo Cataldi (ed.), *'In monasterio reservetur'. Le fonti per la storia dell'Ordine cistercense in Italia dal Medioevo all'Età moderna nelle biblioteche e negli archivi italiani e della Città del Vaticano* (Cesena: Centro Storico Benedettino Italiano, 2018), pp. 291–314 (paper by Enrico Pio Ardolino). Among the monographic studies see Monica Bocchetta, *Biblioteche scomparse: le librerie claustrali degli eremiti del Beato Pietro da Pisa. Ricostruzione storico-bibliografica* (Cargeghe: Documenta, 2016).

Data entry is still in progress, but some religious orders have been fully processed or are at a very advanced stage.[10] About 7,200 lists have been indexed for more than 300,000 items and checked against the most current reference sources for early printing and publishing. As a result, a relevant part of them has been identified as corresponding to 31,212 editions already known that are recorded several times in different lists.[11]

Some cautions are to be taken to find a way in this vast amount of information. It is inconceivable to observe patterns and discover meanings without dominating the numbers, and for this purpose, it is necessary to process them through serial and statistical methods. Otherwise, the 'global' approach that has been claimed before would remain a chimera. In particular, a quantitative analysis focused on the distribution of editions and related copies described in the lists can bring significant elements that may attract the interest of book historians in several respects.

A first issue concerns the problem of lost books. Almost seventy percent of the items in the lists are copies of known editions, while the remaining thirty percent are apparently unrecorded in current bibliographic tools. They can, however, be grouped when showing the same bibliographic information, and, taking due methodological caution to single out possible ghosts, they can be

---

10 Lists of religious orders whose data have been fully indexed in the database are also made available in a printed version in the sub-series *Libri e biblioteche degli Ordini religiosi in Italia alla fine del secolo XVI* within the Vatican Library series *Studi e Testi* (Vatican City: Biblioteca Apostolica Vaticana). The following volumes have so far been published (and their data in the database are therefore ultimative): (1) *Studi e Testi* 475: Samuele Megli and Francesco Salvestrini (eds.), *Congregazione di Santa Maria di Vallombrosa dell'Ordine di san Benedetto* (2013); (2) *Studi e Testi* 487: Cécile Caby and Samuele Megli (eds.), *Congregazione camaldolese dell'Ordine di san Benedetto* (2014); (3) *Studi e Testi 497: Chierici regolari minori*, ed. by Lucia Marinelli, Paola Zito; *Congregazione dell'Oratorio*, ed. by Elisabetta Caldelli, Gennaro Cassiani; *Ordine dei frati scalzi della b. Vergine Maria del Monte Carmelo*, ed. by Giovanni Grosso (2015); (4) *Studi e testi* 522: Monica Bocchetta (ed.), *Congregazione degli Eremiti di san Girolamo del beato Pietro da Pisa. Monaci eremiti di san Girolamo* (2017); (5) *Studi e Testi* 525: Alessandro Serra (ed.), *La Congregazione dell'Indice, l'esecuzione dell'Index del 1596 e gli Ordini regolari in Italia. Documenti*, (2018); (6) *Studi e Testi* 530: Gianna Del Bono (ed.), *Congregazione dei Canonici regolari del ss. Salvatore* (2018); (7) *Studi e Testi 539*: Rocco Benvenuto, Roberto Rusconi (eds.), *Ordine dei Minimi di san Francesco di Paola* (2020); (8) *Studi e Testi 555*: Carmela Compare, Francesca Nepori, Roberto Rusconi (eds.), *Ordine dei Frat Minori Cappuccini I* (2022).
11 Numerical data are updated to 14 September 2021.

used to reconstruct a hypothetical list of editions, described in the lists but unrecorded today because no copies of them have survived.[12]

Some results have already been discussed, for example, in the case of a *Confessionario* by the Dominican theologian Girolamo da Palermo (d. 1595).[13] Data from Edit16, the Italian national census, attests to the partial survival of the work, repeatedly published in Italy in the sixteenth century. In fact, the title page of the oldest known edition of the *Confessionario*, printed in Brescia by Ludovico Sabbio in 1564, presents it as 'nuovamente ristampato con alcuni aggiunti avisi'.[14] The database confirms this evidence by listing six editions, at the moment without any surviving copy, all printed between 1557 and 1563.[15]

There are many other cases concerning very popular religious books subject to the high degree of wear and tear to which this kind of work, more than others, was particularly exposed.[16] For some of these hypothetical lost editions, the number of copies described in book lists might provide some clues and help to identify the most relevant candidates in the 'ocean' of items. Indeed, not checked editions, full of bibliographic data, are approximately 25,000

---

12 The significance of the documentation with regard to the problem of lost books was outlined very early, even before the launch of the database, see Giuseppina Zappella, 'Alla ricerca del libro perduto: supplemento "virtuale" agli annali della tipografia napoletana del Cinquecento', in Vincenzo De Gregorio (ed.), *Bibliologia e critica dantesca. Saggi dedicati a Enzo Esposito, I: Saggi bibliologici* (Ravenna: Longo, 1997), pp. 243–293. Studies on this topic have been encouraged by the new availability of data; see Giovanna Granata, 'Le biblioteche dei religiosi in Italia alla fine del Cinquecento attraverso l'"Inchiesta" della Congregazione dell'Indice. A proposito di libri "scomparsi". Il caso dei Francescani Osservanti di Sicilia', in Maria Grazia Del Fuoco (ed.), *'Ubi neque aerugo neque tinea demolitur'. Studi in onore di Luigi Pellegrini per i suoi settanta anni* (Naples: Liguori, 2006), pp. 329–406; Ugo Rozzo, 'Una fonte integrativa di ISTC. L'inchiesta della Congregazione dell'Indice del 1597–1603', in Borraccini, Rusconi (eds.), *Libri, biblioteche e cultura*, pp. 215–250.

13 Rosa Marisa Borraccini, 'Un Unknown Best-Seller. The *Confessionario* of Girolamo da Palermo', in Bruni, Pettegree (eds.), *Lost Books*, pp. 291–309.

14 Edit16 CNCE 65596, https://edit16.iccu.sbn.it/titolo/CNCE065596; USTC 833364.

15 RICI BIB 41240, https://rici.vatlib.it/BIB/41240, USTC 1793007; RICI BIB 12688, https://rici.vatlib.it/BIB/12688, USTC 1793008; RICI BIB 47123, https://rici.vatlib.it/BIB/47123, USTC 1793009; RICI BIB 13863, https://rici.vatlib.it/BIB/13863, USTC 1793010; RICI BIB 61772, https://rici.vatlib.it/BIB/61772, USTC 1793011; RICI BIB 40744, https://rici.vatlib.it/BIB/40744, USTC 1793012.

16 A list of authors with a higher number of not checked editions compared to the checked editions has been proposed in a methodological paper to filter occurrences of the database by Giovanna Granata, 'On the Track of Lost Editions in Italian Religious Libraries at the end of the Sixteenth Century. A Numerical Analysis of the RICI Database', in Bruni, Pettegree (eds.), *Lost Books*, pp. 324–344.

and almost 3,600 occur more than once. These last ones can be a useful starting point.

The famous late medieval hagiographical collection, the *Legenda aurea* by Jacobus de Voragine (1228/9–1298), is an exemplar study case. The work, widely read in the manuscript era, also had a relevant fortune as a printed text, both in the original Latin version and in vernacular translation.[17] To integrate our knowledge in this regard, the numerical occurrences of the database provide invaluable information.

Seventeen lists include, for example, the Italian version entitled *Legendario delle vite de' santi* printed by Matteo Valentini in 1592, of which, according to Edit16, no copies are available in Italy.[18] With regard to editions by Domenico and Giovanni Battista Guerra, who printed the Italian version by Niccolò Malerbi in 1571, 1578, 1580, 1583, 1585 and 1586, the lists include at least fourteen copies that are described as printed in 1573, and ten as published in 1576; in both cases there is no reference in the Italian census.[19] Finally, nine items suggest that Fioravante Prati published the *Legendario* not only in 1586, 1588, 1590, 1596 and 1600 but also in 1597.[20] It is unlikely to think of the convergence of casual errors in such a relevant number of cases.

A second area of investigation is concerned with the analysis of known editions, which constitute a remarkable sample of early printing and publishing in Europe. Being more than 30,000, as mentioned above, they cover the entire period from the earliest incunabula to the beginning of the seventeenth century, and a vast geographical area. Listed places of publication include the most important European production centres, such as Venice, where a large part of the editions were published (43%), as well as Lyon (9.8%), Paris (8.5%) and Rome (5%). Consequently, the spectrum of printers and publishers, about 2,700, is also vast and includes some minor figures, as well as the most distinguished names of the book world.

---

17   For the critical edition of the Latin version, see Iacopo de Voragine, *Legenda Aurea. Con le miniature del codice Ambrosiano C 240 inf.*, ed. by Giovanni Paolo Maggioni etc. (Florence: Sismel Edizioni del Galluzzo; Milan: Biblioteca Ambrosiana, 2007); concerning the vernacular tradition, see Valerio Marucci, 'Manoscritti e stampe antiche della Legenda aurea di Jacopo da Voragine volgarizzata', *Filologia e critica*, 5 (1980), pp. 30–50 and, for the Italian fortune of the work in the printing era, Linda Pagnotta, *Le edizioni italiane della 'Legenda aurea', 1475–1630* (Florence: Apax libri, 2005).
18   RICI BIB 5389, https://rici.vatlib.it/BIB/5389, USTC 1793013, cfr. Pagnotta, *Le edizioni italiane*, p. 137.
19   RICI BIB 7888, https://rici.vatlib.it/BIB/7888, USTC 1793014; BIB 6823, https://rici.vatlib.it/BIB/6823, USTC 1793015.
20   RICI BIB 20497, https://rici.vatlib.it/BIB/20497, USCT 1793016.

Again, the quantitative analysis provides valuable elements for looking over the data and identifying some general patterns. In particular, it allows assessing in real terms, and not as inferred from the current censuses, the diffusion of an essential category of book production and the scale and degree of its penetration, as well as the printers and publishers' commitment and success in responding to the interests and needs of Italian religious communities.

It is possible to have some hints about the impact of such printers and publishers by considering the occurrence of their editions and related copies on the one hand and the total output of their presses, as is evident from bibliographic tools, on the other. A general view based on both parameters highlights some of the firms as being more effective. This is, for example, the case of the Scoto and the Sessa families (particularly of the heirs of Ottaviano Scoto and the heirs of Melchiorre Sessa), or even of other Venetian printers such as Giovanni Battista Somasco, Domenico Nicolini da Sabbio, Francesco de' Franceschi, the Sign of Speranza, Giovanni Antonio Bertano, Fabio and Agostino Zoppini. For all of them, the editions recorded in the database represent a relevant portion of those resulting from the Edit16 census, and the distribution of copies per edition is also relatively high.[21]

A third research area concerns the cultural identity of Italian religious libraries, particularly the occurrences of authors and works. Books recorded in the Vatican lists cover different thematic domains (including classical and humanistic literature, law, medicine and mathematics), but they are mostly of religious interest. Within this extensive framework, some sub-types and some leading authors stand out. A quantitative analysis based on the distribution of copies by author allows the identification of some relevant features in terms of the impact and importance of their works.

Regarding this aspect, the following section proposes a more detailed picture based on an analysis of a list of authors in decreasing order by the number of copies belonging to both checked and unchecked editions. The investigation is limited to the range of authors with more than 500 occurrences, as shown in Table 10.1.

---

21   The rate of editions from Edit16 recorded in the RICI database is between 60% (Giovanni Battista Somasco) and 85% (brothers Zoppini) and the mean number of copies per edition is from 10 (heirs of Scoto) to 16 (Somasco). An analysis of non-Venetian printers, mainly from Lyon and Paris, has been proposed by Giovanna Granata, 'Books Without Borders. The Presence of the European Printing Press in the Italian Religious Libraries at the End of the Sixteenth Century', in Matthew McLean, Sara Barker (eds.), *International Exchange in the Early Modern Book World* (Leiden: Brill, 2016), pp. 214–238.

TABLE 10.1   List of authors sorted by number of copies

Copies	Authors
5679	Catholic Church
4637	Thomas Aquinas (saint)
3895	Azpilcueta Martín de (1493–1586)
3075	Antoninus of Florence (1389–1459)
3047	Bible (latin)
2797	Council of Trent (1545–1563)
2483	Cicero Marcus Tullius (106–43 a.C.)
2385	Aristotle (384–322 a.C.)
2351	Denis the Carthusian (1402–1471)
2334	Luis de Granada (1504–1588)
2226	Augustine (saint)
1985	Bonaventure (saint)
1955	Fumo Bartolomeo (d. 1555)
1779	Panigarola Francesco (1548–1594)
1736	Duns Scotus John (1265?–1308)
1590	Toledo Francisco (1532–1596)
1573	Berarducci Mauro Antonio (xvith cent.)
1555	Calepino Ambrogio (1435–1510)
1519	Jacobus de Voragine (1228?–1298)
1513	Guevara Antonio de (1481–1545)
1509	De Vio Tommaso (1468–1533)
1422	Angelo da Chivasso (1410?–1495)
1379	Medina Bartolomé de (1527–1580)
1335	Chaves Tomaz de (d. 1570)
1295	Musso Cornelio (1511–1574)
1265	Incarnato Fabio (xvith–xviith cent.)
1246	Javelli Giovanni Crisostomo (1470?–1538)
1227	Estella Diego (1524–1578)
1201	Gregory I (pope)
1170	Tartaret Pierre (xvth cent.)
1140	Jerome (saint)
1126	Nifo Agostino (1473–1545)
1080	Titelmans Franciscus (1502–1537)
1067	Soto Domingo de (1494–1570)
1053	Savonarola Girolamo (1452–1498)
1052	Peter Lombard (1195?–1160?)
1025	Mazzolini Silvestro (1456?–1523)

TABLE 10.1 List of authors sorted by number of copies (*cont.*)

Copies	Authors
1019	Dias Filippe (d. 1601)
995	Pepin Guillaume (d. 1533)
985	Hugo Argentinensis (1200?–1268)
967	Bernard of Clairvaux (saint)
890	Giles of Rome (1243?–1316)
871	John Chrysostom (saint)
867	Ludolph von Sachsen (1300?–1378)
853	Pacifico da Novara (1420–1482?)
851	Calderari Cesare (d. 1588)
789	Caracciolo Roberto (1425–1495)
787	Jean de Jandun (d. 1328)
785	Fiamma Gabriele (1531–1585)
777	D'Angelo Bartolomeo (d. 1584)
772	Durand Guillaume (1230?–1296)
728	Paolo Veneto (1386–1428)
725	Boethius (480?–524?)
674	Vergilius Maro Publius (70–19 a.C.)
669	Nicholas of Lyra (1291–1340)
658	Pérez de Valencia Jaime (1408–1490)
651	Pelbartus of Temesvár (1435?–1504)
640	Forte Giovanni Bernardo (d. 1503?)
636	Menghi Girolamo (d. 1610)
619	De imitatione Christi
606	Ovidius Naso Publius (43 a.C.–17 d.C.)
599	Marcos de Lisboa (1511–1591)
590	Guido de Monte Rocherii (fl. 1333)
587	Anglés José (d. 1586)
586	Razzi Serafino (1531–1613)
586	Ammiani Sebastiano (1503?–1568)
584	Corradone Matteo (d. 1525)
582	Venuti Filippo (1531–1587)
570	Denisse Nicolas (d. 1509)
566	Busti Bernardino (1450?–1513)
563	Bible. New Testament (latin)
558	Burley Walter (1275–1345?)
546	Visdomini Francesco (1516–1573)
544	Verrati Giovanni Maria (d. 1563)

TABLE 10.1 List of authors sorted by number of copies (*cont.*)

Copies	Authors
534	Wild Johann (1495–1554)
530	Pezzi Lorenzo (XVIth cent.)
523	Albertus Magnus (saint)
520	Loarte Gaspar de (d. 1588)
517	Biel Gabriel (1425?–1495)
509	Corpus iuris canonici. Decretales Gregorii IX
504	Vivaldo Martín Alfonso (1545–1605)

2 Analysis of Authors and Works

As is apparent from the top of the list in Table 10.1, higher values can be observed for liturgical or official books, such as the Roman Catechism, recorded under the entry Catholic Church; for several editions of the Latin biblical text; and for the Tridentine decrees that, as expected, are largely widespread. Other entries denote a wide range of authors in the field of scholastic, moral and pastoral theology and in the area of devotional and ascetic literature.

Generally speaking, the prominence of the Thomistic tradition stands out. Saint Thomas Aquinas is, in fact, one of the authors in absolute numbers most cited in the lists (4,637 copies), and no less significant is the position of the Cardinal Thomas De Vio (1,509 copies), the great commentator of the *Summa*, whose exegetical, theological and philosophical works are largely attested.

The importance of Thomism is mirrored, regarding philosophy, by the numerical weight of Aristotle (2,385 copies) and, more generally, by Aristotelianism. Apart from Albertus Magnus (523 copies), some modern commentaries should be noted, mainly represented by Crisostomo Javelli's works (1,246 copies). To them should be added the great names of the Avverroist school of Padua (Paolo Veneto, with 728 copies, and Agostino Nifo, with 1,126 copies), while for medieval Averroism, there is the name of Jean de Jandun (787 copies) and, on the anti-Averroist side, that of Giles of Rome. For him, 890 copies are attested, mainly belonging to editions of his Aristotelian commentaries and the commentary on Peter Lombard's *Sentences*.

Despite the weight of the Aristotelian-Thomistic tradition, a relevant interest in Augustine's work should also be noted (2,226 copies), which attests to his longstanding, powerful influence. In the line of Platonic-Augustinian thought, there are also other authors among the most prominent in the list; in particular, St Bernard (967 copies), the Franciscan theologian par excellence, St Bonaventura (1,985 copies), who comes just after Augustine (2,226 copies), and Duns Scotus, whose weight is also particularly relevant (1,736 copies).

The presence of the Greek Church Father John Chrysostom, who, besides the Latin Fathers Jerome and Gregory the Great, stands out in the list (871 copies), should also be highlighted in this context, as his homiletic work has traditionally been a source for medieval Platonism. However, the presence of Renaissance Neoplatonism appears to be fairly weak, given that the name Marsilio Ficino is far from the top of the list and is out of the range analysed (300 copies).

The long heritage of medieval tradition does not cover all entries on the list; it is also important to note the presence of the 'modern' authors of the second scholasticism who strongly affected the renewal of theological and philosophical thought in early modern Europe. This is the case of Francisco Toledo (1,590 copies), Francisco De Vitoria, whose *Summa sacramentorum* is present through the compendium of Tomaz de Chaves (1,335 copies), Domingo de Soto (1,067 copies), and Bartolomeo de Medina (1,379 copies). Data related to the theologians of Salamanca appear particularly meaningful if we consider the absence of the library lists belonging to Dominicans and Jesuits and seem to represent even more, for the same reason, a strong and widely shared structural element.

This connection of renewal aspects with the chain of tradition is a general feature of the list. Looking at the names, it is evident that some very popular post-Tridentine authors compete and alternate with those from other strands, reflecting the history of religious communities over earlier periods and the persistence of some cultural trends.

Concerning moral theology, for example, both the sixteenth-century Spanish canonist Martin Azpilcueta and the late-medieval archbishop of Florence Antoninus Pierozzi, very close in terms of number of copies, share prominent positions at the beginning of the list (3,895 and 3,075 copies, respectively). A long series of authors of *Summae confessorum* attests to the fortune and evolution of the traditional casuistry: Pacifico da Novara (853 copies), Angelo Carletti da Chivasso (1,422 copies), Silvestro Mazzolini (1,025 copies), Bartolomeo Fumo (1,955), Mauro Antonio Berarducci (1,573 copies); nonetheless, in addition to the Navarro's *Manuale de' confessori et penitenti*, also the *Breve instruttione de' confessori* by Bartolomé de Medina is present, covering a large part of the occurrences of the Dominican theologian.

On the post-Tridentine front, some famous ascetic writers are present among the authors with a higher number of copies, such as Luis de Granada (2,334 copies), Antonio de Guevara (1,513 copies), and Diego Estella (1,227 copies); however, the names of Denis le Chartreux (2,351 copies) and Ludolph von Sachsen (867 copies) remain in the list with relevant data. Devotional works include some classics, such as the *Imitatio Christi* (619 copies) and the *Legenda aurea* by Iacopo de Voragine (1,519 copies), as well as the *Ricordo del ben morire* and the *Consolatione de' penitenti* by the late sixteenth century Dominican Bartolomeo D'Angelo (777 copies).

It is similarly possible to observe the prominent names of sixteenth-century ecclesiastical rhetoric, such as Francesco Panigarola (1,779 copies), Cornelio Musso (1,295 copies), and Gabriele Fiamma (785 copies). At the same time, the late fifteenth-century Italian preacher Roberto Caracciolo and the French Dominican Guillaume Pepin, again a pre-Reformation Catholic preacher, are also quite high in the number of copies (789 and 995 copies).

3   Some Methodological and Conclusive Remarks

This list of authors reconstructs a very general picture resulting from the accumulation of all data. Thus, it risks being abstract, not considering some qualitative and quantitative parameters, such as the uneven contribution of various religious orders due to their cultural identities and their different quantitative weights in relation to the total dataset.

The books of Franciscan Observants in the database amount, for example, to 63,960 items. The 'second' religious order in terms of number of copies, the Canons Regular of the Lateran, counts 37,093 items. Thus, it is highly possible that the strong presence of some authors in the list, for example Bonaventure, is a direct effect of both the Franciscan interest in Bonaventure and the numerical relevance of the Observants' data.

Some doubts can therefore be raised about the significance of the list. The question is whether the framework it provides can be used to reconstruct a common background for religious libraries, or whether it is just an unrealistic numerical model. A second question is how much the various religious orders eventually diverge from this hypothetical canon.

To find an answer, it is necessary to compare the religious-order-specific data after neutralising the numerical differences between them.

The calculation was carried out only for the religious orders most prominent by the number of items in the database. They are, besides the Franciscan

Observants and the Canons Regular of the Lateran mentioned above, the Capuchins (28,880 items), the Carthusians (10,727 items), the Minims (11,539 items), the Benedectines of Cassino (11,533 items) and the Augustinians (10,232 items).

In detail, the number of copies belonging to the different authors of the previously examined list has been normalised, i.e. has been divided by the total number of copies counted for the selected religious orders, thus obtaining the 'religious-order-specific weight' (ROSW) of each author; e.g. as Observant count 1,020 copies for St Thomas Aquinas on a total of 63,960 items, the normalised value of the author (ROSW) for the Observants is 1,020/63,960 = 1.59%.

The calculated ROSWs were used to compute the authors' mean value shown in column 3 of Table 10.2. This value is used as a reference term to compare the behaviour of different religious orders. Columns 4–10 report for each author the ratio of the ROSWs and the mean value. Basically, a unit value means that the normalised specific value (ROSW) of the author is equal to the mean value; an index greater or lower than 1 means that the significance of the author is higher or lower than the mean value.

Some macroscopic results can be observed by looking at the data processing results. First, it is apparent that some indexes are significantly higher than the mean value. As expected, for example, this is the case of Bonaventure and Duns Scotus for Franciscans (Observants and Capuchins); in the same way, Denis le Chartreux and Ludolph von Sachsen have a more distinctive position in Carthusian libraries, as well as Giles of Rome in Augustinian libraries.

On the opposite side, there are authors with a very low index for some religious orders, as is the case of the Portuguese fray Felipe Dias, a famous Franciscan preacher, almost absent from the Cassinesi libraries and even the case of the Franciscan exorcist Girolamo Menghi (1529–1609) for the Carthusian libraries. Again, this is a natural behaviour reflecting the religious orders' cultural trends and their identity-related choices.

A second remark can be made if the sorting criterion is considered. While the list in Table 10.1 is ordered by the absolute number of copies, the criterion in Table 10.2 uses the mean value in Column 3. This implies the inclusion of some other authors in the 'canon'. Their absolute index is lower than 500, but they have a ROSW in the same range as the most common authors. These additional authors, in plain characters, are mainly present in the second part of the table, while the first part is almost the same. This means that the normalising process, by reducing the strong impact of the numerically most significant religious orders, enlarges the list but does not drastically change it, thereby confirming the reliability of the numerical model.

Finally, a third general remark can be raised. As observed, the differences among religious orders as for the specific weight (ROSW) of each author introduce some modifications to the internal organisation of the list, but basically, the main authors are transversal to all of the inspected orders. The mean value is never affected exclusively by just one religious order and they all contribute, at different levels, to determining its value.

A type of bibliographic *koinè* can therefore be envisaged based on these results. Its various modulations outline some differences and peculiarities in the cultural and historical traditions of different religious orders and their libraries. In this bibliographic *koinè*, some authors stand out, pointing to a major (but not exclusive) involvement of some religious orders, as is, for example, the case of Bonaventure. Other authors can have a more marginal role for certain orders, but again, without being completely outside of their cultural paradigm. Finally, a subset of authors has a more neutral position, as the ROSW does not diverge so much from the mean value. This is, for example, the case of Augustine, whose presence is almost a constant for all the orders: a feature whose implications in terms of cultural history are much more complex than numbers can explain and which claims for a deeper and more complete analysis.

The proposed remarks are only a first advancement, not least because they are based on a sample of the documentation now available through the database, which is itself part of the total being processed. However, these remarks already outline some general trends and draw attention to methodological issues and research perspectives.

ITALIAN RELIGIOUS ORDERS AND THEIR BOOKS 215

TABLE 10.2 List of authors sorted by the mean of the ROSWs

Copies	Authors	ROSW's mean	OFMObs (ratio)	OFMCap (ratio)	CRL (ratio)	OCart (ratio)	OM (ratio)	OSBCas (ratio)	OESA (ratio)
5679	Catholic Church	2,70	0,67	0,54	0,68	1,13	0,36	1,53	2,08
4637	Thomas Aquinas (saint)	1,84	0,86	1,43	1,11	0,68	1,38	0,54	1,01
3895	Azpilcueta Martín de (1493–1586)	1,64	1,00	1,11	0,74	0,59	2,14	0,52	0,89
3047	Bible (latin)	1,28	1,05	1,00	1,20	1,08	0,97	0,94	0,76
2351	Denis the Carthusian (1402–1471)	1,18	0,57	1,17	0,60	2,35	1,31	0,57	0,43
3075	Antoninus of Florence (1389–1459)	1,15	1,39	0,95	0,83	0,84	1,12	0,65	1,23
2483	Cicero Marcus Tullius (106–43 a.C.)	1,08	0,52	0,73	0,89	1,33	0,69	2,28	0,55
2334	Luis de Granada (1504–1588)	1,06	0,45	1,60	0,79	1,60	1,34	0,59	0,64
2797	Council of Trent (1545–1563)	1,04	1,40	0,80	0,96	0,60	1,39	0,99	0,86
2226	Augustine (saint)	0,97	0,90	1,00	1,06	1,17	1,00	0,73	1,14
2385	Aristotle (384–322 a.C.)	0,91	0,94	1,16	1,03	0,60	1,18	1,20	0,88
1955	Fumo Bartolomeo (d. 1555)	0,76	1,22	0,75	0,74	0,34	1,73	0,58	1,64
1985	Bonaventure (saint)	0,66	2,11	1,81	0,69	0,81	0,59	0,51	0,49
1573	Berarducci Mauro Antonio (XVIth cent.)	0,64	1,55	0,67	0,56	0,23	2,58	0,22	1,18
1590	Toledo Francisco (1532–1596)	0,63	0,69	1,99	0,81	0,18	1,47	0,73	1,13
1555	Calepino Ambrogio (1435–1510)	0,62	0,79	0,88	1,18	1,34	0,46	1,40	0,95
1379	Medina Bartolomé de (1527–1580)	0,62	0,92	1,04	0,53	0,21	2,11	0,27	1,92
1519	Jacobus de Varagine (1228?–1298)	0,61	1,17	1,30	0,70	1,09	1,21	0,54	0,99
1509	De Vio Tommaso (1468–1533)	0,61	0,69	1,05	0,79	0,69	1,78	0,98	1,02
1513	Guevara Antonio de (1481–1545)	0,60	0,99	1,18	0,89	1,08	1,02	0,94	0,89

TABLE 10.2 List of authors sorted by the mean of the ROSWs (cont.)

Copies	Authors	ROSW's mean	OFMObs (ratio)	OFMCap (ratio)	CRL (ratio)	OCart (ratio)	OM (ratio)	OSBCas (ratio)	OESA (ratio)
1779	Panigarola Francesco (1548–1594)	0,60	2,26	0,65	1,16	0,58	1,04	0,39	0,91
890	Giles of Rome (1243?–1316)	0,55	0,55	0,44	0,60	0,10	0,52	0,41	4,39
1265	Incarnato Fabio (XVIth–XVIIth cent.)	0,55	1,50	0,26	0,31	0,66	2,33	0,82	1,12
1201	Gregory I (pope)	0,51	0,89	1,15	0,63	1,81	1,12	1,04	0,36
1246	Javelli Giovanni Crisostomo (1470?–1538)	0,50	0,80	1,35	1,30	0,35	1,25	0,82	1,13
1140	Jerome (saint)	0,50	0,78	1,22	0,56	1,79	1,23	0,90	0,51
1335	Chaves Tomaz de (d. 1570)	0,49	1,28	0,67	0,82	0,72	1,74	0,67	1,11
1736	Duns Scotus John (1265?–1308)	0,49	3,10	1,21	0,54	0,15	0,95	0,56	0,48
1227	Estella Diego (1524–1578)	0,49	1,09	1,79	0,94	0,70	0,85	0,19	1,43
1295	Musso Cornelio (1511–1574)	0,49	1,23	1,21	1,18	0,78	1,55	0,37	0,68
1126	Nifo Agostino (1473–1545)	0,47	0,72	1,08	0,94	0,53	1,45	0,81	1,47
967	Bernard of Clairvaux (saint)	0,47	0,64	1,02	0,85	1,82	0,83	1,44	0,39
1080	Titelmans Franciscus (1502–1537)	0,46	0,94	1,73	0,91	0,49	0,96	1,51	0,47
1067	Soto Domingo de (1494–1570)	0,45	0,43	1,71	1,08	0,41	1,58	0,69	1,10
1422	Angelo da Chivasso (1410?–1495)	0,45	2,86	0,92	0,54	0,56	0,82	0,55	0,75
1052	Peter Lombard (1195?–1160?)	0,42	1,11	0,97	0,85	0,78	1,08	0,96	1,24
995	Pepin Guillaume (d. 1533)	0,42	1,44	0,75	0,76	0,52	1,48	0,17	1,88
1025	Mazzolini Silvestro (1456?–1523)	0,41	0,84	1,38	0,97	0,69	1,76	0,55	0,81
1019	Dias Filippe (d. 1601)	0,40	1,23	1,79	1,17	0,35	1,01	0,04	1,41
867	Ludolph von Sachsen (1300?–1378)	0,40	0,75	1,17	0,65	2,26	1,17	0,52	0,49

ITALIAN RELIGIOUS ORDERS AND THEIR BOOKS 217

TABLE 10.2 List of authors sorted by the mean of the ROSWs (cont.)

Copies	Authors	ROSW's mean	OFMObs (ratio)	OFMCap (ratio)	CRL (ratio)	OCart (ratio)	OM (ratio)	OSBCas (ratio)	OESA (ratio)
871	John Chrysostom (saint)	0,38	0,81	1,30	1,10	1,16	0,78	1,15	0,70
985	Hugo Argentinensis (1200?–1268)	0,36	1,44	1,03	1,06	0,77	1,10	0,70	0,89
777	D'Angelo Bartolomeo (d. 1584)	0,35	0,85	1,00	0,57	0,61	1,92	0,71	1,33
1053	Savonarola Girolamo (1452–1498)	0,35	1,22	1,27	1,07	0,88	0,91	1,04	0,61
728	Paolo Veneto (1386–1428)	0,34	1,03	0,56	0,95	0,36	0,69	0,51	2,90
1170	Tartaret Pierre (xvth cent.)	0,33	3,38	1,50	0,43	0,00	0,56	0,53	0,60
772	Durand Guillaume (1230?–1296)	0,31	1,24	1,02	0,82	1,01	1,18	0,83	0,90
851	Calderari Cesare (d. 1588)	0,31	1,57	0,86	1,03	0,15	0,79	0,20	2,42
785	Fiamma Gabriele (1531–1585)	0,30	1,02	1,06	1,63	0,43	1,63	0,40	0,84
725	Boethius (480?–524?)	0,29	0,99	0,93	0,92	1,22	0,81	1,62	0,51
789	Caracciolo Roberto (1425–1495)	0,28	1,66	1,07	0,72	0,96	1,53	0,31	0,76
674	Vergilius Maro Publius (70–19 a.C.)	0,28	0,30	0,34	0,84	1,29	0,52	3,14	0,56
787	Jean de Jandun (d. 1328)	0,28	1,22	0,63	1,28	0,14	0,91	0,98	1,85
658	Pérez de Valencia Jaime (1408–1490)	0,27	1,20	1,23	0,85	0,52	1,62	0,45	1,13
563	Bible. New Testament (latin)	0,26	0,90	1,05	0,44	1,58	0,57	1,94	0,53
619	De imitatione Christi	0,26	0,72	1,64	0,49	1,81	0,81	1,15	0,38
606	Ovidius Naso Publius (43 a.C.–17 d.C.)	0,26	0,45	0,30	1,32	0,87	0,57	2,87	0,61
640	Forte Giovanni Bernardo (d. 1503?)	0,25	1,36	1,04	0,67	0,92	0,76	0,93	1,32
853	Pacifico da Novara (1420–1482?)	0,25	2,89	0,52	0,49	0,19	0,98	0,52	1,42
534	Wild Johann (1495–1554)	0,24	0,79	1,42	0,63	0,46	1,35	1,24	1,12

TABLE 10.2 List of authors sorted by the mean of the ROSWs (cont.)

Copies	Authors	ROSW's mean	OFMObs (ratio)	OFMCap (ratio)	CRL (ratio)	OCart (ratio)	OM (ratio)	OSBCas (ratio)	OESA (ratio)
590	Guido de Monte Rocherii (fl. 1333)	0,22	1,17	0,84	0,47	1,29	0,77	0,97	1,49
586	Razzi Serafino (1531–1613)	0,22	1,29	0,36	0,97	0,47	1,58	0,51	1,82
651	Pelbartus of Temesvár (1435?–1504)	0,21	2,34	2,06	0,78	0,39	0,77	0,20	0,46
486	Vincent Ferrer (saint)	0,21	0,85	1,79	0,59	1,09	1,66	0,20	0,82
669	Nicholas of Lyra (1291–1340)	0,21	2,34	1,41	0,89	0,57	0,85	0,49	0,46
520	Loarte Gaspar de (d. 1588)	0,21	0,45	1,38	0,78	1,91	1,07	0,95	0,46
441	Landsberg Johann (1489–1539)	0,21	0,41	1,86	0,45	3,13	0,54	0,42	0,19
582	Venuti Filippo (1531–1587)	0,21	1,30	1,12	0,64	1,97	0,68	0,85	0,43
636	Menghi Girolamo (d. 1610)	0,20	2,13	0,70	1,11	0,05	1,05	0,35	1,62
509	Corpus iuris canonici. Decretales Gregorii IX	0,20	1,76	1,03	0,79	0,47	1,75	0,66	0,54
566	Busti Bernardino (1450?–1513)	0,20	2,08	1,58	0,64	0,80	0,75	0,35	0,79
587	Anglés José (d. 1586)	0,20	2,48	1,04	0,70	0,38	1,58	0,18	0,64
462	Viguier Juan (fl. 1527–1550)	0,20	0,76	1,03	1,35	0,71	1,37	0,58	1,20
517	Biel Gabriel (1425?–1495)	0,20	1,54	1,50	1,02	0,71	0,75	0,66	0,80
523	Albertus Magnus (saint)	0,19	0,92	1,01	1,59	1,29	0,67	0,76	0,75
499	Francisco de Osuna (1497–1540)	0,19	1,71	1,32	0,89	0,00	1,38	0,13	1,56
504	Vivaldo Martín Alfonso (1545–1605)	0,19	1,08	0,38	1,20	0,24	2,73	0,67	0,71
544	Verrati Giovanni Maria (d. 1563)	0,19	1,55	1,02	0,93	0,10	1,21	0,31	1,87
584	Corradone Matteo (d. 1525)	0,19	2,35	0,72	0,48	0,63	0,67	0,58	1,57
477	Morigia Paolo (1525–1604)	0,19	0,63	0,94	0,51	1,80	1,67	0,54	0,92

TABLE 10.2 List of authors sorted by the mean of the ROSWS (cont.)

Copies	Authors	ROSW's mean	OFMObs (ratio)	OFMCap (ratio)	CRL (ratio)	OCart (ratio)	OM (ratio)	OSBCas (ratio)	OESA (ratio)
586	Ammiani Sebastiano (1503?-1568)	0,19	1,76	1,29	1,08	0,49	1,14	0,23	1,03
456	Jansenius Cornelius (1510-1576)	0,19	1,03	1,84	1,05	0,59	1,23	0,55	0,72
457	Petrarca Francesco (1304-1374)	0,19	0,49	0,29	2,03	1,53	0,14	2,16	0,36
474	Marulić Marko (1450-1524)	0,19	1,01	1,18	0,77	1,39	1,24	0,74	0,67
392	Vives Juan Luis (1492-1540)	0,19	0,53	1,05	0,52	1,69	0,51	2,22	0,47
409	Pinto Hector (1528-1584?)	0,19	0,58	1,91	1,53	0,55	1,64	0,00	0,79
432	Terentius Afer Publius (II cent. a.C.)	0,18	0,60	0,23	0,64	1,11	0,47	3,47	0,48
393	Villegas Selvago Alonso de (1534-1594)	0,18	0,87	1,07	0,42	0,96	2,21	0,56	0,90
546	Visdomini Francesco (1516-1573)	0,18	1,55	1,25	1,00	0,20	1,51	0,43	1,07
599	Marcos de Lisboa (1511-1591)	0,18	2,29	3,67	0,19	0,41	0,05	0,24	0,16
440	Eck Johann (1486-1543)	0,18	1,14	1,37	0,90	0,97	1,23	0,85	0,54
475	Corpus iuris canonici. Decretum Gratiani	0,18	1,72	0,94	0,97	0,41	1,82	0,72	0,43
433	Iosephus Flavius (37-100?)	0,18	1,07	0,98	0,99	0,98	0,82	1,20	0,97
341	Cassianus Iohannes (360?-435)	0,18	0,39	0,81	0,59	2,03	1,50	1,40	0,27
483	Barletta Gabriele (d. 1480)	0,18	1,21	0,87	0,89	0,26	1,60	0,24	1,92
428	Horatius Flaccus Quintus (65-8 a.C.)	0,17	0,32	0,58	0,62	1,18	0,45	3,24	0,62
530	Pezzi Lorenzo (XVIth cent.)	0,17	1,64	0,54	0,88	0,75	0,85	1,05	1,29
389	Palacio Paulo de (d. 1582)	0,17	0,94	1,55	1,25	0,27	0,96	0,10	1,93
558	Burley Walter (1275-1345?)	0,17	2,12	0,73	1,34	0,11	0,81	0,76	1,14
570	Denisse Nicolas (d. 1509)	0,17	2,75	1,48	0,84	0,16	0,91	0,46	0,40

CHAPTER 11

Books in the Cloister, Books in the Cells

The Augustinians of Santa Maria del Popolo in Rome and Their Book Collections at the End of the Sixteenth Century

Lucrezia Signorello

The aim of this paper is to present a description of the book collections of Santa Maria del Popolo in Rome (conventual library and friars' books for personal use) derived from the lists sent in the Jubilee year 1600 in response to requests received from the Sacred Congregation of the Index. The study will begin by placing the creation of these inventories in the historical context of the publication of the Clementine Index of prohibited books (1596) and of the actions promoted by the Sacred Congregation of the Index to verify its application. Subsequently, the communications between the Augustinians of the Observant Congregation of Lombardy (to whom the convent of Piazza del Popolo was entrusted) and the Congregation of the Index regarding the lists of their books will be examined. The enrichment of Santa Maria del Popolo's library in the sixteenth century will then be related to the history of this Augustinian community, highlighting its religious and cultural role in the city. The work will also present a quantitative and qualitative analysis of the convent library and of the personal collections of the friars of Santa Maria del Popolo, based on the content of the lists sent in June 1600 to the Congregation of the Index. The paper will conclude with a brief overview of the historical events that affected the convent library over the following centuries causing its gradual dispersion.

1 'The List of All the Books': A Matter of Prerogatives

On 17 May 1596, Clemens VIII issued a reviewed *Index librorum prohibitorum*.[1] The enactment of this index had many consequences, varying from those

---

[1] On the history of censorship in Italy, among the extensive bibliography, see Gigliola Fragnito (ed.), *Church, Censorship and Culture in Early Modern Italy*, transl. Adrian Belton (Cambridge: Cambridge University Press, 2001); Mario Infelise, *I libri proibiti. Da Gutenberg all'Encyclopédie* (Rome: Laterza, 2013); Vittorio Frajese, *La censura in Italia. Dall'Inquisizione alla Polizia* (Rome: Laterza, 2014); Hannah Marcus, *Forbidden Knowledge. Medicine, Science, and Censorship in Early Modern Italy* (Chicago: University of Chicago Press, 2020); Giorgio

related to the promulgation of the previous lists of 1558–1559 and 1564.[2] Among these outcomes were those resulting from the fact that this time the Sacred Congregation of the Index required the preparation of precise and detailed lists of books owned by the Regular Religious Orders in Italy. This request was made to ensure that the Clementine Index had been effectively applied even behind the cloisters' walls. Today, thanks to the preserved documentation, the history of these enforced dynamics of the application of the Clementine Index among the Italian Religious Orders can be retraced, which also highlights the leading role played by the cardinals of the Index, a role that must certainly be considered novel at the time.[3] Previously, in fact, the responsibilities of the Congregation's cardinals had been limited to compiling a list of prohibited or censored books. Its enforcement was instead delegated to the Master of the Sacred Palace and the Holy Inquisition, two much older and more powerful institutions that had acquired expertise in the field of book censorship in various ways.[4]

Caravale, *Libri pericolosi. Censura e cultura italiana in età moderna* (Rome: Laterza, 2022) and Robin Vose, *Index of Prohibited Books. Four Centuries of Struggle over Word and Image for the Greater Glory of God* (London: Reaktion Books, 2022).

2   See Paul F. Grendler, *The Roman Inquisition and the Venetian Press, 1540–1605* (Princeton: Princeton University Press, 1977), pp. 254–285; Gigliola Fragnito, 'L'applicazione dell'indice dei libri proibiti di Clemente VIII', *Archivio Storico Italiano*, 159.1 (2001), pp. 107–149; Gigliola Fragnito, 'The Central and Peripheral Organization of Censorship', in Fragnito (ed.), *Church, Censorship and Culture in Early Modern Italy*, pp. 13–49.

3   In 1998, Pope John Paul II (1920–2005) opened the Archive of the Congregation for the Doctrine of the Faith for consultation. This allowed scholars to freely access the Archive of the Congregation of the Index, which was deposited there in 1917 at the time of its suppression; see Roberto Rusconi, 'Premessa', in Alessandro Serra (ed.), *La Congregazione dell'Indice, l'esecuzione dell'Index del 1596 e gli ordini regolari in Italia. Documenti* (Vatican City: Biblioteca Apostolica Vaticana, 2018), pp. 5–7, esp. 5. On this Archive, see: http://www.acdf.va/content/dottrinadellafede/it/l-archivio-storico/indice.html. This documentation has been analyzed and partially published in Marie-Madeleine Lebreton, Luigi Fiorani (eds.), *Codices 11266–11326. Inventari di biblioteche religiose italiane alla fine del Cinquecento* (Vatican City: Biblioteca Apostolica Vaticana, 1985); Serra (ed.), *La Congregazione dell'Indice*. On this topic, see also Gigliola Fragnito, 'La censura libraria tra Congregazione dell'Indice, Congregazione dell'Inquisizione e Maestro del Sacro Palazzo (1571–1596)', in Ugo Rozzo (ed.), *La censura libraria nell'Europa del secolo XVI* (Udine: Forum, 1997), pp. 163–175; Vittorio Frajese, 'La politica dell'Indice dal Tridentino al Clementino (1571–1596)', *Archivio italiano per la storia della pietà*, 11 (1998), pp. 269–356; Gigliola Fragnito, *La Bibbia al rogo. La censura ecclesiastica e i volgarizzamenti della Scrittura (1471–1605)* (Bologna: Il Mulino, 2015), pp. 227–273.

4   See Vittorio Frajese, 'La congregazione dell'Indice negli anni della concorrenza con il Sant'Uffizio (1593–1603)', *Archivio italiano per la storia della pietà*, 14 (2001), pp. 207–256; Gigliola Fragnito, 'L'Indice clementino e le biblioteche degli ordini religiosi', in Rosa Marisa Borraccini, Roberto Rusconi (eds.), *Libri, biblioteche e cultura degli ordini regolari nell'Italia moderna attraverso la documentazione della Congregazione dell'Indice* (Vatican City: Biblioteca Apostolica Vaticana, 2006), pp. 37–59, esp. 37–38; Vittorio Frajese, *Nascita*

In preparation for the publication of the new list of forbidden books, with the papal brief *Sacrosanctum catholicae fidei* issued on 17 October 1595, the new tasks of the Congregation of the Index were also established: the cardinals and their collaborators were entrusted with the operations relating to the application of the new rules; they also had to interpret the prescriptions contained in the Index and settle disputes that arose during enforcement.[5] Within the Congregation, the cardinals who guided the activity of fulfilling the rules on book censorship were Marcantonio Colonna, Agostino Valier and Simone Tagliavia d'Aragona, as well as the secretary of the Index, the Dominican Paolo Pico.[6] During the first months of the Clementine Index's execution, the regular clergy (along with the laity and the secular clergy) was called to take a census of its libraries, and to return the forbidden and suspended books, or the lists of such volumes, to the Congregation. Most of the Italian regular clergy, sensitive to their own jurisdictional privileges, seemed to oppose the investigation, probably fearing interference in their own affairs.[7] This reluctance led Cardinal

---

dell'Indice. La censura ecclesiastica dal Rinascimento alla Controriforma (Brescia: Morcelliana, 2006) and Gigliola Fragnito, 'La Congregazione dell'Indice', *Archivum Historiae Pontificiae*, 53 (2019), pp. 241–260.

5   Since the Index published at the end of the Council of Trent (1564), the indices of the prohibited books did not consist of a simple list of the books to be censored but also contained general rules for censorship, rules whose application created many problems of interpretation. On this topic, see Fragnito, 'The Central and Peripheral Organization of Censorship'; Fragnito, 'L'applicazione dell'indice'; Fragnito, *La Bibbia al rogo*; Gigliola Fragnito, 'La censura ecclesiastica nell'Italia della Controriforma: organismi centrali e periferici di controllo', in Gigliola Fragnito, Alain Tallon (eds.), *Hétérodoxies croisées. Catholicismes pluriels entre France et Italie, XVIe–XVIIe siècles* (Rome: École française de Rome, 2017), pp. 77–95. For the text of the *Sacrosanctum catholicae fidei*, see Luigi Tomassetti (ed.), *Bullarum diplomatum et privilegiorum sanctorum Romanorum pontificum* (24 vols., Turin: Seb. Franco etc., 1857–1872), x. 231–233.

6   On Cardinal Colonna (1523–1597), see Franca Petrucci, 'Colonna, Marcantonio', in *Dizionario Biografico degli Italiani*, XXVII (Rome: Istituto della Enciclopedia Italiana, 1982), pp. 371–383. On the Venetian Valier (1531–1606), see Giovanni Cipriani, *La mente di un inquisitore. Agostino Valier e l'Opusculum De cautione adhibenda in edendis libris (1589–1604)* (Florence: Nicomp, 2008); Elisabetta Patrizi, *Pastoralità ed educazione. L'episcopato di Agostino Valier nella Verona post-tridentina (1565–1606)* (2 vols., Milan: FrancoAngeli, 2015). On Cardinal Tagliavia (1550–1604), see Giovanni Maria Mazzuchelli, *Gli scrittori d'Italia cioè Notizie storiche, e critiche intorno alle vite, e agli scritti dei letterati italiani* (2 vols., Brescia: Presso a Giambatista Bossini, 1753–1763), II/2. 918 *sub voce*. On Paolo Pico (1563–1614), see Giuseppe Catalani, *De secretario Sacrae Congregationis indicis libri duo* (Rome: Typis Antonii Fulgoni apud S. Eustachium, 1751), pp. 95–96.

7   The edicts of publication of the Index made no distinction between laity, secular clergy and regular clergy; therefore, the superiors of the male and female monastic and conventual institutes had to present to the bishop or the inquisitor the forbidden or suspended books kept in their common libraries and in the individual cells of their institutes, or the lists of

Valier to write several times to the heads of the Religious Orders to immediately enforce the Index. Finally, starting from December 1599, while requests for an extension concerning the lists of suspended books continued to arrive at the Congregation from the Orders, the cardinals of the Index, exasperated by the lack of cooperation of the religious families, iussed a peremptory order to send 'the list of all the books, printed or handwritten, found in public or private libraries of the Italian convents and monasteries'.[8] A new and much more onerous task was thus imposed on the regular clergy, which was supposed to be completed by May 1600, a term later extended to 24 June, for the feast of Saint John the Baptist. With delays and solicitations, the census was concluded only towards the end of the year, although some religious families delivered their lists of books up until 1602. In opposition, some Orders, such as the Dominicans and Jesuits, never responded to the Congregation's requests.[9]

An important result of the investigation promoted by the Congregation of the Index is the numerous book lists sent by various religious families. This documentation is now preserved (for the most part) in the mss. Vat. lat. 11266–11326 of the Vatican Apostolic Library.[10] The census of the book heritage of religious families in Italy was required for disciplinary control purposes, and

these books. Monasteries and convents, especially those endowed with the prerogatives of *nullius dioeceseos*, were rightly afraid that, recognizing the jurisdictional superiority of the bishops, they would lose their autonomy; on this topic, see Fragnito, *La Bibbia al rogo*, pp. 241–246 and Fragnito, 'L'applicazione dell'indice', pp. 126–130.

8   '[la] "nota de tutti li libri, stampati o scritti a mano, che si ritrouano nelle librarie publiche o priuate" dei conventi e monasteri d'Italia', Serra (ed.), *La Congregazione dell'Indice*, p. 17. All translations are my own.

9   See Roberto Rusconi, 'Le biblioteche degli ordini religiosi in Italia intorno all'anno 1600 attraverso l'inchiesta della Congregazione dell'Indice. Problemi e prospettive di una ricerca', in Edoardo Barbieri, Danilo Zardin (eds.), *Libri, biblioteche e cultura nell'Italia del Cinque e Seicento* (Milan: Vita e Pensiero, 2002), pp. 63–84, esp. 66 and Giovanni Petrocelli, 'Considerazioni sugli esiti dell'Inchiesta della Congregazione dell'Indice (1598–1603): il caso lucano', *Bibliothecae.it*, 8.1 (2019), pp. 119–147, esp. 122. On this topic, see also Fragnito, 'L'applicazione dell'indice', pp. 127–130 and Fragnito, *L'Indice clementino*, pp. 37–59.

10 This documentation is currently the object of the extensive research project RICI – *Ricerca sull'Inchiesta della Congregazione dell'Indice*, coordinated by Roberto Rusconi, which provides for the publication of the book lists of the Religious Orders in the collection *Libri e biblioteche degli ordini religiosi in Italia alla fine del secolo XVI* and makes also the data available in an online database, see: https://rici.vatlib.it/. See also Chapter 10 in this volume. It must be stressed that not all the lists sent by the Religious Orders are kept in the *Vaticani Latini* manuscript collection of the Vatican Apostolic Library; on this topic, see Roberto Rusconi, 'L'Ordine dei Frati Minori Cappuccini in Italia e l'inchiesta della S. Congregazione dell'Indice dei libri proibiti al volgere del secolo XVI', in Carmela Compare etc. (eds.), *Ordine dei Frati Minori Cappuccini* (Vatican City: Biblioteca Apostolica Vaticana, 2022), pp. 43–55, esp. 46 and 52–53.

thus to verify (also within ecclesiastical institutions) the conformity of the readings, cultural influences and educational models with the prescriptions of the post-Tridentine Church.[11] However, today it also allows to learn about the book acquisitions of the religious (especially preachers and friars dedicated to the care of souls) as well as the texts used by teachers and students in the internal *studia*. In short, one can take a look inside some of the most important institutions of the Italian ecclesiastical world.[12]

> The richness of these lists appears a priori. Think of the books gathered in these various epochs, the intellectual life and spirituality they reflect, the bibliographies they will complete, from the incunabula to the date so precise of 1600.[13]

The second important aspect, particularly for the history of books and libraries, is the precision required in drawing up the inventories: not only the titles and authors of the registered books (printed or manuscript) had to be given, but also the place of printing, the name of the printer, the print date and the topic of the text in the case of manuscripts without an author.[14] These are the indications that, in fact, Agostino Valier gave to Pedro Balaguer, general of the Mercedarians, on 3 December 1599:

> Reverend father and brother, since in the collections of many religious men and many monasteries there are numerous books that must be censored, which are not easily recognizable by all and must be corrected, therefore by virtue of this, under the penalty of being suspended from

---

11 On this topic, see Romeo De Maio, 'Le biblioteche dei monasteri italiani alla fine del Cinquecento. I modelli culturali della Controriforma', in *Magia, astrologia e religione nel Rinascimento* (Warsaw: Wydawnicwo PAN, 1974), pp. 148–162.

12 On this documentation, see Roberto Rusconi, 'Le biblioteche degli ordini religiosi in Italia alla fine del secolo XVI', *Rivista di storia del cristianesimo*, 1 (2004), pp. 189–199 and Rosa Marisa Borraccini, 'Da strumento di controllo censorio alla "più grande bibliografia nazionale della Controriforma". I codici Vaticani latini 11266–11326', in Maria Guercio etc. (eds.), *Disciplinare la memoria. Strumenti e pratiche nella cultura scritta (secc. XVI–XVIII)* (Bologna: Pàtron, 2014), pp. 177–189.

13 See Marc Dykmans, 'Les bibliothèques des religieux d'Italie en l'an 1600', *Archivum Historiae Pontificiae*, 24 (1986), pp. 385–404, esp. 390.

14 See Petrocelli, 'Considerazioni sugli esiti dell'Inchiesta', p. 121 and Samuele Megli, 'Le liste dei titoli dei libri presenti nei monasteri camaldolesi alla fine del Cinquecento (dall'inchiesta della S. Congregazione dell'Indice dei libri proibiti)', in Livia Martinoli, Ugo Fossa (eds.), *Le fonti per la storia camaldolese nelle Biblioteche Italiane e nella Biblioteca Apostolica Vaticana* (Rome: Biblioteca Nazionale Centrale di Roma, 2015), pp. 19–26, esp. 20.

your office and other arbitrary penalties, by the end of May you will have the procurator of your religion deliver to our Congregation of the Index in Rome the note of all the books, printed or handwritten, that are found in your monasteries in Italy, so that it will be easily known which books must be censored, indicating not only the title and the author, but also the place of printing and the printer.[15]

Although, it should be pointed out that not all notes possess the same degree of accuracy. Consequently, the analysis of book collections from these lists must be done with great care. In fact, the compilers of the lists have not infrequently distorted or omitted some bibliographic data. Sometimes, even the use of Latin or vernacular can mislead the reader because it does not always reflect the language of the work recorded.[16] Despite this, the census remains highly significant: it provides a picture (or a partial one) of the book presence inside the cloisters' walls and often allows to identify, with reasonable accuracy, the editions in the religious libraries, and in some lucky cases even the preserved copies. However, attention must be paid not only to the critical interpretation of these archival sources but also to their historical context: 'the investigation obviously requires strict precautions'.[17] Therefore, when analysing these lists, the reasons that led to their editing and the criteria used to create them must also be taken into consideration.[18]

---

15 'Reuerendo padre come fratello, ritrouandosi molti libri degni di censura appresso diuersi religiosi et in diuersi monasterij, quali non sono facilmente da tutti conosciuti e si deueno emendare, però in uirtù di questa, sotto pena della sospensione dell'offitio et altre arbitrarie pene, per tutto maggio farà presentare in Roma dal procurator della sua Religione la nota de tutti li libri, stampati o scritti a mano, che si ritrouano nei lor monasterii in Italia alla nostra Congregatione dell'Indice, acciò si possa facilmente conoscer quelli che hanno bisogno di censura, esprimendo non solo il titolo del libro et il nome de l'authore ma il luogo anco della stampa e nome del stampatore', Serra (ed.), *La Congregazione dell'Indice*, pp. 130–131, no. 81, esp. 130. On Balaguer (c.1540–1599), see Pedro de San Cecilio, *Annales del Orden de Descalzos de Nuestra Señora de la Merced Redempcion de Cautiuos Christianos* (2 vols., Barcelona: Por Dionisio Hidalgo, 1669), USTC 5058447 and 5058448, I. 189–191; Bruce Taylor, *Structures of Reform. The Mercedarian Order in the Spanish Golden Age* (Leiden: Brill, 2000), p. 427.

16 See Petrocelli, 'Considerazioni sugli esiti dell'Inchiesta', pp. 122–125.

17 See Daniel Mornet, 'Les enseignements des Bibliothèques privées (1750–1780)', *Revue d'Histoire littéraire de la France*, 17.3 (1910), pp. 449–496, esp. 451.

18 See Luca Ceriotti, 'Scheletri di biblioteche, fisionomie di lettori. Gli "inventari di biblioteca" come materiali per una anatomia ricostruttiva della cultura libraria di antico regime', in Barbieri, Zardin (eds.), *Libri, biblioteche e cultura*, pp. 373–432; Edoardo Barbieri, 'Elenchi librari e storia delle biblioteche nella prima età moderna. Alcune osservazioni', in Fabio Forner etc. (eds.), *Margarita amicorum. Studi di cultura europea per Agostino Sottili* (2 vols., Milan: Vita e Pensiero, 2005), I. 81–102; Malcolm Walsby, 'Book Lists and Their Meaning',

2 Between Centre and Periphery: Santa Maria del Popolo and Its Role in the City

Although small in comparison to other contemporaneous Roman libraries, the conventual book collection of Santa Maria del Popolo played a remarkable role in the cultural context of sixteenth-century Rome. Among the library users were ecclesiastics and lay intellectuals, and famous people donated their books to the Augustinians. To understand the composition of the Augustinian library based on the lists sent to the Congregation of the Index in 1600, it is necessary to first outline the history of the convent of Santa Maria del Popolo in the hundred years preceding the issue of the Clementine Index.

The Augustinians have been in charge of the church of Santa Maria del Popolo since the mid-thirteenth century. Here was held in March 1256 the general chapter that had decided the union of the congregations that followed the Augustinian rule in the Order of Saint Augustine (the so-called 'Grand Union'), which was confirmed by Pope Alexander IV with the bull *Licet Ecclesiae Catholicae* of 9 April 1256.[19] The convent of Santa Maria del Popolo had gradually declined during the long years of the Avignon Papacy, following the overall destiny of Rome, which had been compromised by the prolonged absence of the pontiff.[20] The final return of the pope and his court to the Eternal City triggered the beginning of systematic projects of urban planning and building renovation.[21] Located near Porta Flaminia, Santa Maria del Popolo was

---

in Malcolm Walsby, Natasha Constantinidou (eds.), *Documenting the Early Modern Book World. Inventories and Catalogues in Manuscript and Print* (Leiden: Brill, 2013), pp. 1–24.

19   See Paul van Geest, 'The Rule of Saint Augustine', in Krijn Pansters (ed.), *A Companion to Medieval Rules and Customaries* (Leiden: Brill, 2020), pp. 127–154, esp. 146. On the bull of Pope Alexander VII see Alberic de Meijer, 'Licet Ecclesiae Catholicae. I. Text', *Augustiniana*, 6 (1956), pp. 9–13; Rafael Kuiters, 'Licet Ecclesiae Catholicae. II. The Commentary', *Augustiniana*, 6 (1956), pp. 14–36 and Benigno van Luijk, 'Bullarium Ordinis Eremitarum S. Augustini. Periodus formationis 1187–1256 (*finis*)', *Augustiniana*, 14 (1964), pp. 216–249, esp. 239–241, no. 163.

20   See Anna Cavallaro, 'Il XV secolo: da Innocenzo VII (1404–1406) a Martino V (1417–1431)', in Mario D'Onofrio (ed.), *La committenza artistica dei papi a Roma nel Medioevo* (Rome: Viella, 2016), pp. 361–380, esp. 361. On the city of Rome in this historical period, see Silvia Maddalo, In figura Romae. *Immagini di Roma nel libro medioevale* (Rome: Viella, 1990); Jean-Claude Maire Vigueur, *The Forgotten Story. Rome in the Communal Period*, transl. David Fairservice (Rome: Viella, 2016); Walter Angelelli, Serena Romano (eds.), *La linea d'ombra. Roma 1378–1420* (Rome: Viella, 2019) and Daniele Manacorda, *Paesaggi di Roma medievale* (Rome: Viella, 2021).

21   See Maria Chiabò etc. (eds.), *Alle origini della nuova Roma. Martino V (1417–1431)* (Rome: Istituto Storico Italiano per il Medioevo, 1992); Arnold Esch, *Roma dal Medioevo al Rinascimento (1378–1484)*, transl. Maria Paola Arena Samonà (Rome: Viella, 2021).

strategically placed for the religious life, social and urban fabric of the city, next to the entrance for visitors coming from the north to Rome along the Via Flaminia.[22] Among these were popes and emperors, who made their triumphal entries right in front of the Augustinian church, and at the start of the urban route that would lead them to the Vatican.[23] Therefore, it is not surprising that Santa Maria del Popolo was the first Roman Renaissance construction site, a testing ground for the *renovatio Urbis* project of Sixtus IV (Francesco della Rovere), which he also chose as a personal and family monument.[24]

Santa Maria del Popolo became a place to unite visually the universal domination of the church with the della Rovere, a totemic symbol that would associate the della Rovere with Rome and allowed them to co-opt its magnificence and glory as their own. ... The choice of Santa Maria del

---

22 The Via Flaminia, since ancient times, had been one of the most important roads of the Italian peninsula because it connected Rome with northern Italy, and therefore with the Transalpine regions. Its strategic role was also confirmed in the late Middle Ages and then in the Renaissance: pilgrims, kings and emperors had to travel it to reach the Eternal City from the north. On the Via Flaminia, see Gaetano Messineo, *La Via Flaminia. Da Porta del Popolo a Malborghetto* (Rome: Quasar, 1991); Gaetano Messineo, Andrea Carbonara, *Via Flaminia* (Rome: Istituto Poligrafico e Zecca dello Stato. Libreria dello Stato, 1993) and Arnold Esch, 'Die Via Flaminia in der Landschaft: Nachleben einer antiken Straße, mit Hinweisen zur Begehung im Gelände zwischen Soracte und Otricoli', *Antike Welt*, 26.2 (1995), pp. 85–113.

23 See Maria Antonietta Visceglia, *La città rituale. Roma e le sue cerimonie in età moderna* (Rome: Viella, 2002), pp. 64–65. On the road system in Rome in the Middle Ages, see Lia Barelli etc. (eds.), Viae Urbis. *Le strade a Roma nel medioevo* (Rome: Viella, 2023).

24 See Enzo Bentivoglio, Simonetta Valtieri, *Santa Maria del Popolo a Roma. Con una appendice di documenti inediti sulla Chiesa e su Roma* (Rome: Bardi, 1976); *Il '400 a Roma e nel Lazio* (6 vols., Rome: De Luca, 1981–1983), I. Roberto Cannatà etc. (eds.), *Umanesimo e primo Rinascimento in S. Maria del Popolo*; Ilaria Miarelli Mariani, Maria Richiello, *Santa Maria del Popolo. Storia e restauri* (2 vols., Rome: Istituto Poligrafico e Zecca dello Stato, 2009). On Sixtus IV (1414–1484), see Massimo Miglio etc. (eds.), *Un pontificato ed una città. Sisto IV (1471–1484)* (Vatican City: Scuola di Paleografia, Diplomatica e Archivistica, 1986). On the projects of urban planning and building renovation of Rome in the fifteenth century, see *Roma. Le trasformazioni urbane nel Quattrocento* (2 vols., Florence: Leo S. Olschki, 2004). On the building policy of Pope Sixtus IV and his plans for Santa Maria del Popolo, see Fabio Benzi, *Sisto IV Renovator Urbis. Architettura a Roma 1471–1484* (Rome: Officina, 1990), pp. 64–66, 99–107, 197–198; Giulia Petrucci, 'La via Sistina da porta del Popolo al vaticano ed il programma urbanistico di Sisto IV per Borgo (1471–1484)', in *La città del Quattrocento, Storia dell'Urbanistica*, n.s., 4 (1998), pp. 35–57 and Lorenzo Finocchi Ghersi, 'I cantieri sistini di Santa Maria del Popolo e Sant'Agostino a Roma', in Carla Frova etc. (eds.), *La carriera di un uomo di curia nella Roma del Quattrocento. Ambrogio Massari da Cori, agostiniano: cultura umanistica e committenza artistica* (Rome: Viella, 2008), pp. 173–182.

Popolo as a della Rovere monument was also rooted in its location. The church was high in profile and weighty with power. Ninety percent of the documented entries into Rome in the Renaissance used one of two northern approaches: the Via Flaminia leading to the Porta del Popolo, and the Via Triumphalis ending at the gate to Saint Peter's. The position of Santa Maria del Popolo along this path was highly significant and the church derived much of its meaning for the della Rovere from its environment. It was in a very prominent location on a major pilgrimage and supply artery, mentioned fourth in guide books immediately after the historically important Saint Peter's, Saint John Lateran, and Santa Maria Maggiore.[25]

In 1472, Sixtus IV called (with some insistence!) the friars of the Observant Congregation of Lombardy, the most influential among the Augustinians, to take possession of the convent.[26] Exploiting the prestige of the Observance, he relaunched Santa Maria del Popolo by transferring it to a congregation both powerful and learned.[27] However, another element of the pope's project for

---

25   See Lisa Passaglia Bauman, 'Piety and Public Consumption: Domenico, Girolamo, and Julius II della Rovere at Santa Maria del Popolo', in Ian F. Verstegen (ed.), *Patronage and Dynasty. The Rise of the Della Rovere in Renaissance Italy* (Kirksville: Truman State University Press, 2007), pp. 39–62, esp. 40–41.

26   A documentary dossier on this affair can be found in Rome, State Archives, *Congregations suppressed, Augustinians in Santa Maria del Popolo*, register 1, ff. 1r–3r. Regarding the history of the Augustinians and their settlements, see Benigno van Luijk, *Le monde augustinien du XIIIe au XIXe siècle* (Assen: Van Gorcum & Co., 1972); David Gutiérrez, *Storia dell'Ordine di S. Agostino* (3 vols., Rome: Institutum Historicum Ordinis Fratrum S. Augustini, 1972–1987) and Luis Marín de San Martín, *Gli agostiniani. Origini e spiritualità* (Rome: Institutum Historicum Augustinianum, 2013).

27   On the Augustinian Observance, see Katherine Walsh, 'The Observance: Sources for a History of the Observant Reform Movement in the Order of Augustinian Friars in the Fourteenth and Fifteenth Centuries', *Rivista di storia della Chiesa in Italia*, 31.1 (1977), pp. 40–67; Mario Mattei, 'L'Ordine degli Eremitani di S. Agostino e l'Osservanza di Lombardia', in Maria Mencaroni Zoppetti, Erminio Gennaro (eds.), *Società, cultura, luoghi al tempo di Ambrogio da Calepio* (Bergamo: Edizioni dell'Ateneo, 2005), pp. 39–57; Bert Roest, 'Observant Reform in Religious Orders', in Miri Rubin, Walter Simons (eds.), *The Cambridge History of Christianity* (9 vols., Cambridge: Cambridge University Press, 2005–2009), IV. 446–457; Nico Ciampelli, 'Le origini della Congregazione osservante di Lombardia. Il convento di S. Agostino di Crema e i suoi protagonisti. Una ricerca bibliografica e archivistica', *Insula Fulcheria*, 43 (2013), pp. 85–112; James D. Mixson, Bert Roest, *A Companion to Observant Reform in the Late Middle Ages and Beyond* (Leiden: Brill, 2015) and Mario Sensi, 'L'osservanza agostiniana: origini e sviluppi', in Alessandra Bartolomei Romagnoli etc. (eds.), *Angeliche visioni. Veronica da Binasco nella Milano del Rinascimento* (Florence: Edizioni del Galluzzo per la Fondazione Ezio Franceschini, 2016), pp. 71–139.

this church must be also stressed: the presence of one of the most famous Marian icons in the city, 'treasured as an authentic portrait of the Virgin by the hand of Saint Luke'.[28] During his reign, Sixtus IV (who affirmed the authenticity of this icon in 1478) granted numerous privileges to Santa Maria del Popolo, as well as many indulgences to pilgrims who visited it on a feast day associated with the Virgin.[29] Moreover, 'after Sixtus's renovation, its two lengthy façade inscriptions detailed the indulgences possible for visitors and suggested that the church had been built to "prepare the way for the kingdom of heaven"'.[30]

Indeed, 'Santa Maria del Popolo enjoys a double advantage, being at the same time dedicated to the Virgin and administered by a Mendicant Order'.[31] As a consequence, the Augustinian church quickly became a central place for both popular devotion and the self-celebratory aspirations of major figures in the papal court and city's society, a success that lasted through the reigns of Alexander VI, Julius II and Alexander VII (Figure 11.1).[32] Santa Maria del Popolo

---

28   See Alexander Nagel, Christopher S. Wood, *Anachronic Renaissance* (New York: Zone Books, 2010), p. 108. On this icon, see also Anne Dunlop, 'Pinturicchio and the Pilgrims. Devotion and the Past at Santa Maria del Popolo', *Papers of the British School at Rome*, 71 (2003), pp. 259–285; Bram Kempers, 'The Pope's Two Bodies. Julius II, Raphael and Saint Luke's Virgin of Santa Maria del Popolo', in Erik Thunø, Gerhard Wolf (eds.), *The Miraculous Image in the Late Middle Ages and Renaissance* (Rome: "L'Erma" di Bretschneider, 2004), pp. 135–159 and Lisa Pon, *A Printed Icon in Early Modern Italy. Forlì's Madonna of the Fire* (New York: Cambridge University Press, 2015), pp. 30–33, 77–78.

29   See Nagel, Wood, *Anachronic Renaissance*, p. 110.

30   See Passaglia Bauman, 'Piety and Public Consumption', p. 41.

31   See Cécile Troadec, *Roma crescit. Une histoire économique et sociale de Rome au XVe siècle* (Rome: École française de Rome, 2020), p. 435. On this topic, see also Maurice Dejonghe, *Roma santuario mariano* (Bologna: Cappelli, 1969); Giulia Barone, 'Immagini miracolose a Roma alla fine del Medio Evo', in Thunø, Wolf (eds.), *The Miraculous Image*, pp. 123–133 and Giulia Barone, 'Laici e vita religiosa', *Archivio della Società Romana di Storia Patria*, 132 (2009), pp. 133–147, esp. 141–145 [republished in: Giulia Barone, *Vita religiosa e istituzioni politiche nella Roma medievale*, eds. Antonio Montefusco, Andrea Antonio Verardi (Spoleto: Fondazione Centro Italiano di Studi sull'Alto Medioevo, 2022), pp. 147–161].

32   See Nicholas Temple, *Renovatio Urbis. Architecture, Urbanism and Ceremony in the Rome of Julius II* (London: Routledge, 2011). About Santa Maria del Popolo in the fifteenth century, see Anna Esposito, 'Centri di aggregazione: la biblioteca agostiniana di S. Maria del Popolo', in Miglio etc. (eds.), *Un pontificato ed una città*, pp. 569–597; Anna Esposito, 'Gli agostiniani osservanti nel Quattrocento: Santa Maria del Popolo', in Giulia Barone, Umberto Longo (eds.), *Roma religiosa. Monasteri e città (secoli VI–XVI)*, Reti Medievali Rivista, 19.1 (2018), pp. 501–515 and Anna Esposito, 'Presenza degli agostiniani nell'ambito urbanistico e sociale di Roma (secoli XIII–XV)', *Römische Quartalschrift für Christliche Altertumskunde und Kirchengeschichte*, 115.1–2 (2020), pp. 18–28. For the history of the convent in the following century, see Anna Esposito, 'I conventi agostiniani di Roma al tempo del soggiorno di Lutero', in Michael Matheus etc. (eds.), *Martin Lutero a Roma* (Rome: Viella, 2019), pp. 99–115.

therefore came to be, under the pontificate of Alexander VI, the most important cemetery church in the city, where many families chose to place their burials, so that it became 'an elite and privileged resting place'.[33] Thus, the chapels of the Cybo and the Chigi, of the cardinals Girolamo Basso della Rovere and Jorge da Costa were built there, and 'a total of eleven cardinals of various nationalities who died between 1478 and 1508 were buried in the church'.[34]

Less evident but equally significant proofs of its renown can be found in the inventories of the convent's properties, which increased thanks to donations of houses, land, money, liturgical furnishings and books.[35] The inventory

FIGURE 11.1   Giovanni Battista Falda, *Piazza del' Popolo abbellita da N. S. papa Alesandro VII* (Rome: Giovanni Giacomo de Rossi, 1665), Amsterdam, Rijksmuseum, RP-P-1957-653-54-1

---

33   See Jennifer Mara DeSilva, *The Office of Ceremonies and Advancement in Curial Rome, 1466–1528* (Leiden: Brill, 2022), p. 28, n. 41. On this topic, see also Christoph Luitpold Frommel, 'Giulio II e il coro di Santa Maria del Popolo', *Bollettino d'arte*, s. VI, 85.112 (2000), pp. 1–34, esp. 7.

34   See Piers Baker-Bates (etc.), 'Cardinals as Patrons of the Visual Arts', in Mary Hollingsworth etc. (eds.), *A Companion to the Early Modern Cardinal* (Leiden: Brill, 2020), pp. 511–534, esp. 522. On this topic, see also Bentivoglio, Valtieri, *Santa Maria del Popolo a Roma*, pp. 71–131; Anna Cavallaro, 'Introduzione alle cappelle maggiori', in Cannatà etc. (eds.), *Umanesimo e primo Rinascimento in S. Maria del Popolo*, pp. 75–83; Passaglia Bauman, 'Piety and Public Consumption'; Troadec, Roma crescit, pp. 434–435.

35   See Agostino Brigida, *Lucerna del venerabile convento de' reverendi padri agostiniani di Santa Maria del Popolo*, 1858 (Viterbo, Archive of the Augustinian Province of Italy, *Santa Maria del Popolo, Acts of the Convent*, file 2).

created in 1480 by the Augustinian Paolo Olmi and later updated by his brother Paolino da Milano is an exceptional source of information on the establishment and progressive enrichment of the conventual library.[36] This document, in fact, mentions the volumes that the Lombards found in the convent upon their arrival at Santa Maria del Popolo and the manuscripts and printed books that were subsequently added to the collection through donations and testamentary bequests from high prelates and lay people. The first of these gifts was made by Pope Sixtus IV himself, who had transferred to the convent part of the volumes of the Bishop Nicholas of Modruš, who died in 1480.[37] The book collection of Santa Maria del Popolo grew, for instance, due to the added volumes of the Roman lawyer Battista Brendi and of some bishops, including Marino Orsini and Giovanni de Cardellis. The description written by the French humanist Jean Matal, during his *grand tour* visiting numerous public and private libraries in central Italy, dates back to 1542–1546.[38] Finally, the inventory of 1600 inserted among the lists produced by the Observant Congregation of Lombardy in response to the request from the Sacred Congregation of

---

[36] See Esposito, 'Centri di aggregazione', p. 573. The index (preserved in Rome, General Archive O.S.A, *S. Maria del Popolo*, M. 32, ff. 18r–49v, 68v–69v) is published in David Gutiérrez, *De antiquis Ordinis Eremitarum S. Augustini bibliothecis* (Vatican City: Typis Polyglottis Vaticanis, 1955), pp. 264–291. On Paolo Olmi da Bergamo (1414–1484), see Alison Knowles Frazier, *Possible Lives. Authors and Saints in Renaissance Italy* (New York: Columbia University Press, 2005), pp. 241–246 and Paola Farenga, 'La controversia tra canonici regolari e agostiniani attraverso la stampa: Ambrogio, Domenico da Treviso, Paolo Olmi ed Eusebio Corrado', in Frova etc. (eds.), *La carriera di un uomo di curia*, pp. 75–90. On Paolino da Milano (d.1481), see Donato Calvi, *Delle memorie istoriche della Congr. Osser. di Lombardia dell'Ord. Erem. di S. Agostino* (Milan: Nella Stampa di Francesco Vigone, à S. Sebastiano, 1669), USTC 1736614, pp. 115–117.

[37] On Nicholas of Modruš (c.1425–1480), see Luka Špoljarić, *Nicholas of Modruš, 'The Glory of Illyria': Humanist Patriotism and Self-Fashioning in Renaissance Rome* (Budapest: The Central European University, 2013); Han Baltussen, 'Nicholas of Modruš's *De consolatione* (1465–1466): A New Approach to Grief Management', in Susan Broomhall (ed.), *Ordering Emotions in Europe, 1100–1800* (Leiden: Brill, 2015), pp. 105–120; Luka Špoljarić, 'Nicholas of Modruš', in Marco Sgarbi (ed.), *Encyclopedia of Renaissance Philosophy* (Cham: Springer, 2018), pp. 1–3 and Luka Špoljarić, 'Nicholas of Modruš and His *De Bellis Gothorum*: Politics and National History in the Fifteenth-Century Adriatic', *Renaissance Quarterly*, 72.2 (2019), pp. 457–491.

[38] Preserved in Cambridge, University Library, ms. Add. 565, ff. 105r–106r; this book list is published in Lucrezia Signorello, 'La biblioteca agostiniana di Santa Maria del Popolo negli scritti di Jean Matal', *Analecta Augustiniana*, 82 (2019), pp. 99–114, esp. 107–112. On Jean Matal (c.1517–1597), see Anthony Hobson, 'The *Iter Italicum* of Jean Matal', in Richard William Hunt etc. (eds.), *Studies in the Book Trade in Honour of Graham Pollard* (Oxford: The Oxford Bibliographical Society, 1975), pp. 33–61 and Peter Arnold Heuser, *Jean Matal. Humanistischer Jurist und europäischer Friedensdenker (um 1517–1597)* (Cologne: Böhlau, 2003).

the Index constitutes the last overall description of the Augustinian library. These three sources allow us to examine the evolution of the library during the sixteenth century.[39]

3 The Sacred Congregation of the Index and the Augustinian Observant Congregation of Lombardy

Before proceeding with the analysis of the book collection of Santa Maria del Popolo at the end of the sixteenth century, it is appropriate to briefly review the communications between the Augustinian Congregation and the cardinals of the Index. As for other religious families, the Congregation of the Index had to often request the lists relating to the Lombard Observants. On 25 November 1596, Agostino Valier in fact wrote to Costanzo Lodi di San Gervasio, general vicar of the Augustinian Observant Congregation of Lombardy: 'as a good shepherd with all solicitude and zeal, both by virtue of your office and by order of our Congregation of the Index, you will make this Index enforced and respected in all the monasteries subject to your jurisdiction'.[40]

In August 1599, the Congregation of the Index wrote again to the Observant Augustinians, as proved by the receipt of the letter addressed to the general vicar, Maurizio Borrini, by the general procurator Serafino da Como on 23 August.[41] Another letter from Cardinal Tagliavia, dated 25 August, with the order to send the list of suspended books by the end of the year, was not received in Lucca, by Borrini, until 5 November, and he was therefore forced to immediately reply requesting an extension to the deadline for the delivery of the lists.[42] In the following months, however, the Congregation of the Index had decided, as said, to change the type of inventory required. So, on 17 January 1600, Cardinal Valier wrote to Borrini again asking for a list of all the books owned by the Lombard Congregation.[43] The communication was received

---

39 So far, only partial book lists of Santa Maria del Popolo's library created between the seventeenth and nineteenth centuries have been found. On the latter inventory, see Vatican City, Vatican Apostolic Library, ms. Vat. lat. 11285, ff. 10r–27r (RICI, ELE 3364).

40 'come bon pastore con ogni sollicitudine e zelo, sì per debbito de l'officio, come di ordine della nostra Congregatione dell'Indice, farà essequire et osseruare detto Indice in tutti li monasterij soggetti alla sua giurisditione', Serra (ed.), *La Congregazione dell'Indice*, pp. 30–32, no. 4, esp. 30. On Costanzo Lodi di San Gervasio (d.1597), see Calvi, *Delle memorie istoriche*, pp. 346, 382–385.

41 See Serra (ed.), *La Congregazione dell'Indice*, pp. 81–87, no. 48, esp. 85. On Maurizio Borrini (d.1602), see Calvi, *Delle memorie istoriche*, pp. 389–391; on Serafino da Como, see Calvi, *Delle memorie istoriche*, p. 388.

42 See Serra (ed.), *La Congregazione dell'Indice*, pp. 92–94, no. 51 and 125–126, no. 77.

43 Ibid., pp. 147–150, no. 95.

on 25 January by Giacomo Alberici, prior of Santa Maria del Popolo.[44] Borrini replied to Valier on 5 February, assuring him that the lists would be delivered by the deadline.[45] And in fact, by the beginning of the autumn of that year, the lists were sent to the Congregation, since on 10 October Valier confirmed the receipt of the lists (at the same time giving indications for the censorship of expurgable books) to the general vicar of the Lombards Ippolito Zurla, who in the meantime had taken the place of Borrini.[46]

In conclusion, it should be pointed out that the Observant Congregation of Lombardy had been much more prompt than the whole Augustinian Order. Indeed, on 22 November 1602, Cardinal Tagliavia had to write again to urge Ippolito Fabriani, general prior of the Augustinians, to obey the orders of the Congregation of the Index.[47]

4   Books in the Library, Books in the Cells

The ms. Vat. lat. 11285 contains the lists sent by the Observant Congregation of Lombardy, which were collected in June 1600 by command of the general vicar of the Congregation, as can be read on f. 2r:

> Index omnium librorum qui hoc anno 1600 et mense Iunii in monasteriis Congregationis observantiae Lombardiae Ordinis heremitarum Sancti Augustini ex mandato reverendi patris vicarii generalis Congregationis hic notati et descripti reperiuntur.[48]

---

44   Ibid., pp. 153–157, no. 98, esp. 156.
45   Ibid., p. 160, no. 101.
46   Ibid., pp. 178–180, no. 117. On Ippolito Zurla (1540–1601), see Calvi, *Delle memorie istoriche*, pp. 373–375 and Nico Ciampelli, 'Lexicon: I Vicari Generali e i Capitoli della Congregazione Lombarda tra il xv e il xvii secolo', *Insula Fulcheria*, 46 (2016), pp. 303–314, esp. 310.
47   See Serra (ed.), *La Congregazione dell'Indice*, p. 182, no. 119. On Ippolito Fabriani (c.1537–1621), see Benigno van Luijk, 'L'Ordine agostiniano e la riforma monastica. Capitolo 4. I priori generali visitatori 1570–1648', *Augustiniana*, 20 (1970), pp. 235–266, esp. 245–247 and Benigno van Luijk, *L'Ordine Agostiniano e la riforma monastica dal Cinquecento alla vigilia della Rivoluzione francese. Un sommario cronologico-storico* (Heverlee-Leuven: Institut Historique Augustinien, 1973), pp. 107–109. The documentation sent by the Order of the Hermits of Saint Augustine is now gathered together in the mss. Vat. lat. 11285, 11286, 11295 and 11310 of the Vatican Apostolic Library; see Lebreton, Fiorani (eds.), *Codices 11266–11326*, p. xv and Antonella Mazzon, 'Gli Eremitani tra normativa e prassi libraria', in *Libri e biblioteche. Le letture dei frati mendicanti tra Rinascimento ed età moderna* (Spoleto: Fondazione Centro Italiano di Studi sull'Alto Medioevo, 2019), pp. 251–300, esp. 279–281.
48   On this manuscript (RICI, COD 23), see: https://digi.vatlib.it/mss/detail/Vat.lat.11285.

The table of contents at the beginning of the volume includes twenty-five notes on convents and 177 personal lists.[49] At ff. 10r–27r of the Vatican manuscript is the book list of Santa Maria del Popolo: it enumerates a little more than 470 items, although the collection had to be larger, given the absence of the four leaves relating to letters N, O, Q and partially P.[50] The note created by the Augustinians of Piazza del Popolo is quite precise and detailed in recording the bibliographical data, as requested by the Congregation of the Index, but the titles are not always arranged perfectly in the alphabetical order. In addition to the sixteenth-century volumes, there are forty-six books described as manuscripts and over 150 incunabula. Most of the volumes are printed in the Italian peninsula (mainly in Venice and Rome), but there are also numerous editions published in other European cities, especially Lyon, Basel, Cologne and Paris. At the content level, there are remarkable patristic and theological works, such as those of the Bishop of Hippo, attested both among manuscripts and printed volumes (Figure 11.2), as well as those of Augustinian authors including Giles of Rome, Albertus of Padua, Gabriele Buratelli, Thomas of Strasbourg, Paul of Venice and Antonio Dolciati.[51]

There are not only writings of the cornerstones of the Hermits, but also works of the Dominicans, with texts by Thomas Aquinas, Juan de Torquemada, Albertus Magnus and Antoninus of Florence, and of the Franciscans, with works by Joannes Duns Scotus, Roberto Caracciolo and Alexander of Hales. The juridical texts, both canonical and civil, are well represented, with the collections of decretals of Gregory IX, Boniface VIII and Clemens V, the *Decretum Gratiani* and the Justinianian *Corpus iuris civilis*, as are the comments of famous jurists such as Azzone, Federico Petrucci, Pietro d'Ancarano, Bartolo da Sassoferrato, Baldo degli Ubaldi, Antonio da Budrio and Giovanni da Imola. Among the ancient philosophers are Aristotle and Plato, Plotinus, Alexander of Aphrodisias, Ammonius Hermiae, Averroes and Boethius. The inventory

---

49   It should be noted that the manuscript contains some lists not mentioned in the initial table of contents, while some of those indexed have been lost. For an analysis of the Vatican manuscript and the indices contained therein, see Lebreton, Fiorani (eds.), *Codices 11266–11326*, pp. 126–130 and Mazzon, 'Gli Eremitani tra normativa e prassi libraria', pp. 286–289.
50   RICI, ELE 3364.
51   On the Augustinian libraries, see Kenneth William Humphreys, *The Book Provisions of the Mediaeval Friars 1215–1400* (Amsterdam: Erasmus Booksellers, 1964), pp. 67–76; Gutiérrez, *De antiquis Ordinis Eremitarum S. Augustini bibliothecis* and Giorgio Pini, 'Le letture dei maestri dei frati agostiniani: Egidio Romano e Giacomo da Viterbo', in *Libri, biblioteche e letture dei frati mendicanti (secoli XIII–XIV)* (Spoleto: Fondazione Centro Italiano di Studi sull'Alto Medioevo, 2005), pp. 79–113.

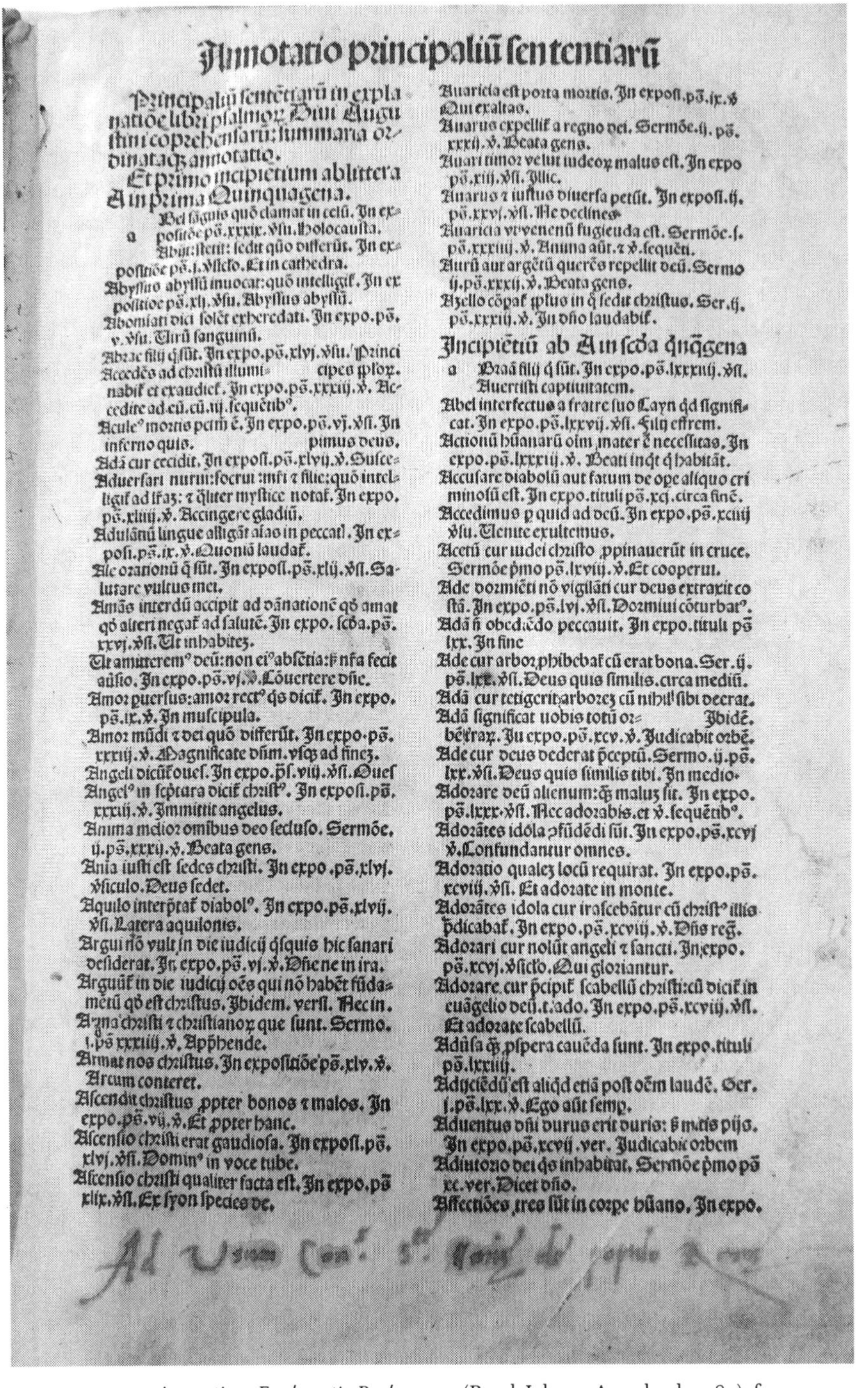
Annotatio principaliũ sententiarũ

Principaliũ sententiarũ in explanatiõe libri psalmorũ Diui Augustini cõprehensarũ: summaria ordinataq; annotatio. Et primo incipientium ablittera A in prima Quinquagena.

FIGURE 11.2 Augustine, *Explanatio Psalmorum* (Basel: Johann Amerbach, 1489), f. a2r, Viterbo, Central Library of the Augustinian Province of Italy, Inc. 11

also includes a number of historiographers (both ancient and modern), so not only Svetonius, Eutropius, Arrian, Justin and Flavius Josephus are listed, but also Biondo Flavio and Bartolomeo Platina. The classics are represented by Virgil, Cicero (both with his philosophical and rhetorical writings) and Seneca, as well as by Terentius and Plautus, Sallust and Apuleius and Pliny and Aulus Gellius. The works of ancient grammarians such as Varro and Lactantius are also included, as are the writings of medieval Italian authors, including Boccaccio, Petrarch, Angelo Poliziano and Leonardo Bruni. In the scientific field, there are Euclid's treatises on geometry, or Ptolemy with his *Geography*, and the medical works of Galen, Rhasis and Avicenna, as well as texts of the more recent authors Benedetto Reguardati and Gaspar Torrella.[52] As was to be expected, the list from 1600 does not include sacristy books and choir books at all.[53] But a comparison with the inventory from 1480 reveals that many of the manuscripts that were part of Santa Maria del Popolo's library are also not included in the list from the end of the sixteenth century, probably due to the greater difficulties involved in describing the contents of handwritten volumes, especially miscellaneous, compared to printed editions.[54] Thus noted, in fact, at the end of a contemporary Franciscan inventory, the anonymous compiler of the list:

> In the aforementioned library, there are many handwritten books that are not comprehensible due to their antiquity. The subject matter is unclear and cannot be read. For this reason, neither the author nor the subject of some works are indicated in this inventory. All that can be said about

---

52 On the composition of the libraries of the Mendicant Orders, see Borraccini, Rusconi (eds.), *Libri, biblioteche e cultura degli ordini regolari* and *Libri e biblioteche. Le letture dei frati mendicanti*.

53 On this topic, see Suzan Folkerts, 'Approaching Lay Readership of Middle Dutch Bibles: On the Uses of Archival Sources and Bible Manuscripts', in Sabrina Corbellini etc. (eds.), *Discovering the Riches of the Word. Religious Reading in Late Medieval and Early Modern Europe* (Leiden: Brill, 2015), pp. 18–43, esp. 29.

54 Regarding the difficulties associated with the registration of manuscript materials in the lists to be sent to the Sacred Congregation of the Index, see Roberto Rusconi, '"O scritti a mano": i libri manoscritti tra inquisizione e descrizione', in Rosa Marisa Borraccini (ed.), *Dalla* notitia librorum *degli inventari agli esemplari. Saggi di indagine su libri e biblioteche dai codici* Vaticani latini *11266–11326* (Macerata: EUM, 2009), pp. 1–26 and Monica Bocchetta, 'I manoscritti degli Osservanti di Tuscia dal censimento della Congregazione dell'Indice dei libri proibiti (cod. *Vaticano latino* 11281)', in Manuel José Pedraza Gracia (dir.), Helena Carvajal González, Camino Sánchez Oliveira (eds.), *Doce siglos de materialidad del libro. Estudios sobre manuscritos e impresos entre los siglos VIII y XIX* (Zaragoza: Prensas de la Universidad de Zaragoza, 2017), pp. 151–167.

these books is that they are twenty-four, as no other information can be given. There are also some leaves detached from the books, without beginning and end, partly printed, partly handwritten and partly not easily understandable. Therefore, this note was written to at least partly obey the orders given.[55]

However, to reconstruct the book presence in Santa Maria del Popolo, the lists of books granted to the friars of the convent for personal use (*ad usum*) must be added. This can be done by documentation attesting to the composition of the Santa Maria del Popolo's family in the Jubilee year 1600. Based on this source, it is possible to identify the book lists quite plausibly linked to these friars in the ms. Vat. lat. 11285.[56] The *Liber familiae* of Santa Maria del Popolo (in which the members of the conventual community are registered year by year from 1473 to 1781) records, on the occasion of the general chapter held in Milan in April 1600, thirty-six names (twenty-two priests, five clerics and nine lay brothers).[57] Excluding the lay brothers, a group not present at all in

---

[55] 'Si trova nella sopra detta libraria molte opere scrite a mano che non se intendono per la vechiaia, non solo se intende di che materia tratono, ma manco si può legere, e dove non è scrito in questo inventario in molti luoghi nel autore, nella materia, è stato per quello si è detto, et i libri de diversi sono numero 24 che per non saper che scrivere altro non si dano se non per numaro. Ed anco si trovano alcune carte fora de i libri senza principio, e senza fine, parte stampate, parte scrite a mano, e parte non se intendono, che per non mancare di quanto si deve si fa questa scritura per non mancare di quanto vien comandato', Vatican City, Vatican Apostolic Library, ms. Vat. lat. 11271, f. 98r. This passage is also mentioned in Rusconi, '"O scritti a mano"', pp. 2–3. The RICI ID of this list (Vatican City, Vatican Apostolic Library, ms. Vat. lat. 11271, ff. 81r–98r) is ELE 2318.

[56] It must be noted that the book lists attributed to the friars of Santa Maria del Popolo in this paper are linked to other convents in Lebreton, Fiorani (eds.), *Codices 11266–11326*, pp. 126–130. The Lebreton and Fiorani's analysis of the ms. Vat. lat. 11285 is, however, not always convincing, since it does not seem to take into account the absence of some leaves from the manuscript. Why, then, is the inventory of Santa Maria del Popolo's library placed at the beginning of the Vatican manuscript, while the friars' book lists are scattered and placed in the middle or at the end of the volume? Probably, when the inventories sent by the Augustinian Observants from convents throughout Italy were bound into a single volume, the lists were placed (at least partially) in disorder. Another hypothesis could be that at the time the lists were sent, these friars were not yet living in Santa Maria del Popolo, but about half of them are attested in the Roman convent in 1599, and some even earlier. A further possibility is that the lists of friars were ordered in the Vatican manuscript according to the friars' affiliation, but this sorting criteria seems excessively complex.

[57] See Rome, State Archives, *Congregations suppressed, Augustinians in Santa Maria del Popolo*, register 1, f. 66v. The same friars (with a few exceptions) are listed in a document

the Vatican manuscript, it is possible to analyse the book collections of the other religious who were part of the community of Santa Maria del Popolo in 1600. The Vatican volume contains the names of four of the five clerics listed in the *Liber familiae*, while sixteen of the remaining twenty-two friars had books for their own use. However, of the twenty lists registered in the index of ms. Vat. lat. 11285 traceable to the members of the community of Santa Maria del Popolo, only fourteen can be examined today because the other notes are missing, as indicated by the Table 11.1, which compares the list of the Augustinian community members of Santa Maria del Popolo enumerated in 1600 in the *Liber familiae* with the lists of books for personal use gathered in ms. Vat. lat. 11285.[58]

The list of books granted for the use of the convent's prior, Aurelio Carminati da Treviglio, who in 1598 had also held the office of general vicar of the Congregation, is large with eighty-eight records.[59] There are patristic works, including those of Augustine, Thomas Aquinas and Bernard, and collections of sermons, such as the *Sermones* by the Franciscan Roberto Caracciolo, and devotional texts.[60] In addition, there are writings relating to the Augustinian Order, such as the *Privilegia fratrum Ordinis eremitarum Sancti Augustini* and the work on the privileges of the Religious Orders by Giovanni Battista Confetti.[61] The list also includes the texts of a Counter-Reformation character

       dated 8 July 1600 concerning the Cerasi Chapel in Santa Maria del Popolo, preserved in Rome, State Archives, *Notaries of the Reverend Apostolic Chamber*, Notary Luzio Calderini, year 1600, vol. 378, ff. 615r–616v, 619r–620r; this document is published in Stefania Macioce, *Michelangelo Merisi da Caravaggio. Documenti, fonti e inventari 1513–1875* (Rome: Ugo Bozzi, 2010), pp. 117–119, doc. 496. On the *Liber familiae* of Santa Maria del Popolo, see Armando Lodolini, 'L'archivio delle corporazioni religiose. II. L'archivio degli agostiniani calzati di S. Maria del Popolo (Roma) (1473–1870)', *Archivi d'Italia*, s. II, 1 (1933–1934), pp. 249–250, esp. 249; Marcello Del Piazzo, 'La Mostra permanente dell'Archivio di Stato di Roma', *Rassegna degli Archivi di Stato*, 22.3 (1962), pp. 281–310, esp. 285, no. 11; Mirella Mombelli Castracane, Maria Grazia Pastura Ruggiero, *Agostiniani in S. Maria del Popolo (1472–1873)* (Rome: 1971), f. 1r (typescript kept in the reading room of the State Archives in Rome, shelfmark: 25/I, no. 2) and Lucrezia Signorello, 'Prosopografia di una famiglia osservante. Il convento romano di Santa Maria del Popolo e il suo *Liber familiae* (1473–1782): il secolo XV', *Analecta Augustiniana*, 86 (2023) [forthcoming].

58   The ELE is the identification number of the Vatican lists used in the RICI database. Please note that the data of three lists have not yet been entered into the database (accessed: October 2023) and therefore their identification numbers are not provided in this table.

59   On Carminati (d.1604), see Calvi, *Delle memorie istoriche*, pp. 385–387. For his book list, see Vatican City, Vatican Apostolic Library, ms. Vat. lat. 11285, ff. 362r–365r (RICI, ELE 3572).

60   On Roberto Caracciolo and the reception of his work, see Giacomo Mariani, *Roberto Caracciolo da Lecce (1425–1495). Life, Works, and Fame of a Renaissance Preacher* (Leiden: Brill, 2022).

61   It is a copy of the edition printed in Florence in 1598 (USTC 823653, CNCE 12746).

TABLE 11.1 Book lists of the friars of Santa Maria del Popolo

Source	*Liber familiae* (April 1600)	ms. Vat. lat. 11285 (June 1600)		
	Name	Registered list	Preserved list	ELE
	Aurelius de Trivilio predicator confessor ac lector sacrae theologiae prior	✓	✓	3572
	Iacobus de Sarnico Bergomensi predicator confessor lector sacrae theologiae ac procurator generalis	✓	✓	3540
	Arcangelus de Como vicarius confessor			
	Camillus de Valico confessor			
	Livius de Rauda confessor predicator ac lector philosophus	✓		
	Clemens de Thaurino predicator confessor ac lector retoricus			
	Gregorius de Bulgaro confessor	✓		
	Thimoteus de Gandino confessor predicator et parocus	✓	✓	3459
	Paulus de Saviliano confessor parocus	✓	✓	3577
	Hilarius de Crema confessor		✓	3539
	Alovisius de Crema confessor	✓	✓	3538
	Alovisius de Calvatono confessor et procurator conventus	✓		
	Aurelius de Cremona confessor predicator et sacrista			
	Paulus Hieronimus de Savona confessor et predicator	✓	✓	3510
	Antonius Maria de Caregiola confessor	✓	✓	–
	Clemens de Valico confessor	✓		
	Hortensius de Bononia			
	Clemens de Bononia confessor	✓		
	Ioannes Maria de Liburno confessor	✓	✓	–
	Guilielmus de Liburno confessor			
	Clemens de Feraria confessor parocus	✓	✓	3530
	Andreas de Controno predicator et confessor	✓	✓	–

TABLE 11.1 Book lists of the friars of Santa Maria del Popolo (*cont.*)

Source	*Liber familiae* (April 1600)	ms. Vat. lat. 11285 (June 1600)		
	Name	Registered list	Preserved list	ELE
Clerici	Stefanus de Tavazano subdiaconus			
	Gabriel de Como diaconus	✓	✓	3590
	Leonellus de Manzolino diaconus	✓	✓	3580
	Benignus de Vercellis subdiaconus	✓		
	Petrus Nicholaus de Tolentino	✓	✓	3598
Conversi et comissi	Peregrinus Pontremulensis			
	Antonius de Turana			
	Ludovicus de Multina			
	Angelus de Multina			
	Venturinus de Como			
	Helius de Trivilio			
	Ioannes Baptista de Desiniano			
	Ioannes Dominicus de Luca			
	Iacobus de Lucca			

such as the *Confirmatione et stabilimento di tutti li dogmi catholici*, an anti-Lutheran work by Luigi Lippomano.[62] Furthermore, there are writings of historians such as Platina, Guicciardini, Giovio and Campana, as well as literary works such as a copy of the first authorized edition of the *Gerusalemme liberata* by Torquato Tasso (Ferrara 1581). Also noteworthy is the mention in the prior's book list of two items (both by Franciscan authors) that bear the indication 'cum licentia' (with license to read).[63] These are the work of Diego de Estella *In Evangelium secundum Lucam enarrationum* (Lyon 1580) and the *Lettioni sopra dogmi*, also known as *Calviniche*, by Francesco Panigarola (Venice 1584).[64] The Clementine Index of prohibited books had in fact banned pre-1581 editions of the first work, while the second, although printed with the *imprimatur*, fell in the category of the biblical vulgarizations and vernacular works of controversy,

---

62 USTC 838228, CNCE 33181. On Lippomano (1500–1559), see Emily Michelson, 'Luigi Lippomano, His Vicars, and the Reform of Verona from the Pulpit', *Church History*, 78.3 (2009), pp. 584–605.
63 See Vatican City, Vatican Apostolic Library, ms. Vat. lat. 11285, f. 363r.
64 The first one is the USTC 156347, while the second is the USTC 846397, CNCE 35191.

which were forbidden because they might become dangerous, albeit involuntary, vehicles of heretical doctrines (which is why the censors rather recommended the *Disceptationes Calvinicae*, a Latin edition of Panigarola's work printed in Milan in 1594).[65] The collection of Giacomo Alberici da Sarnico (Bergamo) is even larger, but its description is less accurate, as it never mentions the printer's name.[66] In the Jubilee year 1600, Alberici held the office of general procurator of the Observant Congregation of Lombardy, having been replaced by Carminati as prior of the convent of Santa Maria del Popolo. His list counts as many as 105 titles, mostly philosophical and theological, such as the writings of Augustine, Thomas Aquinas and Giles of Rome, or the *Theologia Platonica* by Marsilio Ficino. There are also collections of sermons and literary works by classical authors, such as Ovid, or medieval ones like Petrarch, or

---

65   On this topic, see Gigliola Fragnito, '"Zurai non legger mai più". Censura libraria e pratiche linguistiche nella penisola italiana', in Vittoria Bonani (ed.), *Dal torchio alle fiamme. Inquisizione e censura: nuovi contributi dalla più antica Biblioteca Provinciale d'Italia* (Salerno: Biblioteca Provinciale di Salerno, 2005), pp. 81–96; Giorgio Caravale, *Forbidden Prayer. Church Censorship and Devotional Literature in Renaissance Italy*, transl. Peter Dawson (Farnham: Ashgate, 2011) and Gigliola Fragnito, 'Censura romana e usi del volgare', *Philosophical Readings*, 7.3 (2015), pp. 23–27. On Diego de Estella (1524–1578), see Edgar Allison Peers, *Studies of the Spanish Mystics* (2 vols., London: Sheldon Press; New York: Macmillan, 1927–1930), II. 219–249, 436–442; on the prohibition of his text, see Pier Maria Soglian etc., 'La biblioteca di un "intellettuale di provincia". Il canonico Marco Moroni (1520 ca.–1602)', *Bibliothecae.it*, 2.2 (2013), pp. 125–158, esp. 154, n. 62 and Romeo De Maio, *Riforme e miti nella Chiesa del Cinquecento* (Naples: Guida, 1992), p. 366, n. 26. On Panigarola (1548–1594), see Francesco Ghia, Fabrizio Meroi (eds.), *Francesco Panigarola. Predicazione, filosofia e teologia nel secondo Cinquecento* (Florence: Leo S. Olschki, 2013) and Fabio Giunta, *Un'eloquenza militante per la Controriforma. Francesco Panigarola tra politica e religione* (Milan: FrancoAngeli, 2018); on the censorship that involved his *Lettioni sopra dogmi* (first edition printed in Milan in 1582, USTC 846396, CNCE 24449), see Agostino Borromeo, 'San Carlo Borromeo arcivescovo di Milano e la Curia Romana', in *San Carlo e il suo tempo* (2 vols., Rome: Edizioni di Storia e Letteratura, 1986), I. 237–301, esp. 250–253; Fragnito, *La Bibbia al rogo*, pp. 135–137; Gigliola Fragnito, *Proibito capire. La Chiesa e il volgare nella prima età moderna* (Bologna: Il Mulino, 2005), pp. 180–181; Gigliola Fragnito, '"Ogni semplice Chierico, o secolare, anche idiota è habile ad insegnarlo": la circolazione del catechismo negli stati cattolici europei nella seconda metà del Cinquecento', *Rivista Storica Italiana*, 129.1 (2017), pp. 77–97, esp. 91–96 and Samuele Giombi, 'L'esposizione del luogo "super hanc petram" nelle *Lettioni sopra dogmi* (1584) di Francesco Panigarola: un capitolo nella storia dell'esegesi cattolica in età controriformistica', *Rivista di storia della Chiesa in Italia*, 71.2 (2017), pp. 477–490, esp. 480. The Latin edition of Panigarola's work is the USTC 846473, CNCE 47218.

66   On Giacomo Alberici (1554–1610), see Donato Calvi, *Scena letteraria de gli scrittori bergamaschi aperta alla curiosità de suoi concittadini* (2 vols., Bergamo: Per li Figliuoli di Marc'Antonio Rossi, 1664), USTC 1734495, I. 192–193 and Calvi, *Delle memorie istoriche*, pp. 394–396. For his book list, see Vatican City, Vatican Apostolic Library, ms. Vat. lat. 11285, ff. 359v–361r (RICI, ELE 3540).

even contemporary ones such as Giuliano Gosellini. Moreover Alberici's list includes treatises relating to inquisitorial activity, like the *Quaestio de strigibus* by the Pisan Dominican Bartolomeo Spina and the *Compendium concertationis huius seculi sapientium ac theologorum, super erroribus moderni temporis* by the Dominican Jean van den Bundere.[67] Several of the forty-eight entries in the book list of Andrea da Controne, preacher and confessor, are vernacular works.[68] This collection mostly consists of devotional books or texts useful for preaching and the care of souls. Among the Latin volumes is a compendium on the history of the church of Santa Maria del Popolo composed by the aforementioned Giacomo Alberici and published in 1599.[69] Alberici's compendium, both in the Latin edition of 1599 and in the vernacular version of 1600, is also present in the list of Paolo da Savignano, which consists of sixteen records.[70] These include volumes for catechesis, such as the work of Felice Piaci da Colorno, or the *Dottrina cristiana* by Robert Bellarmine.[71] Two-thirds of the twenty-three titles listed in the index of confessor Luigi da Crema are in Latin, and the books surveyed are almost all printed.[72] Among them, only the *Summa* by Cardinal Francisco de Toledo Herrera is explicitly identified as a manuscript. A printed copy of this work is also included in the list of the parish priest Clemente da Ferrara, who recorded only eleven works, all published in the second half of the sixteenth century.[73] This book collection also has the writings of the Spanish canonist Martín de Azpilcueta, one of which is summarized by Pietro Alagona.[74] The list of Paolo Girolamo da Savona, confessor

67 The first one in the edition printed in Rome in 1576 (USTC 857326, CNCE 33932), the second one in the French edition of 1549 (USTC 150188). On Bartolomeo Spina (1474–1546), see Maurizio Bertolotti, 'Le ossa e la pelle dei buoi. Un mito popolare tra agiografia e stregoneria', *Quaderni storici*, 41 (1979), pp. 470–499.
68 For his book list, see Vatican City, Vatican Apostolic Library, ms. Vat. lat. 11285, ff. 399v–400r.
69 Giacomo Alberici, *Historiarum sanctissimae, et gloriosissimae Virginis Deiparae de Populo Almae Urbis compendium* (Rome: Ex Typographia Nicolai Mutij, 1599); USTC 808225, CNCE 650.
70 For his book list, see Vatican City, Vatican Apostolic Library, ms. Vat. lat. 11285, f. 367r (RICI, ELE 3577). The vernacular edition of Alberici's work was printed in Rome in 1600 (USTC 808226, CNCE 651).
71 USTC 852734, CNCE 38960.
72 For his book list, see Vatican City, Vatican Apostolic Library, ms. Vat. lat. 11285, f. 358r–v (RICI, ELE 3538).
73 For his book list, see Vatican City, Vatican Apostolic Library, ms. Vat. lat. 11285, f. 346r (RICI, ELE 3530). The *Summa* is the USTC 859249, CNCE 26862.
74 The last one printed in Rome by Domenico Basa in 1593 (USTC 811764, CNCE 3773). The works of Azpilcueta (1491–1586), Spanish canonist and maternal uncle of Saint Francis Xavier, known more commonly as Navarrus or Doctor Navarrus, had a very wide circulation in Catholic schools; on him, see Vincenzo Lavenia, 'Martín de Azpilcueta (1492–1586). Un profilo', *Archivio italiano per la storia della pietà*, 16 (2003), pp. 15–144.

and preacher, includes seventy-nine works.[75] The vernacular texts are well represented, especially with devotional writings or works related to meditation on the life of Jesus Christ. Among the thirty-two books listed in the collection of Timoteo da Gandino is Boccaccio's *Decameron*, a controversial text in the context of the Catholic Reform, but in the corrected post-Tridentine edition published in Florence by Giunta in 1573.[76] Of the thirty-three entries in the list of the Piedmontese confessor Giovanni Maria da Livorno, the *Eleganze* by Aldo Manuzio 'the Younger', the *Specchio della lingua latina* by Giovanni Andrea Grifoni and the Filippo Venuti's *Dictionarium* are the only works that are not of a theological, religious or philosophical character.[77] The book collection of the confessor Ilario da Crema includes only ten works, mostly concerning the education of the clergy, such as the *Enchiridion sive manuale sacerdotum* by Cosimo Filiarchi.[78] This handbook (and in the same edition) is also recorded in the list of books granted for use to Antonio Maria da Caregiola (Pontremoli), whose collection counts only nine works, for the most part useful for pastoral activities.[79] Nothing can be said about the personal collections of Livius de Rauda, Gregorius de Bulgaro and Clemens de Valico, or even Aloysius de

---

75 For his book list, see Vatican City, Vatican Apostolic Library, ms. Vat. lat. 11285, ff. 320r–322r (RICI, ELE 3510).

76 On this edition (USTC 814874, CNCE 6361), see Infelise, *I libri proibiti*, pp. 46–47. On censorship of Italian literature, see Ugo Rozzo, 'Italian Literature on the Index', in Fragnito (ed.), *Church, Censorship and Culture in Early Modern Italy*, pp. 194–222; Ugo Rozzo, *La letteratura italiana negli Indici del Cinquecento* (Udine: Forum, 2005); Jennifer Helm, *Poetry and Censorship in Counter-Reformation Italy* (Leiden: Brill, 2015); Gigliola Fragnito, *Rinascimento perduto. La letteratura italiana sotto gli occhi dei censori (secoli XV–XVII)* (Bologna: Il Mulino, 2019) and Amedeo Quondam, *Una guerra perduta. Il libro letterario del Rinascimento e la censura della Chiesa* (Rome: Bulzoni, 2022). For the list of Timoteo da Gandino, see Vatican City, Vatican Apostolic Library, ms. Vat. lat. 11285, ff. 278r–279r (RICI, ELE 3459).

77 The first one is the USTC 840395, CNCE 63750; while the second is the USTC 834622, CNCE 21790. For this book list, see Vatican City, Vatican Apostolic Library, ms. Vat. lat. 11285, f. 395r–v.

78 For his book list, see Vatican City, Vatican Apostolic Library, ms. Vat. lat. 11285, f. 359r (RICI, ELE 3539). Actually, the Vatican manuscript contains two book lists bearing the name of Ilario da Crema. Thanks to the analysis of the volume, however, it is possible to identify the one relating to the friar of Santa Maria del Popolo (not listed, it must be noted, in the initial table of contents). The other list is linked to a friar of the same name who may have lived in the convent of San Nicola da Tolentino in Novara, see Lebreton, Fiorani (eds.), *Codices 11266–11326*, p. 129; for this second book list, see Vatican City, Vatican Apostolic Library, ms. Vat. lat. 11285, f. 270r (RICI, ELE 3453). The handbook by Filiarchi is the USTC 829524, CNCE 19006. On Cosimo Filiarchi (1520–1603), see Renzo Nelli, 'Un pistoiese nella letteratura antiturca: Cosimo Filiarchi e i suoi due trattati', *Bullettino Storico Pistoiese*, 116 (2014), pp. 109–128.

79 For his book list, see Vatican City, Vatican Apostolic Library, ms. Vat. lat. 11285, f. 392v (RICI, ELE 3510).

Calvatono and Clemens de Bononia, because their notes, which were once present in the Vatican manuscript, are now lost.[80] Of the lists created by the four clerics of Santa Maria del Popolo, only that of Benignus de Vercellis is missing. The note of the deacon Gabriele da Como includes twenty-four titles.[81] In addition to the usual grammatical texts and those on devotional and pastoral topics, theological and philosophical writings abound. Furthermore, Cicero's *Epistulae ad familiares* and a volume of the *Mirabilia Romae* are also listed.[82] The Bolognese deacon Leonello da Manzolino had twenty-three titles for his personal use: the Bible and the New Testament, liturgical texts, grammars and various dictionaries, including the *Dictionarium* by the Augustinian Ambrogio Calepio.[83] There are also pastoral care books, such as catechisms and a compendium on the seven sacraments, as well as confessional treatises, such as the handbook by Martín de Azpilcueta, the *Interrogatorio* by Agostino da Amatrice and the book by the Dominican Girolamo Savonarola.[84] The *Flagellum daemonum*, written by the Mantuan exorcist Girolamo Menghi, who was active in the second half of the sixteenth century, is also noteworthy.[85] One of the smallest collection is that of Pietro Nicola da Tolentino, consisting of only ten titles, also linked mainly to the liturgy and pastoral activity, with the exception of Palladio's *L'Antichità di Roma* and the *Bellum Iudaicum* by Flavius Josephus.[86]

---

80 Although their lists have not been preserved, the names of these Augustinians can be found in the initial table of contents of the Vatican manuscript, see Vatican City, Vatican Apostolic Library, ms. Vat. lat. 11285, ff. 2r–9r.
81 For his book list, see Vatican City, Vatican Apostolic Library, ms. Vat. lat. 11285, f. 378r–v (RICI, ELE 3590).
82 The last one is the USTC 805228, CNCE 73943.
83 It is a copy of the Venetian edition printed in 1580 (USTC 817821, CNCE 8439). On Calepio (1435–1510), see Mencaroni Zoppetti, Gennaro (eds.), *Società, cultura, luoghi al tempo di Ambrogio da Calepio*. For this book list, see Vatican City, Vatican Apostolic Library, ms. Vat. lat. 11285, f. 369r (RICI, ELE 3580).
84 The *Enchiridion*'s edition is the USTC 811659, CNCE 3787. The *Interrogatorio* by Agostino da Amatrice is the USTC 808076, CNCE 513. The edition of Savonarola's work is the USTC 855295, CNCE 53829. About Girolamo Savonarola (1452–1498), who in 1497 was excommunicated by Pope Alexander VI and the following year was hanged and burned at the stake as a heretic and schismatic, and the ecclesiastical censorship that suffered some of his writings, see Gigliola Fragnito, 'Girolamo Savonarola e la censura ecclesiastica', *Rivista di storia e letteratura religiosa*, 35 (1999), pp. 501–529.
85 Printed in Bologna in 1584 (USTC 842030, CNCE 29334). On Menghi (1529–1609), see Guido Dall'Olio, 'Scourging Demons with Exorcism. Girolamo Menghi's *Flagellum daemonum*', transl. Jan Machielsen, in Jan Machielsen (ed.), *The Science of Demons. Early Modern Authors Facing Witchcraft and the Devil* (London: Routledge, 2020), pp. 224–237.
86 Probably, the first one is the USTC 846300, CNCE 25946, while the second is the vernacular edition printed in Venice in 1555 (USTC 836540, CNCE 36253). For this book list, see Vatican City, Vatican Apostolic Library, ms. Vat. lat. 11285, f. 385v (RICI, ELE 3598). On

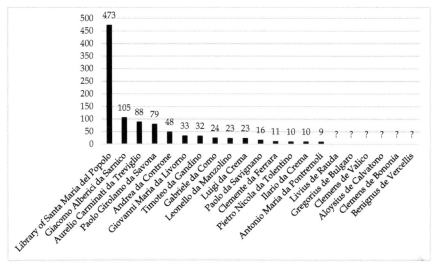

FIGURE 11.3   Consistency of the book collections of Santa Maria del Popolo and the friars of the convent

The *excursus* conducted through the friars' personal collections highlights a large number of books in the cells of the convent of Santa Maria del Popolo in the Jubilee year 1600, roughly equivalent to the number of volumes in the common library (see Figure 11.3).[87] Not only did twenty of the observant friars have a collection for their personal use, but some of them, including the prior of Santa Maria del Popolo Aurelio Carminati, the general procurator of the Congregation Giacomo Alberici and the preacher Paolo Girolamo da Savona (certainly some of the most important Augustinians in the convent), could count on a large number of texts. The analysis of the indexes of the friars' books revealed some common characteristics. The works kept in the Augustinian cells were mostly Italian editions and there were some types of texts recurring in the collections for personal use: the Holy Scriptures, handbooks for confession,

---

Palladio's *L'Antichità di Roma*, see Anna Bortolozzi, 'Architects, Antiquarians, and the Rise of the Image in Renaissance Guidebooks to Ancient Rome', in Anna Blennow, Stefano Fogelberg Rota (eds.), *Rome and the Guidebook Tradition. From the Middle Ages to the 20th Century* (Berlin: De Gruyter, 2019), pp. 115–161, esp. 132–138.

87 See Bernard Dompnier, 'Il libro tra i frati, i libri dei frati', *Franciscana*, 21 (2019), pp. 259–294. Note that the list of the conventual library of Santa Maria del Popolo lacks some leaves and therefore the number of works must be considered incomplete. Moreover, generally the number of entries does not always correspond exactly to the number of editions and manuscripts recorded in the lists. Sometimes, in fact, several printed editions and/or manuscripts are indicated under a single record (author/title), or, conversely, the same multi-volume edition is divided among several entries.

catechesis and preaching, devotional books, collections of sermons, grammatical works and vocabularies. Furthermore, there were inquisitorial texts, such as the *Flagellum daemonum* by the Franciscan Girolamo Menghi and the *Quaestio de strigibus* by the Dominican Bartolomeo Spina. Volumes containing the canons and decrees approved by the Council of Trent were also widespread, as were anti-Protestant treatises, which were one of the manifestations of the Counter-Reformation climate and thus of great relevance at that time. But there were also volumes that reflected the friars' personal interests, such as the literary masterpieces of Petrarch, Boccaccio and Tasso, or some tourist books (such as the *Mirabiliae Romae*) useful to non-Roman friars who came to live in the Eternal City for a few years and wanted to visit the monuments of both apostolic and pagan Rome.[88]

The convent library was also of some importance, despite its incomplete representation. The already extensive book collection described in the inventory of the late fifteenth century was constantly supplemented with several printed editions during the sixteenth century. With almost 500 titles, the library of Santa Maria del Popolo at the end of the sixteenth century turns out to be one of the most consistent within the Lombard Congregation, second only to that of the convent of Sant'Agostino in Cremona (which, according to the Vatican inventory, consisted of about a thousand titles).[89] The composition of the library reflects the regulations of the Augustinian Order regarding studies, as outlined by Giles of Rome in the *Constitutions* of the thirteenth century, and later renewed in the fourteenth and sixteenth centuries, when great space was given to the Thomistic doctrine.[90] Thus, works by Aristotle, Boethius, Peter

---

88   See Kathryne Beebe, *Pilgrim & Preacher. The Audiences and Observant Spirituality of Friar Felix Fabri (1437/8–1502)* (Oxford: Oxford University Press, 2014), pp. 48–50. On this topic, see also Cristina Nardella, *Il fascino di Roma nel Medioevo. Le "Meraviglie di Roma" di maestro Gregorio* (Rome: Viella, 2007); Blennow, Fogelberg Rota (eds.), *Rome and the Guidebook Tradition*.

89   Based on the lists contained in the ms. Vat. lat. 11285. For the list of Sant'Agostino in Cremona, see Vatican City, Vatican Apostolic Library, ms. Vat. lat. 11285, ff. 73r–116v (RICI, ELE 3388). On this convent, see Elisa Chittò, 'Note per la storia del convento di Sant'Agostino di Cremona e i rapporti con l'Osservanza di Lombardia', *Insula Fulcheria*, 43 (2013), pp. 163–182; on its book collection, see *Manoscritti dei secoli XII–XV e incunaboli della biblioteca del Convento di S. Agostino di Cremona* (Cremona: Linograf, 1981).

90   On this topic, see Humphreys, *The Book Provisions*, pp. 67–76; David Gutiérrez, 'Los estudios en la Orden Agustiniana desde la edad media hasta la contemporànea', *Analecta Augustiniana*, 33 (1970), pp. 75–149; Cécile Caby, 'Les ermites de saint Augustin et leurs livres à l'heure de l'humanisme: autour de Guglielmo Becchi e Ambrogio Massari', in Nicole Bériou etc. (eds.), *Entre stabilité et itinérance. Livres et culture des ordres mendiants XIIIᵉ–XVᵉ siècle* (Turnhout: Brepols, 2014), pp. 247–288; Mazzon, 'Gli Eremitani tra normativa e prassi libraria', pp. 251–300 and Matthew Ponesse, 'The Augustinian Rules

Lombard, Thomas of Strasbourg, Alfonso Vargas, Thomas Aquinas and Paul of Venice abound.[91] Along with the books useful to the friars who conducted their advanced studies in the Roman *Studium*, numerous works of philosophy, literature and history of the classical and modern period, as well as several texts of civil and canon law, are listed. The library consisted mostly of incunabula and sixteenth-century printed editions, especially those published in Italy, but there were also a significant number of books from other European cities.[92] However, the collection also had a substantial group of manuscripts, the majority of which containing juridical works. This variety may be related in part to the provenance of the library's books and their former owners. The conventual collection was certainly increased over the decades thanks to donations from prominent members of the clergy and the Roman lay society.[93] Some of the books in the library are identifiable as gifts to the convent from important benefactors.[94] Thanks to the inventory written at the end of the fifteenth century it is in fact possible to reconstruct the dense network of faithful, but also bishops and cardinals, whose books flowed into Santa Maria del Popolo.[95] Among them are the cardinals Marco Barbo and Jorge da Costa, the bishops Marino Orsini and Nicholas of Modruš, and the Roman lawyer Battista Brendi.[96] The cultural role of the Santa Maria del Popolo's library (which was

---

and Constitutions', in Pansters (ed.), *A Companion to Medieval Rules*, pp. 393–428, esp. 418–425.

91 To analyze the organization of the studies of the Augustinian friars, see first of all the contemporary *Constitutions* of the Order 'on the model to follow for studies and students and lecturers of our Order' (*De forma circa studia et studentes ac lectores nostri ordinis servanda*); see *Constitutiones Ordinis fratrum eremitarum Sancti Augustini* (Rome: Antonio Blado, 1581), ff. xxviiv–xxixv. On this topic, see also Ponesse, 'The Augustinian Rules and Constitutions', pp. 418–425.

92 On this topic, see Giovanna Granata, 'Books without Borders: The Presence of the European Printing Press in the Italian Religious Libraries at the End of the Sixteenth Century', in Matthew McLean, Sara K. Barker (eds.), *International Exchange in the Early Modern Book World* (Leiden: Brill, 2016), pp. 214–238.

93 See Natalina Mannino, 'Il ruolo delle biblioteche mendicanti nella formazione dello "Studium Urbis" di Roma', in Bartolomeo Azzaro (ed.), *L'Università di Roma 'La Sapienza' e le Università italiane* (Rome: Gangemi, 2008), pp. 19–28, esp. 20–21.

94 See Lucrezia Signorello, *Catalogo dei manoscritti di Santa Maria del Popolo della Biblioteca Angelica di Roma* (Rome: Istituto Poligrafico e Zecca dello Stato, 2019).

95 See Esposito, 'Centri di aggregazione'.

96 On Marco Barbo (1420–1491), see Annamaria Torroncelli, 'Note per la biblioteca di Marco Barbo', in Concetta Bianca etc. (eds.), *Scrittura, biblioteche e stampa a Roma nel Quattrocento. Aspetti e problemi* (Vatican City: Scuola Vaticana di Paleografia, Diplomatica e Archivistica, 1980), pp. 343–352. About Jorge da Costa (1406–1508), see Christine Maria Grafinger, 'Die Handschriften und Inkunabeln des Kardinal Jorge Da Costa in der Vaticanischen Bibliothek', *Miscellanea Bibliothecae Apostolicae Vaticanae*, 11 (2004),

open not only to the Augustinian friars) is also confirmed by the profile of its users. The inventory of the fifteenth century also records some loan notes of the book collection.[97] These allow us to identify some of the library's users, including prelates, such as the Franciscan Galcerando de Andrea, Bishop of Leighlin, academics, including the well-known humanist Giovanni Pico della Mirandola, or professionals, such as the physician Bernardo Tedallini.[98]

5 From the Inventory to the Copy: A Struggle with History

The virtual reconstruction of Santa Maria del Popolo's library and its analysis, possible thanks to the described inventories, could be expanded and enriched with information on book usage.[99] For this type of investigation, however, ancient inventories are not a sufficient source. Indeed, the presence of a

pp. 413–422, esp. 417–418; Benedetta Cenni, 'Gli incunaboli vaticani di Santa Maria del Popolo e il cardinale Jorge da Costa (1406–1508)', in Cristina Dondi etc. (eds.), *La stampa romana nella città dei papi e in Europa* (Vatican City: Biblioteca Apostolica Vaticana, 2016), pp. 157–180, esp. 157–158. Finally, on Battista Brendi (1405–1482), see Massimo Miglio, 'Brendi, Battista', in *Dizionario Biografico degli Italiani*, XIV (Rome: Istituto della Enciclopedia Italiana, 1972), pp. 141–142 and Anna Modigliani, 'Il commercio a servizio della cultura a Roma nel Quattrocento', in *Roma e lo Studium Urbis. Spazio urbano e cultura dal Quattro al Seicento* (Rome: Ministero per i Beni Culturali e Ambientali. Ufficio Centrale per i Beni Archivistici, 1992), pp. 248–276, esp. 253–254.

97 See Rome, General Archive O.S.A, *S. Maria del Popolo*, M. 32, ff. 68v–69v; published in Gutiérrez, *De antiquis Ordinis Eremitarum S. Augustini bibliothecis*, pp. 288–290.

98 On Galcerando de Andrea (c.1426–1500), see Francis X. Martin, Alberic de Meijer, 'Irish Material in the Augustinian Archives, Rome, 1354–1624', *Archivium Hibernicum*, 19 (1956), pp. 61–134, esp. 103, n. 1 and Francesco Costa, 'Galcerando de Andrea da Licata. Ministro provinciale O.F.M.Conv. e Vescovo', in Diego Ciccarelli, Armando Bisanti (eds.), *Francescanesimo e civiltà siciliana nel Quattrocento* (Palermo: Officina di Studi Medievali, Biblioteca Francescana, 2000), pp. 51–81. On Giovanni Pico della Mirandola (1463–1494) and his book collection, see Outi Merisalo, 'Alla scoperta di biblioteche tardomedievali e della prima età moderna. La Biblioteca di Pico della Mirandola', *Accademie & Biblioteche d'Italia*, n.s., 14.1 (2019), pp. 21–28. On Bernardo Tedallini, see Anna Esposito, 'Note sulla professione medica a Roma. Il ruolo del collegio medico alla fine del Quattrocento', *Roma Moderna e Contemporanea*, 13.1 (2005), pp. 21–52 and Ivana Ait, 'Fra mercato e pratica sanitaria: gli speziali a Roma nel XV secolo', *Studi Storici*, 49.2 (2008), pp. 455–471, esp. 470, n. 60. Tedallini was probably the 'Maestro Bernardo medico nostro' (Master Bernardo our doctor) responsible for the medical care of the friars of Santa Maria del Popolo at the end of the fifteenth century; see Rome, General Archive O.S.A, *S. Maria del Popolo*, M. 1, ff. 3v–4r.

99 This is one of the objectives of my Ph.D. project at the University of Rome Sapienza (tutor Valentina Sestini, co-tutor Paolo Tinti): https://phd.uniroma1.it/web/LUCREZIA-SIGNORELLO_nP1310078_IT.aspx.

text on a library shelf says nothing about its actual use and reading: it must be 'noted that one needed to differentiate between establishing that an individual owned a book and the idea that he might have read it'.[100] Nevertheless, there are other paths to follow, such as analysing the legislation relating to the readings of the friars and their *cursus studiorum*, or the material evidence contained in books.[101] It will therefore be very important to detect the provenance marks of the Augustinian library copies still preserved today in distinguished libraries, such as the Vatican Apostolic Library, the Angelica Library and the National Central Library of Rome.[102] However, to track down and identify these volumes in the contemporary collections, the history of Santa Maria del Popolo's library after the Jubilee year 1600 and up to the present day must be considered. Certainly, the Augustinian book collection of the Popolo never reached the size or importance of its Roman sister institution, the Angelica Library (which was also, unlike that of Santa Maria del Popolo, a public library), but it had some fame and reputation in the following centuries.[103] The book heritage of Santa Maria del Popolo's friars was quoted in the works of some well-known eighteenth-century scholars, such as the *Specimen historicum typographiae Romanae XV saeculi* by François-Xavier Laire.[104] Also the *Catalogus historico-criticus Romanarum editionum saeculi XV* by the Dominican Giovanni Battista Audiffredi mentions the many ancient editions, both Roman and foreign, preserved in the Augustinian library ('quae veteribus

---

100 See Walsby, 'Book Lists and Their Meaning', p. 5.

101 See Borraccini (ed.), *Dalla* notitia librorum *degli inventari agli esemplari*; Bettina Wagner, Marcia Reed (eds.), *Early Printed Books as Material Objects* (Berlin: De Gruyter Saur, 2010) and Rosa Marisa Borraccini, *Segni sui libri. Rilevamento e ricomposizione*, in Roberto Rusconi (ed.), *Il libro antico tra catalogo storico e catalogazione elettronica* (Rome: Scienze e Lettere, 2012), pp. 155–166.

102 On the study of material evidence in books, see Marielisa Rossi, *Provenienze, cataloghi, esemplari. Studi sulle raccolte librarie antiche* (Manziana: Vecchiarelli, 2001); David Pearson, *Provenance Research in Book History. A Handbook* (Oxford: The Bodleian Library, New Castle: Oak Knoll Press, 2019).

103 On the Angelica Library, see Paola F. Munafò, Nicoletta Muratore, *Bibliotheca Angelica publice commoditati dicata* (Rome: Istituto poligrafico dello Stato, 2004); Alfredo Serrai, *Angelo Rocca. Fondatore della prima biblioteca pubblica europea* (Milan: Sylvestre Bonnard, 2004); *La Chiesa, la Biblioteca Angelica, l'Avvocatura generale dello Stato. Il complesso di Sant'Agostino in Campo Marzio* (Rome: Libreria dello Stato, 2009).

104 See François-Xavier Laire, *Specimen historicum typographiae Romanae XV saeculi* (Rome: Sumptibus Venantii Monaldini, 1778). On this French librarian (1738–1801), see Michel Vernus, *Une vie dans l'univers du livre. François-Xavier Laire (1738–1801)* (Besançon: Les Bibliophiles Comtois, 2001) and Graziano Ruffini, La chasse aux livres. *Bibliografia e collezionismo nel viaggio in Italia di Étienne-Charles de Loménie de Brienne e François-Xavier Laire (1789–1790)* (Florence: Firenze University Press, 2012).

cum Romanis, tum exteris editionibus abundat').[105] The manuscripts and early printed books of Santa Maria del Popolo are also described in the unpublished writings of the less famous Augustinian Tommaso Verani, who also dealt with the reorganization and description of the conventual library.[106] Although, after 400 years of history, the book collection of Santa Maria del Popolo was progressively dispersed during the nineteenth century.[107] Many books were taken away during the Napoleonic rule over Rome, as was the case for many other religious libraries. These volumes would have enriched the collections of the two public libraries of the city, the Casanatense Library and the Vatican Library.[108] Another large group of volumes was removed from Santa Maria del Popolo in 1849, when it was decided to save the most precious part of the collection by moving it to the biggest Augustinian centre of the city, the Angelica Library at the convent of Sant'Agostino.[109] In 1873, the process of unification of the Kingdom of Italy led to the confiscation of what remained at Santa Maria

---

105 See Giovanni Battista Audiffredi, *Catalogus historico-criticus Romanarum editionum saeculi XV in quo praeter editiones a Maettario, Orlandio, ac P. Laerio relatas* ... (Rome: Ex Typographio Paleariniano, 1783), p. XXIV. On Audiffredi (1714–1794), see Angela Adriana Cavarra (ed.), *Giovanni Battista Audiffredi (1714–1794)* (Rome: De Luca, 1994) and Franca Sinopoli, 'Giovanni Battista Audiffredi e la realizzazione del modello di biblioteca universale', in Beatrice Alfonzetti (ed.), *Settecento romano. Reti del Classicismo arcadico* (Rome: Viella, 2017), pp. 461–473.

106 See Tommaso Verani to Stefano Borgia (Rome, 15 July 1779), letter preserved in Turin, Central Civic Library, ms. Bosio 125, ff. 360r–366v. On Tommaso Verani (1729–1803), see Benigno van Luijk, 'Les Archives de la Congrégation de Lombardie et du couvent de S. Maria del Popolo à Rome', *Augustiniana*, 18 (1968), pp. 100–115; Giovanna Cantoni Alzati, 'L'erudito Tommaso Verani e la biblioteca agostiniana di Crema nel Settecento', *Insula Fulcheria*, 18 (1988), pp. 147–189; Lucrezia Signorello, 'Vir sane eruditissimus. Tommaso Verani, un agostiniano del Settecento', *Analecta Augustiniana*, 84 (2021), pp. 187–265; Lucrezia Signorello, 'L'*affaire* Laire e le edizioni romane del XV secolo negli scritti scambiati tra Tommaso Verani e Giovanni Battista Audiffredi', *Bibliothecae.it*, 11.1 (2022), pp. 182–221 and Lucrezia Signorello, 'Miseria e nobiltà di due bibliotecari del Settecento italiano. Tommaso Verani e Carlo Carlini tra professione e erudizione', *Nuovi Annali della Scuola Speciale per Archivisti e Bibliotecari*, 36 (2022), pp. 89–139.

107 About that, see Mario Mattei, 'Cronologia delle leggi soppressive dei conventi agostiniani e della loro applicazione in Italia nel corso del XIX secolo', in Luis Marín de San Martín (ed.), *Le soppressioni del secolo XIX e l'Ordine Agostiniano* (Rome: Institutum Historicum Augustinianum, 2010), pp. 95–174.

108 On this topic, see Andreina Rita, *Biblioteche e requisizioni librarie a Roma in età napoleonica. Cronologia e fonti romane* (Vatican City: Biblioteca Apostolica Vaticana, 2012), pp. 101–104.

109 On the collection of Santa Maria del Popolo in the Angelica Library, see Carla Casetti Brach, 'Incunaboli angelicani provenienti da S. Maria del Popolo', *Il Bibliotecario*, 26 (1990), pp. 115–120, esp. 115–116; Elisabetta Sciarra, 'Breve storia del fondo manoscritto della Biblioteca Angelica', *La Bibliofilía*, 111.3 (2009), pp. 251–281, esp. 276–277; Signorello,

del Popolo and the incorporation of its books into the National Library of Rome, which would have been founded a few years later.[110] Due to the many abductions that have already occurred, Ignazio Ciampi and Enrico Narducci, commissioned by the Italian government to inspect the conventual library, described the book collection of Santa Maria del Popolo as follows:

> We found about 4,000 volumes in the library, without ownership notes or shelfmarks, and also without a catalogue. Moreover, these books, some of them valuable for their antiquity and rarity, were in a deplorable state and piled up in a confused manner.[111]

'La biblioteca agostiniana di Santa Maria del Popolo', pp. 103–104; Signorello, *Catalogo dei manoscritti di Santa Maria del Popolo*, pp. 11–15.

110 About the National Library of Rome (inaugurated in 1876 by the Minister of Public Education Ruggiero Bonghi) and its acquisition of the Roman monastic libraries, see Alda Spotti, 'Guida storica ai fondi manoscritti della Biblioteca Nazionale Centrale Vittorio Emanuele II di Roma', in *Biblioteca nazionale centrale di Roma Vittorio Emanuele II. I fondi, le procedure, le storie. Raccolta di studi della Biblioteca* (Rome: Biblioteca Nazionale Centrale di Roma, 1993), pp. 5–31, esp. 16; Carlo M. Fiorentino, *Chiesa e Stato a Roma negli anni della destra storica 1870–1876. Il trasferimento della capitale e la soppressione delle Corporazioni religiose* (Rome: Istituto per la storia del Risorgimento italiano, 1996), pp. 173–251, 359–421; Virginia Carini Dainotti, *La Biblioteca nazionale Vittorio Emanuele al Collegio Romano* (Florence: Leo S. Olschki, 2003); Alberto Petrucciani, 'La biblioteca nazionale e il sistema delle biblioteche: il caso italiano', in Luigi Blanco, Gianna Del Bono (eds.), *Il sapere della nazione. Desiderio Chilovi e le biblioteche pubbliche nel XIX secolo* (Trento: Provincia Autonoma di Trento, Soprintendenza per i Beni Librari e Archivistici, 2007), pp. 141–153; Andrea De Pasquale, *Il lauro dimezzato. Il primo secolo di vita della Biblioteca nazionale centrale di Roma* (Rome: Gangemi, 2020) and Giovanni Solimine, 'Le biblioteche: dalla "guerra dei codici" al "frutto necessario dell'unità nazionale"', in Ester Capuzzo (ed.), *Dalla Roma pontificia alla Roma italiana. Le istituzioni culturali e la città* (Rome: Lithos, 2022), pp. 13–21.

111 'Essi trovarono la Biblioteca medesima ricca di circa 4000 volumi privi d'ogni nota di pertinenza o di collocamento, e priva altresì di catalogo. I detti libri poi, alcuni dei quali, preziosi per antichità e rarità, nel più deplorabile stato e confusamente accumulati', Ignazio Ciampi, Enrico Narducci, *Ispezione delle biblioteche claustrali di Roma*, handwritten report dated 28 February 1873 and addressed to Antonio Scialoja, Italian Minister of Public Education, preserved in Rome, Central State Archives, *Ministry of Education, Directorate General for Higher Education, Libraries and General Affairs, General Archives* (*Universities, Academies and Libraries*), box 127, file 1. On Ignazio Ciampi (1824–1880), see Alessandra Cimmino, 'Ciampi, Ignazio', in *Dizionario Biografico degli Italiani*, XXV (Rome: Istituto della Enciclopedia Italiana, 1981), pp. 128–130. On Enrico Narducci (1832–1893), see Maria Giuseppina Cerri, 'Narducci, Enrico', in *Dizionario Biografico degli Italiani*, LXXVII (Rome: Istituto della Enciclopedia Italiana, 2012), pp. 798–801 and Giovanni Solimine, 'Enrico Narducci e le biblioteche nei primi decenni dell'Italia unita', *Nuovi Annali della Scuola speciale per Archivisti e Bibliotecari*, 8 (1994), pp. 195–218.

The number of books transferred from Santa Maria del Popolo to the Collegio Romano (where the libraries of the Roman ecclesiastical institutions were gathering) was actually 5,880, according to a chart from 1875, and of these only two were manuscripts.[112] Futhermore, contrary to what the report stated, many of them had some kind of provenance marks, like ownership notes and stamps.[113] At this point, the composition of the Augustinian library of Santa Maria del Popolo was lost. Moreover, some volumes of the library were certainly sold on the book antiquarian market during the nineteenth century, as shown for example by the Missal of Anti-Pope John XXIII, formerly in the Astor Collection and currently ms. 34 (88.MG.71) of the Getty Museum of Los Angeles, the incunabulum Byw. H 4.2 (Plato, *Opera*), bequeathed to the Bodleian Libraries by Ingram Bywater, or by an illuminated Augustinian *Manuale* that appeared for sale in 2019 at the antiquarian Günther.[114] The little that had been left to the church of Piazza del Popolo or that had remained in the hands of the Augustinian friars found, between the twentieth century and the beginning of the twenty-first century, a definitive placement in the Central Library of the Augustinian Province of Italy, located in the convent of the Holy Trinity in Viterbo, and in the General Archive O.S.A (Rome).[115]

---

112   The document indicating the number of manuscripts (signed on 24 September 1875 by Ettore Novelli, functionary of the Ministry of Education), preserved in the Central State Archives in Rome and reported in Carini Dainotti, *La Biblioteca nazionale Vittorio Emanuele al Collegio Romano*, pp. 103–105, n. 175, is now unavailable. There is, however, a similar chart signed by Novelli and dated 21 November 1879 (in a copy from 16 February 1881) preserved in Rome, National Central Library of Rome, Historical Archive, pos. 7D *Libraries of the former Religious Congregations*, box 1, file 4 *1875*, subfile 2 *Delivery minutes of books, mss. etc. found in cloisteres' libraries*. On Ettore Novelli (1822–1900), see Gabriele Scalessa, 'Novelli, Ettore', in *Dizionario Biografico degli Italiani*, LXXVIII (Rome: Istituto della Enciclopedia Italiana, 2013), pp. 816–818.
113   See Marina Venier, 'Per dove, fino a dove, da chi: ricostruire il viaggio del libro attraverso i suoi segni. L'esperienza della Biblioteca nazionale centrale di Roma', *La Bibliofilía*, 117.3 (2015), pp. 357–366; https://pda.cerl.org/search?q=maria%20del%20popolo.
114   On this topic, see Venier, 'Per dove, fino a dove, da chi', p. 361. On the Bodleian's incunabulum (USTC 991952, ISTC ip00771000), see: http://textinc.bodleian.ox.ac.uk/catalog/tip00771000 and https://data.cerl.org/mei/00204482. About the Missal of the Getty Museum, illuminated by the Master of the Brussels Initials, see: https://www.getty.edu/art/collection/object/103RWN. Finally, on the *Manuale*, see: https://guenther-rarebooks.com/de/artworks/9515-augustinian-manuale-c.-1493-1500/ (accessed: April 2022).
115   The book collection of the Central Library of the Augustinian Province of Italy (Viterbo) preserves, at least as emerged for the moment, six incunabula coming from the ancient library of Santa Maria del Popolo, which I found in October 2021 and described in the CERL's *Material Evidence in Incunabula* database, see: https://data.cerl.org/mei/_search?query=data.provenance.agent.ownerId:00033679. On the incunabula collection of Viterbo, see: http://www.agostiniani.info/incunaboli/202 and Lucrezia Signorello, '*Disiecta membra*. Frammenti di collezioni antiche nella Biblioteca centrale della Provincia Agostiniana

6 Conclusions

The paper has presented the main features of the book collections of Santa Maria del Popolo in the sixteenth century, based on an inventory created in 1600 to respond to the requests of the Sacred Congregation of the Index. It has also clarified the cultural profile of this conventual community, allowing it to emerge from the titles kept on the library's shelves. To achieve this, the creation and development of the Augustinian library have been contextualized in the Roman panorama of the time, with reference to the role played by this religious center in papal politics and its relations with intellectuals and politicians of the Eternal City. Finally, the consistency and composition of the conventual library have been linked to the regulations of the Augustinian Order for studies and for the book endowment of convents, while highlighting the peculiar characteristics of the collections for personal use, shaped by specific interests, activities and socio-cultural profile of the friars of the Observant Congregation of Lombardy who lived in Santa Maria del Popolo. The analysis of this conventual library confirms once again the richness of a resource that can be certainly considered 'one of the largest bibliographical censuses ever compiled from the age of the scholarly bibliography'.[116] This documentation is undoubtedly both qualitatively and quantitatively impressive, as it provides a snap shot of the book heritage of about thirty Orders.[117] It is a source that allows to investigate, according to different research perspectives, the religious book collections in Italy, especially considering the losses that have affected the ecclesiastical properties during the eighteenth and nineteenth centuries.[118] The virtual reconstruction and the evaluation of these submerged and dispersed libraries, book by book, provide a unique perspective on the people responsible for their constitution and dispersion, and (through them) their historical and cultural context.[119] In conclusion, book collections are unquestionably a valuable

---

d'Italia', *La Bibliofilía*, 125.1 (2023) [forthcoming]. The library of Viterbo also keeps some manuscripts and several sixteenth-century printed books of which I am currently checking the provenance from the convent of Santa Maria del Popolo. At the General Archive O.S.A (Rome), instead, I was able to identify twenty manuscripts formerly belonging to the Augustinians of Santa Maria del Popolo, and in particular, the choir library, composed of sixteen choir books, see: https://manus.iccu.sbn.it/fondo/cnmf/0000002436.

116 See De Maio, *Riforme e miti nella Chiesa del Cinquecento*, p. 381.
117 See Granata, 'Books without Borders', p. 217.
118 On this topic, see Rita, *Biblioteche e requisizioni librarie*; Cristina Dondi etc. (eds.), *How the Secularization of Religious Houses Transformed the Libraries of Europe, 16th–19th Centuries* (Turnhout: Brepols, 2022).
119 See Edoardo Barbieri, 'Dalla descrizione dell'esemplare alla ricostruzione della sua storia (problemi ed esperienze)', in Edoardo Barbieri, *Il libro nella storia. Tre percorsi* (Milan:

resource that scholars can use to shed light on a period; indeed, 'the study of the contents of libraries illuminates the knowledge and the intellectual and spiritual choices of the men who made them'.[120]

CUSL, 2000), pp. 203–280 and Annalisa Anastasio, Lucrezia Signorello, 'Mille libri, cento nomi, una sola biblioteca. Il valore dello studio delle collezioni librarie', in Gianfranco Crupi etc. (eds.), *Prismi* (Milan: Ledizioni, 2022), pp. 101–124.

[120] See Donatella Nebbiai-Dalla Guarda, *Livres, patrimoines, profession. Les bibliothèques de quelques médecins en Italie (XIVe–XVe siècles)*, in *Les élites urbaines au Moyen âge* (Rome: École française de Rome, 1997), pp. 385–441, esp. 385. See also David J. Shaw (ed.), *Books and Their Owners. Provenance Information and the European Cultural Heritage* (London: CERL, 2005).

CHAPTER 12

Benedictine Book Acquisitions in Seventeenth- and Eighteenth-Century Bohemia

A Case of Convents in Broumov and Prague

Jindřich Kolda

'Let it be done that the newly published authors, if they are men of illustrious wisdom, and deal with matter necessary, useful or worthy of knowledge for a literate religious man, should be purchased for the growth of the library'.[1] With these words in 1706, the Benedictine Abbot Othmar Daniel Zinke (1664–1738) defined one of the main tasks in the care of the convent library in Broumov. Still, the statement reveals nothing about how new books were acquired for the Benedictine libraries of the era.[2] Individual strategies and procedures for building order libraries must therefore be sought from different materials than order norms or official statements of religious persons (e.g. accounts, private correspondence, inventories, convent chronicles and the books themselves). This case study focuses on sources from the two oldest monasteries in Bohemia: the male Benedictine abbey of St Wenceslas in Broumov (Braunau), founded around 1322 in connection to the Břevnov mother house (founded around 993); and the female Benedictine convent of St George in Prague Castle, founded around 976 as the first monastic institution functioning in Bohemian territory.[3]

---

1 Národní archiv Praha [National Archives, Prague; hereafter NAP], fond Řád Benediktinů Břevnov [fonds Benedictine Order Břevnov; hereafter RBB], archival box no. 29, shelf mark A VIII 1, *Observantiae monasticae*.
2 Regarding monastic libraries and their building in Central Europe during the early modern period, see, for instance, Ernst Tremp (ed.), *Klosterbibliotheken in der Frühen Neuzeit. Süddeutschland, Österreich, Schweiz* (Wiesbaden: Harrassowitz, 2014) and the volumes of *Studien und Mitteilungen zur Geschichte des Benediktinerordens und seiner Zweige*. See also Christine Beier, 'Producing, Buying and Decorating Books in the Age of Guttenberg. The Role of Monasteries in Central Europe', in Bettina Wagner, Marcia Reed (eds.), *Early Printed Books as Material Objects. Proceeding of the Conference Organized by the IFLA Rare Books and Manuscripts Section Munich, 19–21 August 2009* (Berlin: De Gruyter Saur, 2010), pp. 65–82. For other monastic orders, see Neslihan Şenocak, 'Book Acquisition in the Medieval Franciscan Order', *The Journal of Religious History*, 27.1 (2003), pp. 14–28.
3 Out of the numerous publications on the Břevnov monastery, see Johannes Hofmann (ed.), *Tausend Jahre Benediktiner in den Klöstern Břevnov, Braunau und Rohr* (St Ottilien: EOS, 1993). There is no monograph on St George's. The individual aspects of this female monastery's history are scattered throughout various studies. Of the more recent is Karel Pacovský, 'Úloha svatojiřských abatyší při korunovacích českých královen', *Folia Historica Bohemica*, 32.1–2

Both foundations were endowed with extensive feudal tenures linked with several distinguished Bohemian patrons. Břevnov, for instance, was co-founded by bishop Adalbert (d. 997), one of the earliest Bohemian saints. Likewise, princess Ludmila of Bohemia (d. 921), the first local female saint, and her relatives are buried in the nunnery in Prague. Both abbeys preserved their exclusiveness, albeit primarily titular later on, until the early modern period. In 1420s, because of the Hussite wars, the Břevnov abbots even moved to Broumov where they had their headquarters until the eighteen century. Since the beginning of local recatholisation in 1620s, the abbot at Broumov was one of the most important prelates in the country. The abbess at St George's held the right to crown the wives of Bohemian kings, while the convent itself was very popular among prominent noble families who often entrusted their daughters to God there. Both convents have been closely associated with the beginnings and development of local literature and book culture, owing to the rich medieval tradition of scriptoria, through which several important Bohemian codices were compiled.[4] Furthermore, especially in the seventeenth century, both convents were closely connected when the Broumov abbots acted as spiritual patrons of St George's nuns.

It seems that, at least in the seventeenth and eighteenth centuries, male and female monasteries acquired books differently, depending on their varying freedom of movement outside the monastery walls. Early modern monasticism followed the key concepts of two canonical-legal terms: 'stability of place' and 'enclosure'.[5] St Benedict required stability of place (in chapter 58 of his rules) and granted limited permission to leave a monastery (in chapter 67).[6] The impact of Benedict's requirements can be traced into the nineteenth century: male members of the order were allowed to leave the monastery if needed and if granted permission by their superior, which enabled them to

---

(2017), pp. 151–178. For the enclosure aspects of the convent, see Jindřich Kolda, 'Potridentské překračování hranic klauzury Svatojiřského kláštera na Pražském hradě jako potvrzení "odvěké prestiže"', *Theatrum Historiae*, 22 (2018), pp. 75–100.

4 See Dalibor Havel, 'Glosy a jejich role při odhalování nejstarší vrstvy břevnovského skriptoria', *Studia Historica Brunensia*, 60.1–2 (2013), pp. 25–39; Dalibor Havel, *Počátky latinské písemné kultury v českých zemích. Nejstarší latinské rukopisy a zlomky v Čechách a na Moravě* (Brno: Masarykova Univerzita, 2018). Regarding St George's scriptorium, see the respective studies in Zdeňka Hledíková, *Paleograficko-kodikologické etudy* (Prague: Karolinum, 2021).

5 See Susanne Schul, 'frouwen-Wissen – herren-Wissen? "Geschlecht" als Kategorie des Wissens in mittelhochdeutschen Narrationen', in Andreas Gardt etc. (eds.), *Buchkultur und Wissenvermittlung in Mittelalter und Früher Neuzeit* (Berlin: De Gruyter, 2011), pp. 183–202.

6 'And when they admit him to profession, he shall, in the presence of all, make a promise before God and His Saints, of stability, amendment of manners and obedience', *The Rule of Our Most Holy Father St Benedict, Patriarch of Monks* (London: R. Washbourne, 1875), pp. 239, 241.

have their 'good zeal' outside the walls of their monasteries.[7] The mandatory enclosure of all-female monastic orders from the world outside was probably the most important outcome of the Tridentine decree, *On Regulars and Nuns*, which was added to the older constitution *Periculoso* issued by Boniface VIII in 1298.[8] The enclosure of women dedicated to God was to be respected under all circumstances, often in cooperation with secular institutions, under penalty of excommunication. No nun could leave the convent, and nobody from outside the monastery could enter the enclosure.[9] Pius V's bull, *Circa pastoralis* of 1566, specified that nuns could leave the convent only in three cases: epidemic, leprosy or a devastating fire.[10] These norms implied that the life of female monastic communities, especially of contemplative cloisters, depended primarily on external patronage (e.g. ordinary patrons, founders and their families). In what follows, the different practices of acquiring books by male and female Benedictine communities (in the seventeenth and in the eighteenth centuries) will be discussed using the sources mentioned above.

1 'I Received a List from the Bookstore and Saw a Catalogue at the Book Markets'

The financial potential of early modern wealthy male abbeys to purchase books equaled that of the lay nobility and often even surpassed them.[11] At

---

7   See Christian Rohr, 'Tagungsbericht: Nach Rom gehen – monastische Reisekultur im Mittelalter, 03.09.2014–06.09.2014 St Gallen/Einsiedeln', in *H-Soz-Kult*, 15 November 2014, available online: www.hsozkult.de/conferencereport/id/tagungsberichte-5603 (access: 20 December 2021). The term 'good zeal' (*zelus bonus*) comes from the title of chapter 72 of the Benedict's rule.

8   See, for example, Elisabeth M. Makowski, *Canon Law and Cloistered Women. Periculoso and its Commentators, 1298–1545* (Washington: The Catholic University of America Press, 1997), pp. 21f.

9   James Waterworth (ed.), *The Canons and Decrees of the Sacred and Oecumenical Council of Trent* (London: Dolman, 1848), pp. 236f.

10 'De Clausura & numero Monialium ciuscumque Ordinis, & poenis earundem absque licentia Superiorum, ex causa magni incendij, vel infirmitatis leprae, vel epidimiae tantummodo eis concedenda, e Monasteriis egredientium, concomitantiumque & receptantium, ac Superiorum aliter eis licentiam concendentium. Necnon de eleemosynis pro ipsarum Monialum subuentione colligendis', in [Angelo Maria Cherubini], *Magnum Bullarium Romanum* (Lyon: Laurentius Arnaud, Petrus Borde, 1673), USTC 6095926, pp. 183–184. See Clarence Gallagher, 'The Church and Institutes of Consecrated Life', *The Way*, Supplement 50 (1984), pp. 5–6. The strictest type of enclosure only permitted one to leave a monastic house in a coffin. This was called papal enclosure (*clausura papalis*).

11 The process of book acquisitions and its participants are described in detail in: Jindřich Kolda, 'Správa broumovské konventní knihovny v 17. a 18. století', *Folia Historica Bohemica*, 34.2 (2019), pp. 321–345; Jindřich Kolda, 'Lidé a knihy v broumovském konventu v 17. a 18.

Broumov, the acquisition of books involved a broad network of people, both inside the abbey and out. The hub of the whole network was the abbot, whom the Bohemian Provincial Chapter of 1653 explicitly ordered to provide his community's members with food, clothing, a place to live and books ('in victu, amictu, habitatione ac libris').[12] Since the end of the seventeenth century at the latest, the abbey acquired books by cultivating relationships with a diverse group of people: priors, librarians, provisors, antiquary agents and booksellers *extra muros*.[13] Individual volumes were selected for purchase if they fulfilled two essential criteria: each book had to fall within the established range of the collection, and it had to appeal to the personal preferences or needs of the abbot and other important officials within the monastery. Thus, an extensive and opulent monastic library slowly grew over the years, with almost twenty thousand volumes registered in the 1780s.[14]

The genuinely pansophic collection was divided by theme onto shelves labelled with inscribed boards placed above them: I. *S. scripturae et interpretes;* II. *ss. patres et scriptores eccles.;* III. *Theologi mixti;* IV. *Theologi scholastici;* V. *Theologi dogmat[ici], polem[ici] et varii argumenti;* VI. *Theologi moralesi et pastor[ales];* VII.–IX. *Concionatores;* X. *Ascetae christiani;* XI. *Ascetae monastici;*

  století', in Martina Bolom Kotari, Jindřich Kolda (eds.), *Brána moudrosti otevřená. Knihy a knihovny broumovského kláštera* (Hradec Králové: Gaudeamus, 2020), pp. 67–89.

12 NAP, fond RBB, archival box no. 30, shelf mark A VIII 11/a, *Acta et statuta capitulorum provincialium annis 1631 et 1653*, p. 17. *The Rule of Saint Benedict* does not give any further guidance on this issue (see chapters 2 and 63). The title of this subchapter comes from the abbatial instructions for librarians and confirms the attempts of the male branch of the order to continuously update their library collection ('ut noviter editi scriptores pro bibliotheca de novo comparentur'). See NAP, fond RBB, archival box no. 29, shelf mark A VIII 1, *Observantiae monasticae, 1706*.

13 This network has been reconstructed using the abbots' and priors' correspondence. The heading of this part of the study comes from a letter concerning the offer at the Prague annual book markets in 1750. See NAP, fond RBB, archival box no. 73, shelf mark C v 65, *Grundtmann to Pitr, 21 June, 1750.*

14 The exact number cannot be stated due to the current state of the research. The line of reasoning for the estimate is presented in Zdeněk Zahradník, 'Fond knihovny benediktinského kláštera v Broumově a jeho evidence na přelomu 18. a 19. století', *Východočeské Listy Historické*, 37 (2017), pp. 87–111. Since 2016, 4756 titles from the shelves II, XVIII–XXIII and partly from the closets XII and XXXI have been cataloged. Of this number, 3862 titles were published before 1800. The catalogue is available online: <https://vufind.mzk.cz/Search/Advanced> (accessed 28 June 2023). 161 incunabula from Broumov were catalogued for the MEI database; see Krisztina Rábai, 'The Incunabula Collection of the Benedictine Monastery in Broumov', in Jakub Zouhar (ed.), *Monastic Libraries in East Central and Eastern Europe between the Middle Ages and the Enlightenment* (Brno: Moravská Zemská Knihovna, 2020) pp. 229–249. These corpora form a basis for the hypotheses that will be presented further in the text.

XII. *Concilia, bullae et libri rituales;* XIII. *Ius canonicum;* XIV. *Ius mixtum;* XV. *Ius civile commune;* XVI. *Ius civile particulare;* XVII. *Philosophia generalis;* XVIII. *Philosophia partialis;* XIX. *Historia universalis et ecclessiastica;* XX. *Topographia sacra et acta sanctorum;* XXI. *Historia mixta;* XXII. *Historia profana;* XXIII. *Encicplopaediae, lexica ac.;* XXIV. *Medici;* XXV. *Libri interdicti;* XXVI. *Breviaria;* XXXI. *Grammatica;* XXXII. *Poetica;* XXXIII. *Rhetorica.*[15] This division was typical for large contemporary Benedictine libraries.[16]

Evidence indicates that books were also acquired for smaller collections within the monastery, such as for the library in the provisor's office, for the monastic pharmacy or for the theological school of the order.[17] For instance, the provisor's agenda, which included administration and management within the abbey, required treatises on cattle breeding, gardening, bookkeeping, banking and sections of the Austrian legal code. The library of the monastic *studium* provided, for example, treatises compiled by classic authors and theoretical treatises on literature or drama.[18]

Due to the wide range of required topics, the abbots could not rely solely on books printed locally; that is, only books published by the archiepiscopal printing house or the Jesuit printing house, both located in Prague.[19] Other means

---

15 The bookshelves no. XXVII–XXX were originally not labelled. A board titled 'Miscellanea' or 'Varia' could be given to them according to their contents. These shelves housed, for example, catalogues of books offered by European booksellers and printers (e.g. by the Elseviers), grouped under the shelf mark XXVIII.B.1.

16 See the monastic library of the Benedictine abbey in German Münsterschwarzach, in Friedrich Karl Gottlob Hirsching, *Versuch einer Beschreibung sehenswürdiger Bibliotheken Teutschlands* (Erlangen: Johan Jakob Palm, 1786), I. 189. It is obvious that in the case of the Benedictines, the spirituality of the order did not play a greater role when it came to the book culture. Concerning other orders in Bohemia, like the Jesuits, see Hedvika Kuchařová and Kateřina Valentová-Bobková 'Knihovní fond, jeho struktura a proměny', in Hedvika Kuchařová etc. (eds.), *Knihovna jezuitské koleje v Telči. Katalog výstavy* (Prague: Historický Ústav, 2020), pp. 36–45. Regarding Benedictine theoretical works, see Oliverus Legipont, *Dissertationes Philologico-Bibliographicae* (Nuremberg: Paul Lochner, 1747), pp. 63–64.

17 Kolda, 'Správa', p. 343. For the history of the order's school, see Timotheus Anton Matauschek, *Geschichte des Gymnasiums der Benediktiner in Braunau* (Prague: Carl Bellman, 1863), pp. 11f. As of 1787, 221 books were evidenced in these libraries 'outside the convent'.

18 Státní oblastní archiv Hradec Králové [State Regional Archives Hradec Králové], fond Velkostatek Broumov [fonds Broumov Estate], archival box no. 139, inventory no. 1397, *Y: Inventarium über die ... sowohl in der Prelatur als auch in den Convente befunden Pretiosen* [hereafter *Inventarium über die Pretiosen*].

19 Entries on both of these printing offices can be found in the online Encyclopaedia of (Czech) Books: Petr Voit, 'Arcibiskupská tiskárna - Praha', in *Encyklopedieknihy.cz. Encyklopedie knihy v českém středověku a raném novověku*, available online: <https://www.encyklo

for privately ordering books and texts were employed for the regular members of the order, most frequently for the monks studying for the priesthood (*studiosi*). Hence, the order turned to booksellers and antiquarians to augment their libraries. The role of booksellers as suppliers of recent publications had been growing since the first half of the eighteenth century as their network in central Europe expanded. Before that, the monastery's demand for literature had been largely satisfied by purchases of 'second-hand' books, which formed roughly twenty-three percent of the preserved collection in the Broumov monastic library.[20] Before the mid-eighteenth century, the most significant booksellers the monks collaborated with were Caspar Zacharias Wussin (d.1747) and Gregor Mangold (d.*c*.1747).[21] Both came to Prague in the 1740s from Bavaria.[22] Mangold regularly supplied the Benedictines with the catalogues of German booksellers and sold them books during the St Vitus book fairs in Prague. The books transferred from Prague to Broumov in 1750 included, among others, the ascetic treatise compiled by Michael a S. Catharina, *Trinum perfectum via, veritas, vita*, and Armand Jean de Rancé's recently published handbook on monastic life, *Vortreffliches Werck von der Heyligkeith und denen Pflichten des Clösterliches Lebens*, ordered from Dresden.[23] Still, the Abbot Benno Löbl (1688–1751) hungered for the Latin version of the tract.[24] Early modern Prague was too provincial for such demands, however.

---

    pedieknihy.cz/index.php?title=Arcibiskupsk%C3%A1_tisk%C3%A1rna_%E2%80%93_Praha> (accessed: 28 June 2023); Petr Voit, 'Jezuitská tiskárna - Praha', in *Encyklopedieknihy.cz. Encyklopedie knihy v českém středověku a raném novověku*, available online: <https://www.encyklopedieknihy.cz/index.php?title=Jezuitsk%C3%A1_tisk%C3%A1rna_%E2%80%93_Praha> (accessed: 28 June 2023). Of the 3,862 recently cataloged incunabula and rare books, 820 were published in the Czech Lands, with 495 in Prague.

20   Any provenance mark from outside the order, accompanied by the inscription (*Nunc*) *Monasterii Braunensis O.S.B.*, serves as evidence. The library owned, for example, a volume once owned by the Archduke Ferdinand II (1529–1595), *Catalogus testium veritatis locupletissimus* (Dillingen: Sebald Mayer, 1565), USTC 619858, shelf mark XIX.D.aa.6,1, as well as a volume that used to be in possession of the Jesuit college in Irish Athone: Bartolomeo Mastri, *De Meldula et Bonaventurae Belluti* I. (Venice: s.n., 1688), USTC 1718737, shelf mark XVIII.A.10.

21   Věra Smolová, 'Pražský radní, mědirytec a knihkupec Kašpar Zachariáš Vusín', *Documenta Pragensia*, 10.2 (1990), pp. 291–298.

22   Both were active in Prague between 1743 and 1796. See also Petr Voit, 'Řehoř Mangold', in *Encyklopedieknihy.cz. Encyklopedie knihy v českém středověku a raném novověku*, available online: <https://www.encyklopedieknihy.cz/index.php/Řehoř_Mangold> (accessed 28 June 2023).

23   NAP, fond RBB, archival box no. 73, shelf mark C V 65, *Grundtmann to Pitr, 21 June 1750*. Not a single one of these volumes has been found in Broumov to date. A similar situation holds true for the majority of books mentioned in written sources.

24   NAP, fond RBB, archival box no. 73, shelf mark C V 65, *Grundtmann to Pitr, 21 June 1750*.

Even after 1715, Abbot Othmar, as the head of the local Benedictine province, was forced to send a special resident, Bonifacius the priest, to Vienna. Bonifacius was involved in various issues in the central offices of the Habsburg monarchy, and he was also authorised and responsible for purchasing books. Hence, book expenditures for his monastery averaged yearly between fifty and one hundred guldens, constituting the monastery's second most frequent expense in Vienna (the first being wine). At the beginning of his residency, Bonifacius chose, among numerous booksellers in Vienna, the services of Johann Martin Esslinger (d.1728), who had a wide range of providers and suppliers from territories outside of Central Europe (e.g. Antwerp).[25] Esslinger also offered remarkable services; for example, he delivered purchased books directly to customers.[26] Around 1720, annual book purchases in Vienna numbered between ten and twelve titles. In 1718, the monastery purchased thirty-three titles in forty-six volumes at Esslinger's. These included practical handbooks, perhaps linked to Bauldry's *Ceremoniale*, reissued in 1717. Four copies of *Pharmacopoea Augustana* were presumably intended for the pharmacies of the four monasteries connected with the Břevnov abbey. Most of the items were bought at the price of a few guldens, with the exception of *Corpus Iuris Civilis*, which was acquired for sixty-five guldens.[27]

During the 1730s, the Benedictines sent the German historian Magnoaldus Ziegelbauer (1688–1750) to Vienna as their purchasing officer. Ziegelbauer, apart from his services to the monastery, collected materials for his own academic and scientific research, including the history of the Břevnov monastery.[28]

---

25 C.1700, there were six permanent active bookstores in Vienna, as well as numerous so-called *Buchträger* and *Buchführer*, who operated more informally, see Norbert Bachleitner, Franz M.Eybl, Ernst Fischer, *Geschichte des Buchhandels in Österreich* (Wiesbaden: Harrassowitz Verlag, 2000), pp. 72f. For Esslinger's services (*'Gewölb auf dem Peter-Freythof gegen dem Guldenen väßl über'*), see Isabel Heitjan, 'Wolf Moritz Endters Geschäfte mit Balthasar III. Moretus und Nachfolgern, 1675–1723', *Archiv für Geschichte des Buchwesens*, 29 (1978), col. 1462.

26 See NAP, fond RBB, archival box no. 181, shelf mark G XVII 6, *Registrum expensi et accepti Anno 1715*. The first purchase for the Broumov monastery was evidenced there in April 1712. See NAP, fond RBB, archival box no. 181, shelf mark G XVII 6, *Nro. 20*. Regarding the booksellers, see Bachleitner, Eybl, Fischer, *Geschichte des Buchhandels*, p. 80. For more information on the Vienna purchases, see Kolda, 'Správa', pp. 336–338.

27 11 March 1718, NAP, fond RBB, archival box no. 181, shelf mark G XVII 6, *Anno 1719 – Außzüglein von Johann Martin Eslinger, buchhändler auff den Peters Freyd-Hoff*.

28 Mangoaldus Ziegelbauer, *Epitome historica regii, liberi, exempti, in Regno Bohemiae antiquissimi ... Monasterii Brevnoviensis vulgo S. Margarethae Ordinis S. Benediciti prope Pragam* (Coloniae: 1740). For Ziegelbauer, see Beda Franz Menzel, *Abt Franz Stephan Rautenstrauch von Břevnov - Braunau. Herkunft, Umwelt und Wirkungskreis* (Königstein/Ts.: Königsteiner Institut für Kirchen- und Geistesgeschichte der Sudetenländer, 1969),

Ziegalbauer was in regular contact with Friedrich Grundtmann (1730–1772), the then prior of Břevnov, and kept him informed of the latest news. His letters were often sent with extensive bibliographical registers on select issues. For instance, in November 1739, the issue was the study of Holy Writ; thus, the register contained sixty-two authors, presumably for the needs of the order's students.[29] Besides his regular services, Ziegelbauer also arranged the private purchase of books for Abbot Benno on several occasions.[30] In addition to recent publications, Benno's orders included 'antiquarian' items, such as Johann Baptista Folengius's *Monachi cusinatis* of 1585, 'very rare in German libraries' according to the abbot.[31]

Benedictine channels for book acquisition also included other people and institutions beyond the order. During the 1730s and 1740s, Bavarian bookseller Gotthard Johann Püttner from Hof monitored the central European book market for Benedictines from Bohemia.[32] On several occasions, Püttner surprised the abbots with the high prices of certain books. For example, in 1740, the eight-volume *Annales minorum* (re-edition compiled by English Franciscan Luke Wadding) was available in Leipzig for 120 florins, a sum that equalled the price of all the books bought at the Esslinger's between 1712 and 1720.[33] Presumably, due to Püttner, two books of Ingolstadt provenance found their way to the Broumov library: one from the estate of the deceased local Jesuit Stephan Hueber and the second from the estate of the deceased professor of medicine at the local university, Anton Jonas Kilianstein (d. 1638).[34]

Püttner also bought books for the Benedictines in Leipzig, where he partnered with Lanckischs Erben's company.[35] Evidence from the same period

---

pp. 80–82; Jakub Zouhar, Petr Polehla, *Přehled církevní historiografie na Západě do konce osvícenství* (Červený Kostelec: Pavel Mervart, 2017), pp. 360–362.

29   NAP, fond RBB, archival box no. 73, shelf mark C V 65, *Ziegelbauer to Grundtmann, 11 November 1739*.

30   They included, for instance, the individual volumes of *Universal-Lexicon* by Johann Heinrich Zedler, which began to be published in Leipzig in 1731 (shelf mark XIII.C.1).

31   NAP, fond RBB, archival box no. 73, shelf mark C V 65, *Ziegelbauer to Grundtmann, 13 September 1740*.

32   Püttner was a German publisher and, since 1742, a privileged bookseller in Bayreuth. See J.G. Heinritz, *Zur Geschichte der Stadt Baireuth* (Baireuth: s.n., 1825), II. 49. Püttner was at the same time the publisher, official seller and distributor of the treatise on the history of *Archisterium* by Ziegelbauer. See footnote 28.

33   NAP, fond RBB, archival box no. 73, shelf mark C V 65, *Püttner to Ziegelbauer, 19 November 1740*.

34   Shelf marks XVII.A.11: *Senece omnia opera* (Venice: Bernardinus de Choris, 1492), USTC 991126, and XVIII.A.23,1: *De historia animalium* (Basel: 1534), USTC 600185.

35   For the company, see Christoph Koop, 'Kurzer Entwurf zur Publikationsumgebung des Rechtschaffenen Tantzmeisters', in Hanna Walsdorf etc. (eds.), *Tauberts Rechtschaffener*

reveals Benedictine contacts with the office of Johann Friedrich Gleditsch (d.1744) from Leipzig, and later booksellers Joseph von Kurzböck (1736–1792) and Johann Thomas Trattner (1717–1798) from Vienna.[36] Around the mid-eighteenth century, Trattner headed the largest publishing house in Central Europe and thus played a significant role in Benedictine book acquisitions.[37] The publishing house of Giuseppe Remondini e figli of Venice also sent book offers to the Bohemian Benedictines, as did the Parisian distributors of the Elzevirs, Peez and Bader from Regensburg, Rüdiger from Nuremberg, and Löwe from Wrocław.[38] Moreover, book transmission from Italy to Bohemia increased owing to court agents in Vienna.[39] Because of their involvement, books sent from Rome via Vienna to Broumov, especially the 'banned books', easily received permission for export.[40] However, the manner in which many volumes found their way to the shelves of the library will likely remain a secret forever. Ownership notes found in the Broumov books, for instance, show that older books were sometimes acquired from Silesian ecclesiastical circles, especially the library of the Wrocław cathedral. We know that they arrived to Broumov in the 1660s and 1670s.[41] Yet, it is not known who acquired them (monks, canons, booksellers), nor in what form they were acquired (purchases, gifts, from the estates of the deceased).

Other forms of book acquisitions played a smaller role. These include transfers to the monastic library of private books that had belonged to brethren following their death.[42] Research has identified sixty-nine former owners in the library from the seventeenth and eighteenth centuries, all headed by abbots

---

Tantzmeister (Leipzig 1717). Kontexte – Lektüren – Praktiken (Berlin: Frank & Timme, 2019), p. 198f.

36   On Trattner, see Christoph Augustynowicz and Johannes Frimmel (eds.), *Der Buchdrucker Maria Theresias: Johann Thomas Trattner (1719–1798) und sein Medienimperium* (Wiesbaden: Harrassowitz Verlag, 2019). Trattner's business had branches even in Prague and Brno by the end of the eighteenth century.

37   Bachleitner, Eybl, Fischer, *Geschichte des Buchhandels*, pp. 138f. See Pitr's letters from the 1740s and 1750s in NAP, fond RBB, archival box no. 73, shelf mark C v 65.

38   All can be found in the monastery library in Broumov, shelf mark XXVIII.B.1.

39   NAP, fond RBB, archival box no. 48, shelf mark A XVI 4, *Expens consignation ... von monath Maii bieß monath Augusti 1735*.

40   For instance, NAP, fond RBB, uninvetoried part, Epistolae an. 1761–1785, *Aulich to Rautenstrauch, 27 December 1773*. As of 1801, the inventory of *libri prohibiti* included 391 titles.

41   For instance, shelf marks II.A.32,1, XIII.A.13 or XVII.A.5.

42   See the abbatial instructions for librarians edited in Jindřich Kolda, 'Pravidla pro novověké broumovské knihovníky', in Martina Bolom Kotari, Jindřich Kolda (eds.), *Brána moudrosti otevřená. Knihy a knihovny broumovského kláštera* (Hradec Králové: Gaudeamus, 2020), p. 122.

from the periods 1602 to 1646 and 1663 to 1805.[43] Books were frequent gifts within the Benedictine community as well, usually in commemoration of the crucial moments of a monk's spiritual journey. Such intentions were usually hidden in the inscriptions of the books; for instance: 'I dedicate this little book, in memory of his profession, to congenial man Procopius Dientzenhofer, OSB, in Broumov. Father Cyrillus Wagner, the Rajhrad monastery'.[44] Other means of book transmission, especially for texts of moral theology and pastoral care, occurred when members of the order migrated between monasteries.[45] Novices also would bring some with them to the convent when entering the novitiate. Gifts from people outside of the order were rare and frequently connected with the authors of texts, such as in the case of the Jesuit professor Kaspar Knittel (1644–1702), who gave the monastery a printed volume of his magnum opus *Via regia ad omnes scientias et artes*.[46]

2   'I Cannot Send Anything of Spiritual Writings at This Time'

These words were written to Anna Mechtildis Schönweisin (d. 1691), the Abbess of the Prague Benedictine nuns, by the then Jesuit confessor of the convent at the beginning of 1674.[47] By doing so, he precisely expressed the reading preferences of the convent and revealed that the nuns depended on the outer environment due to their enclosure. During the early modern period, book acquisition opportunities for Benedictine nuns in Bohemia were rare compared to those of the male members of the order. We have records of only occasional activities. In 1666, for instance, Abbess Elisabeth Kestnerowa (1620–1671) purchased new breviaries for her nuns at St George's, but only

---

43 Of the volumes that have been cataloged in Broumov so far, 18.4 percent came from the members of the order.

44 *Pro memoria obtulit hunc Libellum (pl: tit:) Carissimo Domino Procopio Dientzenhofer proff[esui] Brau[nensis] OSB P[ater] Cyrillus Wagner Rayh[radensis] prof[esus]*. In Jan Jiří Středovský, *Rubinus Moraviae* (Brno: Lehmann, 1712), shelf mark XX.F.bb.71,1.

45 In this way, for instance, one medical dissertation (shelf mark XXIV.A.39) from the period of Maria Theresa arrived at the Broumov library together with its owner; it was incorporated into the collection by the then order librarian after the monk's death at the end of the eighteenth century. Furthermore, especially books from other convents of the *archisterium*: Břevnov (for instance, shelf marks XIX.C.bb.29,1,A, XVIII.B.34,1, XXII.E.bb.1,1 or XXIII.a.5,1) and Police nad Metují (for instance, shelf marks XVIII.B.34,1, XVIII.E.bb.5,1, XVIII.G.bb.16,1 or XXII.E.bb.1,1) can be found in Broumov.

46 It was published in Prague in 1682, shelf mark XXIII.G.bb.3,1.

47 NAP, fond Archivy zrušených klášterů [fond Archives of the Abolished Monasteries; hereafter AZK], archival box no. 25, *P. Eucharius to Anna Mechtildis, 6 January 1674*.

for the sisters who lacked manuscript exemplars.[48] The new breviaries were passed ceremonially to the nuns by an unknown canon and a representative of the archbishop, meaning the abbess was side-lined. When acquiring books and the expanding library collections of female Benedictines, most book acquisitions were funded by people active outside the monastery. A record exists from a chronicle of female Benedictine nuns that praises Abbot Thomas Sartorius of the Broumov Monastery, who in 1672 donated to them 'a new book for singing during the holy mass', which took an old medieval gradual out of use.[49] During the 1670s, Christophorus Eucharius, who had been rector of a college in Żagań prior to his arrival to Prague, was in regular contact with several sisters from St George's.[50] According to one letter, Christophorus sent them books for private, devotional reading and encouraged them to read *The imitation of Christ* by Thomas à Kempis.[51] Copies of other early modern bestsellers of spirituality were at the disposal of the nuns, including letters compiled by venerated monks or saints. Among many texts, the following were remarkable: the letters of Pajar, a Jesuit missionary, regarding the veneration of St Francis Xavier in Goa, Portuguese India; and letters written by St Teresa of Ávila praising the Jesuits' support expressed to her for her work.[52] In 1681, Placidus Spáčil, an order choirmaster from Broumov, composed *Parthenologium* for the nuns, which contained the biographies of female Benedictine saints. He urged the nuns: 'as you read these accounts every day, do not marvel at the lives and virtues [of these saints] as much as strenuously imitate them with your minds aflame!'.[53] In 1703, the nuns received a splendid, velour-bound biography of the

---

48   It could have possibly been a reaction (albeit late) to a brief by Paul V of 1616 that specified choral texts and breviaries for the Benedictine order. Its copy is deposited among the written matters of the convent. See NAP, fond AZK, archival box no. 17, inventory no. 735.

49   Archiv Hlavního města Prahy [Prague City Archives], Sbírka rukopisů [Manuscript Collection], book no. 7875, *Kniha pamětní*, p. 26. According to a 'new custom', the Sunday hymn *Salve* was replaced by the hymn *Stabat Mater dolorosa*, sung three times a week.

50   'Eucharius, Christophorus, SJ, ca 1627–1691', in *Historický ústav AV ČR projekt Řeholníci – katalog Clavius*, available online: <http://reholnici.hiu.cas.cz/katalog/l.dll?hal~1000103418> (accessed: 20 December 2021).

51   NAP, fond AZK, archival box no. 25, *P. Eucharius to Anna Mechtildis, 23 September 1674*.

52   Both are found in NAP, fond AZK, archival box no. 15, inventory no. 119 and archival box no. 20, inventory no. 1507. The letters could have been means of informing which order was considered 'the proper one' within early modern *curiae mulierum*.

53   *Quotidie legentes, vitas ac virtutes earum non tam miraremini, quam potius accensis animis strenue imitaremini!* See NAP, fond RBB, archival box no. 105, *Parthenologium Benedictinum ex Vitis Sanctarum, Beatarum, Venerabiliumque Virginum & sub Regula ss. Patriarchae nostri Benedicti ... militantium ... Braunae A. 1681*. The author is identified only by the initials F.P. (Frater Placidus). We know him from the Broumov correspondence of the Austrian Benedictine monk Bernhard Pez. See Thomas Wallnig, Thomas Stockinger

first Bohemian female saint, St Ludmila, who was buried in their convent.[54] Almost fifty years later, the prior of Rajhrad Abbey dedicated to St George's a copy of the first Czech translation of the *Rule of St Benedict*.[55] These cases indicate that most donors came from the Bohemian church environment. They primarily dedicated to the convent's library essential canonical texts and contemplative and formative spiritual works, such as *Geistliche Übungen des Heil[igen] Ignatii*, and handbooks on exemplary monastic life, such as *Kurtzer Begrif der Leben und Tugenden unterschiedlichen Gott verlobten Jungfrauen*, or saints vitae.

In terms of numbers and diversity, St George's library could not compare with the contemporaneus libraries of Bohemia's male monasteries.[56] St George's intellectual decline began during the Hussite wars of the later Middle Ages and continued subsequently into the sixteenth century.[57] Before the Hussite wars, St George's had been a renowned centre of spirituality and book culture. For instance, in the seventeenth century, the most respected codex once owned by St George's, the so-called *Passional of Abbess Kunigunde*, was held in the abbey's reference library along with accounting books and land registers.[58] In 1782 when the monastery was liquidated by Emperor Joseph II, the convent's library registered 435 book entries.[59] Abbess Maria Theresia von Harnach

---

(eds.), *Die gelehrte Korrespondenz der Brüder Pez. Texten, Regesten, Kommentare* (Vienna: Böhlau Verlag 2010), I. 203.

54 NAP, fond AZK, book no. 22, *Rozličný vydání na rok 1703*.

55 Bonaventura Pitr (ed.), *Řehola aneb zákon svatého otce Benedikta opata od téhož svatého arciotce sepsaná a od svatého Řehoře papeže toho jména prvního čtená ...* (Brno: s.n., 1760).

56 For more on this, see e.g. Jindřich Kolda, 'Buchkultur des Ordens der Barmherzigen Brüder im 18. Jahrhundert am Beispiel Kukus, Neustadt an der Mettau, Prag und Feldsberg', in Petr Jelínek (ed.), *Germanische Provinz des Hospitalordens des Hl. Johannes von Gott bis 1780* (Cieszyn: Konwent Bonifratrów, 2018), pp. 127–162. In addition, the Merciful Brothers began building their libraries only after their arrival in the Czech lands in 1620. For an older order, consider the Cistercians: Jindra Pavelková, 'Prameny pro rekonstrukci knihovních fondů klášterů cisterciáckého řádu na Moravě', *Studia Historica Brunensia*, 60.1–2 (2013), pp. 273–279. The number of books in the male monasteries in Velehrad and Žďár-nad-Sázavou exceeded 10,000 and 2000 titles, respectively, in the 1780s, while the library of the female monastery in Brno contained fewer than 500 volumes at the same time.

57 By ca. 1550, only two nuns remained in the monastery. For more, see Jan Zdichynec, 'Ferdinand I. a kláštery v Praze', *Historie – Otázky – Problémy*, 7.2 (2015), p. 105.

58 See NAP, fond AZK, archival box no. 23, inventory no. 2593. During this period, Latin was gradually disappearing from among the languages used in the convent. In the 1680s, Czech rose to prominence, followed by German. For more information on the passional, see Gia Toussaint, *Das Passional der Kunigunde von Böhmen. Bildrhetorik und Spiritualität* (Paderborn: Schöningh, 2003).

59 This number was obtained by adding up the number of titles (ninety-eight) that were taken over by librarians of the Imperial Royal University Library in Prague upon the

(1729–1803), while attempting to protect the library from government commissioners, argued: 'until now [the books] served the nuns who are subordinated to me for their spiritual meditations and retreats'.[60] Therewith, she precisely summarised the library's main mission.

Donor names suggest how St George's acquired its books. Surviving sources indicate three important criteria for library acquisitions. First, the nuns sought the books needed for the daily offices and liturgies required by St Benedict's rule.[61] Second, they bought books that would provide them with devotional texts; these were written almost solely in vernacular languages (Czech and German).[62] Third, the number and quality of the books were warranted by the donors outside the monastery, namely the male ordinaries of convents, patrons and benefactors. One example would be Christophorus, the Benedictine nuns' confessor during the 1670s, who corresponded with a nun named Joanna. Owing to his letters, we know about her reading practices. Moreover, she sent him a book. Unfortunately, we do not know the book's title, but in other letters to Christophorus, Joanna asks him to return it.[63] This suggests that persons

dissolution of the convent. For more on this, see Ondřej Bastl, 'Knihy a listiny zrušeného svatojiřského kláštera', in Petr Kreuz, Vojtěch Šustek (eds.), *Seminář a jeho hosté II. Sborník příspěvků k nedožitým narozeninám doc. PhDr. Rostislava Nového* (Prague: Archiv hlavního města Prahy, 2004), pp. 187–223. For the number of titles that were left to the nuns for temporary use before the dissolution of the monastic house at the end of 1782, see NAP, fond České gubernium – Publicum [fonds Czech Gubernia - Publicum; hereafter CGP], archival box no. 679, *N.37*. Moreover, no female librarian was evidenced among the official posts in the convent during the early modern era, whereas in the case of the male Benedictines from Broumov, this post existed.

60 'Bis her den mir untergebenen Klosterfrauen zu ihren Geistlichen Betrachtungen und Exercitien dienneten', NAP, fond CGP, archival box no. 679 [*N.37*].

61 Spiritual reading was considered the first stage of mental prayer. It served as a basis for meditations and discoursive prayers, next to the spiritual exercises and cues provided by preachers and confessors. The following stages were active contemplations and passive contemplations. For these purposes, the libraries of the Benedictine nuns thus usually included commentaries and meditations upon scripture (*lectio divina*), saints' lives and martyrologies. In central Europe, their authors were typically the Benedictines and Jesuits. See Heater Wolfe, 'Reading Bells and Loose Papers. Reading and Writing Practices of the English Benedictine Nuns of Cambrai and Paris', in: Victoria E. Burke, Jonathan Gibson (eds.), *Early Modern Women's Manuscript Writing: Selected Papers from the Trinity/Trent Colloquium* (Aldershot: Ashgate, 2004), pp. 135–156.

62 Similar leaning towards local languages could be observed across early modern female convents, regardless of the order, its age or region. For instance, see Jolanta Gwoździk, *Biblioteka panien benedyktynek łacińskich we Lwowie (XVI–XVIII wiek)* (Katowice: Wydawnictwo Uniwersytetu Śląskiego, 2001), pp. 108–109; or Caroline Bowden, 'A Distribution of Tyme. Reading and Writing Practices in the English Convents in Exile', *Tulsa Studies in Women's Literature*, 31.1/2 (2012), pp. 99–116. The thematic and genre compositions of the libraries in the contemplative orders were also very similar.

63 NAP, fond AZK, archival box no. 25, *P. Eucharius to Anna Mechtildis, 6 January 1674*.

beyond the cloister were not the only ones distributing books among early modern female monasteries in Bohemia. Besides this, however, we lack further evidence. No single internal document (e.g. a nun profile within the convent necrology) or extant delivered sermon (e.g. on the occasion of the installation of a new abbess or at a funeral) refers to a female reader or scholar, despite specific attributes and characteristics typically being praised.

3   Monastic versus Private Ownership of Books

The previous sections describe the period of book acquisition among Bohemian Benedictines that concluded in the mid-eighteenth century. During this period, entries of book purchases disappeared from the accounting registers of monasteries, even though book production was growing. For example, in the Broumov monastery, the abbots were focused on building their own library collection. By 1795, it already included 5,586 volumes.[64] Nevertheless, the late-eighteenth century saw a particular shift in book purchasing among Benedictines; the centralised purchases were replaced by individual subscriptions. A carefully constructed network of Broumov agents for book purchasing intensified for several decades and came to include other ordinary members of the monastery, reflecting their interests and financial possibilities.[65] St George's buying patterns in this period were somewhat different. The primary providers of new books were the nuns' relatives, whose visits in the monastery's locutorium were ever-more frequent, despite the prohibitions issued by the Council of Trent.[66] At present, we cannot judge whether this was an effect of the general deregulation of monastic discipline influenced by the enlightened reforms of the Habsburg rulers. However, it seems that contemplative female monastic houses started to make a search for a much more active occurrence in society. In 1780s, most likely, the sisters at St George's thought about the establishing of a public school for young girls.[67] Building the contacts with outside world may have been an important part of this idea.

---

64   Zahradník, 'Fond knihovny benediktinského kláštera v Broumově a jeho evidence na přelomu 18. a 19. století', p. 107.
65   Extensive evidence can be found for this in the provisors' correspondence from the 1770s and 1780s. See, for instance, NAP, fond RBB, book no. 146.
66   This was confirmed, for instance, by a brother of one of the nuns, who visited her in the convent in the 1770s. See NAP, fond CGP, archival box no. 680, shelf mark F 2 21/7 [N.1221].
67   The last abbess gave the possibility of girl's education as one of the arguments for resumption of the abolished monastery after the death of Emperor Joseph II, see Österreichisches Staatsarchiv Wien [Austrian State Archives, Vienna], Allgemeines Verwaltungsarchiv [General Archives of the Administration], Bestand Kultus – Katolisch

Lists of books in the cells of male Benedictines at Broumov in 1787 illustrate this shift. Twenty-three monks were resident in the monastery at that time.[68] Records reveal that each monk had books at his disposal in his cell, ranging from a mere four volumes in the case of one senior preacher to up to an impressive 135 registered items in the case of brother Hugo, a new monk and a student at the local Benedictine school. These lists of individual monks' libraries can help elucidate the monks' professions and services within the community. For instance, professors active at the order school had numerous handbooks on treating languages, history, law, mineralogy and theology. We know that the infirmarius Amandus, for example, read Carl von Linné's *Philosophia botanica* and various treatises on chemistry and pharmaceutics. Even brother Cornelius, a joiner and the only local secular monk, was a passionate reader who owned twenty-five volumes. In addition to the religious literature at his disposal, he studied Christian Wolff's tract on mathematics. A total 1,091 listed volumes were possessed by monks, and a further forty-eight volumes belonged only to the monastery.[69] Among the books owned by the Broumov abbey, bibles, missals, catechisms and copies of the rule of St Benedict predominated. These texts constituted the standard Benedictine library, regardless of the interests or responsibilities of individual monks. The extant records indicate that the Broumov abbey had temporarily abandoned acquiring books that appealed to the monks, and thus the library alone was unable to satisfy the members' current tastes.

Around 1784, an inventory was made of the books at St George's, along with a list of the books owned by the nuns. Here, 1,183 books were listed in the cells of twenty-seven nuns. An additional 426 volumes were registered in the rooms of female novices.[70] Thus, more than 1,450 books existed outside the official convent library, three times that of the recorded volumes in the library's inventory. Some repetition occurs among the nuns' personal volumes, as indicated by Sr Maria Gertrudis' register: 'Latin breviaries and to breviaries belonging books, exercise books, German prayer books, meditative and contemplative

---

[fonds Religion – Catholic Affairs], archival box no. 851, inventory no. 620, *161 ex Augusto 803 GS*. However, this idea did not manifest itself in any way in contents of the convent library.

68 See *Inventarium über die Pretiosen*. For more details on the placement of books within the monastery in a given year, see Kolda, 'Správa', pp. 340–343.

69 In connection with the ownership, the books were described as 'dem Geistlichen eygenthumlich zugehörig' and 'dem Kloster zugehörig'. Cited number does not even include all the books; in some cases, the books were more or less dismissed by a note such as 'historische, ascetische, Gebettbüchel, Piezen unbedeutende'. See *Inventarium über die Pretiosen*.

70 Österreichisches Staatsarchiv Wien, Allgemeines Verwaltungsarchiv, Bestand Stiftungshofbuchhaltung, archival box no. 591, *Recognition N.26–N.64*. In case of three nuns, it is evidenced by only books (*Bücher*) without any specification.

books'.[71] Roughly forty percent of the items were devotional manuals and liturgical books. Contemplative texts composed a smaller percentage, likely because these books were available within the convent library. Interestingly, we can trace the nuns' reading preferences through the books connected to individual nuns. St George's possessed thirty French publications that originated from Abbess Maria Josepha von Fürstenberg's estate, for example. In the 1760s, Maria Josepha (1731–1770) published her *Geistliche Fisch-Angel auf der ungestümmen Meer der Welt*, a translation of Pierre Nicole's *Essais de morale*. Each volume of this extensive four-volume work had more than six hundred pages, with meditations urging the reader to practise austerity each day of the year.[72] Abbess Franziska Helena (1648–1720), the daughter of the renowned architect Giovanni Pieroni of Florence, brought several Italian treatises on architecture to the convent as part of her inheritance.[73]

4 Conclusion

In the early modern period, among the male Benedictines in Bohemia, book acquisition was sustained by the initiation and interests of individual monks and sophisticated social networks, including book agents and antiquarians from central Europe. Contrariwise, the nuns were limited to receiving books from donors outside the monastery. The monks were readers of a wide array of subjects. Conversely, the nuns' reading options were limited to mainly religious and educational literature. The current scholarly consensus is that literary production from all over Europe was available to the monks, while the nuns were

---

71 'Latainische Brewir und zum Brewir gehörige Bücher, Exertitien Bücher, teütsche Bettbücher, Betrachtungs- und Meditations Bücher, geistliche Leßbücher', Österreichisches Staatsarchiv Wien, Allgemeines Verwaltungsarchiv, Bestand Stiftungshofbuchhaltung, archival box no. 591, *Recognition N.37*.

72 The original was published in 1671. St George's Convent had the edition of 1745 (see Bastl, 'Knihy a listiny', p. 198). The publication of the book was probably sponsored by the Fürstenberg family, one of the most powerful aristocratic families in the Czech lands and Austria at that time. Translations (from French only?) by Bohemian nuns and the distribution of foreign-language texts within the local environments were probably more extensive than has been believed to date. For the most famous local female translator, Celestine Marie Eleonora Sporck and the text strategies of her family, see Veronika Čapská, 'The (Swéerts-)Sporck and their Subjects. Local and Transcultural Printing and Distribution of Heterodox Books in Eighteenth-Century Bohemia', in Elizabeth Dillenburg etc. (eds.), *Print Culture at the Crossroads. The Book and Central Europe* (Leiden: Brill 2021), pp. 451–471.

73 For instance, *Delle fortificationi libri 5* (Venice: Buonaiuto Lorini, 1597), USTC 838673. See Bastl, 'Knihy a listiny', p. 199.

primarily limited to local book production. These findings are consistent with certain architectural features of the monasteries in question. For example, the rich libraries in male monasteries were built in the centres of the monastic houses.[74] As we know from the letters of monks, most books were read extensively. As for female monasteries, the libraries consisted of a single room with several bookshelves, and large groups of texts were probably never read.[75]

These conclusions are preliminary and reflect what knowledge exists of the setting of Bohemian Benedictine monks during the early modern period. What we know of the local nuns elicits potentially fruitful questions: Abbess Franziska Helena Pieroni assigned the contract for the convent's chapel to the then-unknown and struggling Jan Santini Aichel (1677–1723), now considered an iconic figure of the Bohemian Baroque. How could she have recognised the quality of Santini's project without books on Italian architecture? How could Christophorus Eucharius, a Jesuit rector, have exchanged books with a Benedictine nun if she could only offer him breviaries and hymnbooks? Was this a rare occurrence, or did other nuns have access to a wide range of books? Furthermore, how did a female community's library form the reading habits of its members? These and other questions remain tasks for future research.

Acknowledgements

This study is the result of a project of specific research of the 'International Presentation of the Codicological Research at the FF UHK', supported by the Philosophical Faculty of the University of Hradec Králové in 2021. I would like to thank Luke DeWeese for improving my English.

---

74 For instance, the architectural importance of the monastery's library in Broumov is clear from the artistic rendition of the space in the 1790s. See Andreas Gamerith, 'Die Klosterbibliothek von Broumov. Eine ikonologische Analyse', *Konštantínove Listy*, 12 (2019), pp. 116–128.

75 This holds true for all the non-German books. As for Latin, the nuns were not familiar with the language and had all the Latin texts (like charters and current correspondence with ecclesiastic institutions) translated since the middle of the seventeenth century. As for vernacular books, they possibly had only one reader of French and Italian, as noted. The number of Czech-speaking nuns in the convent had rapidly been decreasing since the second third of the eighteenth century. In 1782, more than 70 volumes (along with 112 Latin manuscripts of medieval origin) remained without their readers at St George's. See lists 1 and 2 in Bastl, 'Knihy a listiny', pp. 196–206.

PART 4

Appropriation of Texts and Books

∴

CHAPTER 13

The Earliest Polish Translation of a Jesuit Catechism

Mirosława Hanusiewicz-Lavallee and Robert Aleksander Maryks

> Questo esercizio d'insegnare la Dottrina Christiana, fra gli altri, è uno dei principali di questa nostra minima Compagnia.
>
> This exercise of teaching the Christian doctrine is, among others, one of the principal of this least Society of ours.
>
> DIEGO DE LEDESMA, *Modo per insegnare la dottrina christiana* (1573)

∴

Catechesis, as a form of ministry of the word directed to those who, already evangelised, responded with faith, was very important already to the founders of the Society of Jesus, or the Jesuits. Their predilection for this ministry resulted in the production of a significant number of popular printed manuals to teach the Christian doctrine, often in the format of a dialogue between a master and a disciple we call catechism. It was a crucial part of the Jesuit agenda to have these manuals issued in many languages and to translate into many more languages. Jesuit bibliographer Carlos Sommervogel (1834–1902) listed in his authoritative *Bibliothèque de la Compagnie de Jésus* more than five hundred catechisms and their translations by Jesuits, not including their many editions.[1] But there must have been even more catechisms in their various translations and editions that Sommervogel did not include.

It seems justified, therefore, that a volume on the book culture in early modern Catholicism include a chapter on the role printed catechisms played in it, for they offer us significant information not only on the book market, printers or ministerial strategies, among others, but also on the formation and development of several European and indigenous languages, as not a few catechisms were among the earliest books published in a given language and contain the

---

1   Carlos Sommervogel (ed.), *Bibliothèque de la Compagnie de Jésus, nouvelle édition* (Louvain: Éditions de la Bibliothèque s.j., Collège philosophique et théologique, 1960).

earliest translations of religious texts, such as prayers and hymns. A good example of such an important text is the *Nauka chrześcijańska albo katechizmik dla dziatek* (Christian doctrine or the little catechism for children), which comprises the translation of a popular catechism by the prominent Jesuit Diego de Ledesma (1519–1575), a Spaniard who taught at the Jesuit flagship school in Rome, the Collegio Romano, and participated in the drafting of the official Jesuit curriculum, the *Ratio studiorum*.[2] He was also a prefect of studies and taught catechetical instruction at the Roman College, when the Polish Jesuit Jakub Wujek (1541–1597), the presumed translator of Ledesma's catechism into Polish, studied there for his doctoral degree in theology in 1565–1567.

Before telling the reader an intriguing story of the formation of the *Nauka chrześcijańska*, we first provide a broader context of the role catechesis and catechism played in Jesuit ministry and then offer some general information about Ledesma's catechism itself.

1 The Formation of Ledesma's Catechism

Even before the formal foundation of the Society of Jesus in 1540, the first companions were appointed in 1538 by Pope Paul III (r.1534–1549) as instructors of Christian doctrine for the children of Roman schools. In the deliberations of 1539 on whether they should form a new religious order, they decided that 'children and anyone else should be taught the Commandments of God', that those instructions should be given for forty days a year, and that such a decision should bind them under mortal sin. This catechesis theme reappears in the petition for approval to the pope, the *Formula of the Institute*; in the General Examen, which is a sort of an autonomous introduction to the Jesuit Constitutions; and in the Constitutions themselves: both the novices and superiors should teach catechism regularly and scholastics (Jesuit students in formation) should study methods of catechesis. A reference to catechesis is also included in the formula of the Jesuit religious vows of the professed.[3]

In the same vein, Superior General Ignatius of Loyola (c.1491–1556) gave instructions to the Jesuits who participated in the Council of Trent in the 1550s that they should not limit themselves to speaking to and advising the bishops:

---

2 *Diccionario histórico de la Compañía de Jesús: Biográfico-temático*, ed. Charles E. O'Neill and Joaquín M.ª Domínguez (4 vols., Rome–Madrid: Institutum Historicum Societatis Iesu–Universidad Pontificia Comillas, 2001) [hereafter DHCJ], III. 2318–2319.

3 DHCJ, I. 713.

> The greatest glory of God is the goal of our Fathers in Trent, and this will be achieved by preaching, hearing confessions, *teaching children*, visiting the poor in hospitals, and exhorting the neighbour.[4]

It could be argued that catechesis for Ignatius was intended as preparation for the sacramental confession, as can be seen in the First Week of his Spiritual Exercises. He focuses therein on the commandments, the precepts of the church, the capital sins, the five senses, works of mercy, the difference between the venial and mortal sins, and how to make a good sacramental confession.[5] Unsurprisingly, then, the first Jesuits, such as Peter Canisius (1521–1597), used catechesis to advocate frequent confession and Communion, a devout practice that at that time was unpopular and controversial in other Catholic circles, even though it had been advocated since the origins of the late-medieval movement of Devotio Moderna, which had a crucial impact on Loyola's spiritual journey and the formation of the *Spiritual Exercises*.[6] It comes as no surprise, therefore, that it is reflected in the Polish adaptation of Ledesma's catechism and perhaps this combination of catechetical instruction with preparation for sacramental confession and Eucharistic devotion can be seen as a distinctive feature of Jesuit catechisms, which is exemplified, among others, in the Polish edition under consideration. Even if Ledesma's popular catechism was translated into other languages, including modern Greek (1595), Lithuanian (1595), English (1597), and French–Huron (1608), we shall focus below exclusively on this Polish edition because of the space limit for our essay within this volume and because we are interested in the specific context of the early modern religious culture in the Commonwealth of Poland–Lithuania that this edited volume deals with.

Loyola's close associate, Jerónimo Nadal (1507–1580), wrote in 1576 that instructors of catechesis should concentrate more on the formation of the will than on the understanding; that the purpose of the catechism was not speculative tradition but practice, lifting souls towards love, which reveals, once again, the foundations of the Jesuit spirituality and ministry in the doctrine

---

4 *Monumenta historica Societatis Jesu. Sancti Ignatii de Loyola Societatis Jesu fundatoris epistolae et instructiones* (12 vols., Madrid: Lopez del Horno, 1903–1911) [hereafter *Ep. Ign.*], I. 386–389.
5 *Ep. Ign.* XII. 666–673.
6 Robert A. Maryks, 'From the IJssel Valley to Paris and Rome via Montserrat: Ignatius of Loyola and Repositioning the Origins of Modern Piety', *Church History and Religious Culture*, 60 (2021), pp. 34–41.

of the Devotio Moderna.[7] One of its main representatives, Thomas à Kempis (1380–1471), the author of the popular *Imitation of Christ*, was among the preferred devotional writers for the early Jesuits, including the Polish ones, as we shall see below.

With such support from the authoritative Jesuits, catechesis became an important tool in both Jesuit missionary and anti-Protestant activities. In Goa in 1542, Francis Xavier (1506–1552) expanded the contents of catechesis to include the Creed and the Our Father, as well as the commandments and some fundamental prayers. He sang them while taking care of the sick, prisoners, slaves and children (a method that captured the imagination of fishermen and peasants who used to sing while they worked). In 1555, Canisius, who, incidentally, was among the first Jesuits to visit Poland and was Ledesma's companion in their trip to German-speaking lands, imitated the format of Martin Luther's (1483–1546) catechism and added 213 questions and answers to his extensive catechism for preachers and teachers (*Summa doctrinae christianae*). In 1556, he simplified it to fifty-nine questions in another catechism for children (*Catechismus minimus*) and expanded it to 223 questions in 1556. For older children, he wrote in 1558 another catechism of medium size (*Parvus catechismus Catholicorum*), with between 112 and 124 questions, divided into two parts, Wisdom and Justice, subdivided into Faith and Creed, Hope and the Our Father, Charity and the Commandments, Sacraments, Sin, and Good Works. It was enormously successful – it was reprinted at least 120 times during his lifetime and imitated up to the nineteenth century.[8]

To add to the variety of Jesuit approaches to catechesis, which was never uniform or imposed from above, other Jesuits published other catechisms, which all together became an inescapable part of the new book culture of early modern Catholicism: Édmond Auger (1563) and Guillaume H. Bougeant (1741) in France; Gaspar Astete (1608) and Jerónimo de Ripalda (1600) in Spain; Marcos Jorge (1561) in Portugal; Lodewijk Makeblyde (1609) and Guillaume de Pretere (1619) in the Netherlands; Matthäus Vogel (1731) in German-speaking lands; Juris Špungianskis (1729) in Latvia; Robert Bellarmine (1614), Alfonso Salmerón (1564), and our Ledesma in the Italian peninsula.

After Canisius's and Bellarmine's, Ledesma's catechism was among the most popular. In our preliminary research (that we still consider inconclusive and hope to expand in the future), we have identified at least eighty-one editions/translations printed before 1800. The oldest edition we were able to retrieve

---

7 *Monumenta Historica Societatis Iesu. Epistolae Hieronymi Nadal* (Rome: Monumenta Historica Societatis Jesu, 1962), v. 846–850.
8 DHCJ, III. 2318–2319.

was printed in Ferrara in 1569, but its editor informs us that several earlier editions had been printed in Rome, Venice, Genoa and Turin, which reads plausible.[9] Besides the main format distinction between what Italian scholar Gilberto Aranci describes as *Dottrina grande* and *Dottrina piccola*, several editions of Ledesma's text were published with different additions or appendices. For example, the 1576 Venetian edition included a series of *lodi*, or religious hymns.[10] The 1577 Spanish edition printed in Callar appends several *coplas*, or brief occasional prayers in a few verses, easy to be sung (and to remember).[11]

At this stage of our study, we have been unable to determine which specific edition of Ledesma's *Dottrina christiana* served as a model for the Polish edition. Still, it is possible that the collection of texts appended to the very translation of Ledesma's catechism was decided by the translators themselves, in the frame of an already established tradition of devotional books that would comprise a catechism, an instruction on how to confess sacramentally, and a series of prayers. We will now explain in more detail how the very first Polish translation of Ledesma's catechism was created and what impact it had on the religious and literary culture in the Commonwealth of Poland–Lithuania. The work combines a fairly strict translation of Ledesma's catechism with additions taken from other sources that give the entire book an original and unique character while also modifying its target readership.

2   Structure and Presumed Readership of the Polish Book *Nauka chrześcijańska albo katechizmik dla dziatek*

In the fifteenth and sixteenth centuries, the common form of catechesis in Poland, Prussia and Lithuania was based on oral instruction involving the Ten Commandments, along with the three main prayers (*Pater noster*, *Credo* and *Ave Maria*), and usually took place during a Mass after the sermon or even *loco sermonis* (instead of a sermon).[12] Therefore, when the first Polish printed

---

9   Diego de Ledesma, *Dottrina christiana per interrogazioni a modo di dialogo, del maestro & discepolo per insegnar alli fanciulli* (Ferrara: Francesco de' Rossi, 1569), USTC 763172.

10   Gilberto Aranci, 'Le "Dottrine" di Giacomo Ledesma s.j. (1524–1575)', *Salesianum*, 53 (1991), pp. 315–382. Diego de Ledesma, *Dottrina christiana, a modo di dialogo del maestro & discepolo per insegnare alli fanciulli* (Venice: Cristoforo Zanetti, 1576), USTC 837698.

11   Diego de Ledesma, *Dotrina por interrogaciones a manera de dialogo, entre el maestro, y discipulo. ... con otras coplas deuotas añadidas, y agora nueuamente impressas* (Callar: Francisco Guarner, 1577), USTC 1793018.

12   Stanisław Bylina, *Religiousness in the Late Middle Ages. Christianity and Traditional Culture in Central and Eastern Europe in the Fourteenth and Fifteenth Centuries* (Berlin: Peter Lang, 2019), pp. 25–30.

Catholic catechism appeared in 1566, its author, Benedykt Herbest (1531–1598), a Jesuit since 1571, expressed some reservations about reading books by laymen, reminding them that faith should be born *ex auditu* (Rom 10:17). Although it was justified, he argued, to produce a Catholic catechism in vernacular vis à vis popular Protestant ones (there were already at least twenty-seven in four vernacular languages used in Poland-Lithuania), he recommended reading it aloud, at least at home, in the presence of the whole family.[13] Of course, it is not the very idea of the devotional book itself that seemed dangerous to Herbest, but rather an individualistic way of reading it that could not be controlled by religious authorities.

As the Jesuit Jakub Wujek, one of the main protagonists of this essay, wrote in the preface to his *Postilla catholica* of 1573, 'daleko jest lepiej i pożyteczniej … rzeczy Boskich z ust kapłańskich i kaznodziejskich przysłuchiwać niźli książki czytać' (It is much better and more advantageous … to learn about Divine matters from the mouth of a priest and preacher than to read books).[14] Therefore, a printed catechism should serve as mnemonic support, a script useful for oral instruction, rather than as a tool for individual religious meditation. Given the views of Herbest and Wujek on the role printed books should play in religious instruction, an analysis of the Polish translation of Diego de Ledesma's *Dottrina christiana* that we offer here becomes even more informative.

This translation, entitled *Nauka chrześcijańska albo katechizmik dla dziatek*, survived in three copies (not in two, as was suggested in the hitherto existing scholarship).[15] They represent three different Krakow editions: one from the Antitrinitarian press of Aleksy Rodecki (d.1606), dated by modern bibliographers c.1600;[16] one issued in 1604; and another one undated.[17] The 1604 edition,

---

13 Benedykt Herbest, *Nauka prawego chrześcijanina* (Krakow: Mateusz Siebeneicher, 1566), USTC 241950, f. Dr–D3r; Waldemar Kowalski, 'The Catechism by Benedykt Herbest. Print and Orality in Religious Education on the Verge of the Modern Epoch', *Questiones Oralitatis*, 5 (2020), pp. 120–121.

14 Jakub Wujek, *Postilla catholica to jest kazania na każdą niedzielę i na kożde święto przez cały rok według wykładu samego prawdziwego Kościoła świętego powszechnego dla pospolitego człowieka teraz nowo a prosto językiem polskim napisana* (Krakow: Mateusz Siebeneicher, 1573), USTC 242157, f. A4r.

15 Margarita Korzo, 'Polski przekład katechizmu Jakuba Ledesmy TJ i jego wpływ na tradycję unicką w XVII w.', *Odrodzenie i Reformacja w Polsce*, 48 (2004), pp. 150–151; Wojciech Pawlik, *Katechizmy w Rzeczypospolitej od XVI do XVIII wieku* (Lublin: Towarzystwo Naukowe KUL, 2010), pp. 97–98.

16 Alodia Kawecka-Gryczowa, *Ariańskie oficyny wydawnicze Rodeckiego i Sternackiego. Dzieje i bibliografia* (Wrocław: Zakład Narodowy im. Ossolińskich, 1974), pp. 40, 43, 161.

17 Two of the copies are preserved in Poland: (1) *Nauka chrześcijańska abo Katechizmik dla dziatek* (Krakow: [A. Rodecki], [c.1600]), USTC 243299, a copy in the Czartoryski Library in Krakow (Cim. 2462 I), USTC provides incorrect information about the translator;

preserved in the Jagiellonian Library, and the undated edition, preserved in the Piarist library in Nitra, share similar typographical features and appear to be the product of the same printer.[18]

However, it is certain that more editions existed. *Catalogus librorum Collegii Posnaniensis*, held in the Uppsala University Library, lists the editions of 1602, 1582 and 1595, none of which have survived to the best of our knowledge.[19] Ledesma's catechism was amongst those most commonly recommended by several Polish provincial church councils (for example, the Krakow councils in 1601, 1609 and 1612 and the Vilnius councils in 1602, 1607 and 1611), so obviously the printers were taking advantage of the demand for this kind of book, legally or otherwise.[20]

But when was the catechism printed for the first time? The manuscript *Historia Societatis Iesu in Polonia ad annum 1572* (The history of the Society of Jesus in Poland until 1572) provides information that, in 1572, Wujek published his translation of Ledesma's catechism and dedicated it to the city council of Poznań (in Greater Poland).[21]

Wujek was one of the most accomplished and distinguished Polish Jesuits in the first decades of their presence in Poland–Lithuania, a rector of the colleges in Poznań, Vilnius and Kolozsvár in Transylvania (modern-day Cluj-Napoca, Romania), an outstanding writer, philologist and patrologist and author of the most influential Catholic translation of the Bible into Polish. Wujek's authorship of the catechism in question is also confirmed in his correspondence. On 17 September 1571, in his letter to the Jesuit superior general Francisco de Borja (1510–1572, in office 1565–1572), Wujek informed him about his current work on Polish postill and mentioned that Ledesma's catechism had already

---

(2) *Nauka chrześcijańska* ([Krakow]: s.n., 1604) USTC 1793019, a copy in the Jagiellonian Library in Krakow (311120 I). One copy of another edition survived in Slovakia, in the Piarist College in Nitra (5184/2017): *Nauka chrześcijańska abo katechizm dla dziatek* ([Krakow]: s.n., s.a.), USTC 1793020.

18 As suggested by Magdalena Komorowska, an expert in early modern printing in Krakow, the typographical features of both these unidentified prints (1604 edition and the undated edition), indicate that they may have been a product of the Drukarnia Łazarzowa (Officina Lazaria), which was run by Bazyli Skalski (c.1570–after 1619) since 1603. We want to thank her for this valuable comment.

19 *Catalogus librorum Collegii Posnaniensis Societatis Iesu per patres Societatis eiusdem editor. Anno reparatae salutis MDCX die XXV Martii factus*, Uppsala University Library, Ms. U 275, f. 267. https://www.alvin-portal.org/alvin/view.jsf?pid=alvin-record:104235 (accessed 15 December 2021).

20 Jan Z. Słowiński, *Katechizmy katolickie w języku polskim od XVI do XVIII wieku* (Lublin: Wydawnictwo KUL, 2005), pp. 238–239.

21 Mieczysław Bednarz, 'Jezuici a religijność polska (1564–1964)', *Nasza Przeszłość*, 20 (1964), pp. 162–163; Korzo, 'Polski przekład katechizmu Jakuba Ledesmy TJ', p. 150.

been translated into Polish. The context and the grammatical forms in plural used in this letter suggest that his translation was done in cooperation with Szymon Wysocki (1546–1622), a young Jesuit from a well-to-do family, a recent graduate of the Roman College, who in the next decades was to become one of the most productive Jesuit translators in Catholic Europe.[22] 'Catechismum seu *Doctrinam Christianam* D. Ledesmae polonicam fecimus: eam in templo recitare solent duo pueri: quae res, ut nova, ita vehementer videtur profitura huic civitati' (We translated the Catechism, or *Doctrina Christiana* of Dr Ledesma into Polish. In the church, two boys usually recite it; though it is new, the city seems to be profiting from it quickly), wrote Wujek to Borja, describing at the same time how Ledesma's catechetic dialogue used to be employed and performed.[23]

It is impossible to provide incontrovertible evidence that the book *Nauka chrześcijańska albo katechizmik dla dziatek*, surviving today in the three previously described seventeenth-century copies, includes the same translation that had been authored by Wujek and Wysocki in about 1571, but there is some strong circumstantial evidence supporting such a hypothesis. First, there is no available information on anyone else translating Ledesma's catechism into Polish, except for these two Jesuits. Second, all surviving copies, as well as Mikalojus Daukša's (after 1527–1613) Samogitian *Kathechismas*, published in 1595 and based on the Polish translation, include (along with Ledesma's catechism) a text entitled *Krótki obyczaj spowiedzi dla tych, którzy często używają tego sakramentu* (A brief way of confessing for those who use this sacrament frequently), which can be, based on external sources, attributed to Wysocki.[24] Third, all these copies include passages that are to be found in Wujek's other translated work, as we indicate below.

Moreover, Ledesma's *Dottrina christiana* was already the second Jesuit catechism translated by Wujek into Polish (in 1570, he translated Canisius's *Parvus catechismus*, of which no copy survived to the best of our knowledge), and it

22 Peter Burke, 'Cultures of Translation in Early Modern Europe', in Peter Burke, Ronnie Po-Chia Hsia (eds.), *Cultural Translation in Early Modern Europe* (Cambridge: Cambridge University Press, 2007), p. 17.
23 Jan Sygański (ed.), 'Korespondencyja księdza Jakóba Wujka z Wągrówca z lat 1569–1596', *Roczniki Towarzystwa Przyjaciół Nauk Poznańskiego*, 44 (1917), p. 317.
24 *Kathechismas arba mokslas kiekwienam krikszczionii priwalus*, trans. Mikalojus Daukša ([Vilnius]: [Typis Academicis Societatis Jesu], 1595), USTC 250361. Jan Wielewicki, *Dziennik spraw domu zakonnego oo. Jezuitów u św. Barbary w Krakowie od r. 1620 do r. 1629 (włącznie)* (Krakow: Uniwersytet Jagielloński, 1899), p. 96; Pedro de Ribadeneyra, Philippe Alegambe, Nathaniel Southwell, *Bibliotheca scriptorum Societatis Iesu* (Rome: Iacobus Antonius de Lazzaris Varesius, 1675), USTC 1737394, p. 744.

is reasonable to assume that both translations were needed for the purpose of religious instruction carried out by the Jesuits in Poznań. Indeed, the manuscript *Acta et historia Collegii Posnaniensis s.J.* (The acts and history of the Jesuit college in Poznań) describes how Wysocki used Ledesma's catechism while instructing youth in the St Stanislaus Church in Poznań.[25] However, *Nauka chrześcijańska albo katechizmik dla dziatek*, which includes the text of Wujek's and Wysocki's presumed translation, was not just a teaching aid for catechesis; it seems to have been designed for a wider readership. This purpose is revealed by the very structure of the *Nauka chrześcijańska* that we are going to present now briefly.

The preface in prose, 'Do czytelnika chrześcijańskiego' (To a Christian reader), repeats certain themes present in the versified (and designed for singing) 'Introduttione alla Dottrina Christiana' (Introduction to the Christian doctrine) or 'Ammonitione alli Padri e Madri' (Admonitions for fathers and mothers), which are included in some of the Italian editions of Ledesma's catechism that we were able to consult.[26] It encourages parents to instil Christian teaching into the young minds of their children, while highlighting the power of early religious instruction. But the Polish preface complements these elements with the new ones by emphasising that religious education is a way to reform the 'rzeczpospolita chrześcijańska' (the Christian republic), where parents should also 'be converted and become as little children' (Mt 18:3).[27] Thus, from the very beginning, the book envisions a double readership: both children and adults.

Some Italian editions of the *Dottrina christiana* published around 1570 include parts designed for singing (like the already mentioned 'Introduttione' or 'Lodi', added at the end) as well as distinctive 'Essortazioni' (Exhortations), which provide instructions for the catechist. The Polish text consistently lacks

---

25   *Acta et historia Collegii Posnaniensis s.I.*, Archiwum Diecezji Warszawskiej, Ms. 440, f. 101r–101v. Quoted in Polish translation by Bronisław Natoński, 'Początki i rozwój Towarzystwa Jezusowego w Polsce', in James Brodrick, *Powstanie i rozwój Towarzystwa Jezusowego*, trans. Włodzimierz Baranowski, Mieczysław Bednarz (2 vols., Krakow: WAM, 1969), I. 467.

26   For example, *Dottrina christiana per interrogationi; Somma della dottrina christiana. Con la sua breve dichiaratione a modo di Dialogo, fra'l Maestro, e Discepolo. Composta per il D. Ledesma, della Compagnia di Giesu* (Genoa: Antonio Bellone, 1570), USTC 837695; *Dottrina christiana, a modo di dialogo del Maestro, et Discepolo, per insegnare alli fanciulli. Composta per il Dottore Giacomo Ledesma della Compagnia di Giesù* (Milan: Pacifico Pontio, 1576), USTC 837692.

27   *Nauka chrześcijańska abo katechizmik dla dziatek* (c.1600), f. A3r. All further quotations are from this edition.

all singing parts and expands 'Essortazioni' into brief moral guidance, which intertwines with subsequent sections of the catechetical dialogue between the master and the disciple. There are very few abridgments of the original dialogue or interpolations, and the latter usually attest to the translators' intent to adapt the original text to the local Polish reality. For example, the Italian mnemonic formula of the third precept of the church: 'Digiunar la quadragesima / Et gli altri giorni comma[n]dati, / Et astenersi dalla carne / Il Venerdi & il Sabbato' (Fast during the Lent and other obligatory days, and abstain from meat on Fridays and Saturdays) was replaced with the more general recommendation: 'Posty przykazane dni swych zachowaj i pokarmów zakazanych w nie nie używaj' (On the days of obligation, observe fasting and do not eat forbidden food).[28] Because fasting days in Poland–Lithuania included Wednesdays, a more universal formula of the precept, without mentioning specific days, seemed more suitable.[29]

The biggest difference between Polish catechism and its Italian models is that it was not designed as a script for teachers, but rather as a book to be read. Therefore, new elements were integrated into Ledesma's catechetical dialogue. One of them was a short text with the separate title *Krótki obyczaj spowiedzi dla tych, którzy często używają tego sakramentu, z włoskiego na polskie przełożony* (A brief way of confessing for those who use this sacrament frequently, translated from Italian into Polish).[30] We identified it as a section of Part II of the first volume of the *Memorial de la vida christiana* by Luis de Granada (1505–1588), which in the Italian translation was entitled *Un breve modo di confessione per le persone che si confessano spesso*.[31] *A brief way of confessing* teaches how to scrupulously examine conscience. The types of sins discussed here (for example, neglecting duties towards the offspring) suggest that the text is not addressed to 'little children', but to adults, who are called to develop a sensitive conscience.

The next section of the book, *Modlitwy ku spowiedzi i przystępowaniu do stołu Pańskiego przynależące* (Prayers appropriate for confession and partaking of the Lord's Table), is a collection of eleven prayers, compiled and translated, it seems, from different sources. It includes four penitential prayers of an

---

28   *Dottrina christiana per interrogationi à modo di Dialogo del Maestro & Discepolo*, f. 28v; *Nauka chrześcijańska abo katechizmik dla dziatek*, f. B12v.
29   Andrzej Kraśnicki, 'Posty w dawnej Polsce', *Collectanea Theologica*, 12 (1931), pp. 225–235.
30   *Nauka chrześcijańska abo katechizmik dla dziatek*, f. f3r–G3v.
31   Luigi di Granata, *Memoriale della vita Christiana, nel quale si tratta tutto quello che deve fare un Christiano dal principio della conversione fin' alla perfettione* (Naples: Giovanni de Boi, 1567), USTC 838878, f. 141v–46v.

unknown origin, commonly printed in Catholic prayer books in the sixteenth and seventeenth centuries,[32] and one Eucharistic prayer based on the elements taken from Mozarabic and Sarum liturgy.[33] It also includes the partial translations of two Eucharistic meditations from the *Memorial de la vida christiana* by Luis de Granada,[34] the Eucharistic prayer of Thomas Aquinas (c.1225–1274), the first Polish translation of his famous hymn *Adoro te devote*,[35] as well as

32 'Modlitwa ku przygotowaniu do spowiedzi', in *Nauka chrześcijańska abo katechizmik dla dziatek*, f. [G4]v–h3r). See Thomas Sailly, 'Oratio praeparatoria ad confessionem sacramentalem' [Inc. 'Conditor caeli et terrae, Rex regum et Dominus dominantium, qui me de nihilo fecisti ad imaginem, et similitudinem tuam ...'], in *Thesaurus precum et exercitiorum spiritualium in usum presertim Sodalitatis Partheniae* (Antwerp: Officina Plantiniana apud Ioannem Moretum, 1609), USTC 1000001, p. 219; 'Modlitwa po spowiedzi' in *Nauka chrześcijańska abo katechizmik dla dziatek*, f. h4r–[h6]v). See 'Precatio post confessionem' [Inc. 'Ita est, Redemptor clementissime, medice humani generis amantissime. Sanasti me sanguinis tui pharmaco preciosissimo ...'], in *Exercitium Christianae pietatis in gratiam studiosorum auctoritate et mandato ... Cardinalis ... Nicolai Radivillii collectum* (Cologne: Arnold Mylius, 1589), USTC 655393, pp. 110–112; 'Druga modlitwa przed spowiedzią' in *Nauka chrześcijańska abo katechizmik dla dziatek*, f. h3r–h4r). See Sailly, 'Oratio ante sacramentalem confessionem' [Inc. 'Suscipe confessionem meam, piissime ac clementissime Domine Iesu Christe ...'], in *Thesaurus precum et exercitiorum spiritualium*, p. 221; 'Druga modlitwa po spowiedzi', in *Nauka chrześcijańska abo katechizmik dla dziatek*, f. h4r–[h6]r. See 'Oratio post confessionem' [Inc. 'Sit tibi, Domine, obsecro, meritis beatae semper Virginis Genetricis tuae Mariae et omnium Sanctorum, grata et accepta ista confessio mea ...'], in *Thesaurus precum et exercitiorum spiritualium*, p. 222.

33 'Druga modlitwa po przyjęciu Ciała Pańskiego', in *Nauka chrześcijańska abo katechizmik dla dziatek*, f. K5r–[K6r]. See Edmund Marten, 'Ave in aeternum, sanctissima Caro Christi, mihi ante omnia et super omnia summa dulcedo. Ave in aeternum caelestis potus, mihi ante omnia et super omnia summa dulcedo', in *De antiquis Ecclesiae ritibus libri tres* (Antwerp: Giovanni Battista Novelli, 1763), p. 152.

34 'Modlitwa przed przystępowaniem', in *Nauka chrześcijańska abo katechizmik dla dziatek*, f. [h7]r–J2r. See Luigi di Granata, 'Inanzi alla sacra communione per suegliare nell'anima timore, & amore di questo santissimo sacramento', in *Seconda parte del Memoriale della vita Christiana ... nel quale si comprendono li tre ultimi trattati gia promessi nella prima parte ... novamente tradotto in lingua Italiana con li luoghi della Sacra Scrittura da un padre della Compagnia di Giesu* (Naples: Giovanni de Boi, 1569), USTC 838907, f. 156v–164r; 'Dziękowanie po przyjęciu Ciała Pańskiego', in *Nauka chrześcijańska abo katechizmik dla dziatek*, f. Kv–K5r. See Luigi di Granata, 'Un' altra molto divota meditatione', in *Seconda parte del Memoriale della vita Christiana*, 175v–177v.

35 'Trzecia modlitwa po przyjęciu Ciała Pańskiego', in *Nauka chrześcijańska abo katechizmik dla dziatek*, f. [K6]r–[K7]r. See Luigi di Granata, 'Oratione di s. Thomasi d'Aquino per dire doppo la sacra communione', in *Seconda parte del Memoriale della vita Christiana*, f. 152v–153r, or Sailly, 'Oratio S. Thomae Aquinatis', in *Thesaurus precum et exercitiorum spiritualium*, p. 122; 'Modlitwa świętego Tomasza z Akwinu przed Naświętszym Sakramentem z rytmów łacińskich na polskie przełożona', in *Nauka chrześcijańska abo*

two Eucharistic meditations from *De imitatione Christi* by Thomas à Kempis. What should be emphasised is that the latter two meditations are evidently taken from the 1571 translation of *De imitatione*, attributed to Wujek by some scholars, which further supports the argument that he was indeed one of the authors of this Polish edition of catechism. It is, however, possible that also this translation was compiled in cooperation with Wysocki.[36]

The mysteries of the rosary, short morning prayers, and the Angelus Domini, table and evening prayers were all meant to organise the day of a Christian, and they concluded the book. Some of them can be found in the Italian editions of the *Dottrina christiana*; others, like the table prayers, appear in a similar form in the popular Polish Jesuit prayer book by Marcin Laterna (1552–1598) *Harfa duchowna* (1585) and do not seem to be translations.

Ledesma's *Dottrina christiana* was usually printed with various additional devotional materials, but typically, these were religious hymns and songs designed to facilitate memorising the catechism. The anthology of texts added by the Polish translators seems rather unique, indicating that the structured book was offered, contrary to its title, not to 'little children', but to mature readers. What is more important, passages from ascetic and mystical literature collected here were conceived for quiet individual meditation and prayer, despite the openly stated (and previously quoted) reservations against this kind of personal reading. Jesuit apostolate, almost from the very beginning, was, in fact, an apostolate also of books. About three decades after *Nauka chrześcijańska* had been published for the first time, one of its translators, Wysocki, wrote it very clearly in a dedicatory letter to a pious Polish lady, Elżbieta Sieniawska (1573–1624): 'Doświadczenie samo, ... by nie było nic inszego, pewnym świadkiem, iż między inszymi do zbawienia i wszelakiej doskonałości chrześcijańskiej dostąpienia śrzodkami jest czytanie ksiąg nabożnych' (If nothing else, the very experience attests to the fact that reading devout books counts among the ways of attaining salvation and Christian perfection).[37]

---

katechizmik dla dziatek, f. [K7]r–[K7]v. See Sailly, 'Rythmus eiusdem sancti Thomae', in *Thesaurus precum et exercitiorum spiritualium*, p. 123.

36 'Druga modlitwa przed przystępowaniem', in *Nauka chrześcijańska abo katechizmik dla dziatek*, J2r–J4r. See Thomas à Kempis, *O naśladowaniu Pana Chrysta i o wzgardzeniu wszelakiej próżności świata tego*, trans. J. Wujek (Krakow: Mateusz Siebeneicher, 1571), USTC 240257, f. 255v–256v; 'Modlitwa trzecia, która też może być mówiona przed przyjęciem Ciała Pańskiego', in *Nauka chrześcijańska abo katechizmik dla dziatek*, f. J4r–Kv. See Thomas à Kempis, *O naśladowaniu Pana Chrysta*, f. 291r–292v.

37 Fulvio Androzzi, *Nauka jako stan wdowi i przystojnie, i chwalebnie może być prowadzony*, trans. Szymon Wysocki (Kalisz: Wojciech Gedeliusz, 1606), USTC 1793017, f. A2r.

3 Conclusion

As we have shown, printed catechisms, especially Jesuit ones, played a significant role in the book culture of early modern Catholicism. Teaching the Christian doctrine to both children and adults while advocating their frequent participation in the church's sacramental life became the Jesuits' unique way of building religious culture in Catholic Europe, including in the Commonwealth of Poland-Lithuania. With the expansion of the Jesuits, who established their presence among recent and new Christian peoples therein, catechism continued to be a crucial means not only in asserting the Catholic doctrine and forming the devout but also in influencing the development of their languages. Remarkably, the Polish translation of Ledesma's *Doctrina christiana* served as a basis for its first translations into Samogitian and East-Lithuanian languages, inspiring Uniate and Orthodox catechisms in the Ruthenian language. But that is another story to be told.

CHAPTER 14

From Bees to Thieves

The Perception of Writing Practices and Intellectual Property in Early Modern Hungary

Gábor Förköli

It is well established in literary history that originality and intellectual property had different meanings in the pre-Romantic era. At that time, poetic and oratorial creation were based on the imitation and emulation of literary antecedents. A further important proviso is that most early modern theories on imitation required authors to dissimulate the very act of borrowing from others by transforming their quotations. Thus, G.W. Pigman identifies three types of intertextual borrowing from this era. The first is a kind of emulation meant to stimulate an aesthetic joy when the reader recognises the imitated original. This, however, was the less common type of intertextual borrowing in theoretical works. More upheld were instructions that limited a procedure to the simple transformation of an original text, or those that required no less than the total dissimulation of the act of borrowing. In his theory of oratorical imitation (*De imitatione oratoria*), the great Lutheran pedagogue, Johannes Sturm, distinguished six methods for hiding that part of a text was a quotation. These methods included expanding or contracting the original quotations (*copia* and *brevitas*), as well as adding or taking away linguistic elements to change the imitated sequence so that it could not be recognised.[1]

Erudite imitation was not considered convenient for every genre of writing, however. The Jesuit Jeremias Drexel was well known for his detailed instructions on notetaking and excerpting, as regrouped in his book *Aurifodina* (Goldmine). Although this practice was conceived to enrich both one's factual knowledge and style through the reading of the best authors, it also enabled one to retrieve the proper quotation and expression quickly as needed. The Jesuit dissuaded young preachers from imitating specific models in their

---

1 G.W. Pigman III, 'Versions of Imitation in the Renaissance', *Renaissance Quarterly*, 33 (1980), pp. 1–32, p. 11. See Colin Burrow, *Imitating Authors. Plato to Futurity* (Oxford: Oxford University Press, 2019), pp. 220–224. The six methods are: *appositio, detractio, transpositio, immutatio, copia* and *brevitas*.

sermons and encouraged them to follow 'nature' on the pulpit instead.[2] These models formed the tastes of young apprentices, but in a more indirect way. In pre-Romantic literature, the most famous metaphor used to describe this complex acquisition process was that of the honeybee, usually attributed to Seneca. It was evoked by some real masters of Renaissance quotation, such as Erasmus and Michel de Montaigne: 'even though a spider emits its web out of its own body, it is less valued than honey, which bees make by collecting the nectar of many different flowers'.[3] This allegory not only implied the superiority of borrowing from other authors over originality but also the necessity of digestion: a bee must process the nectar if it wants to produce honey.

Without this work of absorption or appropriation, the imitator commits plagiarism, or intellectual stealing. Even in early modern vocabulary, this was classified as theft (*furtum*), as Johannes Sturm's choice of word attests.[4] Literary models that followed, such as 'imitation as an act of learning' and 'emulation as an attempt to surpass predecessors', implied two complementary requirements. The first was *copia*, referring to an abundance of models, quotations, phraseological and lexical units to be collected by the imitators. These often resulted in individual and handwritten commonplace collections, prescribed by many Renaissance pedagogues, from Agricola and Erasmus to Sturm. The other requirement was the proper use of these very elements. Although a humanist orator may emphasise his erudition by highlighting the fact that he copiously quotes, his own eloquence depends on his capacity to transform and appropriate the acquired linguistic treasures.[5]

Thus, the generally acceptable lack of rhetorical or poetic originality was no excuse for open plagiarism. While the requirement of transformation

---

2 Jeremias Drexel, *Aurifodina artium et scientiarum omnium. Excerpendi sollertia* (Cologne: Johann Wilhelm Friessen, 1643), USTC 2076194, VD17 1:044695S, p. 306: 'In artibus & scientijs alijs ferè omnibus, imitatio suadetur; hîc [= in sermons] non probatur. In hoc dice[n]di genere ducem habeamus Naturam'.

3 According to Montaigne, the additional element in this process is the judgment (*jugement*, *iudicium*) formed by the user of the quotations: 'Les abeilles pillotent deçà delà les fleurs, mais elles en font apres le miel, qui est tout leur; ce n'est plus thin ny marjolaine: ainsi les pieces empruntées d'autruy, il les transformera et confondera, pour en faire un ouvrage tout sien: à sçavoir son jugement'. Michel Eyquem de Montaigne, *Les Essais*, eds. Pierre Villey, Verdun-Louis Saulnier (Paris: Presses Universitaires de France, 1965), I. 152. About the origin and the different versions of the metaphor from Seneca through Macrobius to John of Salisbury and Renaissance authors, like Petrarch and Erasmus, see Ann Moss, *Printed Commonplace-Books and the Structuring of Renaissance Thought* (Oxford: Clarendon Press, 1996), pp. 11–21, 29–30, 51–52, 87, 97–98, 105.

4 Burrow, *Imitating Authors*, p. 221.

5 See also Brian Cummings, 'Encyclopaedic Erasmus', *Renaissance Studies*, 28 (2014), pp. 183–204.

concerned linguistic expression or style, often designated with the term *verbum* or *voces*, humanist imitation relied on the copiousness of factual knowledge (*res*). The concept of intellectual property in cases of *res* was problematic. When writing about controversial subjects, such as theology or canon law, authors had to convince the reader that they claimed nothing original and were faithful to a tradition. Individual judgment over historical exempla, theological arguments and articles of law were what distinguished an author from a mere compiler of quotations. This way of thinking has been documented as early as the late Middle Age.[6] Further, the metaphor of the digesting bee also implies the necessary use of personal judgment rather than the simple linguistic transformation of a borrowed text.[7]

This chapter focuses on situations in which the originality of words (*verba*) and of arguments (*res*) were both questioned by parties engaged in confessional disputes in early modern Hungary. The first hypothesis of this essay is that the more developed the institutions of literature were, the more difficult it was for authors to commit intellectual theft by omitting transformative procedures required by the usual norms and by quoting texts without good faith. The second hypothesis is that, at least in early modern Hungary, granting that a work was original or declaring it plagiarism could depend on the confession of both the author and the person assessing the text.

1 A Bee or a Thief? The Case of Péter Pázmány

Hungary is the perfect place to observe the shifting and transitional views on intellectual property in the early modern era. Even thought it had a relatively rich production of printed works, especially on topics of religious controversy, it still had no university until 1635, no society of letters, no larger supra-confessional community of readers and no centralised system of printing privileges.[8] Due to the Ottoman conquest, the medieval Kingdom of Hungary

---

[6] An interesting monograph about the publishing practices of Jean Gerson (1363–1429), the famous theologian of Paris is enlightening in this respect: Gerson criticised the experts of canon law who only quoted previous authorities without judging the concrete case which they were supposed to address using their personal experience: Daniel Hobbins, *Authorship and Publicity before Print. Jean Gerson and the Transformation of Late Medieval Learning* (Philadelphia: University of Pennsylvania Press, 2009), pp. 51–71.

[7] See note 3.

[8] On learned readers in Hungary, and the confessional division of the *Respublica Litteraria*, see Gábor Almási, *The Uses of Humanism. Johannes Sambucus (1531–1585), Andreas Dudith (1533–1589) and the Republic of Letters in East Central Europe* (Leiden: Brill, 2009), pp. 329–355. Regarding the privileges, Queen Isabella Jagiellon, the regent of the Eastern Kingdom

broke into ethnically, politically and religiously divided regions. The areas that remained under Christian control (the Kingdom of Hungary ruled by the Habsburgs and the Eastern Kingdom, which became the Principality of Transylvania) harboured different Christian denominations that often had a rebellious attitude towards lay or clerical powers. Thus, it was difficult to regulate what could or could not be published in print. Although this chaos sometimes offered a good opportunity for controversial publications, there was no authority to support the interests of printers, not to mention authors, whose rights were much less protected, if at all, in the early modern era all over in Europe.[9]

Views on and the vocabulary for intellectual theft were unstable in this era, and at times they could be astonishing. For example, around 1630, Mátyás Nyéki Vörös (1575–1654), a Jesuit poet from Győr, copied in his notebook a mock-epitaph for the Hungarian humanist, Johannes Sambucus (1531–1584). Sambucus, who earned his living as a physician in the imperial court of Vienna, is considered to have been more an erudite manuscript collector than a professional philologist. He often commissioned other scholars to edit the works in his possession. He published numerous editions of antique and early modern texts, including *The Hungarian History* by Antonio Bonfini (1427/34–1502), the Italian historiographer of kings Mathias and Vladislaus II. Sambucus often commissioned more qualified scholars to do the real work in terms of textual criticism,

---

of Hungary, and her son King John Sigismund tried to regulate printing in their country. The rare instances of Hungarian printing privileges were issued by them for various Bible editions. The bibliography of Hungarian books printed between 1473 and 1670 (Gedeon Borsa et al., *Régi magyarországi nyomtatványok* (4 vols., Budapest: Akadémiai Kiadó, 1971–2012), abbreviated as RMNy) lists such privileges for a Hungarian translation of the five books of Moses (*A Biblianac elsö resze, az az Mosesnec ött könyue*, Cluj: Heltai and Hoffgreff, 1551), USTC 305097, RMNy 90, and for the books of Valentin Wagner, the printer of the Saxon town Braşov (*Geistliche Lieder und Psalmen durch D.M. L[uther] und andere gelerte Leuth gemacht* [Braşov: Wagner, 1556]), USTC 305144, RMNy 131; *Novum Testamentum Graecae ac Latinae iuxta postremam D. Erasmi Rot. translationem* ([Braşov: Wagner, 1557]), USTC 305151, RMNy 138. Later, a part of the Eastern Kingdom became the Principality of Transylvania, and it seems that its rulers wanted to continue these policies but did not have much success. For example, Christopher Báthory, who governed in the name of his brother Stephen, King of Poland, issued a privilege valid for thirty years for an Old Church Slavonic Gospel Book used by the Orthodox Romanians of Transylvania (*Tetroevangilie* [Alba Iulia: Lorinţ, 1579]), USTC 305469, RMNy 435. After these efforts, the practice of privileges faded away.

9 About the rights of printers and the rights (or lack thereof) of authors in the early modern era, see Lucien Febvre, Henri-Jean Martin, *The Coming of the Book. The Impact of Printing 1450–1800*, transl. David Gerard (London: Atlantic Highlands, Humanities Press, 1976), pp. 159–166.

but he still put his name on the title page as editor and as a trademark.[10] In the epigram, the author accused Sambucus of stealing Bonfini's history, but research indicates that the accusation was unjustified. Thus, it serves as an illustration of the profound confusion that reigned in matters of intellectual property during the early modern period in Hungary:

> Ad sepulchrum Sambuci
> Ad tu venturo sis ut diuturnior aevo,
> Carmina digna tuo canimus, Sambuce, sepulchro,
> Historiae fur Hungaricae, non auctor et auctor,
> Et sine doctrina doctor, non arbor et arbor.
> Sambucus iacet hic nulliscius, omnisciusq[ue]
> Expue qui transis, cineriq[ue] imminge Viator.[11]

> On the tomb of Sambucus
> May you last longer than the future eternity,
> let's sing a song appropriate for your tomb, Sambucus,
> thief of the History of Hungary, author and non-author,
> doctor without doctrine, tree and not a tree.
> Here lies Sambucus [i.e. elder tree],
> the knower of nothing and the knower of everything.
> You, passenger passing by,
> spit and urinate onto the ashes.

This exceptionally harsh poem implies that to base one's philological work on someone else's text and to publish it is theft, and that to do so to appear as an author is a repugnant act. But did Sambucus actually steal Bonfini's history? It is true that when Sambucus published his work, an edition that contained

---

10   Gábor Almási, Farkas Gábor Kiss, *Humanistes du Bassin des Carpates II. Johannes Sambucus*, Europa Humanistica 14 (Turnout: Brepols, 2014), pp. v–lxxiv; in English: Gábor Almási, Gábor Farkas Kiss, 'In Search of Sambucus. His Philology, Publications and Friends', in Christian Gastgeber, Elisabeth Klecker (eds.), *Johannes Sambucus / János Zsámboki / Ján Sambucus (1531–1584). Philologe, Sammler und Historiograph am Habsburgerhof* (Vienna: Praesens Verlag, 2018), pp. 35–126. Apart from his contribution to philology, Sambucus is also known to be the author of an emblem book and to be a pioneer of this genre in Central Europe: Arnoud S.Q. Visser, *Joannes Sambucus and the Learned Image. The Use of Emblem in Late-Renaissance Humanism* (Leiden: Brill, 2005).

11   Budapest, National Széchényi Library, Quart. Lat., 2940, f. 159r. Nyéki Vörös used an emblem book created by a magistrate from Sopron to write down his annotations: Christoph Lackner, *Coronae Hungariae emblematica descriptio* (Lauingen: Jacob Winter, 1615), USTC 2068836; VD17 12:195003H.

the first three sections of the book already existed, which had been edited by Martin Brenner in Basel in 1543.[12] Sambucus had the distinction of publishing the first complete edition in 1568, in the same town. He honestly acknowledged on the title page that he used Brenner's version to edit the first three sections of the text before providing the remaining parts of the full work.[13] Thus, it appears that the epitaph distorted these facts to forge an accusation of plagiarism, but the motivation for doing so remains unclear. The denominational difference between the protestant Sambucus and the Jesuit Vörös may be the reason. Although scholarship describes Sambucus as a Nicodemite who dissimulated his true opinion about religious matters, his Lutheran sympathies came to light after Viennese intellectual life, especially at the university, became less tolerant in the late 1570s. In 1583, Sambucus was fined for having his child baptised by a Protestant minister, and as an author, he encountered censorship.[14] Thus, the mock-epitaph might reveal an interesting pattern: the openly admitted editing and publishing of a text, which would normally be considered acceptable in a community of learning, was judged as plagiarism or intellectual theft due to the religious controversy and prejudice it involved.[15]

The influence of confessional differences affected Jesuit Péter Pázmány (1570–1637), the leader of the Hungarian Counter-Reformation. Pázmány spent his noviciate in Krakow and Jarosław in Poland. Having completed the philosophical curriculum in Vienna, he went to study theology in Rome as a pupil of Robert Bellarmine. His first book written in Hungarian against the Protestant interpretation of the Ottoman threat was published in 1603; this marked the beginning of an incessant controversy with the Protestants in the Hungarian Kingdom and in Transylvania.[16] Pázmány was responsible for several important

---

12 Antonius Bonfinius, *Rerum Ungaricarum decades tres*, ed. Martin Brenner (Basel: Robert Winter, 1543), USTC 611995, VD16 B 6592.
13 Antonius Bonfinius, *Rerum Ungaricarum decades quatuor cum dimidia*, ed. Joannes Sambucus (Basel: Johannes Oporinus, 1568), USTC 611992, VD16 B 6593.
14 Almási, *The Uses of Humanism*, pp. 345–350.
15 The author of the mock-epitaph was the Transylvanian Ferenc Hunyadi (c. 1550–1600) whose collected poems were published in a critical edition after the submission of this chapter. Originally, his criticism on Sambucus was motivated by the fact that his supplements to Bonfini's history revealed a strong bias towards the Habsburg narrative while commenting on the rivalry between King Ferdinand I and King John Szapolyai. See Franciscus Hunyadi, *Francisci Hunniadini poemata Latina omnia*, ed. Dávid Molnár (Budapest: L'Harmattan, 2022), pp. 60–61, pp. 263–264.
16 Its critical edition: Péter Pázmány, *Felelet Magyari István sárvári prédikátornak az ország romlása okairul írt könyvére* (1603), ed. Emil Hargittay, in: *Pázmány Péter művei* (11 vols., Budapest: Universitas Kiadó, 1975–), I. The treatise was a reaction to the following book, which blamed not only Catholicism but also bad military policies for the failure against Ottoman expansion: István Magyari, *Az orszagokban valo soc romlasoknac okairol* (Sárvár:

families in the Hungarian aristocracy, who formerly embraced a Protestant confession, converting to Catholicism. This attracted attention from the Habsburg monarchy and the leadership in Rome, who appreciated the Hungarian Counter-Reformation. In 1616, Pázmány left the Society of Jesus after being appointed archbishop of Esztergom, the head of the Hungarian Catholic Church. In 1629, he was appointed cardinal.[17]

Pázmány's religiously controversial works were notorious for their ironic, witty and harsh style. His satirical vein was the strongest when he wrote his *Öt szép levél* (Five fair letters, 1609), in which he impersonated an ignorant Calvinist minister addressing letters to his superior about controversial questions.[18] Pázmány's preaching was so influential that Catholic authors continued to imitate his sermons a century after his death. He was both a victim of plagiarism and accused of plagiarism, or at least of copying ecclesiastical authorities out of intellectual laziness.[19] In his works, Pázmány connected his late humanist erudition to an agenda of vernacular literature aimed at a larger public. Although he used several quotations from authoritative texts, especially the Church Fathers, he did not want his works to be mere amalgams of common places; he intended to create a unified style. As such, he translated Latin quotations almost every time he introduced one.

As a translator, Pázmány laid down strict principles for himself. One of his main contributions to the Hungarian letters was his translation of *Imitatio Christi* by Thomas à Kempis. The foreword of this book is often quoted to

---

Manlius, 1602), USTC 871530, RMNy 890. About this debate: Ágoston Keisz, 'Magyari és Pázmány vitája', in Emil Hargittay (ed.), *Pázmány Péter és kora* (Piliscsaba: PPKE BTK, 2001), pp. 219–249.

17 These classic biographies are still used by researchers: Vilmos Frankl [Fraknói], *Pázmány Péter és kora* (3 vols., Pest: Ráth Mór, 1868–1872); Vilmos Fraknói, *Pázmány Péter (1570–1637)*, Magyar Történeti Életrajzok (Budapest: Méhner Vilmos, 1886); recently in English: Paul Shore, Péter Tusor, 'Péter Pázmány. Cardinal, Archbishop of Esztergom, Primate of Hungary', *Journal of Jesuit Studies*, 7 (2020), pp. 526–544.

18 Its critical edition: Péter Pázmány, *Egy keresztyén prédikátortúl, S.T.D.P.P. az kassai nevezetes tanítóhoz, Alvinczi Péter uramhoz íratott öt szép levél (1609) – Egy tudakozó prédikátor nevével íratott öt levél (1613)*, ed. Csaba Péter Horváth, Pázmány Péter művei, X.

19 He composed his sermon book at the end of his life: Péter Pázmány, *A romai anyaszentegyház szokásából minden vasarnapokra es egy-nehany innepekre rendelt evangeliomokrúl predikacziok* (Pozsony: Societas Jesu, 1636), USTC 870393, RMNy 1659. Recently, the research has been very much focused on Pázmány's posterity and compilers using his sermons. I only quote two monographs: Ibolya Maczák, *Elorzott szavak. Szövegalkotás 17–18. századi prédikációkban* (Szigetmonostor: WZ Könyvek, 2010); Ibolya Maczák, *Kölcsönzés és kompozíció: Szövegalkotás 17–18. századi szerzők prédikációiban* (Budapest: MTA–PPKE Barokk Irodalom és Lelkiség Kutatócsoport, 2019, Pázmány Irodalmi Műhely: Lelkiségtörténeti Tanulmányok 23).

illustrate Pázmány's thoughts about the relationship between an original text and its translation. He explains that he intended to create a text, suggesting that 'it had originally been written by a Hungarian and in Hungarian'.[20] This statement also clarifies the polemics that broke out over the authorship and the originality of two of Pázmány's other works: a successful prayer book, which he published four times (1606, 1610, 1625, 1631),[21] and his chef-d'oeuvre *Kalauz* or *Hodoegus* (Guide to divine truth), published three times during his lifetime (1613, 1623, 1637). In this work, he summarised the Catholic doctrine and the anti-Protestant controversy.[22]

The first book was a comprehensive prayer book that covered almost everything that could be useful for devotional life. It contained prayers for the morning, for going to bed, to be recited before and after confession and for communion, and which were adapted to different situations, ages and status, not to mention the seven penitential psalms and several litanies. Although Pázmány published several orations of the book himself, and Catholic tradition assumes his authorship, the major part of Pázmány's prayerbook was a compilation for which he was mainly responsible for the choice and, eventually, the translation

---

20 This work has not been published in the new series of Pázmány's critical edition, therefore I quote an older, complete edition of his works: Rajmond Rapaics etc. (eds.), *Pázmány Péter összes munkái* (7 vols., Budapest: M. Kir. Tud.-Egyetemi Nyomda, 1894–1905), I. 208: 'mint-ha először magyar embertül, magyarúl iratott volna'. About Pázmány's views on vernacular letters, see Emil Hargittay, 'A Campianus-fordítás és Pázmány írói pályakezdése', *Irodalomtörténeti Közlemények*, 103 (1999), pp. 661–665; Csilla Gábor, 'A szóllásnak módját úgy ejteném ... Pázmány Péter és az anyanyelvűség programja', *Nyelvünk és Kultúránk*, 32 (2002), pp. 102–106.

21 Péter Pázmány, *Keresztyeni imadsagos koenyv, melybe szep aytatos keoneorgesek, haladasok es tanusagoc foglaltatnac* (Graz: Wildmanstadt, 1606), USTC 871380, RMNy 945. For the further three editions, see RMNy 1003, 1345, 1513. This figure does not include the numerous posthumous editions. The following article lists thirty-two editions until the nineteenth century: Judit Bogár, 'Pázmány Péter Imádságos könyvének kiadásai és a reprezentáció', in Orsolya Báthory, Franciska Kónya (eds.), *Egyház és reprezentació a régi Magyarországon* (Budapest: MTA-PPKE Barokk Irodalom és Lelkiség Kutatócsoport, 2016), pp. 59–77. A critical edition is based on the version of 1631: Péter Pázmány, *Imádságos könyv (1631)*, eds. Rita Sz. Bajáki, Emil Hargittay, *Pázmány Péter művei*, III; annotations are in a separate volume: Péter Pázmány, *Imádságos könyv (1631). Jegyzetek a szövegkiadáshoz*, eds. Rita Sz. Bajáki, Judit Bogár, *Pázmány Péter művei*, VI.

22 Péter Pázmány, *Isteni igazsagra vezerloe kalauz* (Bratislava: Typ. Archiepiscopalis, 1613), USTC 871211, RMNy 1059. In each edition, the title is slightly different: *Igassagra vezerlö Kalauz* (Bratislava: Typ. Societatis Jesu, 1623), USTC 871214, RMNy 1293; the Hellenised title *Hodoegus* appears in the third edition: *Hodoegus. Igazsagra-vezerlö kalauz* (Bratislava, Societas Jesu, 1637), USTC 870435, RMNy 1697. A facsimile is based on this last edition: ed. Péter Kőszeghy, intr. Emil Hargittay (Budapest: Balassi Kiadó–MTA Irodalomtudományi Intézete, 2000).

of texts. He of course had to include basic texts such as the Lord's Prayer, the Hail Mary or prayers attributed to famous saints, like a thanksgiving formula addressed to the guardian angel by St Augustine or the prayer of St Bridget for a godly death. Certain prayers attested a continuous Hungarian textual tradition, such as Psalm 50. Pázmány's book identified its translator on the margin as Bálint Balassi (1554–1594), the most important Renaissance poet of the Hungarian language.[23] Balassi was a Protestant nobleman who only converted to Catholicism at the end of his life, under the influence of the Jesuit Sándor Dobokay. Pázmány probably wanted to honour both Balassi's conversion and his significance as a poet by including his translation of the psalm amongst many other traditional devotional texts.

Pázmány was appalled when he saw in 1610 that a large part of his prayerbook had been republished the year prior by a Lutheran minister of Eperjes (Prešov), János Mihálykó (before 1591–after 1613).[24] The pastor had selected texts almost exclusively from Pázmány's prayerbook but put his own name, without other acknowledgements, on the title page. Furthermore, Mihálykó carefully omitted controversial Catholic content, including the litanies and the Hail Mary. In total, only twenty-five pages of the work's 221 contained texts not taken from Pázmány's book.[25] Mihálykó's plagiarism did not pass unnoticed. When Pázmány published his prayerbook for the second time the following year, he wrote a short remark about it in the introduction:

> Last year, a less inspired preacher of Eperjes (Prešov) published a major part of my previous prayer book under his own name in Bártfa (Bardejov). When I managed to get a copy, I remembered what I had read several times in the following section by Martin Luther who claims that they [the Lutherans] inherited everything that is good [in their faith] from those who are in the Roman faith: 'we acknowledge that in papacy, there are many good things which descended to us, namely the true Scripture, the true Baptism, the true Eucharist, the true keys for the remission of sins, the true office of preaching, the true catechism, and the true core of Christianity' (Tom. 2. Lat. Wittenberg, 1557, edited by Lufft, page 229: *Epistola ad duos plebanos*). Therefore, I was not offended by the work

---

23   Pázmány, *Keresztyeni imadsagos koenyv* (1606), f. 180v.
24   János Mihálykó, *Kereztién istenes es aitatos imadsagok, ez mostani nyomorúlt és veszedelmes üdökben minden kereztién és istenfélö embernek felötte szükségesek és haznosok* (Bardejov: Klöz, 1609), USTC 871183, RMNy 976.
25   For a detailed comparison, see Rita Bajáki, 'Pázmány Imádságos könyvének utóéletéhez', in Emil Hargittay (ed.), *Pázmány Péter és kora* (Piliscsaba: PPKE BTK, 2001, Pázmány Irodalmi Műhely: Tanulmányok 2), pp. 285–291, especially pp. 286–287.

of this preacher; moreover, I wanted to thank him for his effort. But as I began to read it, I noticed that he had mutilated it at several places, and he had used his maculated, patchwork-like taste to repair [the alleged defects of] my work. ... Thus, I do not acknowledge the work of this preacher of Eperjes, and I even besmirch it for its many deficiencies, and I refuse to recognise it as mine.[26]

The witty remark is interesting for two reasons. First, the Latin quotation he takes from Luther to use against the Lutherans is presented in a tendentious way. The original text was written against Anabaptists, and Luther only spoke about certain Catholic doctrines and practices as acceptable. There are also some issues with the indication of the source. I found no Latin edition of Luther's complete works from 1557, but there is a German edition from the same year with a matching page number.[27] Either the Latin edition has been lost, or Pázmány made a mistake by designating the edition to be a Latin book. The possibility that Pázmány translated the phrase from German himself could explain why his version differs from what we can find in other texts that quote the same section, as Luther's phrase seems to have been a standard argument in the hand of Catholic apologists. For instance, Miklós Telegdi (1535–1586), an

---

26 Pázmány, *Imádságos könyv* (1631): *Jegyzetek*, pp. 59–60: 'Az el múlt esztendöben egy csekély indúlattúl el ragadtatot Eperjesi Predikátor, maga neuéuel, nagy részét ki Nyomtatá Bártfán az elébbi imadságos könyuecskémnek: Midön azért kezemhez jutot vólna az eo Nyomtatása, eszemben juta az mit Luther Mártonban nem egyszer oluastam vala, tudny illik hogy az Romai hiten valóktúl származot eo reájok az mi jó nálok vagyon, Testamur in Papatu esse multa bona, quae inde ad nos fluxerunt, Ibi enim est vera scriptura, verus Baptismus, vera Eucharistia, verae claues ad peccati remissionem, verum officium praedicandi, verus Catechismus, immo verus Christianitatis nucleus, Tom. 2. Lat. Wittemb. anno 1557. per Lufft. edit. fol. 229. Epistola ad duos Plebanos: és ez okon nem csak nehéz neuen nem vöm az Predikátor munkáját, de söt vgyan megis akarom vala köszönny az jámbornak fáradságát. Mikor pedig oluasny kezdettem vólna, eszembe vöm hogy sok helyen meg szaggatta, és az eo foltos teczésének rongyáual béis tatarazta az én irásomat. ... Annak okáért nem hogy jauallanám ezt az Eperjesi Predikátor munkáját, de söt inkab az benne való sok fogyatkozásokért gyalázom, és enymnek nem ismérem'.

27 Georgius Rorarius (ed.), *Der ander Teil der Buecher D. Mart. Luth. Darin alle Streitschriften sampt etlichen Sendbrieuen an Fürsten und Stedte etc. zusamen gebracht sind, Wider allerley Secten, so zu seiner zeit reine Christliche lere angefochten haben* (Wittenberg: Hans Lufft, 1557), USTC 632739, ff. 229v–230r: 'Wir erkennen aber, das unter dem Bapsthum viel Christliches gutes, ja alles Christich gut sey, und auch daselbst herkomen sey an uns, nemlich, wir erkennen, das im Bapsthum die rechte heilige Schrifft sey, rechte Tauffe, recht Sacrament des altars, rechte Schlüssel zur vergebung der sünde, rechte Predigampt, rechter Catechismus, als das Vater unser, zehen Gebor, die Artickel des glaubens'. See also the modern edition of the text: *D. Martin Luthers Werke. Kritische Gesammtausgabe* (73 vols., Weimar: Hermann Böhlau, 1883–1939), XXVI. 144–174.

influential Catholic preacher, used it to dispute a Protestant polemist, Péter Bornemisza (1535–1584), who claimed that the Reformation had refuted every single doctrine of Catholicism.[28]

Pázmány intentionally misinterpreted Luther's text to lampoon Protestants, but his remark was not simply ironic. When he claimed that he would have been happy with Mihálykó's new publication had he not mutilated his text, he spoke seriously; or at least, his word was taken seriously by his Catholic readers. This interpretation is supported by several examples. Prior research has demonstrated how other Catholics reworked and republished Pázmány's prayerbook without making the slightest effort to conceal the fact of borrowing. In 1622, while Pázmány was still alive, the Franciscan Márton Kopcsányi (1579–1638) published a prayerbook that copied Pázmány's structure and sometimes even his texts. Ádám Batthyány (1610–1659), an aristocrat whose family converted to Catholicism by the personal intervention of Pázmány himself, published an excerpted version of the book in Vienna in 1654 under his own name and with the new title, *Lelki kard, avagy imádságoskönyv* (Spiritual sword).[29] It is also a well-known fact that Pázmány's sermons were abundantly recycled in later Catholic compilations, namely those by András Illyés (1637–1712), the elected bishop of Transylvania, by the Franciscan Didák Kelemen (1683–1744) and

---

28 Miklós Telegdi, *Feleleti Bornemisza Peternec Feitegetés nevü könyvére* (Nagyszombat: Telegdi, 1580), USTC 395514, RMNy 476, p. 115: 'fatemur in Papatu veram esse scripturam sacram, verum Baptismum, verum sacramentum altaris, veras claves ad remissionem peccatorum, verum praedicandi officium, verum cathechismum, ut sunt oratio dominica, Decem praecepta, articuli fidei: Dico insuper sub Papatu veram Christianitatem. imo verum nucleum Christianitatis esse'. About this debate and the quotation, see Kornél Rupp, 'Bornemisza és Telegdi theologiai álláspontja: Bornemisza "Fejtegetés" czimű könyve alapján', *Protestáns Szemle*, 10 (1898), pp. 1–27, 129–149.

29 Márton Kopcsányi, *Keresztyen imadsagos keonyvecke* (Vienna: Gelbhaar, 1622), USTC 871575, RMNy 1260 (he had already published a prayerbook in 1616, but there is no extant copy of this edition: USTC 871564, RMNy 1103); Ádám Batthyány, *Lelki kard, avagy imádságoskönyv* (Vienna: Cosmerovius, 1654), USTC 1770173, RMNy 2508A. About the relationship between Pázmány and the Batthyány family: Béla Iványi, István Fazekas, András Koltai, *Pázmány Péter és a Batthyányak* (Budapest: Szent István Társulat, 2008). About the Catholic posterity of Pázmány's prayerbook, see Rita Bajáki and Judit Bogár, 'Pázmány Imádságos könyvének hatása', in Ibolya Maczák (ed.), *Jubileumi emlékkönyv Pázmány Péter egyetemalapításának 375. évfordulója tiszteletére* (Budapest: Pázmány Péter Katolikus Egyetem, 2010), pp. 195–201; Rita Bajáki, 'Pázmány Péter és Kopcsányi Márton imakönyve', in Judit Bogár (ed.), *Régi magyar imakönyvek és imádságok* (Piliscsaba: PPKE BTK, 2012), pp. 11–22; Rita Bajáki, 'Dialógus az imakönyvekben. A hitbéli vitákon történő felülemelkedés ünnepi pillanatai', in Csilla Gábor, Anna Farmati (eds.), *A dialógus formái a magyar régiségben* (Kolozsvár: Egyetemi Műhely Kiadó-Bolyai Társaság, 2021), pp. 215–224.

several others.[30] I would like to add to this scholarship my own finding, a particularly intriguing example because Pázmány was personally involved in the case. The Hungarian bishop Bálint Lépes (1570–1623) was a successful politician, courtier and the Hungarian chancellor of the Habsburg monarch. In 1614, the *papal nuncio* and Melchior Khesl, the archbishop of Vienna, denounced him for his scandalous lifestyle. The exact nature of his misconduct is unclear, but his disgrace might explain why he devoted himself to religious literature.[31] To restore his reputation, he translated into Hungarian Gabriele d'Inchino's monumental sermons on the four last things (Death, Judgment, Hell and Heaven).[32] The Hungarian text was published in two large volumes, the second of which was dedicated to Pázmány, then the recently appointed archbishop.[33] The Hungarian version was not a simple translation: Lépes included his own additions in the book, such as religious poems, hymns and historical examples. Surprisingly, he copied Pázmány as well, without proper credit. In the beginning of his *Hodoegus*, Pázmány used the arguments of natural theology to prove the existence of God to the alleged atheists and freethinkers of his time. To gain the reader's admiration, he demonstrated his knowledge in natural philosophy, zoology and astronomy to describe the wonders of Creation. In his translation, Lépes merged Pázmány's section about the wonders of nature with Gabriele d'Inchino's description of the world during the Last Judgment.[34] Had Lépes thought that his act of plagiarism (if it may be considered as such) would offend Pázmány, his superior, he may not have committed it so openly. I propose that he must have been convinced that he was honouring Pázmány's text and promoting religious truth.

---

30   Maczák, *Elorzott szavak*; Maczák, *Kölcsönzés és kompozíció*.
31   István Bitskey, 'Lépes Bálint és az olasz seicento stílus', in József Jankovics (ed.), *Klaniczay-emlékkönyv. Tanulmányok Klaniczay Tibor emlékezetére* (Budapest: Balassi Kiadó, 1994), pp. 334–343, 334–335.
32   Gabriele d'Inchino, *Conciones de quatuor hominis novissimis*, transl. Antonio Dulcken (Cologne: Joannes Crithius, 1609), USTC 2041032, VD17 12:192851F.
33   Gabriele d'Inchino, *Az halando es iteletre menendeo tellyes emberi nemzetnek fényes tüköre*, transl. Bálint Lépes (Prague: Sessius, 1616), USTC 871524, RMNy 1119; *Pokoltól rettenteo es mennyei bodogsagra edesgeteo tükör*, transl. Bálint Lépes (Prague: Sessius, 1617), USTC 871526, RMNy 1146.
34   For the details, see Gábor Förköli, 'A Kalauz helye a magyar vallásos antropológia történetében: Pázmány Péter érvei a katolikus Lépes Bálint és a református Margitai Láni Péter műveiben', in Ibolya Maczák (ed.), *Útmutató. Tanulmányok Pázmány Péter Kalauzáról* (Budapest: MTA-PPKE Barokk Irodalom és Lelkiség Kutatócsoport, 2016, Pázmány Irodalmi Műhely: Lelkiségtörténeti Tanulmányok 14), pp. 9–29, 19–24.

2 Intellectual Property and Catholic Tradition in Pázmány's Work

Pázmány explained that true doctrine was a common good, and nobody could claim ownership. He expounded this idea in the preface of *Hodoegus*. This volume, which integrated many of his previous works, was meant to transmit the integrity of Catholic doctrine in the vernacular and to crown Pázmány's *oeuvre*. Pázmány targeted three kinds of enemies: freethinkers, whom he described as atheists; followers of other religions, especially Islam; and Protestants, who were the focus of most chapters. Pázmány had learnt much from his Roman master, Bellarmine, whose *Controversiae* clearly inspired his student. However, Pázmány did not imitate the structure of Bellarmine's work, instead basing most of his arguments on the authority of the Church Fathers who constituted a common ground between Catholics and Protestants.

In the preface, Pázmány likened his use of ecclesiastical authorities to the work of a bee that collects nectar from a variety of flowers, in contrast to the spinning of a spider, which creates a web from its own body.[35] This antique common place supported two claims. The first is the more obvious: Pázmány did not say anything new, but rather repeated what had been said by previous Catholic authorities albeit in a different manner. The second is less explicit: the reformers of the faith in Pázmány's era claimed the same false doctrines as the heretics of antiquity.[36] It is remarkable that in the second edition from 1623, Pázmány felt the need to considerably augment this section with new arguments and quotations, including this one from St Paul: 'Eadem vobis scribere, mihi quidem non pigrum, vobis autem necessarium' (Philippians 3:1: 'To write the same things to you, to me indeed is not grievous, but for you it is safe').[37] This raises the question: what happened between the two editions?

After the first edition of Pázmány's book, more than one Protestant polemist claimed that the book contained nothing new compared to other Catholic works. A Calvinist minister of Debrecen, István Milotai Nyilas (1571–1623), referred readers to well-known Protestant theology handbooks in case they

---

35 Pázmány, *Isteni igazsagra vezerleo kalauz*, f. a2r–v (edition of 1613); *Igassagra vezerlö kalauz*, ff. a1v–a2r (edition of 1623).

36 Because of this identification, Pázmány chose to use the authority of the Church Fathers who addressed the equivalent heresies in their age: István Bitskey, 'Ókeresztény szerzők Pázmány Kalauzában', in József Jankovics etc. (eds.), *A magyar művelődés és a kereszténység. A IV. Nemzetközi Hungarológiai Kongresszus előadásai: Róma–Nápoly, 1996. szeptember 9–14*, vol. 2 (Budapest–Szeged: Nemzetközi Magyar Filológiai Társaság, 1998), pp. 710–716.

37 Pázmány, *Igassagra vezerlö kalauz*, ff. a2r (edition of 1623).

wished to answer Pázmány's allegations.[38] Others asserted that the only thing Pázmány did was quote his teacher, Bellarmine, and since Protestants had already answered Bellarmine's accusations, their works could thus respond to each of Pázmány's arguments.[39] This opinion was shared by two Lutherans from Csepreg in Western Hungary: a deacon named Imre Zvonarics (cc. 1575–1621) and the teacher Benedek Nagy (d. c.1617). The Protestants were concerned with Pázmány because he had successfully converted aristocratic families to Catholicism, and Protestant communities in Hungary depended to a large extent on patronage.

At the beginning of the polemic in 1614, Zvonarics replied to Pázmány's *Hodoegus* by translating a collection of common places by Matthias Hafenreffer, a theologian from Tübingen. In a preliminary text signed by István Klaszekovits (c.1545–1620), Zvonarics' superintendent (the Protestant bishop) and other ministers accused Pázmány of not being able to formulate his arguments without the help of other Jesuit works.[40] The debate was extremely harsh and abounded in defamatory claims. To give justice to the tone of the polemics, it is necessary to remark that, apart from the charge of plagiarism, its other main topic was Luther's origin. The Protestant party was offended by the Jesuit claim that Luther was conceived from his mother's union with the Devil. Pázmány responded to the accusations with a book entitled *Csepregi mesterseg* (Machinations from Csepreg). He used the pseudonym Miklós Szyl, but it was obvious to Zvonarics that Pázmány was the author.[41] The Zvonarics then co-authored a new book in 1615 with Benedek Nagy, titled *Pazman Peter pironsagi* (Péter Pázmány's shameful acts). This work accused the Jesuit of plagiarising Bellarmine's arguments to refute the Augsburg Confession and the Formula of

---

38   Milotai Nyilas's work is lost. Its content can be reconstructed from Pázmány's answer: Péter Pázmány, *Roevid felelet ket calvinista keonyvecskere, mellyeknek eggyke okát adgya, miért nem felelnek az calvinista praedikátorok az Kalauzra, masika Itinerarium catholicumnak neveztetik* (Vienna: Gelbhaar, 1620), USTC 871572, RMNy 1203, see József Barcza, 'Újabb szempontok a Pázmány vitához', *Református Egyház*, 30 (1978), pp. 154–160.

39   A remark about these accusations made by Vilmos Frankl (later known as Fraknói) misled the historiography for a long period of time, and Bellarmine's *Controversiae* was often said to be the main model of the *Hodoegus*: Frankl, *Pázmány Péter és kora*, I. 113–114. This misunderstanding has been elucidated by many researchers; for a summary of these results, see Emil Hargittay, *Pázmány Péter írói módszere. A Kalauz és a vitairatok újraírása* (Budapest: Universitas Kiadó, 2019), pp. 43–46.

40   Matthias Hafenreffer, *Az szent irasbeli hitunk againak bizonyos moddal es rendel harom konyvekre valo osztasa* (Keresztúr: Farkas, 1614), USTC 871406, RMNy 1072, f. C1r.

41   Miklós Szyl, *Csepregi mesterseg, az az Hafenreffernek magyarrá fordítot könyve eleiben függyesztet leveleknek czegéres cziganysági és orczaszégyenítő hazugsági* (Vienna: [Margarete Formica?], 1614), USTC 871560, RMNy 1061.

Concord. The two authors first quoted the *Csepregi mesterseg*, then responded to Pázmány's allegation as follows:

> The superintendent wrongfully claims that the *Hodoegus* had been composed out of the concordant works of many Jesuits. No one else's hand has part in it, but the one's whose name is on the title page, etc. Response: Why are you speaking wrongfully and vainly, when you even took the title *Guide* from some German work? Furthermore, do you not confess yourself in your hideous work about Csepreg that every horrible thing you spit onto Luther comes from other people's writings, and you did not say anything about him by yourself? In addition, I must say that anything you wanted to put onto the Augsburg Confession and the Formula of Concord with your dirty hands, you pulled them out of Bellarmine's quiver, although you must have been informed that his lies had been refuted long ago. And if you, master Pázmány, consider the *Guide* to be your beloved offspring because you assembled it into a poor bricolage, all you have achieved is like a patchwork, an ugly, and inornate mantle made by a tailor who stole various pieces of textile.[42]

In 1616, Pázmány responded to these charges in his *Disgrace of Csepreg*, re-emphasising that religious truth is a common good and that he could not 'pull the answer out of thin air nor bring it out of [his] mother's womb' simply because he needed arguments in favour of the Catholic faith. He also stressed that although he referred to Bellarmine, his text was different from his master's both in terms of content and manner of expression.[43]

---

[42] Imre Zvonarics, Benedek Nagy, *Pazman Peter pironsagi* (Keresztúr: Farkas, 1615), USTC 871409, RMNy 1091, p. 256: 'Nem igazan iria, ugy mond Attendens, hogy az Kalauz sok Iesuitaknak egyenlö munkaiabol keszettetet. Senki keze szennie ninczen abban, hanem egyedül chak aze, az kinek nevet viseli, etc. F. Mit szollasz heltele[n] heiaba, ha az Kalauz nevetis valami Nemet irasbol kaptad? Söt ez Czepregi timarsagodbannis meg vallod, hogy az minemü szörnyüseget Lutherre keröedel, magadtul sem[m]it erröl nem mondottal, hanem mas emberek irasibol iedzetted fel? Ennek fölötte azt mondom, hogy valamit az Augustana Confessiora, az Concordia könyvre, es Lutherre akaral szurkos kezzel kenni, ezt iobbara Bellarminus tegzeböl vonyad elö, noha lehet hiredde, hogy ennekis regen torkaban vertek sok izben az borsos levet. Ha penig azert tartod edes szülöttednek Pazman Uram az Kalauzt, hogy im te tatarosztad gonoszul poklul egybe, chak anni ditsereted ebbenis, mint az mely szabo sok fele dirib darab posztot lopogat, es vegre valami disztelen cziunya foltos dolmant raggat belöle'.

[43] Péter Pázmány, *Csepregi szegyenvallas, az az roevid felelet, melyben az csepregi hiusagoknak köszegi tóldalékit veröfényre hozza Pazmany Peter* (Prague: Sessius, 1616), USTC 871725, RMNy 1120, p. 238: 'Mert ugyanis ujomból nem szophattam, sem Anyám méheböl nem hoztam magammal'.

Pazman Peter pironsagi also accused Pázmány of stealing the title 'guide' (later the Hellenised *Hodoegus*) from German books. Although the authors did not address so, several Protestant works in the Holy Roman Empire used the title *Wegweiser*, including the work of Calvinist Johannes Pistorius and Lutheran Balthasar Mentzer's book, which attacked Pistorius for his Calvinism, and Lutheran Georg Hanfelt's book about the Lord's Supper.[44] Pistorius' *Wegweiser* was also published as the appendix to an anonymous pamphlet against Catholic celibacy, *Deß Römischen Bapsts, seiner Geistlichen Clerisey und Societet der Jesuiten Unreine Schlaffkammer*, directed most pointedly against Jesuits.[45] Of these, the Lutheran Mentzer's anti-Calvinist works were preserved in the Güssing Protestant school's collection at the centre of the Batthyány family's estate (in present Austria).[46] This means that once again, the accusations out of Csepreg had a strong denominational aspect: if Pázmány committed plagiarism, it was even more serious because it was a Catholic who stole the title from Protestant works.

The metaphors of patchwork and bricolage that the Zvonarics and Nagy employed to admonish Pázmány implied a superficial work and an assembly of disparate elements. In sum, they were the opposite of what Pázmány used the metaphor of the bee collecting nectar to describe as digestion and appropriation. Remarkably, the Zvonarics and Nagy used the same vocabulary to describe Pázmány's book as Pázmány did when he accused Mihálykó of stealing his prayerbook. They described book as the result of theft; 'patchwork' or 'mending with rags' (*rongy, foltozás*) and 'repairing a bad roof or renovating a house' or 'bricolage' (*tatarozás*). Although this coincidence has not yet been pointed out in the literature, I believe it could provide an argument for linking the two debates.

---

44 Georg Hanfelt, *Wegweiser inn der Lehr vom H[eiligen] Abendmal* (Neustadt an der Hardt: Harnisch, 1582), USTC 706261, VD16 H 525; Balthasar Mentzer, *Evangelischer Wegweiser. Das ist: Widerlegunge deß von Johanne Pistorio in Truck verfertigten Buchs, so er genennet: Wegweiser vor alle verführte Christen* (Marburg: Egenolff, 1603), USTC 2000530, VD17 39:148272D; Johann Pistorius, *Wegweiser vor alle verführte Christen. Das ist: Kurtzer, doch gründtlicher, warhaffter, auß einiger H. Schrifft genommener bericht, von vierzehen fürnembsten zwischen den Catholischen und den Newglaubigen in der Religion streitig gemachten Articulen* (Münster: Raßfeldt, 1605), USTC 2092288, VD17 23:678591W.

45 Huldreych Geer zur Freyenstadt, *Deß Römischen Bapsts, seiner Geistlichen Clerisey und Societet der Jesuiten, Unreine Schlaffkammer* (s.l.: s.n., 1608), USTC 2014550, VD17 23:320484Z. The name of the author is a pseudonym.

46 István Monok, *A humanizmus és a protestantizmus áttűnései a Magyar Királyság és Erdély olvasmányműveltségében* (Budapest: Kossuth Kiadó-Eszterházy Károly Egyetem, 2020), p. 164.

It could be that the Lutheran participants of this second polemic wanted to reopen the case of Mihálykó's prayerbook by raising the same allegations against Pázmány. Mihálykó was a known Lutheran pastor even for the Zvonarics and Nagy in Csepreg, and he likewise paid attention to the Transdanubian Lutherans. For instance, Mihálykó completed a handwritten copy of the colloquy of Csepreg, a religious debate that took place in the summer of 1591 between orthodox Lutherans and the so-called 'crypto-Calvinists' about the correct interpretation of the Lord's Supper.[47] His network within the Hungarian Lutheran community was certainly strengthened by the fact that in 1613 he worked as minister to the Thurzó family in their castle of Spiš (Spišský hrad, Slovakia).[48] It is not surprising that he dedicated the first edition of his prayerbook to Erzsébet Czobor, the spouse of György Thurzó (1567–1616), who held the title of palatine, viceroy of Hungary. Mihálykó was also present on the book market with his translations of German religious meditations and sermons, some of which were financed by the Thurzó family.[49] After a couple of reprints in Levoča, Mihálykó's prayerbook was also published in Csepreg in 1630. This was certainly an important event for Hungarian Lutherans because it was the first time that the editors included Protestant religious songs as an annex, some of which could have been composed by Mihálykó himself.[50]

---

47 The manuscript, dated to 8 August 1591, was found at the archives of Prešov: József Hörk, 'A csepregi kollokvium', *Protestáns Egyházi és Iskolai Lap*, 24 (1881), pp. 1194–1197, 1224–1128.
48 His correspondence with the Thurzó family: Jenő Zoványi, 'Pauli Simon postilláinak fordítója', *Magyar Könyvszemle*, 64 (1940), pp. 272–274; Bálint Ila, 'A Thurzó-levéltár egyháztörténeti adatai', *Magyar Protestáns Egyháztörténeti Adattár*, 15 (1934), pp. 1–265, 25–27.
49 Jakob Zader, *Az örök eletnek szep es gyönyörüseges nyari udeieröl valo könyueczke*, transl. János Mihálykó (Bardejov: Klöss, 1603), USTC 871176, RMNy 894: translation from Zader's *Sommer-Spiegel des ewigen Lebens*; Simon Pauli, *Magyarazattia az evangeliomoknak, mellyek az apostaloknak és egyéb szenteknek napiaira rendeltettek*, transl. János Mihálykó (Bardejov: Klöss, 1608), USTC 871182, RMNy 967: translation of the *Dispositio et enarratio evangeliorum dominicalium et festivalium* by Simon Pauli, the superintendent of Rostock; the work was dedicated to Zsuzsanna Thurzó, the sister of the palatine; Lukas Pollio, *Hét praedicátio az Isten fiainak örök eletekröl* (Bardejov: Klöss, 1612), USTC 871184, RMNy 1030: translation from *Vom ewigen Leben der Kinder Gottes sieben Predigten* by Lukas Pollio, a Lutheran minister of Wrocław; the book was dedicated to Erzsébet Czobor, the wife of the palatine.
50 Levoča: Schulz, 1620 (USTC 871470, RMNy 1229, no extant copy); János Mihálykó, *Keresztyeni istenes és aijtatis imadsagok* (Levoča: Brewer, 1629), USTC 871486, RMNy 1442 (the unique copy in Matica Slovenská of Martin, Slovakia); *Keresztyeni istenes és ahítatos imadsagoc .... Ezek mellé adattattanac egynéhány szép isteni dicséretec és sóltári enekec, most uyjonnan kibocsáttattac* (Csepreg: Farkas, 1630), USTC 871276 , RMNy 1459 (the religious songs fill 270 pages, increasing the original volume of the prayerbook by more than double).

Today, very few extant copies are known from these editions of Mihálykó's prayerbook. It can be assumed that the Zvonarics and Nagy were well aware of Pázmány's complaint against Mihálykó regarding the plagiarised prayers and the minister's superficial compiling method. It is not unlikely then that the authors from Csepreg intentionally used a similar vocabulary to turn Pázmány's accusations against him. Presumably, they felt the necessity of doing so because Mihálykó himself did not explicitly react to Pázmány's accusations, and the plagiarised prayers were not removed from later editions. Moreover, when Mihálykó's prayerbook was published once again in 1640 in Bardejov, the editors augmented it with additional prayers.[51] They thus 'plagiarised' by crossing denominational borders again but carefully stayed within the boundaries of Protestantism. This time, they used the prayers of Andreas Musculus, whose book had been translated into Hungarian by the Calvinist János Kecskeméti C. (d. after 1627) in 1624.[52]

The Lutherans of Western Hungary were not completely satisfied with the impact of the Hungarian translation of Hafenreffer's work. György Thurzó made special efforts to hire a professor in Wittenberg to refute Pázmány's *Guide*. After György's death in 1616, his son Imre took over the project. Their candidate for the commission was Balthasar Meisner, who almost assumed the task. After the tragic death of the young Imre, his widowed mother, Erzsébet Czobor, commissioned a team to translate the *Guide* into Latin under the leadership of Zvonarics's superintendent, István Klaszekovits. The translation was then sent to Wittenberg, where Friedrich Balduin, another professor, finally published an answer to Pázmány at Erzsébet Czobor's expense (*Phosphorus veri catholicismi*, Wittenberg, 1626).[53]

---

51   János Mihálykó, *Keresztyeni istenes es aitatos imadsagok* (Bardejov: Klöss, 1640), USTC 870559, RMNy 1818. There was a similar edition published in Levoča in 1642 as well (USTC 870687, RMNy 1942).

52   The original: Andreas Musculus, *Precationes ex veteribus orthodoxis doctoribus* (Frankfurt an der Oder: Johann Eichorn, 1561), USTC 2213227, VD16 ZV 26230; Hungarian translation: Andreas Musculus, *Szép és aytatos imadsagos könyveczke*, transl. János Kecskeméti C. (Bardejov: Klöss, 1624), USTC 871194, RMNy 1295. The fact that some of these prayers were added to Mihálykó's book was a source of error in the Hungarian bibliography. For a long time, some researchers supposed that Mihálykó's prayerbook had been a translation of Musculus' work. See Tivadar Thienemann, 'A XVI. és XVII. századi irodalmunk német eredetű művei (Első közlemény)', *Irodalomtörténeti Közlemények*, 32 (1922), pp. 63–92, 88–89. The error was elucidated by Bajáki, 'Pázmány Imádságos könyvének utóéletéhez', pp. 288–290.

53   István Gyurás SJ, 'Pázmány Kalauzának latin fordítása és a wittenbergi válasz', in László Lukács SJ, Ferenc Szabó SJ (eds.), *Pázmány Péter emlékezete. Halálának 350. évfordulóján* (Rome: Tipografia Ugo Detti, 1987), pp. 389–398; László Barta, 'Adalékok a Kalauzra adott wittenbergi válasz készítéséhez', in Emil Hargittay (ed.), *Pázmány Péter és kora* (Piliscsaba: PPPKE BTK, 2001), pp. 268–273.

3 Conclusion

Plagiarism was but one aspect of many raised in the course of confessional polemics, yet it was constantly brought to attention. Pázmány's example demonstrates that a charge of plagiarism did not necessarily mean respect for intellectual property. In the preface of his prayerbook, Pázmány accused Mihálykó of committing intellectual theft, but in the very same text, the Jesuit put a quotation from Luther into a tendentiously misinterpreted context. In cases of textual transmission or borrowing, the vague contours of intellectual property left a wide gap for diverse interpretation. Even if one was to publish someone else's text, to use it in a compilation, imitate it or outright plagiarise it would be noticed. The moral judgment of such practices, however, depended on personal sympathies and denominational differences. Mihálykó probably did not expect a Catholic readership for his prayerbook that contained texts phrased by a Jesuit because of geographic distance, the lack of a unified book market and the fragmentation of literary networks. Paradoxically, it was the religious controversy of the time that created a supra-confessional reading community, at least amongst clergymen, in which plagiarism could be unveiled and denounced.

PART 5

The Interplay of Word and Image

CHAPTER 15

Framing the French Protestant Threat in Richard Rowlands Verstegan's *Théâtre des cruautés des hereticques de nostre temps* (1588)

Claire Konieczny

Many scholars recognise Richard Rowlands Verstegan's *Theatrum crudelitatum haereticorum nostri temporis* (1587) as one of the most iconic and compelling printed illustrated Catholic martyrologies of the late sixteenth century.[1] Interestingly, Verstegan's original Latin work was only ever translated into one other language: French. This French translation first appeared in 1588 under the title *Théâtre des cruautés des hereticques de nostre temps*.[2] Verstegan scholars indicate that the choice to translate the work specifically in to French was to support the cause of the French Catholic League, a radically anti-Protestant Catholic organization founded in 1585 during the latter years of the French

1   Richard Rowlands Verstegan, *Theatrum crudelitatum haereticorum nostri temporis* (Antwerp: Adrian Hubert, 1587), USTC 88365. The copy used to produce this article is held at the Johns Hopkins University Sheridan Libraries, call no. 274.06 V616 1587 c.1. For scholars who have recognized Verstegan's importance, see: Paul Arblaster, *Antwerp & the World. Richard Verstegan and the International Culture of Catholic Reformation* (Leuven: Leuven University Press, 2004); Anne Dillon, *The Construction of Martyrdom in the English Catholic Community, 1535–1603* (Aldershot: Ashgate, 2002); A.G. Petti, 'Richard Verstegan and Catholic Martyrologies of the Later Elizabethan Period', *Recusant History*, 5 (1959), pp. 64–90; Charles Ruelens, 'Un publiciste catholique du XVIe siècle: Richard Verstegan', *Revue Catholique: Receuil religieux, philosophique, scientifique, historique et littéraire*, 3 (1854), pp. 447–490; and Romana Zacchi, Massimiliano Morini (eds.), *Richard Rowlands Verstegan: A Versatile Man in an Age of Turmoil* (Turnhout: Brepols, 2012).
2   Richard Rowlands Verstegan, *Théâtre des cruautés des hereticques de nostre temps* (Antwerp: Adrian Hubert, 1588), USTC 13611. The copy used to produce this article is also at the Johns Hopkins University Sheridan Libraries, call no. 272 V616 1588 c.1. A few notes here. First, there is much debate surrounding the original date of publication of the French translation of Verstegan's original Latin work; please see my forthcoming article, 'The Catholic Martyrological Tradition of the Reformation and the Early Editions of Richard Rowlands Verstegan's *Théâtre des cruautés* (1588)' in *The Papers of the Bibliographical Society of America* for clarification regarding the publication history. Second, throughout this article I have chosen (as other Verstegan scholars have done) to slightly modernise the spelling of the French edition's title; instead of 'cruautez', as is written for the original title, I write 'cruautés'. Finally, I will refer to these works as the *Theatrum crudelitatum* or the *Theatrum*, and the *Théâtre des cruautés* or the *Théâtre*, respectively, throughout the article.

Wars of Religion (1562–1629).³ While Verstegan scholars write of his personal involvement with the League as proof of the French translation's propaganda purposes, there is little scholarship on how the translation itself specifically supports the expressed goals of the League – namely, that of eradicating all trace of Protestantism in France. In this article I provide a detailed analysis of the French translation in order to show how the wording of the translation itself supports the causes of the French Catholic League.

1   The *Theatrum*

I will first provide a brief overview of the *Theatrum*'s content before analysing its French translation. Simply explained, Verstegan conceived his text as a Catholic martyrology, championing the commitment of European Catholic martyrs to the faith during the Reformation in the face of persecution. The work is divided into sections based on the geographical locations and time periods of Catholic persecution at the hands of Protestants. Placed first is England under Henry VIII, from his conversion in 1534 to his death in 1547. Second is France in the early years of the Wars of Religion (mostly during the 1560s). Third are the Low Countries in the early years of the Protestant revolts, with Verstegan covering instances of persecution mainly in the 1560s. Finally, Verstegan addresses England again, this time under the rule of Elizabeth, from her ascension to the throne in 1558 until the publication of his work in 1587. A typical page of the *Theatrum* consists of an engraving on the right-hand side, a title above and a short poem below, and an explanation of the image on the left-hand side. Capital letters link a specific portion of the explanatory text to a specific part of the image, as a single illustration usually represents multiple

---

3   For Verstegan scholars who support the idea that the *Théâtre* catered specifically to the needs of the French Catholic League, refer to footnote one. Second, many scholars traditionally date the end of the Wars of Religion to the signing of the Edict of Nantes in 1598. However, other scholars attribute the true end to the wars to the signing of the Edict of Alès in 1629, signed after the Huguenot rebellions of the 1620s. For more on this dating, see Mack P. Holt, *The French Wars of Religion, 1562–1629* (Cambridge: Cambridge University Press, 1995); Kathleen Perry Long, 'Violent Words for Violent Times. Théodore Agrippa d'Aubigné's *Les Tragiques*', in Jeff Kendrick, Katherine S. Maynard (eds.), *Polemic and Literature Surrounding the French Wars of Religion* (Berlin: De Gruyter, 2019), among others. Third, there was an earlier attempt to found the Catholic League, in 1576, but its power was successfully diffused and rendered largely ineffective by the French king, Henri III. The second Catholic League was founded in 1585 and lasted until ca. 1594. For more see Holt, *French Wars of Religion*, and Ann W. Ramsey, *Liturgy, Politics, and Salvation. The Catholic League in Paris and the Nature of Catholic Reform, 1540–1630* (Rochester: University of Rochester Press, 1999).

FRAMING THE FRENCH PROTESTANT THREAT   311

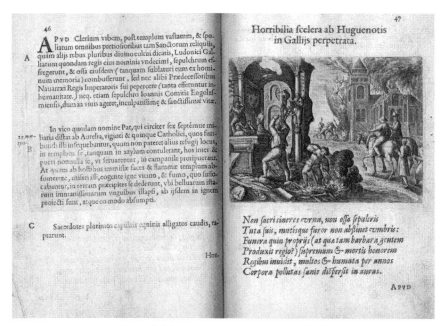

FIGURE 15.1   A typical spread of the *Theatrum*, pp. 46–47. Special Collections, George Peabody
Library, The Sheridan Libraries, Johns Hopkins University, 272 V616 1588 c. 1

acts of persecution. The section on the Huguenots in France actually occupies the bulk of the text, with twelve engravings comprising this part. Three engravings refer to the Catholics under Henry VIII, five are dedicated to the Catholic situation in the Low Countries, and Verstegan allots Elizabeth's reign in England eight images. The French translation maintains the original layout and structure of Verstegan's Latin text.

2   Two *Théâtres*?

Before delving into an analysis of the translation, one element of the French work needs to be explained: that there is not one French translation, but rather *two* distinct French translations of Verstegan's original Latin work. Two publications of Verstegan's text in French were produced in 1588, though the exact date of the publication of each translation is not known.[4] The two translations

---

4   It is possible that the second translation was commissioned after a major League victory, the Day of the Barricades (12 May 1588), when the moderate French King Henri III was forced to

were not published concurrently, given the publisher's (Adrien Hubert's) note at the end of the second translation. In this note, Hubert writes that the first translation of the work was not translated well into French, and thus a second was commissioned.[5] The identities of both French translators remain unknown. Paul Arblaster proposes that the first translation is Verstegan's own, but this suggestion is by no means certain.[6]

The first French translation of 1588 mirrors the Latin original in its physical presentation; that is, like the Latin original, a typical spread of the work contains an explanation of the engraving on the left-hand page, with the corresponding image on the right-hand page, a title above the illustration, and a short poem below the image. As with the Latin work, capital letters link parts of the description on the left to specific parts of the engraving on the right.

The second French publication of Verstegan's work in 1588 differs significantly from both the Latin original and the first French translation. The most striking difference is that this second translation contains no engravings; it is a words-only translation. Nevertheless, the capital letters that relay the reader to

---

flee Paris, effectively rendering him powerless. One should note that this is merely a speculative view; the only evidence I have to support this idea is that the occurrence of the Day of the Barricades in mid-1588 would have allowed for more than enough time for the publication of the first translation. In addition, perhaps the League, emboldened by its ousting of the French king, wished to capture the momentum for its cause by producing a pointed piece of propaganda – the second translation of Verstegan's *Theatrum*.

5 The full note, contained in the second 1588 French edition after the second translation, reads as follows: 'Amy lecteur il y quelque temps que ce theatre de la cruauté des Heretiques, ayant esté imprimé en latin auroit esté fort heureusement recueilli non seulement en Flandres mais aussi en Alemaigne & Italie, & en quelques parties de l'Espagne: cela donna subject à nos Flamans de le traduire en François pour le faire voyr à la France, qui estoit l'un des plus irreprochables tesmoins de ces cruautez. Toutefois comme cette langue leur estoit estrangere, aussi faut il confesser qu'il y commirent d'estranges fautes. Car leur François en quelques endroits escorché du Latin & autres lieux mal cousu & pirement tissu, degousta ceux qui cognoissoient la naifveté & gentillesse de cette langue. Joint qu'ils avoient fait graver des vers au pied des planches, où si la Rithme estoit facheuese, c'esoit encores pis de la raison. Dequoy estant adverti je communiquay la traduction à un François qui negotioit par deça & que l'on reputoit homme assez bien entendu en cette langue. Lequel marri des fautes commises fit un prologue à ce theatre que nous te presentons, ensemble les vers & les arguments de chacune figure. Et neantmoins il nous a fallu laisser le ravage de nos Flamans, a fin que voyant l'un, tu juges de l'autre. Je te prie le prendre de bonne part, & d'aussi bon coeur que je le presente au public: car je ne suis meu d'autre pensee.' The Newberry Library holds in its collections a 1588 edition containing only one translation, call no. Case D 78.943, corroborating the fact that there were two publications of the work in 1588. The edition of the *Théâtre* used to produce this article held at Hopkins is in fact the second edition of 1588, the edition that contains both translations.

6 See Arblaster, *Antwerp & the World*, pp. 32, 41.

FRAMING THE FRENCH PROTESTANT THREAT 313

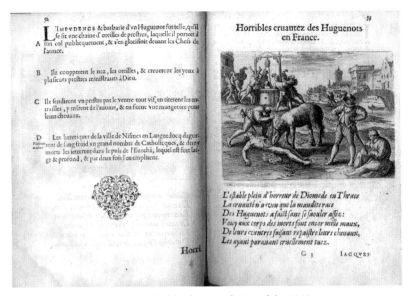

FIGURE 15.2   A typical spread of the first translation of the *Théâtre*, pp. 52–53. Special Collections, George Peabody Library, The Sheridan Libraries, Johns Hopkins University, 272 V616 1588 c. 1

certain parts of the images are still present in this translation. Confusingly, this second translation was not published as a unique work; it instead accompanied the first translation. Most often, the second translation is bound in the same volume as the first, with the second translation placed at the end of the first. Another notable difference in this second translation is that the poems are not at all like those of the original Latin work or the first French translation. I will provide specific examples below; however, in general the second translation's poems merely reiterate the explanatory text in verse, rather than provide a new, poetical take on the idea of Catholic persecution or Protestant cruelty, as is the case with the original Latin work and the first French translation. While the poems differ greatly compared to the two other texts, the second translation does closely follow the prose descriptions, with only a few minor differences in diction and syntax. Finally, and perhaps most interestingly, this second translation contains its own prologue, an element unique to this work.[7]

---

7   For more detail regarding the publication history of these two translations, please see A.F. Allison and D.M. Rogers, *The Contemporary Printed Literature of the English Counter-Reformation between 1558 and 1640* (New York, Routledge, 2016) and my forthcoming article, 'The Early Editions of Richard Rowlands Verstegan's *Théâtre des cruautés* (1588)' in *The Papers of the Bibliographical Society of America*.

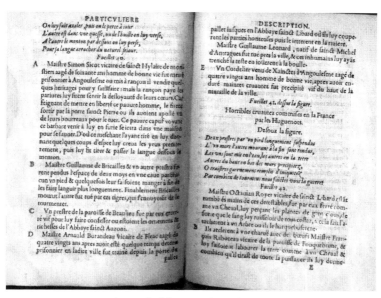

FIGURE 15.3 A typical spread of the second translation of Verstegan's *Théâtre*, n.p. Notice that while the images are lacking, the capital letters linking the text to the engraving are still present. Special Collections, George Peabody Library, The Sheridan Libraries, Johns Hopkins University, 272 V616 1588 c. 1

The first translation, most similar to the Latin original, is usually considered the better of the two translations. Most scholars dismiss the second translation as a poorly executed work, or fail entirely to mention it. Romana Zacchi neglects to include any mention of it in her short history of the work's editions; Arblaster only states that the second translation was made to better suit the propaganda of the Catholic League; Frank Lestringant heavily criticises the second translator and translation, stating that the second translation was hastily written and that the translator's work (especially his poems) is mediocre at best.[8] Despite his critiques, Lestringant does find some merit in the work of the second translator, writing that the prologue to the second translation, an element found neither in the original Latin work nor the first French translation, is close to a written masterpiece.[9]

While the second translation is usually dismissed by Verstegan scholars, I propose that it merits closer study on several counts. First, this second

---

8 See: Romana Zacchi, 'Words and Images. Verstegan's "Theatre of Cruelties"', in Zacchi, Morini (eds.), *Richard Rowlands Verstegan* (Turnhout: Brepols, 2012), pp. 53–75; Arblaster, *Antwerp & the World*, p. 43; and Frank Lestringant (ed.), *Le Théâtre des cruautes de Richard Verstegan (1587)* (Paris: Editions Chandeigne, 1995), p. 39.

9 *Le Théâtre des cruautes de Richard Verstegan*, p. 39.

translation is most relevant to the subject of this article, as scholars suggest that it was specifically adapted to the needs of the French Catholic League; scholars propose that the anonymous second translator was most likely a member or sympathiser of the League.[10] As I will show, this is perhaps most clearly indicated by the second translation's unique prologue. Second, while not carried throughout the whole of the second translation, there are specific mentions of names – mostly French Protestant leaders – in the second translation that are found neither in the original *Theatrum* nor in its first French translation. The mention of these particular figures indicates that the translator wished to inflame the audiences' sentiments against certain Huguenot personages. Third, there are intriguing questions surrounding the reader's usage of this second translation, and how its presence affected one's experience of the text. Lestringant, for example, suggests that the second translation reinforced the reading of the text as a personal spiritual meditation, as readers would flip back and forth between the two versions, an idea that will be explored further in the following sections.[11]

3 The (Second) *Théâtre* and the French Catholic League

At the time in which the two French translations were published, the French Catholic League was an influential force in France. It openly advocated against the reigning house of Valois, for a Catholic successor to the throne (the Catholic Cardinal Charles de Bourbon, uncle to the heir apparent and Huguenot Henri de Navarre), and for the eradication of all French Protestants, known as the Huguenots, in the nation.[12] Having lived in Paris before permanently settling in Antwerp later in his life, scholars speculate that Verstegan worked for the League during his time in Paris and that he maintained those ties whilst living in Antwerp.[13] Indeed, Arblaster and Charles Ruelens suggest that Verstegan departed for Paris almost directly after the publication of the *Theatrum* in 1587 in order to promote the text's use both in the city and throughout France, which was perhaps a catalyst to the work's being subsequently translated

---

10   See: Arblaster, *Antwerp & the World*, p. 43; Ruelens, 'Un publiciste catholique', p. 484; and *Théâtre des cruautés de Richard Verstegan*, pp. 9, 40.
11   *Théâtre des cruautés de Richard Verstegan*, pp. 39–40.
12   For more on this history see Holt, *French Wars of Religion*.
13   Verstegan was born in England, but as an outspoken Catholic was forced to flee during Elizabeth's reign. Verstegan subsequently lived in various cities throughout Europe, including Rouen, Paris, and Rome; he finally settled in Antwerp. For more on Verstegan's life, see Arblaster, *Antwerp & the World*.

into French.[14] Verstegan's work, with its gruesome and shocking depictions of Protestant cruelty, would have been the perfect piece of propaganda for the League to advocate for its uncompromising policies.

However, one must pose the questions: why does the second translation exist? Would not the first translation have been sufficient for the League's purposes? In order to better understand the reasons for the second translation's existence and how it better supports the League's goals, one must look closely at the elements unique to the second translation, namely: the second translation's prologue; its mention of specific leaders of the Huguenot movement; the differences in its poems; and the lack of engravings.

The second translation's prologue, formally entitled 'Prologue of tragedies depicted in the heretical theatre of cruelties', both fully reflects the French Catholic League's intentions and it also impresses the reader with a sense of urgency, that French Catholics cannot wait to fight against the French Protestants; the time to fight is *now*.[15] While no direct comparison can be made between Verstegan's original Latin prologue and the prologue to the second translation – the second translation's prologue being its own unique writing – Verstegan's original prologue lacks the burning sense of urgency present in the second translator's writings.

The second translator uses numerous persuasive techniques to convince his readers to act immediately to fight against the Huguenots. Perhaps most prominently, the second translator plays on the idea that the *Théâtre*, rather than being a simple text, is in fact a *pièce de théâtre*, a play. Zacchi explores the role of the theatre in the context of the Latin original and the first French translation, but she does not study the second translation.[16] I will apply Zacchi's approach to the second translation here in order to show that the second translator wishes his readers to be moved to action against the Huguenots, as promoted by the Catholic League.

It is clear from the opening lines of the prologue that the second translator desires his readers to think of the *Théâtre* as a play. He opens his prologue with these words: 'Sirs, we erected this Theatre in order to show you the miserable tragedies that the heretics acted out in our Europe, and to show you

---

14 See Arblaster, *Antwerp & the World*, p. 42, and Ruelens, 'Un publiciste catholique', pp. 447–490.

15 'Prologue des tragedies répresentees au theatre de la cruauté des heretiques', f. A1r. All translations of Verstegan's texts are my own, as no English translation exists. I have also chosen to slightly modernize the spelling in citations in the footnotes coming from the *Theatrum* and the *Théâtre*, such as changing 'i's to 'j's, when appropriate, and 'u's to 'v's, when needed.

16 See Zacchi, 'Words and Images', pp. 53–75.

that which they committed and perpetrated'.[17] The translator continues this rhetoric of theatre throughout the prologue, often using the verb 'to see' (*voir*) instead of 'to read' (*lire*) to describe the audience's experience, naming the work a 'spectacle' and a 'tragédie', calling the people mentioned in the work 'actors' (*joueurs*), referring to the four different sections of the work as 'acts'. He further compares the text to ancient theatrical traditions, most notably the Greek one.[18]

The translator's heavy emphasis on the work as a *pièce de théâtre* plays directly into Zacchi's idea that the reader of the *Théâtre* is not simply a reader, but rather an eyewitness to the events described and pictured in the work.[19] Indeed, considering the second translator's insistence on theatre, one might recall the etymology of the word 'theatre', which derives from the Greek word *theasthai*, meaning 'to watch' or 'to behold'; the reader of this work is one who beholds the events described in the texts. As an eyewitness to these atrocities, the reader (spectator?) has an obligation to act, to fight against the Protestants. This call to action is not simply implied in the prologue, but the author directly addresses the reader, asking,

> What would you say if one day, as spectators, one made you come on stage in order to play the role of a martyr, or of someone suffering tortures? O how the time threatens us! All is ready and waiting, the Church prepares for it, the Catholics awaiting.[20]

The reader understands that this theatre is in fact reality, a reality in which he will be asked to play a part. In addition, the writer closes the prologue with a sense of urgency, that immediate action must be taken against the Huguenots. He writes that France, before 'such a beautiful and flourishing Kingdom that was in the past the heart and soul of Christianity' lies now in ruins, nothing

---

17 'Messieurs, nous avons dressé ce Theatre, affin de vous representer les miserables tragedies que les heretiques ont jouées en nostre Europe, & pour vous faire voir ce qu'ils on commis & perpeté'. Verstegan, *Théâtre*, second translation prologue, f. A1r.
18 Ibid.
19 See Zacchi, 'Words and Images', pp. 53–75. Dillon, too, in *Construction of Martyrdom*, notes that the detailed nature of Verstegan's images gives 'readers access to events of war and religious persecution ... as if they had witnessed the events themselves', p. 274. While Dillon is not referencing the nature of theatre of the work in this quote, it does convey the idea that the engravings themselves provide an eyewitness experience.
20 'Que dires vous si de spectateurs on vous fait un jour cette grace, de monter sur ce theatre à fin de jouer le roolle d'un martir, & d'un patient? O le temps nous en menace fort, tout y est appareillé, l'Eglise s'y prepare, les Catholiques si attendent ....' Verstegan, *Théâtre*, second translation prologue, f. B3r.

more than 'a dead body', and that 'already we hear the ruins of the temples that they make in England, and we see the fires spreading to the monasteries', threatening that this same fate imminently menaces France should Catholics not act.[21] The spectators of this *Théâtre* are seeing it play out before their eyes, both in the text and in actuality. In order to stop this tragedy from continuing, readers must become actors in life's play by taking up the cause of the French Catholic League and fighting against the Protestants.

In addition to underlining the reader's role as an actor and active witness, the prologue also touches on the idea that the work will emotionally move the audience, thereby inciting the reader to action. The second translator states that this work was not 'invented to please you [the reader]', but to 'elicit tears from your eyes, cries from your mouths, sighs from your hearts, and sobbing from your chests'.[22] Indeed, the translator believes that it is impossible to read this work and not be emotionally moved, writing that the reader will not be so

> Only if you are without eyes, without a mouth, without a heart, and without a chest, and only if not a single drop of humanity resides in you. Or if you have eyes that are those of moles, if your mouths are like those of fish, and your hearts are made of diamonds, and your chests are like boulders, settled and immobile against the waves.[23]

Only in these cases (i.e. if the reader is quite literally bereft of all humanity) will he not be moved when reading this *Théâtre*. In order to effectively move the reader to action against the Protestants, to support the Catholic League, the *Théâtre* will emotionally move him by showing him the tortures that the Catholics have endured at the hands of the Protestants.

In addition to the prologue, the second translation differs noticeably from both the Latin original and the first translation in the fact that it mentions specific names of Huguenot leaders; these names are neither in the Latin original nor the first French translation. For example, the first image regarding the maltreatment of the Catholics in France states in the Latin and first French

---

21   'Un si beau & si florissant Royaume qui estoit autre fois le coeur & l'ame de la Chrestienté'; 'un corps mort'; 'desja nous entendons les ruynes des temples que l'on fait en Angleterre, & voyons les feuz espandus par les monasteres ....', ibid., f. C3r.
22   'Inventé pour vous donner du plaisir'; 'tirer les larmers de voz yeux, les plaintes de vos bouches, les soupirs de vos coeurs, & les sanglots de vox poitrines', ibid., f. A1v.
23   'Si ce n'est que vous soyez sans yeux, sans bouche, sans coeur, & sans poitrine, & qu'il ne reside en vous aucune humanité. Où si vous avez des yeux que ce soient yeux de Taupes, que vos bouches soient bouches de poissons, vos coeurs soient diamants, & voz poitrines quelques Rochers plantez sans s'esmouvoir au milieu des undes', ibid.

translation that 'the city of Angoulême was encircled by the Huguenots', whereas the second translation states 'the city of Angoulême having been besieged by the Admiral [Gaspard de Coligny], with the King of Navarre [Henri], and his mother [Jeanne d'Albret] present there'.[24] This is not the sole instance wherein the second translator adds names not found in either of the previous versions of the text. When describing the situation in England under Henry VIII, for example, the translator adds an entirely new paragraph to the description of the first plate that contains strong invectives against Théodore de Bèze, the leader of the Calvinist church at the time.[25] As Calvinism was the branch of Protestantism most popular in France, the French Huguenots often looked to Bèze for guidance in religious matters. Of Bèze the second translator writes:

> That Calvin never approved of this in his time, strongly and firmly criticizing it; and however this great Patriarch of the Church of Geneva, Bèze, this good successor from his seat, approves, receives, and recommends this Jezebel of England [Elizabeth], the one who is stained with innumerable whores, and pretends that she is the leader of the Church.[26]

In a different description regarding the state of Catholics in France, the second translator specifically states that it was 'by the order of the Queen of Navarre [Jeanne d'Albret], mother of the King of Navarre [Henri]' that captured Catholics, who had been set free after nine months of imprisonment, be tracked down the night after their release and be killed.[27]

The addition of names of specific Protestant leaders would have helped direct the readers' anger at these prominent Protestant (indeed, Huguenot) figures. While the *Theatrum* and the first *Théâtre* contain many names of specific Catholics who suffered persecution, the Protestants who perpetrated these

---

24 'Civitas Engolisma obsidione Huguenotorum arcata', Verstegan, *Theatrum*, p. 32. 'La ville d'Engoulême pressee par les Huguenotz', Verstegan, *Théâtre*, p. 32. 'La Ville d'Angoulesme ayant esté assiegee par l'Admiral, le Roy de Navarre & sa mere y estans presens', Verstegan *Théâtre*, second translation, f. A2v.

25 The original description, without the wording against Bèze, is found in Verstegan, *Theatrum*, pp. 24–25 and Verstegan, *Théâtre*, pp. 24–25.

26 'Ce que Calvin n'a jamais approuvé de son temps ains la improuvé fort & ferme, & toutefois ce grand Patriarche de l'Eglise de Geneve Beze, ce bon successeur de sa chaire aprouve & reçoit & recommande cette Jezabel d'Angleterre [Elizabeth] masculee de putasseries innumerables, & soustient qu'elle est chef de l'Eglise …', Verstegan, *Théâtre*, second translation, f. C4v.

27 'Par le commandement de la Royne de Navarre mere du Roy de Navarre', Verstegan, *Théâtre*, second translation, f. E3v. The original description, lacking this detail, can be found in Verstegan, *Theatrum*, pp. 50–51 and Verstegan, *Théâtre*, pp. 50–51.

persecutions remain unnamed. The second translation provides the reader with named French Calvinists (mostly leaders of this movement) in order to help direct the reader's anger and disgust at a specific enemy. The reader's fury against 'Protestants' in general, as promoted by the *Theatrum* and the first translation, is perhaps too vague; in reading the second translation, the audience would have distinct figures at whom they could channel their animosity and fight against.

Interestingly, the second translation only contains these short additions in the first two sections of the work, those that describe Catholic maltreatment under Henry VIII and in France during the early years of the Wars of Religion. Indeed, the second translator names figures only connected to the Huguenots; even though he is mentioned in the section regarding England, Bèze was an important figure to the Huguenots. The fact that the second translator only mentions personages connected to French Protestantism indicates the French Catholic League's hand in its publication. As a work of League propaganda, the second translator provides readers with a list of specific people against whom they should fight: Bèze; Henri de Navarre; the admiral Gaspard de Coligny; and the queen of Navarre and Henri's mother, Jeanne d'Albret. While some of these figures died before the publication of Verstegan's work (Coligny and Jeanne d'Albret), the reader is nevertheless reminded of the history surrounding Catholic persecution at the hands of these Huguenot leaders.

Yet another noticeable diversion in the second translation is this version's poems. Lestringant notes that unlike the first two publications, the second translator's verses are often more concrete and realistic, as opposed to poetic; however, Lestringant does not provide specific examples.[28] I would like to suggest that the second translator's poems, as ones that reiterate the descriptive prose, function to provoke the reader's emotions to a fever-pitch of anger against the Huguenots. In doing so, the second translator would incite the reader to fight against the French Calvinists and to support the League's goals.

Specific examples are perhaps the best way to illustrate this point. In one engraving regarding Catholic persecution, Verstegan details in prose how the Huguenots boiled a man's hands in oil until the flesh fell off, then subsequently forced him to drink the boiling oil before finally shooting him. In the same image, Verstegan writes how they also castrated a different man, enclosed him in a coffin with holes in the lid, and then poured boiling oil on him through the holes, and also how the Huguenots ripped a man's tongue out and then killed him. Still in the same engraving, Verstegan further writes of another

---

28   *Théâtre des cruautés de Richard Verstegan*, p. 39.

man whose feet were burned with hot irons and then his throat was slit.[29] Accompanying the prose and image is the following poem in the Latin original and first French translation:

> The wolf, with the good shepherd his gluttonous entrails
> Fills, to better after devour the flocks,
> Because to taste the good whets all of his appetite:
> And the heretic attacks the leader and good priest
> To better lead his own into the darkness of horror,
> To which they are pushed by the cunning evil spirit.[30]

In the second translation, however, the author writes:

> One, with his hands burned in boiling oil,
> But not so much that he dies of it, with great gulps,
> They make him drink the oil, then they disembowel him,
> The other lays in a coffin, where they pour the oil on him,
> To the other they pierce him under the chin,
> In order to rip out the tongue from its natural resting place.[31]

This example clearly demonstrates that the second translation's poems merely restate the prose descriptions. By repeating yet again the Huguenots' methods of torturing the Catholics, the second translator forces the reader to contemplate such horrors *ad nauseum*. The second translation's poems truly cement the horrific nature of Catholic persecution in the mind of the reader, conceivably convincing the reader of the League's expressed goal that Huguenots cannot be allowed to live in the Kingdom of France.

Aside from the words themselves, the mere presence of the second translation, and specifically its lack of engravings, would have transformed the reader's

---

29 The descriptions can be found in Verstegan, *Theatrum*, pp. 38–39, Verstegan, *Théâtre*, pp. 38–39, and Verstegan, *Théâtre*, second translation, f. D4r–D4v.

30 'Pastorem lupus aggreditur, quo tutiùs omnes/ Diripiat praedator oves custode remoto:/ Sic caput invadit primùm, rerúmque magistros/ Impietas, facili tum caetera membra labore/ Expugnat, legísque sacrae monitoribus orbat,/ Spargat ut incautae furtim mendacia plebi', Verstegan, *Theatrum*, p. 39. 'Le loup, du bon berger ses gloutonnes entrailles/ Remplit, pour mieux aprés devorer les ouailes,/ Car à gaster les bons tend tou son apetit:/ Et l'heretique assaut le chef & bon pasteur/ Pour mieux mener les siens en tenebres d'horreur,/ A quoy in sont poussex par le maling esprit', Verstegan, *Théâtre*, p. 39.

31 'L'un dans l'huile bouillant à ses mains eschaudees,/ Et d'autant qu'il n'en meurt, avec grandes ondees,/ On luy fait avaler, puis on le perce à jour/ L'autre est dans une quesse, ou de l'huille on luy verse,/ A l'autre le menton par dessous on luy perse,/ Pour sa langue arracher du naturel sejour', Verstegan, *Théâtre*, second translation, f. D4r–D4v.

experience of the *Théâtre*. As mentioned briefly above, Lestringant suggests that the second translation would have transformed the reader's experience into a spiritual exercise.[32] I would like to expand further on Lestringant's idea and propose that the second translation not only creates a spiritual experience but also demands the reader's active engagement with the text, which would in turn lead to a stronger commitment to the Catholic faith, perhaps even to the Catholic League. The second translation was printed without the appropriate accompanying images, but it still contained the capital letters referring to specific parts of the images (see Figure 15.3). In order to properly read the second translation, therefore, the reader would be obliged to move back and forth between the first and second translations (recall that the two were sold together), matching the second translation's descriptions with the correct depictions. This would have no doubt been a time-consuming task, one that would have required great effort on the part of the reader.

In thus turning a passive reading of the work into a meticulous activity, the second translation forces the reader to become actively engaged in the text; the reader can no longer simply turn the page, but rather he is required to mindfully match description and engraving. Moreover, the act of sending the reader back to the image compels the reader to look at the image again – an image containing appallingly detailed representations of Protestants torturing and killing Catholics. Both of these actions would have cemented the subject matter of the work in the mind of the reader as well as aroused yet again the reader's sentiments against the Protestants. The second translation in effect forces the reader to witness these atrocities not once, but rather twice, both visually and through the written word.

4 Conclusion

This article provides an analysis of the second French translation of Verstegan's *Theatrum crudelitatum* in an effort to show exactly how this translation supported the French Catholic League's goals and attempted to move readers to assist in the League's endeavours. The fact that a second French translation exists, published in short order after the first, indicates a specific reason for its publication: to better suit the needs of the League. In the ever-changing political and religious climate of late sixteenth century France, this second translation (the translation itself, with its novel prologue and differences in wording) served to better reflect the needs of the Catholic League at the time.

---

32   *Le Théâtre des cruautés de Richard Verstegan*, pp. 39–40.

CHAPTER 16

Meditative Emblems in the Polish-Lithuanian Commonwealth (1570–1775)

Alicja Bielak

This paper presents meditative emblem books as a segment of Catholic book production in the Polish-Lithuanian Commonwealth of the seventeenth and eighteenth century. Like Protestant catechisms, these emblem books were intended to propagate a certain kind of spirituality. Approximately fifty such books have been identified during this research. They were written between c.1570 and 1780; that is, from when the *Symbolica vitae Christi meditatio* (Symbolic meditation on the life of Christ) was designed by Tomasz Treter (first draft between 1569–1575; printed in 1612) to the publication of the last known edition of *Hebdomada sancta* (Holy week) by the Jesuit Świętosław Zygmunt Niwicki (1775). The books in question were published in the Polish-Lithuanian Commonwealth, with exception of two works printed in Augsburg and Naples. The first of these was a translation into German of *Hebdomada sancta* (see Table 16.1, no. 40, 41) by Niwicki, while the second was written by a Polish Dominican, Wojciech Margoński, who was active in Italy. I based my selection on the fundamental bibliography by Paulina Buchwald-Pelcowa and complemented this with my own archival findings.[1] I have included illustrated rosaries because they fulfil the requirements of both meditative and emblematic literature.[2]

In my research, I focused on texts written primarily in Polish and Latin (by authors who identified themselves as Poles or Lithuanians) and on the circulation of these texts in print. Therefore, I have excluded publications from Silesia and Pomerania. My research has yielded over twenty hand-crafted books with pasted or sewn-in engravings and handwritten prayers or meditations, all

---

1 Paulina Buchwald-Pelcowa, *Emblematy w drukach polskich i Polski dotyczących XVI–XVIII wieku. Bibliografia* (Wrocław: Ossolineum, 1981).
2 On the emblematic nature of these rosaries see Anna Paulina Pawłowska, 'Emblematyczność w polskich drukach różańcowych w pierwszej połowie XVII wieku', *Terminus*, 14 (2012), pp. 137–156. The several editions of anonymous work *Ogród różany, abo opisanie porządne dwu szczepow wonney Rożej Hierychuntskiey* and *Sposób mówienia psałterzyka Panny Maryjej abo różanki* by Walerian Litwanides, OP (or Litwinkowic, wrongly: Adrianowicz, Andrzejowicz, 1574–1635) (absent in Buchwald-Pelcowa's bibliography), see Table 16.1.

created in cloisters in the seventeenth and eighteenth centuries. This handiwork practice confirms the recognition of the relationship between meditation and emblems by contemporary audiences.

I excluded manuscripts from my analysis, with two notable exceptions (Table 16.1, no. 1 and 30) because they were drafts of future publications. The first, a sketch of *Symbolica vitae Christi meditatio* by Treter, marks the first known attempt towards meditative (and religious in general) emblems in Polish literature. The collection awaited publication until 1612, but it began to take shape in 1569, just six years after the publication of the first ever religious emblem book by Georgette de Montenay. Treter's collection contains seventy-eight sketched emblems (both icons and subscriptions), from which fifty-one were published in 1612.[3] The second manuscript is a collection of nude emblems (without icons) praising Mary by the Carmelite, Sebastianus a Matre Dei (Stanisław Rulcz). The manuscript was accepted for publication by the Prior General of the Carmelite Order, Domenico della Trinità, on 19 May 1662, but for unknown reasons it never reached the press.[4]

As many as seventy-two percent of the publications analysed were composed by Catholic clerics, of which almost forty percent were Jesuits. The Dominicans were the next most highly represented religious order, with four authors (Walerian Litwanides, Wojciech Margoński, Hiacynkt Sierakowski, anonymous author of *Sposób mówienia psałterzyka*) and nineteen editions of illustrated rosaries (36 percent of all listed editions). The following orders had one or two representatives each: Carmelites (Sebastianus a Matre Dei), Paulites (Ambroży Nieszporkowic, Augustyn Bentkowicz as translator), Benedictines (Bonifacio Pfaffenzeller as translator.) Only two editions of emblematic meditations by Jan Gerhard can be classified as Protestant works. Their author and Aaron Bliwernica (minister to the Polish-speaking community in Toruń), their translator, were both Lutherans. Thus, Lutheran writings constituted only four percent of all listed editions.[5] Most of the handcrafted books of the meditative

---

3 About the first draft of *Symbolica vitae Christi meditatio* held now in Biblioteca Civica Angelo Mai in Bergamo (Italy) see Alicja Bielak, 'Nowo odnaleziony autograf Tomasza Tretera. Notatnik z projektem księgi emblematów', *Terminus*, 3 (2021), pp. 259–307.
4 See Edward Ozorowski, 'Sebastian od Matki Bożej (Sebastianus a Matre Dei) (XVII w.) karmelita bosy', in Hieronim Wyczawski (ed.), *Słownik polskich teologów katolickich* (vol. 1–4, Warsaw: Akademia Teologii Katolickiej, 1983); Valentino Macca, 'L'immacolata e la congregazione d'Italia dei Carmeliti Scalzi', *Ephemerides Carmeliticae*, 7.1 (1956), pp. 46–50; W. Pawlak, '*Firmamentum symbolicum* Sebastiana od Matki Bożej', in idem, *Respublica litteraria pisarzy nowołacińskich XVI–XVII wieku. Studia i szkice*, Lublin 2022, p. 211–260.
5 Johannes Gerhard, *Rozmyślania nabożne*, transl. Aaron Bliwernica (Toruń: Christian Bek, 1682), USTC 1793021. A year later, another edition came out, considered by Paulina Buchwald-Pelcowa to be the same as the previous one, but with a changed title page: See Buchwald-Pelcowa,

emblems mentioned above were authored by Catholics, which demonstrates their dominance over these kind of writings in Poland.[6]

Significantly, lay priests (Tomasz Treter, Paweł Mirowski, Stanisław Grochowski) and noblemen (Mikołaj Krzysztof Chalecki, Aleksander Teodor Lacki, Adrian Wieszczycki, Jan Kościesza Żaba) were among the authors and writers of this type of literature, indicating the popularity of the genre among the laity. This was certainly related to devotional practices, popularised mainly by Jesuits and Dominicans among the nobility, and the socio-political dimension of patronage, which engaged elites in religious life through foundations, the erection of court chapels, financial support for religious orders, participation in religious confraternities and pilgrimages.[7]

The involvement of the Dominicans in promoting religious emblems needs to be commented on. This study emphasises the role of the Jesuits and, more broadly, the popularisation of post-Tridentine piety among the laity. The St Dominic order, for example, was linked with a pre-Reformation devotion that centred around Mary. Monastic rosary confraternities were established in Poland in the fifteenth century, and from 1629 each convent was expected to conduct public rosary devotions (in the beginning three times a week, then on daily basis). These reforms increased the demand for publications that facilitated the recitation of the rosary. As such, meditative books became part of a broader trend of the Catholic Reformation that aimed to internalise Catholic orthodoxy.[8]

Descriptions of *emblemata sacra* as a genre or any recommendations on how to create such descriptions are absent from the compendia of rhetoric from the era. Only a brief remark can be found in *L'art des emblèmes* (1662) by

---

Emblematy w drukach polskich, p. 90. On the use of emblems in Protestant books with meditations: See Peter C. Erb, 'Emblems in Some German Protestant Books of Meditation. Implications for the Index Emblematicus', in Peter M. Daly (ed.), *The European Emblem. Towards an Index Emblematicus* (Waterloo, Ontario: Wilfrid Laurier University Press, 1980); Karel Porteman, 'Cat's concept of the emblem and the role of occasional meditation', in *Emblematica*, 6 (1992), pp. 70–82.

6 Some of them had been already edited. See Radosław Grześkowiak etc. (eds.), *Karmelitańskie adaptacje Pia Desideria Hermana Hugona z XVII i XVIII w.* (Warsaw: Neriton, 2021); Radosław Grześkowiak, Jakub Niedźwiedź (eds.), Mikołaj Mieleszko, *Emblemata* (Warsaw: Neriton, 2010).

7 Alina Nowicka-Jeżowa, 'Pokolenia trydenckie między tradycją a wyzwaniami przyszłości', in Justyna Dąbkowska-Kujko (ed.), *Formowanie kultury katolickiej w dobie potrydenckiej. Powszechność i narodowość katolicyzmu polskiego* (Warsaw: Wydawnictwa Uniwersytetu Warszawskiego, 2016), pp. 21–102.

8 Piotr Stolarski, *Friars on the Frontier. Catholic Renewal and the Dominican Order in Southeastern Poland, 1594–1648* (Farnham: Ashgate, 2010), pp. 137–169.

Claude-François Ménestrier, who distinguished the group of *emblemata sacra* within emblematics. He pointed to *Pia desideria* by Hermann Hugo, a Flemish Jesuit and poet, and to 'seventeen emblems of the heart' (i.e. *Cor Iesu Amanti Sacrum* by Hieronymus Wierix) as examples of this phenomenon. The French theoretician stated that 'the entire Mystical Life is agreeably represented in these emblems'.[9] Therefore, it is impossible to apply to *emblemata sacra* the genetic theory usually implemented in literary studies, and any mechanisms or common features must be deduced form the works themselves or from their prefaces. It is clear, however, that not all religious emblem collections were arranged according to meditative structure, nor were they characterised by meditative content. For example, although there exists a large group of emblematic pseudo-biographies of saints, their purpose was commemorative and laudatory rather than devotional.[10]

In this chapter, I examine religious emblems that consist of a graphic component and a meditation in verse or prose in the subscription (prosaic subscriptions were more common). More precise criteria for the genre are impossible to establish because they would have to be disregarded too often. Even though many non-illustrated meditations were surely written as commentaries on existing emblems, they are not easy to identify; as such, they will serve only

---

9   Claude-François Menestrier, *L'art des emblèmes* (Leon: Benoist Coral, 1662), USTC 6156746, ff. C1v–C2r. Translation after: Ralph Dekoninck etc., 'Catalogue of the Exhibition', in *Emblemata Sacra. Emblem Books from Maurits Sabbe Library Katholieke Universiteit Leuven* (Philadelphia: Saint Joseph Press, 2006), p. 41 (more on the sacred emblems see Ibid. 14–50). In the titles of emblematic collections and in the prefaces to them, the term *emblema sacra* began to appear, such as: Andrew Willet's *Sacrorum emblematum centuria una* (Cambridge: John Legate, 1592), USTC 512287; Daniel Cramer's *Emblemata sacra* (Frankfurt: Sumptibus Lucae Jennisi, 1622), USTC 2110481; and Guillelmus Hesius', *Emblemata sacra de fide, spe, charitate* (Antwerp: Balthasar Moretus, 1636), USTC 1003217.

10   Eg. Jan Sebastian Piskorski, *Flores vitae b[eatae] Salomeae* (Krakow: Typis Universitatis, 1691), USTC 1793022; Paulo Zetel, *Philosophia sacra, sive vita divi Stanislai Kostka, Soc. Jesu, positionibus moralibus et philosophicis illustrata* (Dilingen: Joannes Mauritius Korner, 1715). In both cases mentioned, each illustration depicting an episode from a saint's life also includes an hieroglyphical symbol that comments on the scene. Mario Praz pointed it out as an error that the illustrated lives of saints are labelled as emblematic collections in many catalogues when in fact they are not, e.g. *Vita Beati Patris Ignatii Loiolae Societatis Jesu fundatoris* (Rome: s.n., 1610), USTC 1506737. At the same time, he noted that in some cases this type of classification was motivated by the title of the work, e.g. *S. Francisci Vitae et miraculorum epitome emblematis et carmine expressa* (Antwerp: Ioannes Galleus, 1632); *Emblêmes sacrés sur la vie, et miracles de Sainct François. Expliquez en vers françois* (Paris: Jean Messager, 1637); or *Idea vitae teresianae iconibus symbolicis expressa* (Antwerp: s.n., s.a.), USTC 17930343, by Hubert a S. Joanne Babtista. See Mario Praz, *Studies in Seventeenth-Century Imagery* (Rome: Edizioni di Storia e Letteratura, 2007), p. 326.

as context in this chapter.[11] Some exceptions have been included in the list of meditative emblems (see Table 16.1), such as collections lacking a graphic element (*emblemata nuda*). These cases are: translations and adaptations of Herman Hugo's *Pia desideria* by Aleksander Teodor Lacki, Stanisław Skibicki and Jan Kościesza Żaba (no. 37, 49, 50) and of Jan David's *Paradisus sponsi et sponsae* by Stanisław Grochowski (no. 2 and 6); works that were explicitly called emblems but were published without engravings for financial reasons; and works that had engravings in at least one edition (e.g. no. 37–39, 42, 50–51).

Apart from the presence of a graphic element, the key to selection was the meditative purpose and structure of the emblem books. In this study, I regard meditation as a devotional practice often supported by texts (also called meditations) that engaged the imagination, emotions, reason and will to enhance the spiritual development of the *meditans*. Such texts were formative, and artistic principles were not crucial in their production (e.g. redundancy in both content and stylistic elements helped readers to focus on the topic and memorise it). Therefore, early modern meditation itself cannot be defined and analysed as a literary genre, but rather as a method of prayer or thinking directed at moving epistemic powers to refashion the inner-self.[12] The most influential in combining emblematic and meditative traditions was the Ignatian method of meditation.

The meditative purpose of the works analysed in this paper was frequently indicated by the authors themselves, who gave their subscriptions titles such as 'reflexions' (*refleksyje*), 'pious considerations' (*piae cogitationes*) or, more often, described the books as collections of 'meditations' (*rozmyślania*).[13] In

---

11   In Table 16.1, I have included translations of emblem collections (no. 45, 46), works that are explicitly called emblems but which do not have engravings for financial reasons (no. 48) and works that had engravings in former editions (no. 35–37, 40, 48–49).

12   Louis L. Martz, *The Poetry of Meditation* (New Haven–London: Yale University Press, 1962), pp. 13–15; Marc Fumaroli, *L'école du silence. Le sentiment des images au XVII*^{e} *siècle* (Paris: Flammarion, 1988); Pierre Hadot, *The Inner Citadel. The Meditations of Marcus Aurelius* (Cambridge, Mass.: Harvard University Press, 2001).

13   See Karol Piotr Sawicki, *Prawdziwe zwierciadło niewinności* (Krakow: Jakub Matyaszkiewicz, 1725), pp. 3, 11, 19, 27, 35; Ambroży Nieszporkowic, *Officina emblematum quae praecipuos Virgis [et] Matris dei Mariae titulos [et] elogia complectuntur* (Krakow: Jerzy & Mikołaj Schedel, 1680), USTC 1793023, f.)(2r.; for example the preface in *Sposób mówienia psałterzyka Panny Maryjej abo różanki ostatni raz dostateczniej opisany i poprawiony* (Krakow: Marcin Horteryn, 1617), USTC 258252, f. A1v: 'Umyśliłem … sposób uczynku zacnego, a iż tak rzekę, chrześcijańskiego mówienia wianka różanego Matki Syna Bożego Panny Maryi z rozmyślaniem tajemnic i z niektórymi modlitwami króciuchno wydać' ('I have decided to publish … a method for a good deed, so to speak, the Christian performance of the Rose Wreath of the Mother of the Son of God, Our Lady Mary, with meditation on the mysteries and certain prayers in brief').

some instances, a text's meditative purpose was only discovered during its analysis, thanks to the presence of fragments regarding *compositio loci*, which was typical for Ignatian meditation, or fragments devoted to the stimulation of the reader's epistemic powers to examine their conscience or follow the virtuous role models depicted in the engravings.

The most popular theme of meditative emblem books in Europe was the love between the Soul and Amor Divinus (sometimes depicted as Christ himself) and cordial emblems.[14] Polish-Lithuanian emblem production often exhibited the strong influence of Marian devotion. For example, the works of Mikołaj Krzysztof Chalecki (analysed below) and Sebastianus a Matre Dei (Table 16.1, no. 27, 30, 41) are collections of meditative emblems dedicated to the Virgin Mary, which focus on the symbolic interpretations of Marian symbols. Rosary emblems propagated by the Dominicans form a separate but associated group. The Passion and other Christological themes are also present in a large number of emblem collections (Hińcza, 19–20, 23; Mirowski, 30; Niwicki, 39–41, 44, 52–53). The works of Hińcza, who based his *Chwała z Krzyża* (Glory of the cross) on the *Regia via crucis* by Benedictus van Haeften, exhibits a special interest in the symbol of the cross (i.e. inspirations are evident in emblematic icons made by an anonymous Polish engraver). Finally, examples of parenetic literature that fit into the *speculum* genres were also present (Karol Sawicki recommended meditating on the life of Aloysius Gonzaga, table 16.1, no. 45–56).

During the Reformation, prayer books became a subject of controversy and a tool of confessional warfare.[15] While humanistic emblematic literature was considered non-confessional, in the Polish-Lithuanian Commonwealth meditative emblems sought to convey confessional content and teach confessional orthodoxy.[16] This is not surprising given that the first religious emblem book, *Emblèmes ou devises chrestiennes* (1567) by Georgette de Montenay, marked the beginning of the exploitation of the genre for religious propaganda. Both de Montenay (as the author of the subscriptions) and Pierre Woieriot (the engraver) used emblems to allude to Lyon's political and religious situation in

---

14   Dekoninck etc., *Catalogue of the Exhibition*, pp. 41–54.
15   Maximilian von Habsburg, *Catholic and Protestant Translations of the Imitatio Christi, 1425–1650. From Late Medieval Classic to Early Modern Bestseller* (Farnham: Ashgate, 2011), pp. 145–148; Scott H. Hendrix, *Early Protestant Spirituality* (New York: Paulist Press, 2009), p. 201; Kao Chaoluan, *Reformation of Prayerbooks. The Humanist Transformation of Early Modern Piety in Germany and England* (Göttingen: Vandenhoeck & Ruprecht, 2018), pp. 50–55.
16   Arnoud Visser, 'Escaping the Reformation in the Republic of Letters. Confessional Silence in Latin Emblem Books' in *Church History and Religious Culture*, 88.2 (2008), pp. 139–167.

the 1560s and 1570s, when the Reformation established itself in France after the Colloque de Poissy of 1561. Biblical quotations and supra-confessional symbols and motives gained a confessional dimension (e.g. a building depicted by Woeiriot in Emblem 43, *Multi sunt vocati*, has been identified as the old Paradise Temple of Lyon where Protestants gathered between 1564 and 1567).[17]

I focus on illustrated meditative books for two reasons: their persuasive potential and, in consequence, their role as a tool of religious formation. The end of the sixteenth century and the religious crisis associated with the Reformation greatly popularised meditation, reflecting processes of individualisation and internalisation.[18] This context is indispensable for understanding meditative emblems as books for religious formation that propagated the monastic practice of meditation among laypeople.

1 Meditative Emblems as Tools of Formation

The Society of Jesus famously used emblems both as artistic and persuasive means of communication. This started with the success of Jerónimo Nadal's *Adnotationes et meditationes in Evangelia* (1595). While initially meant for the youngest students of Jesuit colleges, it quickly became a bestseller and began to be used during extracontinental missions to help overcome language barriers.[19] Missionaries explained each fragment of the engraving according to Nadal's recommendations, using his short inscriptions marked with corresponding letters. Further, the book's visual attractiveness encouraged readers to purchase and peruse it. The Jesuits cared greatly about the execution of illustrations in their books, employing superior artists and printers.[20] The most popular meditative emblems had their engravings executed by professional engravers, such as those who collaborated with the famous Plantin-Moretus

---

17   Alison Adams, *Webs of Allusion. French Protestant Emblem Books of the Sixteenth Century* (Geneva: Droz, 2003), pp. 9–118; Pascal Joudrier, *Un 'miroir' calviniste les emblèmes, ou devises chrestiennes de Georgette de Montenay et Pierre Woeiriot 1567/1571* (Geneva: Droz, 2021), pp. 54–80.

18   Klára Erdei, 'Méditation et culpabilasation. Une spiritualité du péché', in *Méditation en prose à la Renaissance* (Paris: Presses de l'École normale supérieure, 1990), pp. 19–27.

19   See Nicolas Standaert, 'Ignatian Visual Meditation in Seventeenth-Century China', in Halvor Eifring (ed.), *Meditation and Culture. The Interplay of Practice and Context* (London: Bloomsbury, 2015), pp. 24–26.

20   Dirk Imhof, 'An Author's Wishes Versus a Publisher's Possibilities. The Illustration of Thomas Sailly's Prayer Books Printed by the Plantin Press in Antwerp c.1600', in Feike Dietz etc. (eds.), *Illustrated Religious Texts in the North of Europe, 1500–1800* (Aldershot: Routledge, 2014), pp. 205–220.

printing house, which merited the highest acclaim for its illustrations among European printing centres of the time.[21] The missionary Matteo Ricci wrote in a letter from the Chinese province of Fujian that Nadal's book 'is of even greater use than the Bible, in the sense that while we are in the middle of talking we can also place right in front of their eyes things that with words alone we would not have been able to make clear'.[22]

As early as the mid-sixteenth century, when the effectiveness of preaching and catechesis in rural Catholic countries or areas invaded by 'heretics' was noticed, these regions began to be referred to as 'nostra India' (our Indies) or 'las otras Indias' (other Indies). In his *Rhetorica cristiana* (1579), Diego de Valades advised that recommendations arising from the Indian experience should be used by all preachers. In the late sixteenth century, it was decided that several missions should be established in all Jesuit provinces. Moreover, in 1647, it was established that each province must have its own prefect, not only the non-European ones. The goal of the mission set by the Jesuit General Claudio Acquaviva was to fight ignorance in theological matters, which was also spreading in Europe.[23] This way, engravings and engraved books, which had proven so successful in teaching on transcontinental assignments, became an important persuasive missionary tool also in European and Christian states.

Because Jesuits ran most schools in the Polish-Lithuanian Commonwealth, their students were trained to create emblems and were well-acquainted with their purposes.[24] This educational type of emblem was celebratory: the students were expected to laud their patrons and sponsors and commemorate a bishop's ordination. The Jesuit Mikołaj Mieleszko, the first translator of Herman Hugo's emblematic collection *Pia desideria* into Polish, attributed the success of the publication to the addition of emblems. He believed that thinking in images was highly effective: 'What satisfies the eye enters the mind more

---

21 Among the engravers involved with the Plantiniana and collaborating with the Jesuits, one should mention: Boëtius à Bolswert, Théodore Galle, Marten de Vos, Jan and Hieronymus Wierix. See Karen L. Bowen, Dirk Imhof, 'Reputation and Wage. The Case of Engravers Who Worked for the Plantin-Moretus Press', *Simiolus*, 30.3/4 (2003), pp. 161–195.

22 Standaert, *Ignatian Visual Meditation*, pp. 24–26 (fn. 8).

23 See Adriano Prosperi, '"Otras Indias": Missionari della controriforma tra contadini e selvaggi', in *Scienze, credenze occulte, livelli di cultura* (Firenze: L.S. Olschki Editore), pp. 205–234; idem, 'The Missionary', in Rosario Villari (ed.), *Baroque Personae* (Chicago: University of Chicago Press, 1995), pp. 178–181.

24 Barbara Milewska-Waźbińska, 'The Literary Heritage of Jesuits of the Polish-Lithuanian Commonwealth', *Journal of Jesuit Studies*, 5 (2018), pp. 421–440.

swiftly'.[25] A similar belief was expressed by Fabian Birkowski (1566–1636), a preacher on the court of King Władysław IV of Poland, in his famous sermon *O świętych obrazach, jako mają być szanowane* (On holy images and how they should be respected):

> When a simpleton sees the story of Christ's birth or an image of another mystery of salvation, it acts as both his teacher and his book; and the lively representation will teach and move him more than the preacher's words.[26]

Now popular in Catholic circles, emblematic works broke down confessional barriers and also reached Protestant artists and readers across Europe. The emblems by Francis Quarles, for example, who drew from Herman Hugo's works (*Pia desideria* and *Typus mundi*), followed the tradition of Protestant meditation formulated by Joseph Hall (*Arte of divine meditation*, 1606).[27] According to Calvinist philosopher Théodore de Bèze, emblems are desirable when they illustrate pious things worth meditation.[28]

The publishing boom for meditative emblems may also have influenced the rising popularity of meditation among laypeople. In the case of Jesuit meditation, faith in the power of images transcended the didacticism of *Biblia*

---

25   Mieleszko, *Emblemata*, p. 76: 'Prędzej bowiem do rozumu wchodzi, czego się i samo oko do woli napatrzy'. The text remained in manuscript until the 2010s.

26   Fabian Birkowski, 'O świętych obrazach, jako mają być szanowane kazanie', in idem, *Głos krwie b. Jozafata Kunczewica ... kazania czworo* (Krakow: Andrzej Piotrkowczyk, 1629), USTC 258416, p. 72: 'Bo gdy prostaczek obaczy historyją Narodzenia Pańskiego abo innej tajemnice odkupienia malowanie, to stoi mu za doktora i za księgę i ta reprezentacyja żywa więcej go drugdy uczy i wzrusza aniż słowa kaznodziejskie'. After: Pawłowska, 'Emblematyczność w polskich drukach różańcowych', p. 154.

27   Höltgen, *Emblem and Meditation*, p. 58.

28   Théodore Beze, *Icones, id est verae imagines virorum doctrina simul et pietate illustrium* (Geneva: Johannes Laon, 1580), USTC 450822, f. *3r. William E. Engel, 'Mnemonic Emblems and the Humanist Discourse of Knowledge', in Peter Daly etc. (eds.), *Aspects of Renaissance and Baroque Symbol Theory, 1500–1700* (New York: AMS Press, 1999), pp. 128–129. About Protestant emblem books, see Adams, *Webs of Allusion*; Julie Barr, 'I Am the Light of the World. Light as a Motif in Protestant and French Emblems', in Ralph Dekoninck etc. (eds.), *Emblemata sacra. Rhétorique et herméneutique du discours sacré dans la littérature en images* (Turnhout: Brepols, 2007), pp. 465–481; Huston Diehl, 'Graven Images. Protestant Emblem Books in England', *Renaissance Quarterly*, 39 (1986), pp. 49–64; Sabine Mödersheim, *'Domini doctrina coronat'. Die geistliche Emblematik Daniel Cramers (1568–1637)* (Bern: Peter Lang, 1994); Dietmar Peil, *Zur »angewandten Emblematik« in protestantischen Erbauungsbüchern. Dilherr – Arndt – Francisci – Scriver* (Heidelberg: Carl Winter Universitatsverlag, 1978).

pauperum and the like, entering the domain of psychology and epistemology. Philosophical treatises employed the metaphor of fine arts to explain human epistemological mechanism. When writing about cognition and the mental images generated during meditation, Spanish Jesuit philosopher and reviver of scholastics Francisco Suárez used a metaphor of painting: the soul learns of things in imaginations, and then through spiritual power, taking the imagination as an exemplar, reproduces or literally 'depicts' (*depingit*) the thing in the intellect.[29] Thus, *meditans*, like the painter, should paint the meditated scene in their soul with all possible details. Vivid, sensory literary imagery was intended to move the intellect, the memory and, ultimately, the affects and the will.

According to European devotion, *enargeia* was an instrument for evoking the inner reality (accessible only to the interior sight) and the epistemic principle of internal, religious practices. A telling example of connecting the imagination with the process of painting can be found in eighteenth-century handwritten meditations dedicated to a 'female *meditans*' (*Dla rekoletki*), who was advised to 'see through imagination the Lucifer much scarier and uglier than the one [she] saw in paintings'.[30] What is distinctive about Ignatius Loyola's method is that *compositio loci* and *applicatio sensuum* were designed to move all five traditionally recognised senses simultaneously. The first principle, which preceded every meditation, focused on sight. Using memory and imagination, the *meditans* was to create in his or her mind the scenery of the meditated situation or concept. The second principle referred to all human cognitive powers (*quinque imaginarios sensus*) to create the illusion of physical participation in the contemplated events.[31]

From its beginnings, meditation was intended as an individual practice that could be conducted outside the church, thus it became an ideal tool for

---

29 Francisco Suárez, *Commentaria una cum quaestionibus in libros Aristotelis 'De anima',* 3, [*d. 8–d. 14*], ed. Salvador Castellote, transl. C. Baciero, L. Baciero (Madrid: 1991), p. 96.

30 Biblioteka Diecezjalna w Sandomierzu A 189, [Rekolekcje], [Sandomierz? 18th century], pp. 110–111 (*punctum* 1): 'Obacz przez imaginacyją Lucypera, daleko bardziej, niżeś go kiedy malowanego widziała, brzydszego i straszniejszego, ogniami w oczach, piorunami w uszach pałającego ...'.

31 Anna Kapuścińska, 'Theatrum meditationis. Ignacjanizm i jezuityzm w duchowej i literackiej kulturze I Rzeczpospolitej – źródła, inspiracje, idee', in Nowicka-Jeżowa (ed.), *Drogi duchowe katolicyzmu*, pp. 138–143. About Jesuit image theory in the context of epistemology, see especially Walter S. Melion, *The Meditative Art. Studies in the Northern Devotional Print, 1550–1625* (Philadelphia: Saint Joseph's University Press, 2010); and Ralph Dekoninck, *'Ad imaginem'. Statuts, fonctions et usages de l'image dans la littérature spirituelle jésuite du XVII*ᵉ *siècle* (Geneva: Droz, 2005); Agnès Guiderdoni, 'Meditative Images and the Psychology of Soul', in R. Falkenburg etc. (eds.), *Image and Imagination of the Religious Self in Late Medieval and Early Modern Europe* (Turnhout: Brepols Press, 2008), pp. 1–36.

purposeful spiritual direction.[32] In the second half of the sixteenth century, it became an inter-denominational personal piety practice, with both Catholics and Protestants pursuing it.[33] Still, the Jesuits popularised it among laypeople as a reaction to a religious crisis.

As argued by Louis L. Martz, seventeenth-century meditation was very close to mystical contemplation, in which the contemplative would feel that he or she knew God and could receive messages from the transcendental world. At the same time, it was more practical and accessible than the mystical experience because it was a method (that is, it could be trained) of a deliberate, 'diligent and forcible application of the understanding, to seeke, and knowe' with the aim to exercise virtue and avoid sin in daily life.[34] However, the mystical potential of meditative images worried some Protestants because they were not subject to supervision.[35] 'Imaginative meditation' also turned out to be problematic for the Jesuits; they began to face accusations of being *alumbrados* who were popularising mystical illumination with the spread of the meditative formula.[36] For example, Piotr Skarga (1536–1612), a member of the first generation of Jesuits and a leading representative of Catholic Reformation in Poland, believed that the faithful only needed oral prayer, and that in terms of ascetic practices, only the purgative way (*via purgativa*) was available to them. His writings for laypeople did not include recommendations on meditation or any mentions of direct contact or unity with God (*via illuminativa* or *via unitiva*, respectively). Rather, Skarga focused on preaching about the communal prayer.[37]

The situation changed in the second half of the sixteenth century.[38] This shift is reflected by authors who specifically defined their intended readers in their forewords or in the titles of their meditations and piety handbooks. Examples

---

32   Ronald K. Rittgers, *The Reformation of Suffering. Pastoral Theology and Lay Piety in Late Medieval and Early Modern Germany* (Oxford: Oxford University Press, 2012).

33   Klára Erdei, *Auf dem Wege zu sich selbst: die Meditation im 16. Jahrhundert. Eine Funktionsanalytische Gattungsbeschreibung* (Wiesbaden: Harrassowitz, 1990), pp. 1–64.

34   Vincenzo Bruno, *An Abridgment of Meditations of the Life, Passion, Death, and Resurrection of Our Lord and Saviour Jesus Christ*, transl. Richard Gibbons (St. Omer: s.n., 1614), USTC 3006328, quote after: Martz, *The Poetry of Meditation*, p. 14; see also pp. 16–20.

35   David Freedberg, *The Power of Images. Studies In The History And Theory Of Response* (Chicago-London: The University of Chicago Press, 1989), p. 187–188; James Simpson, 'The Rule of Medieval Imagination', in Jeremy Dimmick etc. (eds.), *Images, Idolatry, and Iconoclasm. Textuality and the Visual Image* (Oxford: Oxford University Press, 2002), p. 11.

36   Wietse de Boer, 'The Early Jesuits and the Catholic Debate about Sacred Images', in Wietse de Boer etc. (eds.), *Jesuit Image Theory* (Leiden: Brill, 2016), pp. 65–68.

37   Konrad Górski, *Od religijności do mistyki. Zarys dziejów życia wewnętrznego w Polsce*, vol. 1, 966–1795 (Lublin: Towarzystwo Naukowe KUL, 1962), p. 124.

38   Ewa Poprawa-Kaczyńska, 'Ignacjański "modus meditandi" w kulturze religijnej późnego baroku', in Czesław Hernas etc. (eds.), *Religijność literatury polskiego baroku* (Lublin: Towarzystwo Naukowe Katolickiego Uniwersytetu Lubelskiego, 1995), p. 68.

include *Łatwy sposób rozmyślania dla panów* (An easy way of meditating for noblemen) by Jesuit Mikołaj Łęczycki, and *Akademia pobożności z przydatkiem nie tylko zakonnym osobom do doskonałości potrzebna* (The academy of piety which is needed for perfection not only by monastic persons) by influential Polish Dominican reformer, Mikołaj Mościcki (1559–1632).[39] Nevertheless, concerns about the possibility of the faithful going beyond dogma were valid. This factor likely contributed to the fact that the Jesuits increasingly included in their books a theoretical framework to guide the meditation process, as well as engravings that provided the reader with ready-made imagery to keep his or her imagination in check.[40]

Illustrated meditations attempted to explain dogmatics and teach meditative life and the specificity of Jesuit piety to a broader audience.[41] Such inclusive references to the public can be found in the book subtitles and forewords to meditative emblems:

> It is not only the duty of monastic people, but also all Christians to spread the glory of dear God; (Anonymous, 1636)[42]

> not only spiritual people, but all the estates of Christ's tireless realm may find broad, holy and salvific lessons here. Anyone can safely … open it even thrice daily. (Paweł Mirowski, 1656)[43]

While collections in Latin were more often addressed to men (due to women's limited opportunities to learn Latin), collections written in Polish were often intended for female readers. For example, Niwicki's 1692 Latin edition of *Hebdomada sancta* was dedicated to Wojciech Konstantyn Breza, but the

---

39   Mikołaj Łęczycki, *Łatwy sposób rozmyślania dla panów, zebrany z książek wielebnego księdza Mikołaja Lancicego SJ* (Lublin: Drukarnia Societatis Iesu, 1751); Mikołaj Mościcki, *Akademia pobożności z przydatkiem nie tylko zakonnym osobom do doskonałości potrzebna* (Krakow: Walerian Piątkowski, 1628), USTC 258380.

40   Ralph Dekoninck, 'Jesuit Emblematics between Theory and Practice', in *Jesuit Historiography Online*, http://dx.doi.org/10.1163/2468-7723_jho_COM_192540 (first published online: 2016, access: 5 January 2022); Joseph de Guibert, *The Jesuits, their Spiritual Doctrine and Practice. A Historical Study*, transl. William J. Young (St Louis, Missouri: The Institute of Jesuit Studies, 1986), pp. 298–299, 304–305.

41   Jeffrey Chipps Smith, *Sensuous Worship. Jesuits and the Art of the Early Catholic Reformation in Germany* (Princeton-Oxford: Princeton University Press, 2002), pp. 23–7, 40–52.

42   *Sposób mówienia psałterzyka*, p. A₁v: 'Gdyż nie tylko ludzi zakonnych, ale i chrześcijańskich powinność ta jest, aby oni chwałę miłego Boga krzewili'.

43   Paweł Mirowski, *Młotek duchowny w sercach ludzkich tor Chrystusów drelujący* (Gdańsk: Friedrich David Rhete, 1656), USTC 1793035, f. [ ]2r–v: 'Mają tu nie tylko duchowni, ale i wszytkie stany pracowitego toru Chrystusowego dość szeroką, świątobliwą a zbawienną naukę … Może tej beśpiecznie kożdy … i po trzykroć na dzień otwierać'.

Polish version from the same year was devoted to his wife, Teresa Konstancja of Bnin neé Opalińska (1645–1703). Another vernacular version (1758) was also dedicated to a noblewoman, Helena Ogińska (1700–1790). Women's ownership of such literature is indicated by inventories, manuscript provenances and dedications.[44] Interestingly, vernacularisation impacted both the language used and the topics explored in these texts directed at female readers. The authors referred to their female readers' maternal love for their children, reminding them that they could empathise with Mary and to imagine what a mother watching her own child die would have felt. They even included feminine gender forms. In *Prawdziwe zwierciadło niewinności* (The true mirror of innocence), for example, the Jesuit theologian Karol Sawicki criticised people who looked in the mirror instead of looking to and imitating the actions of virtuous people (by reading parenetic literature such as *specula*). According to Sawicki, they looked in the mirror to feed their own vanity:

> Scrutiny falls on those male [*spektatorów*] and female spectators [*spektatorki*] and their eyes and pupils who sit all day in front of a mirror to such an extent that it is doubtful where one would find them: in the room or in the mirror?[45]

Some authors mentioned the gender of the audience even in the prefaces, encouraging women to read the book. For example, the preface of the Polish version of *Allegoriae* by Chalecki reads: 'intended for pious men and female circles ... insatiable with the love of God'.[46] Out of the forty-nine books examined in the present study, as many as eight contain a dedication to a woman protector, which constitutes over a half of all writings dedicated to laypeople (manuscripts not included).[47] Furthermore, educational literature was also ordered by women. For example, the greatest protector of Polish Baroque religious emblems was King Jan III Sobieski's sister, Katarzyna Radziwiłł (née Sobieska), who ordered the creation of as many as five meditative emblem collections.[48]

---

44   Stanisław Siess-Krzyszkowski etc. (eds.), *Katalog księgozbioru Konstancji Sapieżyny (1697–1756)*, https://www.estreicher.uj.edu.pl/inne/sapiezyna.

45   Sawicki, *Prawdziwe zwierciadło*, f. A2r: '... cenzura pada na tych spektatorów i spektatorki, na oczy i źrzenice, co całe dni prawie w zwierciedle przesiedzą, tak że wątpliwość być może, gdzie ich szukać? Czy w pokoju, czy w zwierciedle?'.

46   Mikołaj Krzysztof Chalecki, *Allegoriae albo kwiecia modł gorących wynalezione dla unurzenia dusze w Bogu* (Vilnius: Leon Mamonicz, 1618), USTC 250434, f. A2r: 'płci nabożnej męzkiej i niewieściej gromadzie'.

47   A lot of editions do not have any dedications, for example all anonymous editions (10) of rosaries entitled *Sposób mówienia psałteryka ...* (Table 16.1, no. 2–6, 9–11, 14–15, 22).

48   Radosław Grześkowiak, Jakub Niedźwiedź, 'Introduction', in Mieleszko, *Emblematy*, pp. 62–64.

2   Confessional Disputes

The first Polish-Lithuanian meditative emblem book was *Symbolica vitae Christi meditatio* by Tomasz Treter (Treterus, 1547–1610), who studied with the Jesuits and was a secretary to a key Catholic reformer, Cardinal Stanislas Hosius (1504–1579). Treter's role, as well as the time and place of the book's creation (immediately after the Council of Trent and several years after Hosius introduced the Jesuits to Poland), likely shaped the controversial and confessional nature of the collection. Direct statements against Protestants and ecclesiological assertions on the necessity of belonging to the Catholic Church can be found within it: 'To be at peace with God means to refrain from sin and agree in all that pertains to faith and religion with the Catholic Church, which is the mystical body of Jesus Christ himself'.[49] The church is described according to distinctive adjectives in line with the Nicene-Constantinopolitan Creed as the 'one, holy, catholic church'. The word 'heretic' in turn appears twenty-nine times in total (including one instance of 'heresiarch'), and the word 'heresy' appears five times. Luther is mentioned four times as 'the antichrist of Eisleben' and 'monster, not man'; Calvin is described two times as 'the antichrist of Geneva'; and Zwingli is once called 'the antichrist of Zurich'.

The collection comprises 103 emblems arranged into pairs (at the end, there is an additional emblem: a call to the reader to imitate the virtues of Jesus shown in the collection). The emblematic icons of the first emblem in each pair depict a scene from Jesus' life, while the icons of the second emblem in the pair transfer the biblical episode into symbolic language and, following the mechanism of *imitatio Christi*, draw moral lessons out of Christ's actions. This creates a list of 51 virtues and behaviours which 'every Christian should fulfil'. The emblem *Conscientae securitas* (Security of conscience) is a call to fighting for good conscience, persisting in belief and shunning 'castaways from faith', which echoes the First Letter of Paul to Timothy (Tim 1:18–19):

> we see and lament that it happened to many heretics in our century who … through their greed are paving a wide road for their conscience from faith to infidelity; they have been transported from Christ born in Bethlehem to [an antichrist] from Eisleben or Geneva, or Zurich, or finally any other antichrist whose word they worship instead of God's and the holy Gospel.[50]

---

49   Tomasz Treter, *Symbolica vitae Christi meditatio* (Braniewo: Georg Schönfels, 1612), USTC 2055155, p. 185: 'Pacem cum Deo habere est a peccatis abstinere et in omnibus his quae ad fidem religionemque pertinent cum Ecclesia Catholica, quae corpus ipsius est mysticum, consentire et concordare'.

50   Ibid., p. [71, wrongly: 67]: 'nostro seculo multis haereticis evenisse videmus et ingemiscimus, qui dum a concupiscentia sua abstracti et illecti, largam, conscientiis suis viam

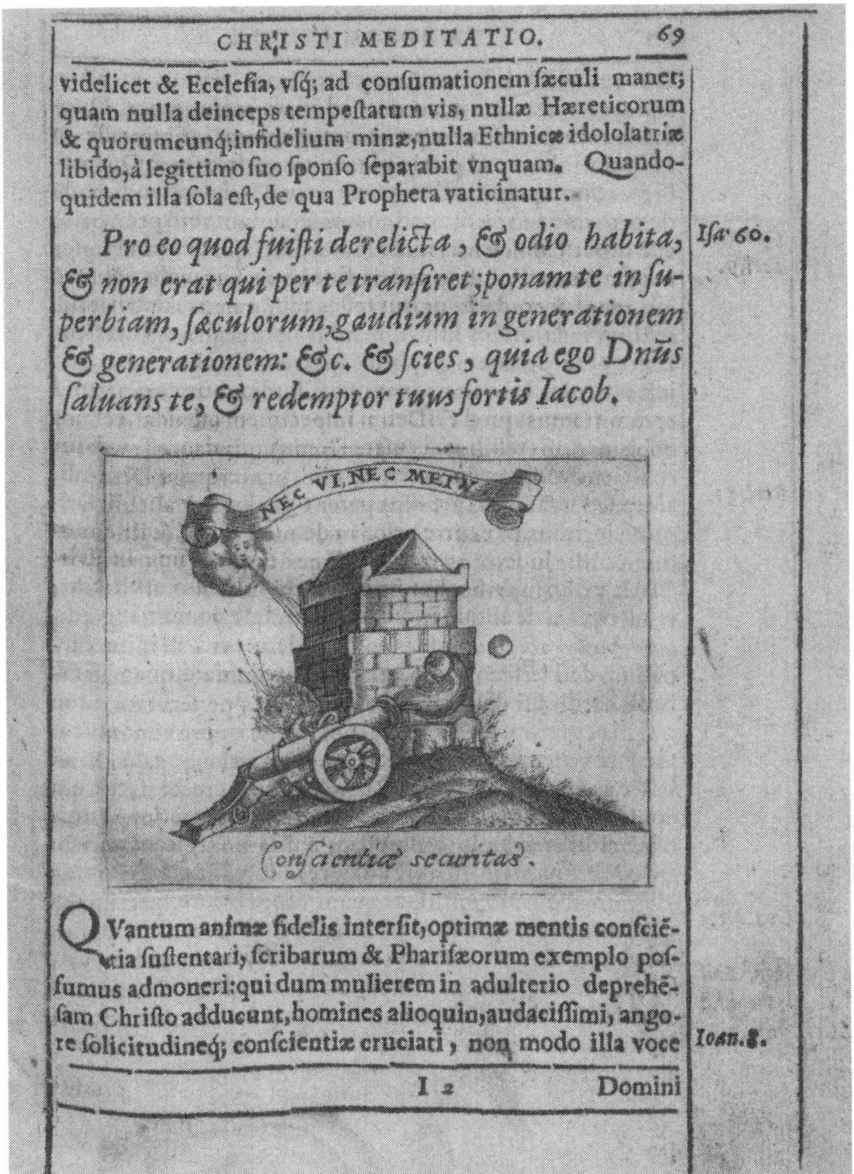
CHRISTI MEDITATIO. 69

videlicet & Eccleſia, vſq; ad conſumationem ſæculi manet; quam nulla deinceps tempeſtatum vis, nullæ Hæreticorum & quorumcunq; infidelium minæ, nulla Ethnicæ idololatriæ libido, à legittimo ſuo ſponſo ſeparabit vnquam. Quandoquidem illa ſola eſt, de qua Propheta vaticinatur.

Pro eo quod fuiſti derelicta, & odio habita, & non erat qui per te tranſiret; ponam te in ſuperbiam, ſæculorum, gaudium in generationem & generationem: &c. & ſcies, quia ego Dn̄s ſaluans te, & redemptor tuus fortis Iacob. Iſa. 60.

QVantum animæ fidelis interſit, optimæ mentis conſciẽtia ſuſtentari, ſcribarum & Phariſæorum exemplo poſſumus admoneri: qui dum mulierem in adulterio deprehẽſam Chriſto adducunt, homines alioquin, audaciſſimi, angore ſolicitudineq; conſcientiæ cruciati, non modo illa voce Ioan. 8.

I 2 Domini

FIGURE 16.1 Tomasz Treter, *Symbolica vitae Christi meditatio* (Braniewo: Georg Schönfels, 1612), p. 139. Krakow, Biblioteka Jagiellońska, 35699 I

The list alludes to Luther, Calvin and Zwingli. After condemning the covetousness of 'antichrists' who strayed into infidelity, Treter encourages his readers to hide 'in that confined chamber' depicted in the emblematic icon, 'full of the fear of God and love for Him', to self-examine in the internal 'tabernacle of the mind' (to which the subject of meditation wants to be transformed: 'let me become the jar in which Aaron placed the Manna') and atone with tears and repentance if necessary.[51]

Another emblem, *Oboedientia* (Obedience), was again addressed to the collective of the faithful and promoted obedience to two superior authorities: priests and lay rulers. Treter thought this to be a guarantee of social order. When people rebelled against any of these powers, 'chaos worse than in Babylon' ensues and Protestants are to be blamed for it:

> On these lands where we hear that [the order] was changed and reversed, where political authority has impudently appropriated what belongs to priests, there is greater disarray than in Babylon; there is no one who would see it and not lament it. This fruit of foolishness seems to be born by those who preferred to follow the impure teachings of Luther or Calvin instead of the Word of God and Christ's gospel.[52]

In the 1600s, the rhetoric of open religious battle was employed less frequently, and emblem collections were addressed to the general Christian community. The authors of such seemingly non-confessional collections referred to Christian meditative traditions from pre-Reformation times, accentuating the personal dimension of this spiritual experience of meditation. In their forewords, they distanced themselves from 'scholarly theological debates'.[53] Texts from the movement of *devotio moderna* proved especially helpful in that task. A telling example of such a manoeuvre is Paweł Mirowski's 1656 *Młotek duchowny* (The spiritual hammer), which is in fact a loose translation of Thomas à Kempis'

---

sternunt a fide ad perfidiam, a Christo in Bethleem nato, ad Islebiensem, vel Genevensem, vel Tygurinum, vel quemcunque; tandem alium Antichristum, cuius verborum pro Dei verbo et Sancto Evangelio colunt ....'

51   Ibid., p. 47: 'Utinam vas illud, in quo manna Aaron recondidit, ego efficiar'. See also ibid., p. [71, wrongly: 67]'.

52   Treter, *Symbolica vitae Christi meditatio*, p. 140: 'Caeterum in quibus eum terris commutatum et inversum audimus, dum politicus Magistratus ea quae sacerdotum propria sunt sibi ausu temerario vendicat, in iis plus quam Babylonicam rerum omnium esse confusionem, nullus est qui non videat et ingemiscat. Hunc fructum amentiae suae refere videntur illi, qui pro verbo Dei Christique Evangelio, impurum Lutherii vel Calvini dogma sequi maluerunt ....'

53   See Jakub Wujek, *O naśladowaniu Pana Chrystusa i o wzgardzie wszelakiej próżności świata tego* (Krakow: Jakub Siebeneicher, 1586), USTC 242595, f. +2r: 'No one quarrels or debates about faith here, but faithful *Christians* are guided to better their lives and consistently practice their Christian virtues'.

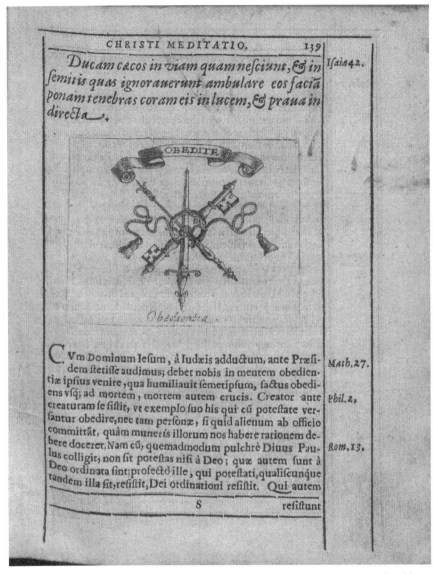

FIGURE 16.2 Tomasz Treter, *Symbolica vitae Christi meditatio* (Braniewo: Georg Schönfels, 1612), p. 69. Krakow, Biblioteka Jagiellońska, 35699 I

Imitatio Christi, with complex emblematic icons added.[54] As far back as the fifteenth century, Thomas à Kempis' work served as a devotional text intended

---

54 Agnieszka Pabian, *Symbolika rycin ilustrujących. 'Młotek duchowny w sercach ludzkich tor Chrystusowi drelujący', wydany w Gdańsku w 1656 r.*, Warsaw: Faculty of Historical and Social Sciences at Cardinal Stefan Wyszyński University in Warsaw (unpublished M.A. thesis),

for laypeople and during the Reformation it continued to be valued and recommended by all denominations. Later, Mirowski simplified the terminology in the work, supplemented it with quotations from the Church Fathers and, most importantly, made the collection more attractive by embellishing it with emblematic engravings. In his foreword to the reader, Mirowski purports to be a pious simpleton who prefers *docta ignorantia* over scientific disputes: 'Rather than showing off with your reason, pretend to be ignorant'.[55] According to him, avoiding 'philosophal [sic] disputes' is an expression of humility and stands in line with Jesus' premise from Matthew 11:25 ('thou hast hid these things from the wise and prudent, and hast revealed them to the little ones'). Mirowski glorifies the God-fearing 'humble peasant' over 'a puffed-up bladder of a philosopher who, forgetting himself, idles in the heavenly spheres'.[56] These recommendations appear as broader notions in much emblematic literature, such as *Altum sapere periculosum* (It is dangerous to be high-minded) by Anton van Schoonhoven, Flemish jurist and philologist. Van Schoonhoven openly attacked theological debates in his emblem, which represented hybris and inappropriate curiosity with the figures of Phaethon and Icarus, respectively. Predestination, free will and primal sin are discussed as the effects of interlocutors having too much time; van Schoonhoven suggests that the interlocutors should develop their faith rather than gain dubious knowledge.[57]

To avoid the confessional dimension (and its associated disputes), Mirowski wrote that Thomas à Kempis' book was a message from God himself to all Christians. In truth, Mirowski himself was highly qualified for theological disputes as a Doctor of Theology at the University of Krakow and a one-time student of the University of Padua.[58]

It should be emphasised that the book *Imitatio Christi* itself became the subject of confessional battles, which was reflected in the emergence of varying editorial traditions. Depending on the editor's denomination, the arrangement of the

---

2016; Alicja Bielak, 'The "Spiritual Hammer" (1656) as an emblematic translation of the "Imitatio Christi" by Thomas à Kempis', *Central European Cultures*, 1.2 (2021), pp. 29–58.

55   Mirowski, *Młotek duchowny*, f. [ ]7r: 'Nie wyjeżdżaj przed swaty rozumem, ale raczej pisz się nieukiem'.
56   Ibid., f. [ ]6v: 'Wolę zaprawdę pokornego chłopka przy bojaźni Bożej niż nadęty pęcherz filozofski, który samego siebie zapomniawszy, po niebieskich się obrotach wałkuni'.
57   Visser, *Escaping the Reformation*, pp. 150–152.
58   Paulus Mirovius, *Quaestio theologica, de processione Spiritus p. ex prima parte angelici Doctoris ad disputandum publice proposita* (Krakow: Franciszek Cezary, 1634), USTC 256638. See Bielak, 'The "Spiritual Hammer"', pp. 29–58.

MEDITATIVE EMBLEMS 341

FIGURE 16.3   Paweł Mirowski, *Młotek duchowny w sercach ludzkich tor Chrystusów drelujący* (Gdańsk: Friedrich David Rhete, 1656), f. T1r. Warsaw, Biblioteka Uniwersytecka, Sd.712.788

content would change: the fourth book, on the sacrament of Communion, would be included or omitted according to the denomination in question.[59] The fourth book contained the most of Mirowski's additions, starting with the text and ending with the illustration. He also added a statement to Thomas à Kempis' text (included both in the motto and the subscription to the emblem) that a mass is a heavenly feast attended by the angels and God himself. Mirowski completed the chapter with an engraving of the Paschal candle as the symbol of Christ: a light that burns out and dies while showing people the way (1 Cor. 6:17). He also added an image of the Arch of the Covenant as a predecessor of the altar alongside a high priest's hat, an incense boat and a thurible. To the left, the Archangel Gabriel holds a trial over a dog and a pig; according to the Gospel of Matthew (7:6), these symbolise those who cannot recognise holiness. Thus, besides establishing the holiness of the Catholic Eucharist, Mirowski implies that the dog and pig symbolise heretics.[60]

Another example of the legacy of confessional disputes came from the pen of a Lithuanian nobleman, Mikołaj Krzysztof Chalecki (1589–1653). Interestingly, he was only a second-generation Catholic, as his father Dymitr Chalecki (1550–1598) converted from Orthodox Christianity to Catholicism. In his *Binarius Chalecianus sive duo manipuli liliorum* (Chalecki's *binarius* or two bundles of lilies, 1641), Chalecki aimed to pay homage to the Virgin Mary and present an auspicious eschatological perspective to the reader.[61] He organised twenty-four emblems around a floral theme of the lily and divided the book into two parts (twelve emblems each): 'Lily in the abyss of God' (*Lilium in abysso Dei*) and 'Lily in the sunlight' (*Lilium in aprico*). The guide explaining the meaning of the symbols was Amor Divinus. Chalecki's praises of the Virgin Mary resembled the order of the Litany of Loreto. It is worth mentioning that to imitate the Italian Loreto, which he visited during his studies abroad, Chalecki built a Chapel of the Holiest Virgin Mary and a chapel of the Holy Cross in Valkininkai (Lithuania). What is more, research has demonstrated a structural and lexical relationship between *Binarius* and the Orthodox Christian hymn *Akathist to Holy Mary*, sung at the icon of Our Lady of the Gate of Dawn in Vilnius in the mid-1600s (and used by Unitarians, Orthodox Christians and

---

59 von Habsburg, *Catholic and Protestant Translations*, pp. 178–183.
60 Pabian, *Symbolika rycin ilustrujących. 'Młotek duchowny w sercach ludzkich tor Chrystusowi drelujący'*, pp. 15–17.
61 Jolita Liškevičienė, 'Religinė vaizduotė didiko Mikalojaus Kristupo Chaleckio kūryboje', in Jolita Liškevičienė (ed.), *Mikalojaus Kristupo Chaleckio Embleminių Meditacijų Knygos. Alegorijos (1618) ir Dvinaris (1642)* (Vilnius: Vilniaus dailės akademijos leidykla, 2020), 27 (for more biographical information see ibidem: pp. 19–31).

Roman Catholics).[62] The hymn inextricably links Christology and Mariology. The Lithuanian nobleman's work can be counted as the legacy of a series of responses by Catholics to Protestants' denials of Mary's holiness from the most tense periods of confessional disputes. Among the most important treatises in this domain are Peter Canisius's *De Maria, Virgine incomparabili et Dei Genitrice sacrosancta* (1577), in which he established the main themes of post-Tridentine Mariology and codified ways of expressing veneration for Mary, as well as Francisco Suárez's twenty-three disputations on the mysteries of the life of Christ, *De mysteriis vitae Christi* (1592).[63] As proven by Ona Daukšienė even here, in a mystical work of emblematic meditations, one can identify the echoes of the confessional conflict. *Binarius* discussed the mysteries of God and assumed that they exceeded the human capabilities of understanding. The Lithuanian noble explained this at the start, referring to Thomas Aquinas' hymn *Pange lingua*, which expresses reverent wonder over the Eucharist and contains the phrase *sola fides*. Chalecki talked about a paralysing astonishment towards the mystery of incarnation: 'Under the weight of the mystery, the senses are weakened, the mind is darkened, understanding dies, the school of angels falls silent; faith alone [*sola fides*] suffices'.[64] This demonstrates that the argument of *sola fide*, a key component of the Reformed doctrine, was ironically twisted by Chalecki to the benefit of the Catholic cause by referencing the authority of Thomas Aquinas and applicating it in a contemplative mental prayer.

3 Teaching Meditation by Training Eyes

Apart from these manifest examples of consolidating post-Tridentine piety and echoes of the confessional disputes between Catholics and Protestants, one can observe certain techniques of creating meditational and mystical reader

---

[62] Ona Dilytė-Čiurinskienė, 'Chaleckio *Dvinario* slėpiniai. Suasmenintas potridentinės mariologijos manifestas', in Jolita Liškevičienė (ed.), *Mikalojaus Kristupo Chaleckio Embleminių Meditacijų Knygos: Alegorijos (1618) ir Dvinaris (1642)* (Vilnius: Vilniaus dailės akademijos leidykla, 2020), pp. 529–531.

[63] Ona Daukšienė, 'Sola fides sufficit. Poleminiai elementai Chaleckio Dvinaryje (Binarius Chalecianus, 1642)', *Senoji Lietuvos literatūra* 4 (2018), p. 115; Ona Dilytė-Čiurinskienė, 'Chaleckio Dvinario slėpiniai Suasmenintas potridentinės mariologijos manifestas', pp. 543–551.

[64] Mikołaj Krzysztof Chalecki, *Binarius Chalecianus sive duo manipuli liliorum* (Vilnius: Officina Typographica Patrum Basilianorum, 1642), USTC 250788, f. A1v: 'A pondere mysterii sensus hebescit, ratio tenebrescit, intellectus emoritur, angelorum schola mutescit; sola fides sufficit' (see Daukšienė, 'Sola fides sufficit', pp. 121–123).

experiences. Forewords to meditative emblems reveal particular care for the audience's reading conditions. For example, the lack of leisure time among laypeople was taken into account. Writers responded by trying to encapsulate messages in fewer words. The author of *Sposób mówienia psałterzyka Panny Maryjej* justified the short descriptions of his emblematic rosary by saying that 'hard-working people' would have to skip parts of the book, saying that 'some hard-working people not only cannot read everything that others have written, but they even have to omit smaller things due to home occupations'.[65] Therefore, it is better to condense the content accompanying the engravings 'because the duty to spread the glory of good God belongs not only to monastic people, but also [all] Christians'.[66] In the first half of the seventeenth century, Polish-language rosary prayers supplemented with emblems proved extremely popular, as they were connected to rosary brotherhoods active in Poland.[67] At the same time, the Catholic clergy began accepting other forms of piety outside mass, including more individualist ones.[68] Most publications came from the circle of the Krakow Dominican convent. One Dominican, Hieronim Sierakowski, recommended his emblematic book with rosary meditations to his readers by stressing that it is a key form of piety in the Catholic Church, second only to mass.[69] Another author of rosaries and a commentator, Walerian Litwanides (1574–1635, Table 16.1, no. 15–16, 48), allowed for the presence of engravings during personal meditation and included a sample cycle in his handbook on rosaries.[70]

The educative aims of Jesuits to teach meditation to laypeople led to the publication of Polish-language meditation collections. The best examples are

---

65 *Sposób mówienia psałterzyka*, f. A1v: 'pracowite niektóre ludzie, którzy nie tylko żeby mieli tak wiele jako od drugich napisano jest czytać, ale snadź i co mniejszego przez zabawy domowe opuszczać muszą'.

66 Ibid.: 'Gdyż nie tylko ludzi zakonnych, ale i chrześcijańskich powinność ta jest, aby oni chwałę miłego Boga krzewili'.

67 On emblem rosaries cf. Pawłowska, 'Emblematyczność w polskich drukach różańcowych', pp. 137–156.

68 See Jędrzej Kitowicz, *Opis obyczajów za panowania Augusta III* (Warsaw: PIW, 1985), pp. 33–35. Rosary meditations became most popular in seventeenth century in Polish-Lithuanian Commonwealth (see Table 16.1, no. 4–5, 7–9, 12–18, 21–22, 25–26, 48).

69 Sierakowski, *Wieniec różany*, f. B1r–v. In many situations, prayer handbooks replaced the preacher as proven explicitly in the title of a work by a Jesuit, Tomasz Młodzianowski (1622–1686): *Rozmyślania albo lekcyja duchowna miasto kazania na wszystkie święta uroczystsze* [*Meditations or Spiritual Lessons Instead of Sermons for All Greater Holidays*] (Poznań: Collegium Societatis Iesu, 1699), USTC 1777921.

70 Walerian Litwanides, *Ogród różany abo Opisanie porządne dwu szczepów wonnej Różej Hierychuntskiey to jest o dwu świętych różańcach dwojga bractw Blogosla[wionej] Panny Maryjey i Naświęt[szego] Imienia P[ana] Iezusowego* (Krakow: Franciszek Cezary, 1627), USTC 258374, pp. 30–45.

FIGURE 16.4
Hiacynt Sierakowski, *Wieniec różany Królowej Niebieskiej Naświętszej Bogarodzice Panny Maryjej* ([Poznań: Wojciech Regulus], 1644), between pp. 37–38. Warsaw, Biblioteka Narodowa, XVII.3.416

works by Marcin Hińcza (1592–1663), a Jesuit and propagator of contemplative prayer who authored a number of ascetic books dedicated to his female noble protectors. The fact that the Jesuit order followed the rules of *accomodatio* (tailoring to the audience) and *familiaritatis* both in its writings and interactions with the faithful resulted in a wide selection of emblem books, which could be matched to one's social status, gender and skill.[71] Hińcza expressed such intentions explicitly in the foreword to his work: 'although you do not know how to meditate, you can read carefully and apply it to yourself and your estate; however close or far from learning you are, you can learn by reading'.[72] The Jesuit was successful in adapting his emblems to diverse circumstances and audiences. He dedicated his *Plęsy aniołów* (Frolics with angels, 1638) to nobleman Jan Daniłowicz and his bride Zofia of Tęczyn on the occasion of their marriage. The angels' joyful dance around the Christ child was inspired by wedding dances. At the same time, based on texts by the Church Fathers, it explained the cosmic order of the stars dancing around Jesus. The collection also associated the wedding with the mystery of incarnation, viewed as a marriage between humans and divine nature. This subject was especially promoted by Catholics in the face of the Protestant Reformation.

---

71 Schloesser, *Accommodation*, pp. 347–372.
72 Marcin Hińcza, *Dziecię Pan Jezus, to jest Nabożne rozmyślania o dzieciństwie Pana Jezusowym* (Lublin: Paweł Konrad, 1631), USTC 258501, p. 7. For a broader description of Hińcza's emblem works see Alicja Bielak (ed.), *Plęsy Aniołów Jezusowi narodzonemu, naświętszego Krzyża tańce by Marcin Hińcza* (Warsaw: IBL PAN, 2019).

FIGURE 16.5 Marcin Hińcza, *Plęsy Aniołów Jezusowi narodzonemu, Naświetszęgo Krzyża tańce* (Krakow: Franciszek Cezary, 1636[1638]), between pp. 142–143. Warsaw, Biblioteka Uniwerystecka, Sd 4g.2.2.31

Each emblem of *Plęsy* is composed of an icon (a counterpart of the *applicatio sensuum* stage in Ignatian meditation), an ekphrasis of the image which serves as the motto, and an elaborate meditative subscription consisting of questions and answers. The reader starts by reading the soul's soliloquy and is led by spiritual guides through the stages of atonement and *reformatio*. The questions performatise the process of looking for and identifying meaning in the emblematic icons. Questions are followed by numbered answers given by a spiritual guide, angels or, towards the end of the work, Jesus himself. Although the numbers are not present in the engraving, this resembles Jerónimo Nadal's, Jan David's and Antoine Sucquet's method to mark parts of the engraving with letters and elaborate on them with corresponding meditation points. Hińcza explains all of this in the instructions at the beginning of his work, which encourage the reader to move around the structure of the book freely to avoid the boredom caused by linear reading. Rather than learning in order, the reader can peruse the book as they please:

> In order that you do not become discouraged by the length, and that you can more easily understand how things are tied to spiritual lessons, I have given you numbers which will show you how each question relates to an answer in every frolic.[73]

The functionality of Hińcza's incredibly reader-friendly and strongly didactic system resembles the arrangement of catechisms. However, it is characterised by a greater persuasive strength because the reader-viewer (*lector-inspector*) is immersed in an engraving each time, needing to guess its meaning. This engages both the senses and reasoning abilities. The parallel points of questions and answers mimic the structure of logical reasoning, specifically the enthymeme. The renaissance tradition of using the paradox referring to the Christ child was broadly discussed by the Jesuit theologian Jacob Masen in his *Ars nova argutiarum* (The new art of wit, 1649). The enthymematic logical structure consisted of omitting one premise (out of the two that form classical logic reasoning) and proceeding directly from the antecedent (*protasis*) to the consequent (*epitasis*) as the conclusion rather than the second premise.[74]

---

73   Hińcza, *Plęsy aniołów*, p. 68: 'Długość żeby cię w czytaniu nie odrażała i żebyś łacniej mógł zrozumieć, jako się rzeczy i nauki duchowne powiązały, przydałem ci liczbę, którać pokaże, jako się pytanie z odpowiedzią wiąże w każdym Plęsie'.

74   This mechanism was described in detail in Alicja Bielak, '"Teach Me, Reveal the Secret to My Heart". The Role of a Spiritual Guide in the Meditative Works of Marcin Hińcza', in Ralph Dekoninck etc. (eds.), *Quid Est Secretum? Visual Representation of Secrets in*

Dogmas are explained through inventive concepts adapted for the Polish noble reader, as required by the Jesuit principle of acculturation.[75]

At the same time, the book functions as an extraordinary epistemic machine: the paradox resulting from various interpretations of the emblematic icon surprises the reader with the conclusion, which improves understanding and memorisation. For example, in one engraving, angels hold *arma Christi* while dancing around the Christ child. Hińcza draws parallels between the whipping cane and a cane sugar lollipop, as well as a toy horse for the child. Elsewhere, he addresses his female readers and highlights the role of the mother in detailed descriptions of childcare (such as swaddling or breastfeeding), only to later confront them with scenes of the crucifixion. These juxtapositions were intended to provoke strong emotions. Affect was also engaged by a first-person narrative, imperative exclamations directed at the reader (e.g. 'notice', 'look', 'see in your heart'), sensual descriptions according to the principles of *enargeia* or apostrophes to the characters depicted in the icons (as if they were present alongside the reader). The sensually and emotionally affected reader would find relief and a theological explanation once he or she turned several pages to search for an ekphrasis with a corresponding number to clarify the meaning of the image. Further, Marcin Hińcza promoted a type of sensual-affective prayer suitable for those already in the stage of spiritual growth (*via illuminativa*).[76] He also constructed comparisons and metaphors according to the method of acculturation, which was particular to the Jesuits and followed the recommendation of *familiaritas* given to extracontinental missionaries.[77]

Apart from such performative techniques, Polish emblem books also included direct epistemological commentary. Here, I will use the example of a lay author who both expressed himself through meditative and ascetic literary work and explained its philosophical and theological basis. Mikołaj Krzysztof Chalecki, voivode of Nowogródek, studied with the Jesuits in Vilnus and completed his education on *eloquentia sacra*. He then wrote two collections of emblematic

---

Early Modern Europe, 1500–1700 (Leiden: Brill, 2020), pp. 191–228. See similar mechanism in Silvestro Pietrasanta's emblems described by Walter S. Melion, 'Analogies known and unknown in Silvestro Pietrasanta, s.j.'s 'De symbolis heroïcis', *Emblematica*, 3 (2019), pp. 55–114.

75 About acculturation in the Polish translations of *Pia desideria*, see Radosław Grześkowiak, 'Zwyczajem kawalerów ziemskich postępuje z nią Oblubieniec. Pierwotna dedykacja *Pobożnych pragnień* Aleksandra Teodora Lackiego jako autorski projekt lektury emblematów Hermana Hugona', *Pamiętnik Literacki*, 106.1 (2015), pp. 199–227.

76 Guibert, *The Jesuits*, pp. 605–606.

77 Kapuścińska, *Theatrum meditationis*, p. 206.

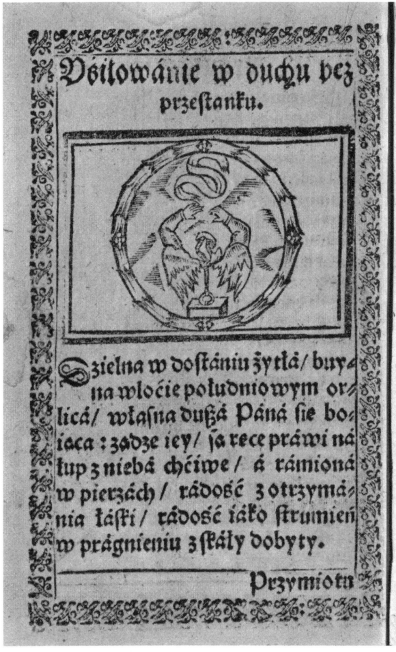

FIGURE 16.6   Mikołaj Krzysztof Chalecki, *Allegoriae albo Kwiecia módł gorących wynalezione dla unurzenia dusze w Bogu* (Vilnius: Leon Mamonicz, 1618), f. B3v. Vilnius, Vilniaus universiteto biblioteka, III 15155

meditations: *Allegoriae* (published in Polish and Latin in 1618) and the mentioned *Binarius* (1641). According to one elegy, he died holding *Binarius* in his left hand and a rosary in his right.[78]

In his first oeuvre *Allegoriae*, Chalecki often prioritised the sense of sight, which was common for religious emblem books, and followed Gregory the Great's famous formula 'per visibilia invisibilia demonstramus':

> *Allegoriae* is the name given to these books. It signifies that in the similitudes of many things hidden from the senses, knowledge is clearly shown through an intelligible medium, and the uncovered mysteries of the meditations of God are exposed to every one's view.[79]

By using 'similarities' to things that could be perceived by the senses, Chalecki taught the reader about mysteries by stimulating their sense of sight, which was assumed to be the most powerful. In the Latin edition of *Allegoriae*, the Vilnius Academy professor and propagator of the Catholic Reformation Laurentius Boyer (1561–1619), hiding under an anagram pseudonym, rendered the main objective of the book in Greek as 'a dialogue between God and Love', with Chalecki's verses and 'soul-captivating images'.[80] In the Latin version, Chalecki explained in detail why he used engravings to first stimulate physical eyesight as the strongest of the senses and then to cleanse internal sight:

> Therefore, the balm for the eyes (ἐγκάθαρσις) is the purest internal cleansing towards elevation and the only medicine for the soul whose eyes can see well, meaning that they can identify any debris in the eye or any enemy of the spirit.[81]

---

78 Mikołaj Krzysztof Chalecki, *Kompendium retoryczne*, eds. Jarosław Nowaszczuk etc., transl. Jarosław Nowaszczuk (Szczecin: Wydawnictwo Naukowe Uniwersytetu Szczecińskiego, 2011), pp. 9–12.

79 Chalecki, *Allegoriae*, ff. A2v–A3r: 'Allegoriae nazwisko tym książk[om] dane. To jest w podobieństwach siłu rzeczy od zmysłów utajonych przez środek pojęty nauka podana wyraźna i na widok kożdego myśli o Bogu z tajemnic wyrwanych zabawa wystawiona'.

80 Mikołaj Krzysztof Chalecki, *Allegoriae*, f. A5r; see Jolita Liškevičienė, 'Religinė vaizduotė didiko Mikalojaus Kristupo Chaleckio kūryboje', 44.

81 Chalecki, *Allegoriae*, f. A2r: 'Quare elevationis purissima ἐγκάθαρσις, collyrium est, et unica mentis medicina, cuius oculus vere cernit, id est, separat faeces, et omne spiritui inimicum'. See a commentary in Liškevičienė (ed.), *Mikalojaus Kristupo Chaleckio Embleminių Meditacijų Knygos*, pp. 44–45, 153–154 (by Tomas Veteikis).

Thanks to the 'balm', the soul was supposed to recognise 'any enemy'. This followed the Ignatian objective of meditation, namely the distinction between good and bad spirits. Chalecki stimulated his reader's sense of sight to activate the internal sight: the eyes of the soul. Emblematic icons were therefore intended to correspond with mental images during meditation. This was compared to the process of painting in that the *meditans* should paint in their hearts. Jesuit writer Marcin Laterna, the author of the prayerbook *Harfa duchowna* (The spiritual harp), explained that 'insatiable gluttony will not grip you so easily if you piously paint an image of the naked Jesus in your heart'.[82]

According to such mystics as St Bonaventure, the perfection of sight was strictly connected with spiritual development. One should start by contemplating the created world as a mirror of God. In Polish meditative emblems, one can see such exercises in deciphering the *invisibilia* through the *visibilia*. In Hińcza's *Chwała z krzyża* (Glory of the cross), thirty-three meditations with emblematic icons compare such objects as a school board, a throne, weapons, a shield, a chest, a tree, keys and a lute to the holy cross. The Marian emblems in the *Binarius*, meanwhile, focus on the Marian symbols of lilies. To reach a union with God, exercises should be followed in pure contemplation. Mikołaj Mościcki, a Dominican who encouraged laypeople to practise spiritual exercises, described contemplation as the final stage of spiritual perfection: the moment when a person does not search with his or her mind anymore, but immediately watches and sees that it is a 'free vision'.[83]

Chalecki's collections concluded with the unification of the soul with God, which adhered to the ages-old mystical traditions of *unio mystica* or contemplative mental prayer, during which the *meditans* acquires the ability to gaze continuously at God and the intellect and reposes with complacency.[84] Such a conclusion was also present in Polish translations of *Pia desideria* that fulfilled the model of *triplicia via* and in works by Marcin Hińcza, Stanisław Skibicki and Świętosław Zygmunt Niwicki. The latter author's *Hebdomada sancta* (first edition: 1692) was written in the first-person singular and focused on an intimate and emotional relationship with Christ. Each meditation began with the

---

82   Marcin Laterna, *Harfa duchowna, to jest dziesięć rozdziałów modlitw katolickich* (Krakow: A. Piotrkowczyk, 1604), p. 333: 'Nie chwyci się ciebie tak łatwie i łakomstwo nienasycone, kiedy nagiego Jezusa w sercu twym nabożnie sobie wymalujesz'.
83   Mikołaj z Mościsk, *Elementarzyk ćwiczenia duchownego* (Częstochowa: Paulini, 1722), p. 271; Jerzy Misiurek, *Historia i teologia polskiej duchowości katolickiej* (Lublin: Redakcja Wydawnictw KUL, 1994) I. 70–71; Stolarski, *Friars on the Frontier*, pp. 50–51.
84   Guibert, *The Jesuits*, p. 606.

repentance of the heart (*contritio cordis*), followed by a phase of union with Christ (*unio cum Christo*) and thanksgiving (*gratiarum actio*), gratitude (*gratitudo*), supplication (*supplicatio*) and, finally, an act of love and sorrow (*actus amoris et doloris*). Marcin Hińcza's *Plęsy* describe a direct conversation with Christ to provide a spiritual model for the reader and encourage them to pursue *imitatio Christi*.

Clearly, in addition to *imitatio Christi* piety, Polish-Lithuanian collections of emblematic meditations promoted the idea of spousal love popularised in European literature by Herman Hugo's *Pia desideria*. However, they also developed this theme in an original way. Seventeenth-century meditative emblem collections in the Polish-Lithuanian Commonwealth accepted such meditative or even mystical forms of piety and encouraged their readers to pursue them. This was evidenced not only by borrowings from foreign literature (e.g. translations by Aleksander Teodor Lacki and Jan Kościesza Żaba that maintained Herman Hugo's three-stage journey towards God from atonement [*via purgativa*] through illumination [*via illuminativa*] to unity with God [*via unitiva*]) but also by the very layout of meditations by local authors, ending with the soul's (the reader's *porte parole*) direct contact with God.[85]

4   Conclusion

The relatively large number of illustrated meditative works printed in the Polish-Lithuanian Commonwealth between the late sixteenth and the mid-seventeenth century, as well as the existence of multiple editions, testify to the popularity of the meditation and emblem amalgamate phenomenon. These books were not only intended for the clergy but also for laypeople. Despite their apparent non-confessional character, the collections sometimes contained controversial topics that were significant in a time of confessional divisions during the Reformation period. Tomasz Treter chastised 'heretics'; Paweł Mirowski added an emblematic icon that symbolised Catholic mass to his

---

85   See titlepage of the Jan Kościesza Żaba, *Pobożne żądania* (Vilnius: Drukarnia Akademicka Soc. Iesu, 1754): 'Jęczenia duszy pokutującej' (The moanings of a penitent soul) = *Gemitus Animae poenitentis*, 'Żądze duszy świętej' (The desires of the holy soul) = *Vota Animae sanctae*, and 'Wzdychania duszy kochającej' (The sighs of the loving soul) = *Suspiria Animae amantis*. See Grześkowiak, 'Zwyczajem kawalerów ziemskich postępuje z nią Oblubieniec', pp. 203–204. On the popularity of the metaphorical three-stage path to God in emblematics, see Praz, *Studies in Seventeenth-Century Imagery*, pp. 82–168.

adaptation of Thomas à Kempis' *Imitatio Christi*; Krzysztof Chalecki intertextually alluded to the Protestant doctrine *sola fide* by using it for his mystical meditation. References to pre-Reformation Christian texts (by authors such as Aquinas or Thomas à Kempis, and to ascetic writings from the *devotio moderna* movement) were significant. They suggested that devotional works were to be treated as tools of religious propaganda, which was consistent with the expanded idea of mission work by the Jesuits, who were the main proponents of the genre.

Authors strove to make their emblem books as attractive as they could by providing illustrations and adapting the form and content of the meditations for lay readers. Furthermore, the books' prefaces often demonstrated acculturative methods and a tendency to popularise piety among noblemen and women. These principles manifested themselves in frequent decisions to publish in Polish, as well as changes in language (e.g. feminine grammatical forms for female readers) and imagery (e.g. spousal or parental love towards Christ or the baby Jesus). Most notably in the seventeenth century, writers used such literature to give laypeople access to meditative (e.g. rosary prayers, Marcin Hińcza's works) and even mystical experiences characteristic of contemplation (Niwicki, Chalecki). The literature's formative function was also visible in how it addressed readers, who were repeatedly encouraged to look at the accompanying engravings or examine one's conscience and think about how to improve. In addition, the prefaces and main bodies of the books contained numerous instructions and tips on how to perform meditative prayer correctly.

The topics addressed in these emblematic meditations published within the Polish-Lithuanian Commonwealth were not limited to the theme of love between the soul and *Amor Divinus*, which was made famous with the success of Herman Hugo's *Pia desideria*. Rather, the most frequent themes were rosaries, Marian praises and meditations on the life of Jesus, as well as ordinary objects to be analysed as concealing the knowledge of God. Although the Jesuits surely initiated and popularised fusing emblems and meditations, Polish-Lithuanian book production shows that the Dominicans and laity were also active co-creators of this amalgamate literature.

To complete their view of the broader phenomenon of Polish meditative emblem books, researchers should now turn to documents intended for strictly personal use. These include meditative manuscripts with glued-in engravings, which are currently stored in monastery libraries and the archives of noble families.

TABLE 16.1 Meditative emblem collections published in the Polish-Lithuanian Commonwealth (ca. 1569–1775)

No.	Date of print	Author	Title	Place of print	Printer	Icon's inventor	Icon's engraver	Dedication	Author's confession	Topic	Remarks
1	1569–1574	Tomasz Treter (1547–1610)	*Imprese*	—	—	Tomasz Treter	—	—	Catholic (priest)	Meditations on the life of Christ, symbols	Manuscript draft of *Symbolica vitae Christi* (no. 3). Held in the Biblioteca Civica Angelo Mai di Bergamo (MM 378)
2	1608	Stanisław Grochowski (1542–1612)	*Pięćdziesiąt punktów rozmyślaniu Męki Pana Jezusowej służących*	Krakow	Mikołaj Lob	—	—	—	Catholic (priest)	Meditation on divine love	USTC 1793024 Translation of the *Paradisvs sponsi et sponae* (Antwerp 1607) by Jan David, SJ
3	1612	Tomasz Treter (1547–1610)	*Symbolica vitae Christi meditatio*	Brunsberga	Georg Schönfels	Tomasz Treter	Błażej Treter	Szymon Rudnicki	Catholic (priest)	Meditations on the life of Christ, symbols	USTC 2055155

MEDITATIVE EMBLEMS 355

TABLE 16.1 Meditative emblem collections published in the Polish-Lithuanian Commonwealth (*cont.*)

No.	Date of print	Author	Title	Place of print	Printer	Icon's inventor	Icon's engraver	Dedication	Author's confession	Topic	Remarks
4	1602	Confraternity of the Holy Rosary (Krakow Dominicans?)	*Sposób mówienia psałterzyka Panny Maryjej abo różanki*	Krakow	Wojciech Kobyliński	?	?	–	Catholic (Dominican)	Rosary	USTC 1793025
5	1610	Confraternity of the Holy Rosary (Krakow Dominicans?)	*Sposób mówienia psałterzyka Panny Maryjej abo różanki*	Krakow	Wojciech Kobyliński	?	?	–	Catholic	Rosary	USTC 258842
6	1611	Stanisław Grochowski (1542–1612)	*Pięćdziesiąt punktów rozmyślaniu Męki Pana Jezusowej służących*	Krakow	Bazyli Skalski	–	–	–	Catholic (priest)	Meditation on divine love	USTC 258166 Translation of the *Paradisus sponsi et sponae* (Antwerp 1607) by Jan David, SJ
7	1613	Confraternity of the Holy Rosary (Krakow Dominicans?)	*Sposób mówienia psałterzyka Panny Maryjej abo różanki*	Krakow	Wojciech Kobyliński	?	?	–	Catholic	Rosary	USTC 1793026

TABLE 16.1 Meditative emblem collections published in the Polish-Lithuanian Commonwealth (*cont.*)

No.	Date of print	Author	Title	Place of print	Printer	Icon's inventor	Icon's engraver	Dedication	Author's confession	Topic	Remarks
8	1616	Confraternity of the Holy Rosary (Krakow Dominicans?)	*Sposób mówienia psałterzyka Panny Maryjej abo różanki*	Krakow	Marcin Horteryn	?	?	–	Catholic	Rosary	USTC 1793027
9	1617	Confraternity of the Holy Rosary (Krakow Dominicans?)	*Sposób mówienia psałterzyka Panny Maryjej abo różanki*	Krakow	Marcin Horteryn	?	?	–	Catholic	Rosary	USTC 258252
10	1618	Mikołaj Krzysztof Chalecki (1589–1653)	*Allegoriae, sive Sinthemata per quae amor creatus cum amato supernaturali symbolizant, et in unum velut aque duae confluunt*	Vilnius	Leon Mamonicz	?	?	płci męskiej i niewieści (Dusza/ czytelnik)	Catholic (lay, noble)	Meditations on symbols	USTC 250445
11	1618	Mikołaj Krzysztof Chalecki (1589–1653)	*Allegoriae albo Kwiecia modł gorących wynalezione dla unurzenia dusze w Bogu*	Vilnius	Leon Mamonicz	?	?	płci męskiej i niewieści (Dusza/ czytelnik)	Catholic (lay, noble)	Meditations on symbols	USTC 250434 Polish version of *Allegoriae, sive Sinthemata…* (no. 8)

MEDITATIVE EMBLEMS 357

TABLE 16.1 Meditative emblem collections published in the Polish-Lithuanian Commonwealth (*cont.*)

No.	Date of print	Author	Title	Place of print	Printer	Icon's inventor	Icon's engraver	Dedication	Author's confession	Topic	Remarks
12	1620	Confraternity of the Holy Rosary (Krakow Dominicans?)	*Sposób mówienia psałterzyka Panny Maryjej abo różanki*	Krakow	Marcin Horteryn	?	?	–	Catholic	Rosary	USTC 1793028
13	1622	Confraternity of the Holy Rosary (Krakow Dominicans?)	*Sposób mówienia psałterzyka Panny Maryjej abo różanki*	Krakow	Marcin Horteryn	?	?	–	Catholic	Rosary	USTC 1793029
14	1626	Confraternity of the Holy Rosary (Krakow Dominicans?)	*Sposób mówienia psałterzyka Panny Maryjej abo różanki*	Krakow	Andrzej Piotrkowczyk	?	?	–	Catholic	Rosary	USTC 1793030
15	1627	Walerian Litwanides, OP (or Litwinkowic, wrongly: Adrianowicz, Andrzejowicz, 1574–1635)	*Ogród różany, abo Opisanie porządne dwu szczepów wonnej rożej hierychuntskiej*	Krakow	Franciszek Cezary	?	?	Matka Boska, bracia i siostry	Catholic (Dominican)	Rosary	USTC 258374

TABLE 16.1 Meditative emblem collections published in the Polish-Lithuanian Commonwealth (*cont.*)

No.	Date of print	Author	Title	Place of print	Printer	Icon's inventor	Icon's engraver	Dedication	Author's confession	Topic	Remarks
16	1629	Walerian Litwanides, OP (or Litwinkowic, wrongly: Adrianowicz, Andrzejowicz, 1574–1635)	*Pius modus recitandi publice per Choros SS. Rosarium B.V. Mariae*	Krakow	Antoni Wosiński	?	?	alumni of Krakow University	Catholic (Dominican)	Rosary	USTC 255770
17	1630	Confraternity of the Holy Rosary (Krakow Dominicans?)	*Sposób mówienia psatterzyka Panny Maryjej abo różanki*	Krakow	Andrzej Piotrkowczyk	?	?	–	Catholic	Rosary	USTC 1793031
18	1634	Confraternity of the Holy Rosary (Krakow Dominicans?)	*Sposób mówienia psatterzyka Panny Maryjej abo różanki*	Krakow	Andrzej Piotrkowczyk	?	?	–	Catholic	Rosary	USTC 1793032
19	1636 (in fact: 1638)	Marcin Hińcza, SJ (1592–1668)	*Plęsy aniołów Jezusowi narodzonemu, naświętszego Krzyża tańce*	Krakow	Franciszek Cezary	?	Egidius van Schoor	Jan Daniłowicz & Zofia z Tęczyna	Catholic (Jesuit)	Passion meditations, meditations on symbols	USTC 258541 Cf. no. 10 (1638 edition has a changed titlepage)
20	1638	Marcin Hińcza, SJ (1592–1668)	*Plęsy Jezusa z aniołami, naświętszego Krzyża tańce*	Krakow	Franciszek Cezary	?	Egidius van Schoor	Jan Daniłowicz i Zofia z Tęczyna	Catholic (Jesuit)	Passion ameditations, meditations on symbols	USTC 258537

TABLE 16.1 Meditative emblem collections published in the Polish-Lithuanian Commonwealth (*cont.*)

No.	Date of print	Author	Title	Place of print	Printer	Icon's inventor	Icon's engraver	Dedication	Author's confession	Topic	Remarks
21	1639 [post 5 II]	Wojciech Margoński, OP (?–1640)	*Rosae salutiferae in amohenissimo sanctissimi rosarii Beatiss. Virginis Mariae Horto plantatae*	Naples	Widow of Lazzaro Scoriggio	?	?	Pope Urban VIII	Catholic (Dominican)	Rosary	USTC 4011277
22	1639 [post 19 II]	Wojciech Margoński, OP (?–1640)	*Rosae salutiferae in amohenissimos sanctissimi rosarii Beatiss. Virginis Mariae horto plantatae*	Naples	Widow of Lazzaro Scoriggio	?	?	Pope Urban VIII	Catholic (Dominican)	Rosary	USTC 4011277
23	1641	Marcin Hińcza, SJ (1592–1668)	*Chwała z Krzyża której i sobie, i nam nabył Jezus Ukrzyżowany*	Krakow	Andrzej Piotrkowczyk	?	?	Katarzyna Zamojska, neé Ostrogska (c.1600–1642)	Catholic (Jesuit)	Passion meditations, meditations on symbols	USTC 258584 and 258585 Icons inspired by Benedictus van Haeften's *Regia via Crucis*
24	1642	Mikołaj Krzysztof Chalecki (1589–1653)	*Binarius Chalecianus sive duo manipuli liliorum*	Vilnius	Officina Typographica Patrum Basilianum	?	?	–	Catholic (lay, noble)	Meditations on Marian symbols	USTC 250788

TABLE 16.1 Meditative emblem collections published in the Polish-Lithuanian Commonwealth (cont.)

No.	Date of print	Author	Title	Place of print	Printer	Icon's inventor	Icon's engraver	Dedication	Author's confession	Topic	Remarks
25	1643	Confraternity of the Holy Rosary (Krakow Dominicans?)	*Sposób mówienia psałterzyka Panny Maryjej abo różanki*	Krakow	Andrzej Piotrkowczyk	?	?	—	Catholic	Rosary	USTC 1793033
26	1644	Hiacynt Sierakowski, OP (?–1656)	*Wieniec różany Królowej Niebieskiej Naświętszej Bogarodzice Panny Maryjej z piętnastu różanych kwiatów tajemnic Pana Chrystusa uwity*	Poznań?	Wojciech Regulus?	?	?	Confraternity of the rosary	Catholic (Dominican)	Rosary	USTC 1793034 The same engravins as in: *Rosae Salutiferae* by Wojciech Margoński
27	1646	Walerian Lithuanides, OP (mylnie: Adrianowicz, Andrzejowicz, 1574–1635)	*Ogród różany, abo Opisanie porządne dwu szczepów wonnej rożej hierychuntskiey*	Vilnius	Drukarnia Ojców Jezuitów	—	—	Zofia Chodkiewicz, neé Drucka-Horska (c.1600–1657)	Catholic (Dominican)	Rosary	USTC 250914

TABLE 16.1   Meditative emblem collections published in the Polish-Lithuanian Commonwealth (cont.)

No.	Date of print	Author	Title	Place of print	Printer	Icon's inventor	Icon's engraver	Dedication	Author's confession	Topic	Remarks
28	1650	Adrian Wieszczycki (c.1612–after 1654)	Ogród rozkoszny miłości Bożej wesołemi lilijami, purpurowemi różami, niesmiertelnemi amarantami dostatnie obfitujący, z których misternie uwity ofiarowała wieniec	Krakow	Walerian Piątkowski	?	?	Władysław Dominik Zasławski (1618–1656)	Catholic (lay)	Rosary	USTC 258751
29	1652	Sebastianus a Matre Dei, OC (Stanisław Szulc, ?–?)	Firmamentum symbolicum in quo Deiparae elogia, quibus, velut firmamentum stellis, est exornata, symbolice depinguntur	Lublin	Georg Förster	Thomas, Jan van Yperen (1617–1678)	Aernout Loemans (1632–1656)	Tomasz Ujejski	Catholic (Carmelite)	Meditations on symbols, praises of Mary	USTC 1777908

TABLE 16.1 Meditative emblem collections published in the Polish-Lithuanian Commonwealth (*cont.*)

No.	Date of print	Author	Title	Place of print	Printer	Icon's inventor	Icon's engraver	Dedication	Author's confession	Topic	Remarks
30	1656	[Paweł Mirowski] (?–?)	*Młotek duchowny w sercach ludzkich tor Chrystusów dreluiący*	Gdańsk	David Friedrich Rhetius	David Friedrich ?	?	–	Catholic (priest)	Meditations on the life of Christ, meditations on symbols	USTC 1793035 Adaptation of the *Imitatio Christi* by Thomas à Kempis
31	1657	Herman Hugo, SJ (1588–1629)	*Piorum desideriorum libri tres*	Gdańsk	Jacobus Weissius	Boetius Bolswert	Baptista Pravicinus (frontispiece)	'Omnium gentium'	Catholic (Jesuit)	Meditations on the Divine Love	USTC 2605594
32	ante 1662	Sebastianus a Matre Dei, OC (Stanisław Szulc, ?–?)	*Situlae symbolicae e puteo aquarum viventium tam potum quam mirabilia ab ipso contenta extrahentes, sive Novae et breves materiae ex diversis confectae symbolis pro concionibus efformandis in festivitatibus decem Virginis Deiparae Mariae*	–	–	–	–	Virgin Mary	Catholic (Carmelite)	Meditations, emblems on Mary	Manuscript accepted for publication by the general of Carmelite order, Domenico della Trinità on 19 May 1662 (never published). Held in the Archivio Generale – Ordine dei Carmelitani Scalzi, Roma (A 342b)

TABLE 16.1 Meditative emblem collections published in the Polish-Lithuanian Commonwealth (*cont.*)

No.	Date of print	Author	Title	Place of print	Printer	Icon's inventor	Icon's engraver	Dedication	Author's confession	Topic	Remarks
33	1673	Herman Hugo, SJ (1588–1629), transl. Alexander Teodor Lacki (1614–c.1683)	*Pobożne pragnienia*	Krakow	Heirs of Krzysztof Schedel († 1653)	–	–	Konstancja Krystyna Wielopolska, neé Komorowska	Catholic (Jesuit), author; Catholic (lay noble), translator	Meditations on the Divine Love	USTC 1773049 and 1771722 Translation of *Pia desideria* by Herman Hugo. Initially dedicated to Gryzelda Wiśniowiecka (1623–1672), change because of her death)
34	1680	Ambroży Nieszporkowic, OSPPE (1643–1703)	*Officina emblematum, quae praecipuos Virginis, et Matris Dei Mariae titulos et elogia complectuntur*	Krakow	Franciszek Cezary	–	–	Augustyn Benkowicz, OSPPE	Catholic (Paulite)	Praise of the Virgin Mary	USTC 1793036

TABLE 16.1 Meditative emblem collections published in the Polish-Lithuanian Commonwealth (*cont.*)

No.	Date of print	Author	Title	Place of print	Printer	Icon's inventor	Icon's engraver	Dedication	Author's confession	Topic	Remarks
35	1682	Gerhard Johann (1582–1637), transl. Aaaron Bliwernica (Bliwernitz, ?–?)	*Rozmyślania nabożne*	Toruń	Christian Bekk	?	?	Town council	Lutheran, author, Lutheran pastor, translator	Meditations on the history of the Holy Family, meditations on symbols	USTC 1793037 Translation of Johann Gerhard's *Ein und Funfzig Christliche Andachten Zur Ubung wahrer Gottseligkeit*
36	1683	Gerhard Johann (1582–1637), transl. Aaaron Bliwernica (Bliwernitz, ?–?)	*Nabożne rozmyślania*	Toruń	Christian Bekk	?	?	Town council	Lutheran	Meditations on the history of the Holy Family, meditations on symbols	USTC 1793038 Translation of Johann Gerhard's *Ein und Funfzig Christliche Andachten Zur Ubung wahrer Gottseligkeit*. Edition identical to the No. 25 (changed titlepage and 1 engraving less)

TABLE 16.1   Meditative emblem collections published in the Polish-Lithuanian Commonwealth (*cont.*)

No.	Date of print	Author	Title	Place of print	Printer	Icon's inventor	Icon's engraver	Dedication	Author's confession	Topic	Remarks
37	1685	Stanisław Skibicki, SJ (1607–1690)	*Dusze pod cieniem Drzewa Żywota ukrzyżowanego Jezusa siedzącej z ranami i boleściami jego nabożna zabawa*	Kalisz	Kolegium Societatis Jesu	–		–	Catholic (Jesuit)	Passion meditations, divine love	USTC 1793039
38	1691	Ambroży Nieszporkowic, OSPPE (1643–1703)	*Officina emblematum quae praecipuos Virgis [et] Matris Dei Mariae titulos [et] elogia complectuntur [etc.]*	Krakow	Jerzy & Mikołaj Schedel	–		Augustyn Benkowicz, OSPPE (1675–1681)	Catholic (Paulite)	Praise of the Virgin Mary, meditations on symbols	USTC 1793040
39	1692	Świętosław Zygmunt Niwicki, SJ (1640–1702)	*Hebdomada sancta: seu Christus Rex, Iudex, Mediator, Pater, Benefactor, Redemptor, Sponsus*	Gdańsk	Janssonius van Waesberghe	Świętosław Zygmunt Niwicki, SJ	Karol Scottus	Wojciech Konstanty Breza (c.1620–1698)	Catholic (Jesuit)	Meditations on Christ for the whole weekend	USTC 2558480

TABLE 16.1 Meditative emblem collections published in the Polish-Lithuanian Commonwealth (*cont.*)

No.	Date of print	Author	Title	Place of print	Printer	Icon's inventor	Icon's engraver	Dedication	Author's confession	Topic	Remarks
40	1692	Świętosław Zygmunt Niwicki, SJ (1640–1702)	*Tydzień święty albo Chrystus Król, Sędzia, Pośrednik, Ociec, Dobrodziej, Zbawiciel, Oblubieniec*	Gdańsk	Janssonius van Waesberghe	–	–	Teresa Konstancja neé Opalińska of Bnin (1645–1703)	Catholic (Jesuit)	Meditations on Christ for the whole weekend	USTC 1793034¹
41	1696	Świętosław Zygmunt Niwicki, SJ (1640–1702); transl. Bonifacio Pfaffenzeller, OSB	*Die heiligen Wochen oder Christus der Konig etc.*	Ausburg	Jacob Bottler	–	–	Christoph Wentzel von Nostitz	Catholic (Jesuit), author, Catholic (Benedictine), translator	Meditations on Christ for the whole weekend	USTC 263540⁶
42	1697	Herman Hugo, SJ (1588–1629), transl. Alexander Teodor Lacki (1614–c.1683)	*Pobożne pragnienia trzema księgami zebrane*	Krakow	Jerzy Romuald Schedel	–	–	–	Catholic (Jesuit), author; Catholic (lay noble), translator	Meditations on the Divine Love	USTC 1793034²

MEDITATIVE EMBLEMS   367

TABLE 16.1   Meditative emblem collections published in the Polish-Lithuanian Commonwealth (*cont.*)

No.	Date of print	Author	Title	Place of print	Printer	Icon's inventor	Icon's engraver	Dedication	Author's confession	Topic	Remarks
43	1698	Sebastianus a Matre Dei, OC (Stanisław Szulc, ?–?)	*Coelum symbolicum in quo sacra elogia, quibus, velut firmamentem stellis*	Gdańsk	Sumptu Fischeriano	Jan van Yperen Thomas (1617–1678)	Aernout Loemans (1632–1656)	Tomasz Ujejski	Catholic (Carmelite)	Praise of the Virgin Mary	USTC 2582288 Edition identical to the *Firmamentum symbolicum in quo Deiparae elogia* (title page changed)
44	1723	Świętosław Zygmunt Niwicki, SJ (1640–1702); transl. Bonifacio Pfaffenzeller, OSB	*Die heiligen Wochen oder Christus der König etc.*	Augsburg	Jacob Botter	–	–	Jesus and Mother Mary	Catholic (Jesuit), author; Catholic (Benedictine), translator	Meditations on Christ for the whole weekend	
45	1725	Karol Piotr Sawicki, SJ (1661–1733)	*Prawdziwe zwierciadło niewinności to jest Życie czyste, niewinne, anielskie błogosławionego Alojzego Gonzagi*	Poznań	Drukarnia Kollegium Societatis Iesu	?	Michał Niedbałowicz	Janusz Aleksander Sanguszko (1712–1775)	Catholic (Jesuit)	Emblematic biography of Luigi Gonzaga	

TABLE 16.1 Meditative emblem collections published in the Polish-Lithuanian Commonwealth (*cont.*)

No.	Date of print	Author	Title	Place of print	Printer	Icon's inventor	Icon's engraver	Dedication	Author's confession	Topic	Remarks
46	1733	Karol Piotr Sawicki, SJ (1661–1733)	*Prawdziwe zwierciadło niewinności to jest Życie czyste, niewinne, anielskie błogosławionego Alojzego Gonzagi*	Krakow	Jakub Matyaszkiewicz	?	Michał Niedbałowicz	"Wszystkim na przeglądanie się codzienne i na poprawę życia wystawione"	Catholic (Jesuit)	Emblematic biography of Luigi Gonzaga	Without 'refleksyje' (reflexions) present in former edition
47	1737	Herman Hugo, SJ (1588–1629); Aleksander Teodor Lacki (1614–c.1683)	*Pobożne pragnienia*	Krakow	Jakub Matyaszkiewicz	–	–	–	Catholic (Jesuit), author Catholic (lay), translator	Meditations on the Divine Love	Identical to 1697 edition, no. 33 (changed titlepage)
48	1741	Walerian Bartłomiej Litwanides, OP (mylnie: Adrianowicz, Andrzejowicz, 1574–1635)	*Ogród różany dwojakim różowym kwiatem przyozdobiony*	Brunsberga	Typografia Brunsberska	–	–	–	Catholic (Dominican)	Rosary	

TABLE 16.1 Meditative emblem collections published in the Polish-Lithuanian Commonwealth (*cont.*)

No.	Date of print	Author	Title	Place of print	Printer	Icon's inventor	Icon's engraver	Dedication	Author's confession	Topic	Remarks
49	1744	Herman Hugo, SJ (1588–1629); (transl.) Jan Kościesza Żaba (?–1754)	*Pobożne pragnienia*	Supraśl	Druk. oo. Bazylianów	–	–	Ignacy & Helena Ogińscy	Catholic (Jesuit), author; Catholic (lay), translator	Meditations on the Divine Love	Translation of *Pia desideria* by Herman Hugo
50	1754	Herman Hugo, SJ (1588–1629); (tranl.) Jan Kościesza Żaba (?–1754)	*Pobożne żądania*	Vilnius	Drukarnia Akademicka Soc. Iesu	–	–	–	Catholic (Jesuit)	Meditations on the Divine Love	Translation of *Pia desideria* by Herman Hugo
51	1755	Jesuits of Jarosław	*Mater dolorum et gratiarum, septem vulneribus, velut fontibus miraculorum, in icone jaroslaviensi conspicua*	Lviv	Collegium Leopoliensis Societatis Iesu	?	Jerzy Wysłowski & Michał Żukowski	Bishop Wacław Hieronim Sierakowski (1700–1780)	Catholic (Jesuit)	Meditations on Mary	

TABLE 16.1 Meditative emblem collections published in the Polish-Lithuanian Commonwealth (cont.)

No.	Date of print	Author	Title	Place of print	Printer	Icon's inventor	Icon's engraver	Dedication	Author's confession	Topic	Remarks
52	1758	Świętosław Zygmunt Niwicki, SJ (1640–1702), transl. anonymous noble	Tydzień święty albo Chrystus Król, Sędzia, Pośrednik, Ociec, Dobrodziej, Zbawiciel, Oblubieniec	Vilnius	Aegidius Jansonius Waesberg	–	–	Helena Ogińska, neé Ogińska (1700–1790)	Catholic (Jesuit)	Meditations on Christ	
53	1775	Świętosław Zygmunt Niwicki, SJ (1640–1702)	Hebdomada sancta seu Christus Rex, Judex, Mediator, Pater, Benefactor, Redemptor, Sponsus	Gdańsk	J.H. Floerke	–	–	Wojciech Konstanty Breza (?–1698)	Catholic (Jesuit)	Meditations on Christ	

Legend: – – lack; ? – unknown

Acknowledgements

Research is funded by National Science Centre (NCN), Poland, within the project *Polish Meditative Emblems in the 16th Through 18th Century: Sources, Realizations, and Aims* (Preludium, no. 2018/31/N/HS2/01187).

CHAPTER 17

Supralibros as a Creed

Ownership Stamps on Books Belonging to Tomasz Treter, Canonicus et Custos Varmiensis

Justyna Kiliańczyk-Zięba

Marking the ownership of a volume on its binding was a practice that took a long time to become customary among book buyers and binding commissioners.[1] Bindings primarily identified the possessors of the books they protected by displaying their names, often proclaimed in longer inscriptions or represented only by initials, as well as accompanied by mottos. Verbal formulas in turn could be combined with or supplanted by visual representations, which (for the most part) evolved from the pictorial vocabulary of mediaeval heraldry.

Coats of arms of noble owners can easily be found on bindings made in fifteenth and sixteenth centuries, particularly in German lands and workshops of bookbinders active in the Kingdom of Poland. Signs of ownership of non-nobles are less common. Nevertheless, merchants' marks (*Hausmarken*) used by tradesmen and craftsmen, as well as burgher arms (*Bürgerwappen*) of more prosperous individuals, can be noted on some of the bindings covering volumes that once belonged to the commoners.[2] In the sixteenth century, these signs of identification and ownership, which had originated in the tradition of heraldic recognition, began to be displayed along (or even replaced with) *imprese*, personal devices, 'expressing some personality trait, thought or

---

1 Paul Needham, *Twelve Centuries of Bookbindings 400–1600* (New York, London: Oxford University Press, 1979), p. 92.
2 Kamila Follprecht, 'Gmerki mieszczan krakowskich', *Krakowski Rocznik Archiwalny*, 9 (2003), pp. 46–62; Stefan K. Kuczyński, 'Quelques remarques sur les armoires bourgeoises de Pologne', in Hervé Pinoteau etc. (eds.), *Les armoires non nobles en Europe XIIIe–XVIIIe s. Académie Internationale d'Héraldique, IIIe Colloque International d'Héraldique, Montmorency 19–23 Septembre 1983* (Paris: Le Léopard d'Or, 1986), pp. 55–62; James Douglas Farquhar, 'Identity in an Anonymous Age: Bruges Manuscript Illuminators and their Signs', *Viator. Medieval and Renaissance Studies*, 11 (1980), pp. 371–384; Detlef Mauss, 'Der Rubrikator PW', *Gutenberg Jahrbuch*, 52 (1997), pp. 107–110; Maria Koczerska, 'De manu, signo et nomine, czyli o krakowskich notariuszach publicznych w późnym średniowieczu', in Danuta Gawinowa etc. (eds.), *Kultura średniowieczna i staropolska. Studia ofiarowane Aleksandrowi Gieysztorowi w pięćdziesięciolecie pracy naukowej* (Warsaw: PWN, 1991), pp. 191–206.

intention of their bearers, through ingenious coupling of a typically quite concise image with an equally brief motto'.[3] For the meaning of the composition to become apparent, these two elements were to be read in conjunction with each other. Perhaps the best-known examples of bindings exhibiting stamps, which can be classed as *imprese*, are the 'plaquette bindings' manufactured in the 1540s in Rome for Apollonio Filareto (an eagle with a Virgilian motto) and Giovanni Battista Grimaldi (Apollo and Pegasus accompanied by a Greek inscription), and those made for the French collector Claude Gouffier (the figure of a term paired with a motto 'Hic terminus haeret').[4] As far as I know, in the Kingdom of Poland, *imprese* first appear on bookbindings in the early sixteenth century, stamped on volumes bound for men of learning, professors at the Krakow University.[5]

The ownership signs displayed on book covers are sometimes referred to as supralibros (superlibros) due to their placement (on the binding, both protecting and adorning the volume). In my text, I use this term as designating signs on bindings that declared ownership of the volume, whether they were verbal (names, mottos, etc.), pictorial (e.g. armorial bearings) or a combination of the two (e.g. *imprese*). Admittedly, supralibros is a term rarely used in book historical discourse by authors writing in English, where the armorial stamp, ownership stamp and central panel dominate. For my purposes, this term is

---

[3] Dorigen Caldwell, *The Sixteenth-Century Italian Impresa in Theory and Practice* (New York: AMS Press, 2004), p. xi. For other definitions and their discussion, see Mario Praz, *Studies in Seventeenth-Century Imagery* (London: Warburg Institute–University of London, 1939), p. 50; Kristen Lippincott, 'The Genesis and Significance of the Fifteenth-Century Italian Impresa', in Sydney Anglo (ed.), *Chivalry in the Renaissance* (Woodbridge: The Boydell Press, 1990), pp. 51–54; Caldwell, *The Sixteenth-Century Italian Impresa*; Laura De Girolami Cheney, 'The Impresa in the Italian Renaissance', in Peter M. Daly (ed.), *Companion to Emblem Studies* (New York: AMS Press, 2008), pp. 251–266.

[4] Anthony Hobson, *Apollo and Pegasus. An Enquiry into the Formation and Dispersal of a Renaissance Library* (Amsterdam: Van Heusden, 1975); Needham, *Twelve Centuries*, pp. 163–167, 228; Jean Guillaume, 'Hic Terminus Haeret: Du Terme d'Erasme à la devise de Claude Gouffier: la fortune d'un emblème à la Renaissance', *Journal of the Warburg and Courtauld Institutes*, 44 (1981), pp. 186–192.

[5] Kazimierz Piekarski, *Superexlibrisy polskie od XV do XVIII wieku* (Krakow: Drukarnia W.L. Anczyca i Spółki, 1929), plates 32–35; Arkadiusz Wagner, *Superekslibris polski. Studium o kulturze bibliofilskiej i sztuce od średniowiecza do połowy XVII wieku* (Toruń: Wydawnictwo Naukowe Uniwersytetu Mikołaja Kopernika, 2016), pp. 208, 214, 235; Justyna Kiliańczyk-Zięba, '*Imprese* of Non-Noble Intellectuals as Ownership Stamps on Bookbindings. An Example from Sixteenth-Century Poland', *Emblematica*, 5 (2021), pp. 55–81.

most convenient, denoting the main function (proclamation of ownership) and placement (on the binding) of specific signs.[6]

There are various ways to examine supralibros. The most straightforward approach is cataloguing them and identifying their early owners for the purpose of provenance research. Supralibros can also be studied as material objects, for example for techniques used to execute them (as they were stamped, painted, cut or burnt in, engraved and embroidered) and their placement (on both covers and on book spine, on clasps and on centre as well as corner furniture).[7] They are often regarded as works of art whose forms reflect how certain decorative styles and general aesthetic trends of the day spread in the mediaeval and early modern world: despite the fact that the majority of binders are traditionally minded, supralibros pursued various styles, and they were designed and created in accordance with contemporary developments in visual arts.[8] In this study, however, I propose a slightly different approach to the ownership marks that bookbindings were furnished with. I will focus on two supralibros that elaborate on the same iconographical theme. These supralibros marked the books of Tomasz Treter (Treterus, 1547–1610), a secretary of Cardinal Stanislas Hosius (Hozjusz, 1504–1579), a canon of Santa Maria in Trastevere in Rome and (towards the end of his life) a *canonicus et custos Varmiensis*. When discussing Treter's supralibros, I will provide preiconographic descriptions and attempt at identifying motives, themes and concepts that were incorporated in these compositions.[9] This will be an attempt to discover and interpret 'symbolical values' of supralibros, which served not only to identify the owners of the books they were applied to, but also to convey meanings. My iconological investigations abstain from aesthetic considerations, and for the most part, ignore the materiality of supralibros. Nevertheless, they are connected to social-historical influences that affected 'devices on books'.[10]

---

6   See David Pearson, *Provenance Research in Book History. A Handbook* (London: Bodleian Library, 1994), p. 97. For a discussion of relevant terminology, see Wagner, *Superekslibris polski*, pp. 37–62.

7   For the techniques of binding and decorating books, see e.g. Mirjam M. Foot, *The History of Bookbinding as a Mirror of Society* (London: The British Library, 1998), pp. 3–50, as well as numerous other studies by the same author.

8   Mirjam M. Foot, *The History of Bookbinding*, p. 51.

9   Erwin Panofsky, *Studies in Iconology. Humanistic Themes in the Art of the Renaissance* (New York: Oxford University Press, 1939), pp. 6–11.

10 Roelof van Straten, *An Introduction to Iconography. Symbols, Allusions and Meaning in the Visual Arts* (New York: Routledge, 1994), p. 12; about perspectives opened up by the methodologies such as 'actor-network theory' and 'theory of art', see the compact introduction

The identification and possession signs displayed on the books of Tomasz Treter are noteworthy in several key respects. First, they document non-hereditary personal devices of a man who spent many years close to the papal curia and the most influential figures of the early modern Catholic Church, first and foremost his patron, Cardinal Hosius.[11] Second, they were certainly adopted and used consciously because Treter was an author of emblems and an artist who was the *inventor* or *auctor intellectualis* of numerous projects. Third, we are fortunate to have contemporary interpretations of these supralibros' symbolism, either from Treter himself or from his milieu. Forth, these stamps mark and distinguish volumes from a substantial library, amassed by the canon in Frombork (Frauenburg), Warmia (Ermland), between the sixteenth and seventeenth centuries. Treter's collection was looted and dispersed, but perhaps identifying and studying his supralibrios will help to uncover more of the volumes that once belonged to the canon.

1   Life, Works and Library

Tomasz Treter was the son of a bookbinder from Poznań.[12] Smart and diligent, he was educated first in his hometown, and later in the Jesuit College at Braniewo (Braunsberg) in Warmia, the Society's earliest school in Poland-Lithuania, established in 1565 primarily through the efforts of Hosius, the

---

by Grażyna Jurkowlaniec etc., *Art History Empowering Medieval and Early Modern Things*, in Grażyna Jurkowlaniec etc. (eds.), *The Agency of Things in Medieval and Early Modern Art. Materials, Power and Manipulation* (New York: Routledge, 2017), pp. 3–14.

11   Characterising, even briefly, activities and achievements of Hosius falls beyond the scope of this article. From extensive literature on the subject, see e.g. Anton Eichhorn, *Der ermlandische Bischof und Cardinal Stanislaw Hosius* (2 vols., Meinz: Franz Kirchheim, 1854–1855); Jadwiga A. Kalinowska, *Stanisław Hozjusz jako humanista (1504–1579). Studium z dziejów kultury renesansowej* (Olsztyn: Wydawnictwo Hosianum, 2004); Stanisław Achremczyk etc. (eds.), *Kardynał Stanisław Hozjusz (1504–1579). Osoba, myśl, dzieło, czasy i znaczenie* (Olsztyn: Wydawnictwo Hosianum, 2005).

12   After nineteenth-century scholars, such as Anton Eichhorn and Franz Hipler, the greatest contributions to the knowledge of Treter's biography were: Józef Umiński, 'Zapomniany rysownik i rytownik polski XVI w., ks. Tomasz Treter i jego *Theatrum virtutum D. Stanislai Hosii*', *Collectanea Theologica*, 13 (1932), pp. 13–59; Tadeusz Chrzanowski, *Działalność artystyczna Tomasza Tretera* (Warsaw: Państwowe Wydawnictwo Naukowe, 1984); Tadeusz Chrzanowski, 'Uzupełnienia do biografii Tomasza Tretera', *Rocznik Historii Sztuki*, 15 (1985), pp. 129–162.

then bishop of Warmia.[13] In 1569, Tomasz was accepted into the service of this prominent prelate of post-Tridentine church, and in the summer of that year, he embarked with his patron on the journey to Italy. With time, Treter grew to become a trusted secretary of the cardinal, and during his long Roman sojourns, he was to rub elbows with influential figures active in the Eternal City: diplomats, intellectuals, writers and patrons of the arts. In Rome, Treter studied theology and law, and also worked for Hosius as a draughtsman, painter, engraver, monument and print designer and Neo-Latin poet. A versatile and talented amateur, Treter produced a large body of work that varied in both subject matter and function. It often combined the verbal and the visual, evidencing his lifelong interest in emblematic forms. The most monumental of these endeavours was *Theatrum virtutum Stanislai Hosii*, a cycle of approximately a hundred illustrations and odes, which recounted Hosius's life and praised his virtues.[14] Others include allegoric prints (e.g. *Typus Ecclesiae Catholicae*), a cycle *Regum Poloniae icones* and an emblem book *Symbolica vitae Christi meditatio*.[15] Shortly before Hosius's death in 1579, Treter became a canon of Santa Maria in Trastevere, where he proposed an iconographic programme for

---

13   Jan Korewa, *Z dziejów diecezji warmińskiej w XVI wieku. Geneza braniewskiego Hozjanum. Przyczynek do dziejów zespolenia Warmii z Rzeczpospolitą (1549–1564)* (Poznań: Księgarnia św. Wojciecha, 1965); Ludwik Piechnik, 'Gimnazjum w Braniewie w XVI w.', *Nasza Przeszłość*, 7 (1958), pp. 5–72.

14   Treter first drafted 'an emblematic biography' of his late protector in 1580; in 1588, *Theatrum virtutum* was published in Rome, but as a series of prints only. See Karol Bayer, 'Rysunki oryginalne Tomasza Tretera kanonika warmińskiego z drugiej połowy XVI w.', *Biblioteka Warszawska*, 4 (1868), pp. 467–470; Chrzanowski, *Działalność*, pp. 84–116; Magdalena Górska, *Polonia–Respublica–Patria. Personifikacja Polski w sztuce XVI–XVIII wieku* (Wrocław: Wydawnictwo Uniwersytetu Wrocławskiego, 2005), pp. 178–180; Joanna Talbierska, *Grafika XVII wieku w Polsce. Funkcje, ośrodki, artyści, dzieła* (Warsaw: Neriton, 2011), pp. 107–108.

15   From the growing body of literature concerning Treter's work, see: Grażyna Jurkowlaniec, *Sprawczość rycin. Rzymska twórczość graficzna Tomasza Tretera i jej europejskie oddziaływanie* (Krakow: Universitas, 2017), but also Karolina Mroziewicz, '*Regum Poloniae icones* Tomasza Tretera ze zbiorów Biblioteki Królewskiej w Sztokholmie i szwedzkie wątki w losach serii', *Folia Historiae Artium*, 15 (2017), pp. 25–34; Tomasz Treter, *Symboliczne medytacje nad życiem Chrystusa*, transl. Anna Treter (Warsaw: Wydział Polonistyki UW, 2020); Alicja Bielak, '*Symbolica vitae Christi meditatio* Tomasza Tretera jako siedemnastowieczna realizacja emblematycznych medytacji. Źródła graficzne i zamysł zbioru', *Terminus*, 20 (2018), pp. 411–462; Alicja Bielak, 'Nowo odnaleziony autograf Tomasza Tretera. Notatnik z projektem księgi emblematów', *Terminus*, 34 (2021), pp. 259–307.

the sumptuously rebuilt Altemps Chapel.[16] In the years that followed, the 'piccolo canonico polacco' travelled between Italy and Poland before finally leaving Rome for good in 1593. Afterwards, Treter lived in Frombork as a chancellor of the Warmia chapter, in a house where he had 'every wall and every ceiling coffer' decorated with 'impressive emblems and clever mottos' and where he amassed an ample, well-kept library.[17]

The collection remained in Warmia only briefly: in 1626 and at the beginning of the eighteenth century, it was looted by the Swedes, and subsequently the books once owned by Treter were distributed among Swedish libraries, including the Uppsala Universitetsbibliotek and Kungliga Biblioteket in Stockholm.[18] It is in these two collections that books marked with Treter's supralibros have been identified. The Uppsala University Library has preserved Jerónimo Osório's *Opera*, while the National Library of Sweden holds a larger collection of volumes bound for Treter, the most impressive of which are two monumental folios of works by pope Gregory I, with deluxe bindings executed in Gdańsk (Danzig), tooled in blind and high-quality gold.[19]

---

16   See Grażyna Jurkowlaniec, 'Cult and Patronage. The Madonna della Clemenza, the Altemps and a Polish Canon in Rome', *Zeitschrift für Kunstgeschichte*, 72.1 (2009), pp. 69–98.

17   'Omnis paries, omne lacunar, speciosis emblematis et ingeniosis lemmatis eruditionem spirat'. See Georg Schönfels, 'Typographus ad bonae mentis lectorem', in Tomasz Treter, *Symbolica vitae Christi meditatio* (Braniewo: Georg Schönfels, 1612), USTC 2055155, f.)(5r.–)(5v.

18   Otto Walde, *Storhetstidens litterara krigsbyten. En kulturhistoriskbibliografisk studie* (Uppsala: Almqvist & Wiksell, 1916–1920), I. 32, 97–99. Krystyna Korzon, 'Fragment treterianów w Ossolineum', *Ze Skarbca Kultury*, 35 (1990), pp. 155–173. Walde, p. 99, also mentions a copy of Cassiodorus, *Variarum libri XII* (Lyon 1595), now in the Royal Library in Copenhagen, inscribed 'Thomas Treterus Custos Varmiensis. Emptus Braunsbergae 26 Junij 1601'.

19   Walde, *Storhetstidens*, p. 98. Jerónimo Osório, *Opera* (Rome: Bartolomeo Bonfadino, 1592), copy at the Uppsala University Library, call no. 1500 t. Polen Fol. 19, USTC 845594; copy annotated in Treter's hand: 'Emptus Varmiae a Joanne Krause Bibliopola Gedanensis 26 Maji 1600. Constat florenis Polonicis quinque'. See Adam Heymowski, 'Reliures armoriées polonaises de l'époque des Jagiellon et des Vasa dans les collections suédoises', in Krystyna Dymkowska, Joanna Pasztalaniec-Jarzyńska (eds.), *VIIIe Congrès International des Bibliophiles, Varsovie, 23–29 juillet 1973* (Warsaw: Biblioteka Narodowa, 1985), p. 157; Sten G. Lindberg, *Reliures polonaises dans les bibliotheques suedoises de l'âge gothique, de la renaissance et de la reforme*, in Dymkowska, Jarzyńska, *Congrès*, p. 119. Gregorius I, *Opera omnia* (Antwerp: Gerard Smits, 1572), KB liste VIII B: 26, USTC 404668; copy annotated: 'Ligata et curata Gedani 1598 constaterunt mihi florenis 10 Polonicis'. See Lindberg in *Reliures*, pp. 85–86, 98, 119, il. 40; Wagner, *Superekslibris polski*, p. 380, plate XV.

FIGURE 17.1 Upper cover of Gregorius I, *Opera omnia*, vol. 1 (Antwerp 1572). Stockholm, Kungliga Biblioteket, KB liste VIII B: 26
PHOTO COURTESY OF WOLFGANG UNDORF

2 The Brazen Serpent

On these volumes, one cover (usually the upper cover) has a stamp with an oval enclosed by a thick, ornamental frame. The stamp depicts a fierce reptile coiled around a tau-shaped cross, its wings stretched and mouth revealing a protruding tongue. The image is surrounded by the legend THOMAS TRETERVS CVSTOS VARMIEN<SIS>.

The other supralibros (regularly stamped on the lower cover) is a similar medallion composition. It has an elaborate cartouche enclosing a *pictura* that shows a cross with its vertical beam entwined by a snake and mounted by the IHS monogram encircled by light rays. Above the image, a brief urging 'HOC SAPE' (Understand this!) is inscribed.[20]

FIGURE 17.2   Supralibros of Tomasz Treter, upper cover of Jerónimo Osório, *Opera* (Rome 1592), Uppsala Universitetsbibliotek, call no. 1500 t. Polen Fol. 19

20   A device in Claude Paradin *Devises Heroïques* (Lyon 1557) is erroneously presented as an immediate source for Treter's *impresa* in Carlo Bertelli, 'Di un cardinale dell'impero

FIGURE 17.3   Supralibros of Tomasz Treter, lower cover of Jerónimo Osório, *Opera* (Rome 1592), Uppsala Universitetsbibliotek, call no. 1500 t. Polen Fol. 19

Both stamps represent and interpret the same iconographical theme: the brazen serpent, a subject taken from the Book of Numbers (21: 4–9), which tells the story of Israelites who rebelled against Moses during the exodus from Egypt. God sent a plague of snakes to punish their disobedience, and many people died. The cure revealed to Moses was a 'serpent of brass', placed on a pole for the stricken Israelites to look at and be cured. Because of the typological reference inspired by Christ's own words ('as Moses lifted up the serpent in the wilderness, even so must the Son of man be lifted up: That whosoever believeth in him should not perish, but have eternal life', Jn 3: 14–15), the Old Testament subject (the story and its visual representation) became widely understood as a prototype of Christ's

e di un canonico Polacco in S. Maria in Trastevere', *Paragone–Arte*, 327 (1977), pp. 89–128 (p. 100). Repeated in Chrzanowski, *Działalność*, p. 149.

sacrifice, a prefiguration of salvation and redemption.[21] By the mid-sixteenth century, the brazen serpent had emerged as an independent scene in contemporary figurative arts, while the interpretations of the Old Testament episode were recurring in polemical writings of the time, as Catholics and Protestants analysed the narrative and its meaning with renewed interest. The Lutheran doctrinal discourse viewed the crucifixion as the central event in the history of humanity, and faith in the redeeming power of Christ's passion was stressed as being of the greatest importance for individual salvation. Luther used the story of the brazen serpent and its typological interpretation to visually explain the doctrine of justification by faith (*iustificatio ex fide*) and to clearly determine his stance on image worship. For the reformer and his followers, Moses's serpent became a symbol of justification by faith: the stricken Israelites, for whom the only cure was trust in God's word personified in the serpent of brass resembled the Christians, for whom the only hope of salvation is their faith in the crucified Christ.[22] Catholics cited the Old Testament episode first and foremost as historical proof of the legitimacy of image-making, arguing that, unlike Jews, who were inclined to idolatry, Christians understood that the image is merely a sign referring to the model.[23] Importantly, Hosius also explained the subject, for example, in his widely disseminated *Confessio catholicae fidei Christiana* (a treatise reprinted throughout his life more than thirty times):

> The church is rightly raising a monument of crucified Christ in the most eminent place of temple, in such a manner that it could be seen by everyone; that way as those that were bitten by snakes could look at the brazen serpent that Moses lifted up in in the desert and be cured, so these who want to be cured of their sin wounds left by Satan the serpent, would look up at the One, who agreed to die for us hanged at the cross, so that, thanks to Him, we could receive hope of remission of our sins.[24]

---

21   Donald L. Ehresmann, 'The Brazen Serpent, a Reformation Motif in the Works of Lucas Cranach the Elder and his Workshop', *Marsyas. Studies in the History of Art*, 13 (1966–1967), pp. 32–47; Molly Faries, 'A Drawing of the Brazen Serpent by Michiel Coxie', *Revue belge d'archéologie et d'historie de l'art*, 44 (1975), pp. 131–141; Jefferson C. Harrison, 'The Brazen Serpent by Maarten van Heemskerck. Aspects of its Style and Meaning', *Record of the Art Museum. Princeton University*, 49. 2 (1990), pp. 16–29; Alicia Craig Faxon, Nancy Frazier, 'Crucifixion', in Helene E. Roberts (ed.), *Encyclopedia of Comparative Iconography. Themes Depicted in the Work of Art* (Chicago, London: Fitzroy Dearborn, 1998), I. 189–198.

22   See Faries, 'A Drawing of the Brazen Serpent', pp. 137–38, and Ehresmann, 'The Brazen Serpent', pp. 32–47.

23   Eleanor A. Saunders, 'A Commentary on Iconoclasm in Several Print Series by Maarten van Heemskerck', *Simiolus*, 10 (1978–79), pp. 59–83.

24   'Verum et in medio templi cuiusque in eminentiori loco, ut ab omnibus conspici possit, Christi crucifixi statuam erexit, quo sicut in serpentem aeneum, quem in deserto Moyses

The Catholic theologians also promoted the brazen serpent as a symbol of Eucharist, that is, the figure of Christ's true and real presence in transubstantiated bread and wine. The meaning of the Old Testament scene might also converge on temperance, following the exegesis proposed by Philo of Alexandria, and often quoted in the early modern period.

The new chapter in the history of the interpretation of the brazen serpent was written during the thirteen years of Gregory XIII's papacy, precisely during the time when Treter lived in Rome, close to the curia's affairs. The family coat of arms of Boncompagni, elected a pope in 1572, was a winged dragon without a tail. Boncompagni's Draco evoked interpretations associating it with the demonic serpent and with Satan, posing a political, 'public relations' problem for Gregory XIII. The pope and his family sought to neutralize the negative connotation of the Boncompagnis coat of arms. Their campaign to counter defamatory interpretations drew many intellectuals and artists, who reimagined the Draco in positive terms in numerous works, including drawings, pamphlets, printed volumes and decorations of the Vatican buildings.[25] Many of these depicted the pope's dragon as a brazen serpent.[26]

While living in Rome, Treter must have been aware of the efforts of the Boncompagnis and the authors of verbal and visual works who (in view of gaining the pope's grace) were seeking to shift and modify the traditional perceptions of the Draco. All this information about the new lease of life of the brazen serpent, all this talking and publishing, could only have reinforced Tomasz's conviction that he once had made the right decision in choosing the old symbol as his sign of recognition and identification; 'once', because Treter started to use the image of the brazen serpent as his personal badge not in Rome, but before his voyage to Italy and before Boncompagni's elevation to the papacy.[27]

---

exaltavit, qui morsi a serpentibus intuebantur, sanabantur, sic qui vellent a morsibus peccatorum sanari, quos intulit serpens diabolus, in eum intuerentur, qui pro nobis in cruce pendens mori dignatus est, certa cum spe remissionis peccatorum illius merito consequendae', Stanisław Hosius, *Confessio catholicae fidei Christiana* (Mainz: Franz Behem, 1557), f. xIIr, USTC 624569.

25 Marco Ruffini, 'A Dragon for the Pope. Politics and Emblematics at the court of Gregory XIII', *Memoirs of the American Academy in Rome*, 54 (2009), pp. 83–105. Perhaps most influential being Principio Fabrizi's *Delle allusioni, imprese, et emblemi* (Rome 1588), manuscript composed in 1579, with numerous interpretative ideas.

26 Yvan Loskoutoff, *Un art de la réforme catholique*, vol. 2: *La symbolique du pape Grégoire XIII (1572–1585) et des Boncompagni* (Paris: Honoré Champion, 2018), pp. 107–132.

27 However, since Ugo Boncompagni was Hosius's friend from their university period in Bologna, Treter might have known the coat of arms of this Italian family already at the time when he studied in Braniewo and joined the cardinal's household. See Jadwiga Ambrozja Kalinowska, 'Podróże Stanisława Hozjusza. Zarys problematyki', in: Danuta Quirini-Popławska, Łukasz Burkiewicz (eds.), *Itinera clericorum. Kulturotwórcze i religijne aspekty podróży duchownych*, pp. 287–300.

SUPRALIBROS AS A CREED

FIGURE 17.4   Tomasz Treter's seal stamped on a letter of 1569. Olsztyn, Archiwum Archidiecezji Warmińskiej, Ms AB 62

Already in his young years, Treter stamped his letters with a non-armorial seal that depicted a shield with a winged snake twisted around a cross; the shield was flanked by the legend THOMAS TRETERVS.

Treter used this signet ring until his death. This is evidenced by the seals preserved in the canon's letters: the earliest letter sealed by the signet ring with Treter's non-heraldic sign described above was sent in 1569 (the year Treter embarked on his first journey to Rome), and the most recent examples come from 1605 to 1610. To authenticate his correspondence in the last years of his life (and possibly earlier as well, but there are no documents confirming such a supposition), the canon also used a signet ring different, but with the

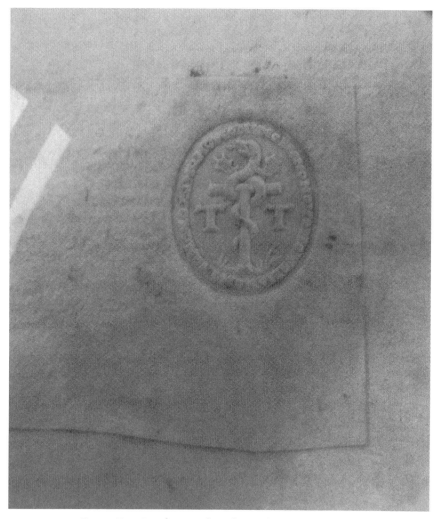

FIGURE 17.5   Tomasz Treter's seal stamped on a letter of 1604. Krakow, Biblioteka XX Czartoryskich (Muzeum Narodowe), Ms 1625

representation also repeating the brazen serpent theme: this new seal (known from letters sent between 1605 and 1610) depicted a tau cross entwined by a winged snake, raising among plants. In the seal composition, this living cross was flanked by two letters T: Treter's initials, but perhaps also a visual allusion to Golgotha where Christ's cross stood between crosses of two criminals.[28]

28   In Archiwum Archidiecezji Warmińskiej in Olsztyn, Ms D 62; in Biblioteka Książąt Czartoryskich (Oddział Muzeum Narodowego) in Krakow, Ms 1625, 1626, 1628.

The brazen serpent image was used as well as Treter's sign of authorisation or workmanship, constituting a part of elaborate designs. A striking example is a manuscript *Lectionarium sanctorum Ecclesiae S. Mariae in Transtiberim*, copied and illuminated by Treter, the frontispiece of which features an architectural title border with the canon's personal sign displayed at the bottom.[29]

Burgher arms were non-noble badges of identity, which were usually personal in nature, but could be passed down within a family. Often, they depicted (in place of a heraldic charge) an identifiable item. Those who adopted and used such *insignia* clearly recognized the potential of heraldic representation as an allegoric medium and at least some burgher arms were presented and interpreted by their educated bearers and viewers as symbolic images.[30] Treter's non-armorial sign (as stamped on his letters or displayed on the covers of his books) depicted not an item, but a scene, and one that has long served as a symbol of layered Christological significance. There is little doubt that it must have acted as a badge of identity, a sign of recognition and ownership, as well as a device that (at least for some viewers) resonated the symbolical tradition of interlaced threads recapitulated above.

Bürgerwappen could resemble *imprese* lacking a motto.[31] However, it is only rarely possible to observe how the symbolic capacities of the entities depicted in any given burgher arms could have been handled and the components of the original device elaborated upon to reinterpret it into an *impresa*, that is a composition devised (and understood) as expressing ideas in an individual's mind, their sentiments, aspirations and ambitions.[32] Supralibros on books that once belonged to the Warmia canon are an example of such a manipulation. The stamp that is displayed on the front covers of Treter's volumes constitutes a transposition of the canon's burgher arms as was presented on his signet rings: the brazen serpent, a biblical *figura*, with crucifixion implicit in it, is displayed in this supralibros with the priest's name and title. However, the other of Treter's supralibros (the one usually placed on the bottom cover of his books) enhances the legibility of the original idea by associating the

---

29   Chrzanowski, *Działalność*, pp. 135–143; Chrzanowski, *Uzupełnienia*, p. 146.
30   Pedro F. Campa, 'The Space between Heraldry and the Emblem. The Case of Spain', in Peter M. Daly (ed.), *Emblem Scholarship. Directions and Developments. A Tribute to Gabriel Hornstein* (Turnhout: Brepols, 2005), pp. 55–57; Magdalena Górska, 'Symbolika heraldyczna a teoria impresy. Przykład *Orbis Polonus* Szymona Okolskiego', *Rocznik Polskiego Towarzystwa Heraldycznego*, new series 13 (2014), pp. 35–49. On controversies pertaining to *imprese* without mottos, see Lippincott, p. 58; Caldwell, *The Sixteenth-Century Italian Impresa*, pp. 16–17, 36–37, 218–219.
31   Lippincott, 'The Genesis', p. 52.
32   On theories and practices of *imprese*, see Caldwell, *The Sixteenth-Century Italian Impresa*.

representation of the brazen serpent with further symbolic material. The picture is more complex, as it merges the depiction of the snake with that of Christogram surrounded with a radiant glory. Such a *pictura* reveals in encapsulated form the parallel notion of deliverance through faith in God's chosen image (the Moses' serpent) and of salvation through Christ and his sacrifice on the cross. Moreover, the image was associated with a verbal component other than just a label naming the owner of the device. The motto 'HOC SAPE' (Understand this!) not only transforms the composition into a full *impresa*, an amalgamate of word and image. It also urges the viewer to contemplate and comprehend the meaning of the symbol it accompanies.

3   Device as a Creed

By definition, any given *impresa* can elicit a wide range of interpretations: 'without the confirmation of the inventor or the bearer, all suggestions as to meaning could only be supposition'.[33] In the case of Treter's device, we are fortunate to have additional clarification of its significance, an exegesis that most likely comes from someone familiar with the meaning hidden within this badge of identity. It is found in Treter's posthumously published emblem book, *Symbolica vitae Christi meditatio*.

This volume is a collection of verbal-visual wholes, in which engravings interact with Bible quotations serving as mottoes, and with prose commentaries.[34] Treter drafted these meditative compositions during his Roman years already (between 1569 and 1579), in an environment of unparalleled visual richness, and liberally employing iconographical models from contemporary emblem books.[35] Towards the end of his life, in Warmia, Tomasz oversaw the publication of the work being prepared by his nephew, Błażej Treter. The volume was printed in Braniewo by Georg Schönfels in 1612, two years after the author's death.

Each of the verbal-visual compositions in *Symbolica vitae Christi meditatio* consists of an engraving with a motto and a prose commentary. Compositions are organized in pairs, grouped together under a single heading. Yet, the

---

[33] Caldwell, *The Sixteenth-Century Italian Impresa*, p. 222.
[34] On various structural forms of emblems, see e.g. David Graham, 'Emblema Multiplex. Towards a Typology of Emblematic Forms, Structures and Functions', in Peter M. Daly (ed.), *Emblem Scholarship*, pp. 131–157; Peter M. Daly, *The Emblem in Early Modern Europe. Contributions to the Theory of the Emblem* (London: Routledge, 2014), pp. 131–150.
[35] Three collections have so far been identified as his sources: Claude Paradin' *Devises heroïques*, *Emblemata* by Hadrianus Junius – Adriaen de Jonghe, and *Picta poesis, ut pictura poesis erit* by Aneau Barthélemy. See Bielak, '*Symbolica vitae Christi meditatio* Tomasza Tretera', p. 414.

FIGURE 17.6 Tomasz Treter, *Symbolica vitae Christi meditatio* (Braniewo: Georg Schönfels, 1612), pp. [Gg3v–Gg4r]. Warsaw, Biblioteka Narodowa, SD XVII.3.2721

volume's final facing pages (preceded by indexes and errata, and thus appearing to belong to the paratextual materials rather than the main body of the book), display a different emblematic structure.[36]

On the left-hand side of the opening, beneath the heading 'In Symbolum T.T.', the 'HOC SAPE' *impresa* is displayed, and it is unclear if the brazen serpent crest on the facing page belongs under the same *inscriptio*. Below the pictures, multiple verses are printed in Roman and Italic typefaces. Two of these are anagrams that rearrange the letters from the canon's name, repeatedly emphasising the idea of 'overcoming fate'.[37] However, the first distich printed right underneath the 'HOC SAPE' *impresa* seems to provide its exegesis. It reads:

---

36 They also seem to echo the custom pervading the books produced in early modern Poland-Lithuania, that of preceding the work presented in an edition by a heraldic blason, a verbal-visual composition, where the woodcut displays a coat of arms of the work's author or patron, and an epigram follows, interpreting the heraldic representation, at the same time praising its bearer. See Bartłomiej Czarski, *Stemmaty w staropolskich książkach, czyli rzecz o poezji heraldycznej* (Warsaw: Muzeum Pałac w Wilanowie, 2012).

37 *In Anagramma euisdem*: Sors levis rebus dominatur imis: / Prosperis tollit, levat haec sinistris. / Tu teras sortem: monet hoc volumen / Voxque Treteri. [*In the anagram of the same one*: The variable fate rules the lowest: / Sometimes it brings fortune, sometimes misfortune. / Overcome the fate! This is this book's admonition, /And Treter's.] *Anagramma*. *Tu sortem teras*: Ludit in humanis sors fallacissima rebus: / Quod parit illa, perit; quod struit illa, ruit: / Divitias parit his, aliis molitur honores, / Sors ubi Morsve rotam verterit,

> Seps morsu mortem, crux icto sepe salutem;
> Hoc sapis? Hoc, iam, quid sit sapuisse capis.
>
> The snake means death from a bite, the cross, salvation from the snake's bite.
> Do you understand this? So you understand what is wisdom.

The tightly constructed epigram interprets the image, but its brevity suggests that it is also a statement of the bearer's faith and a summary of Christianity's basic beliefs.[38] It is even more striking when we consider that *symbolum* as 'the creed' was the most important usage of the term during the Middle Ages and into the Renaissance.[39] Presumably, Treter and the people assisting him in preparation of the volume published in 1612 were well aware of this tradition and practice. It is perhaps no coincidence that Tomasz's *impresa* (and his burgher arms) was included in his emblem book and printed under the heading 'Symbolum T.T.'

I say 'Treter and the people assisting him', as I suppose it was not the canon who penned all the epigrams linked to the representations of the brazen serpent in the 1612 book. While the verses quoted above could have been written by Tomasz Treter, the distich printed below them refers to the canon as deceased already, and elucidates not on his *impresa*, but praises the parenetic value of Treter's *Symbolica vitae Christi meditatio*:

> Quem vivus sapuit probitate Treterus Jesum,
> Hoc post fata libro nos sapuisse docet.
>
> Late Treter teaches us in this book about Jesus,
> whom he came to know when living thanks to his righteousness.

---

    omne labat. / Docta quod at pietas dedit aere perennius exstat. / Tu pie TV SORTEM docte TRETERE teras. [*Anagram. Defeat the fate*: Deceptive Fate plays with human affairs: / What it creates gets lost, what it builds, falls into ruin. / It sends wealth to some, honors to others; / But when Fate or Death spins the wheel, everything is gone. / While, what a learned piety offers is stronger than bronze. / You, devout Treter, defeat the Fate wisely.]

38 Placing the verbs *sapis* and *capis* in immediate vicinity seems to echo St Augustine's paronomasia (*Contra Iulianum* (*opus imperfectum*), 5,44): 'Si ergo vis Manicheos vel devitare vel vincere, hoc sape, hoc cape intellegendo si potes, credendo si non potes, quoniam ex bonis orta sunt mala, nec est aliquid malitia nisi boni indigentia'. The phrase 'seps morsu mortem' may be an allusion not only to snakes that attacked Israelites, but also Satan who tempted Eve to bite the fruit from the tree of the knowledge of good and evil.

39 Elizabeth See Watson, *Achille Bocchi and the Emblematic Book as Symbolic Form* (Cambridge: Cambridge University Press, 1993), pp. 106–107.

Similarly, the couplet underneath the representation on the right-hand page mentions Treter as no longer alive:

Cernit acuta draco custodis digma Treteri,
Virus at huic adimens crux super astra c<ur>at.

Draco sees the subtle sign of custos Treter,
while the cross that renders venom harmless, rules over the stars.

Interestingly, this distich seems to identify the brazen serpent with the Draco, the family coat of arms of Gregory XIII, at the same time suggesting the line of associations between the Old Testament subject and Christ's passion, as well as between Treter's burger arms and Boncompagni's crest.[40] As such, it interprets Treter's device as engendering layered readings, which is consistent with the claims of *imprese* theoreticians, who repeatedly stated that these compositions should allow for syncretic readings, and that (with time and use) they should acquire new meanings, absorbing rather than replacing earlier ones.[41] A successful *impresa* would also convey an overt, more obvious meaning, while inviting less evident interpretations, not apparent but intelligible to the initiated. The components of the device could also be recombined and elaborated upon to form variants of the original composition that highlight specific aspects of the original idea.[42]

4   Conclusions

When focusing on early modern Polish bindings, it is possible to see how book possessors who had their ownership stamps cut were abandoning heraldic motifs in favour of alternate structures and symbolic representations.[43] Treter's

---

40   On the tradition that Treter was ennobled by Gregory XII and received the privilege to use the Boncompagnis's Draco, see Justyna Kiliańczyk-Zięba, 'Wąż Miedziany i rzekoma nobilitacja. Przyczynek do biografii Tomasza Tretera', *Terminus*, 2 (2023) [forthcoming].
41   Watson, *Achille Bocchi*, pp. 37–38.
42   Claudia Rousseau, 'The Yoke impresa of Leo X', *Mitteilungen des Kunsthistorischen Instituts in Florenz*, 33 (1989), pp. 113–114.
43   A large number of illustrations showing supralibros belonging to Polish collectors are to be found in: Kazimierz Piekarski, *Superexlibrisy polskie*; Maria Sipayłło, *Polskie superexlibrisy XV–XVIII wieku w zbiorach Biblioteki Uniwersyteckiej w Warszawie* (Warsaw: PAX, 1988); Maria Cubrzyńska-Leonarczyk, *Polskie superekslibrisy XVI–XVIII wieku w zbiorach Biblioteki Uniwersyteckiej w Warszawie. Centuria druga* (Warsaw: Biblioteka Narodowa, 2001); and in a recently published monograph Wagner, *Superekslibris polski*, where an

supralibros are, in turn, a striking example of how badges of identity with roots in the mediaeval tradition of heraldic recognition came to express ideas about the owners of the volumes they marked. In other words, how they were reinterpreted into *imprese*, signs imbued with 'a unique sort of reciprocity between the reality and the ideal self-image of the bearer'.[44] Tomasz Treter's burgher arms and his *impresa* stamped on the bindings of his library were badges of identity whose literary and iconographic points of reference encompassed the continuous tradition of vocabulary of heraldic devices, as well as a more intellectual sphere, informed by current artistic trends and forms of decoration for cultural élites. Neither of the supralibros was overly obscure or controversial, and they worked as a pair on Treter's binding, as if they were an obverse (both theological and identifying a person) and a symbolical reverse. *Litterati*, such as Treter (and those responsible for the epigrams on the final pages of *Symbolica vitae Christi meditatio*), were most likely to have the knowledge needed to decipher and explain the signs found on the books belonging to the Warmia canon. For those who did not understand their significance or did not have the advantage of a guide to their complexities, 'devices on books' might nevertheless serve simply as signs of identification and ownership woven into the ornamentation of the bindings they marked.

Acknowledgements

I wish to thank Bartłomiej Czarski and Wojciech Ryczek for their help with translating Treter's epigrams from Latin. To both of them, but also to Magdalena Górska and Magdalena Komorowska, I am grateful for sharing their erudition with me. The research for this chapter has been supported by a grant from the Priority Research Area Heritage under the Strategic Programme Excellence Initiative at Jagiellonian University.

---

elaborate apparatus of footnotes and a bibliography list numerous publications reproducing photographs of Polish mediaeval and early modern bookbindings.

44   Rousseau, 'The Yoke impresa', p. 113.

Index

Acquaviva, Claudio   60, 61, 330
Agostino da Amatrice   244
Alagona, Pietro   242
Alberici, Giacomo   233, 241, 242, 245
Albertus Magnus   210, 234
Albertus of Padua   234
Albrecht Hohenzollern, duke of Prussia   129
Alexander of Aphrodisias   234
Alexander of Hales   234
Alexander IV, pope   266
Alexander VI, pope   229, 230
Alexander VII, pope   229
Alfonso de Castro   192, 193, 195
Allen, William   53, 54, 57–60, 62–67, 69–73
Alvise de Calvatone (Aloysius de Calvatono)   234–244
Amandus, Johannes   126
Ambrose, St   36, 187, 190
Ammonius Hermiae   234
Anastatius of Sinai   23
Andrea da Controne   242
Anemoecius Wolfgang   160
Anonymus Neveleti   185
Anselm of Canterbury   23
Antonio da Budrio   234
Antonio de Guevara   212
Antonius Wilhelm   168
Apel, Jakob   169
Äpinus, Johannes   125
Apuleius   236
Aranci, Gilberto   279
Arbusow, Leonid   187
Aristotle (Aristoteles)   171, 172, 190, 210, 234, 246
Arrianus Flavius   236
Astete, Gaspar   49, 50, 278
Auger, Édmond   278
Augustine, St   187, 192, 210, 211, 214, 226, 233, 238, 241, 296
Averroes   234
Avicenna   236
Azpilcueta, Martín de   211, 242, 244
Azzone   234

Balaguer, Pedro   224, 225
Balassi, Bálint   296

Balduin, Friedrich   305
Baldung, Hans   123
Barbara Zapolya, queen of Poland   128
Baronio, Cesare   20
Barré, Antonio   90
Barrera, Alonso de la   46, 47
Bartolo da Sassoferrato   234
Basa, Domenico   21, 22, 26, 28, 29, 31, 33–36, 87, 89–92
Basso della Rovere, Girolamo   230
Batthyány, Ádám   298, 303
Bauer, Albert   185
Bellarmine, Robert   27, 242, 278, 293, 300–302, 331
Belorado, Lucas de   46
Benigno da Vercelli   244
Bentkowicz, Augustyn   324
Berarducci, Mauro Antonio   211
Bernard, St   211, 238
Bertano, Giovanni Antonio   207
Bessarion   27
Beyer Hartmann   160
Bèze Théodore de   160, 319, 320, 331
Biondo, Flavio   236
Birkowski, Fabian   331
Blado, Antonio   21, 23, 90
Bliwernica, Aaron   324
Boccaccio, Giovanni   236, 246
Bochius, Johannes
Bock, Hieronymus   153
Boeschenstein, Johann   95
Boethius   234, 246
Boldewan, Johann   125
Bona Sforza   128
Bonaventure, St   211–214
Boncompagni, Ugo. *See* Gregory XIII, pope
Bonfini, Antonio   291, 292
Boniface VIII, pope   234, 257
Borja, Francisco de   281, 282
Bornemisza, Péte   298
Borrini, Maurizio   232, 233
Bougeant, Guillaume H.   278
Boyer, Laurentius   350
Brendi, Battista   231, 247
Brenner, Martin   293
Breza, Wojciech Konstantyn   334

Bridget, St   296
Briesemann, Johannes von   125
Bröcker, Heinrich   187
Bruni, Leonardo   236
Bryling, Nikolaus   168
Buchwald-Pelcowa, Paulina   324
Buendía, Gaspar de   50
Bugenhagen, Johann   125, 151, 160
Bundere, Jean van den   242
Buratelli, Gabriele   234

Calepio, Ambrogio   244
Calvin, John   55, 319, 336, 338
Camerarius, Joachim   160
Campana, Cesare   240
Canisius, Peter   277, 278
Caracciolo, Roberto   212, 234, 238
Cardellis, Giovanni de   231
Cardona, Juan Bautista   148
Carga, Giovanni   24, 25, 33
Carletti, Angelo da Chivasso   211
Carminati, Aurelio da Treviglio   238, 241, 245
Cervini, Erennio   24, 25
Cervini, Marcello   17, 25, 36
Chalecki, Dymitr   342
Chalecki, Mikołaj Krzysztof   325, 328, 335, 342, 343, 348, 350, 351, 353
Charles V, emperor   118, 127, 193
Chaves, Tomaz de   211
Chigi, family   230
Cholinus, Maternus   9
Chytraeus, David   168
Cicero Marcus Tullius   236, 244
Clemens de Bononia   244
Clemens de Valico   243
Clemens V, pope   234
Clemens VIII, pope   220
Clemente da Ferrara   242
Coattino, Francesco   91, 92
Cochlaeus, Johannes   194
Colonna, Marcantonio   222
Confetti, Giovanni Battista   238
Cordus, Euricius   151, 153, 160
Costa, Jorge da   230, 247
Cox, Leonard   128
Cranach, Lucas   123
Cybo, family   230
Czobor, Erzsébet   304, 305

D'Angelo Bartolomeo   212
Da Palestrina, Giovanni Pierluigi   28, 76, 80, 81, 85, 86, 97
Daniłowicz, Jan   345
Daniłowicz, Zofia   345
Dantyszek, Jan   129, 134
Daukša, Mikalojus   282
Davanzati, Bernardo   64, 65
David, Jan   327, 347
de Rancé, Armand Jean   260
De Vio, Thomas (Caietanus)   210
Dedelow, Bernhard   125
Denis le Chartreux   212, 213
Dias, Felipe   213
Dobokay, Sándor   296
Dolciati, Antonio   234
Domenico della Trinità   324
Dorico, Valerio   91
Drexel, Jeremias   288
Dryander, Johann   153
Duns Scotus Joannes   211, 213, 234

Eck, Johannes   108–113, 115
Eder, Wolfgang   70–72
Egenolph, Christian   168
Eliano, Vittorio   27
Elizabeth I, queen of England   52, 53, 55, 56, 57, 59, 62–69, 73, 319
Elzevirs, family   263
Erasmus of Rotterdam   298, 299, 129, 130, 138, 140, 141, 153, 160, 172
Erastus, Thomas   160
Erytraeus, Valentin   160
Espinosa, Juan Bautista de   46
Esslinger, Johann Martin   261, 262
Estella, Diego   212, 240
Eucharius, Christophorus   265, 271
Euclid   236
Eutropius   236

Faber, Nikolaus   168
Fabriani, Ippolito   233
Fabricius, Georg   160
Ferdinand I, emperor   194
Fiamma, Gabriele   212
Ficino, Marsilio   211, 241
Filareto, Apollonio   373
Folengius, Johann Baptista   262
Foxe, John   52

INDEX

Francis Xavier, St   265, 278
Francisco de Vitoria   211
Frederick Jagiellon   127
Freig, Johannes Thomas   160
Fritsch, Ambrosius   168
Frizzoli, Lorenzo   90
Froben, Johann   153, 160, 168
Froschauer, Christoph   153, 168
Frycz Modrzewski, Andrzej   160
Fumo, Bartolomeo   211

Gabriele da Como   244
Galen   236
Galletti, Fabrizio   21, 22
Gardano, Alessandro   91
Gellius Aulus   236
Gerhard, Johann   324
Gesner, Conrad   153, 160
Giles of Rome   210, 213, 234, 241, 246
Giovanni da Imola   234
Giovanni Maria da Livorno   234
Giovio, Paolo   240
Girolamo da Palermo   205
Giunta, family   32, 64, 79, 234
Gleditsch, Johann Friedrich   263
Goclenius, Rudolph   160
Gonzaga, Aloysius   238
Górski, Stanisław   135
Gosellini, Giuliano   242
Gouffier, Claude   373
Granada, Luis de   212, 284, 285
Granjon, Robert   28, 24, 35, 76, 87, 88, 90–94, 97, 98
Grassis, Paris de   84, 85
Grbic, Matija   160
Gregorius de Bulgaro   243
Gregory I (the Great), pope   377
Gregory IX, pope   234
Gregory VII, pope   23
Gregory XIII, pope (Boncompagni, Ugo)   19–29, 31, 33, 34, 36, 75, 76, 80–82, 85–89, 92–94, 97, 98
Grifoni, Giovanni Andrea   243
Grimaldi, Giovanni Battista   373
Grochowski, Stanisław   323, 327
Gronenberg, Simon   168
Grundtmann, Friedrich   262
Guerra, Giovanni Battista   206

Guicciardini, Francesco   240
Guidetti, Giovanni   75, 76, 82, 84–87, 89–98
Gustavus II Adolphus, king of Sweden   143
Gwalther, Rudolf   153, 160

Haeften, Benedictus van   328
Hafenreffer, Matthias   301, 305
Haimo   192
Hall, Joseph   331
Hanfelt, Georg   303
Hantzsch, Georg   168
Haro, Pedro López de   46
Haultin, Pierre   26
Hegge, Jakob   125
Henri III, king of France   66, 67, 68, 69, 73, 315, 319, 320
Henri I, duke of Guise   60
Henri IV, king of France (Henri of Navarre)   66, 69
Henry VIII, king of England   52, 54, 56, 62, 67, 73, 310, 311, 319, 320
Herentals, Thomas van   108, 121
Hermann V von Wied   194
Herwagen, Johann   168
Hey, Lucas van der   104–106
Hińcza, Marcin   328, 345, 347, 248, 351–353
Hosius (Hozjusz), Stanislaw   53, 60, 336, 374–376, 381
Hubert, Adrien   312
Huerta, Alonso de la   46
Hugo, Hermann   326
Hutten, Ulrich van   160

Ilario da Crema   243
Illyés, András   298
Ilmanowski, Kasper   172
Inchino, Gabriele d'   299
Infantas, Fernando de las   81, 86

Josephus Flavius   236, 244
Julius II, pope   84, 229
Julius III, pope   92
Justinus Marcus Junianus
Jacobus de Voragine   192, 206, 212
Jan III Sobieski, king of Poland   335
Javelli, Crisostomo   210
Jean de Jandun   210
Jerome, St   23, 172, 175, 189, 190, 211

Joanna, Benedictine nun 267
Jobin, Bernhard 168
John Chrysostom, St 23, 27, 33, 160, 211
Jorge, Marcos 278
Joris, David 104
Joseph II, emperor 266
Junius, Melchior 168, 168
Justinian, emperor 189, 190

Karnkowski, Stanisław 160
Keckermann, Bartholomaeus 160
Kecskeméti, C. János 305
Kelemen, Didák 298
Kestnerowa, Elisabeth 264
Ketelhut, Christian 125
Khesl, Melchior 299
Kilianstein, Anton Jonas 262
Kirchhofer, Theodor 187
Klaszekovits, István 301, 305
Knaust, Heinrich 160
Knittel, Kaspar 264
Knopke, Andreas 125
Kopcsányi, Márton 298
Krzycki, Andrzej 124, 127–130, 133, 136–140
Kuricke, Johannes 125

Lacki, Aleksander Teodor 352
Lactantius 236
Lanckisch, Friedrich 262
Łaski, Jan, archbishop, primate of Poland 133, 136
Laterna, Marcin 286
Łęczycki, Mikołaj 334
Ledesma, Diego de 12, 275–287
León, Juan de 46
Leonello da Manzolino 244
Lépes, Bálint 299
Lippomano, Luigi 240
Lipsius, Martin 153
Litwanides, Walerian 324, 344
Livius de Rauda 243
Löbl, Benno 260, 262
Lodi, Costanzo 232
Lorich, Reinhard 160
Lorraine Charles, Cardinal de Vaudemont 66–67
Löwe, Gottlieb 263
Loyola, Ignatius 276–277, 332
Lubrański, Jan 127–128

Ludmila of Bohemia, St 256
Ludolph von Sachsen 212–213
Lufft, Hans 296
Luigi da Crema 242
Luther, Martin 2, 5, 8, 11, 55, 105–107, 112–140, 147, 157, 192–193, 278, 296–298, 302, 306, 336, 338
Lycosthenes, Conrad 160

Magnus, Johannes 92
Magnus, Olaus 92
Makeblyde, Lodewijk 278
Malerbi, Niccolò 206
Mangold, Gregor 260
Manuzio, Aldo 243
Manuzio, Paolo 17, 21–23, 36, 92
Marcus, Hannah 177
Margoński, Wojciech 323–324
Maria Gertrudis, nun in Prague 269
Martínez de Angulo, Juana 50
Martínez, Sebastián 50
Martz, Louis L. 333
Mary Stuart, queen of Scotland 62, 65–69, 72
Masen, Jacob 347
Massano, Ioanne Francisco 97
Mata, Alonso de la 49
Matal, Jean 231
Mathias I, king of Hungary 291
Mazzolini, Silvestro 211
Medici, Ferdinando de' 34, 65
Medina, Bartolomé 211
Meffreth 189–190
Meisner, Balthasar 305
Melanchthon, Philipp 149–153, 160, 168
Ménestrier, Claude-François 326
Menghi, Girolamo 213
Mentzer, Balthasar 303
Merbecke, John 77
Michael a S. Catharina 260
Micyllus, Jacob 160
Mihálykó, János 296, 298, 303–306
Milotai, Nyilas István 300
Mirowski, Paweł 325, 328, 334, 338–340, 342, 352
Misenus, Andreas 160
Möller, Roloff 126
Montaigne, Michel Eyquem de 289
Montenay, Georgette de 324, 328
Morone, Giovanni 33

INDEX

Mościcki, Mikołaj   334, 351
Moses   380–381
Münster, Sebastian   160
Müntzer, Thomas   78
Musculus, Andreas   305
Musculus, Wolfgang   160
Musso, Cornelio   212

Na'matallah, Ignatius   34
Nadal, Jerónimo   227, 329–330, 347
Nagy, Benedek   301, 303–305
Nausea, Friedrich   194
Naveda, Juan de   45–47
Neander, Michael   160
Neira, Pedro García de   45–46
Neri, Filippo   20
Never, Heinrich   126
Nicolaus, Busch   185
Nicole, Pierre   270
Nicolini da Sabbio, Domenico   207
Nieszporkowic, Ambroży   324
Nimptsch, Hans   126
Niwicki, Świętosław Zygmunt   323
Novotný, Amandus   126
Nyéki, Vörös Mátyás   291–293

Oecolampadius, Johannes   117, 160, 171, 175
Ogińska, Helena   335
Oldendorp, Johann   126
Olmi, Paolo   231
Opalińska, Teresa Konstancja   335
Oporinus, Johannes   168
Orsini, Marino   231, 147

Pachomius   23
Pacifico da Novara   227
Palladio, Andrea   244
Pallotta, Giovanni Evangelista   85
Panigarola, Francesco   212, 240–241
Paolino da Milano   231
Paolo da Savignano   242
Paolo Girolamo da Savona   242
Paolo Veneto   210
Paul, St   300
Paulino, Stefano   97
Pázmány, Péter   288–306
Peez, Johann Conrad   263
Pelbartus of Temesvar   190
Pepin, Guillaume   212

Pérez de Aguilar, Sebastián   41
Perna, Petrus   168
Persons, Robert   52–74
Peter Lombard   210
Petrucci, Federico   234
Pfaffenzeller, Bonifacio   324
Philip II, king of Spain   28–29, 37, 41, 53, 59
Philo of Alexandria   382
Piaci, Felice   242
Piccolomini, Enea Silvio   186
Pico della Mirandola, Giovanni   248
Pico, Paolo   222
Pieroni von Galliano, Giovanni   270
Pieroni von Galliano, Helena Franziska   271
Pierozzi, Antonino   211
Pietro d'Ancarano   234
Pietro Nicola da Tolentino   244
Pirckheimer, Willibald   160
Pistorius, Johannes   303
Pius II, pope. See Piccolomini, Enea Silvio
Pius IV, pope   17, 21, 27–28, 36
Pius V, pope   18–19, 27, 79–80, 257
Plantin, Christophe   29, 88
Plato   234
Plautus Titus Maccius   236
Plaza, Juan de la   41
Pletho Georgius   160
Plinius Secundus Gaius   236
Plotinus   234
Poliziano, Angelo   236
Pollini, Girolamo   63–66
Possevino, Antonio   34
Prati, Fioravante   206
Pretere, Guillaume de   278
Ptolemy (Ptolemaeus Claudius)   189–191, 236
Pürstinger, Berthold   193
Püttner, Gotthard Johann   262

Quarles, Francis   331

Radziwiłł, Katarzyna   335
Raimondi, Giovanni Battista   34–35, 81
Rålamb, Claes   144
Rambau, Hans   168
Ramírez, Hernán   50–51
Ramírez, María   50
Ramus, Petrus   160, 168
Reguardati, Benedetto   236
Remondini, Giuseppe   263

Reuchlin, Johannes   95
Reyes, Baltasar de los   48
Rhasis   236
Rhau, Georg   151
Rhode, Paul   126
Ribadeneira, Pedro de   54–55, 60–66
Ricci, Matteo   330
Rihel, Wendel   168
Ripalda, Jerónimo de   278
Rishton, Edward   56
Roberto, Francisco   47
Rodecki, Aleksy   280
Rodríguez, Miguel   47
Rorarius, Georgius   297
Rotterodamus, Erasmus. *See* Erasmus

Sabbio, Ludovico   205, 207
Sallustius Crispus Gaius   236
Salmerón, Alfonso   278
Sambucus, Johannes   290–293
Sander, Nicholas   52–74
Santini Aichel, Jan   271
Santori Giulio Antonio   33
Santoro Guilio Antonio   88
Sarcerius, Erasmus   160
Sartorius, Thomas   265
Savonarola, Girolamo   244
Sawicki, Karol   328, 335
Schönfels, Georg   402
Schönweisin von Eckstein, Anna Mechtildis   264
Scoto, Ottaviano, heirs of   207
Sebastianus a Matre Dei   324, 328
Seneca Lucius Annaeus   236, 289
Serafino da Como   232
Sessa, Melchiorre heirs of   207
Seyfried, Johann   126
Sieniawska, Elżbieta   286
Sierakowski, Hiacynt   324
Sigismund I, king of Poland   127–129, 131, 136
Sirleto, Guglielmo   19, 22–26, 33
Sixtus IV, pope   227–229, 231
Sixtus V, pope   20, 22, 24, 35, 36, 85, 93
Skarga, Piotr   333
Skibicki, Stanisław   327, 351
Slüter, Joachim (Jochim Slyter)   126
Socrates   171, 172
Somasco, Giovanni Battista   207
Sommervogel, Carlos   275

Spáčil, Placidus   265
Speratus, Paul   125
Spiegel, Jacob   160
Spina, Bartolomeo   242
Špungianskis, Juris   278
Steinmann, Johannes   168
Stoppelberg, Hans   126
Sturm, Johannes   160, 288–289
Suárez, Francisco   332, 343
Suawe, Peter   125
Sucquet, Antoine   347
Svetonius Tranquillus Gaius   236
Szulc, Stanisław. *See* Sebastianus a Matre Dei
Szyl, Miklós. *See* Pázmány Péter

Tagliavia de Aragón, Simone   222, 232–233
Tasso, Torquato   240, 246
Telegdi, Miklós   297
Terentius Afer Publius   236
Teresa of Ávila   265
Theodoret of Cyrus   27
Thomas à Kempis   265, 278, 286, 294, 338–340, 342, 353
Thomas Aquinas, St   234, 238, 241, 247, 285, 343, 353
Thurzó, György   304
Thurzó, Zsuzsanna   304
Tinto, Alberto   35
Titelmans, Franciscus   108, 121
Toledo de Herrera, Francisco   242
Toledo, Francisco   211
Tomicki, Piotr   127
Torquemada, Juan de   234
Torrella, Gaspar   236
Tosi, Bartolomeo   26
Traiani, Giovanni Domenico   25–26
Trattner, Johann Thomas   263
Treter, Błażej   386
Treter, Tomasz   323–325, 336–338, 352, 372, 372–390

Ueckermünde, Georg von   125

Valades, Diego de   330
Valente, Diogo   94
Valentini, Matteo   206
Valier, Agostino   222
Valk-Falk, Endel   188
Vallejo, Alonso de   42

INDEX

Vega, Antonio de la 46
Venuti, Filipo 243
Verdussen, family 9
Verstegan, Richard Rowlands 12, 54, 58, 69, 309–322
Vettori, Piero 26
Vincent de Beauvais 185
Viviani, Gaspare 25–27, 31, 33, 35, 92
Vladislaus II Jagiellon, king of Hungary and of Bohemia 291
Vogel, Matthäus 278
Vögelin, Ernest 168
Volker, Honemann 194
von Fürstenberg, Maria Josepha 270
von Harnach, Maria Theresia 266
von Kurzböck, Joseph 263
von Linné, Carl 269
Vuković, Božidar (Dionigi della Vecchia) 23
Vuković, Giovanni Vicenzo 23–24, 26

Wadding, Luke 24
Wierix, Hieronymus 326
Wietor, Hieronim 136

Wilhelm V, duke of Bavaria 70–72, 77, 85
Willich, Jodocus
Witzel, Georg 193
Woieriot, Pierre 328
Wolff, Christian 268
Wollenwever, Jürgen 126
Wolter von Plettenberg 182
Wujek, Jakub 276, 281–283, 286
Wussin, Caspar Zacharias 260
Wysocki, Szymon 282–283, 286
Wyssenbach, Rudolf 168

Zanetti, Francesco 24, 26–28, 33, 36
Ziegelbauer, Magnoaldus 261
Zinke, Othmar Daniel 255
Zoilo, Annibale 97
Zoppini, Fabio and Agostino 207
Zsámboky, János. *See* Sambucus, Johannes
Zurla, Ippolito 233
Zvonarics, György 301–305
Zvonarics, Imre 301–305
Zwingli, Ulrich 111, 117, 336, 338
Żaba, Jan Kościesza 327, 325, 352